A History of Islam in America

Muslims began arriving in the New World long before the rise of the Atlantic slave trade. The first arrivals date to the turn of the sixteenth century when European explorers and colonists crossed the Atlantic in search of new horizons and trading routes. Kambiz GhaneaBassiri's fascinating book traces the history of Muslims in the United States and their different waves of immigration and conversion across five centuries, through colonial and antebellum America, through world wars and civil rights struggles, to the contemporary era. The book tells the often deeply moving stories of individual Muslims and their lives as immigrants and citizens within the broad context of the American religious experience, showing how that experience has been integral to the evolution of American Muslim institutions and practices. This is a unique and intelligent portrayal of a diverse religious community and its relationship with America. It will serve as a strong antidote to the current politicized dichotomy between Islam and the West, which has come to dominate the study of Muslims in America and further afield.

Kambiz GhaneaBassiri is Associate Professor of Religion and Humanities at Reed College in Portland, Oregon. He is the author of *Competing Visions of Islam in the United States: A Study of Los Angeles* (1997) and has served on the editorial board of *The Encyclopedia of Islam in the United States* (2007) and the *Encyclopedia of Muslim-American History* (2010).

For
Kamala and Daryush

A History of Islam in America

*From the New World to the
New World Order*

KAMBIZ GHANEABASSIRI

Reed College, Oregon

CAMBRIDGE UNIVERSITY PRESS
Cambridge, New York, Melbourne, Madrid, Cape Town,
Singapore, São Paulo, Delhi, Mexico City

Cambridge University Press
32 Avenue of the Americas, New York, NY 10013-2473, USA

www.cambridge.org
Information on this title: www.cambridge.org/9780521614870

First published 2010
Reprinted 2010, 2011 (thrice), 2013

A catalog record for this publication is available from the British Library.

Library of Congress Cataloging in Publication Data

GhaneaBassiri, Kambiz.
  A history of Islam in America : from the new world to the new world order /
Kambiz GhaneaBassiri.
    p. cm.
  Includes bibliographical references and index.
  ISBN 978-0-521-84964-7 (hardback)
  1. Islam – United States – History.   2. Muslims – United States.   I. Title.
  BP67.U6G43   2010
  297.0973–dc22   2010006223

ISBN 978-0-521-84964-7 Hardback
ISBN 978-0-521-61487-0 Paperback

Contents

Illustrations

Acknowledgments

During the years that I have worked on this book, I benefited from more conversations with colleagues and American Muslims than I could acknowledge here. In its proposal stage, this book benefited from the feedback of professors Patrice Brodeur, Carl Ernst, and William Hutchison. I was deeply saddened that Professor Hutchison passed away in 2006 and was unable to see its publication.

To my colleagues in the religion department at Reed College – Ken Brashier, Michael Foat, and Steve Wasserstrom – I owe special thanks for their support particularly during my long leave, which significantly stressed an already small department. The interlibrary loan office at Reed generously availed me of numerous obscure sources scattered throughout the country. Thanks also to Nasrin Marzban, Kathryn Lofton, and Taly Lind for helping me access sources that were not available through interlibrary loan. Thanks to my students in an undergraduate and a graduate course on the history of Islam in America at Reed; I learned much from their critical engagement with the sources and ideas that shaped this book.

I am extremely grateful to Peter Skerry, Leila Ahmed, Juliane Hammer, Christopher White, and especially Steven Wasserstrom for graciously commenting on a full draft of the present book. Thanks to Paul Silverstein, Jacqueline Dirks, Laura Leibman, Kathryn Lofton, Kamyar GhaneaBassiri, David Ranz, and Rowena Vrabel for reviewing drafts of varying chapters of the book. In addition to those who read all or portions of this book at different stages, I am indebted to Kaveh Bassiri, Imad Damaj, Margaret Jacob, Murray Last, Jan Mieszkowski, Darius Rejali, Marc Schneiberg, Lamin Sanneh, John Slifko, and John Urang for engaging with me in conversations about American Muslims and for helping hone some of my ideas and arguments. I alone, however, am responsible for any mistakes or shortcomings in the book.

I wish to express my gratitude to my student assistants who helped with the research for this book: Karima Abedine, Osman Balkan, Vahid Brown, William Brown, Nicholas Callaway, Audrey June Davidson, Samuel Kigar, Miranda Meadow, Sarah Robberson, and Angélique Thomas. Angélique, Audrey, Karima, Sam, and Will not only helped with research but also assisted me in preparing the manuscript. In particular, Will's competent assistance and encouragement were indispensible to my successful completion of the draft for reviewers before the end of my leave.

Many of the arguments made about the historical development of Islam since 1965 in the last two chapters of the book were tested through extensive interviews and oral histories gathered for the Portland Muslim History Project, which I directed in 2005. I am grateful to Dr. Diana Eck and the Harvard Pluralism Project and Colin Diver, president of Reed College, for funding this study and to the local Portland Muslim community for allowing us to inquire into the lives of their institutions. Reed students Anne Marie Armentrout, Jonathan Grass, Miranda Meadow, Muntasir Sattar, and Akbar Mumtaz conducted interviews for this study and wrote brief histories of different Muslim institutions in Portland. Anne Marie, Jon, and Miranda each wrote an extensive research report for this project – all of which has helped enrich aspects of the present study.

I completed this book in large part because of the Carnegie Corporation of New York's Carnegie Scholars award program (2006–2008). This grant allowed me time away from my teaching and administrative duties so that I could focus on writing. I am also grateful to my dean, Peter Steinberger, and the staff of his office, Christine Mack and Karen Perkins-Butzien, for administering the Stillman Drake and Summer Scholarship awards that helped fund the material and research assistance I received for this project.

Given the large scope of this study and the fact that it is one of the first historical studies of its kind, completing it took me much longer than I had anticipated. I am grateful to my editor, Marigold Acland, for her understanding and patience.

My wife and our children have been an enormous support and a constant source of encouragement throughout the long process that culminated in the pages at hand. Words cannot adequately express my love and gratitude for them. This book is dedicated to them.

Introduction

The history of Islam in America begins in the context of rivalries and encounters of the Atlantic world that shaped the American republic. The presence of Muslims in the territories that eventually formed the United States of America dates back to the earliest arrivals of Europeans in the Americas.[1] Muslims neither came to America in large numbers at that time nor did they play a primary role in colonizing the Americas. They were, however, deeply embedded in the commercial and political rivalries that led to the establishment of the Atlantic world. Given the enormous impact the European discovery of the Americas has had on the modern world, it is easy to forget that during the fifteenth and sixteenth centuries, European empires navigated the Atlantic in order to establish new trade routes that would circumvent the Mediterranean and Middle Eastern trade routes dominated at that time by Muslim empires. Subsequently, as Europeans conquered and colonized the Americas, an Atlantic world emerged relating Africa, Europe, and the Americas through a triangle of mercantile relations and imperial networks. Muslims from North and West Africa were active participants in this triangle, and many of them ended up in America as slaves. Since that time, there has been a continuous presence of Muslims in America.

---

[1] Some popular histories of Muslims in America claim that Muslims came to the Americas as early as the late ninth century. Such claims are based on dubious readings of ancient Muslim geographers' mention of Muslims' maritime excursions off the Atlantic coast of the Iberian peninsula and Northwest Africa. They tell us more about some American Muslims' desire to establish their own American foundation myths than about the activities of ancient Muslim sailors. For an example of such claims, see Jerald F. Dirks, *Muslims in American History: A Forgotten Legacy* (Beltsville, MD: Amana Publications, 2006), 28–38.

At the turn of the twenty-first century, the United States is home to about three million Muslims[2] who arguably comprise the most diverse Muslim population in any single country in the world. Not only have Muslims of varying ethnic and sectarian orientation from every corner of the world immigrated to the United States, but Americans of African, European, Latin, and Native American ancestries have converted to Islam as well. There are also a number of new religious movements within Islam in the United States (e.g., the Moorish Science Temple and the Nation of Islam). The United States is undoubtedly a microcosm of the world's Muslim population.

This book analyzes the abiding presence and diversity of Muslims in the United States by reference to its historical context. It demonstrates how Muslims have participated in American history by narrating the ways in which they have defined themselves and their religion in relation to changing conceptions of race, religious pluralism, and national identity in the United States. Given the enormous diversity found within the Muslim population in the United States, no one narrative can capture the

---

[2] The question of how many Muslims are in the United States is controversial. Since the U.S. Census does not ask questions about individuals' religious beliefs or affiliations, there is no official estimate of the number of Muslims in the United States. Estimates differ widely. As American Muslims have sought to become more politically active, the number of Muslims in the United States has become politicized. American Muslim leaders cite larger numbers to attract political attention to American Muslims as a voting block. Other groups that feel politically threatened by increased American Muslim political activity cite smaller numbers. In 2002, for example, a researcher for the Council of American-Islam Relations estimated that there are between 3,225,390 and 5,055,390 American Muslims (Mohamed Nimer, *The North American Muslim Resource Guide: Muslim Community Life in the United States and Canada* (New York: Routledge, 2002), 27), while the American Jewish Committee put the number of American Muslims around 1,886,000 (Tom W. Smith, "Estimating the Muslim Population in the United States" http://www.ajc.org/site/apps/nl/content3.asp?c=ijITI2PHKoG&b=843637&ct=1044159, accessed June 25, 2009). In my estimate, I rely mainly on polls conducted in the last decade by Gallup, the Pew Research Center, and American Religious Identification Survey. For an overview of these polling results see Pew Research Center, "Muslim Americans: Middle Class and Mostly Mainstream" (2007). In the absence of census data or any other type of concrete evidence, these surveys represent the only available scientific attempts at estimating the number of Muslims in the United States. Since they rely mainly on telephone surveys and many Muslims may be reluctant to discuss their religious affiliation over the phone (given the stigmatization of Islam in contemporary America), I have placed more stock in the larger estimate of the 2007 Pew Research Center study (2,350,000) and have rounded this up to the nearest million. Another reason for my rounding up these estimates is to account for cultural Muslims who would be reluctant to self-identify as Muslims because they do not regularly practice Islam but nonetheless would commemorate major events in their lives, such as weddings and deaths, in accordance with Islamic laws and customs.

varying experiences of American Muslims. As the following pages will lay bare, there is no single American Muslim experience. This absence of uniformity, however, should not be taken to mean that there is no historical continuity in Muslims' experiences in the United States. Muslims who found themselves in this country, whether as slaves, immigrants, or converts, have had to define themselves and to interpret their varying religious understandings and practices in relation to the dominant laws, conceptions of religion, and political and cultural institutions that have shaped American society through the years. They also have had to grapple with the diversity of Islamic beliefs and practices that they faced in the United States as they, as a minority group, formed relations with co-religionists from varying parts of the world. This experience of dealing with American social, political, and legal norms on the one hand and with diversity of Muslim beliefs and practices on the other has helped shape the contours of American Islamic history.

In rendering the story of how Muslims interpreted their roles and practiced their religion in the United States, I try to focus (the availability of sources permitting) on the communal relations they formed and the institutions they developed. It is my contention that nowhere is the contours of American Islamic history better seen than in varying Muslims' experiences of community and institution building in the United States. At each period of American history discussed in the following chapters, from colonial times to the present, Muslims in the United States have formed communal relations with both Muslims and non-Muslims, and whenever possible, they have sought to institutionalize these communal relations through the founding of local and national organizations designed to fulfill their religious and cultural needs and aspirations. Many of these organizations proved ephemeral and left scant records. Others, however, endured and played a role in shaping Muslims' experiences in the United States. Over the years, through the dynamic process of American Muslim community and institution building, American Muslims have effectively brought America (as a national concept) and Islam (as a lived religion) into relation with one another. The historical import of these local and national institutions and communal relations has been vividly evidenced in recent years in the way in which American Muslims have relied on them to weather the backlash from 9/11. It is thus not surprising (as I will discuss later in the epilogue) that the events of 9/11 and its aftermath accelerated American Muslim institution building and pushed American Muslims further into public life and civil service within their respective communities.

It is worth repeating that my emphasis on the historical context of American Islam[3] is not meant to suggest that there is a distinct American Muslim experience, but rather it is intended as an argument for a *relational* understanding of American religious history and modern Islamic history. American Muslims stand at the intersection of these histories, and their lived historical experiences give the lie to the notion that Islamic culture is intrinsically distinct from American culture. The phenomenon of American Islam blatantly contests the binary opposition assumed in the oft-repeated phrase, "Islam and the West." This binary opposition has shaped not only how policy makers, pundits, and the general public think about the relationship between the United States and the Muslim-majority world, but it has also influenced much of the scholarship on Islam in America, which up until recently has been primarily sociological and anthropological, focusing on questions of assimilation and identity formation. The few historical studies have focused primarily on African American Muslims[4] and on non-Muslim Americans' perceptions of Islam.[5] Operating on the implicit assumption that Islam and "the West" are essentially different, the bulk of the scholarship on Islam in America, whether immigrant or indigenous, however, has focused on how Muslims are faring in the United States rather than how they have actively participated in American history. Scholars have inquired, for instance, into how Muslims in the United States deal with the mixing of sexes, liberal democracy, religious bigotry, and, of course, the wearing of the veil. These inquiries have commonly centered on the question of how Muslims identify themselves in this inherently foreign society.[6] One popular book on American Islam, for example, set out to answer such questions as:

[3] I use American Islam not to refer to a type of Islam but to the variety of efforts through which self-proclaimed Muslims have sought to root their understandings of Islam within the social, political, cultural, and economic life of this country. As such, I do not understand American Islam to be either exceptionally unique or an adulterated form of Islam. Rather, I use it as a descriptive category for the variety of Islamic beliefs and practices that have developed in relation to the legal, social, political, and cultural norms of this country.

[4] See, for examples, Michael Gomez, *Black Crescent: The Experience and Legacy of African Muslims in the Americas* (Cambridge: Cambridge University Press, 2005) and Richard Brent Turner, *Islam in the African-American Experience*, 2nd ed. (Bloomington, IN: Indiana University Press, 2003).

[5] See, for examples, Timothy Marr, *The Cultural Roots of American Islamicism* (Cambridge: Cambridge University Press, 2006) and Thomas S. Kidd, *American Christians and Islam: Evangelical Culture and Muslims from the Colonial Period to the Age of Terrorism* (Princeton, NJ: Princeton University Press, 2009).

[6] See, for examples, Yvonne Yazbeck Haddad and Adair T. Lummis, *Islamic Values in the United States: A Comparative Study* (New York: Oxford University Press, 1987);

Can Muslims become part and parcel of a pluralistic American society without sacrificing or losing their identity? Can Muslims be Muslims in a non-Muslim state that is not governed by Islamic law? [Conversely, i]s the American legal system capable of allowing for particular Muslim religious and cultural differences[7] within the Constitution's broader universal claims? Do the secular and/or Judeo-Christian values of American society make this impossible?[8]

The methodology implied in these emblematic questions is that by pinpointing an American Islamic identity one can assess the "Americanness" or "Islamicness" of Islam in America and thus know how "successfully" Muslims are coping with life in the United States. The answer to this question has obvious political implications given the contemporary preoccupation with "political Islam" or Islamism. Knowing how well American Muslims balance being both "American" and "Islamic" helps determine whether they ought to be regarded as a disruptive source in American society or, rather, as another thread in the colorful fabric of American society. For many scholars of Islam, there is a degree of *déjà vu* to such queries insofar as they echo similar questions asked by nineteenth- and twentieth-century Orientalists who sought to assess the compatibility of Islam with European modernity. In sum, determining whether or not a modern Islam or an American Islamic identity exists has been a stepping-stone toward assessing the degree of conflict we may expect between a "modern West" and a "Muslim Orient," between American society and the Muslims within it.

It should be noted that the binary opposition of "Islam and the West" has not only framed the way immigrant Muslims' experiences have been examined in the United States but also the study of African American

---

Yvonne Yazbeck Haddad and John Esposito, *Muslims on the Americanization Path?* (New York: Oxford University Press, 1998); Jane I. Smith, *Islam in America* (New York: Columbia University Press, 1999) (Columbia University Press published a second edition of Smith's book as the present book went into production); Jocelyne Cesari, *When Islam and Democracy Meet: Muslims in Europe and in the United States* (New York: Palgrave Macmillan, 2004). For examples of scholarly works that counter this predominant trend in the study of Islam in America, see Bruce B. Lawrence, *New Faiths, Old Fears: Muslims and Other Asian Immigrants in American Religious Life* (New York: Columbia University Press, 2002) and Edward E. Curtis, IV, ed. *The Columbia Sourcebook of Muslims in the United States* (New York: Columbia University Press, 2008). As the title of Lawrence's book suggests, it addresses the question of assimilation, but rather than examining how American Muslims self-identify, it focuses on how American society and American Muslims have adapted to one another.

[7] The veil is discussed explicitly as a symbol of these differences in the second part of the book, "North American Pluralism and the Challenge of the Veil."

[8] Haddad and Esposito, *Americanization Path?*, 3.

Muslims. Early scholars of the rise of Islam in black America generally explained the separatist tendencies of African American Muslim nationalist organizations, such as the Moorish Science Temple and the Nation of Islam, in terms of their appropriation of Islam. As such, they overlooked the distinctly American influences, which as I will discuss in Chapter 5, shaped these institutions. In this scholarly literature, Islam as the binary opposite of "the West" helped explain the separatist tendency of "black Muslims." Assuming that integration is the expected norm in America and that Islam is strange to the American experience, this scholarship attributed the black nationalism of the twentieth century to the outside influence of Islam, and it helped bring national focus to the Nation of Islam as the prototypical black nationalist organization of the twentieth century.[9]

Another discernable objective of much of the scholarship on Muslims in the United States has been to teach non-Muslim Americans about Islam in order to counter xenophobia and to make the case for American political, social, and cultural establishments to include Muslims within their purview. The above-cited book, for example, proclaims that Americans need to "realize that Muslims are 'us.'"[10] The most comprehensive textbook on American Islam to date argues: "That task [of making Muslims political and economic equals] will be easier to the degree that Americans know more about, and can come to better appreciate, the religion of Islam as a vital contributor to its religious landscape. This book is intended as one way to facilitate that task."[11]

The methodology employed to fulfill this task is noteworthy insofar as it is representative of the methodology that, up until recently, dominated American Islamic Studies in general. Such studies of Islam in America aim to "present the perspectives of as many American Muslims as possible and allow their voices to determine the important issues and illuminate

---

[9] Two influential examples of such scholarship are C. Eric Lincoln, *The Black Muslims in America*, 3rd ed. (Grand Rapids, MI: W.B. Eerdsmans, 1994), originally published by Beacon Press in 1961; and Essien Udosen Essien-Udom, *Black Nationalism: A Search for an Identity in America* (Chicago, IL: The University of Chicago Press, 1962). For other similar critiques of this scholarship see Susan Nance, "Mystery of the Moorish Science Temple: Southern Blacks and American Alternative Spirituality in 1920s Chicago" in *Religion and American Culture*, 12, no. 2 (2002), 125, and Sherman A. Jackson, *Islam and the Blackamerican: Looking toward the Third Resurrection* (New York: Oxford University Press, 2005), 121–128. Jackson's critique is aimed at the later work of Richard Brent Turner (1997) and is at times unduly harsh for reading certain malicious intents in Turner's work that are not evident in Turner's text.

[10] Haddad and Esposito, *Americanization Path?*, 3.

[11] Smith, *Islam in America*, xvi.

the presentation of material."[12] This approach, while *indispensable* for attaining an authentic understanding of how Muslims are self-identifying in the United States, is not conducive to an analytical interpretation of the phenomenon of Islam in America. By simply re-representing American Muslim representations of themselves and allowing their voices to determine the issues, this methodology stymies the self-reflexivity needed for critical analysis.[13] It leaves the burden of evaluating the context and categories of scholarly analysis on the shoulders of the scholar's subjects rather than the scholar himself. In doing so, this approach ironically fails to achieve its goal of debunking a superficial and politicized East-West dichotomy, which the phenomenon of an American Islam so blatantly contests. The irony is that by privileging Muslim voices in analyses of Islam in America, Islam and America are perpetuated as reified, mutually exclusive categories. The privileging of Muslim voices in scholarly explanations of American Islam necessarily devalues, if not excludes, the significance of other American voices (e.g., non-Muslim American immigrant voices, Christian African-American voices, mainline Protestant voices), which, through their interaction with American Muslim voices, have helped shape the historical phenomenon of American Islam. In short, scholarly burrowing into American Muslim articulations of their religious identity has dimmed the significance of the larger American and Islamic socio-historical context on which American Muslims have been acting for nearly four centuries.

Many scholars of Islam in the United States have sought to overcome the dichotomies between "Islam and the West," "Islam and Democracy," or "Islam and Modernity" that have long shaped much of the popular and scholarly discourses on modern Islam by familiarizing Americans or "Westerners" with "Islamic" beliefs, practices, and voices.[14] In addressing this audience and its preconceptions about Islam, they have ended up evoking these conceptual dichotomies even while working to counter them. They have not reframed the discourse but have situated American Islam within it. In contrast to these approaches to the study of Islam in the United States, the organizing principle of this book is that American

---

[12] Ibid., xii.
[13] I am not suggesting that Muslims cannot offer critical analysis of American Islam. My criticism applies to the uncritical representation of their understandings of American Islam as "analysis" in the existing scholarship.
[14] I have in mind here particularly the works of Jane I. Smith, Yvonne Haddad, and John Esposito. Out of all these scholars, Professor Yvonne Haddad's pioneering work did the most in the 1980s and 1990s to bring the study of Islam in America into the academy.

Muslim history is a history of Muslim and non-Muslim American encounters and exchanges. These encounters and exchanges highlight how Islam and "the West," far from being mutually exclusive categories, are lived traditions that have been varyingly thought and re-thought in relation to one another and to their respective historical contexts.

Decades of research and scores of researchers will be required before we know as much about the history of Muslims in the United States as we now do about the history of Jews, Catholics, or members of any Protestant denomination in this country. The present study is not intended as a synthetic culmination of the current state of the study of Islam in America. Nor did I set out to write an encyclopedic history.[15] The contribution of this book lies in its development of an analytical, historical framework and periodization for the study of American Islam that underscores the *relational* nature of American religious history and modern Islamic history. It is intended as a commencement, an invitation to further historical inquiry into the presence of Muslims in America. To this end, I deliberately cite at length from many of the primary sources I have consulted, and I conservatively allow the available data for each epoch to drive my arguments rather than offer a theory of American Islam, whose polysemy we could begin to understand only after more years of research. My hope in adopting such an approach has been to demonstrate how the emerging subfield of American Islamic history not only challenges the predominant narratives through which Islam and "the West" or Islam and modernity are conceived but also provides fertile ground for the future development of new and innovative analyses.

---

[15] Those interested in an encyclopedic work could consult Edward E. Curtis, IV, ed. *Encyclopedia of Muslim-American History* (New York: Facts on File, forthcoming).

I

Islam in the "New World"

The Historical Setting

In the late nineteenth century, Robert Bayles, president of the Market and Fulton National Bank of New York City, reviewed historical records of his ancestry. He discovered that family heirlooms, including a bronze pan, a copy of the Qur'an, and a copper teapot probably belonged to Anthony Jansen van Salee, also known as Anthony Jansen van Vaes and Anthony "the Turk."[1] Bayles would have known that "Turk" was the contemporary and derogatory term for Muslim (regardless of ethnicity);[2] "van Salee" and "van Vaes" signified that Anthony was "from Salé" or "from Fez," Morocco. Anthony immigrated to New Amsterdam some time around 1630 as a colonist for the Dutch West India Company. There, in what eventually became New York City, he settled down as a farmer and at times dealt in real estate. Upon his demise, he left behind four daughters, the youngest of whom, Eva, was an ancestor of Mr. Bayles.

Anthony at some unknown time was joined by Abraham Jansen van Salee, a possible brother or half-brother, who was also referred to as "the Turk" and "the Mulatto."[3] Anthony may be the first settler from a Muslim

[1] Edward Lee McClain, *The Washington Ancestry and Records of the McClain, Johnson, and Forty Other Colonial American Families*, vol. 3 (Greenfield, OH: Privately Printed, 1932), 71.

[2] On the derogatory use of the term "Turk" in New Netherland, see Jaap Jacobs, *New Netherland: A Dutch Colony in Seventeenth-Century America* (Leiden: Brill, 2005), 449.

[3] Hazel Van Dyke Roberts, "Anthony Jansen van Salee 1607–1676," *New York Genealogical and Biographical Record* 103, no. 1 (January 1972), 25–27; Teunis G. Bergen, *In Alphabetical Order, of the Early Settlers of Kings County, Long Island, N.Y., from Its First Settlement by Europeans to 1700* (New York: S. W. Green's Son, 1881), 154; McClain,

background[4] in the territories that eventually formed the United States, but
he was not the first person of Muslim heritage to traverse America. From the
time Christopher Columbus crossed the Atlantic, West and North Africans
served as involuntary servants to Europeans arriving in the Americas.
The most notable of them in early American history was Estevanico de
Dorantes, "a black Arab originally from Azamor," Morocco.[5] Estevanico
is recognized as possibly the first African and the first person of Muslim
heritage[6] to travel in the Southwest United States and the first non-native
to enter the Zuni Pueblos in New Mexico and Arizona.

However scant, the history of Islam in America reminds us of the
neglected fact that the early making of the "New World," long before the
rise of the Atlantic slave trade, included Africans alongside Europeans
and Native Americans. West Europeans "discovered" the Americas while
in search of new trade routes from the Atlantic Ocean to the Indian
Ocean. It is too often forgotten that European voyages of discovery in
the Americas in the sixteenth and seventeenth centuries were in large part
intended to find new mercantile routes to circumvent the overland and
maritime routes through rival Muslim empires – mainly the Ottoman
(1299–1923) and Mamluk (1250–1517) Empires. Prior to Columbus,
fifteenth-century Iberians established trading posts along the western and

---

The Washington Ancestry, 89 and 100; and Henry B. Hoff, "Frans Abramse van Salee
   and His Descendants: A Colonial Black Family in New York and New Jersey," *New York
   Genealogical and Biographical Record* 121, no. 2 (April 1990), 65–66.
[4] While Anthony Jansen may have had a Muslim upbringing as one would expect given
   his background, the extant sources, short of calling him a Turk, do not identify him
   as Muslim. It seems that his daughter, Eva, had been baptized. See Van Dyke Roberts,
   "Anthony Jansen van Salee 1607–1676," 17. Also, when the colonial council banished
   him and his wife, Grietjen Reyniers, from New Netherland on April 7, 1639, it was
   said that they had broken their promise "to conduct themselves quietly and piously as
   behooves Christians." See *New York Historical Manuscripts: Dutch, Council Minutes,
   1638–1649*, vol. 4, trans. and annot. Arnold J. F. van Laer (Baltimore, MD: Genealogical
   Publishing Co., 1974), 47.
[5] Alvar Núñez Cabeza de Vaca, *Relación de los Naufragios y Comentarios de Alvar Núñez
   Cabeza de Vaca*, vol. 1 (Madrid: Librería General de Victoriano Suárez, 1906), 144.
[6] Estevanico's religious identity is not known. As Rolena Adorno and Patrick Charles Pautz
   have noted, although Estevanico Cabeza de Vaca referred to Estevanico as an Arabic-
   speaking native of Azemmour, he also identified him as a Christian. His explicit identification as a Christian may have had to do with a 1526 royal decree that required all owners
   of Spanish-speaking black Africans to acquire special permission to take their slaves to the
   Indies. See Álvar Núñez Cabeza de Vaca, *The Narrative of Cabeza de Vaca*, ed. and trans.
   Rolena Adorno and Patrick Charles Pautz, vol. 1 (Lincoln, NE: University of Nebraska
   Press, 1999), 96n4.

southern coasts of Africa in order to circumvent Moorish[7] merchants plying the routes between sub-Saharan Africa and Europe. In short, European exploration and colonization of the Americas and of West and North Africa were coeval and correlates of the same imperial projects fueled by the rivalries between varying European states (the Portuguese, the Spanish, the English, the French, and the Dutch) on the one hand and between European and Muslim states (Moors, Ottomans, and Mamluks) on the other.

The mercantile relations and imperial networks Europeans created between Europe, Africa, and the Americas led to epic changes in global commerce, state administration, international relations, and conceptions of alterity. We do not know much about the actual religious practices and beliefs of early explorers and settlers, such as Estevanico and Anthony Jansen van Salee, who came from the Muslim-majority world. Nonetheless, their lives personify the interrelations between the Muslim-majority world, Northwest Africa, Western Europe, and the Americas that shaped the Atlantic world. Estevanico left Spain with his master, Andrés Dorantes, on an expedition led by Pamfilo de Narváez to the northern Gulf Coast around 1527. The expedition went awry. Estevanico and Dorantes survived the wreck of the expedition with one Alonso del Castillo. Together they crisscrossed the Gulf Coast for some six years, occasionally as lost wanderers but usually as captives among the natives. With another survivor of the Narváez expedition, the famed explorer Álvar Núñez Cabeza de Vaca, they spent eight years journeying from the Gulf Coast to western Mexico. During this time, they often acted as medicine men among the natives, Estevanico at times serving as an intermediary between the Spanish and the Native Americans. "These people were convinced that we came from heaven," claimed Cabeza de Vaca.

We walked all day without eating until nighttime, and even then we ate so little to their astonishment. We never sat down to rest having been so inured by hard work that we didn't feel tired. We had a lot of authority and clout with them, and in order to preserve this we seldom spoke to them. The Negro [Estevanico] always spoke to them and informed us of the paths to travel, the towns in the area, and other matters that we wanted to know.[8]

---

[7] The term Moor was used in this period to refer to people of Arab and Berber descent who originally came from Northwest Africa (modern day Morocco, Tunisia, Algeria, and Mauritania) and were widely supposed to have dark or black skin.

[8] Cabeza de Vaca, *Relación*, 119.

The familiarity Estevanico gained with the natives and the region as a result of his intermediary role made him a valuable asset to the Spanish Empire. When the wandering explorers finally reached a Spanish colony, the Spanish Viceroy in Mexico, Antonio de Mendoza, purchased Estevanico from Dorantes, and appointed him to act as a scout and a guide to a new expedition to the northern frontier of Mexico, searching for the fabled gold-paved Seven Cities of Cíbola. Estevanico traveled ahead by a few days and sent reports back with some of the natives who accompanied him. Legend has it that in the Zuni settlements he was welcomed as a medicine man of sorts and given gifts of turquoise and women, but when, in 1539, he reached the Pueblo of Háwikuh in New Mexico, he was killed by the natives.[9]

Anthony Jansen van Salee worked for the Dutch Empire, which in the early modern period rivaled Estevanico's imperial patrons. Anthony was in all likelihood the son of Jan Jansz van Haarlem, a Dutch privateer and raider of Spanish galleons in the Mediterranean. Jan Jansz van Haarlem was captured in 1618 by one of the Moorish states along the North African (Barbary) coast and, soon after, found privateering with the Moors more profitable than with the Dutch. He "turned Turk" and became Admiral Murat Reis in the fleet of Moulay Zaydan of Morocco in Salé.[10] Anthony is believed to have been the son of this Murat Reis and a Moroccan woman. Based on the thin record of Anthony's life, it appears that he settled in New Netherland as part of a larger effort by the staunchly Calvinist Dutch empire "to inflict damage on the colonial resources" of its Catholic, Iberian rivals in America.[11] He lived a prosperous, albeit controversial, life in New Netherland until he died in 1676.[12]

---

[9] My account of Estevanico's life is based on Cabeza de Vaca's *Relación*, in particular 59–69, 77, 82–86, 113–119, 126–127, and 144; Cabeza de Vaca, *Narrative of Cabeza de Vaca*, 1, 2, 12–13, 14, 19, 22, 98–101, 104, 106, 110–112, 118, 147–148, 153, 159, 160, 164, 176; Pedro de Castañada, "The Narrative of the Expedition of Coronado," ed. Frederick W. Hodge in *Original Narratives of Early American History: Spanish Explorers in the Southern United States, 1528–1543*, ed. J. Franklin Jameson (New York: Charles Scribner's Sons, 1907), 285–290; J. Fred Rippy, "The Negro and the Spanish Pioneer in the New World," *Journal of Negro History* 6, no. 2 (April 1921), 183–189.

[10] See Peter Lamborn Wilson, *Pirate Utopias: Moorish Corsairs and European Renegadoes*, 2nd ed. (Brooklyn, NY: Autonomedia, 2003), 96–97. According to Wilson, Jansz was captured by Barbary Corsairs and thereafter he "apostasized" in Algiers. Wilson does not give the exact date of Jansz's conversion, but he says that Jansz was sailing with the fleet in Salee by 1619.

[11] Jacobs, *New Netherland*, 2.

[12] On the controversies surrounding Anthony's life, see Leo Hershkowitz, "The Troublesome Turk: An Illustration of Judicial Process in New Amsterdam," *New York History* 46

Commercial and political rivalries between the Portuguese, Spanish, French, Dutch, and English helped shape the modern Americas. Europeans were not the only actors in these rivalries as Anthony and Estevanico remind us. Native Americans, Moors, and black Africans played an important role in shaping this part of the world, and they did so not just as involuntary laborers or conquered peoples but also as independent actors, working within their means to survive in a rapidly globalizing world. While clearly not at the forefront of the forces that shaped modern America, they signify confluences between Europe, Africa, and the Americas at the onset of the history of American Islam.[13] This chapter narrates the early history of Muslims in colonial and antebellum America in the context of the way in which these new relations were negotiated commercially, conceptually, and religiously by Anglo-American Christians and African Muslims. Chapter 2 focuses more on how African Muslim slaves, both individually and collectively, practiced their religion in this new context.

SCOPE OF THE PRESENT NARRATIVE

There are two points to keep in mind while reading the following narrative. First, inasmuch as this is a book on the history of Islam in America, my discussion of American conceptions of Islam focuses on the representation of living Muslims in colonial and antebellum America and not on broader American literary and political images of Islam in this period. The latter fortunately have been the subject of illuminating studies in recent years.[14] This is, however, only tangentially related to Muslims in America, who constitute the subject of the book in hand.

(1965), 299–310; and Van Dyke Roberts, "Anthony Jansen van Salee 1607–1676," 16–28.

[13] See John Kelly Thornton, *Africans and African Americans and the Making of the Atlantic World*, 2nd ed. (Cambridge: Cambridge University Press, 1999), 1–9.

[14] Timothy Marr, *The Cultural Roots of American Islamicism* (Cambridge: Cambridge University Press, 2006); Fuad Shaban, *Islam and Arabs in Early American Thought: The Roots of Orientalism in America* (Durham, NC: Acorn Press, 1991); Robert J. Allison, *The Crescent Obscured: The United States and the Muslim World, 1776–1815* (New York: Oxford University Press, 1995); and Mohammed Sharafuddin, *Islam and Romantic Orientalism: Literary Encounters with the Orient* (London: I. B. Tauris Publishers, 1994). On American imagining of, and encounters with, the Middle East as "the Holy Land," see Burke O. Long, *Imagining the Holy Land: Maps, Models, and Fantasy Travels* (Bloomington, IN: Indiana University Press, 2003); Hilton Obenzinger, *American Palestine: Melville, Twain, and the Holy Land Mania* (Princeton, NJ: Princeton University Press, 1999); and John Davis, *The Landscape of Belief: Encountering the*

Second, there seem to have been interactions, possibly of some historical significance, between African Muslim runaways and Native Americans. Advertisements in Savannah, Georgia, for example, mentioned runaways with Muslim names who had taken refuge with Native Americans. One "Mahomet" was said to have been seen three years after his flight "at a settlement near the Indian Line on Ogechee."[15] Some, seeking the origins of a group of people from Appalachia known as the Melungeons, have hypothesized that Moorish and Ottoman Muslims whom English and Spanish explorers brought with them as slaves and war captives to the southeastern coast of seventeenth-century America went inland along with a number of Europeans to settle among the natives in Appalachia. They are said to have been later joined by black Africans to eventually form the community that by the mid-nineteenth century (at the latest) were identified by Euro-Americans as a "tri-racial" people called the Melungeons.[16] The evidence on which these hypotheses rest, however, is allusive, and the available research is for the most part non-scholarly or, at best, suggestive. A lot more scholarship will have to be done before we can incorporate the interactions between African Muslims and Native Americans in narratives of the early history of Islam in America.[17]

Holy Land in Nineteenth-Century American Art and Culture (Princeton, NJ: Princeton University Press, 1996).

[15] *Savannah Georgia Gazette*, August 31, 1774, cited in Michael Gomez, "Muslims in Early America," *Journal of Southern History* 60, no. 4 (Nov. 1994), 688.

[16] An anonymous article published in 1849 stated that "The legend of their history, which they carefully preserve, is this. A great many years ago, these mountains were settled by a society of Portuguese adventurers, men and women – who came from the *long-shore* parts of Virginia, that they might be freed from the restraints and drawbacks imposed upon them by any form of government…These intermixed with the Indians, and subsequently their descendants (after the first advances of the whites into this part of the state) with the negroes and the whites, thus forming the present race of Melungens (sic)." "Melungens" in *Littell's Living Age* 20, no. 254 (March 31, 1849), 618. Tim Hashaw states that this article was apparently reprinted from the *Knoxville Register* (September 6, 1848), *Children of Perdition: Melungeons and the Struggle of Mixed America* (Macon, GA: Mercer University Press, 2006), 3n1. Will Allen Dromgoole recorded an anonymous Tennessee legislator saying in 1890 that "a Malungion isn't a nigger, and he isn't an Indian, and he isn't a white man. God only knows what he is." "The Malungeons" in *The Arena* 3 (March 1891), 472, reproduced in Wayne Winkler, *Walking Toward the Sunset: The Melungeons of Appalachia* (Macon, GA: Mercer University Press, 2004), 273.

[17] For existing discussions of the possible Muslim origins of the Melungeons, see Michael Gomez, *Black Crescent: The Experience and Legacy of African Muslims in the Americas* (Cambridge: Cambridge University Press, 2005), 186–194; Elizabeth Hirschman, *Melungeons: The Last Lost Tribe in America* (Macon, GA: Mercer University Press,

SLAVE BIOGRAPHIES AND THE HISTORIOGRAPHY OF
ISLAM IN AMERICA

Most Muslims in antebellum America were of North and West African ancestry. As such, they arrived as victims of the processes by which Mediterranean and African commercial and political relations were being imported into the "New World." A few, like Anthony Jansen van Salee, benefited from these processes; some, like Estevanico, became the stuff of legends. Most, in any event, debarked in shackles. Unsurprisingly, then, they left few extant records; future research in this nascent field seems certain to uncover more.

The history of Islam in America must be located in the transcontinental context of early American history. From this perspective, extant biographies of early Muslims in America instructively connect Muslim Africa, Western Europe, and America. It should be noted at the outset that scholarship on African Muslims in colonial and antebellum America has been largely biographical.[18] These biographies have been of particular interest to some contemporary African American Muslims not only because they root Islam within early African American culture but also because they substantiate – in part – the claim made by Muslim black nationalist groups, such as the Moorish Science Temple and the Nation of Islam, that Islam was "the original religion" of black Americans of which they were "stripped" during slavery. The extraordinary lives of these men, however,

---

2005), 117–126; Joseph M. Scolnick, Jr. and N. Brent Kennedy, ed., *From Anatolia to Appalachia: A Turkish American Dialogue* (Macon, GA: Mercer University Press, 2003); N. Brent Kennedy, *The Melungeons: The Resurrection of a Proud People, An Untold Story of Ethnic Cleansing in America*, 2nd ed., rev. and corr. ed. (Macon, GA: Mercer University Press, 1997), 108–136; Winkler, *Walking Toward the Sunset*, 242–247; and Clinton Alfred Weslager, *Delaware's Forgotten Folk: The Story of the Moors and Nanticokes* (Philadelphia, PA: University of Philadelphia Press, 1943), 25–39. As an example of how loosely mixed race Americans in the nineteenth century had been given Islamic markers, see Hugo P. Leaming, "The Ben Ishmael Tribe: A Fugitive 'Nation' of the Old Northwest," in *The Ethnic Frontier: Essays in the History of Group Survival in Chicago and the Midwest*, ed. Melvin G. Holli and Peter d'A. Jones (Grand Rapids, MI: Wm. B. Eerdmans Publishing Company, 1977), 98–141. For a refutation of Leaming's view, see Nathaniel Deutsch's critical history of the "Ben Ishmael Tribe." Nathaniel Deutsch, *Inventing America's "Worst" Family: Eugenics, Islam, and the Fall and Rise of the Tribe of Ishmael* (Berkeley, CA: University of California Press, 2009), 11–15.

[18] See for examples, Douglas Grant, *The Fortunate Slave: An Illustration of African Slavery in the Early Eighteenth Century* (London: Oxford University Press, 1968); Terry Alford, *Prince among Slaves: The True Story of an African Prince Sold into Slavery in the American South* (New York: Oxford University Press, 1977), and Allan D. Austin, *African Muslims in Antebellum America: Transatlantic Stories and Spiritual Struggles* (New York: Routledge, 1997).

should not distract present attention from the larger social, political, and economic interconnections of the Atlantic world. Indeed, their lives draw attention to those interconnections by vividly personifying them.

Reading the early history of Islam in America exclusively through biographies can lead to misunderstandings. The first of these is quantitative. These individuals represent only a tiny fraction of the Muslims in antebellum America. Although there is no conclusive way of assessing the number of Muslims who were transported as slaves to the territories that became the United States, based on the size of the Muslim population in the region from which slaves were taken to America, scholars estimate that "tens of thousands" of African Muslims lived in colonial and antebellum America.[19] Surviving biographical data detail the lives of very few Muslims who, as a result of a combination of serendipity and their own extraordinary backgrounds, were sufficiently prominent to be memorialized in white America.

When centered on the biographies of extraordinary individuals, the history of Islam in colonial and antebellum America is reduced to little more than quaint stories of a "fortunate slave" or a "prince among slaves." These stories capture the imagination – as do those of Anthony Jansen and Estevanico – but do little to reshape larger narratives of American, Islamic, or African history.[20] While the fact remains that most of our evidence for the early history of Islam in America is spotty and biographical, the recent work of Michael Gomez, a historian of the African diaspora, has begun to demonstrate that this history need not be limited to personalized accounts.[21] An examination of historical evidence from regions in Africa from which slaves were purchased could be combined with American sources that identify slaves by either African names or Muslim nationalities. Such sources as runaway slave advertisements or slave ledgers help flesh out larger contexts of the early Muslims in America. Gomez's scholarship, in particular, adds the African dimension

---

[19] Gomez, *Black Crescent*, 166; Austin, *African Muslim: Transatlantic Stories*, 22.

[20] For a discussion of how stories of African "kings" in France and England captured the literary imagination of West Europeans around the eighteenth century, see Philip D. Curtin, *Africa Remembered: Narratives by West Africans from the Era of the Slave Trade* (Madison, WI: University of Wisconsin Press, 1967), 5–7.

[21] Gomez, "Muslims in Early America"; Michael Gomez, "Prayin' on duh Bead: Islam in Early America," in *Exchanging Our Country Marks: The Transformation of African Identities in the Colonial and Antebellum South* (Chapel Hill, NC: University of North Carolina Press, 1998), 54–87; Gomez, *Black Crescent*. See also Sylviane A. Diouf, *Servants of Allah: African Muslims Enslaved in the Americas* (New York: New York University Press, 1998).

of this larger historical context. What he finds is that African Muslims during the late eighteenth and early nineteenth centuries were increasingly involved in the Atlantic slave trade. One reason for their growing numbers was mainly the jihads of this period. These West African jihads were led by Muslim reformers who dramatically increased the presence of Islam in West Africa and sought to purify West African Islam from native practices, which these reformers deemed superstitious and heretical. They resulted in the establishment of a number of Muslim states in sub-Saharan Africa, the best-known of which is the Sokoto Caliphate established by the Fulbe scholar-warrior, 'Usman dan Fodio.[22] Non-Muslim war captives taken during these jihads were generally sold into slavery, and, as Gomez has argued, it appears that these jihads were "responsible for nearly all of the captives coming from the interior" of West Africa. This, in turn, helps explain one scholar's estimate that 75 percent of the Africans sold into the Atlantic slave trade between 1690 and 1800 came from the interior.[23]

The African trade in humans, of course, did not begin with the Atlantic slave trade or with the West African jihads of the eighteenth and nineteenth centuries. Slavery had a long and horrifically profitable history in Africa, with routes that traversed the Sahara, the Mediterranean Sea, and the Indian Ocean to reach markets in North Africa, the Middle East, Europe, and the Indian subcontinent, respectively.[24] The domination of the Atlantic slave trade changed the nature of the slave market in Africa, making it, by the time of the West African jihads, an engine of the continent's economy.[25] As a consequence, West African Muslim states established in this period depended heavily on the Atlantic slave trade and sought to monopolize its slave exports.[26]

While jihads stimulated the selling of non-Muslims into slavery, these jihads, as Gomez has observed, were not "one long, uninterrupted

[22] For a discussion of 'Usman dan Fodio and the Sokoto Calphate, see Murray Last, *The Sokoto Caliphate* (Harlow: Longmans, 1967); Mervyn Hiskett, *The Sword of the Truth: The Life and Times of the Shehu Usuman dan Fodio* (New York: Oxford University Press, 1973); and Joseph Smaldone, *Warfare in the Sokoto Caliphate: Historical and Sociological Perspectives* (Cambridge: Cambridge University Press, 1977).

[23] Gomez, "Muslims in Early America," 680; Walter Rodney, *A History of the Upper Guinea Coast, 1545–1800* (Oxford: Clarendon Press, 1970), 244–255, cited in Gomez, "Muslims in Early America," 679 and 680.

[24] For a historical survey of slavery in Africa, see Paul E. Lovejoy, *Transformations in Slavery: A History of Slavery in Africa*, 2nd ed. (Cambridge: Cambridge University Press, 2000).

[25] Ibid., 21.

[26] Ibid., 104.

Muslim march to victory. Non-Muslim populations fought back; in particular, the incursions into Muslim-ruled territory by Kundi Burama of Wassaulu lasted from the 1760s into the 1780s and wreaked havoc among the community of the Muslim faithful."[27] It seems that most African Muslims transported to America in the late eighteenth and early nineteenth centuries arrived at this fate as a result of wars between conquering Muslim reformers and their opponents in West Africa. Biographies of the few enslaved African Muslims, as Gomez's work has demonstrated, substantiate this conclusion. In what follows, I turn to a critical examination of their lives in the context of early American history.

DE-NEGROFICATION OF ENSLAVED AFRICAN MUSLIMS

One of the most striking aspects of the sources on the early history of Islam in America is the way in which African Muslims are disassociated in them from contemporary, popular perceptions of the "typical" Muslim or black African. To refer to these processes by which prejudicial patterns of cultural stereotypes are interrupted in shorthand, I employ the terms "de-negrofication" and "de-Islamicization." Some scholars have referred to the disassociation of individual black Africans in America from Africa or the "typical" black African as "de-Africanization,"[28] but as we shall see, their disassociation from Africa or African cultures was not as significant as their disassociation from Negroid attributes and stereotypes. For this reason, de-negrofication may be a more apt descriptive for us to employ. Thomas Bluett, the biographer of Job Ben Solomon (Ayuba ibn Sulayman), a Fulbe Muslim of some rank from Bundu who was captured by Mandingo bandits and sold to the English on the Gambia River, wrote of Job that "his Countenance was exceedingly pleasant, yet grave and composed; his hair [was] long, black, and curled, being very different from that of the Negroes commonly brought from *Africa*."[29] 'Umar ibn Said, a Fulbe from Futa Toro who was captured around 1807 when

---

[27] Gomez, "Muslims in Early America," 680.

[28] See for examples, Austin, *African Muslims: Transatlantic Stories*, 15; and Zahid H. Bukhari et al., ed., *Muslims' Place in the American Public Square: Hope, Fears, and Aspirations* (Walnut Creek, CA: AltaMira Press, 2004), xvii.

[29] Thomas Bluett, *Some Memoirs of the Life of Job, the Son of Solomon, the High Priest of Boonda in Africa* (London: Printed for Richard Ford, at the Angel in the Poultry, 1744), 46. A digitized version of this work can be found at the UNC Library's "Documenting the American South" web site: http://docsouth.unc.edu/neh/bluett/menu.html (accessed August 28, 2009).

FIGURE I. Ambrotype of 'Umar ibn Said. From the North Carolina Collection in the Photograph Archives of the University of North Carolina at Chapel Hill.

Bundu, Kaarta, and Khasso joined forces to counter the Muslim jihads and invaded Futa Toro in 1806–1807[30] was regularly referred to as an "Arabian prince."[31] The author of an anonymous article in *Farmer and Mechanic* (1888), sidestepping geography, magically transported this Fulbe from West Africa to Arabia to make 'Umar "a hereditary prince of the Foulah tribe in Arabia." It also made him a specimen of "white beauty": "His hair was straight. His features and form were as perfect as those of an Apollo Belvidere.... [H]e was no ordinary person, and was certainly not a negro."[32] Observers less inclined toward mythic depictions of 'Umar described him as "a fine looking man, copper colored, though an African."[33]

Descriptions of Ibrahima 'Abdul Rahman, who claimed to be the son of the famous Ibrahima Sori (the *Almamy* or religious and political leader

[30] Gomez, "Muslims in Early America," 690–691.
[31] See, for example, Louis T. Moore, "Prince of Arabia," *Greensboro Daily News*, February 13, 1927, reprinted in *African Muslims: A Sourcebook*, ed. Austin, 493–498.
[32] "Prince Omeroh," in *African Muslims: A Sourcebook*, ed. Austin, 489.
[33] J. F. Foard, "A True Story of an African Prince in a Southern Home," published in *African Muslims: A Sourcebook*, ed. Austin, 478.

of the Futa Jallon around 1751–1784),[34] differed depending on the way
in which he was intended to be received by the public. Those who sought
to evoke pity for 'Abdul Rahman's plight de-negrofied him, as Cyrus
Griffin, the editor of the *Southern Galaxy*, did:

That Prince ['Abul Rahman's slave name] is a Moor, there can be but little doubt.
He is six feet in height; and though sixty-five years of age he has the vigor of the
meridian of life. When he arrived in this country, his hair hung in flowing ringlets
far below his shoulders. Much against his will, his master compelled him to sub-
mit to sheers, and this ornament, which the Moor would part with in his own
county only with his life, since that time he has entirely neglected. It has become
coarse, and in some degree curly. His skin, also, by long service in the sun, and the
privations of bondage, has been materially changed; and his whole appearance
indicates the Foolah rather than the Moor. But Prince states explicitly, and with
an air of pride, that not a drop of negro blood runs in his veins. He places the
negro in a scale being infinitely below the Moor.[35]

Once 'Abdul Rahman and his wife, Isabella, were redeemed from slavery
with the help of John Quincy Adams's administration, they toured the
North for ten months in 1828 to raise money for the ransom of their
adult children before being transported by the American Colonization
Society to Liberia. In parts of the South, 'Abdul Rahman's tour raised concerns about the Adams administration using 'Abdul Rahman as "a traveling emancipator"[36] to agitate against slavery in its presidential campaign

---

[34] R. Cornevin, "Futa Djallon," in *The Encyclopaedia of Islam*, ed. Clifford E. Bosworth et
al., 2nd ed. (Leiden: Brill, 1986), vol. 2, 959a.

[35] Cyrus Griffin, "The Unfortunate Moor," *Natchez Southern Galaxy*, December 13,
1827, reprinted in *African Muslims: A Sourcebook*, ed. Austin, 135. Elsewhere Griffin
writes: "Prince is a Moor. Of this, however, his present appearance suggests a doubt. The
objection is that '*he is too dark for a Moor and his hair is short and curly*.' It is true such
is his present appearance; but it was materially different on his arrival in this country. His
hair was at that time, soft and very long, to a degree that precludes the possibility of his
being a negro. His complexion, too has undergone a change. Although modern physiol-
ogy does not allow color to be a necessary effect of climate, still one fact is certain that a
constant exposure to a vertical sun for many years, together with the privations incident
to the lower order of community, and an inattention to cleanliness, will produce a very
material change in the complexion. It is true his lips are thicker than are usually, those of
the Moor; but the animal frame is not that of the negro; his eyes, and, in fact, his entire
physiognomy is unlike that of any negro we have ever seen. And if the facial angle be
an infallible criterion the point is established, his being equal and perhaps greater, than
most of the whites." Griffin, *Natchez Southern Galaxy*, June 5, 1828, reprinted in *African
Muslims: A Sourcebook*, ed. Austin, 139–140.

[36] Andrew Marschalk, "Mr. Adams and the emancipation of Slaves and the Violation of
the Faith of the Administration," *Natchez Statesman and Gazette*, October 16, 1828;
reprinted in *African Muslims: A Sourcebook*, ed. Austin, 202.

against Andrew Jackson, a southern slave owner. 'Abdul Rahman's story was so well known that a handbill distributed in Louisiana four days before the election in 1828 read:

LOUISANIANS! (sic) Remember that ANDREW JACKSON IS A MAN OF THE SOUTH, A SLAVE HOLDER, A COTTON PLANTER. Recollect the iniquitous and profligate PLOT of ADAMS and CLAY to excite the prejudices of your Northern brethren against the SOUTH by employing an emancipated NEGRO TO ELECTIONEER FOR THEM.[37]

The southern papers, in an attempt to slander Adams, depicted 'Abdul Rahman as a "savage negro" in order to diminish any pity he may have gained in the public eye.

In his journey through the free states he has artfully concealed the fact, of which in Mississippi he used to boast, that he himself in Africa owned 2000 slaves whom he could kill and whip (and did kill, torture, and whip) as he pleased.... He neglected to dry the weeping eyes of the Bostonians by telling the fact to which hundreds can testify, that Mr. Foster had continually to keep an eye upon him and to curb his sanguinary temper to prevent him from exercising cruelty on his fellow servants. He neglected to tell that his African schemes of torture and his blood thirsty disposition caused him to be viewed by the negores of the neighborhood as the *bug bear or negro devil*, whose very name would terrify the unruly into obedience.[38]

African Muslims were painfully aware of the oppressive linkage slavery reinforced between one's color and humanity. In the 1850s, Mahommah Gardo Baquaqua, an enslaved Muslim from an elite merchant family in Djougou, observed that "some persons suppose that the African has none of the finer feelings of humanity within his breast, and that the milk of human kindness runs not through his composition; this is an error, an error of the grossest kind;... the only difference is their color, and that has been arranged by him who made the world and all that therein is."[39] Nicholas Said, born Muhammad ibn Sa'id in Kouka in the kingdom of Borno, similarly commented that "Africa has been, through prejudice and ignorance, so sadly misrepresented, that anything like intelligence, industry, etc., is

---

[37] As reprinted in *New Orleans Louisiana Advertiser*, November 4, 1828, reprinted in *African Muslims: A Sourcebook*, ed. Austin, 226.

[38] P. K. Wagner, "To the Freemen of Louisiana," *New Orleans Louisiana Advertiser*, October 25, 1828, 2; reprinted in *African Muslims: A Sourcebook*, ed. Austin, 216–217.

[39] Robin Law and Paul E. Lovejoy, eds., *The Biography of Mahommah Gardo Baquaqua: His Passage from Slavery to Freedom in Africa and America* (Princeton, NJ: Markus Wiener Publishers, 2003), 145–146; *African Muslims: A Sourcebook*, ed. Austin, 622.

believed not to exist among its natives."[40] Other African Muslims did not
share in Baquaqua's and Said's sober attitude toward skin color; they sought
to disassociate themselves from Negroid stereotypes and complied with
whites' de-negrofication of them. The journal of the South Carolina Royal
Council records a petition from 1753 on behalf of individuals captured
in 1736 by the Portuguese in a battle for "Maguson."[41] A Captain Henry
Daubrig purchased their freedom on the condition that they would serve
him in South Carolina for five years. Once in South Carolina, however, they
were sold to Daniel LaRoche, for whom they slaved for fifteen years. Their
petition was written in "Arabick" by "Abel Conder" ('Abd al-Qadir?) and
"Mahamut" (Mahmud), requesting to be freed from slavery because they
were "Moors" from "Sali on the Barbary Coast" and not black Africans.[42]
Cyrus Griffin of the *Southern Galaxy* wrote that 'Abdul Rahman claimed
that "not a drop of negro blood runs in his veins."[43] Similar assertions were
attributed to 'Umar ibn Said: "Some thought occasionally that Moreau was
of negro extraction. He always emphasized the fact that he was an Arabian
and not a native of Africa."[44]

In their collaboration with whites' de-negrofication of them, African
Muslims were in part acting out of self-interest. They hoped that such
complicity could gain them better treatment and possibly passage back
to Africa. Furthermore, as Gomez has suggested, they may have been
"deeply affected by racist views of whites toward other Africans" and
thus sought to "deny any similarity to them."[45] At the same time, African
Muslims also displayed a certain sense of superiority. Most of the documented African Muslims in antebellum America, in fact, derived from
noble and literate backgrounds, levels of cultivation that attracted the
attention of white Americans. In *A Twelvemonth's Residence in the
West Indies*, for example, Richard Madden prefaced his discussion
of the African Muslims he had met in Jamaica by stating that "[t]he
Mandingos are said to be superior in intelligence to the other classes.

[40] Said, *The Autobiography of Nicholas Said*, 13–14.
[41] This was most likely the Portuguese fort city of Mazagan, which stood where El Jadida
stands today. Mazagan was recaptured by Moroccans in 1769.
[42] *South Carolina Council Journal*, note 21 (March 3, 1753), 298–299; James W. Hagy,
"Muslim Slaves, Abducted Moors, African Jews, Misnamed Turks, and an Asiatic Greek
Lady: Some Examples of Non-European Religious and Ethnic Diversity in South Carolina
Prior to 1861," *Carologue: Bulletin of the South Carolina Historical Society* 9 (1993),
25–26; and Gomez, *Black Crescent*, 149.
[43] Alford, *Prince among Slaves*, 73.
[44] Moore, "Prince of Arabia," cited, 494.
[45] Gomez, "Muslims in Early America," 704.

Many of them read and write Arabic; and my own experience confirms the account of Bryan Edwards[46] as to their priding themselves on their mental superiority over the other negroes."[47] These enslaved Muslims, then, emerged from elites of West African societies, and thus it is not surprising that they elevated themselves over other black Africans. There is also evidence that as Muslims they held themselves above black pagans and perhaps even white Christians. 'Abdul Rahman, for example, rebuked white Christians: "I tell you the Testament very good law, you no follow it; you no pray often enough; you greedy after money." "You good man, you join the religion?" "See, you want more land, more neegurs; you make neegur work hard." He explained that in his country, there is a superior order. "I tell you, man own slaves – he join the religion – he very good – he make he slaves work till noon – go to church – then till the sun go down they work for themselves – they raise cotton, sheep, cattle, plenty, plenty."[48] Georgia Bryan Conrad, on a visit to the Spalding plantation in Sapelo Island, Georgia, observed that Bilali Muhammad's family, from Timbo, "held themselves aloof from the others as if they were conscious of their own superiority."[49] During the War of 1812, when British troops landed on the shores of South Carolina, Bilali is reported to have offered to help his master defend the plantation with the retort that "I will answer for every Negro of the true faith but not for these Christian dogs of yours."[50] 'Umar ibn Said was also said to have been "very religious and never associated with the other negro slaves."[51] William B. Hodgson, who had served in the U.S. consulates of Algiers, Constantinople, and Tunis and who was a founding member of the American Oriental Society, a member of the American Philosophical and Ethnological Societies,[52] and a friend

[46] See Bryan Edwards, *The History, Civil and Commercial, of the British Colonies in the West Indies*, 2nd ed., vol. 2 (London: J. Stockdale, 1794), 65.

[47] R. R. Madden, *A Twelvemonth's Residence in the West Indies, During the Transition from Slavery to Apprenticeship*, vol. 1 (London: James Cochrane and Co., 1835), 127. See also Madden, "Letter IX, to J. F. Savory, March 30, 1835," in *Twelvemonth's*, vol. I, 98–102, reprinted in *African Muslims: A Sourcebook*, ed. Austin, 547.

[48] Cyrus Griffin, *Natchez Southern Galaxy*, May 29, June 5 and 12, and July 5, 1828, reprinted in *African Muslims: A Sourcebook*, ed. Austin, 142–143.

[49] Georgia Bryan Conrad, "Reminiscences of a Southern Woman," *Southern Workman* 30, no. 5 (May 1901), 252.

[50] Ella May Thornton, *Law Library Journal*, XLVIII (1955): 228–229, reprinted in *African Muslims: A Sourcebook*, ed. Austin, 291.

[51] Calvin Leonard, "The Story of Prince Omeroh," a Greensboro (NC) newspaper, March 25, 1934, reprinted in *African Muslims: A Sourcebook*, ed. Austin, 500.

[52] Austin, *African Muslims: Transatlantic Stories*, 111.

of James Hamilton Couper, the owner of another enslaved Bilali, Salih Bilali of Massina, in his *Notes on Northern Africa* made similar observations about the Fulbe (or Fula) in general: "The Foulahs of every region represent themselves to be *white* men, and proudly assert their superiority to the black tribes among whom they live."[53]

Enslaved African Muslims' sense of superiority can be attributed both to their own background as slaveholders and to the West African jihads of the eighteenth and nineteenth centuries which pitted Muslims against non-Muslims in an effort to purge West Africa of paganism. As Michael Gomez has argued, enslaved African Muslims' sense of superiority resulted in a significant stratification of African American society. "Vis-à-vis other Africans, and consistent with the record in Brazil and the Caribbean," Gomez writes, "Muslims were generally viewed by slaveholders as 'more intelligent, more reasonable, more physically attractive, more dignified people.'"[54] Ulrich Bolnell Phillips cites slaveholders' preference for the Senegalese, "who had a strong Arabic strain in their ancestry" to employ as "commanders over other negroes."[55] In 1803, Dr. Collins described the predominantly Muslim Senegalese as a "handsome race of people, in features resembling the whites.... Many of them converse in the Arabic language, and some are sufficiently instructed even to write it. They are excellent for the care of cattle and horses, and for domestic services; though little qualified for the ruder labours of the field."[56] Another reason for slave owners' preference of Muslims may have been that they came from Senegambia, a region known for its expert knowledge of rice and indigo cultivation.[57]

In other words, African Muslims cooperated in their own denegrofication both for "racial" benefits they stood to gain, and out of the intrinsic sense of superiority to which they felt entitled by virtue of their ethnic and religious backgrounds.

---

[53] William B. Hodgson, *Notes on Northern Africa: The Sahara and Soudan* (New York: Wiley and Putnam, 1844), 50.

[54] Gomez, *The Black Crescent*, 173–184. See also Newbell N. Puckett, *Folk Beliefs of the Southern Negro* (Chapel Hill, NC: University of North Carolina Press, 1926), 528–529 and Charles Lyell, *Second Visit to the United States of America*, 2 vols. (New York: Harper and Brothers, 1849), vol. 1, 266.

[55] Ulrich Bonnell Phillips, *American Negro Slavery: A Survey of the Supply, Employment and Control of Negro Labor as Determined by the Plantation Régime* (New York: D. Appleton and Company, 1929), 42.

[56] Dr. Collins, *Practical Rules for the Management and Medical Treatment of Negro Slaves in the Sugar Colonies* (London: J. Barfield, 1803), 41–42.

[57] Gomez, "Muslims in Early America," 700.

Further benefits could have been accrued by labeling an African slave a "Moor." This term originally denoted Muslims of Arab and Berber background in Northwest Africa (modern day Morocco, Tunisia, Algeria, and Mauritania) who conquered Southern Spain in the eighth century. They were generally supposed to have dark or black skin even though "white Moors" were also recognized. In eighteenth- and nineteenth-century America, Moors were more specifically associated with the inhabitants of independent and semi-independent states of the Barbary Coast, which played an important role in the Mediterranean trade. Pirating and privateering had been a common practice in which both Europeans and North Africans engaged for centuries. States used both diplomatic and military means to safeguard their merchant vessels in the Mediterranean from pirates and privateers. The American public at the turn of the nineteenth century was well aware of the so-called Barbary States (Algiers, Tunis, Tripoli, and the Kingdom of Morocco) and their corsairs in the Mediterranean Sea. The first merchant ship flying an American flag was seized on October 11, 1784 after several delays by the newly independent nation to form its own treaty with Sultan Sidi Muhammad ibn 'Abdullah of Morocco (r. 1757–1790). Thereafter, several other American ships were captured and members of their crews held for ransom. For the next three decades the United States' relationship with the Barbary States was negotiated through a series of amity treaties, U.S. tributes paid to the Barbary States, and military clashes that came to be known as the "Barbary Wars."[58] A number of Americans who fell victim to the corsairs of North Africa wrote about their experiences as "white, Christian slaves" in Muslim Africa.[59] This genre of captivity narrative had captured the American imagination at the turn of the nineteenth century to such an extent that some literary entrepreneurs published fictional Barbary captivity narratives.[60]

[58] For discussion of U.S.-Barbary relations in this period, see Frank Lambert, *The Barbary Wars: American Independence in the Atlantic World* (New York: Hill and Wang, 2005); Richard B. Parker, *Uncles Sam in Barbary: A Diplomatic History* (Gainesville, FL: University Press of Florida, 2004); and Allison, *The Crescent Obscured.*

[59] For examples and an excellent overview of this genre of early American writings, see Paul Baepler, ed., *White Slaves, African Masters: An Anthology of American Barbary Captivity Narratives* (Chicago, IL: University of Chicago Press, 1999).

[60] See, for examples, Lucinda Martin [Maria Martin], *History of the Captivity And Sufferings of Mrs. Maria Martin, Who Was Six Years a Slave in Algiers: Two of Which She Was Confined in a Dark and Dismal Dungeon, Loaded with Irons* (Boston, MA: W. Carary, 1807); Mary Velnet, *The Captivity and Sufferings of Mrs. Mary Velnet, Who Was Seven Years a Slave in Tripoli, Three of Which She Was Confined in a Dungeon, Loaded with Irons, and Four Times Put to the Most Cruel Tortures Ever Invented by Man. To Which Is Added, The Lunatic Governor, and Adelaide, or the Triumph of Constancy, a*

Against this historical backdrop, enslaved Moors in the United States proved diplomatically valuable in U.S.-Barbary relations and to American trade in the Mediterranean. Andrew Marschalk realized this when he sent 'Abdul Rahman's Arabic letter to Thomas B. Reed, a U.S. senator from Mississippi, to forward to the "Emperor of Morocco" via the U.S. State Department. In his cover to 'Abdul Rahman's letter, Marschalk misidentified 'Abdul Rahman as belonging to "the royal family of Morocco." 'Abdul Rahman's letter itself seems to have been composed solely of some verses from the Qur'an; these verses were presumably all that he was able to write in Arabic after three decades of slaving in the United States. Thomas Mullowny, the U.S. consul in Tangier, recognized that the letter was intended to prove that 'Abdul Rahman was Muslim and showed it to the Pasha of the Moroccan ruler, who wanted the "Moor" to be freed and agreed to pay for all of his expenses. Mullowny advised the State Department to have 'Abdul Rahman sent to Morocco because "his liberty would give me an important power," presumably in negotiating the release of American captives and castaways from the Barbary shores and assuring the safe access for American ships to Mediterranean ports.[61] Later, when the Adams administration came under attack (ironically through the pen of Marschalk himself), for using 'Abdul Rahman as a tool against Andrew Jackson, Cyrus Griffin wrote in his own defense that he had suggested to Marschalk "the necessity of informing the President of the mistake, as there would be less reason for the interference of the government; (if indeed, the government would interfere at all, of which I had strong doubts) in relation to a personage, however, important, from the interior of Africa, than a native of one of the Barbary states, with which it was the highest importance that we maintain friendly relations."[62]

In considering 'Abdul Rahman's case, I do not want to overstate the importance of enslaved Moors for U.S.-Barbary relations. There is no

---

Tale (Boston, MA: T. Abbott, 1828); Thomas Nicholson, *An Affecting Narrative of the Captivity and Sufferings of Thomas Nicholson [a Native of New Jersey] Who Has Been Six Years a Prisoner Among the Algerines, and from Whom He Fortunately Made His Escape a Few Months Previous to Commodore Decatur's Late Expedition. To Which Is Added, A Concise Description of Algiers of the Customs, Manners, Etc of the Natives – and Some Particulars of Commodore Decatur's Late Expedition, Against the Barbary Powers* (Boston, MA: Printed for G. Walker, 1816); cited in Baepler, *White Slaves*, 11.

[61] Alford, *Prince among Slaves*, 98–101.

[62] Cyrus Griffin, *Daily National Intelligencer*, November 27, 1828, 3, orig. pub. in *Natchez Southern Galaxy*, October 23, 1828; reprinted in *African Muslims: A Sourcebook*, ed. Austin, 204.

evidence of the government interfering with the slave labor that black Muslims from Northwest Africa provided in the United States. Even when Secretary of State Henry Clay agreed to use Treasury funds to bring 'Abdul Rahman to Washington, D.C. "for the purpose of making favorable impressions on behalf of the United States," he made sure to attain the consent of 'Abdul Rahman's master and agreed to deny 'Abdul Rahman his liberty in the United States.[63] Incidentally, it was because of this stipulation that Marschalk and other Southerners were later angered by 'Abdul Rahman's tour with the American Colonization Society in the North and accused the Adams administration of lying and treating him as a tool against Andrew Jackson.

DE-ISLAMICIZATION OF ENSLAVED AFRICAN MUSLIMS

In addition to being de-negrofied, contemporary reports on early African Muslims in America also *de-Islamicized* them by either disassociating them from the negative stereotypes of Islam prevalent at the time or by presenting them as converts to Christianity. Islam was generally associated with licentiousness and despotism under the Ottoman Empire, which was a waning but nonetheless formidable rival of western European states in the eighteenth and nineteenth centuries. Thomas Bluett thus wrote about Job: "'tis known he was *Mahometan*, but more moderate in his Sentiments than most of that Religion are. He did not believe a sensual Paradise, nor many other ridiculous and vain Traditions, which pass current among the Generality of the *Turks*."[64] While 'Abdul Rahman was still in the South, it was said that "although he adheres strictly to the religion of his country (Mahometism) he expresses the greatest respect for the Christian religion."[65] In another place, he was said to be "still, *nominally* at least, a Mohamedan," but "friendly disposed toward the Christian religion."[66] When he arrived in the North, however, touring various cities to raise funds for the manumission of his children under the auspices of the American Colonization Society, he was presented

---

[63] Alford, *Prince among Slaves*, 107. See also Andrew Marschalk, "The Captive African Restored to Liberty: Letter from a Gentleman of Natchez to a Lady of Cincinnati," Natchez, April 7, 1828, reprinted in *African Muslims: A Sourcebook*, ed. Austin, 149–151.

[64] Bluett, *Some Memoirs of the Life of Job*, 51.

[65] This letter was reprinted several times. Marschalk, *Freedom's Journal of New York City*, March 16, 1828, 57, 61, reprinted in *African Muslims: A Sourcebook*, ed. Austin, 149–151.

[66] Griffin to Gurley, Natchez, December 13, 1827, reprinted in *African Muslims: A Sourcebook*, 134–136.

as a convert to Christianity who had been baptized in the Baptist church.[67] Individual enslaved African Muslims complied with their de-Islamicization, just as they did with their de-negrofication, in order to improve their lot in antebellum America. When Rev. Thomas Gallaudet sent 'Abdul Rahman an Arabic New Testament and an Arabic translation of Hugo Grotius' apology for Christianity, *On the Truth of the Christian Religion*,[68] 'Abdul Rahman read the writing on the wall; the American Colonization Society intended to help Christianize Africa through the colonization of African Americans in Liberia. 'Abdul Rahman replied to the Reverend (who later became his keenest advocate) that "after I take this book home, I hope I shall get many to become Christians.... I shall not go to fight them but to beg them. I go to give them light, I will show them the way for the Christian religion."[69] 'Abdul Rahman's purported conversion to Christianity and his promise to help its propagation in Africa was most likely a ploy to boost support for the manumission of his children, for once he was back in Africa, it was reported that 'Abdul Rahman "died in the faith of his fathers – a Mahometan."[70]

In the above-mentioned campaign against the Adams administration in which 'Abdul Rahman had become a tool, Southern papers sought to vilify 'Abdul Rahman by (re-) Islamicizing him just as they negrofied him. That is, they associated him once again with the negative stereotypes of Islam: "The said negro was ... educated in Arabic literature and bro'tup in the Mahometan faith, a faith which he has never relinquished.... Such is the blood thirsty, tyrannical Mahometan negro, who is now travelling himself and suite, up and down through the free states in pomp, with the President's passport in his pocket."[71]

Of the African Muslims in antebellum America who surmounted racial barriers to be memorialized in white society, only Bilali Muhammad and

[67] See for example, Thomas Gallaudet, *Springfield (MA) Hampden Journal*, October 8, 1828, 3, reprinted in *African Muslims: A Sourcebook*, 168; and "Abduhl Rahahman," *New York Journal of Commerce*, October 16, 1828, reprinted in *African Muslims: A Sourcebook*, ed. Austin, 170.

[68] Alford, *Prince among Slaves*, 155.

[69] *Freedom's Journal of New York City*, June 20, 1828, orig. pub. in the *Connecticut Observer*; reprinted in *African Muslims: A Sourcebook*, ed. Austin, 157.

[70] H. Niles et al., ed. *Niles' Weekly Register Containing Political, Historical Geographical, Scientifical, Statistical, Economical, and Biographical Documents, Essays and Facts, Together with Notices of the Arts and Manufactures, and a Record of the Events of the Times from September, 1829, to March, 1830*, vol. 37, 181. See also Alford, *Prince among Slaves*, 283.

[71] P. K. Wagner, *New Orleans Louisiana Advertiser*, October 35, 1828, 2, reprinted in *African Muslims: A Sourcebook*, ed. Austin, 216–217.

Salih Bilali, who slaved on the coastal plantations of Georgia, were not portrayed as Christian converts. Both of these individuals were presented as adherents of Islam and as African survivals in America. Unsurprisingly, neither ever lived freely in the antebellum South or had the opportunity to return to Africa. In other words, neither they nor the white Americans who wrote about them had much to gain by de-Islamicizing or de-negrofying them.

AFRICAN MUSLIM SLAVES AS LIMINAL FIGURES

The de-negrofication and de-Islamicization of African Muslims in the extant sources for the early history of Islam in America demonstrate the fluidity of racial and religious identities as sociopolitical constructs. From the above discussion, it is clear that there were cultural, religious, political, and economic stakes in the way in which the bodies and beliefs of African Muslims were represented in antebellum America. In depicting these enslaved African Muslims as exceptions to the prevailing negative stereotypes of blacks and Muslims, our sources redefined them as liminal figures who stood at shifting communal boundaries defined by race and religion. The concept of liminality was advanced in anthropology by Victor Turner, who defined "liminal entities" as being "neither here nor there; they are betwixt and between the positions assigned and arrayed by law, custom, convention, and ceremonial."[72] As such, liminality is generally associated with rites of passage through which individuals transition from one position in the community to another (e.g., from childhood to adulthood or from being an outsider to becoming an initiated insider). There is, however, another aspect to the concept that points not to individuals' transitions from one state to another within a community but to the transition of the community itself from one mode of self-identification to another. As Robert Dannin has explained, "[t]he anthropological concept of *liminality* expresses the idea that all societies incorporate the seed of their own denial to a greater or lesser extent."[73] The liminal person, who stands between and betwixt categories through which communities organize themselves, on the one hand, reinforces existing communal categories by transitioning through her liminal state and entering into a new state or category of belonging within the community, but her state

---

[72] Victor Turner, *The Ritual Process: Structure and Anti-Structure* (New York: Aldine de Gruyter, 1969), 95, see also 94–130.
[73] Robert Dannin, *Black Pilgrimage to Islam* (New York: Oxford University Press), 16.

of liminality also points to the shortcoming and inadequacies of existing structures that reduce her to invisibility or non-being while she is in her liminal state. To give a concrete example, puberty as a liminal state of transition reinforces the structural distinction made in some societies between childhood and adulthood, but it also points to the arbitrariness of these social distinctions that make no room for the adolescent undergoing puberty. The way communities structure themselves, however, could change by celebrating the liminal person or empowering her to the point where her liminal state comes into being as one of the categories communities use to structure themselves. As such, the liminal persons would effect a change in the way in which members of the community self-identify. In other words, the intermediary position of the liminal person need not only point to individuals' transition from one state to another within the community but it could also encompass the community's transition from one mode of self-identification to another.

Anglo-Americans' representation of enslaved African Muslims in antebellum America as liminal figures, though intended to rethink racial and religious categories in antebellum American society, was not instrumental in actually doing so. Their numbers were not significant to have such an enormous impact on American society. Nonetheless, as liminal figures, African Muslims provided an avenue by which some Anglo-Americans advanced a different understanding of an English or American community in which the existing boundaries between races and religions were temporarily blurred, mainly, for commercial and missionary purposes. These white, Protestant Anglo-Americans sought to use the "semi-civilized" African Muslims whom they encountered in bondage to advance trade into the African interior and to Christianize the continent.

LIMINALITY OF ENSLAVED AFRICAN MUSLIMS AND COMMERCE

An example of the commercial benefits Anglo-Americans stood to gain from the liminality of enslaved African Muslims is found in the Royal African Company's employment of Job Ben Solomon. Job was taken captive by Mandingo bandits while he was on his way home, ironically, after having traded two of his father's slaves for some cows. He was sold to the English on the Gambia River and ended up in Maryland where he managed to dispatch a letter in Arabic to his father. This letter came to the attention of James Oglethorpe, the founder of Georgia, who issued a bond for Job's release and passage to England. In England,

Job became acquainted with the gentry and even met the royal family. In 1734, he was elected an honorary member to the prestigious Spalding's Gentleman Society, assuring himself a place among such notables as Sir Isaac Newton and Alexander Pope.[74] In England's high society, Job was courted, particularly by John, the second Duke of Montague, to help the Royal African Company expand its trade in gold and Arabic gum in the African inlands. He thus returned to Africa as an agent of the Royal African Company. The Royal African Company instructed its agents to treat him well and to send someone along with him on his return to his own country so that "a trade and Correspondence between the nation of those parts and our highest Factory" may be established.[75] Trade in sub-Saharan Africa in the eighteenth century was dominated by the French. One of the strategies used by the French to bolster their commercial hegemony in the region was to form solid ties with local elites by bringing them to Paris and impressing them with the achievements of French society. The grand reception Job received, particularly at the hand of the Duke of Montague, aimed to duplicate the success the French had achieved through this strategy.[76] Job's efforts to open trade between the Royal African Company and the African interior were also a matter of some popular interest. One of his letters to the physician Sir Hans Sloane, in which he indicated that "he has been in the country where the Gum arabick grows ... and can assist the English in that Trade" and that he is willing to assist further the English trade in gold, was widely distributed in not only English but also colonial newspapers.[77]

Job was not a passive partner. By agreeing to assist the English, Job not only assured his passage home as a trading agent of the Royal African Company, he also negotiated with the Royal African Company to guarantee "that if any of his Religion should at any time be Sold to any of our Factors, That upon application for their Redemption and upon paying two other good slaves for one, they may be restored to their Liberty."[78]

In the early nineteenth century, American philanthropists and entrepreneurs also recognized in 'Abdul Rahman the potential to advance

---

[74] See Austin, *African Muslims: Transatlantic Stories*, 56; Grant, *The Fortunate Slave*, 101.

[75] Grant, *The Fortunate Slave*, 110–111.

[76] Ibid., 159.

[77] See, for example, reprints of his letter to Sir Hans Sloane in *The Boston Weekly News-Letter* (January 6, 1737); *American Weekly Mercury* (March 17, 1736–24, March 1737); *Virginia Gazette* (January 28, 1737); and *New England Weekly Journal* (February 1, 1737).

[78] Grant, *The Fortunate Slave*, 110.

American trade in Africa. In the notice of 'Abdul Rahman's demise published in the *African Repository*, the mouthpiece of the American Colonization Society, it was stated that

> in the death of this individual, the Colony sustained a great loss; for it was his intention to visit his native country, and remain there until he could raise funds to liberate his children; he was then to return and reside in the Colony [of Liberia], after having made arrangements for opening a direct communication from his own country to this place so as to divert at least a portion of the trade from Sierra Leone into this channel.[79]

By diverting the trade between the African inlands and Sierra Leone to Liberia, Americans sought to diminish the commercial influence of the British whose control over Sierra Leone began in 1808 and lasted until 1961. Indeed, it was not until Reverend Gallaudet was able to enlist the support of the New York businessman, philanthropist, and owner of the *Journal of Commerce*, Arthur Tappan, that the American Colonization Society began to collect large enough donation for the purchase of 'Abdul Rahman's children and their fare back to Africa.[80] Gallaudet astutely tapped Tappan because of the businessman's desire to train "some coloured youths to go to Africa, even to its very interior, to become *Commerical Agents,* & possibly (inter nos) to induce the Government of the United States to appoint a Consul to reside, if practicable, at Timbo."[81] Like Job, 'Abdul Rahman willingly participated in the scheme to advance trade between his homeland and the country of his enslavers. In one of his letters from Africa, he assured his sponsors that "as soon as the rains are over, if God be with me, I shall try to bring my countrymen to the Colony, and to open the trade."[82]

THE INTERPLAY BETWEEN MISSIONS AND COMMERCE

At the most basic level, the missionary purpose of portraying African Muslims in antebellum America as liminal figures was the same as its

---

[79] John D. Legare, "An Account of an Agricultural Excursion Made into the South of Georgia in the Winter of 1832, by the Editor," *Southern Agriculturist* VI (March 1833), 138–147, reprinted in *African Muslims: A Sourcebook*, ed. Austin, 238.

[80] Alford, *Prince among Slaves*, 159f.

[81] Letter from Thomas Gallaudet to Gurley, November 8, 1828, American Colonization Society Papers, Manuscripts Division, the Library of Congress, Washington, D.C., cited in Alford, *Prince among Slaves*, 160.

[82] 'Abdul Rahaman, Letter from Monrovia, Liberia, May 5, 1829, extract in *African Repository* (July 1829), 158, reprinted in *African Muslims: A Sourcebook.*, ed. Austin, 237.

commercial purpose; it was to sell a product – the product being Christianity in this case. African Muslims who were de-Islamicized or had genuinely converted to Christianity were seen as "instruments"[83] who could promote Christianity alongside trade in Africa. In the minds of most nineteenth-century Euro-Americans, Christianity and commerce went hand in hand. John Comaroff and Jean Comaroff's observations on the relationship between commerce and conversion in the nineteenth century, though made in regard to British evangelists in South Africa, are equally applicable to American aspirations for the African American colony of Liberia:

Saving the savage meant teaching the savage to save. It meant, too, that he be taught to recast his inefficient mode of production so that, using God's gifts, he might bring forth the greatest possible abundance. Only then would black communities be animated by the spirit of commerce that – along with the Gospel of Christ – promoted exchange on a worldwide scale. Only then might they be part of the sacred economy of civilized society.[84]

In this "sacred economy," Christianity valued commodity as a divine gift thus changing individuals' relationship with property. As such, Christianity placed a burden on commercial activity. Commerce was not only to amass wealth but also to shape how individuals relate to the material world. Reverend Gallaudet made the Christian expectations of commerce clear when he indicated that through 'Abdul Rahman "we may be able to extend our commercial relations to the very heart of Africa, and the influence of our institutions also. As christians (sic) we must especially rejoice that an opportunity will be afforded for diffusing the blessings of christianity (sic) to that dark and benighted region."[85]

Cyrus Griffin, in commending 'Abdul Rahman to the American Colonization Society wrote:

I cannot persuade myself but that you will seize with avidity an instrument that appears so completely adapted to your wants. Is it impossible – is it *improbable* that 'Abdul Rahahman may become the chief pioneer of civilization to unenlightened Africa – that, armed with the Bible, he may be the foremost of that band of pilgrims who shall roll back the mighty waves of

[83] Griffin, "The Unfortunate Moor" in *African Muslims: A Sourcebook*, ed. Austin, 136.

[84] John L. Comaroff and Jean Comaroff, *Of Revelation and Revolution: The Dialectics of Modernity on a South African Frontier*, vol. 2 (Chicago, IL: The University of Chicago Press, 1997), 166.

[85] "Abduhl Rahahman," *New York Journal of Commerce*, October 16, 1828, reprinted in *African Muslims: A Sourcebook*, 175.

darkness and superstition, and plant the cross of the Redeemer upon the furthermost mountains of Kong![86]

After meeting with leaders of the American Colonization Society and with President John Quincy Adams and Secretary of State Henry Clay, the secretary of the society, Ralph Randolph Gurley, agreed with Griffin that 'Abdul Rahman could be instrumental to the society's efforts to spread Christianity and "civilization" in Africa by sending African American colonists to Liberia. Gurley wrote, "We have repeatedly conversed with Prince, since his arrival in our City [Washington, D.C.]; nor have our expectations concerning him, in any respect been disappointing. He is intelligent, modest, and obliging."[87]

Around 1850, W. L. Judd, who was responsible for baptizing Mahommah Gardo Baquaqua in Haiti, sought to train him for missionary work in Africa hoping that he would serve "as a messenger of mercy to the dark land of his birth."[88] Judd explained his recruitment of Baquaqua for missionary work to the American Baptist Free Mission Society by arguing that missions to Africa could only be successful with the aid of natives. White Americans and Europeans have been trying to Christianize Africa for years, Judd argued, "but they go there to die ... Missionaries, therefore, must be sought among the colored inhabitants of the West India Islands. Descended from natives of Africa, and always accustomed to a tropical climate, they can go to the land of their fathers with comparative safety."[89]

The analogy between proselytization and commerce is particularly apt at this time because the modern era witnessed the growing commodification of religion through the mass printing and worldwide distribution of religious texts. Christian missionaries translated and distributed copies of the New Testament and other Christian texts wherever they went. Recall that 'Abdul Rahman was given Arabic translations of the New Testament and Grotius's *On the Truth of the Christian Religion*. He pledged to Reverend Thomas H. Gallaudet "to take home the two

---

[86] Griffin, "The Unfortunate Moor," in *African Muslims: A Sourcebook*, ed. Austin, 136.

[87] Griffin, "Abduhl Rahahman, The Unfortunate Moorish Prince," *African Repository*, May 1828, 77–81, reprinted in *African Muslims: A Sourcebook*, ed. Austin, 145 and n. 40 on 248.

[88] Judd's description of the baptism is reprinted in *African Muslims: A Sourcebook*, ed. Austin, 594, orig. pub. in the *Christian Contributor*. Also cited in *The Adventures of Mahommah Gardo Baquaqua*, see *African Muslims: A Sourcebook*, ed. Austin, 638.

[89] Judd, in the *Christian Contributor*, reprinted in *African Muslims: A Sourcebook*, ed. Austin, 592.

books, the Arabic Testament and that you sent me" and through the printed texts persuade young Africans to follow Christianity. At the request of the Secretary of the Royal Society, Cromwell Mortimer, the Society for Promoting Christian Knowledge asked one of its associates, the Arabist George Sale, who published an acclaimed English translation of the Qur'an in 1733, to provide Job Ben Solomon Arabic copies of the Pentateuch, the New Testament, and the Psalter to carry back "to his own Country in the Midland parts of Africa."[90] The Society itself had printed the New Testament and the Psalter that Job carried to Africa presumably to help spread Christianity there. Job reciprocated by writing three copies of the Qur'an from memory for his English patrons.[91]

There were other instances of the export of Christianity in the form of the printed Bible. Theodore Dwight, Secretary of the Ethnological Society of New York, informed Reverend Daniel Bliss, President of the Syrian Protestant College (which later became the American University of Beirut) that he knew of a slave in North Carolina ('Umar ibn Said) who was literate in Arabic and suspected that others from his native land also knew Arabic. Dwight also knew of another enslaved African Muslim, Lamine Kaba (or "Lamen Kaba"), who was literate in Arabic. Lamine Kaba was a formally trained Muslim scholar who taught about fifty-five of his own pupils for five years in Kaba, Guinea. He was kidnapped and sold into slavery during an excursion to the coast to purchase paper. As a slave, Lamine went from master to master until his last owner liberated him in 1834. Like 'Abdul Rahman, he supposedly converted to Christianity and came under the care of the American Colonization Society, giving lectures in places such as New York City to raise money for his own repatriation and for the Society's efforts to colonize free African Americans in Liberia.[92] Dwight had interviewed Kaba extensively about the Arabic education system in his native land. In his exchanges with Daniel Bliss, Dwight informed Bliss that there are numerous West Africans literate in Arabic. This led Bliss to arrange for Arabic Bibles to be sent to Liberia for distribution in the interior. Included in the Bibles was a questionnaire in Arabic that sought more information about the populations that spoke

[90] Grant, *The Fortunate Slave*, 107–108.
[91] Bluett, *Some Memoirs of the Life of Job*, 88–89.
[92] Theodore Dwight, Jr., *The People of Africa: A Series of Papers on their Character, Condition, and Future Prospects*, ed. Henry M. Schieffelin (New York: Anson D.F. Randolph, 1871), 44–61. See also "Colonization Meeting in New York" (held in mid-May), in *African Repository*, XI (July 1835), 205, reprinted in *African Muslims: A Sourcebook*, ed. Austin, 411.

Arabic and their religious affiliations. The distribution of the Bibles and
the return of the surveys were facilitated by Joseph Roberts, who was at
the time the President of Liberia College and had earlier served as the first
president of Liberia (1848–1856 and again in 1872–1876).[93]

'Umar himself was also given at least two copies of the Bible in Arabic,
one of which he gifted to Lamine Kaba.[94] Those who knew 'Umar believed
that his reading of the Bible in Arabic was instrumental in his supposed
conversion to Christianity (see Chapter 2). In 1819, John Louis Taylor,
Chief Justice of the North Carolina Supreme Court, wrote Francis Scott
Key, the author of the *Star-Spangled Banner* and a prominent member of
the American Colonization Society, to request an Arabic Bible for 'Umar.
Taylor noted that "a person of his ['Umar's] enlargement of merit could
not but peruse it without perceiving its authenticity and divine origin."[95]
'Umar himself is reported to have said in a letter to Lamine Kaba that his
master "read the Bible for me until my eyes were opened."[96]

MISSIONARY DEALINGS WITH DIVERSITY

In addition to its economic dimensions, the proselytization of Protestantism
among Africans raised many questions for Anglo-Americans about
Protestant identity and existing conceptions of religious difference. Anglo-
Americans' encounter with African Muslim slaves influenced some of the
responses to these questions. Thomas Bluett's encounter and friendship
with Job Ben Solomon is a telling example. Bluett was a minister in the
Society for the Propagation of the Gospel in Foreign Parts (S.P.G.).[97] The
S.P.G. was chartered by William III in 1701 for the purpose of promot-
ing the Anglican Church in English colonies and countering the influence
of the Catholic Church, Deists, and Nonconformist Protestants (such as
Puritans, Quakers, Anabaptists, and Presbyterians). It was also intended

---

[93] George E. Post, "Arabic-Speaking Negro Mohammedans in Africa," *African Repository*
(May 1869), 129–133, reprinted from *Missionary Herald* (April 1869), 114–117,
reprinted in *African Muslims: A Sourcebook*, ed. Austin, 485–486.

[94] Ralph R. Gurley, "Secretary's Report," *African Repository*, XIII (July 1837), 201–205,
reprinted in *African Muslims: A Sourcebook*, ed. Austin, 470.

[95] "Letter from John Louis Taylor to Francis Scott Key," October 10, 1819, published in
African Muslims: A Sourcebook, ed. Austin, 455.

[96] Gurley, "Secretary's Report," reprinted in *African Muslims: A Sourcebook*, ed. Austin,
470.

[97] According to Douglas Grant, Bluett was ordained in the Anglican Chruch in 1727. He
was involved with the mission maintained by the S.P.G. in Dover, Kent County, but did
not serve as a missionary for the Society until 1745. Grant, *Fortunate Slave*, 83.

to promote the conversion of "infidels and heathens" to Christianity throughout the English colonies. The evangelicalism of the S.P.G. was rooted in Enlightenment ideas of the inherent equality and rationality of all mankind, which in their eyes made every human a candidate for conversion. In line with Enlightenment thought, the S.P.G. attributed disparities in wealth and technological and cultural achievements of varying societies to their environments rather than the innate ability of their members. For this reason, the S.P.G. was particularly concerned with how the expansion of the English Empire into the "wilderness of America," without the expansion of the Church, would affect the colonists and the fate of the Empire. Thomas Bray, who was most influential in the establishment of the S.P.G., in *A Memorial, Representing the Present State of Religion on the Continent of North-America* (1701), described the English colonies as being "at a Crisis ... so infidelity and Heresie seem to make their utmost Efforts to withdraw people from religion" (p. 5). In another report on the state of religion in the Anglo-American Colonies, he associated the neglect of religion with the decline of the Empire; he warned that "as Contempt of Religion and the Law is a sure mark of a declining Nation, so new Colonies and Societies of Men must soon fall to pieces, and dwindle to nothing, unless their Governors and Magistrates interpose, to season betimes the Minds of such a new People with a sense of Religion, and with good and vertuous (sic) Principles."[98]

Most Anglo-Americans at the turn of the eighteenth century, however, did not share in the Enlightenment values of the S.P.G. In 1730, David Humphreys, Secretary to the S.P.G., wrote in *An Historical Account of the Incorporated Society for the Propagation of the Gospel in Foreign Parts*, that the "greatest Obstruction [to the conversion of 'the Negroes'] is the Masters themselves do not consider enough, the Obligation which lies upon them, to have their Slaves instructed. Some have been so weak as to argue, the *Negroes* had no Souls; others, that they grew worse by being taught, and made Christians; I would not mention these, if they were not popular Arguments now" (pp. 235–236). Already "by 1706 at least six colonial legislatures had passed acts denying that baptism altered the condition of a slave 'as to his bondage or freedome'."[99] Nonetheless doubts lingered. As

---

[98] Thomas Bray, *Apostolic Charity, Its Nature and Excellence Consider'd in a Discourse Upon Dan. 12. 3...to Which Is Prefixt a General View of the English Colonies in America, with Respect to Religion; in Order to Shew What Provision Is Wanting for the Propagation of Christianity in Those Parts* (London: William Hawes, 1699).

[99] Albert J. Raboteau, *Slave Religion: The "Invisible Institution" in the Antebellum South* (New York: Oxford University Press, 1978), 99.

late as 1729, appeals were sent to England on the subject only to have the Crown-Attorney and Solicitor-General confirm the colonial legislations.[100]

The S.P.G. in the early eighteenth century sought to overcome the obstacle slaveholders presented to the conversion of slaves in two ways. First, it argued that the status of the slave did not change with his conversion. If anything, the slave became a more productive slave after conversion:

Christianity and the embracing of the Gospel, does not make the least Alteration in Civil Property....The Freedom which Christianity gives, is a Freedom from the Bondage of Sin and Satan, and from the Dominion of Mens (sic) Lusts and Passions and inordinate Desires; but as to their *outward* Condition, whatever that was before ... their being baptized, and becoming Christians, makes no manner of Change in it.... And so far is Christianity from discharging Men from Duties of the Station and Condition in which it found them, that it lays them under stronger Obligations to perform those Duties with the greatest Diligence and Fidelity, not only from the Fear of Men, but from a Sense of Duty to God, and the Belief and Expectation of a future Account.[101]

Second, it sought to persuade slaveholders of the Enlightenment idea of the inherent equality of all mankind. "Let me beseech you to consider *Them*," wrote the Anglican Bishop of London to slaveholders in English Plantations,

not barely as Slaves, and upon the same Level with labouring Beasts, but as *Men*-Slaves and *Women*-Slaves, who have the same Frame and Faculties with your selves, and have Souls capable of being made eternally happy, and Reason and Understanding to receive Instruction in order to it. If they came from abroad, let it not be said, that they are as far from the Knowledge of Christ in a Christian Country, as when they dwelt among Pagan Idolaters, If they have been born among you, and have never breathed any Air but that of a Christian Country, let them not be as much Strangers to Christ, as if they had been transplanted, as soon as born, into a Country of Pagan Idolaters.[102]

The last statement by the Bishop evinces the reinterpretation of the self necessitated by missions in light of encounters with others. To

[100] Charles Vernon Bruner, "The Religious Instruction of the Slaves in the Ante-bellum South" (Ph.D. dissertation, George Peabody College of Teachers, 1933), 35; mentioned in Raboteau, *Slave Religion*, 344n9.

[101] "A letter by the Bishop of London to the masters and mistresses of families in the English Plantations abroad," dated May 19, 1727, cited in David Humphreys, *An Historical Account of the Incorporated Society for the Propagation of the Gospel in Foreign Parts–to the Year 1728* (London, 1730), 265–266.

[102] "A letter by the Bishop of London to the masters and mistresses of families in the English Plantations abroad," cited in Humphreys, *An Historical Account*, 269.

slaveholders in Anglo-American colonies, slaves were no different than chattel. The Bishop and the S.P.G., however, were concerned with what it meant to self-identify as a Christian nation but to allow, even promote, paganism among certain members of the nation. In *An Address to Serious Christians Among Our Selves, to Assist the Society for Propagating the Gospel, in Carrying Out on the Work of Instructing the Negroes in Our Plantations Abroad*, the Bishop of London wrote:

The Souls for which I am now pleading have a more particular Claim to our Regard, as they are truly Part of our own Nation, and live under the same Government with our selves, and, which is more, contribute much by their Labour to the Support of our Government, and the Increase of the Trade and Wealth of this Kingdom.[103]

Thomas Bray also expressed the ethics of separating Christianity from commerce. Could Christians ethically accept material benefit from non-Christians without extending to them the benefits of the Church? Bray wrote:

[Missionary work] is a Work of Gratitude due from such a Nation as this: A Nation so enrich'd by the Commerce and Commodities of so many Barbarous and Pagan Countries. Surely, *since we have in so plentiful a manner been made partakers of their Carnal Things, it is our Duty also to Minister to them in Spiritual things.*[104]

In their call for the propagation of the Gospel, the S.P.G. generally adopted a paternalistic attitude toward English colonists and non-Christians in America. Bray, in a sermon to ordained missionaries to be sent to North American plantations, stated that

Turning many to Righteousness, ought to be the Care and Concern of every Christian Church and Nation; and this out of a grateful Return for that Blessed Light of the Gospel ... by which Christians may be ... so much distinguished from the deplorable State of those Barbarous and Savage Nations, where Ignorance of the True God and Religion overspreads their Country.... But especially this is a Care and Concern incumbent upon such a Church and Nation as ours. A Church so pure in its Doctrine, and so Heavenly in its Worship, as in that respect is the fittest in the World to be the Model to the New Acquisitions which shall be gain'd to the Church of Christ.[105]

---

[103] Humphreys, *An Historical Account*, 255.
[104] Bray, *Apostolic Charity*, 12.
[105] Ibid., 10–11.

Missions, in other words, did double duty. On the one hand, they were a means for fulfilling a religious duty to others less fortunate. On the other, they impressed upon the English and non-English alike the superiority of the nation and church.

For Thomas Bluett, who had become well acquainted with the enslaved African Muslim, Job Ben Solomon, this mode of English self-identification did not appear empirically justifiable. Bluett was a minor missionary in the S.P.G. and had very little influence on his contemporaries. Nonetheless, the theological conclusions he drew from his encounter with Job Ben Solomon demonstrate one of the ways in which the perceived liminality of African Muslims, such as Job, whom Bluett described as an "African Gentleman," (p. 10) led to rethinking of English self-identity and a reevaluation of the purpose and means of missionary work in the colonies of the British Empire. Bluett's conclusions, by recognizing some similarities between his and Job's understandings of religion, also anticipated the identification of Islam as a "semi-civilized" religion in nineteenth-century debates in the United States on the enslavement of Africans.

For Bluett, Job was too familiar to fit the Bishop of London's description of the heathen or "savage man" who possessed a soul and rational faculties, waiting to be delivered from "the Pagan Darkness and Superstition in which [he] was bred and ... [partake in] the Light of the Gospel."[106] Bluett explained that Job's "Notions of God, Providence, and a future State were in the main very just and reasonable."[107] Unlike the "noble savage" of eighteenth-century European imagination, who participated unknowingly in the divine design, Job interpreted his life in theological terms similar to Bluett's. "JOB used to comfort himself in his Captivity; and upon proper Occasions, in Conversation, would speak very justly and devoutly of the Care of God over his Creatures, and particularly of the remarkable Changes of his own Circumstances; all of which he piously ascribed to an unseen Hand. [Indeed, h]e frequently compared himself to *Joseph*."[108]

In Bluett's biography, Job's liminality as an "African gentleman" challenged conventional understandings of English self-identity and of Anglican missions in British colonies; Bluett subtly reinterpreted these

---

[106] "A letter by the Bishop of London to the masters and mistresses of families in the English Plantations abroad," cited in Humphreys, *An Historical Account*, 257–258.
[107] Bluett, *Some Memoirs of the Life of Job*, 52.
[108] Ibid., 58.

through a theology of Providence and hospitality in the concluding observations of his biography of Job. He reflected on Job's capture in Africa, enslavement in America, and redemption from slavery in England to instantiate his interpretation of Providence:

Chance being as unable to govern a World as to make one; we may safely and on good Grounds infer, that the various Occurences in human Life, however inconsiderable or perplex'd they may appear to us, are neither beneath the Care, nor inextricable to the Wisdom of him who rules the Universe: No: they have all their proper Places in the great Scheme; and all conspire in a regular Gradation, to bring about their several Ends, in Subservience to the whole.[109]

In Bluett's theology, cultural differences were reconciled through a divine design for a noble purpose; differences were made familiar by identifying the distinct roles they play in God's design for the world. Bluett wrote:

It would be Presumption in us to affirm positively what God is about to do at any Time; but may we not be allowed humbly to hope that one End of JOB's Captivity, and happy Deliverance, was the Benefit and Improvement of himself and his People? His knowledge is now extended to a Degree which he could never have arrived at in his own Country; and the Instruments which he carried over, are well adjusted to the Exigencies of his Countrymen. Who can tell, but that thro' him a whole Nation may be made happy? The Figure which he makes in those Parts, as Presumptive High-priest, and the Interest which he has with the King of the Country, considering the singular obligations he is under to the *English*, may possibly, in good time, be of considerable Service to us also; and we have reason to hope this, from the repeated Assurances we had from JOB, that he would upon all Occasions, use his best Endeavours to promote the *English* Trade before any other.[110]

The hospitable reception of liminal figures or, to use Bluett's own words, "distressed Strangers," is a human activity that reaffirms God's absolute control over the world:

There is something singularly sublime, and even God-like, in this benevolent Disposition toward strangers. The common Parent of the Universe pours out his Blessings daily upon all Mankind, in all Places of the Earth; the Just and the Unjust, the Rich and the Poor, all the Classes, all the Families of human Creatures subsist by his Bounty, and have their Share of his Universal Favours. The good hospitable Man, in his low Sphere, imitates his Maker, and deals about him to his Fellow Mortals with great Chearfulness.[111]

---

[109] Ibid., 55–56.
[110] Ibid., 59–60.
[111] Ibid., 61–62.

Since God is the Creator of and the Provider for all of humanity, to be hospitable to others, to provide and to care for them, is an act of divine imitation. Hospitality is thus an emulative means of affirming God's absolute providence and a practical theological tool for dealing with differences among humans.

Through this theology of Providence and hospitality, which Bluett advanced in relation to his encounter with Job, he envisioned an English colonial identity that was markedly different from Bray's conception of the English as a people "pure in Doctrine," "Heavenly in Worship," and "the fittest in the World to be the Model to the New Acquisitions." Bluett wrote,

Such a happy Temper of Mind [that views hospitality as an act of divine imitation] appeared eminently in those worthy Gentlemen that promoted and encouraged a Subscription for the Relief of JOB; and we hope there are many such Instances of Hospitality among us, which is one very honourable Part of the Character of the *English*.[112]

Bluett did not explicitly attribute his vision of the English to his encounter with Job, but in light of his admiring characterization of Job as an "African Gentleman," it would have been impossible for him to uphold the conventional, binary opposition expressed by Bray between the civilized Christian and the barbarous non-Christian.

ENSLAVED AFRICAN MUSLIMS AND DEBATES ON THE
ROLE OF CHRISTIANITY AND SLAVERY IN FASHIONING
AMERICA'S NATIONAL IDENTITY

Bluett's recognition of similarities between his and Job's views of the divine anticipated the way in which Americans' liminal conceptions of African Muslims configured African Islam as a "semi-civilizing" force in abolitionist arguments of antebellum America. Moreover, by converging commercial and religious interests in his theology of providence and hospitality, Bluett delivered Job as an example of how the adoption of Africans as trading partners rather than slaves could help the English and the Africans alike. While Bray and the S.P.G. argued that the commercial success of English plantations ethically obligated them to save the souls of the natives and black slaves, Bluett put forth an economic argument for hospitality that surreptitiously challenged the institution of slavery.

[112] Ibid., 62–63.

Bluett's stance on slavery is unknown, and it is difficult to say if the above statement unfairly credits him with a sound moral compass. His sympathetic biography of Job certainly suggests that he may very well have been ahead of his time. In line with the growing influence of capitalist ideology, abolitionists in the nineteenth century explicitly advanced what Bluett indirectly argued through his discussion of providence and hospitality. In 1828, a representative article in the New York *Journal of Commerce* stated that there was a "higher motive" to helping 'Abdul Rahman and his family return to Africa; "a commercial intercourse, that may be opened, will strike at the root of the slave trade. It has already, as has been stated. Let us make it for the interest of Africans to pay for their purchases in the productions of their country."[113]

Throughout the antebellum period, African Muslims played a noteworthy role as liminal figures in debates surrounding the role of Christianity and slavery in fashioning America's national identity. This was particularly the case because in the nineteenth century more and more Christian Americans related to others through missionary ideology. As the popular story of "Salem (Selim), the Algerine convert" demonstrates, the non-Christian world was perceived as a fertile field hungering for the "civilizing" rays of Christianity, and enslaved African Muslims provided an opening for the realization of this goal. Selim's life story was fit for fiction and is worth recounting in some detail because of the way it exemplifies an important way in which Muslims, who became slaves in America as a result of the triangular rivalries and encounters between Europe, Africa, and the Americas, were configured in nineteenth-century Americans' missionary self-understanding.[114] Despite the literary embellishments found in published accounts of Selim's life, the fact that some of the major figures with whom he was said to have interacted were locally significant figures[115] who lived at the same time and place as Selim lends credence to the narrative of his life. Reverend Benjamin H. Rice first wrote a sketch

---

[113] "'Abdul Rahahman," *New York Journal of Commerce* (October 16, 1828), reprinted in *African Muslims: A Sourcebook*, ed. Austin, 174–175.

[114] A genre in early American fiction used Muslim characters and Muslim pseudonyms to address cultural and political issues facing the nascent Republic. An example of such works relevant to the story of Selim is *The Algerine Spy in Pennsylvania; or, Letters Written by a Native of Algiers on the Affairs of the United States of America, from the Close of the Year 1783 to the Meeting of the Conventions* (Philadelphia, PA: Prichard and Hall, 1787). For a critical discussion of *The Algerine Spy*, see Marr, *The Cultural Roots of American Islamicism*, 37–43.

[115] Reverend John Craig, for example, who was said to have converted Selim to Christianity, came to Augusta, Virginia in September 1740 to serve as the region's Presbyterian

of his eventful life and conversion to Christianity in *The Panoplist and Missionary Magazine* (1816). Bishop William Meade also included Selim in his popular book on *Old Churches, Ministers, and Families of Virginia* (1857). Meade reprinted Rice's biography of Selim with an appendix that included evidence of his later life when he met Virginia's Governor John Page (1802–1805), who kept a portrait of Selim in the parlor of his mansion at Rosewell. Selim's story was also reprinted in *Graham's Magazine*.[116]

Selim's life intersected tragically with the Seven Years' War (1756–1763), which began in the Ohio Valley and was known in America as the French and Indian War. Britain emerged from this war as the mightiest imperial power in the world. In North America, the British gained all the French territories east of the Mississippi, while Spain received Louisiana as compensation for its support of the French during the war. Meade and Rice, however, were not interested in how Selim, who had been a student in Constantinople when he was captured and transported to Louisiana, contended with imperial warfare to end up in Virginia. They were primarily interested in his incredible conversion to Christianity in America, which made his life story, in Meade's words, "edifying in a religious point of view."[117]

---

minister. He died in 1774. See Jos. A. Waddell, *The Annals of Augusta County, Virginia* (Richmond, VA: Wm. Ellis Jones, 1886), 20–21. August County court records also mention the presence of a Samuel Givins (who was said to have found Selim in the woods around 1755) in Augusta County in 1752. See Lyman Chalkley, *Chronicles of the Scotch-Irish Settlement in Virginia Extracted from the Original Court Records of Augusta County, 1745–1800* (Rosslyn, VA: The Commonwealth Printing Co., 1912), 55. Also, Charles Willson Peale, who was said to have done a portrait of Selim for Governor John Page, knew Page, whose portrait he had also painted.

[116] Benjamin H. Rice, "The Converted Algerine," *The Panoplist and Missionary Magazine* 12, no. 12 (December 1816), 544–551. This article was published anonymously in *The Panoplist*, where it was written that the narrative "was committed to writing by an aged clergyman in Virginia, and is communicated for publication by a missionary of known character. Its authenticity could be relied on." In attributing the article to Benjamin H. Rice (1782–1856), I follow Bishop William Meade, *Old Churches, Ministers and Families of Virginia*, (Philadelphia, PA: J.B. Lippincott Company, 1891; orig. pub. 1857), 341. In *The Annals of Augusta County, Virginia, from 1736 to 1871*, 2nd ed. (Staunton, VA: C Russell Caldwell, Publisher, 1902), 202, Jos. A. Waddell mentions Meade's rendition of the article but attributes it to Rev. David Rice, "a Presbyterian minister who removed from Virginia to Kentucky before the year 1800." Meade's narrative of Selim's life was reprinted under the title "Selim, or the Algerine in Virginia" in *Graham's American Monthly Magazine of Literature, Art, and Fashion* 51, no. 5 (November, 1857), 433–438.

[117] Meade, *Old Chruches*, 333.

Selim was "born of wealthy and respectable parents in Algiers" at a time when Algiers was a more or less autonomous city within the Ottoman Empire. His parents had sent him to Constantinople at a young age for his education. Some time in the 1750s, during a return trip to Constantinople from Algiers, he was captured by a Spanish privateer at Malta. The Spanish, who were in alliance with France, Austria, and Russia against Prussia in the European sphere and against Great Britain in the "New World," took Selim to Gibraltar where he was transferred to a French slaver heading for New Orleans. Selim lived for "some time among the French," presumably as a slave, before "they sent him up the rivers Mississippi and Ohio to the Shawnee towns."[118] The French had formed an alliance with the Shawnee against the British. They left Selim with their native allies as a prisoner of war, where he came across an English woman prisoner, from whom he inquired about the location of English settlements in order to plan an escape from French territories. He successfully escaped from the natives and managed to walk to Augusta County, Virginia, where sometime around 1755 a hunter named Samuel Givins found him naked and emaciated in the woods.

Givins turned Selim over to a Captain (later Colonel) Dickerson who, in Rice's romantic, populist rendering of the American frontier, took care of him "with a generosity that is more common with rough backwoodsmen...than among the opulent sons of luxury and ease."[119] While in the company of Dickerson, Selim met a Presbyterian frontier minister by the name of John Craig. He asked if he could lodge with Craig and receive religious instruction from him. For Craig, this request indicated the providential purpose of Selim's travails. He, it was explained, "cheerfully undertook the agreeable work he seemed called to by an extraordinary Providence."[120] There was, however, more than Providence at work here; almost immediately after his baptism and public profession of Christianity, Selim asked Craig to help him fund his return to his family. Once he returned to Algiers, his father, upon discovering that he had converted to Christianity, disowned him and threw him out of the house. Selim somehow managed to return to Virginia in a "state of insanity."[121] He wandered in Virginia, living off Americans' hospitality. He met Governor John Page and at one point

---

[118] Ibid., 343; Rice, "Converted Algerine," 547.
[119] Meade, *Old Churches*, 342; Rice, "Converted Algerine," 546.
[120] Meade, *Old Churches*, 345; Rice, "Converted Algerine," 549.
[121] Meade, *Old Churches*, 346; Rice, "Converted Algerine," 549–550.

even traveled with him to Philadelphia where Page attended a meeting of the U.S. Congress. There it is said that the famed American artist, Charles Willson Peale,[122] drew a portrait of Selim, which Page kept on the wall of his Parlour, "among many others of higher degree" as a praiseworthy sign of what Bishop Meade attributed to this American statesman's humility and true republicanism, despite his residence in "the proud mansion of his forefather."[123]

Given the degree to which missionary ideology affected how nineteenth-century American Christians viewed themselves and their relation with the rest of the world, both proponents and opponents of slavery couched their arguments not just in what Christianity demanded but also in what made practical sense for the spread of Christianity. On the one hand, proponents of slavery generally ignored the presence of Muslims among slaves and focused on how slavery brought Christianity and civilization to the "savage" Africans. On the other hand, opponents of slavery pointed to African Muslims as evidence of the presence of limited forms of civilization among Africans that was being degraded through slavery rather than being advanced through Christianization.

Moral opposition to slavery increased throughout the United States in the first third of the nineteenth century. In the South, when sentiments against slavery turned into legislative action against the institution itself, slavery was gradually redefined from a "necessary evil" into a "positive good." The turning point could be seen in a review of the legislative debate on slavery in Virginia (1832) by Professor Thomas R. Dew of William and Mary. Dew warned that any abolitionist legislation that followed the rebel slave Nat Turner's revolt "would necessarily appear to be the result of [this] most inhuman massacre," leading other slaves to follow Nat Turner's example. "No plan of abolition could act suddenly on the whole mass of slave population." Dew suggested that Virginia consult with other slaveholding states before it took any action on slavery and warned the South of the material consequences it could face if it succumbed to moral opposition to slavery. The later defense of slavery as a "positive good" was carried out most vocally by John C. Calhoun, who served as Vice President under John Quincy Adams (1825–1829) and Andrew Jackson (1829–1833) and as a senator from

---

[122] A presumed sketch of this portrait is in Meade, *Old Churches*, inserted between pages 340 and 341 and in "Selim" in *Graham's Magazine*, 433.
[123] Meade, *Old Churches*, 333.

South Carolina (1833–1850). Calhoun declared that "abolition and the Union cannot coexist."[124] Changing the "existing relations between the two races" would result in "drenching the country and the other of the races." In addition to such negative reasons for maintaining slavery, Calhoun argued that slavery was a "positive good": "Never before has the black race of Central Africa, from the dawn of history to the present day, attained a condition so civilized and so improved, not only physically, but morally and intellectually." He also appealed to history: "There never has yet existed a wealthy and civilized society in which one portion of the community did not, in point of fact, live on the labor of the other." Furthermore, he found slavery to be a better form of life than the "wretched condition of the pauper in the poorhouse[s]" of industrializing cities of the North.

The notion of slavery as a positive good swept over much of the South in the mid-nineteenth century, accentuating the question of how slave holding could be done properly. One of the plantations that was held up as an example for other slaveholders was the well known Hopeton plantation, where Salih Bilali was a head driver. In 1832, John Legare, the editor of *Southern Agriculturist* (one of the largest regional monthly magazines, published out of Nashville, Tennessee) decided to visit the plantation, which he hoped "will have some influence on our planters to go and do likewise." He reported, "Disobedience, running away, and riotous conduct are scarcely known on the [Hopeton] plantation, and the necessity for punishment is very small, and almost confined to very slight inflictions for neglect of work. Regular, firm and mild discipline is held to be at once the most efficacious as well as humane system. The extremes of indulgence and severity are equally fatal to the happiness and good conduct of a gang."[125] Charles Lyell described Hopeton as "a favorable specimen of a well-managed estate,"[126] and Fedrika Bremmer

[124] John C. Calhoun, "Slavery a Positive Good," speech to U.S. Senate, February 6, 1837, in Calhoun, *The Works of John C. Calhoun*, ed. Richard Kenner Crallé (New York: D. Appleton, 1888), vol. 2, 626–633.

[125] John Legare, "Account of an Agricultural Excursion Made into the South of Georgia in the Winter of 1832; by the Editor," *Southern Agriculturist* 6 (April 1833), 157–178; (May 1833), 243, 249–253; (July 1833), 358–363; (November 1833), 571–574, 576–577; 7 (June 1833), 281–287, reprinted in *African Muslims: A Sourcebook*, ed. Austin, 349–350.

[126] Charles Lyell, *A Second Visit to the United States of North America*, vol. 1 (New York: Harper, 1849), 244–245, 248–249, 252–253, 261–271, 291, 273, reprinted in *African Muslims: A Sourcebook*, ed. Austin, 367.

called its owner, James H. Couper "one of the greatest planters in the south of the United States."[127]

Couper, himself, was an advocate of colonization and viewed it as a means to end slavery. A visitor to his plantation recalled that he "regard[ed] slavery in America as a school for the children of Africa....it is the only means of imparting to Africa the blessings of Christianity and Civilization."[128] The racist and paternalistic assumptions of Couper were more overtly articulated by the English geologist, Charles Lyell, who wrote about Hopeton in 1846.

Throughout the upper country there is a large preponderance of Anglo-Saxons, and a little reflection will satisfy the reader how much the education of a race which starts originally from so low a stage of intellectual, social, moral, and spiritual development, as the African negro, must depend not on learning to read and write, but on the amount to familiar intercourse which they enjoy with individuals of a more advanced race.... each generation is acquiring habits of greater cleanliness and propriety of behavior, while some are learning mechanical arts, and every year many of them becoming converts to Christianity.[129]

For its advocates, slavery was seen as a providential means for the Christianization of Africa. "The Creator of men formed them for labor under guidance," wrote another visitor to Hopeton, "and there is probably a providential intention of producing good Christian men and women out of it in time."[130]

Proponents of slavery who visited Hopeton made little of the fact that its head driver was an African Muslim. Lyell described him as "a man of superior intelligence and higher cast of features" and "a strict Mahometan," but Lyell was more interested in his progeny who, because of their contact with whites, had "exchanged the Koran for the Bible" and thus were de-negrofied by Lyell as having "countenances of a more European cast than those of ordinary negroes."[131] For opponents of slavery, however, in the mid-nineteenth century, the fact that many West

[127] Fredrika Bremmer, *Homes of the New World: Impressions of America*, vol. 2 (New York: Harpers and Brothers, 1854), 488–491, reprinted in *African Muslims: A Sourcebook*, ed. Asutin, 376.

[128] Ibid.

[129] Lyell, *A Second Visit*, 244–245, 248–249, 252–253, 261–271, 291, 273, reprinted in *African Muslims: A Sourcebook*, ed. Austin, 373.

[130] Amelia M. Murray, *Letters from the United States, Cuba, and Canada* (New York: Putnam, 1856), reprinted in *African Muslims: A Sourcebook*, ed. Austin, 382.

[131] Lyell, *A Second Visit*, 244–245, 248–249, 252–253, 261–271, 291, 273, reprinted in *African Muslims: A Sourcebook*, ed. Austin, 371.

Africans were Muslims and that a number of slaves in America were Muslim was evidence of the falsity of racist and paternalistic arguments in defense of slavery. These opponents of slavery viewed Islam as the religion of a semi-civilized people. The fact that there were black Africans who adhered to Islam demonstrated that "the black race" was not "naturally uncivilized." They simply lacked the means and resources to become fully civilized. Captain Basil Hall, a celebrated British traveler who had been to Africa and visited the Couper plantation to learn more about American management of cotton and rice plantations and also about the treatment of slaves, declared "that as far as my own experience has gone, I have invariably noticed that precisely in proportion as the negro has a fair chance given him, so he proves himself equal in capacity as the white man."[132]

Opponents of slavery who wrote about African Muslims had their own paternalistic and racist attitudes toward Africans. Reverend William L. Judd who baptized Baquaqua wrote, "The best, if not the only means of removing that prejudice against the colored man, which is his curse and our shame, is, aiding him to rise in intelligence and virtue."[133] Even when they recognized varying aspects of what they defined as civilization in African Muslim society, they identified them as partial achievements on a scale of evolution toward "civilization": "The Foulahs, or Falatas," reported the *Wilmington Chronicle* in January 1847, "are known as the descendants of the Arabian Mahomedans who migrated to Western Africa in the seventh century. They carried with them the literature of Arabia, as well as the religion of their great Prophet, and have retained both. The Foulahs stand in the scale of civilization at the head of all the African tribes."[134] Theodore Dwight, first secretary of the American Ethnological Society, was one of the most vocal spokespersons for why Americans should check their prejudices against Africans given the presence of educated African Muslims both in Africa and America:

Where is the excuse for looking only at ten millions, more or less, of slaves and descendants of slaves in America, and entirely neglecting to inquire into the condition and character, the history and capacities of the hundred or more millions

---

[132] Hall, *Travels in North America*, vol. 2, reprinted in *African Muslims: A Sourcebook*, ed. Austin, 329.

[133] William L. Judd, "The Free Mission Society of Haiti," in *Facts for Baptist Churches*, ed. Andrew Foss and Edward Mathews (Utica, NY: American Baptist Free Mission Society, 1850), 391; reprinted in *African Muslims: A Sourcebook*, ed. Austin, 591.

[134] *Wilmington Chronicle* (January 22, 1847), reprinted in *African Muslims: A Sourcebook*, ed. Austin, 473.

of negroes in their native country, who have had some opportunity to show what they are capable of?

Dwight followed this statement with an assertion that Christians had mistreated educated and venerable blacks in America:

It will certainly bring more compunction to the hearts of the humane among us, to learn that the race which we have been accustomed to despise as well as to ill treat, still lie under a load of evils perpetuated by the prejudices prevailing even among many of the most enlightened Christians; and it will be surprising to be told, that among the victims of the slave-trade among us have been men of learning and pure and exalted characters, who have been treated like beasts of the field by those who claimed a purer religion.[135]

Dwight offered enslaved African Muslims, such as Job Ben Solomon, 'Abdul Rahman, 'Umar ibn Said, and Lamine Kaba, as examples of "learning" and "exalted character" among blacks.[136] He faulted Americans for denying "negroes those intellectual faculties and moral qualities which the Creator has bestowed on the entire human family" by remaining ignorant of the African history and culture that was being exposed at the time by travelers such as Bowen, Livingston, and Barth. The works of these authors, he wrote, "prove that millions of pagan negroes, in different parts of that continent, have been for ages in the practice of some of the most important arts of life, dwelling in comfort and generally at peace; while many other millions have been raised to a considerable degree of civilization by Mohammedism, and long existed in powerful independent states."[137]

For this reason, Dwight took particular interest in Lamine Kaba who as a literate and religiously learned slave could teach Euro-Americans about Africa. He reproduced a list of thirty books that Lamine, who was an Islamic scholar, had studied in Africa. These books represented an advanced curriculum in Islamic Studies in West Africa. Elsewhere in the North Atlantic, Reverend G. C. Renouard, Foreign Secretary of the Royal Geographic Society of London, showed similar interest in Abu Bakr al-Saddiq in Jamaica:

---

[135] Theodore Dwight, "Condition and Character of Negroes in Africa," *The Methodist Quarterly Review* (January 1864), 79–80, reprinted in *African Muslims: A Sourcebook*, ed. Austin, 423.

[136] Dwight, "Condition and Character," 77–90, reprinted in *African Muslims: A Sourcebook*, ed. Austin, 421–433.

[137] Dwight, "Condition and Character," 77, reprinted in *African Muslims: A Sourcebook*, ed. Austin, 421.

The Korán he must have known almost by heart, as he declared he had never seen a copy of it from the time he left Ghónah till one was put into his hands by the writer of this paper. He was not old enough, he said, when captured, to enter on a course of logic and rhetoric, or to study the commentaries on the Korán; but he knew the names of the most celebrated commentators. This is a plain proof of the superior civilization of the negroes in the interior over those near the coast; and, however incredible at first sight, it is confirmed by Burckhardt's account of the Shaïkhīyah Arabs in Meroë,[138] and the well-written Arabic despatches from Bello's court,[139] now in the records of the Foreign Office.[140]

At a series of lectures before the Royal Institution of Great Britain, which were published both in the United States and Britain, Reginald Bosworth Smith drew similar conclusions about the "civilizing" influence of Islam in West Africa from his reading of nineteenth-century travelogues:[141]

Christian travelers, with every wish to think otherwise, have remarked that the negro who accepts Mohammedanism acquires at once a sense of the dignity of human nature not commonly found even among those who have been brought to accept Christianity. It is also pertinent to observe here, that such progress as any large part of the Negro race has hitherto made is in exact proportion to the time that has elapsed since their conversion, or to the degree of fervour with which they originally embraced, or have since clung to, Islam.[142]

The degree to which Dwight, Renouard, Bosworth Smith and others recognized signs of culture and learning among African Muslims was measured in relation to ideas of progress and civility among Euro-Americans. Like most of their contemporaries, these individuals had no

---

[138] J. L. Burckhardt, *Travels in Nubia* (London, 1819).

[139] Muhammad Bello, son of 'Usman dan Fodio, whom he succeeded in 1817 to become the head of the Sokoto Caliphate.

[140] Abú Bekr eṣ Ṣiddík, "Routes in North Africa," communicated by Rev. G. C. Renouard, *Journal of the Royal Geographical Society of London* 6 (1836), 110, reprinted in *African Muslims: A Sourcebook*, ed. Austin, 562.

[141] Some of the travelogues that Bosworth Smith mentioned by name include William G. Browne, *Travels in Africa, Egypt, and Syria from the Year 1792 to 1798* (London: printed for T. Caddell Junior and W. Davies by T. N. Longman and O. Rees, 1799); Mungo Parks, *Travels in the Interior Districts of Africa: Performed in the Years 1795, 1796, and 1797 with an Account of a Subsequent Mission to that Country in 1805*, 2nd ed. (London: printed for John Murray by William Bulmer and Co., 1817); Henry Barth, *Travels and Discoveries in North and Central Africa, Being a Journal of an Expedition Undertaken Under the Auspices of Her Majesty's Brittanic Government in the Years 1849–1855*, 3 vols. (New York: Harper and Bros., 1857); David Livingstone, *Narrative of an Expedition to the Zambesi and its Tributaries; and of the Discovery of the Lakes Shirwa and Nyassa, 1858–1864* (New York: Harper and Bros., 1866).

[142] R. Bosworth Smith, *Mohammed and Mohammedanism*, 2nd ed. (London: Smith, Elder, & Co., 1874; New York: Harper and Bros., 1875), Lecture I, 32.

particular penchant for Islam. Dwight referred to Islam as "the religion of the false prophet"[143] and attributed what he found to be valuable in it to what the "Koran copied from the Hebrew Scriptures."[144] Bosworth Smith asserted that "it is undeniable that a vague and hearsay acquaintance with the Old Testament, the Talmud, and the New Testament … influenced Mohammed much."[145] For most of these individuals, Islam was an instrument for shaming American Christians who supported slavery and institutional racism. One critic of laws banning the education of people of African ancestry in Southern states wrote, "These barbarians [i.e., Arab Muslims] did not dream of excluding their sacred book from their schools [for black children], as some more enlightened states have done."[146]

Other opponents of slavery viewed Islam as a "civilizing" force that primed West Africans for evangelization:

These [Arabic-speaking] would appear to be superior in culture and civilization to surrounding peoples. They profess the religion of Mohammed, shorn of much of its bigotry and intolerance. They are spreading this religion, by preaching and conquest, through an unknown but vast region of the interior of that mysterious continent. The way is open for evangelizing them through the Arabic language, by means of men who should be trained for the purpose in an Arabic department of the Liberia College.… It may be that a process is going on in Central Africa similar to that by which the many languages and races of the Graeco-Roman empire were all merged into one, and made susceptible of evangelization through the Greek tongue. If, indeed, it be the plan of Providence that these many barbarous nations of Africa are to be consolidated under one aggressive empire of ideas and faith, erroneous and imperfect though they be, we shall recognize the wisdom and foresight which thus prepare the way for evangelization through the medium of one copious, cultivated, expressive tongue, in the place of leaving to the Church the difficult task of translating and preaching in *many barbarous languages*, incapable of expressing the finer forms of thought, and denoting the separation of the people into many hostile tribes, quite forbidding the freedom of travel and commercial intercourse, and the progress of Christian missions.[147]

---

[143] "Condition and Character of Negroes in Africa," *Methodist Quarterly Review* (January 1864), 77–90, reprinted in *African Muslims: A Sourcebook*, ed. Austin, 426.

[144] "Condition and Character of Negroes in Africa," reprinted in *African Muslims: A Sourcebook*, ed. Austin, 422.

[145] Smith, *Mohammed and Mohammedanism*, 12.

[146] Mathew B. Grier, "Uncle Moreau," *North Carolina Presbyterian* (July 23, 1859), reprinted in *African Muslims: A Sourcebook*, ed. Austin, 481. Grier was 'Umar ibn Said's Presbyterian pastor.

[147] Post, "Arabic-Speaking Negro Mohammedans in Africa," reprinted in *African Repository* (May 1869), 129–133 and in *African Muslims: A Sourcebook*, ed. Austin, 486–487.

AFRICAN ISLAM IN BLACK NATIONALIST AND CIVILIZATIONALIST DISCOURSES

The nascent admiration of Islam as a partially "civilizing" religion in Africa came to fruition in the history of Islam in America in the twentieth century among African Americans who joined the Moorish Science Temple and the Nation of Islam. These groups (see Chapter 4) claimed Islam as the "original" religion of "the lost-found nation" of African America. The change in the characterization of Islam from a "civilizing" force in Africa to the "original" religion of African America was enabled by the significant influence that European conceptions of civilization and progress had on African Americans.[148] In an 1828 gathering in honor of 'Abdul Rahman, for example, African American citizens of Boston offered toasts wishing for "Christianity, industry, prudence, and economy, [to] characterize every descendant of Africa; and may they one day rise above the obloquy of their foes, transcendent." "May the sons and daughters of Africa soon become a civilized Christian-like people and shine forth to the world as conspicuous as their more highly favoured neighbors."[149] Baquaqua wrote of his homeland, "Africa is rich in every respect (except in knowledge.) The knowledge of the white man is needed, but not his vices. The religion of the white man is needed, but more of it, more of the spirit of true religion, such as the Bible teaches, 'love to God and love to man.'"[150]

As these quotes demonstrate, the discourse on civilizational progress in the nineteenth century viewed civilization as an amalgam of race, religion, and progress. Skin color, faith, and economic standings were all viewed and variously weighed as indicators of one's potential for civilizational progress. Consequently, in the aftermath of the Civil War and the emancipation of slaves, many African Americans believed that blacks could not attain equality with whites unless they could lay claim to a prosperous African Civilization. Believing firmly that "we shall never receive the respect of other races until we establish a powerful

---

[148] Wilson Jeremiah Moses, *The Golden Age of Black Nationalism, 1850–1925* (New York: Oxford University Press, 1978), 20–22.

[149] "Public Dinner in Boston," orig. pub. in *American Traveller*, quoted in *Freedom's Journal of New York City* (October 24, 1828), reprinted in *African Muslims: A Sourcebook*, ed. Austin, 165–166.

[150] Baquaqua, *The Adventures of Mahommah Gardo Baquaqua*, ed. Samuel Moore, reprinted in *African Muslims: A Sourcebook*, 613; and Baquaqua, *The Autobiography of Mahommah Gardo Baquaqua*, ed. Law and Lovejoy, 128–129.

nationality,"[151] pan-Africanists and black nationalists concentrated
their efforts on "Negro improvement" and "racial uplift." One of the
most important figures of nineteenth-century black nationalism and
pan-Africanism was Edward Wilmot Blyden (1832–1912), the author
of *Christianity, Islam, and the Negro Race* (1887). This collection of
Blyden's essays and lectures was widely read and reviewed[152] as white
America struggled to incorporate its emancipated citizens into mainstream society, politics, and economy. Blyden himself favored the return
of African Americans to Africa, which is suggestive of the type of audience that found his message appealing (e.g., supporters of the American
Colonization Society). Blyden was also influential among missionaries
who believed that the failure of Christianity to spread in sub-Saharan
Africa as rapidly as Islam was mainly the result of the subordinate position of blacks in white, Christian societies.[153]

Blyden's intellectual journey helps explain the connection between
antebellum discussions of Islam as a "civilizing" religion in Africa and
the appropriation of Islam as the national religion of African Americans
by such groups as the Moorish Science Temple and the Nation of
Islam in the early twentieth century.[154] Blyden was born in 1832 in
St. Thomas in the Danish West Indies, where he met an American
pastor by the name of John P. Knox. Knox was very impressed by
Blyden's scholastic abilities and encouraged him to become a minister.
He brought Blyden to the United States in 1850 to study at Rutgers'
Theological College, but Rutgers denied Blyden admission on account
of his skin color. After becoming acquainted with some members of
the American Colonization Society, Blyden decided to immigrate
to Liberia in 1851 as a missionary in order to "bring those barbarous tribes under civilized and enlightened influences."[155] In Liberia,
he studied theology and biblical languages and became an ordained

---

[151] As reported in *New York Colonization Journal* 12 (July 1862), quoted in Hollis R. Lynch,
Edward Wilmot Blyden: Pan-Negro Patriot, 1832–1912 (London: Oxford University
Press), 28–29.

[152] Lynch, *Edward Wilmot Blyden*, 74.

[153] Bernard Lewis, *Race and Slavery in the Middle East: A Historical Enquiry* (New
York: Oxford University Press, 1990), 101–102.

[154] For a review of Blyden's life and thought in relation to the later development of Islam
among African Americans in the twentieth century, see Edward E. Curtis, IV, *Islam
in Black America: Identity, Liberation, and Difference in African-American Islamic
Thought* (Albany, NY: State University of New York Press, 2002), 22f.

[155] Lynch, *Edward Wilmot Blyden*, 6, cited in Curtis, *Islam in Black America*, 24.

Presbyterian minister. He went on to have a distinguished career as an author, academic, and statesman.[156]

According to one account, "in the spring of 1866, Professor Blyden, of the Liberia College, being deeply interested in the fact of the existence of this [Arabic-speaking] element in the population of Western Africa, visited Syria, and spent the summer in the study of Arabic" at the Syrian Protestant College.[157] When back in West Africa, Blyden acquainted himself with Muslims and found that West African Muslims had done more to attain what he envisaged for African nationalism than their Christian counterparts. In an essay on "Mohammedanism and the Negro Race" published in 1875 in *Fraser's Magazine*, Blyden wrote:

It is not a fact that "when the sun goes down, all Africa dances," but it might be a fact if it were not for the influence of Islam.... When we left a Pagan and entered a Mohammedan community, we at once noticed that we had entered a moral atmosphere widely separated from, and loftier far than, the one we had left....The Koran...has furnished to the adherents of its teachings in Africa a ground of union which has contributed vastly to their progress. Hausas, Foulahs, Mandingoes, Soosoos, Akus, can all read the same books and mingle in worship together, and there is to all one common authority and one ultimate umpirage.... Wherever the Negro is found in Christian lands, his leading trait is not docility, as has been often alleged, but servility. He is slow and unprogressive.... [T]here is no Christian community of Negroes anywhere which is self-reliant and independent. Haiti and Liberia, so-called Negro Republics, are merely struggling for existence, and hold their own by the tolerance of the civilized powers. On the other hand, there are numerous Negro Mohammedan communities and states in Africa which are self-reliant, productive, independent and dominant, supporting, without the countenance or patronage of the parent country, Arabia, whence they derived them, their political, literary and ecclesiastical institutions.[158]

Christianity, Islam, and the Negro Race, in which the above article was reprinted, was in many ways a culmination of intellectual efforts aimed at explaining what Blyden viewed as the shortcomings of Christianity vis-à-vis Islam in helping Africans progress. Blyden's answer was that Christianity, though originally founded among Semites,

[156] Curtis, *Islam in Black America*, 21–25. For a biography of Blyden, see Lynch, *Edward Wilmot Blyden*.

[157] Post, "Arabic-Speaking Negro Mohammedans," reprinted in *African Muslims: A Sourcebook*, ed. Austin, 486.

[158] Edward Wilmot Blyden, *Christianity, Islam and the Negro Race* (Edinburgh: Edinburgh University Press, 1887), 6–10.

had become an essentially European religion, while Islam never took on any specific racial coloring. Furthermore, Christianity came to Africans with their enslavement. "If the Mohammedan Negro had at any time to choose between the Koran and the sword," Blyden wrote, "when he chose the former, he was allowed to wield the latter as the equal of any other Muslim; but no amount of allegiance to the Gospel relieved the Christian Negro from the degradation of wearing the chain which he received with it, or rescued him from the political and, in a measure, ecclesiastical proscription which he still undergoes in all the countries of his exile."[159]

Blyden never converted to Islam,[160] and even though his characterizations of Christianity and Islam in relation to blacks struck a cord with many Americans of African and European descent who were concerned about the "race problem" in postbellum America, most found his laudatory treatment of Islam suspect. A review in *The Independent* captured the general reaction of his sympathizers in the United States: "…there has probably been no one in this country who would altogether accept Dr. Blyden's picture of Islamism. But however this may be, there can be no question that so much of his testimony as bears on the evangelization of Africa is substantially true."[161]

More recently, scholars have also criticized Blyden for his romantic view of Islam as a color-blind religion. "Edward Wilmot Blyden created the first paradigm of … 'the myth of a race-blind Islam'," writes one scholar of African American Islam.[162] Another scholar called it "the myth of Islamic racial innocence," which "mythologized and idealized Islam provid[ing] a stick with which to chastise Western failings."[163] From the perspective of a nineteenth-century black nationalist, however, such critiques were beside the point. Blyden was not concerned with the global practice or history of Islam. During his time in Syria and Egypt in 1866, he made little to no effort to acquaint himself with local Muslim customs or to inquire into their history and beliefs.[164] His

---

[159] Blyden, *Christianity, Islam and Negro Race*, 13.

[160] Blyden's commitment to Christianity is sometimes obscured in light of his fierce criticism of Christianity. For a discussion of this issue, see Sherman Jackson, *Islam and the Blackamerican: Looking toward the Third Resurrection* (New York: Oxford University Press, 2005), 62–63.

[161] *The Independent* (January 19, 1888), 17.

[162] Richard Brent Turner, *Islam in the African-American Experience*, 2nd ed. (Bloomington, IN: Indiana University Press, 2003), 55.

[163] Lewis, *Race and Slavery*, 101.

[164] Curtis, *Islam in Black America*, 27–28.

interest in Islam was ideological. Politically, he was interested in Islam as an instrument of black nationalism that could bolster self-reliance and "civilizational" progress among blacks. As a scholar, he was interested in the history, sociology, beliefs, and practice of Islam as the religion of independent black states in West Africa, who had attained aspects of self-reliance and "civilization" to which he aspired for his race. When he wrote about Islam, he wrote primarily about the religion he saw among the West African Muslim elites whom he admired and not about Islam as a global or popular religion. He reproached, for example, a popular revolt by African Muslims against the Futa Jallon aristocracy, known as the Hubbu movement,[165] as "the unprincipled activity of these vagabonds who would extinguish the interior traffic [in goods with Sierra Leone]" resulting from the "cupidity of a lawless horde."[166] Similarly, he criticized Arab Muslims for their involvement in the slave trade.[167]

SUMMARY

Blyden's portrayal of Islam synthesizes many of the historical themes of this chapter and adumbrates future developments in African American Islam in the first half of the twentieth century. African Muslims enslaved in colonial and antebellum America stood at the intersection of the encounters and rivalries between Europe, Africa, and America which shaped the Atlantic World. Their lives are for the most part unknown. Those for whom we have some historical record represent a handful of the estimated tens of thousands of African Muslim slaves who came to the United States. They were not, however, isolated figures; rather their life stories instantiate major historical events of their time. This chapter narrated a story of their lives in the context of early American history to demonstrate how African Muslims were perceived as liminal figures – neither savage nor civilized – through whom Anglo-Americans

---

[165] The name of this movement is derived from the Arabic phrase, *nuhibbu rasul allah hubban wahidan*, which means, "We love the Messenger of God singularly." See Edward Wilmot Blyden, "Report on Expedition to Falaba, January to March 1872" (with an Appendix Respecting Dr. Livingstone), in *Proceedings of the Royal Geographical Society of London* 12, no. 2 (1873), 123. For an overview of the movement see Lamin Sanneh, *The Crown and the Turban: Muslims and West African Pluralism* (Boulder, CO: Westview Press, 1997), 92–94; and Roger Botte, "*Révolte, pouvoir, religion: Les Hubbu du Fūta-Jallon (Guinée)*," *Journal of African History* 29, no. 3 (1988), 391–413.

[166] Blyden, "Report on Expedition to Falaba," 124.

[167] Curtis, *Islam in Black America*, 32.

re-conceptualized existing racial and religious boundaries of their community primarily for commercial and evangelizing purposes.

As economic "progress" and Protestantism came to stand for "civilization" in the minds of most Americans, the recognition that "semi-civilized" African Muslims could contribute to "civilization" by advancing trade with the African interior and by evangelizing in Africa led some Americans to question the principles of the "Christian civilization" that tolerated their enslavement. Some African Muslims, like Job Ben Solomon and 'Abdul Rahman, willingly played the liminal role ascribed to them by the predominant civilizationalist narrative of their time. They purported to advance trade with their countrymen and to evangelize them in exchange for their freedom and return to Africa.

Following emancipation, the liminal status of African Muslims that resulted in an understanding of Islam as a "partially civilizing" force in Africa became more than a means of questioning the principles of a racist "Christian civilization." It became, as seen in the writings of the influential black nationalist Edward Wilmot Blyden, a means of positively conceiving black identity and African civilization outside the oppressive frame of "Christian civilization." For Blyden, who never became Muslim himself, and for most of his contemporaries, Islam as a civilizing force in Africa and a boon to black nationalist aspirations was for the most part an academic issue. It was not until the first Great Migration of southern blacks to the metropolises of the Midwest and the Northeast around the time of World War I and the 1920s that we encounter organized efforts to uphold Islam as the national religion of black Americans by such groups as the Moorish Science Temple and later the Nation of Islam.

2

Islamic Beliefs and Practice in Colonial and Antebellum America

The preceding chapter contextualized the early history of Islam in America within the rivalries and encounters of the Atlantic world that formed the American Republic. It demonstrated how the perceived liminality of African Muslims provided avenues for European Americans to advance their commercial and missionary interests and to re-evaluate the morality of a "civilized" Christian country that permitted slavery. In doing so, it placed the early history of Muslims in America within larger narratives of the rise of mercantile capitalism, the military and economic ascendancy of Western European states, and the formation of an American national identity. The present chapter covers the same historical period but examines another side of the early history of Islam in America. It tells the story of the role Islam played in the lives of African Muslims in colonial and antebellum America. The following chapter shifts focus from the passive, liminal role Muslims played in reaction to forces external to them. This was a moment for them to re-evaluate and reconfigure Islamic beliefs and practices in an American idiom to form new communal relations and to make sense of their historical context.

As the reader has already gathered, the limitations and paucity of the available sources and the fledgling state of historical scholarship on Islam in America restricts any account of the role of Islamic beliefs and practices in colonial and antebellum America to the tentative rather than the conclusive. As seen in the previous chapter, nearly all sources for the early history of Islam in America were written either by white, American Protestants who knew little about Islam and West Africa or by Muslim "converts" to Christianity who were writing for a European American, Protestant audience. With the exception of the Georgia Writers' Project

Drums and Shadows (discussed below), none of our sources expressed
interest in the practice of Islam as such in colonial or antebellum America.
That being said, the extant sources do allow us to make some general
observations with a reasonable degree of confidence.

NO SINGLE HISTORICAL TRAJECTORY OR EXPERIENCE

There are few constants and no single, dominant trajectory in the historical record of Muslims in America in this period. Muslims in colonial
and antebellum America came from a variety of ethnic, educational, and
economic backgrounds. In America, their experiences varied depending
on when, where, and how they were transported to these shores. The
overwhelming majority of Muslims in colonial and antebellum America
hailed from West Africa. The Atlantic slave trade that brought them to
the "New World" transformed the kinship, tribal, and religious bonds
through which Africans had navigated their worlds. The work of the
historian of the African diaspora, Michael Gomez, shows that the largest concentration of Muslims was found along the coast of Georgia
and South Carolina.[1] One possible reason for this was that the plantations in this region were large and isolated, which helped insulate their
inhabitants from outside influences.[2] Another likely reason was that
Charleston, and to some extent Savannah, were major slave ports that
provided slave labor for the large-scale cultivation of rice and indigo,
a trade for which the agricultural skills of slaves from Senegambia and
Sierra Leon (both areas with a significant Muslim presence) were in great
demand.[3] Yet, even in Georgia and South Carolina, African Muslims had
widely varying experiences depending on their background and on who
purchased them. Bilali Muhammad, for example, became the driver on
Thomas Spalding's plantation on Sapelo Island, while 'Umar ibn Said felt
so abused by his first master who purchased him at Charleston that he
ran away to Fayetteville, North Carolina. Elsewhere in the South, Yarrow
Mamout was essentially an indentured servant who was set free once he

---

[1] See Michael Gomez, "Prayin' on duh Bead: Islam in Early America," in *Exchanging our
Country Marks: The Transformation of African Identities in the Colonial and Antebellum
South* (Chapel Hill, NC: University of North Carolina Press, 1998), 54–87.
[2] The isolation of this region has long been noted by scholars of African American Studies,
who have studied the region for African retentions. For a classic study, see Charles Joyner,
Down by the Riverside: A South Carolina Slave Community (Urbana and Chicago,
IL: University of Illinois Press, 1984).
[3] Michael Gomez, *Black Crescent: The Experience and Legacy of African Muslims in the
Americas* (Cambridge: Cambridge University Press, 2005), 150.

completed making all the bricks for a house his master planned to build. He became a property owner in Georgetown, held stock in the Bank of Columbia, and had his likeness memorialized by the famed artist Charles Willson Peale in 1819 and later in 1822 by James Alexander Simpson.[4] 'Abdul Rahman, on the other hand, was manumitted on behest of the State Department after nearly thirty years of slaving and travelled on the American Colonization Society's fundraising circuit in order to purchase his children's freedom. Job Ben Solomon's life in the Atlantic slave trade led him to become an agent for the Royal African Company and have his biography penned for the Duke of Montague by Thomas Bluett while his translator, Lahamin Jay or Lamine Njai, who had been captured with him but sold to a different master, led a life of anonymity.

Just as there was no uniform African Muslim experience in colonial and antebellum America, there was no singular interpretation nor practice of Islam. In some instances, Islamic beliefs and practices were means of self-identification that distinguished, and at times even isolated, African Muslims from other enslaved Africans or white Americans. Job Ben Solomon, for example, was known to "often leave the Cattle, and withdraw into the Woods to pray; but a white Boy frequently watched him, and whilst he was at his Devotion would mock him, and throw Dirt in his Face."[5] When Job was asked by his English patrons to sit for a portrait, he at first refused given Islamic sensibilities toward the portrayal of human images as a potential form of idolatry. He only consented to the portrait once he was told that "we wanted his [picture] for no other End but to keep us in mind of him." Job asked the artist, Mr. Hoare, to paint him in his "Country Dress." Mr. Hoare replied that he could not depict

---

[4] Allan Austin, *African Muslims in Antebellum America: Transatlantic Stories and Spiritual Struggles* (New York: Routledge, 1997), 30–32; pages 45–49 of Peale's unpublished diary for 1819, held at the American Philosophical Society Library, cited in Allan Austin, *African Muslims in Antebellum America: A Sourcebook* (New York: Garland Publishing, Inc, 1984), 69–70 and 108 fts. 7–9; David M. Cole, *The Development of Banking in the District of Columbia* (New York: The William-Frederick Press, 1959), 6–10; and Kathleen M. Lesko, Valerie Babb, and Carroll R. Gibbs, *Black Georgetown Remembered: A History of Its Black Community from the Founding of "The Town of George" to the Present Historic District* (Washington, D.C.: Georgetown University Press, 1991), 11–12 and 136–137. According to Kathleen M. Lesko et al., Yarrow Mamout's house and land was located at 3330–3332 Dent Place in the area that today constitutes Northwest Washington, D.C.

[5] Thomas Bluett, *Some Memoirs of the Life of Job, the Son of Solomon, the High Priest of Boonda in Africa; Who Was a Slave About Two Years in Maryland; and Afterwards Being Brought to England, Was Set Free, and Sent to His Native Land in the Year 1734* (London: Richard Ford, 1744), 19–20.

what he has not seen. Job took this opportunity to draw a distinction between his and his patron's religions: "If you can't draw a Dress you never saw, why do some of you [Christian] Painters presume to draw God, whom no one ever saw?"[6]

Abstinence from alcohol and pork products both set Muslims apart and attracted attention to them. Thomas Bluett took an interest in Job and identified him as a "Mahometan" upon "his refusing a Glass of Wine" and hearing him pronounce a phrase he had written in Arabic that contained the words "Allah" and "Mahommed."[7] The Georgian plantation owner, James Hamilton Couper, described his head slave driver, Salih Bilali, as a "strict Mahometan; [who] abstains from spirituous liquors, and keeps the various fasts, particularly that of the Rhamadan. He is singularly exempt from all feeling of superstition; and holds in great contempt, the African belief in fetishes and evil spirits."[8] According to Charles Willson Peale, the "acquaintances of [Yarrow Mamout] often banter him about eating Bacon and drinking Whiskey – but Yarrow says 'it is no good to eat Hog – & drink whiskey is very bad'."[9] A biographical account distinguished 'Abdul Rahman from other slaves by pointing to the fact that his master, Thomas Foster, "has never known him intoxicated, (he makes no use of ardent spirits)."[10]

Some Muslims in colonial and antebellum America self-identified primarily in religious – rather than racial – terms as members of a larger Muslim community (the *umma*) that stood in contradistinction to the Christian community into which they were transported. When British troops were about to embark on Sapelo Island, Bilali Muhammad, for example, reportedly proclaimed to his master, that were the plantation to come under attack, "I will answer for every Negro of the true faith, but not for the *Christian dogs* you own."[11] Nicholas Said's autobiography shows that such religious-based distinctions harkened back to Africa: "The Christians considered and treated them [i.e., Muslims] as infidels, and they, in turn, look upon the Christians, from a religious point of view, as no

[6] Ibid., 50–51 and 44.
[7] Ibid., 21.
[8] "Letter of James Hamilton Couper, Esq.," published in Austin, *African Muslims: A Sourcebook*, 321.
[9] Pp. 45–49 of Peale's unpublished diary for 1819, held at the American Philosophical Society Library, cited in *African Muslims: A Sourcebook*, 70.
[10] Cyrus Griffin, "The Unfortunate Moor," *Natchez Southern Galaxy*, December 13, 1827, reprinted in *African Muslims: A Sourcebook*, 134.
[11] Caroline Couper Lovell, *The Golden Isles of Georgia* (Boston, MA: Little, Brown, and Co., 1933), 104.

better than dogs (*giour*), and here the matter ended by mutual consent."[12] 'Umar ibn Said likewise negatively self-identified as a Muslim when he identified his purchasers as "Christians" who took him to "the Christian country" where they spoke to him in "a Christian language."[13]

In at least three of 'Abdul Rahman's Arabic manuscripts, two of which were copies of the first chapter of the Qur'an, *al-Fatiha*, and the third a self-introduction, he inscribed "the sheikh, the jurist said/says to Mecca and Medina."[14] The precise meaning of this statement is unclear. It could be that he was indicating that he utters these words in the direction of Mecca and Medina. Since Muslims recite *al-Fatiha* in ritual prayers, which are performed in the direction of Mecca and Medina, this is certainly a possibility. His reference to himself as a sheikh (an elder or a master) and a learned jurist, however, appears odd, particularly since there is no hint of him having played a religious leadership role elsewhere in his biography. 'Abdul Rahman's Arabic was rather poor, which makes it difficult to ascertain what he meant to write. Nevertheless, his act of writing in Arabic at the request of white Christians, coupled with his reference to Mecca and Medina and to Muhammad as "His prophet" in these Arabic manuscripts marked him as belonging to a distinctive, larger community with a separate geographical and religious axis than that of those surrounding him.

RELIGIOUS OBSERVANCE AND COMMUNITY BUILDING

Evidence of religious observance among African Muslims in colonial and antebellum America has led some to conclude that these enslaved Muslims maintained their "cultural and religious distinctiveness" and rejected "adaptation," and in the process "made it evident that neither the white Christian world nor a creolized identity and culture appealed to them."[15]

---

[12] Nicholas Said, *The Autobiography of Nicholas Said, A Native of Bornou, Eastern Soudan, Central Africa* (Memphis, TN: Shotwell and Co., 1873), 69–70.

[13] See John Franklin Jameson, ed., "Autobiography of 'Umar ibn Said, Slave in North Carolina, 1831," *American Historical Review* 30, no. 4 (July 1925), reprinted in *African Muslims: A Sourcebook*, 464–468. A digitized version of Said's "Autobiography" is available at the University of North Carolina Library's "Documenting the American South" web site: http://docsouth.unc.edu/nc/"Umarsaid/menu.html (accessed August 28, 2009).

[14] Copies of these manuscripts can be found in *African Muslims: A Sourcebook*, 133, 158, and 190.

[15] Sylviane A. Diouf, *Servants of Allah: African Muslims Enslaved in the Americas* (New York: New York University Press, 1998), 71–106, quote on 106. It should be noted that Diouf is commenting on the experiences of Muslims in the Americas as a whole. In South America and the Caribbean there is more conclusive evidence of the existence of a Muslim community in the nineteenth century than in North America. Diouf, however,

For these scholars resistance to syncretism and white Christian hegemony unified the African Muslim experience in this period. The extant evidence, however, does not support this conclusion. How we understand the historical import of individual acts of religious observance among early Muslims in America depends on two interrelated questions. On the one hand, there is the historical question of whether or not the existing evidence permits us to conclude that there was a Muslim *community* in colonial or antebellum America. On the other, there is the hermeneutical question of how we should interpret the significance of Islamic acts of worship under the oppressive conditions of racism and slavery.

Our best source for surmising whether or not there was a distinct Muslim community in antebellum America is a series of short interviews with descendents of African Muslim slaves conducted by the Georgia Writers' Project of the Works Progress Administration during the 1930s. These interviews are particularly important for the rare glimpse they provide into the lives of Muslim women in antebellum America. The fact that some Muslim husbands and wives lived together on the plantations on Georgia's coastal islands apparently contributed to the modicum of a Muslim community one gleans from reading the interviewees' proud recollections of their Muslim grandparents. In assessing this data, Michael Gomez has been more cautious than others. When he refers to them as a "community of believers," Gomez cautiously concedes that his was not so much of a portrayal of a community as "an incomplete but substantive picture of individuals who pursued their religion with diligence and purpose."[16]

Inasmuch as existing evidence does not complete our picture of a *community*, we must turn our attention to the more interpretive question of the historical significance of Muslim beliefs and practices in colonial and antebellum America. Most students of African American Islam interpret the observance of Islamic precepts under the hardship of slavery as a unifying experience of "resistance" or "subaltern agency." Accordingly, it is reasonable to posit the existence of a Muslim community in places like the coastal islands of Georgia, where a few practicing Muslims lived on the same plantations together. The practice of Islam as a form of resistance under such conditions would necessitate the formation of a distinct Muslim community through which African Muslims would strive

    does not distinguish the regions in her blanket statement. Allan Austin also refers to the Muslims of Sapelo Island as an "*umma* – the only known antebellum African Muslim community in the United States." Austin, *African Muslims: Transatlantic Stories*, 6.

[16] Gomez, *Black Crescent*, 152–153.

to maintain their own identities. Adopting this line of reasoning, Richard Brent Turner has argued in his popular textbook on *Islam in the African-American Experience* that "signification (the issue of naming and identity) is...the interpretive thread that runs through the historical narrative of Islam in black America." The concept of signification, Turner explains, "refers to the process by which names, signs, and stereotypes were given to non-European realities and peoples during the western conquest and exploration of the world." It was the means by which "the West" identified and wrote the history of the non-Western world. In this context, Turner states that Islam, since slavery, has been a means for resisting the signification of blacks as inferior, "offering black Americans the chance to signify themselves, giving them new names and new political and cultural identities."[17] For Turner, and most other scholars of African American Islam, the practice of Islam in colonial and antebellum America foreshadows the formation of communal identities, though few agree with Sylviane Diouf's assertion that enslaved Muslims in America completely rejected "adaptation" and "creolization."

The historical significance of documentable Islamic beliefs and practices in this period is often framed in terms of "retentions" or "survivals" from Africa that endured the Middle Passage and slavery to influence African American life and culture in America. Indeed most of the scholarship on African American Islam has been in large part preoccupied with this question,[18] which stems from a seminal debate in the study of African American culture and religion known as the Herskovits-Frazier debate. On one side of the debate is the position associated with Melville Herskovits, who argued that Africanisms survived in America and played an important role in shaping African American religion and culture.[19] On the other side is the position associated with E. Franklin Frazier, who argued that the institutions of slavery stripped Africans of their culture and identity, making the survival of any Africanisms in the "New World" inconsequential to the development of African American religion and

[17] Richard Brent Turner, *Islam in the African-American Experience*, 2nd ed. (Bloomington, IN: Indiana University Press, 2003), 2–3.

[18] See for examples, Diouf, *Servants of Allah*; Gomez, *Exchanging Our Country Marks*, 59–87; and Austin, *African Muslims: Transatlantic Stories*.

[19] Melville J. Herskovits, *The Myth of the Negro Past* (Boston, MA: Beacon, 1958); Melville J. Herskovits, "African Gods and Catholic Saints in New World Negro Belief," in *The New World Negro*, ed. Frances S. Herskovits (Bloomington, IN: Indiana University Press, 1966), 168–174; Melville J. Herskovits, "What Has Africa Given America?," in *The New World Negro*, 321–329; Melville J. Herskovits and Frances S. Herskovits, *Rebel Destiny* (New York: McGraw-Hill, 1934).

culture.[20] Since the inception of this debate in the mid-twentieth century, scholars of African American religion and culture have offered varying reiterations and fusions of these positions, which have ultimately resulted in a general consensus that "this is not a debate with a winner and a loser."[21] Rather, there is evidence in support of both positions and interpretive excesses on both sides, which the other side corrects. Nonetheless, the Herzkovits-Frazier debate has remained relevant in African American Studies because of its political implications for how we interpret African American history in the larger context of American history. At the time of the civil rights struggle against Jim Crow laws, when this debate raged, Herzkovits' argument for African retentions implied that African Americans resisted the dominant culture and had their own distinct historical trajectory, while the argument for the extinction of Africanisms suggested the inclusion and incorporation of African American community in the historical narrative of the dominant culture.[22]

As important as the question of African survivals is for the study of African American culture and for American historiography, it is of limited utility in the quest to understand the role Islam played in the lives of Muslims in early American history. By interpreting the presence of Islamic beliefs and practices in colonial and antebellum America either as modes of resistance or African survivals, Islam is reduced to an identity or a rigid set of beliefs or practices (the Five Pillars of Islam). Islam, however, is not static. On the contrary, just as any other religion, it is polyvalent and dynamic. Its role in individual and communal lives cannot be expressed in terms of a concrete set of beliefs and practices. The significance of Islam for any individual Muslim or a community of Muslims is shaped by a complex dialectic between laws extrapolated by Muslim jurists from the Qur'an and the traditions of Prophet Muhammad, individualized understandings of God, communal norms and customs, and changing historical circumstances. To be sure, some African Muslims self-identified as Muslims and distinguished themselves by observing the Five Pillars. The telling feature of the early history of Islam in America, in any event, resides neither in the subaltern quality of Islam nor in the

[20] E. Franklin Frazier, "Rejoinder [to Herskovits] by E. Franklin Frazier," *American Sociological Review* 8, no. 4 (1943), 394–402.

[21] Albert J. Raboteau, *Slave Religion: The "Invisible Institutions" in the Antebellum South* (New York: Oxford University Press, 1978), 86f.

[22] For a discussion of the political implication of the Herzkovits-Frazier debate, see James L. Matory, *Black Atlantic Religion: Tradition, Transnationalism, and Matriarchy in the Afro-Brazilian Candomblé* (Princeton: Princeton University Press, 2005), 277–284.

retention of Islamic beliefs and practices but rather in the re-evaluation and reconfiguration of Islamic beliefs and practices in light of African Muslims' changing historical circumstances.

When we acknowledge the polyvalence and dynamism of religious beliefs and practices, it becomes apparent that Islam did not shape a distinct Muslim community in colonial and antebellum America but rather was a way through which Muslims made sense of their new experiences and encounters and formed new individual and communal relations. This polysemous aspect of religion in colonial and antebellum African America has been widely recognized in the scholarship on the topic, and it is usually discussed in terms of *syncretism* or the mixing of religions. However, as John Thornton has argued, "the merging of religions requires something more than simply mixing forms and ideas from one religion with those of another."[23] Such syncretism presumes an endeavor "to find common ground," and given the vast changes and diversity found in the eighteenth and nineteenth century in the Atlantic world, there were multiple resources to which people of different religious backgrounds could resort in order to find common ground. Recoiling from establishing common grounds was also an option that was exercised, but we should be wary of viewing this as a form of heroic resistance to slavery or European American hegemony. The islands off the Georgia coast, where we find most of our evidence for the isolated practice of Islam, are also where some African Muslims, like Bilali Muhammad and Salih Bilali, served as slave drivers. In other words, they accommodated slavery. According to some accounts, when the British anchored off the shore of Sapelo Island during the War of 1812, Bilali Muhammad was placed in "direct charge of about five hundred of his fellows and invariably gave a good account of his stewardship."[24] His master, Thomas Spalding, entrusted him with a load of muskets and authorized him to train other slaves in their use to defend the plantation.[25]

The polyvalence of Muslim religious beliefs and practices was particularly suited for finding common ground between both Christianity and Islam and Islam and other African religions in America. To begin with, Muslims from West Africa were no strangers to religious polysemy.

[23] John Kelly Thornton, *Africans and African Americans and the Making of the Atlantic World*, 2nd ed. (Cambridge: Cambridge University Press, 1999), 235.

[24] Ella May Thornton, "Bilali–His Book," *Law Library Journal* XLVIII (1955), 228–229, cited in *African Muslims: A Sourcebook*, 291.

[25] B. G. Martin, "Sapelo Island's Arabic Document: The 'Bilali Diary' in Context," *Georgia Historical Quarterly* LXXVII, no. 3 (Fall 1994), 592–593.

Normative Islamic practices (i.e., Islamic practices based strictly on Islamic law) and indigenous religious practices have a long and complicated history of coexistence in West Africa. The fifteenth-century Songhay ruler Askia Muhammad ibn Abi Bakr (r. 1493–1528) described his encounter with them:

I entered lands after Sunni 'Alī, who had amassed wealth and slaves from diverse sources, and I took possession of all of that.... I asked about the circumstances of some of them and about their country and behold they pronounced the *shahāda*: "There is no god save God; Muḥammad is the Messenger of God." But in spite of that they believe that there are beings who can bring them benefit or do them harm other than God, Mighty and Exalted is He. They have idols and they say: "The fox has said so and so and thus it will be," and "If the thing is thus then it will be so and so." They venerate certain trees and make sacrifices to them. They have their shrines (*buyūt mu'aẓẓama*) and they do not appoint a ruler or undertake any matter either great or small except at the command of the custodians of their shrines.[26]

At the turn of the nineteenth century, the famed Fulbe reformer and founder of the Sokoto Caliphate, 'Usman dan Fodio, took up arms (jihad) against those whom he and his ilk called "syncretists" or "mixers" (*mukhallitun*) in order to purify West African Islam from what they regarded as indigenous adulterations.[27] No doubt many of the African Muslims who were brought to America, particularly those enslaved prior to the jihads of the turn of the nineteenth century, were religious heirs of the people described by Askia or the *mukhallitun* persecuted by 'Usman dan Fodio. One of the interviewees of the Georgia Writers' Project, for example, recalled her Muslim grandmother, who regularly observed her ritual prayers, performing "set-ups":

Yes'm, Gran Hestuh tell me uh set-ups. Dey kill a wite chicken wen dey hab set-ups tuh keep duh spirits way. She say a wite chicken is duh only ting dat will keep duh spirits way an she alluz keep wite chicken fuh dat in yahd. Lak dis. Hestuh, she hav frien and frien die. Ebry ebenin friens spirit come back an call tuh hestuh. Hestuh know ef she keep it up, she die too. Hestuh den kills wite chicken, tro it

---

[26] Muhammad ibn 'Abd al-Karīm al-Maghīlī, *Sharī'a in Songhay: The Replies of al-Maghīlī to the Questions of Askia al-Ḥājj Muḥammad*, ed. and trans. John O. Hunwick (Oxford: Oxford University Press, 1985), 77–78, in English text, 22–23 in Arabic text.

[27] Ismaël Hamet, "Nour-El-Eulbab (Lumière des Coeurs) de Cheikh Otmane ben Mohammed ben Otmane dit Ibn-Foudiou," *Revue Africaine* 41 (1897), 301, and 42 (1898), 58–59, cited in *African Spirituality: Forms, Meanings, and Expressions*, ed. Jacob K. Olupona (New York: Crossroad, 2000), 284.

out uh doze, and shut doe quick. Wen she tro it out, she say, "Heah, spirit, mob away – dohn come back no mo."[28]

Another interviewee recalled that her religiously observant, Muslim grandmother conjured.

She talk plenty bout cunjuh. Say dat wen a pusson bin made tuh swell up frum a ebil spell, dey go tuh hab somebody tuh pray and drag fuhrum. Ef yuh hab a pain aw a misery in duh leg aw ahm, you kill a black chicken an split it open an slap it weah duh pain is an dat will cuo duh pain.[29]

While these enslaved Muslims' worldviews and religious lives were informed by and to a large degree shaped by normative Islam, Islam was not the exclusive religion they lived. Furthermore, Islam also exercised an influence in the religious lives of West Africans who did not self-identify as Muslims. Muslim holy men, known as marabouts (derived from *mura-bit* in Arabic), were sought out by Muslims and non-Muslims alike to effect cures and offer supernatural protection through talismans and prayers. There is evidence that such practices continued among Africans in colonial and antebellum America.

One, however, need not look to such objects as Qur'anic talismans to find proof of Muslims creating common ground with non-Muslims in colonial and antebellum America. African Muslims' normative acts of worship also connected them on the one hand with a larger Muslim com-munity (the *umma*) and on the other with the immediate community of Muslims and non-Muslims surrounding them. In Islam, individuals are held directly accountable to God, and many Islamic observances, such as the daily ritual prayers or the fast of Ramadan, could be carried out in-dividually. The presence of a Muslim community creates social structures and expectations that encourage individuals to observe these acts, but the presence of a community is not necessary for the acts to be legally valid or spiritually efficacious. When a Muslim performs these acts individu-ally, knowing that Muslims in other parts of the world are carrying out the same acts in more or less the same fashion and around the same time, they not only bring themselves physically and religiously into relation

---

[28] Interview with Shad Hall, Georgia Writers' Project–Savannah Unit (Work Projects Administration), *Drums and Shadows: Survival Studies among the Georgia Coastal Negroes*, ed. Mary Granger (1940; New York: Anchor Books–Doubleday, 1972 ed.), 159.

[29] Interview with Rosa Grant, Georgia Writers' Project–Savannah Unit, *Drums and Shadows*, 137.

with God but also with other members of the *umma*. Consequently the localized practice of Islam is imbued with universal significance, while concomitantly the universality of the practice among Muslims worldwide imputes Islamic value to (or Islamicizes) the local context in which it is performed.

A concrete example should help to explain what I mean. In recalling her grandmother Ryna to interviewers from the Georgia Writers' Project in the 1930s, Rosa Grant of Possum Point, Georgia said, "Friday wuz duh day she call huh prayuh day. Den she use tuh make bread."[30] Islamic law enjoins Muslim men to congregate, listen to a sermon and perform a ritual prayer together at noon on Fridays. While this duty is incumbent upon men, women are also allowed to attend congregational prayers when they are not menstruating. Even though it does not seem from this account that Ryna performed congregational Friday prayers, her recognition of Friday as the day of prayer and her decision to mark the day with a personal prayer indexes a sense of belonging to a larger, universal Muslim community separate from her immediate community. At the same time, her commemoration of the day with bread baking connects her to her immediate community. Ryna's adaptation of the Friday prayer, which normally brings individual Muslims into congregational relation, brought Ryna religiously into a communal relation with a Muslim *umma* that was physically absent and into a communal relation with her local non-Muslim cohort.

Another normative Islamic practice observed throughout the Muslim world that brought Muslims and non-Muslims into communal relations in antebellum America was *sadaqa* or *saraka*. Katie Brown of Sapelo Island recalled that her grandmother, Magret, who was one of Bilali Muhammad's African-born daughters, made

funny flat cake she call 'saraka.' She make um sam day ebry yeah, an it big day. Wen dey finish, she call us in, all duh chillum, an put in hans lill flat cake an we eats it. Yes'm, I membuh how she make it. She wash rice, an po off all duh watuh. She let wet rice sit all night, an in mawnin rice is all swell. She tak dat rice an put it in wooden mawtuh, an beat it tuh paste wid wodden pestle. She add honey, sometime shuguh, an make it in flat cake wid uh hans. 'Saraka' she call um.[31]

Saraka is derived from the Arabic word *sadaqa*, which refers to voluntary alms. In West Africa, according to Sylviane Diouf, the Fulbe of Guinea,

---

[30] Interview with Rosa Grant, Georgia Writers' Project–Savannah Unit, *Drums and Shadows*, 137, cited in *African Muslims: A Sourcebook*, 395.
[31] Interview with Katie Brown, Georgia Writers' Project–Savannah Unit, *Drums and Shadows*, 155.

Senegal and Mali have retained the use of the Arabic *sadaqa*. Among other ethnic groups, however, different pronunciations have been adopted. The Wolof of Senegal pronounce it *sarakh*, the Mandingo of Senegal and the Bambara of Mali *sarakha*. The Malinke of Guinea and the Hausa of Nigeria, like Katie Brown, call it *saraka*.[32] The Dyula of Côte d'Ivoire also refer to it as *saraka* and translate it into French as *sacrifice*.[33]

The use of *sadaqa* in Islamic sources dates back to the Qur'an where it is mentioned both as an obligatory (9:103) and voluntary (58:13) form of charity. In later Islamic discourses, it mainly refers to voluntary alms (*sadaqat al-tatawwu'*) offered to people of one's own choosing, with the intent to please God or to attain divine reward. According to Islamic law, *sadaqa* should be given with the intent of attaining divine rewards in the hereafter, but in practice Muslims often give *sadaqa* to attain divine favor in the here and now in the form of an answered prayer, the expatiation of sin, and assurance of general well-being for one's self, family, or community against calamity or evil.[34]

Enslaved African Muslims in America may have given *sadaqa* for any or all of the above personal reasons. Our sources do not offer any clues regarding their personal intent. What is notable in our sources, however, is the communal dimension of *saraka*.[35] In Katie Brown's above recollection of the practice, *saraka* marked an annual day of giving, a "big day," when children were given rice cakes. Shad Hall remembered her grandmother, Hestuh, another of Bilali Muhammad's African-born daughters, offering *saraka* on a monthly basis:

She make strange cake, fus ub ebry munt. She call it 'saraka.' She make it out of uh meal an honey. She put meal in bilin watuh an take it right out. Den she mix it wid honey, and make it in flat cakes. Sometime she make it out uh rice. Duh cake made, she call us all in an deah she hab great big fannuh full an she gib us each cake. Den we all stand roun table, and she says, "Ameen, Ameen, Ameen," an we all eats cake.[36]

[32] Diouf, "*Ṣadaqa* among African Muslims Enslaved in the Americas," *Journal of Islamic Studies* 10, no. 1 (1999), 27.

[33] Robert Launay, *Beyond the Stream: Islam and Society in a West African Town* (Berkley, CA: University of California Press, 1992), 196.

[34] For a general discussion of *sadaqa* in the Islamic law and society, see T. H. Weir and A. Zysow, "Sadaka" in *Encyclopaedia of Islam*, 2nd ed. (Leiden: Brill) and Amy Singer, *Charity in Islamic Societies* (Cambridge: Cambridge University Press, 2008), in particular 17–26.

[35] For an excellent ethnographic discussion of the communal dimensions of this practice in West Africa, see Launay, *Beyond the Stream*, 211–218.

[36] Interview with Shad Hall, Georgia Writers' Project–Savannah Unit, *Drums and Shadows*, 159.

That both Shad and Katie confuse *saraka* with the name of a sweet cake suggests that the giving of sweet cakes to children may have been the only form of voluntary almsgiving practiced by their Muslim ancestors. The absence of other adults in their memories, particularly male adults, is also notable. Both Magret's and Hestuh's offerings were most likely intended to receive an answer to some sort of personal prayer, in line with the traditional use of *sadaqa* among Muslims. This is evidenced by Hestuh's utterance of amen at the time of her offering. Usually, when *sadaqa* is offered to members of one's own community, it is intended to reinforce communal relations or to expand communal boundaries to include others.[37] That both Magret and Hestuh gave *sadaqa* to kids marks a way by which they were forging new relations with the next generation with whom they did not have clear kinship or tribal ties. As such, this Islamic practice became a way by which these women were able to form *new* communal boundaries. The fact that their grandchildren did not associate the practice with Islam and thought *sadaqa* referred to the cake itself rather than the practice of almsgiving suggests that their use of this practice was not intended necessarily to create an Islamic community but rather to Islamically sanction the existing community in which they participated.

It is worth noting that while the observance of some Islamic practices by Muslim men mentioned earlier set them apart from non-Muslims, these women's religious practices, though deemed distinctive, did not distinguish them from others. It is difficult to know whether or not this disparity is attributable to differences in gender roles among Muslims on the plantation. The making of rice cakes was not exclusive to female Muslims. Ben Sullivan, for example, recalled "it wuz muh fathuh Belali dat made rice cakes."[38] There is no mention, however, of Bilali or any other Muslim man offering *saraka*.

Whatever role gender difference may have played in Muslims interactions with non-Muslims, it seems clear from our sources that not all Muslim practices had the effect of isolating Muslims from non-Muslims. At harvest time, for example, Rosa Grant recalled her grandmother, Ryna, saying that they "stay up all night an shout. At sun-up dey all sing an pray and say dey live bettuh an be mo thankful duh nex yeah."[39] From Rosa's description of Ryna's prayers at sunrise, it is clear that her grandmother

[37] Launay, *Beyond the Stream*, 214–218.
[38] Interview with Ben Sullivan, Georgia Writers' Project–Savannah Unit, *Drums and Shadows*, 173.
[39] Interview with Rosa Grant, Georgia Writers' Project–Savannah Unit, *Drums and Shadows*, 137.

observed the Islamic ritual prayer: "Ebry mawnin at sun-up she kneel on duh flo in uh ruhm an bow obuh an tech uh head tu duh flo tree time. Den she say a prayuh. I dohn membuh jis wut she say, but one wud she say use tuh make us chillum laugh. I membuh it wuz 'ashamnegad.' Wen she finish prayin she say 'Ameen, ameen, ameen.'"[40] Did Ryna perform the Islamic ritual prayer as she had on other mornings after the all-night "ring shout"[41] that marked harvest time? Perhaps. Another interviewee of the Georgia Writers' Project at Possum Point recalled that harvest time "sho wuz a big time. We hab a big feas. All night we shouts an in duh mawnin right at sunrise we pray an bow low tuh duh sun. Muh great-gran – she name Peggy – I membuh she pray ebry day, at sunrise, at noon, an at sunset. She kneel down wen she pray an at duh en she bow low tree times, facin duh sun."[42] The fact that Rosa recalls laughing at her grandmother for uttering Arabic words in her prayer suggests that the majority of the participants in these harvest celebrations were probably not Muslim. Otherwise, Ryna's utterance of Arabic words would not have seemed so strange to her granddaughter. Nonetheless, it appears that their Islamic practices were part and parcel of the slave community's everyday life.

ISLAMIC OBSERVANCES AS AN ASPECT OF EVERYDAY LIFE

The memories of other interviewees of the Georgia Writers' Project re-inforce this sense that Islamic practices were *distinctive* but nonetheless *a feature of everyday life* among the Muslims on the Georgia sea islands' large plantations, to about twenty of whom *Drums and Shadows* refers.

"Muh gran wuz Hestuh, Belali's daughtuh," recalled Shad Hall of Sapelo Island. "She say Belali an all he fambly come on same boat frum Africa. Belali hab plenty daughtuhs, Medina, Yaruba, Fatima, Bentoo, Hestuh, Magret, and Chaalut.... Hestuh and all ub um sho pray on duh bead. Dey weah duh string uh beads on duh wais. Sometime duh string on duh neck. Dey pray at sun-up and face duh sun on duh knees an bow tuh it tree times, kneeling on a lill mat."[43] Shad Hall here

[40] Interview with Rosa Grant, Georgia Writers' Project–Savannah Unit, *Drums and Shadows*, 136–37.

[41] For a description of "ring shouts" in the Sea Islands, see Raboteau, *Slave Religion*, 68–75.

[42] Interview with Alec Anderson, Georgia Writers' Project–Savannah Unit, *Drums and Shadows*, 134.

[43] Interview with Shad Hall, Georgia Writers' Project–Savannah Unit, *Drums and Shadows*, 158.

refers to two different rituals. The prayer with beads is a form of *dhikr* ("remembrance"), a supererogatory act of worship that entails recalling verbally the names of God or calling praises on God for spiritual elevation and divine reward. The bead is used to count the praises uttered. The prayer on a mat, which involves bowing and kneeling, is the proscribed daily ritual prayer, which is usually performed five times a day, but when traveling or facing certain types of hardship, Islamic law allows the noon and afternoon prayers and the evening and night prayers to be combined, thus reducing the times of the ritual prayers to three.[44]

Katie Brown, another descendent of Bilali, recalls, "Magret [another of Bilali's daughters] an uh daughtu Cotto use tuh say dat Belali an he wife Phoebe pray on duh bead. Dey wuz bery phticluh bout duh time dey pray and dey bery regluh bout duh hour. Wen duh sun come up, wen it straight obuh head an wen it set, das duh time dey pray. Dey bow tuh duh sun an hab lill mat tuh kneel on. Duh bead is on a long string. Belali he pull bead an he say, 'Belambi, Hakabara, Mahamadu.' Phoebe she say, 'Ameen, Ameen.'"[45] The Arabic words which Katie Brown misconstrues here as "Belami, Hakabara, Mahamadu" may have been *bismillah* ("in the name of God"), *allahu akbar* ("God is greater"), and *alhamdu li-llah* ("praise belongs to God"). The latter two phrases are often said repeatedly with a prayer bead. In mainland Georgia, near Darien, Rachel Grant recalled, "Muh gran,... I membuh she use tuh pray ebry day at sunrise, at middle day and den at sunset. She alluz face duh sun an wen she finish prayin she alluz bow tuh duh sun."[46]

Ben Sullivan's memory of enslaved African Muslims' sartorial and religious practices is perhaps the best example of how Islamic practices were a distinctive but nonetheless quotidian aspect of antebellum life on some plantations on the islands of Georgia:

---

[44] We do not know if these enslaved Muslims themselves had a deliberate reason for praying three times a day. There are reports of certain radical, Sunni Muslim communities in the "deep-rural" areas of Northeast Kano (and beyond) who believe that ritual prayers should be performed only three times a day. This practice most likely dates to precolonial times and is based on the belief that it is closer to the practice of Prophet Muhammad's time. Praying three times a day, however, was not a common practice among most eighteenth- and nineteenth-century West Africans. Personal correspondence with Murray Last (December 19, 2009).

[45] Interview with Katie Brown, Georgia Writers' Project–Savannah Unit, *Drums and Shadows*, 154.

[46] Interview with Rachel Grant, Georgia Writers' Project–Savannah Unit, *Drums and Shadows*, 134.

Ole Israel he pray a lot wid a book he hab wut he hide, an he take a lill mat an he say he prayuhs on it. He pray wen duh sun go up and wne duh sun go down. Dey ain non but ole Israel wut pray on a mat. He hab he own mat. Now ole man Israel he hab shahp feechuh an a long pointed beahd, an he wuz bery tall. He alluz tie he head up in a wite clawt an seem he keep a lot uh clawt on han, fuh I membuh, yuh could see em hangin roun duh stable dryin.... I membuh a ole uhmun name Daphne. He didn't tie he head up lak ole man Israel. He wea loose wite veil on he head.... He weah one ring in he eah fuh he eyes. I have reference to it bein kine uh pruhtection tuh he eyes. Wen he pray, he bow two aw tree times in duh middle uh duh prayuh.[47]

Ben Sullivan's assertion that no one but Israel prayed on a mat contradicts other recollections in interviews from the Georgia Writers' Project. This inconsistency seems to support the notion that even though Islamic practices were distinctive, they were recurrent enough to be overlooked. What made Israel's Islamic observances stand out in Ben Sullivan's mind was most likely his uncommon appearance as a tall man with a pointed beard, sharp features, and a headdress.

RELIGIO-MAGICAL PRACTICES

I mentioned earlier that Muslim magical practices played a formative role in bringing Muslims and non-Muslims into communal relations in West Africa. It appears from some of the Arabic manuscripts written by African Muslims played a similar role in colonial and antebellum America. Eighteenth- and nineteenth-century West African Muslim societies were semi-literate societies in which writing had great religio-magical significance. Throughout sub-Saharan Africa, Arabic-Islamic writing was used in amulets and talismans that provided protection from calamities or adverse spirits and individuals.[48] Marabouts regularly produced and sold amulets with Arabic inscriptions to both a Muslim and non-Muslim clientele. In *A Voyage to the River Sierra Leone on the Coast of Africa* (1788), the British merchant John Mathews described these amulets, which were often referred to as *gris-gris*:

In the power and efficacy of charms, which they call griggories [*gris-gris*], they have an unlimited faith. These are made of goat's skin, either with the hair on, or drest like Morocco leather, into various shapes and sizes, from the bigness

---

[47] Interview with Ben Sullivan, Georgia Writers' Project–Savannah Unit, *Drums and Shadows*, 171.

[48] Jack Goody, "Introduction" and "Restricted Literacy in Northern Ghana" in *Literacy in Traditional Societies*, ed. Jack Goody (Cambridge: Cambridge University Press,

of a shilling to the size and form of a sheep's heart, and stuffed with some kind of powder, and bits of paper on which are written in Arabic sentences from the Alcoran; these they wear tied round their neck, waist, legs, and arms.... Every griggory is assigned its particular office; one is to preserve him from shot, one from poison, another from fire, others from being drowned; and when a man happens to be killed, burned, or drowned, they only say his griggory was not so good as to the person's who occasioned his death. (132–33)

Gris-gris was widely used by Africans and African Americans in co-lonial and antebellum America.[49] Antoine Le Page du Pratz, a plantation director for the Company of the Indies in Louisiana, wrote in 1758 that slaves "are very superstitious and attached to their beliefs and to trinkets that they call *gris-gris*; and they must not be taken from them nor can one talk about them, otherwise they would think themselves lost if these things were taken from them."[50] I have not found evidence of the actual employment of African Muslims for the production of amulets in the regions that eventually formed the United States. Regardless, an exam-ination of the few Arabic writings enslaved African Muslims left behind suggests the likely possibility of them producing or disseminating Arabic-Islamic inscriptions as talismans in colonial and antebellum America. Such practices were certainly present among Muslims in the Caribbean and Brazil during this period.[51]

One example of the talismanic use of Arabic-Islamic writings in ante-bellum America is a thirteen-page manuscript preserved in a letter pouch, which has been attributed to Bilali Muhammad of Sapelo Island. This manuscript titled the "Ben Ali Diary" was believed to be Bilali's autobiog-raphy and was known well enough for Joel Chandler Harris to create a fictional caricature of "Ben Ali" in *The Story of Aaron (so named), the Son of Ben Ali* (1896). When the "Ben Ali Diary" was examined more closely, it became evident that it contained a hodgepodge of excerpts from a popular eleventh-century Maliki legal treatise, *al-Risala*, by 'Abd Allah

1968), 16–19 and 199–264; Mervyn Hiskett, *The Development of Islam in West Africa* (New York: Longman, 1984), 314–319; and David Owusu-Ansah, "Prayer, Amulets, and Healing," in *The History of Islam in Africa*, ed. Nehemia Levtzion and Randall L. Pouwels (Athens, OH: Ohio University Press, 2000), 477–488.

[49] Yvonne P. Chireau, *Black Magic: Religion and the African American Conjuring Tradition* (Berkeley, CA: University of California Press, 2003), 34 and 46–51. Diouf, *Servants of Allah*, 128–134.

[50] Antoine Simone le Page du Pratz, *Histoire de la Louisianne*, (Paris, 1758) vol. I, 334, cited in Diouf, *Servants of Allah*, 130. Project Gutenberg has digitized an English translation of this work: http://www.gutenberg.org/dirs/etext05/8lsna10.txt (accessed March 15, 2010).

[51] Diouf, *Servants of Allah*, 131–134 and Chireau, *Black Magic*, 34.

ibn Abi Zayd al-Qayrawani (d. 1011) alongside recurring devotional formulas, such as the *shahada*: "I bear witness that there is no deity but God and Muhammad is the Messenger of God."[52] B. G. Martin's inquiry into the paper on which this text was written has revealed that the "diary" was written on "an Italian '*tre lune*' paper, a well-known and common kind of paper, exported widely from the late eighteenth century until well into the nineteenth century from Venice, Trieste, and Livorno to Egypt and North Africa."[53] How this paper reached the hands of Bilali in the United States is a mystery. It was not impossible for him to have had brought the text with him. Charles William Day mentions that in a shipment of "recaptured negroes" from Africa to Trinidad, most of the youngsters "had amulets very neatly sewn up in leather, suspended either round their necks or loins."[54] Another possibility is that Bilali acquired this text somewhere along the way, perhaps in the Bahamas where he slaved for ten years before being shipped to Charleston around 1802, where he and some members of his family were purchased by Thomas Spalding of Sapelo Island.[55] In any case, it was one of his prized possessions, which he at some point before his death entrusted to a Presbyterian minister and popular author of children's books, Francis R. Goulding, at Darien, Georgia where he spent the last years of his life.[56] Goulding, like other Americans mentioned in Chapter 1, probably took interest in this Arabic manuscript as evidence of Islam's "civilizing" influence in Africa. However, the recurring devotional formulas and the nonsensical ordering of the phrases in the document, coupled with the fact that the document was preserved in a leather pouch, strongly suggests that Bilali's so-called diary was actually a talismanic text. The manuscript's poor Arabic grammar and orthography is also in line with the Arabic writings commonly found in these amulets in West Africa.[57] Muslim scholars in Kano who were shown the "Ben Ali Diary" in 1939–40 in order to decipher it apparently acknowledged its magical qualities by declaring it "the work of jinn (spirits)."[58]

---

[52] Joseph Greenberg, "The Decipherment of the 'Ben-Ali Diary,' A Preliminary Statement," *Journal of Negro History* 25 (July 1940), 372–374, reprinted in *African Muslims: A Sourcebook*, 288–290; Martin, "Sapelo Island's Arabic Document."

[53] Martin, "Sapelo Island's Arabic Document," 600.

[54] Charles William Day, *Five Years' Residence in the West Indies* (London: Colburn and Co., 1852, 2 vols.), vol. I, 275.

[55] Martin, "Sapelo Island's Arabic Document," 591.

[56] Ibid., 593 and Austin, *African Muslims: A Sourcebook*, 275.

[57] David Owusu-Ansah, *Islamic Talismanic Tradition in Nineteenth-century Asante* (Lewiston, NY: Edwin Mellen, 1991), 42.

[58] Greenberg, "The Decipherment of the 'Ben-Ali Diary,'" cited in *African Muslims: A Sourcebook*, 289.

John Hunwick, an authority on the history of West African Islam, has argued that 'Umar ibn Said's 1819 manuscript addressed to his owner's brother, John Owen and the Christians of Raleigh, North Carolina, "should [also] perhaps be seen as something of a talisman"[59] that was intended to repatriate 'Umar to Africa. According to Hunwick's analysis, the key phrase in 'Umar's text is one of the few original phrases he penned himself, which Hunwick translates from 'Umar's broken Arabic as: "Indeed I wish to be seen in our land called Āfrikā in a place of the sea/river (*al-baḥr*) called K-bā [Gambia]." "The rest of the document," Hunwick surmises, "is … padding for this expressed wish, which is buried deep among Qur'ānic and other quotations." That the intended audience of his writing could not read what he had written was beside the point since it was the religio-magical efficacy of the words themselves that was significant.[60]

'Umar appears to have been recognized by other Africans in the United States as a marabout of sorts. Both the content and the mid-level knowledge of Arabic and Islamic sources evidenced in his writings supports this conclusion. Marabouts were holy men who were not learned scholars.[61] 'Umar's two-page "letter" to John Owen and the Christians of Raleigh, North Carolina is the second longest of his manuscripts after his autobiography (discussed below).[62] It consists of varying verses from the Qur'an and excerpts from didactic texts widely memorized in West and North African Islamic schools, such as Abu Muhammad al-Qasim ibn 'Ali al-Hariri's (d. 1052) versification of Arabic grammar, *Mulhat al-i'rab*. Many of the Qur'anic verses penned by 'Umar in this "letter" are among those commonly used in amulets. A near contemporary of 'Umar, George E. Post of the Syrian Protestant College (renamed the American University of Beirut in 1920), also attested to the talismanic nature of 'Umar's manuscript in an 1869 article for the American Colonization Society's *African Repository*, where he described the letter

---

[59] John Hunwick, "'I Wish to Be Seen in Our Land Called Āfrikā': 'Umar b. Sayyid's Appeal to Be Released from Slavery (1819)," *Journal of Arabic and Islamic Studies* 5 (2003), 73.

[60] Ibid., 67–68.

[61] According to some reports, 'Umar ibn Said was referred to as "a pray-God to the king" by other Africans; see Austin, *African Muslims: A Sourcebook*, 450 and 461. As John Hunwick has explained, this suggests that he was "a marabout who would offer prayers on a ruler's behalf…a position [that] does not require extensive learning, but rather a good memory of the Qur'ān." Hunwick, "'I Wish to Be Seen in Our Land Called Āfrikā,'" 66.

[62] For copies of a number of 'Umar's manuscripts, see Austin, *African Muslims: A Sourcebook*, 456–463.

as a "bombastic collection of sentences from the Koran ... followed by some Cabalistic sentences."[63]

'Umar's use of the powerful symbol of the pentacle is further evidence of the talismanic quality of this text. The pentacle in Islamic talismanic practices is believed to be the "seal of Solomon" and "to represent the secret 100th name of God and to have miraculous powers."[64] It appears on a number of 'Umar's manuscripts, including an Arabic translation of the Lord's Prayer.[65]

'Umar's abovementioned "letter" to John Owen also contains a geometric arabesque with the phrase, "sheikh general Jim Owen," inscribed in its center. Jim Owen was 'Umar's master. A similar geometrical design appears on another of his manuscripts with the names of members of Owen's family.[66] Given that in his autobiography 'Umar praises Jim and John Owen as "righteous men" who "give me to eat what they eat and give me to wear what they wear,"[67] it could be that he wrote their names in these texts in order to provide them with talismanic protection. This hypothesis is corroborated by a 1927 biography of 'Umar which recalled that "the Arabian prince would spend a great portion of his hours at Owen Hill, writing quaint sentences in Arabic on paper. He would then nail the messages to the pine trees on the plantation. Later when asked the contents of the message he had thus placed, he replied with a good natured chuckle that they were appeals to the neighbors not to take him from his good master."[68]

It seems that African Muslims employed the religio-magical powers of Arabic-Islamic writings to fulfill their wishes and prayers, on the one hand, and, on the other, to negotiate their relations with non-Muslims. In both Bilali's and 'Umar's cases, their writings brought them into ingratiating relations with whites. We do not know why Bilali chose Reverend

---

[63] George E. Post, "Arabic-Speaking Negro Mohammedans in Africa," *African Repository* (May 1869), 129–133, reprinted from *Missionary Herald* (April 1869), 114–117, reprinted in *African Muslims: A Sourcebook*, 484.

[64] Hunwick, "'I Wish to Be Seen in Our Land Called Āfrikā,'" 73. On the use of the pentacle as the Seal of Solomon, see Edmond Doutté, *Magie et religion dans l'Afrique du Nord* (Algiers: A. Jourdan, 1909), 156–158.

[65] See a photocopy of the manuscript in *African Muslims: A Sourcebook*, 462.

[66] Ibid., 463.

[67] 'Umar ibn Said, "The Life of 'Umar ibn Said (1831)," reprinted in Marc Shell and Werner Sollors, eds., *The Multilingual Anthology of American Literature: A Reader of Original Texts with English Translations* (New York: New York University Press, 2000), 80 in Arabic. My translation.

[68] Louis T. Moore, "Prince of Arabia," *Greensboro Daily News*, February 13, 1927, reprinted in *African Muslims: A Sourcebook*, 498.

Goulding to entrust with his "amulet," so we could only guess at what this act signified about their relationship. 'Umar's writings, on the other hand, have left us with some clues. He clearly appreciated his master and sought talismanic protection for him and his family even while he himself may have longed to return to Africa. Through the religio-magical powers of Arabic-Islamic writings, these African Muslims appear to have blunted the sharp distinction between black and white, slave and master in antebellum America in order to enter into varying forms of communal relations with non-Muslim whites. The nature of these relations remains a mystery, but what is clear is that Islamic beliefs and practices availed African Muslims of means with which they could negotiate their encounters with non-Muslims and bring them into their own world and in the process adapt themselves to their new context.

CONVERSION TO CHRISTIANITY

Conversion to Christianity was arguably the most widespread method by which African Muslims reconfigured their religious practices and beliefs to adapt to their new context and to form new communal relations. While we do not know exactly when and how (or even whether) the open practice of Islam completely ceased in nineteenth-century United States, it is clear from our sources that the American-born children of African Muslims did not practice Islam nor did they self-identify as Muslims.[69] A visitor to the Couper plantation in Hopeton, Georgia reported that Salih Bilali's children had "exchanged the Koran for the Bible."[70] 'Abdul Rahman had married an African American Baptist woman, and at least one of his sons was said to have become a preacher.[71]

Even though the religious revival in the latter half of the eighteenth century led to the conversion of many urban blacks and household slaves to Christianity, particularly at the hand of Baptists and Methodists, the great majority of slaves in the rural south remained outside of the church until the 1830s and 1840s. This is when a concerted effort was made to establish plantation missions in the South, both to save the souls of

---

[69] Bilali Muhammad's daughters mentioned by Georgia Writers' Project's interviewees were African-born and were transported to the United States with their parents.

[70] Charles Lyell, *A Second Visit to the United States of North America*, 3rd ed. (New York: Harper, 1855), 266.

[71] *Springfield Hampden Journal*, October 8, 1828, 3, cited in *African Muslims; A Sourcebook*, 168.

slaves and their masters and to Christianize the racist social order of the South.[72] "The process by which Christianity began to compete with and eventually overtake Islam," Michael Gomez explains, "can be viewed in the Sapelo community." Based on a 1992 interview with a descendent of African Muslims in Georgia's Sapelo Island, he writes, "The progeny of African-born Muslims ... eventually began attending the Tuesday, Thursday, and Sunday night 'prayer houses' held by each community on the island.... With the establishment of the First African Baptist Church in May of 1866, however, the open and collective pursuit of Islam became increasingly rare, although it is difficult to say when, exactly, it ended on the island."[73] The same interviewee informed Gomez that her great-grandmother, who was Bilali's great granddaughter, while "very active" in the Sunday school of the First African Baptist Church until she died in 1922, frequently stole away into the woods to pray. Did she go into the woods to conceal her observance of Islamic prayers?[74]

While the practice of Islam petered out among second-generation African Americans, the conversion of Muslims to Christianity had already begun with the first-generation arrivals. It is difficult to pin down the significance of conversion to Christianity for Muslims in the United States. A superficial reading of our sources would suggest that their conversion was opportunistic. As we saw in Chapter 1, the conversions of Selim, 'Abdul Rahman and Lamine Kaba were all associated with a desire for repatriation to Africa. Selim appealed to Reverend John Craig for religious instruction and immediately after his baptism asked the reverend to help him fund his trip back to Algiers. 'Abdul Rahman and Lamine both responded to the American Colonization Society's evangelical zeal to establish a Christian colony in Africa. They were baptized and promised to evangelize if the Society returned to their homeland. Mahommah Gardo Baquaqua also converted to Christianity "to be enabled to return to his native land, to instruct his own people in the ways of the Gospel of Christ."[75] Reports of some Muslims reverting to Islam once they arrived in Africa further corroborates the notion that they pretended to convert

---

[72] Raboteau, *Slave Religion*, 152f.

[73] Gomez, *Black Crescent*, 160.

[74] Michael Gomez, "Muslims in Early America," *Journal of Southern History* 60, no. 4 (Nov. 1994), 708 and Gomez, *Black Crescent*, 162.

[75] Robin Law and Paul E. Lovejoy, eds., *The Biography of Mahommah Gardo Baquaqua: His Passage from Slavery to Freedom in Africa and America* (Princeton, NJ: Markus Wiener Publishers, 2003), 92.

to Christianity or to comply with their de-Islamicization, because of the opportunity it provided to return to their homeland.[76]

These stories seemingly suggest that African Muslims' conversions were disingenuous. They were strategic acts of dissimulation that were necessary within a political structure that dehumanized blacks and deemed African religions backward and superstitious. This may very well have been the case for some African Muslims, but a careful examination of our sources allows for the more likely possibility that what was viewed by non-Muslim whites as conversion to Christianity was in actuality the re-evaluation and reconfiguration of Islamic beliefs and practices for a racial and religious context that was both highly diverse and oppressive.

Religious conversion is popularly conceived as the sincere and decisive adoption of a new faith accompanied by concrete changes in religious praxis, worldview, and lifestyle. It is thus widely assumed that one cannot confess to Christianity and cite the Qur'an or perform Muslim rituals. While this assumption holds true in theory, in the way in which religion is lived the world over, we cannot identify a causal relation between a specific set of beliefs and a particular set of practices in the same way that we could identify causes and effects in the natural world. Religion, as a living practice rather than a set of doctrines and laws, is messy. When we acknowledge this messy reality of "lived religion," it becomes very difficult to ascertain what, exactly, conversion meant to early Muslims in America. I do not mean to suggest that Muslim "converts" to Christianity in colonial and antebellum America did not understand what their baptism signified or that they underwent the acts of conversion without knowing what they were getting themselves into. Most Muslims would have had some knowledge of Christianity based on what the Qur'an and the Islamic tradition teach about Jesus and his followers.[77] They would have recognized Jesus as a revered prophet of God who along with Abraham, David, Moses, and Muhammad was given a written revelation, *al-Injil* ("the Gospels"), through which he was called by God to bring humanity onto God: "And We sent, in the footpath of the prophets, Jesus, son of Mary, confirming what was between his hand from the Torah and We gave to him the Gospel, in which there is guidance and light, and confirming what was between his hands

---

[76] See the report regarding 'Abdul Rahman's reversion to Islam in Africa cited in Chapter 1, p. 28.

[77] See Tarif Khalidi, ed. and trans. *The Muslim Jesus: Sayings and Stories in Islamic Literature* (Cambridge, MA: Harvard University Press, 2001).

from the Torah, as a guidance and an admonition unto the godfear-
ing" (Qur'an 5:46). Following Islamic teachings, Muslims in colonial
and antebellum America would have recognized the God of Christianity
as the same God as their own, but they would have considered belief
in the divinity of Jesus and the Trinity a form of human corruption
(Qur'an 4:171), which God sought to correct through the revelation of
the Qur'an to Prophet Muhammad. Like the Qur'an, they would have
referred to Jesus as the Messiah (Qur'an 3:45) and recognized him as
the Word of God (Qur'an 4:171). Indeed, as Job Ben Solomon's chastise-
ment of Christians for their audacity to paint the likeness of God (cited
earlier) demonstrates, most African Muslims would have been familiar
with Christianity in its Islamic version. And as Nicholas Said's conversion narrative demonstrates, many Muslims were fully aware of what
conversion to Christianity entailed. Nicholas was a slave to a Russian
prince at the time of his conversion. His account of the experience is
singular in its level of detail and remarkable for its self-reflexivity. It
deserves to be cited in full:

Hitherto, ever since my advent into Christendom, I had remained a consistent
Islam (sic), repeating the requisite number of prayers daily, and at the time
required, refraining from the use of pork, wine, etc., and rolling my eyes in holy
horror at the frequent infractions of the Koran that I constantly had occasion
to witness. But His Excellency [i.e., his former Russian master, Prince Nicholas
Vassilievitch Troubetzkoÿ (1831–1889) (Nikolai Vasilevich Trubetskoi)] made
up, his mind to turn me from the error of my ways, and devoted himself assidu-
ously to the accomplishment of his purpose. Whenever he went to prayers, he
made me stand before him, *bon gré, mal gré*, and imitate every action of his, such
as kneeling, bowing, making the sign of the cross, etc., and I used to enjoy myself
hugely, cutting capers and going through all sorts of pantomimic performances
when he thought I was acting in a very devotional manner. One day, as I was
indulging extensively in my favorite amusement, the Prince happened to turn,
and caught me in my most striking attitude, whereupon he gave, me a *striking* reminder of what was decent and respectful on such solemn occasions, by
administering to my ears a good boxing and depriving me of my dinner. Finally,
my, prejudices gave way, however, and I consented to embrace the Greek faith,
the State religion of Russia. I was baptized in Riga on the 12th of November,
1855, leaving my Mohammedan name of *Mohammed Ali Ben Said* at the font,
and bearing therefrom the Christian name of Nicholas. This performance ended,
I thought the job was complete, but the next day the *papa*, or priest who had me
baptized, sent for me, and on getting where he was, I found myself in a beautiful chapel, handsomely paved with marble of different colors. He caused me
to kneel before an immense *tableau* of the Saviour for hours, asking pardons for
my past sins. As the marble was harder than my knees, I was in perfect agony
during the greater portion of the time, and became so enraged with the papa,

that I fear I committed more sins during that space of time than I had done in days before. If fact, I am not sure but that a few ungainly Mohammedan asperities of language bubbled up to my lips. But I managed to get through without any overt act of rebellion. When I had become a confirmed Christian, the Prince presented me with a solid gold cross, and a chain of the same metal to suspend it around my neck by, in prevailing Russian fashion; and, as he had never allowed me to associate with the rest of his domestics, I began to consider myself quite a superior being.[78]

Nicholas clearly understood what conversion to Orthodox Christianity meant, how it ought to have, and in many ways did, change his life. He was aware of the opportunities it afforded him and of how it ingratiated him to his master. He understood what was expected of him as a Christian even though he did not wholeheartedly accept the confessional demands of Christianity. His narrative shows that enslaved Muslims likely understood what their conversion to Christianity meant to Christians, but they did not interpret their baptisms in the same way that their baptizers did.

Nicholas, like other Africans in America in this period, lived in a *poly-religious* world in which the same religious beliefs and practices were subject to widely varied meanings. Their polyvalence helped bridge individual differences in ethnicity, race, and religion, without eliminating these markers of difference. Encounters between religions in this period did not result in the syncretizing of Islam and Christianity nor did they result in religious pluralism defined as the accepted social form of religious diversity. Poly-religious beliefs and practices resulted from people of varying racial, religious, and cultural backgrounds coming into relation with one another. In Nicholas's case, his grappling with religious differences eventually led to his involvement in the universalizing, clairvoyant eclecticism that flourished in America's nineteenth-century "spiritual hothouse."[79] Late in his life he declared, "I was a Mohammedan; I am now, in belief, a Christian and a Swedenborgian."[80] He made no further mention of his involvement with the influential teachings of the Swedish scientist, philosopher, mystic, theologian, and biblical exegete, Emanuel Swedenborg (1688–1772), but the affiliation signals his participation in

---

[78] Said, *Autobiography of Nicholas Said*, 143–146.
[79] Jon Butler, *Awash in a Sea of Faith: Christianizing the American People* (Cambridge, MA: Harvard University Press, 1990), 225f.
[80] Said, *Autobiography of Nicholas Said*, 70. Unfortunately, Nicholas Said does not provide any explanation of how or why he became a Swedenborgian. The Swedenborgian church is based on the spiritual visions and teachings of the scientist, philosopher, theologian, mystic, biblical exegete, Emanuel Swedenborg (1688–1772).

what Catherine Albanese, a historian of American religion, has called "metaphysical religion," an eclectic and highly spiritual form of religion that dissolves traditional religious differences by appealing to individualistic intuitions, visions, clairvoyance, and monism.[81]

A few more examples from the lives of Muslims in colonial and antebellum America will better illustrate my argument regarding how the polyvalence of Islamic beliefs and practices helped bridge racial, ethnic, and religious differences without eradicating them. On 29 December 1828, Condy Raquet, a former U.S. *chargé d'affaires* in Brazil, met 'Abdul Rahman in Philadelphia and asked him to inscribe the Lord's Prayer in Arabic. 'Abdul Rahman instead wrote down the first chapter of the Qur'an – *al-Fatiha*.[82] This act could be interpreted as subversive or as a subtle form of resistance, ironically issued from a man who had consented to help spread Christianity to Africa and who had married a Christian woman whom he reportedly accompanied to church.[83] A more likely interpretation, however, is that in the poly-religious context of slave life in antebellum America, *al-Fatiha* was functionally polysemous for 'Abdul Rahman. *Al-Fatiha*, like the Lord's Prayer, is a scriptural prayer memorized for ritual recitation in daily prayer. By writing down *al-Fatiha* when asked to inscribe the Lord's Prayer, 'Abdul Rahman was writing the Lord's Prayer that he knew and in the process founding common ground with Condy Raquet and ascribing a new sphere of meaning to both *al-Fatiha* and the Lord's Prayer.[84]

'Umar ibn Said, who explicitly self-identified as a Christian convert, likewise understood *al-Fatiha* to be interchangeable with the Lord's Prayer. In his autobiography, he wrote (in broken Arabic):

At first, [as a] Muhammad[an]. When praying, [I] said: 'Praise belongs to God, the Lord of the worlds; the Compassionate, the Merciful; Sovereign of the Day of Judgment; It is You that we worship and it is from You that we seek help; Guide us on the straight path; The path of those whom you have favored with grace; Not of those with whom you are angry; Nor of those who have strayed. Amen.'

---

[81] Catherine L. Albanese, *A Republic of Mind and Spirit: A Cultural History of American Metaphysical Religion* (New Haven, CT: Yale University Press, 2007), 6–10.

[82] Photocopy available in *African Muslims: A Sourcebook*, 190.

[83] Thomas Gallaudet, *Springfield (MA) Hampden Journal*, October 8, 1828, 3, reprinted in *African Muslims: A Sourcebook*, 168 and 187 (the article on p. 187 was reprinted in *Providence Manufacturer's and Farmer's Journal*, August 21, 1828).

[84] Since all that exists of 'Abdul Rahman's Arabic writings are copies of *al-Fatiha*, it is possible that this was all that he could recall writing in Arabic. Even if this was the case, it does not change the fact that he saw the Lord's Prayer and *al-Fatiha* as essentially interchangeable.

Yet now, when praying, the saying of our Lord Jesus the Messiah: 'Our Father, who art in heaven, hallowed be thy name, thy Kingdom come, thy Will be done, on earth as it is in Heaven. Give us this day our daily bread and forgive us our trespasses as we forgive those who trespass against us, and lead us not into temptation but deliver us from the evil one for thine is the Kingdom, the power, and the glory for ever and ever. Amen.'[85]

Both *al-Fatiha* and the Lord's Prayer are scriptural prayers recited daily. By presenting them as interchangeable practices of Islam and Christianity, 'Umar did not syncretize these two religions; rather, he established a poly-religious common ground that maintained the distinctness of each religion while at the same time allowing him to step in and out of both. While he made a distinction between the prayer formula he used to use as a Muslim and the words he used later to pray as a Christian, the act of praying to God itself remained essentially the same to him.

Similarly, 'Umar presents the Qur'an and the Gospels as functional equivalents of one another as different forms of the same divine guidance: "I am 'Umar who loves to read the scripture, the Great Qur'an. General Jim Own along with his wife read the Gospels. They read the Gospels to me a lot."[86] We have already seen that the Gospels (*al-Injil*) in Islam is regarded as the scripture revealed to Jesus just as the Qur'an is the scripture revealed to Muhammad and the Torah to Moses. The main difference is that Muslims believe that all revelations received by prophets prior to Muhammad were corrupted by their followers and that the Qur'an supersedes them all. It is thus noteworthy that 'Umar used the term from Muslim discourses on Christianity, *al-Injil*, to refer to the Bible. 'Umar had been given an Arabic translation of the Bible, so he would have known from its title page that Christians themselves refer to their scripture in Arabic as *al-kitab al-muqaddas* ('the Holy Book').[87] Were he to have had acknowledged the Christian scripture as *the* Holy Book, he would have rendered a secondary status to the Qur'an. He was not however, interested in scriptural rivalry. Rather, he apparently sought common ground with Christians within his own Islamic worldview. While acknowledging, in his autobiography, that he and his master's family were brought up with different scriptures – "I am 'Umar who loves to read the scripture, the Great Qur'an. General Jim Own

---

[85] 'Umar ibn Said, "The Life of 'Umar ibn Said (1831)," reprinted in Shell and Sollors, *Multilingual Anthology of American Literature*, 88–89 in Arabic. My translation.

[86] Ibid., 86–87 in Arabic. My translation.

[87] See copies of two pages from 'Umar ibn Said's Arabic Bible, on which he wrote with his own hand, in *African Muslims: A Sourcebook*, 452–453.

along with his wife read the Gospels" – he asked, "God, our Lord, our Creator, and our Ruler, the Restorer of our state...Open my heart to the Gospels, to the path of guidance." He followed this with a phrase from the Qur'an, "Praise belongs to God, the Lord of the Worlds" (Qur'an 1:2, 6:45, 40:65), and then went on to quote the Gospels, "Because the Law (*shar'*) was made for Moses and grace (*al-ni'ma*) and truth (*al-haqq*) were for Jesus the Messiah"[88] (John 1:17). 'Umar simultaneously stepped in and out of both Islam and Christianity by appealing to a shared conception of God, as the Creator, Lord, and Ruler of all of existence. Tellingly, 'Umar cites a verse from the Gospel of John that would not offend Muslim sensibilities, ignoring both preceding and proceeding verses that describe Jesus as the Son of God or as the Word having been made flesh. While obviously cognizant of the differences between Islam and Christianity, his focus on their commonality allowed him to enter into a communal relation of sorts with the Owens.

Most white Protestants in colonial and antebellum America were unaware of the multiple religious worlds in which African Muslims participated, but a few did notice their interchanging of Islamic and Christian concepts. The preacher and historian Charles Colcock Jones wrote in *The Religious Instruction of the Negro in the United States* (1842): "The Mohammedan Africans remaining of the old stock of importations, although accustomed to hear the Gospel preached, have been known to accommodate Christianity to Mohammedanism. 'God,' say they, 'is *Allah*, and Jesus Christ is *Mohammed* – the religion is the same, but different countries have different names."[89] The British abolitionist Richard Robert Madden, in his account of his residence in the West Indies, also documented the multiple religious worlds in which African Muslims participated in the "New World". He was dismayed to receive a letter from a seventy-six-year-old African Muslim convert to Christianity "who is so anxious to convert his country man from the Mussulman creed, commencing in these terms, 'In the name of God, merciful and omnipotent, the blessings of God, the peace of his prophet Mahomet!' So much for the old African's renunciation of Islamism," wrote Madden. Commenting on a letter from another enslaved African, who, after having received "the

[88] 'Umar ibn Said, "The Life of 'Umar ibn Said (1831)," reprinted in Shell and Sollors, *Multilingual Anthology of American Literature*, 88–91. My translation.

[89] Charles Colcock Jones, *The Religious Instruction of the Negroes in the United States* (Savannah, GA: Thomas Purse, 1842), 125. A digitized copy of Jones' work is available at the UNC Library's "Documenting the American South" website: http://docsouth.unc.edu/church/jones/menu.html.

Testament, both of the old and the new law of our Lord the Saviour, in the Arabic language," was now "very anxious to get a prayer-book, the psalms, and an Arabic grammar – also a copy of the Alcoran," Madden wrote:

> Now, the latter part of the request, I think, looks like the yearning of one who was not quite weaned from the recollections of his old religion. I do not mean to say there was any hypocrisy in the new profession of either of these persons; I only mean to state my belief, that all the proselytes I have seen in Mahometan countries, have rather ingrafted the doctrines of Christianity on the stem of Mahometanism, than plucked up the latter, root and branch, to make way for the former. I have elsewhere stated, that so vague are their notions of the character of the religion they last adopt, that they think it compatible with the doctrines both of it and of their former creed, to believe in each.[90]

Madden's experiences with African Muslim "converts" took place mostly in Jamaica but his observations apply equally to the U.S. context. On another occasion, Madden boasted of having tricked three freed African Muslims "converts" to Christianity to divulge their "true" religion by taking "up a book, as if by accident, and … repeating the well-known Mussulman Salaam to the prophet Allah Illah, Mahommed rasur allah! In an instant," he boasted, "I had a Mussulman trio, long and loud."[91] Madden reported that one of the three men, Benjamin Cockrane,

> would have inflicted the whole of the "perspicuous book" of Islam on me, if I had not taken advantage of the opportunity for giving him and his companions a reproof for pretending to be that which they were not. Few, very few, indeed, of the native Africans who have been instructed in their creed or their superstition, which you please, have given up their early rites and observances for those of the religion of the country they were brought to. But this they do not acknowledge, because they are afraid to do so.[92]

In Madden's analysis of these men's religion, there is a clear disjuncture between their beliefs and their behavior. In line with popular understandings of conversion, he assumes that one who professes to be a Christian would not perform Muslim rites. Therefore, he self-righteously scolds these men for their false pretensions. It is, however, unlikely that these

---

[90] R. R. Madden, *A Twelvemonth's Residence in the West Indies, During the Transition from Slavery to Apprenticeship*, vol. II (London: James Cochrane and Co., 1835), 206–207, reprinted in *African Muslims: A Sourcebook*, 541.

[91] Madden, "Letter IX, to J. F. Savory, March 30, 1835," in *Twelvemonth's*, vol. I, 98–102, reprinted in *African Muslims: A Sourcebook*, 549.

[92] Ibid., 549.

men, by self-identifying with what they valued in Christianity and performing Christian rituals, were forgoing Islam. Or that they *only* associated themselves with Christianity out of fear. On the contrary, they were
founding poly-religious common ground on which they could enter into
relations with whites while still holding them accountable to God. One of
the men whom Madden claimed he had tricked into revealing his "true"
religious colors, for example, argued that given that God is the Creator of
all humans, blacks and whites should have the same freedoms:

Since he got free he try to serve God every day for so much goodness to him. An
why for no? who made the white man's heart? – God. And who made the black
man's heart? – God. Why should not black man serve God as well as white man?
and everyday him get up and go where him choose, and do what him like; very
much goodness to be thankful for to him good Father.[93]

While fear and dissimulation may have played some role in how African
Muslims related to Christianity, it was most likely this egalitarian dimension of Christian and Islamic conceptions of a Creator-God that allowed
them to participate in both religions simultaneously.

For 'Umar ibn Said, the association made, in both Islam and Christianity,
between belief in God and righteous behavior helped shape his judgment
of his masters and identify the whites with whom he formed a more
intimate relation. He ran away from his first master, who abused him;
he described his first master in his autobiography as "a weak small, bad
man named Johnson, a true infidel (*kafir jiddan*), who did not fear God
at all."[94] By contrast, he described his later master, Jim Owen, and his
brother as "righteous men who give me to eat whatever they eat and give
me to dress whatever they dress" and attributed their righteous behavior to their religiosity: "Jim along with his brother read the Gospels to
me."[95] The shared notion in Islam and Christianity that religion *is* morality, then, helped relate 'Umar to his white, Christian masters while at the
same time allowing him to hold them accountable for their actions.

Divine Providence played a similar role among some enslaved African
Muslims. The first four pages of 'Umar's thirteen-page autobiography is a more-or-less accurate transcription of the 67th chapter of the
Qur'an, *al-Mulk. Mulk* means "possession" or "property" in Arabic, and
when applied to God's relation with the world, it also refers to divine

[93] Ibid., 549.
[94] 'Umar ibn Said, "The Life of 'Umar ibn Said (1831)," reprinted in Shell and Sollors,
    Multilingual Anthology of American Literature, 76–77 in Arabic. My translation.
[95] Ibid., 80–81. My translation.

providence. Theologically, this chapter of the Qur'an underscores God's sovereignty over every aspect of life and warns those who ignore divine guidance or who assume that God is not aware of their every thought and action and that God is the All-knowing and vigilant judge of humanity. The chapter *al-Mulk*, as previously mentioned, is often used in talismanic writings and thus may also have a magical purpose in 'Umar's autobiography. It seems unlikely, however, that this would have been its primary purpose in this manuscript. Neither theology nor magic could alone explain why a slave would begin his autobiography by citing God's own words on divine providence. Here again we see how the polyvalence of Islam helped Muslims form relations with others, including those who legally possessed their body and labor. On the one hand, 'Umar denied his human master's power over him by acknowledging God's power over all things. By placing his life in God's hands he also avails himself of divine protection. Divine providence also softens the inhumanity of slavery, which allows us to fathom why 'Umar would have regarded the Owens, whose chattel he was, as "righteous men." While Christian slavers evoked divine providence to justify slavery, 'Umar invoked God's *mulk* to endure slavery. The slave and the slaver met on the plain of providence and held each other accountable before God.

Providence also seems to have played an important role in the way in which Mahommah Gardo Baquaqua endured slavery and held slavers accountable. He was purchased in Brazil by a sea captain. During a voyage from Rio de Janeiro to New York, upon discovering "that at New York there was no slavery," he devised to walk off his master's ship and into freedom when the ship embarked. "That was the happiest time in my life," he wrote later, "even now my heart thrills with joyous delight when I think of that voyage, and believe that the God of all mercies ordered all for my good; how thankful I was."[96] His celebration of God's providential plan for him, however, was premature, for that evening his master went to hit him on the head when he could not light the lamp at the binnacle. He protected his head by raising his forearm. This enraged his master who beat him mercilessly and tied him up at the bow of the ship. When reflecting upon the abuse he endured, Baquaqua took solace in providence and the punishment God will enact on his master on Judgment Day:

[96] Samuel Moore, ed., *An Interesting Narrative. Biography of Mahommah G. Baquaqua, A Native of Zoogoo, in the Interior of Africa* (Detroit, MI: By the author, 1854), published in *African Muslims: A Sourcebook*, 632.

Slavery is bad, slavery is wrong. This captain did a great many cruel things which would be horrible to relate.... But the day is coming when his power will be vested in another, and of his stewardship he must render an account; alas what account can he render of the crimes committed upon the writhing bodies of the poor pitiless wretches he had under his charge, when his kingship shall cease and the great account is called for; how shall he answer? And what will be his doom? – That will only be known when the great book is opened. May God pardon him (in his infinite mercy) for the tortures inflicted upon his fellow creatures, although of a different complexion.[97]

There is a possibility that these sentiments expressed in *An Interesting Narrative. Biography of Mahommah G. Baquaqua* were not actually his because, as indicated on the title page, the book was "written and revised from his own Words, by Samuel Moore, Esq." Allan Austin, in his analysis of the text, attributes the writing primarily to Moore, whom he considers to have been "simplistically Eurocentric in his interpretation of Baquaqua's words," and he belittles the text as a product of "the naïveté of both men."[98] Africanists Robin Law and Paul E. Lovejoy, however, have argued that Baquaqua was the author of the text and that "'written' here evidently means 'written down' rather than 'composed,' the implication being that Moore put into writing an account given orally by Baquaqua." Law and Lovejoy offer as evidence for their position the fact that Moore indicated that he made readable "the imperfect English spoken by Mahommah,"[99] the fact that the only known contemporary review of the book by a person familiar with Baquaqua described it as "an autobiography, but revised and prepared for publication by Samuel Moore,"[100] and the fact that information Baquaqua provides about nineteenth-century life in Djougou "seems both plausible and valuable."[101] This is not the place to render a final judgment on the authenticity of Baquaqua's text. Austin's assessment of the text as inauthentic seems to be based on its enormously positive presentation of Christianity and the hope it represents for Africa, while Law and Lovejoy seem to have been mainly concerned with the data it provides about life

---

[97] Moore, *Biography of Mahommah G. Baquaqua*, published in *African Muslims: A Sourcebook* Austin, *African Muslims: A Sourcebook*, 633.

[98] Austin, *African Muslims: Transatlantic Stories*, 160.

[99] P. 5 of Baquaqua's original *Biography*, reprinted in Law and Lovejoy, *Biography of Mahommah Gardo Baquaqua*, 92.

[100] Law and Lovejoy, *Biography of Mahommah Gardo Baquaqua*, appendix 4, "Review of the *Biography*, published in *The American Baptist*, 2 November 1854," 251; see p. 9 for their argument regarding the plausibility of Baquaqua's information.

[101] Law and Lovejoy, *Biography of Mahommah Gardo Baquaqua*, 19.

in Africa and the African diaspora in the nineteenth century. For our purposes, what is noteworthy is that providence and divine judgment become the ground on which Moore and Baquaqua meet, crossing religious and racial boundaries, in order to make sense of slavery and to render a religious judgment on it.

Another account of a former African Muslim slave and a white Christian finding common ground through providence could be found in another Moore's, Francis Moore's, account of his trade mission with Job Ben Solomon on behalf of the Royal African Company. During this trip to Job's homeland, Job ran into the people who had robbed him and sold him into slavery. He at first sought to take revenge, but was persuaded by Moore to interrogate them incognito instead. He discovered in the course of their conversation that their king was later accidently killed by the pistol he received as part of the price for Job. Moore reported:

> At the Closing of this Story *Job* was so very much transported, that he immediately fell on his Knees, and returned Thanks to *Mahomet* for making this Man die by the very Goods for which he sold him into Slavery; and then turning to me, he said, "Mr. *Moore*, you see now God Almighty was displeas'd at this Man's making me a Slave, and therefore made him die by the very Pistol for which he sold me; yet I ought to forgive him," *says he*, "because had I not been sold, I should neither have known any thing of the *English* Tongue, nor have had any of the fine, useful and valuable Things I now carry over, nor have known that in the World there is such a Place as *England*, nor such noble, good and generous People as Queen *Caroline*, Prince *William*, the Duke of *Montague*, the Earl of *Pembroke*, Mr *Holden*, Mr *Oglethorpe*, and the Royal *African* Company."[102]

As was the case with Baquaqua, we cannot be absolutely certain that what Moore reports of Job's interpretation of his ordeals is accurate, but there is also no reason to doubt such a politic response from Job. In the cases of 'Umar, Baquaqua, and Job, the notion of providence played a significant role in the way in which they interpreted their lives under slavery and the way in which they held others, particularly whites, accountable for their actions in order to enter into relations with them.

SUMMARY

While the practice of Islam seems to have died out among second-generation African Americans in the nineteenth century, Islamic beliefs and

---

[102] Francis Moore, *Travels into the Inland Parts of Africa: Containing a Description of the Several Nations* (London: Edward Cave, 1738), 206–207.

practices were a vital part of the way in which many enslaved Africans interpreted their American context and negotiated their relations with black non-Muslims and white Christians. Generally speaking, Islamic beliefs and practices provided means by which Muslims in colonial and antebellum America sought poly-religious common ground with others. Islam was re-evaluated and reconfigured to define new poly-religious communal relations that crossed racial and religious boundaries.

The polysemy of Islamic beliefs and the polyvalence of religious praxis, more generally, paved the way for a poly-religious world in which Muslims participated in varying distinct religious practices at the same time, stepping in and out of Christianity, Islam, and indigenous African religions, and in the process redefining them for their new contexts and relations.

Some African Muslims in colonial and antebellum America may have created a separate community. However, the evidence allows only a weaker conclusion that Islamic practices and beliefs were re-evaluated and reconfigured to create new communal relations with both non-Muslim blacks and white Christians. The most prominent example of this re-evaluation and reconfiguration of Islam took a form that was generally recognized as conversion to Christianity, but in actuality was an effort to create poly-religious common ground between Islam and Christianity in order to make sense of the horrors of slavery on the one hand and on the other to hold its participants accountable to one another before God.

While the re-evaluation and reconfiguration of Islamic beliefs and praxis in the poly-religious world of colonial and antebellum America in and of itself were not syncretistic, they helped form a poly-religious common ground on which Muslims related to other religions, setting the stage for postbellum religious practices more properly characterized as syncretistic. The most prominent examples of such syncretistic religions are the Moorish Science Temple and the Nation of Islam, which were founded in the North in the 1920s and 1930s, respectively. But the syncretism of Islam with Christianity and indigenous African religions was also found in more mainstream circles of the African American South. Preacher Little and his sermon in a church on Sapelo Island in the 1930s, described by the Georgia Writers' Project, appear to be a case in point:

The church was filled with a tense quietness. The preacher came from behind the platform and stood silently behind the pulpit desk, looking dramatically over his congregation. He was tall and spare, with brown skin, narrow face, and a thin pointed beard, a Mohammedan looking Negro. He wore a black skull cap, which we learned later was not ritualistic but was worn to protect his head from the draught. This was Preacher Little who, we were afterward told, was an itinerant preacher, not a native to the island but a type native to the district. His text, read in a loud, commanding voice, was "You ah the salt of the earth; but if the salt has lost its savory, wherewith shall it be salt; it is then no good and should be trompled intuh earth." … The sermon that followed, however, was in no way connected with the text. Preacher Little divided his sermon into three parts and lectured his congregation on "straying frum duh paat." What he said was not really coherent. Words stood out, phrases rang in our ears, quotations from the Bible resounded at random but that was the beginning and the end. The impelling element was the sound of Preacher Little's voice…. Regular stumping of the feet began; the vibration penetrated into every corner. It was impossible not to think of the beating of the drum.[103]

As others have also observed, Preacher Little appears as "the embodiment of a certain Islamic-Christian synthesis,"[104] and his sermon on "straying from the path" resonates in frequently used parts of the Bible (Psalm 44:18, Romans 3:12) and the Qur'an (1:6–7). The congregation's rhythmic response, of course, has resonance in African religions. If the common ground African Muslims sought to establish in places like Sapelo Island set the stage for this later synthesis of Islam, Christianity, and the indigenous religions of Africa, the exact means and institutions by which this synthesis was passed on to future generations is unknown and deserves careful study.

[103] Georgia Writers' Project–Savannah Unit, *Drums and Shadows*, 161.
[104] Gomez, "Muslims in Early America," 707.

3

Conflating Race, Religion, and Progress

Social Change, National Identity, and Islam in the Post–Civil War Era

> We are all a little wild here with numberless projects of social reform; not a reading man but has a draft of a new community in his waistcoat pocket.
>
> Ralph Waldo Emerson (1840)

The poly-religious common ground African Muslims sought with white Christians and non-Muslim Africans, though distinctive, was symptomatic of the times. Emerson's description of religious life in America in a letter to the historian and essayist Thomas Carlyle (1795–1881) captured the experimentalist, adaptive, heterogeneous, spiritualist, and individualistic ethos of religious life in antebellum America. The religious issues facing African Muslims were unique in many ways because of slavery and institutionalized racism, but as Nicholas Said's embrace of the teachings of the scientist, mystic, philosopher, exegete, and visionary Emanuel Swedenborg reminds us, not all African Muslims were cut off from the socio-religious reform movements to which Emerson referred.[1] Americans sought to adapt their religious lives to Enlightenment ideals and the founding principles of their new republic, and they were not

---

[1] Jon Butler, *Awash in a Sea of Faith: Christianizing the American People* (Cambridge, MA: Harvard University Press, 1990), 225f. For a discussion of Emanuel Swedenborg's influence on the religious movements that emerged in antebellum America see Catherine Albanese, *A Republic of Mind and Spirit: A Cultural History of American Metaphysical Religion* (New Haven, CT: Yale University Press, 2007), 140–144; and Ralph Waldo Emerson's essay on Swedenborg in his *Representative Men: Seven Lectures* (Boston, MA: Phillips, Sampson, and Company, 1850), 95–145. This latter book was inspired by Thomas Carlyle's *On Heroes, Hero-Worship, and the Heroic in History* (1840), which has a chapter on "The Hero as Prophet. Mahomet: Islam." I am indebted to Steve Wasserstrom for bringing this relation to my attention.

wanting in prophets, visionaries, fraternities, or volunteer associations. Mormons, Shakers, Evangelicals, Theosophists, Transcendentalists, Freemasons, Adventists, and Millenarians (just to name a few) all offered their own interpretations of religion and communal life.

The rapid growth of immigration to the United States in the latter half of the nineteenth century further altered America's religious landscape. In 1775, Catholics numbered about 25,000. By 1860, an estimated 3 million Catholics lived in the United States, and by 1900 their number rose to 12 million. Most of them immigrated to the United States from Southern Europe. Many, however, became citizens of the United States as U.S. boundaries expanded westward into former French and Spanish colonies. In 1776, Jews numbered around 2,000. By 1860, there were about 150,000 Jews in the United States, and by the early 1900s their number had risen to 2 million.[2] The Gold Rush and demand for agricultural and industrial labor also brought large numbers of immigrants from China (and later Japan) to the United States. Between 1850 and 1900, some 300,000 Chinese immigrants came to the United States.[3] As I will discuss in the following chapter, the first two decades of the twentieth century also saw the immigration of some 60,000 Muslims from Anatolia, the Levant, Eastern Europe, and South Asia.

The western expansion of the United States also brought more Native Americans within the boundaries of the country and increased their rate of contact and conflict with European Americans. The North's victory in the Civil War preserved the Union, but it offered no lasting solution to the integration of newly freed African Americans into the social, political, and economic life of the country. Both churches and fraternal orders played a crucial role in the development of a distinct African American society and culture following the Civil War. They served as places where African Americans could exercise self-governance, publically celebrate their citizenship, form mutual bonds of fellowship, and come to one another's aid. Many blacks withdrew from white churches and established their own congregations. New black denominations emerged, and older black denominations originally founded in the North came to establish churches in the South. Prince Hall Masonry, which was founded by a free black Freemason named Prince Hall in Boston in 1775, formed branches in the

---

[2] Bret E. Carrol, *Routledge Historical Atlas of Religion in America* (New York: Routledge, 2000), 90–95, 108.

[3] Stephan Thernstrom, Ann Orlov, and Oscar Handlin, eds., *Harvard Encyclopedia of American Ethnic Groups* (Cambridge, MA: Harvard University Press, 1980), 223.

South during the Reconstruction Era, while black southerners formed hundreds of other lodges and fraternal orders.[4]

The postbellum era was indeed a time of great social change. Increased ethnic and racial diversity and the heterogeneity of religious life in America, coupled with a bloody Civil War, called for the rethinking of the essential character of America. These questions were further complicated by greater access to information about other people's religions and ways of life. Many factors, in addition to the emancipation of slaves, increased immigration from abroad, and the colonization of Native American territories, decreased the distance between European American Protestants and others. Industrialization brought a great amount of wealth and jobs to American cities, further fueling domestic and international migration into the burgeoning cities of the Northeast and the Midwest. As industry replaced agriculture as the engine of America's economy, America became more urban and its urban centers became more diverse.

Furthermore, the steam engine and railroads facilitated travel throughout the world. The increasing globalization of commerce made rapid transportation available not only in Europe and North America but wherever European interests were found. The world was getting smaller. The vastness of the British Empire gave an advantage to Anglophones. It is thus not surprising that when Jules Verne wrote about a fictional trip "around the world in eighty days" in 1873, he adopted an English protagonist who completed his travels by traversing the British Empire and the United States. The decreasing of distances between peoples made possible by steam ships and railroads was not lost on Americans. In fact, what Verne imagined in 1873 had already been completed in 1870 by an eccentric American entrepreneur, George Francis Train, who wrote that "Jules Verne wrote fiction ... of my fact."[5] In the latter part of the nineteenth century, missionaries, travelers, pilgrims to the Holy Land, soldiers, and merchants brought news, artifacts, and merchandise back to the United States from such diverse places as Italy, Greece, Egypt, China, Japan, India, West Africa, Syria, North Africa, Anatolia, and Persia.

Increased contact with cultural, religious, and ethnic differences stimulated the growth of new disciplines, such as ethnology, comparative philology, and comparative religion. The practitioners of these disciplines

---

[4] Albert J. Raboteau, *Canaan Land: A Religious History of African Americans* (Oxford: Oxford University Press, 2001), 68–71.

[5] Train traveled around the world four times. His 1870 trip was his second trip and took eighty days. His shortest trip was in 1892 and lasted sixty days. George Francis Train,

sought to translate both the cultures and the texts of other societies into Western European and American vernaculars, making it all the more necessary for any construction of American identity at this time to grapple with what Americans believed they knew about other people's collective identities. In short, the transcontinental encounters and exchanges that led to the founding of the Atlantic world in the sixteenth and seventeenth centuries came into their own in late-nineteenth-century America.

RESPONSES TO DIVERSITY

There was a myriad of responses to what it meant to be American in the face of the rapid diversification, urbanization, and industrialization of the United States in the latter part of the nineteenth century. What was significant in these responses for the history of Islam in America was the way in which they conflated industrial development, commercial capitalism, egalitarian Enlightenment ideals, science, rationality, the white race, and Protestant Christianity to argue for the superiority of Anglo-American, liberal Protestantism. In what follows, I refer to this in shorthand as the conflation of race, religion, and progress. "Progress" here denotes the positive value that was attributed to industrial development, capitalism, and Enlightenment thought as civilizing forces in the evolutionary history of mankind. I should note that talking about these categories in terms of "conflations," though helpful today, would have been anachronistic in the late nineteenth and early twentieth centuries. Race, religion, and progress were not seen as distinct analytical categories that could be conflated. Rather, they were defined in relation to one another at this time to define a singular national identity.

In the antebellum period, Anglo-American Protestants had not felt a necessity to assert their preeminence in society. Their cultural, political, and economic dominance was palpable in virtually all aspects of American life. They constituted what historians have called "the establishment." Ethnic, racial, and religious minorities were "outsiders" who, as discussed in the previous chapter, could enter into relation with the establishment by trying to establish some sort of common ground. The emancipation of slaves along with increased immigration, industrialization, and urbanization altered not only the social and religious landscape of America but also its economic and political power structures. Not only was there more ethnic, racial, and religious diversity in the country but

My Life in Many States and in Foreign Lands: Dictated in My Seventy-Fourth Year (New York: D. Appleton and Company, 1902), x.

there were new classes of elites emerging from these varying communities in urban centers throughout the United States. Industrial capitalism also allowed for the emergence of a *nouveau riche*, cosmopolitan class, the likes of the famed Scottish industrialist Andrew Carnegie. This new post–Civil War era was characterized more by religious competition than poly-religious practices, and the competition was over the cultural authority to define America's national identity and to lay claim to its economic, industrial, and scientific advancements. The conflation of race, religion, and progress was thus a means by which nineteenth-century Anglo-American Protestants, awash in ethnic, racial, and religious diversity, sought to hold on to their dominant position in society by defining America as an essentially white, Protestant country, uniquely committed to progress.

The triumphant articulation of a white, Protestant American national identity through the conflation of race, religion, and progress is important for narrating the history of Islam in America at the turn of the twentieth century for two reasons. First, this conflation functioned as a matrix into which others could define their own identities in order to lay claim to America's progress and to help reshape America's national identity. As the next chapter will illustrate, early immigrants from South Asia and the Levant self-identified as members of the "white race" and, in the case of Christian Levantine immigrants, touted their association with the homeland of Jesus Christ as a means of becoming legal citizens and participating in America's modernity. Ironically insofar as such efforts were successful (particularly for lighter-skinned, Levantine Arabs), an establishment venture that was intended to maintain the social and cultural authority of the Protestants in actuality abetted the diversification of America by allowing for the inclusion of some non-Anglo, non-Protestants from the Muslim-majority world into American society as citizens.

Secondly, in the context of European imperialism, a similar discourse around race, religion, and progress was employed to justify the colonization of much of the Muslim-majority world as a "civilizing" or "modernizing" project, the ethos of which Rudyard Kipling captured in the title of one of his poems, "The White Man's Burden."[6] The first Muslim missionaries who immigrated to the United States in this period were intimately familiar with the way in which race, religion, and progress were conflated to support the colonization and oppression of dark-skinned non-Europeans. These Muslim missionaries did not challenge

---

[6] For two classic discussions of these processes, see Edward W. Said, *Orientalism* (New York: Vintage Books, 1979) and Timothy Mitchell, *Colonizing Egypt* (Berkeley, CA: University of California Press, 1988).

the soundness of the conflation of race, religion, and progress through which an American national identity was articulated. As I will discuss in the latter half of this chapter, the earliest Muslim missionaries in the United States had to grapple with this conflation in order to articulate Islam's place within it. Chapter 5 will show how, later, Muslim missionaries' decision to proselytize in America was in large part influenced by a desire to turn the table on white Christians by arguing for the superiority of Islam as a race-blind religion, particularly suited for progress and modernity. They found their firmest footing in America among African Americans who had migrated to the North in search of a share in America's progress but were disappointed by the racism they encountered.

WHOSE COUNTRY?

The conflation of race, religion, and progress was already present in the development of the conception of "civilization" in earlier encounters between Anglo-American Protestants and African Muslims discussed in Chapter 1. In the late nineteenth century, under the influence of social evolutionary ideas developed around the works of such thinkers as Charles Darwin (1809–1882) and Herbert Spencer (1820–1906), this notion reached a triumphant pitch.[7] The Congregationalist minister Josiah Strong, for example, wrote in his best-selling book, *Our Country: Its Possible Future and Its Present Crisis* (1885):

If the dangers of immigration [from southern Europe], which have been pointed out, can be successfully met for the next few years, until it has passed its climax, it may be expected to add value to the amalgam which will constitute the new Anglo-Saxon race of the New World. Concerning our future, Herbert Spencer says: "One great result is, I think, tolerably clear. From biological truths it is to be inferred that the eventual mixture of the allied varieties of the Aryan race, forming the population, will produce a more powerful type of man than has hitherto existed, and a type of man more plastic, more adaptable, more capable of undergoing the modifications needful for complete social life. I think, whatever difficulties they may have to surmount, and whatever tribulations they may have to pass through, the Americans may reasonably look forward to a time when they will have produced a civilization grander than any the world has known."[8]

[7] It should be noted that Darwin himself disavowed any relation between his biological findings and the evolutionary social theories espoused by Spencer and others at the time.
[8] Josiah Strong, *Our Country: Its Possible Future and Its Present Crisis* (New York: The Baker and Tayor Co., 1885), 172.

Strong attributed Spencer's prediction of American triumph to "two great ideas" forged out of the Enlightenment and the Protestant Reformation: *civil liberty* and *spiritual Christianity*:

The noblest races have always been lovers of liberty ... but it was left to the Anglo-Saxon branch fully to recognize the right of the individual to himself, and formally to declare it the foundation stone of government. The other great idea of which the Anglo-Saxon is the exponent is that of pure *spiritual* Christianity. It was no accident that the great reformation of the sixteenth century originated among a Teutonic, rather than a Latin people. It was the fire of liberty burning in the Saxon heart that flamed up against the absolutism of the Pope. Speaking roughly, the peoples of Europe which are Celtic are Catholic, and those which are Teutonic are Protestant; and where the Teutonic race was purest, there Protestantism spread with the greatest rapidity.... That means that most of the spiritual Christianity in the world is found among Anglo-Saxons and their converts; for this is the great missionary race.[9]

Strong further pointed to the "successes" of the Anglo-Saxons in commerce, industry, and empire-building as providential affirmation of Anglo-Saxon superiority:

This mighty Anglo-Saxon race, though comprising only one-fifteenth part of mankind, now rules more then one-third of the earth's surface, and more than one-fourth of its people.... Does it not look as if God were not only preparing in our Anglo-Saxon civilization the die with which to stamp the peoples of the earth, but as if he were also massing behind that die the mighty power with which to press it?... The physical changes accompanied by mental, which are taking place in the people of the United States are apparently to adapt men to the demands of a higher civilization.... "At the present day," says Mr. Darwin, "civilized nations are everywhere supplanting barbarous nations...; and they succeed mainly, though not exclusively, through their arts which are the products of the intellect?" Thus the Finns were supplanted by the Aryan races of Europe and Asia, the Tartars by the Russians, and thus the aborigines of North America, Australia and New Zealand are now disappearing before the all-conquering Anglo-Saxons. It would seem as if these inferior tribes were only precursors of a superior race, voices in the wilderness crying: "Prepare ye the way of the Lord!"[10]

Strong's vision for America struck a chord with popular nativist opposition to the increased ethnic and religious diversification of the United States at this time. "Neither he nor most of his readers felt any doubt about just who it was that *our* [in *Our Country*] referred to."[11]

---

[9] Ibid., 159–160.

[10] Ibid., 161–176.

[11] William R. Hutchison, *Religious Pluralism in America: The Contentious History of a Founding Ideal* (New Haven, CT: Yale University Press, 2004), 139.

Later in life, Strong, who was one of the founders of the liberal Social
Gospel Movement, which sought to apply Jesus' teachings to the social
challenges of industrialism and urban life, retreated from his hyper-
optimistic rhetoric and its implicitly biological notion of race. To be
fair, Strong's appeal to race, even between the covers of *Our Country*,
was not consistent. "Anglo-Saxon" was an ambiguous racial category in
Our Country. People like Strong often conflated "race" with "nation."
"Anglo-Saxon" did not always designate a biological race; it also served
as an assimilative place holder for the providential spread of Protestant
Christianity to all peoples in the world.[12] The Anglo-Saxon race and
Protestantism were the cultural and moral sources through which he
sought to address the social perils he identified in a rapidly diversifying
and industrializing America. These perils included "Romanism," polygamy (Mormonism), intemperance, rapid urbanization, socialism, and
the mammon.

WHICH RELIGION? LET'S COMPARE THEM!

There were other, milder articulations of Anglo-American superiority that were also influenced by pseudo-scientific social evolutionary
theories, but these were more likely to see Protestantism as fulfilling
rather than supplanting other religions. The most influential advocate
of such a position was James Freeman Clarke, a Unitarian minister who
in 1867 was appointed to the faculty of Harvard Divinity School to
teach "Comparative Theology," which entailed lectures on "world religions." He was most likely "this country's first academic lecturer on the
subject." In 1871, Clarke published *Ten Great Religions: An Essay in
Comparative Theology*, which went through numerous editions and
"became by all odds the most widely read American work on the history
and comparison of world religions past and present."[13] Comparative
theology viewed itself as akin to ethnology and evolutionary biology
as an impartial mode of scientific inquiry. Its practitioners saw themselves as students of different religious beliefs and practices with the
aim of defining what is "Religion," in the singular. "It may be called
a science," Clarke wrote, "since it consists in the study of the facts of

[12] Ralph E. Luker, *The Social Gospel in Black and White: American Racial Reform, 1885–
1912* (Chapel Hill, NC: University of North Carolina Press, 1998), 268–275.
[13] Sydney E. Ahlstrom, *The American Protestant Encounter with World Religions* (Beloit,
WI: Beloit College, 1962), 27–28.

human history, and their relation to each other. It does not dogmatize; it observes."[14] Despite claims to objectivity, the results of these observations were for the most part foregone conclusions: "It will be seen that each of the great ethnic religions [*note the plural*] is full on one side, but empty on the other while Christianity is full all around. Christianity is adapted to take their place, not because they are false, but because they are true as far as they go."[15] Clarke defined "ethnic religions" as "religions, each of which has always been confined within the boundaries of a particular race or family of mankind, and has never made proselytes or converts, except accidentally, outside of it."[16] According to this definition, Islam, a religion that expanded around the globe, should have been considered a "universal religion." Clarke, however, contested that while this may appear to be the case, "Mohammedanism has never sought to make *converts*, but only *subjects*; it has not asked for belief, but merely for submission"[17] (emphasis his). Similarly, Clarke argued that while Buddhism "has shown some tendencies toward catholicity" because it "has extended itself over the whole of the eastern half of Asia," it only "includes a variety of nationalities, it is doubtful if it includes any variety of races. All the Buddhists," he wrote, "appear to belong to the great Mongol family."[18]

Far from an objective exercise in the scientific study of religion, Clarke's comparative theology was committed to rationalizing the superiority of Protestantism in a country of increasing religious diversity. Clarke identified non-Protestant religions as "partial religions" in an evolutionary scale that was informed by pseudo-scientific theories about race and its relation to moral behavior and civilizational progress. "Now we find that each race, beside its special moral qualities, seems also to have special religious qualities which cause it to tend toward some one kind of religions more than to another kind."[19] According to this view, there was a natural connection between the races and religions of the world, which led Clarke to conclude that Protestantism, as the "universal religion" endowed with rational principles and truth, was necessarily a product of Northern Europeans and their descendents:

[14] James Freeman Clarke, *Ten Great Religions: An Essay in Comparative Theology* (Boston, MA: James R. Osgood and Company, 1871), 3.

[15] Ibid., 29.

[16] Ibid., 15.

[17] Ibid., 18.

[18] Ibid., 20.

[19] Ibid., 16–17.

In the South of Europe the Catholic Church, by its ingenious organization and its complex arrangements, introduced into life discipline and culture. In the North of Europe Protestant Christianity, by its appeal to the individual soul, awakens conscience and stimulates to individual and national progress. The nations of Southern Europe accepted Christianity mainly as a religion of sentiment and feeling; the nations of Northern Europe, as a religion of truth and principle. God adapted Christianity to the needs of these Northern races; but he also adapted these races, with their original instincts and their primitive religion, to the needs of Christianity. Without them, we do not see how there could be such a thing in Europe to-day as Protestantism.[20]

The superiority of Protestantism for Clarke was demonstrated, just as it was for Strong, by Northern Europeans' "civilizational" progress toward such Enlightenment ideals as universal brotherhood and individual liberty on the one hand, and by its sheer power on the other.

The North [of Europe] developed individual freedom, the South social organization. The North gave force, the South culture.... But in modern civilization a third element has been added, which has brought these two powers of Northern freedom and Southern culture into equipoise and harmony. This new element is Christianity, which develops, at the same time, the sense of personal responsibility, by teaching the individual destiny and worth of every soul, and also the mutual dependence and interlacing brotherhood of all human society. This Christian element in modern civilization saves it from the double danger of a relapse into barbarism on the one hand, and a too refined luxury on the other. The nations of Europe, to-day, which are the most advanced in civilization, literature, and art, are also the most deeply pervaded with the love of freedom; and the most civilized nations on the globe, instead of being the most effeminate, are also the most powerful.[21]

Non-Northern Europeans and their "partial religions," according to Clarke, were the "decaying soil" in which the "universal religion" of Protestantism "must root itself."[22] Clarke explained: "When the Papacy became a tyranny, and the Renaissance called for free thought, it suddenly put forth Protestantism, as the tree by the water-side sends forth its shoots in due season."[23] The power and progress of Anglo-Saxon Protestants in the latter half of the nineteenth century was proof that that season had come.

[20] Ibid., 395.
[21] Ibid., 359–360.
[22] Ibid., 2.
[23] Ibid., 29–30.

CONSERVATIVE REACTIONS

While liberal Protestants took for granted that "civilizational progress" could be used as an empirical measure of the veracity and utility of religion, more conservative Protestants objected to the fact that such a measure privileged human activity over scriptural authority and doctrinal fidelity. They maintained that the Protestant establishment, rather than adapting to religious diversity and reforming in response to the social changes of the time, should stick to the business of saving souls through Christ. To cite but one example, Reverend S. H. Kellogg, a Presbyterian missionary to India and the author of *A Handbook of Comparative Religion* (1899), took liberal Protestants, such as Clarke, to task on this issue:

As Christians, we do well also to keep in mind that not only is the fashionable modern view as to the evolutionary religious progress of mankind, and the relation of the various ethnic religions to Christianity, contradicted by the facts of history, but also, no less certainly, is it in the most direct opposition to the teachings of those Scriptures which as Christians we profess to receive as the Word of God. In both the Old and the New Testaments, there is much about the religions which surrounded the writers of the various books; and never once do those writers, speaking 'as they were moved by the Holy Ghost' exhibit that broad 'sympathy' with the ethnic religions which, we are now taught by many, it is the first duty of the intelligent Christian to cherish.[24]

For Kellogg and ilk, the Bible, not evolutionary progress nor rationally or socially determined truths, was the litmus test for the veracity of religion: "Nothing could be more explicit than the words of the apostle with regard to Jesus Christ: 'In none other is there salvation: for neither is there any other name under heaven, that is given among men, wherein we must be saved'" (Acts 4:12).[25]

For Clarke and other liberal Protestants, however, such a position did not take into account what they regarded as the reality of human nature. In Clarke's view, all of humanity innately sought God, and to assume that non-Christian searches for God were utterly false was disrespectful of humanity's inborn religious nature and irreverent of divine providence. He wrote:

[Such a view] supposes man to be the easy and universal dupe of fraud. But these religions do not rest on such a sandy foundation, but on the feeling of dependence,

---

[24] Samuel H. Kellogg, *A Handbook of Comparative Religion* (Philadelphia, PA: Westminster Press, 1899), 160.

[25] Ibid., 172f, quote on 177.

the sense of accountability, the recognition of spiritual realities very near to this world of matter, and the need of looking up and worshiping some unseen power higher and better than ourselves. A decent respect for the opinions of mankind forbids us to ascribe pagan religions to priestcraft as their chief source. And a reverence for Divine Providence brings us to the same conclusion. Can it be that God has left himself without a witness in the world, except among the Hebrews? This narrow creed excludes God from any communion with the great majority of human beings. The Father of the human race is represented as selecting a few of his children to keep near himself, and as leaving all the rest to perish in their ignorance and error.[26]

Clarke's respect for others' religious understandings and his recognition of the human as "eminently a religious being," were not only ways by which he sought to make theological sense of religious diversity, but also attempts to assure the preeminence of Protestantism by adapting it to a modernizing world that was coming increasingly under the influence of science and non-religious theories of progress. The notion that non-Christian religions are completely false, he wrote,

contradicts that law of progress which alone gives meaning and unity to history. Instead of progress, it teaches degeneracy and failure. But elsewhere [in the natural world], we see progress, not recession. Geology shows us higher forms of life succeeding to the lower. Botany exhibits the lichens and mosses preparing a soil for more complex forms of vegetation. Civil history shows the savage state giving way to the semi-civilized, and that to the civilized. If heathen religions are a step, a preparation for Christianity, then this law of degrees [i.e., evolution] appears also in religion.... Then we can understand why Christ's coming was delayed till the fullness of the time had come. But otherwise all, in this most important sphere of human life, is in disorder, without unity, progress, meaning, or providence.[27]

Clarke's scientist discourse was intended to counter the rise of scientific positivism and moral relativism, which in his view asserted "that man passes from a theological stage to one of metaphysics, and from that to one of science, from which later and higher epoch both theology and philosophy are excluded."[28] Clarke's underscoring of the rationally determined innateness of religion and his assertion that Protestantism is directly related to contemporary progress of humanity was intended to demonstrate the continued relevance of religion (read Protestantism) in the new, modern United States of America:

---

[26] Clarke, *Ten Great Religions*, 7–8.
[27] Ibid., 9.
[28] Ibid., 489.

FIGURE 2. A session of the 1893 World's Parliament of Religions. From John Henry Barrows's *The World's Parliament of Religions* (1893).

[Protestant] Christianity blossoms out into modern science, literature, art,.... Christianity, the spirit of faith, hope, and love, is the deep fountain of modern civilization....We cannot, indeed, here *prove* that Christianity is the cause of these features peculiar to modern life; but we find it everywhere associated with them, and so we can say that it only, of all the religions of mankind, has been capable of accompanying man in his progress from evil to good, from good to better.[29]

THE WORLD'S PARLIAMENT OF RELIGIONS (1893)

By making the shared humanity of adherents of different religions the basis of Protestant encounters with other religions and by ranking religions according to an evolutionary scale of "civilizational progress," Clarke posited an understanding of religious diversity that captured postbellum liberal Protestant America's understanding of itself and its place in history. Following the Civil War, the United States constitutionally affirmed its founding belief in the equality of *all* men through the passage of the 13th–15th Amendments, which outlawed slavery and granted citizenship to former slaves and voting rights to black men. Nonetheless, most Americans valued humanity as measured by a civilizational scale of "progress."

Perhaps nowhere was white America's self-understanding after the Civil War better synthesized and more publically demonstrated than at

[29] Ibid., 30.

the 1893 World's Columbian Exposition of Chicago. The Columbian Exposition was a triumphalist celebration of American industry and progress on the 400-year anniversary of Christopher Columbus's arrival in the "New World." Other massive world fairs had taken place in London (1886) and Paris (1889) and Philadelphia (1876), but the Chicago fair was deliberately organized to exceed all of them in extravagance and publicity. The fair was divided into two contrasting parts. At one end was the White City, which displayed the marvels of American industry, wealth, and ingenuity; at the other was the Midway, a vast display of people of varying races and ethnicities, imported from all over the world, placed in simulated village settings, and ordered on an evolutionary scale to demonstrate the progress of humanity toward the (fittingly named) White City.[30]

The perceived relation between race, religion, and progress was unmistakable in the spatial ordering of the Midway. The Teutonic and Celtic races represented by German and Irish villages were situated closest to the White City. In the middle were the "semi-civilized" worlds of Muslims and other West and East Asians.[31] Then, at the opposite end of the White City, in the words of a contemporary literary critic, Denton J. Snider, "we descend to the savage races, the African of Dahomey and the North American Indian, each of which has its place."[32] Newspapers underscored the didactic message of the fair's evolutionary ordering of space and time. "What an opportunity," wrote the *Chicago Tribune*, "was here afforded to the scientific mind to descend the spiral of evolution, tracing humanity in its highest phases down almost to its animalistic origins."[33]

Indelible impressions left by the contrast between the White City and the Midway on fairgoers were captured in a contemporary novel titled, *Sweet Clover*:

That Midway is just a representation of matter, and this great White City is an emblem of mind. In the Midway it's some dirty and all barbaric. It deafens you with noise; the worst folks in there are avaricious and bad; and the best are just children in their ignorance, and when you're feelin' bewildered with the smells and sounds and sights, always changin' like one o' these kaleidoscopes, and when you come out o' that mile-long babel [i.e., the Midway] where you've been

[30] See Robert W. Rydell, *All the World's a Fair: Visions of Empire at American International Expositions, 1876–1916* (Chicago, IL: University of Chicago Press, 1984), 38–71.

[31] Ibid., 65.

[32] Denton J. Snider, *World's Fair Studies* (Chicago, IL: Sigma Publishing Company, 1895), 256.

[33] "Through the Looking Glass," *Chicago Daily Tribune*, November 1, 1893, 9.

elbowed and cheated, you pass under a bridge – and all of a sudden you are in a great, beautiful silence [i.e., the White City]. The angels on the Woman's Buildin' smile down and bless you, and you know that in what seemed like one step, you've passed out o' darkness and into light.[34]

What the World's Columbian Exposition in particular and the European and American world fairs of the era more generally demonstrated for contemporaries was the *power* of their countries to order the world and to reproduce others' realities.[35] The Columbian Exposition was triumphalist in its display of the United States' image of itself and smug in its ability to "empirically" and "scientifically" demonstrate U.S. superiority in a simulated world, complete with "natives" from every corner of the world who gaily played out their traditional roles for America's education and amusement.

The president of the World's Congresses at the Columbian Exposition, Charles C. Bonney, a lay member of the Swedenborgian Church, decided that one of the congresses should be on "world religions" in order to demonstrate the contributions religion, as an innate aspect of human experience, has made to humanity's evolutionary progress. Bonney selected John Henry Barrows, a minister at Chicago's First Presbyterian Church, to chair this congress, which came to be known as the World's Parliament of Religions. Barrows invited representatives of varying religions from different parts of the world to take part in the congress, but Protestants ended up comprising about 65 percent of the final delegate count.[36]

The Parliament was organized with the same sense of triumphalism present at the rest of the Exposition. The underlying assumption of the Parliament was that an "empirical" and "scientific" examination of the world's religions would show the superiority of America's liberal Protestant understandings of religion as an individualistic and spiritual connection with a loving and beneficent deity that shapes humans' moral and social behavior. In his welcome address, Bonney asserted that "[i]n this Congress the word 'Religion' means the love and worship of God and the love and service of man. We believe the scripture that 'of a truth God is no respecter of persons, but in every nation he that feareth God

---

[34] Clara Louisa Burnham, *Sweet Clover* (Chicago, IL: Laird and Lee, 1893), 201, cited in Rydell, *All the World's a Fair*, 67.

[35] See Mitchell, *Colonising Egypt*, 1–34.

[36] Richard H. Seager, *The Dawn of Religious Pluralism: Voices From the World's Parliament of Religions, 1893* (La Salle, IL: Open Court Publishing, 1993), 35.

and worketh righteousness is accepted of him'," (Acts 10:34–35).[37] He further exclaimed that "the members of this Congress meet, as men, on a common ground of perfect equality.... But no attempt is here made to treat all religions as of equal merit."[38] Barrows, in his introductory comments, went on to assert that the very fact that the Parliament was planned and realized by American Protestant Christians, who possess the ability, the foresight, and the religion "fitted to the needs of all men," demonstrates the superiority of their faith: "Christendom may proudly hold up this Congress of the Faiths as a torch of truth and of love which may prove the morning star of the twentieth century. There is a true and noble sense in which America is a Christian nation....Justice Ameer Ali, of Calcutta,...has expressed the opinion that only in this Western republic would such a congress as this have been undertaken and achieved."[39]

Even though they had invited others to come and speak to them about the values found in their varying religions, Barrows and other organizers saw the Parliament as a form of missionary work.[40] They believed that once they had spoken of the value of their faith and of its contribution to human progress – as evidenced by the industrial, scientific, and aesthetic wonders on display at the White City – they would convince others of the superiority of their religion. Moreover, by demonstrating the important contributions religions more generally had made to human progress over time, the organizers also wanted to demonstrate to their fellow citizens the relevance of religion – properly understood – to the material progress of their nation on display at the Columbian Exposition.

In the World's Parliament of Religions we see the ideas of Clarke and his ilk reaching their logical conclusion; the valuing of others' quest for the divine ultimately meant that adherents of other religions should be allowed to speak for themselves. Barrows defined the Parliament as a place "wherein devout men of all faiths may speak for themselves without

---

[37] Charles Carroll Bonney, "Words of Welcome," reprinted in Seager, *Dawn of Religious Pluralism*, 17.

[38] Ibid., 21.

[39] John Henry Barrows, "Words of Welcome," reprinted in Seager, *Dawn of Religious Pluralism*, 24–25.

[40] James Freeman Clarke's explanation of Comparative Theology demonstrates this point: "Finally, this department of Comparative Theology shows the relation of each partial religion to human civilization, and observes how each religion of the world is a step in the progress of humanity. It shows that both the position and the negative side of a religion make it a preparation for a higher religion, and that the universal religion must root itself in the decaying soil of partial religions. And in this sense Comparative Theology becomes the science of missions." Clarke, *Ten Great Religions*, 2.

hindrance, without criticism and without compromise, and tell what they believe and why they believe it."[41] Similarly, Bonney asserted that "the very basis of our convocation is the idea that the representatives of each religion sincerely believe that it is the truest and the best of all; and that they will, therefore, hear with perfect candor and without fear the convictions of other sincere souls on the great questions of the immortal life."[42] In this sense, the Parliament was a true watershed. It was, as some have correctly observed, a major turning point in American religious history.[43] The national newspaper coverage of the Parliament popularized ecumenism and the notion that there is some value in other religions, and argued that religion in the singular, a "universal religion," has to *account for* rather than *eradicate* diversity of religious opinions among humans. It also allowed average Americans to come face to face with members of other religious traditions, some of whom, such as Vivekananda, a young Hindu reformer, stayed in the United States and lectured on the universal teachings of their religion to small but receptive audiences among American seekers of spirituality.

During the Parliament, Americans heard from members of other religious traditions who were as smug about the veracity of their religions as liberal Protestants. Before entering this discussion, however, it is important to note the voices that were not heard. No Mormon was officially invited to participate in the Parliament. Most of the women who spoke at the Parliament were of liberal Protestant denominations, either Universalists or Unitarians. Several Jewish women also spoke, but no women from other religious traditions were represented. The voices of African Americans and Native Americans were conspicuously underrepresented. There was one brief, anthropological paper on Native Americans, and only two African Americans spoke.[44] These limited African American voices were particularly significant because they belied the triumphalist spirit of the Exposition. Bishop Benjamin Arnett of the African Methodist Episcopal Church told the Parliament in a congratulatory tone that "We have gathered from the East, from the West, from the North, from the South this day to celebrate the triumph of human freedom on the American continent. For there is not one slave within all of our borders." But he also sought to curb the triumphalism of the

[41] Barrows, "Words of Welcome," reprinted in Seager, *Dawn of Religious Pluralism*, 25.

[42] Bonney, "Words of Welcome," reprinted in Seager, *Dawn of Religious Pluralism*, 21.

[43] Seager, "Pluralism and the American Mainstream: The View from the World's Parliament of Religions," *Harvard Theological Review* 82, n. 3 (July 1989), 301–324, esp. 304n7.

[44] Seager, *Dawn of Religious Pluralism*, 6–7.

Parliament by reminding his audience of the evils committed in the name of Christianity in America:

We know what has been done in the name of Christianity, in the name of religion, in the name of God. We were stolen from our native land in the name of religion, chained as captives, and brought to this continent in the name of the liberty of the gospel; they bound our limbs with fetters in the name of the liberty of the gospel; they bound our limbs with fetters in the name of the Nazarene in order to save our souls; they sold us to teach the principles of religion; they sealed the Bible to increase our faith in God; pious prayers were offered for those who chained our fathers, who stole our mothers, who sold our brothers for paltry gold, all in the name of Christianity, to save our poor souls. When the price of flesh went down the interest in our souls became small; when the slave trade was abolished by the strong hand of true Christianity, then false Christianity had no interest in our souls at all.[45]

An aging Frederick Douglass, the only other African American to speak at the Parliament, was not on the schedule but was asked as an audience member to address the Parliament extemporaneously on the anniversary of the Emancipation Proclamation. In his own brilliant rhetoric, he sardonically drew the audience's attention to the fact that they were in a bubble, secluded from the religious prejudices of the world that surrounded them. "I did not come here to speak," he told visitors of the Parliament.

I am somewhat in the condition of a man who attended a missionary meeting in London. "Give me a subject," he said, when called upon for a speech, "and I will address you." Said his friends, sitting behind him: "Pitch into the Roman Catholics." I take it that it would be very dangerous in this meeting to pitch into the Roman Catholics, for we are all Catholics, ready to strike hands with all manner of men, from all the nations of the earth, not disposed to draw the line anywhere absolutely.[46]

Douglass concluded his speech by asserting that, in the age of Jim Crow, he was more concerned with "human rights" than "human religions." By distinguishing the two concepts, Douglass struck an open blow to the Parliament's attempt to demonstrate that the two concepts were necessarily related to one another in American Protestantism. He questioned "whether this great nation of ours is great enough to live up to its own convictions, carry out its own declaration of independence, and execute the provisions of its own constitution."[47]

---

[45] Benjamin William Arnett, "Christianity and the Negro," reprinted in Seager, *Dawn of Religious Pluralism*, 140.

[46] Frederick Douglass, "Impromptu Comments," reprinted in Seager, *Dawn of Religious Pluralism*, 135.

[47] Ibid., 135–136.

This contrast in the way in which blacks and whites experienced the Columbian Exposition and the World's Parliament of Religions underscores the fact that the "common ground of perfect equality" which Bonney sought to create religiously had no real index in the social and political world of late-nineteenth-century America. There were no African American Muslim voices from the Parliament, but, as we saw in the previous chapter, some African Muslims, like 'Umar ibn Said, also sought to establish common religious ground with their white masters in order to hold them morally accountable to God. One could imagine that had they been present at the Parliament, they too would have been keenly aware of the disparity in power between blacks and whites and of the hypocritical gap between confessed religious ideals and sociopolitical realities. This, after all, was a time of Anglo-Saxon, Protestant triumphalism, popular nativism, Jim Crow, and an increase in racial violence, especially lynching. It was also a time of grave social change brought on by the rise of industrial cities and the slums that accompanied them. The World's Parliament of Religions was a historical turning point in the history of religious pluralism in the United States, but it was also an aberration in its own time. Its goals and aims did not correspond to the reality of contemporary American society which was marked by social unrest and antagonistic competition between races, ethnicities, and religions. It is thus not surprising that soon after the Columbian Exposition the Parliament was for the most part forgotten until the 1980s, when interest in religious pluralism was rekindled in light of the arrival of new immigrant religions from Asia and Africa in the 1960s and 1970s.[48]

MOHAMMED ALEXANDER RUSSELL WEBB: THEOSOPHY, THE PARLIAMENT, AND INDIAN ISLAM

While the steps taken at the Parliament to allow the practitioners of other religions to speak for themselves was too radical for most Americans in the 1890s, there were a few Americans, mainly Theosophists, who were assimilating science and "Eastern" religions into a new "Western" religious

---

[48] Seager, "Pluralism and the American Mainstream," 303–308. Despite the fact that the Parliament slipped from the minds of most Americans at the turn of the twentieth century, there were some marginal ventures that sought to realize the pluralistic ideals of the Parliament at such places as Greenacre in Maine. See Leigh E. Schmidt, "Cosmopolitan Piety: Sympathy, Comparative Religions, and Nineteenth Century Liberalism" in *Practicing Protestants: Histories of Christian Life in America, 1630–1965*, ed. Laurie F. Maffly-Kipp, Leigh E. Schmidt, and Mark Valeri (Baltimore, MD: John Hopkins University Press, 2006), 218.

FIGURE 3. Mohammed Alexander Russell Webb. From *Neely's History of the Parliament of Religions and Religious Congresses at the World's Columbian Exposition* (1893).

discourse. In this process, Theosophists were in conversation both with native practitioners of "Eastern" religions and with scholars of comparative philology and comparative religion.[49] They served as intermediaries between liberal Protestants and the exotic "East," providing the intellectual means and social networks through which the imagined religious

---

[49] For a concise authoritative overview of the Theosophical Society and its impact on Western esoteric thought, see Kocku von Stuckard, *Western Esotericism: A Brief History of Secret Knowledge* (London: Equinox, 2005), 122–132.

other could be culturally and socially encountered in the flesh. Indeed, many of the Asian scholars of Buddhism and Hinduism who attended the Parliament were Theosophists, and there were a number of American Theosophist delegates at the Parliament. The one representative of Islam at the Parliament, Mohammed Alexander Russell Webb, was an American diplomat and a Theosophist who formally converted to Islam around 1888 and went on to found the first American Muslim mission – the short-lived American Islamic Propaganda – in New York City in 1892.[50]

Webb's religious journey represents an important counter-establishment response to the social changes and increased religious diversity of his time. Webb, like most of his contemporary Theosophists, was spiritual in the sense that he believed in an immortal soul and spiritual existence, but was deeply resentful of the Christian church. Early in life he rejected Christianity and embarked on a personal search for "religion" by studying Theosophical literature on varying "Eastern" religions. He eventually settled on Islam and decided to propagate its teachings in America in an effort to define an alternate American national identity, one that was anti-ecclesiastical and promoted free thought. He gained financial and moral support for his mission from a few Muslim merchants in India who, like their American counterparts, were also at this time awash in religious diversity and sociopolitical change brought about by British colonial rule. Some of these Indian Muslims saw in Webb a "white hope" who could assist in reviving a spirit of education and progress among Muslims in India (discussed below). In sum, Webb's extraordinary life journey exemplified personally how Islamic and American religious histories intersected at the turn of the twentieth century.

Webb was born to a Presbyterian family in Hudson, New York in 1846. He reported that as an adolescent, he was disillusioned by the church and "orthodox Christianity." In typical romantic fashion, he recalled enjoying the "sermons preached by God Himself through the murmuring brooks, the gorgeous flowers and the joyous birds" more than the "abstruse discourses of the minister."[51] After graduating from Claverack College, Webb moved to Missouri to work as a journalist and eventually became the editor of the *Missouri Republican*. While working

---

[50] Albanese, *A Republic of Mind and Spirit*, 332; Umar F. Abd-Allah, *A Muslim in Victorian America: The Life of Alexander Russell Webb* (Oxford: Oxford University Press, 2004), 66.

[51] Mohammed Alexander Russell Webb, *The Three Lectures of Mohammed Alexander Russell Webb, Esq., Delivered at Madras, Hyderabad (Deccan) and Bombay, with a Brief Sketch of His Life* (Madras: Hassan Ali, Lawrence Asylum Press, 1892), 24.

as a journalist, he explained: "After trying in vain to find something in the Christian system to satisfy the longings of my soul and meet the demands of reason, I drifted into materialism, and for several years had no religion at all."[52] He dabbled in Spiritualism and the occult.[53] In 1881 he joined the Pioneer Theosophical Society of St. Louis.[54] He studied "Oriental religions" through Theosophical literature and works popular with Theosophists, such as Paul Carus's *The Gospel of Buddha*.[55] When he explained his conversion to Muslim audiences in India, Webb, aware that other Muslims would most likely disapprove of his association with Theosophy, mentioned that he had read Theosophical literature but never divulged that he became a Theosophist. He told his Muslim audiences in India that "I will not weary you with details [of my conversion] further than to say that at that time I had access to a most excellent library of about 13,000 volumes, from four to seven hours a day at my disposal, and that I was intensely in earnest in my efforts to solve the mysteries of life and death, and to know what relation the religious systems of the world bore to these mysteries."[56] The latter part of this statement regarding his questioning of the mysteries of life and death and the relation between religions and these mysteries clearly hinted at his continued involvement with the Theosophical Society, and long after his conversion, contemporary members of the Theosophical Society counted him – though coolly – as one of them.[57]

Webb was convinced that Theosophy was compatible with Islam. "My adoption of Islam" he wrote, "was not the result of misguided sentiment, blind credulity or sudden emotional impulse." After some years of studying "Oriental religions" through a Theosophical lens, Webb arrived at a personal theory of religion and then went out to find the religion that matched his theory:

After I had fully satisfied myself of the immortality of the soul, and that the conditions of the life beyond the grave were regulated by the thoughts, deeds and acts of the earth life; that man was, in a sense, his own savior and redeemer, and that the intercession of anyone between him and his God could be of no benefit to him, I began to compare the various religions, in order to ascertain which was

[52] Ibid., 24.
[53] "Hopes to Islamize America," *Chicago Daily Tribune*, December 21, 1892, 2.
[54] *The Path* 8 (1893–1894), 27.
[55] Webb, *The Three Lectures*, 12; Abd-Allah, *A Muslim in Victorian America*, 57.
[56] Webb, *The Three Lectures*, 24.
[57] *The Path* 8 (1893–1894), 27, 112; *Lucifer: A Theosophical Magazine* 11 (September 1892–February 1893), 428–429.

the best and most efficacious as a means of securing happiness in the next life. To do this it was necessary to apply to each system, not only the tests of reason, but certain truths which I had learned during my long course of study and experiment outside the lines of orthodoxy, and in fields which priest and preacher usually avoid. And now let us see what Islam really is, and I think the reader will readily understand why I accept it.[58]

Webb's readings in apologies for Islam by John Davenport and Godfrey Higgins[59] and in English translations of works by such Muslim mystics as Abu Hamid al-Ghazzali (d. 1111), Mushrif al-Din Sa'di (d. 1292), and Jalal al-Din Rumi (d.1273),[60] led him to see Islam as an instantiation of "rational" or "universal" religion (outside "orthodoxy" or "priestcraft"). When Webb, who was a lifelong supporter of the Democratic Party, was offered the opportunity to serve as a diplomat in Grover Cleveland's first administration (1885–1889), he consciously sought an appointment in the "East" to further pursue his study of "Oriental religions." He was assigned to head the U.S. diplomatic mission in the Philippines in 1887.[61]

The rational, seemingly disciplined process through which Webb discovered his religion before actually encountering that religion in practice demonstrates the appeal Theosophy held for liberal Protestants who wished to make sense of religious difference in an age of science and increased contact between peoples of varying religions. Like Webb, the organizers of the World's Parliament of Religions had deduced what was universally religious and went out to affirm empirically their definition of religion by showcasing adherents of other religions who could confirm their view. Neither Webb nor the Parliament took other religions very seriously as alternative ethical worldviews that related dynamically to their historical contexts to shape communal and individual lives. Having decided what constitutes "religion," Webb searched in Islamic writings for teachings that would substantiate his point of view.

Reality, however, proved to be a mixed bag of affirmation and rebuke for Webb, just as it was for the organizers of the Parliament. While

[58] Webb, *Islam in America: A Brief Statement of Mohammedanism and an Outline of the American Islamic Propaganda* (New York: Oriental Publishing Company, 1893), 14.

[59] John Davenport, *An Apology for Mohammed and the Koran* (London: J. Davy and Sons, 1869) and Godfrey Higgins, *An Apology for the Life and Character of the Celebrated Prophet of Arabia Called Mohamed or the Illustrious* (London: Rowland Hunter et al., 1829).

[60] Abd-Allah, *A Muslim in Victorian America*, 136, 168, 191, and 201; "The Death of the Prophet," *Moslem World*, November 1893, 4, cited in Abd-Allah, *A Muslim in Victorian America*, 191; and Webb, *Islam in America*, 26–27.

[61] Abd-Allah, *A Muslim in Victorian America*, 4, 87, and 104–106.

traveling among Muslims in India and elsewhere, Webb found much that he admired, but he also met people who repelled him either because they imitated British or "Western" materialist cultural practices or because, in his view, they insisted on the rote observance of Islamic law. Of the former he wrote, "Why these poor, addle-pated people will sacrifice their manhood and play lick-spittle to a lot of beefy, whiskey soaked brutes who despise them I cannot imagine."[62] The latter he regarded as "fanatical Mussluman…Poor, benighted creatures! They have no more idea of the spirit of Islam than the cows or horses."[63] Here Webb echoes the common distinction made in Protestant thought between spiritual and legalistic religions. Spiritual religions are dynamic while nomocentric religions are ossified and doctrinaire. Meeting "Eastern" Muslims who did not reject materialism nor shared his Theosophical view of a spiritual Islam did not turn Webb away from his new faith. On the contrary, the neophyte firmly believed that Theosophy had brought him to a deeper understanding of Islam than the Muslims to whom he lectured in India:

I certainly cannot hope to tell anyone here anything which he does not already know of Islam as an exoteric religious system…. Now I am fully aware of the fact that there are many professed Mussulmans who do not know that there is a philosophic side to their religion; and perhaps it is just as well that they do not, for such knowledge might, possibly, lead them away from the plain, safe and simple truths already within their grasp, and out into the broad and dangerous ocean of metaphysical speculation where their frail mental barks would be wrecked upon the rocks of doubt and despair.[64]

Webb rationalized the "exoteric" dimensions of Islam as laws that could be shown to be "thoroughly applicable to all the needs of humanity" rather than a set of divine injunctions. He focused on "the spirit that prevails among the Moslems of the higher [spiritual] class" and on an unnamed "spiritual truth" that Muhammad taught and which he claimed in typical esoteric fashion "every man who knows anything of the spiritual side of religion ought to know."[65]

Webb obviously believed in the superiority of his Theosophical or metaphysical understanding of Islam just as the organizers of the Parliament

---

[62] Mohammed Alexander Russell Webb, *Yankee Muslim*, ed. and intro. Brent D. Singleton (Rockville, MD: Borgo-Wildside Press, 2007), 170.

[63] Ibid., 174.

[64] Webb, *The Three Lectures*, 40.

[65] Webb, "The Spirit of Islam," reprinted in Seager, *Dawn of Religious Pluralism*, 275–276.

believed in the superiority of liberal Protestantism. He was one of the representatives of "Eastern" religions at the Parliament who contested the white, Protestant triumphalism of the fair.[66] In a description of his American Islamic Propaganda prior to the Parliament, he made his anti-church sentiments plain and sung a triumphant praise of Islam:

The plainly apparent decay of church Christianity and the defection from that system of many of the most intelligent and progressive people in nearly all large American cities seem to encourage the belief that the time has now arrived for the spread of the true faith from the Eastern to the Western Hemisphere. Its adoption as the universal religion seems only a question of a comparatively short time.[67]

In his address to the Parliament, Webb also rejected Christian claims to universality and rationality and attributed these qualities to Islam:

I wish...I could impress upon your minds the feelings of millions of Mussulmans in India, Turkey, and Egypt, who are looking to this Parliament of Religions with the deepest, the fondest hope. There is not a Mussulman on earth who does not believe that ultimately Islam will be the universal faith.... I have not returned to the United States to make you all Mussulmans in spite of yourselves....But I have faith in the American intellect, in the American intelligence, and in the American love of fair play, and will defy any intelligent man to understand Islam and not love it.[68]

In his alternative vision for America and his optimistic outlook of his mission, Webb misread the depth of prejudice among most Americans against Islam. The audience listened to him in the spirit of tolerance called for by the occasion, but it did so reluctantly. According to the *Chicago Tribune*, "He met with a reception wherein hisses and cheers were equally mingled. Cries of 'Shame' greeted him when he spoke of polygamy, but there was enthusiastic approval when he said that the Mussulman daily offers his prayers to the same God that the Christian adores."[69]

Webb's audience may not have afforded him the same courtesy they gave their foreign-born guests because this white, American diplomat's conversion to Islam challenged the Parliament's and nineteenth-century

---

[66] Another representative of "Eastern" religions, Vivekananda, told the Parliament: "If the Parliament of Religions has shown anything to the world it is this: It has proved to the world that holiness, purity and charity are not the exclusive possessions of any church in the world, and that every system has produced men and women of the most exalted character." Seager, *Dawn of Religious Pluralism*, 337.

[67] *Moslem World* (May 12, 1893).

[68] Webb, "The Spirit of Islam," reprinted in Seager, *Dawn of Religious Pluralism*, 270–273.

[69] "Discourses on Religion of Islam," *Chicago Daily Tribune*, September 21, 1893, 9.

America's deep-seated belief in the enviable superiority of America and its Protestant faith. The audience's applause for Webb's claim that Muslims and Christians pray to the same God shows that the Parliament's attendees sought to reaffirm what they already knew rather than to encounter difference seriously. Webb was the familiar in strange clothing. Newspaper accounts of Webb's two addresses to the Parliament made a point of estranging him from his compatriots by drawing attention to his "odd" appearance: "his head surmounted by a red fez and his bushy brown beard."[70]

Most visitors to the Parliament would have known Webb as an American diplomat who converted to Islam and had been commissioned by Muslims from the "East" to establish Islam in the United States. Six months before he spoke at the Parliament, the *New York Times* described his mission: "He is the American Mohammedan whom the wealthy Mussulmans of India and the East have sent to introduce the faith of Islam – the Religion of the Sword, as some have called it – among the 'civilized' Christians of the West."[71] The *Chicago Tribune* also wrote condescendingly of his mission: "The proposed Moslem propaganda in this country offers a new fad for those curiously constructed beings who are always chasing after new and strange doctrines."[72]

Webb himself defined his mission as an effort to promote rational inquiry into religion by educating "thinking Americans" about the teachings of Prophet Muhammad and by dispelling unjustified prejudices against Islam. He wrote that his aim was not "to make proselytes for Islam, but to arouse and encourage among English-speaking Christians a spirit of calm, persistent and unprejudiced investigation to be applied to their own as well as other systems of religion."[73] His goal was to lay the groundwork for Muslim missionaries from India who would later come to formally convert Americans.[74] Webb outlined the anticipated components of his mission in a monograph addressed to the American public:

The first step in this great work will be the establishment of a weekly journal devoted to the elucidation of Islamic doctrines and laws, and the discussion of matters bearing thereon as well as to record news items of interest to Mussulmans in all parts of the world. It is expected that this journal will be the means of

---

[70] Ibid., 9.
[71] "Muhammed Webb's Mission," *New York Times*, February 25, 1893.
[72] "The Moslem Propaganda," *Chicago Daily Tribune*, December 25, 1892, 12.
[73] Webb, *Islam in America*, 7.
[74] Ibid., 67.

creating and encouraging direct intercourse between the Mohammedan world and the more intelligent masses of our country.... Besides the journal a free lecture room and library will be opened to the public where those who desire to do so, can study Islamic literature and converse with the learned Moulvis [religious scholars] who are expected to arrive in New York in August or September [of 1893]. A book publishing house will also be established which will print and circulate Islamic books and pamphlets.[75]

Webb managed to realize all of the above goals but only for a brief period of time (about four years). In 1893, he founded the American Moslem Brotherhood and the Moslem Publishing Company, both located at 30 East 23rd Street in New York City. On October 7, 1893, about two weeks after he had delivered his speeches at the World's Parliament of Religions, he opened a lecture hall in New York City at 458 West 20th Street. The lecture hall was open to the public and made the mission's literature available to the public gratis. Regular meetings were held on Friday nights and informal lectures offered on Sundays.[76] It was Webb's plan to establish small study circles throughout the United States to discuss Islam. He began publishing a 16-page journal called *The Moslem World* on May 12, 1893.[77] Later, he published *The Voice of Islam*, and at one point, as a result of financial difficulties, the two journals were combined in *The Moslem World and Voice of Islam*. In December 1895, a *New York Times* reporter who was given a copy of the journal, which Webb put together at his home office on the top floor of the barn of his modest house in Ulster Park, New York, described it as "a neatly printed little paper of four pages, with three columns on each page."[78]

For Webb the promotion of Islam went hand in hand with free thought and rational inquiry into religion. He felt that Islam and its prophet had been "so persistently and grossly misrepresented and misunderstood by Christians" that only "broad-minded Americans" unfettered from "the chains that bind them to the church" could "give Islamic doctrines a fair, unprejudiced and honest investigation."[79] For his Indian Muslim sponsors, however, Webb's conversion to Islam and his desire to propagate Islam in America represented a "white hope" who could revive a nationalist sense of pride and progress among Indian Muslims under British

---

[75] Ibid., 67–68.
[76] "For the Faith of Islam," *New York Times*, October 8, 1893.
[77] "The Islamic Propaganda," *New York Times*, May 28, 1893, 4.
[78] "Fall of Islam in America," *New York Times*, December 1, 1895, 21.
[79] Webb, *Islam in America*, 9–10.

colonial rule. One of the most ardent supporters of Webb's mission in Bombay, Budruddin Abdulla Kur, explained:

We see this day in India a rare and pitiable phenomenon of a powerful nation of sixty millions of Mussulmans absorbed in apathy and lethargy, and steeped in ignorance, in so far at least as secular education is concerned. Now, who can rouse such a vast number of our Mahomedan brethren to a sense of their duty in educational matters in a surer and a better way than the civilized English and American Mussulmans? For these people can easily make us realise our degraded and fallen condition, and bring about a revival of learning in our community. I have not the least doubt that the noble instincts of the English race, when permeated with the sublime doctrines of Islam, will influence and appeal to the imagination of the Indian Mussulmans to cast aside their languor and the sleep of centuries and take a new place in the roll-call of nations.... For the educational development and progress of the Indian Mussulman in their present helpless condition, my eyes are hopefully riveted in India upon the grace of the British Government and in the West upon the civilized American and English converts, whose help and fresh zeal will be of inestimable value in the noble cause of regeneration and revival.[80]

In the late nineteenth century, Kur was not alone among upper-class Indian Muslims in expressing anxious concerns about the welfare of Muslims in British India. In the aftermath of the Sepoy mutiny-rebellion of 1857, the British government formally took power over India from the East India Company, whose administrative policies were largely blamed for the mutiny-rebellion. Among the most pressing tasks before the crown's viceroy was the reform of the British Indian army and civil-bureaucracy. The colonial government reserved all senior positions exclusively for British officials. For more menial positions, it began to recruit Indians from new social classes who were unlikely to have loyalties to the old Mughal dynasty or the varying regional dynasties that emerged throughout India in the eighteenth century. The crown also adopted a policy of mixing Indians from varying socio-religious groups in army regiments in an effort to "counterpoise natives against natives."[81]

These policies resulted in racial tension between the British and Indians and promoted rivalries between Indian socio-religious communities. Consequently, many elite Indian Muslims became very concerned about their future under the British Raj. Their concerns were further exacerbated by a sense of shortcoming in the face of Western Europeans'

[80] Budruddin Abdulla Kur, "Letter to the Editor" in *The Times of India* (November 22, 1892) cited in *Yankee Muslim*, ed. Singleton, 290.
[81] Sugata Bose and Ayesha Jalal, *Modern South Asia: History, Culture, Political Economy* (London: Routledge, 1998), 98.

military, scientific, and technological advancements in the modern era. Like Kur, the eminent Indian Muslim reformer, Sayyid Ahmad Khan (1817–1898) (among others) believed that the future of Islam in India was at stake. Khan worried that individual Muslims who advanced in India under the new British government would lose their Islam and thus, at a time when socio-religious rivalries demanded group solidarity, they would not wish to contribute to the advancement of Indian Muslims as a community. "So if we desire the progress of the Muslim *qaum* [i.e., nation] and its welfare and prosperity," Khan wrote, "it is our duty to strive at the same time for them [i.e., Muslims] to remain Muslims, because if they do not remain Muslims and then progress, this progress will not be the progress of our *qaum*."[82] Khan also expressed a concern about Muslims "well acquainted with English and interested in English sciences" being "thrown into doubt about the truth of the principles of Islam."[83] To address these problems, he sought to reinterpret Islamic theology, arguing for a natural affinity between Islam, reason, and science. He believed that this "reality" of Islam had been overshadowed in modern times by adherences to centuries-old dogmas. Like Kur, he saw education as the principle means by which Indian Muslims could advance within British India and still maintain their distinct social identity. To this end, he founded the Muhammadan Anglo Oriental College in 1875, which later became the Aligarh Muslim University.

Given how widespread concerns about the plight of Muslims were under the British Raj, it is easy to see why Kur and others who supported Webb's mission hoped that the conversion of white Anglophones to Islam would contribute to an Islamic revival in India. Just as the liminality of African Muslims discussed in Chapter 1 allowed Americans to cross racial and religious boundaries in order to pursue their missionary and commercial interests in Africa, Webb's liminal status as a "Yankee Mohammedan"[84] allowed the Indian Muslims who had enlisted him to spread Islam in the United States to cross racial and religious boundaries to pursue not only their missionary aims but also their community-building agendas in British India (and

---

[82] An article by Sayyid Ahmad Khan, published in *Tahdhib al-akhlāq*, vol. 3, cited in Christian W. Troll, *Sayyid Ahmad Khan: Reinterpretation of Muslim Theology*, 303.

[83] Sayyid Ahmad Khan, "Lecutre on Islam" given in Lahore on February 2, 1884 before the Anjuman-i himayat-i Islam ('the Association for the Support of Islam') in Troll, *Sayyid Ahmad Khan*, 314–15.

[84] *Daily Inter Ocean*, September 21, 1893, cited in Seager, *Dawn of Religious Pluralism*, 278 and Singleton, "Introduction," in *Yankee Muslim*, 9.

perhaps even their commercial interests, given that his mission was supported predominantly by Muslim merchants).[85]

Unfortunately, Webb's mission in the United States was short lived in part due to lack of funding. The prosperous Calcutta merchant, Abdullah Arab, who learned about Webb's plans for a Muslim mission in the United States through Kur and who travelled to the Philippines to negotiate with Webb the financial terms of such a mission, had only managed to send Webb $11,427.51. This amount, according to Webb, amounted to a quarter of what he had been promised by way of salary and housing benefits alone.[86] By the end of 1895, Webb claimed to have spent nearly twice the amount of money he received from abroad on his Propaganda. The extra money, he claimed, was raised "here in various ways, by subscriptions, advertisements, &c."[87]

Webb also had difficulty gaining followers among the white, middle-class Americans whom he targeted. Most of these Americans were not interested in Islam. A *New York Times* article described his efforts to convert American Christians to Islam as "a highly-impudent and a highly-ridiculous performance" that "does not appear feasible except to himself and his Mohammedan backers."[88] Prejudices against Islam also ran so deep that even Theosophists, who counted among the free-thinking truth-seekers whom Webb had told his Muslim audiences in India were primed for the message of Islam, were highly skeptical and disapproved of Webb's mission. One of the founding presidents of the Theosophical Society, Henry Steel Olcott, who was one of the more sympathetic Theosophists toward Webb's mission, nonetheless described Islam as "that iron body of bigoted intolerance" whose "sweet indwelling spirit" Webb was trying to release through Theosophy.[89] Another Theosophist remarked, "In fact, we are thoroughly disappointed in trying to find the *why* of Mr. Webb's conversion.... On the whole, we do not think that an Islamism of unsupported statements will be much of an appeal to freethinkers."[90] Some Theosophists thought that Islam was too dogmatically monotheistic: "Islamism seems to many to exact a belief in *a* God, and the conception of *a* God demands that that being shall be separate from those who

---

[85] Webb, *Islam in America*, 68–69; Abd-Allah, *A Muslim in Victorian America*, 60–65; and "Fall of Islam in America," *New York Times*, December 1, 1895, 21.

[86] "Mohammed Webb's Account," *New York Times*, March 27, 1896.

[87] "Fall of Islam in America," *New York Times*, December 1, 1895, 21.

[88] "The Islamic Propaganda," *New York Times*, May 28, 1893, 4.

[89] *Lucifer* 11 (September 1892-February 1893), 513.

[90] Ibid., 440.

believe in him. This view does not appeal to many Western Theosophists, because they assert that there can be no God different or separate from man."[91] Given the hostile atmosphere he faced and the scandals that arose in his organization, it is likely that even the people who gathered around Webb to help with his mission seem to have been motivated by inaccurate newspapers reports of the large sums of money Webb had brought with him from "the Orient."[92]

By 1897, Webb's mission was officially defunct. In 1899, he moved his family to Rutherford, New Jersey where he bought the *Rutherford News* and served as its editor. In 1901, he sold the paper and left journalism as a profession. In that same year, Sultan 'Abd al-Hamid II appointed him Honorary Consul General of the Ottoman Empire at New York as an acknowledgment of his services on behalf of Islam. He was also honored with the title "Bey."[93] Webb remained a Theosophist Muslim and was active in the local politics of Rutherford until he died on October 1, 1916. He did not, however, raise his children as Muslim. His wife belonged to the local Unitarian Church whose pastor, Elizabeth Padgham, performed the funeral rites for Webb.

THE PARLIAMENT'S "TROJAN HORSE EFFECT" AND ISLAM

The inclusionary religious beliefs and practices of the World's Parliament of Religions – fashioned as we have seen by liberal Protestant thought on the one hand and by metaphysical religions (such as the Theosophical Society) on the other – had what William Hutchison has called a "Trojan Horse effect" on nineteenth-century American Protestant claims to "universal religion."[94] Most of the Parliament's attendees were too busy celebrating American Protestant triumphs to notice the irony in Webb, and followers of other "Eastern" religions, claiming their religion as the "universal religion" of an enlightened and rational humanity. Nonetheless, the gathering's inclusionary practices, to use Hutchison's language again, left the door ajar. Following the Parliament, Vivekananda, who adamantly questioned American Protestants' triumphalism at the Parliament, went

---

[91] *The Path* 8 (1893–1894), 112–114.
[92] See, for examples, the relations of John H. Lant and Nefeesa M. T. Keep with Webb's propaganda as they are portrayed in the following *New York Times* articles: "Muhammed Webb Locked Out," July 14, 1894, 5; "Nefeesa Keep Breakfasts," July 16, 1894, 1; "Fall of Islam in America," December 1, 1895, 21.
[93] "Sultan Honors an American," *New York Times*, October 1, 1901.
[94] Hutchison, *Religious Pluralism in America*, 181–182.

on to offer numerous lectures about the universal and "scientific" dimensions of Hindu metaphysics in the Vedas. Soon after, one of his followers,
Abhedananda, established an American branch of Vivekananda's Vedanta
Society in 1898.[95] Baha'is, the followers of a messianic religion that
emerged among Shi'is in mid-nineteenth-century Iran, also began arriving
in the United States as early as 1894[96] to promote their faith in "the West"
as a universal, rational religion, particularly suited for modernity.[97]

Both the Vedanta Society and the Baha'i Faith made converts in the
United States. According to the decennial census of "religious bodies"
conducted between 1906 and 1936 by the Bureau of Census, there were
340 members of the Vedanta Society and 1,280 Baha'is in the United
States in 1906. By 1936, their numbers, though still modest, had doubled
to reach 628 and 2,584, respectively. Both of these religious communities
have had a continuous history of activity in the United States since their
introduction in the 1890s.

It is worthwhile to contrast the relative success of these groups
with the failure of Webb's mission. All of these missionary ventures
promoted an alternate "universal religion" in America among middle
and upper-middle class Americans who were spiritual seekers adverse
to the Christian church, but only Webb's venture became defunct.
Undoubtedly, Webb's mission failed in large part for financial reasons
and for its lack of sustained institutional support. It also seems clear,
however, that another reason for the failure of his mission was the fact
that he was proselytizing Islam and arguing for Islam as *the* "universal
religion" of humanity. The social stigma surrounding Islam among white
Americans was too great to overcome. As the hisses Webb heard during
his lecture at the Parliament evidence, the opening in the gate left ajar
by inclusive Protestant beliefs and practices and the universalizing discourses of metaphysical religions was not wide enough to accommodate
Islam in the same way that it was able to accommodate other groups
such as the Vedanta Society and the Baha'i movement. Most Americans
resented and ridiculed him because of the inverse space his liminality as

---

[95] U.S. Department of Commerce and Labor, Bureau of the Census, *Religious Bodies: 1906*
(Washington, D.C.: Government Printing Office, 1910), 658.

[96] Peter Smith, "The American Bahá'í Community, 1894–1917: A Preliminary Survey," in
Studies in Bábí & Bahá'í History, vol. 1, ed. Moojan Momen (Los Angeles, CA: Kalimat
Press, 1982), 85–224.

[97] For a discussion of this topic, see Juan Cole, *Modernity and the Millennium: The Genesis
of the Baha'i Faith in the Nineteenth-century Middle East* (New York: Columbia
University Press, 1998).

FIGURE 4. The Royal Musicians of Hindustan. Inayat Khan is the third musician from the left. Courtesy of the International Headquarters of the Sufi Movement, the Netherlands.

a "Yankee Mohammedan" broached for Islam in the United States at a time when America was celebrating its triumphs as an Anglo-Saxon, Protestant nation.

INAYAT KHAN AND THE SUFI ORDER OF THE WEST

The missionary of Muslim background who was able to get his foot through the door was Inayat Khan, whose universalist, esoteric interpretation of Sufism stripped the Sufi tradition from Islam in order to gain him acceptance in the United States. Although Inayat Khan's teachings were inspired by the Islamic tradition, he did not explicitly promote Islam. Inayat Khan was an Indian musician who came from a courtly musical family. He claimed to have been initiated into the Nizamiyya branch of the Chistiyya Sufi order by Muhammad Abu Hashim Madani (d. 1907). He arrived in New York on September 13, 1910 along with his brother and cousin. Soon after their arrival, Khan and his relatives gave a performance at Columbia University. In their audience was Ruth St. Denis (1877–1968), a founding figure in American dance, who was known for her interpretations of Oriental dances. The Khans joined her troupe and accompanied her on a national tour as the Royal Musicians. Somewhere along his journey, Inayat Khan came to be regarded as a Sufi teacher, no doubt by the same "masses of intelligent people" Mohammed Alexander Webb hoped to convert and whom he described as "drifting away from the Christian churches and forming themselves into free-thought societies, ethical cultural societies, non-sectarians societies and numerous other organizations the purpose of which is to seek religious truth."[98]

At the end of his tour in San Francisco in 1911, Inayat Khan was invited by Swami Trigunatita and Swami Paramananda to lecture on Indian music at the Vedanta Society Hindu Temple. There he met Ada Martin (1871–1947), who concluded from the meeting that Inayat Khan fulfilled a vision she claimed to have had in the spring of 1910 of "a very great and illuminated intelligence."[99] Khan is said to have noticed in her a "soul who was drinking in all I said."[100] Later he had a vision of a room being filled with light that led him to believe that he was to initiate her as his first "Western" disciple into what eventually became the Sufi Order of the West. Inayat Khan gave her a new personal name, Rabi'a, after the famous eighth-century Sufi saint, Rabi'a al-Adawiyya (d. 801). Martin's initiation was followed by others, but Martin became Inayat Khan's favored disciple (*murid*), and when he left for Europe in 1912 she served as his representative in the United States. Inayat Khan returned briefly to the United States in 1923 to visit with his American disciples under the tutelage of Ada Martin. By that time he was the spiritual head of an inter-national organization known as the Sufi Order of the West headquartered in Geneva, Switzerland. He died in 1927. Following Inayat Khan's death there were a number of schisms among his followers, some of whom, like Samuel Lewis (also known as Sufi Sam), went on to found their own spiritual organizations. None of the groups founded upon Inayat Khan's teachings consider themselves specifically Islamic, even though they call themselves Sufi and employ Sufi terminology and rituals. They focus on

---

[98] Webb, *The Three Lectures*, 51. Many of the individuals who joined Inayat Khan's Order or listened to his lectures were involved in such societies. See Zia Inayat-Khan, "A Hybrid Sufi Order at the Crossroads of Modernity: The Sufi Order and Sufi Movement of Pir-o-Murshid Inayat Khan" (Ph.D. dissertation, Duke University, 2006) 22F and 63–81.

[99] *Notes for an Autobiography of Murshid Rabia Martin* (unpublished), cited in Andrew Rawlinson, *The Book of Enlightened Masters: Western Teachers in Eastern Traditions* (La Salle, IL: Open Court, 1997), 436.

[100] Inayat Khan et al., *Biography of Pir-o-Murshid Inayat Khan* (Madras: East-West Publications, 1979), 85.

what they regard as the universal wisdom found within the Sufi tradition, which they believe happened to be associated with Islam as a matter of historical accident. Initiates in these groups are not required to convert to Islam.[101]

Inayat Khan's spiritual message was informed by an enduring axiological division of the world into a spiritual, mystical, emotive "East" and a materialist, positivist, rational "West." Inayat Khan fashioned himself as a bridge between these worlds. In his redacted autobiography, he lauded the individual liberties and freedoms found in the United States and described America as "the sum-total of modern progress." "With all the modern spirit in America," he wrote, "I found among the people love for knowledge, search for truth, and tendency to unity."[102] Clearly, the more inclusionary theologies and practices of liberal Protestantism and universalizing discourses on metaphysical unity of religions had paved the way for Inayat Khan in certain cosmopolitan circles in the United States. This road, however, was not without its bumps. Inayat Khan lamented that the "commercialism" and "the reign of materialism" in "the West" made working for a "spiritual Cause...like travelling in a hilly land, not like sailing in the sea, which is smooth and level."[103] Commercialism, however, was not the only difficulty he encountered. He also confronted the conflation of race, religion, and progress in the United States:

There is still to be found in America a prejudice against colour which is particularly shown to the Negroes.... They think Negroes are too backward in evolution to associate with....An ordinary man in America confuses an Indian with brown skin with the Negro. Even if he does not think that he is a Negro, still he is accustomed to look with contempt at a dark skin, in spite of the many most unclean, ignorant and illmannered (sic) specimens of white people who are to be found there on the spot.[104]

At one point in 1923, Inayat Khan was detained and questioned by immigration officials at Ellis Island because "the quota of Indians was completed for that month." He was freed after a few hours when one

[101] I have relied on the following sources for my biography of Inayat Khan: Carl W. Ernst and Bruce B. Lawrence, *Sufi Martyrs of Love: The Chishti Order in South Asia and Beyond* (New York: Macmillan, 2002), 141–142; Zia Inayat-Khan, "A Hybrid Sufi Order," 64f; Inayat Khan, *Biography*, 83–88 and 106–119; and the entries on Sufi Order and Sufi Movement and on Rabia Martin in Rawlinson, *The Book of Enlightened Masters*, 543–553 and 436–438.
[102] Inayat Khan, *Biography*, 84.
[103] Ibid., 112.
[104] Ibid., 87–88.

of his disciples, Marya Gushing, interceded on his behalf. "I was glad to have had that experience," he later wrote, "to see to what extent materialism has affected nations."[105]

Inayat Khan was also keenly aware of the prejudice against Islam in the early 1900s:

> The prejudice against Islam that exists in the West was another difficulty for me. Many think Sufism to be a mystical side of Islam, and the thought was supported by the encyclopedias, which speak of Sufism as having sprung from Islam, and they were confirmed in this by knowing that I am Moslim (sic) by birth. Naturally I could not tell them that it is a Universal Message of the time, for every man is not ready to understand this.[106]

Inayat Khan deliberately disassociated his teachings from Islam and framed his message in the context of the more acceptable discourse of "universal religion," shaped by liberal Protestant theology and metaphysical interpretations of religion. By adopting the discourse of "universal religion," he was able to transcend his race and the stigma of Islam, which by now he no longer regarded as *his* religion but the accidental religion of his birth. In one of the earliest biographies of him, he was portrayed as a man who outgrew the legalism of his Islamic heritage and discovered the "inner truth" of existence through esoteric Sufism.[107] Inayat Khan and his followers carefully guarded the liminal status the concept of "universal religion" attributed to him. He eschewed, for example, any political activity at a time when, as I discussed earlier, there was a growing call for Muslim nationalism and discontent with British colonial rule in his homeland:

> When Gandhi proclaimed non-cooperation I heard its silent echo in the heart of Great Britain. Besides, the Khilafet Movement[108] had stirred up the minds of the people there. I felt a hidden influence coming from every corner, resenting against any activity which had a sympathetic connection with the East. I then felt that

---

[105] Ibid., 106.
[106] Ibid., 113.
[107] See "Biography of the Author" in Inayat Khan, *Sufi Message of Spiritual Liberty* (London: The Theosophical Publishing Society, 1914), 7–15.
[108] The Khilafat Movement was a pan-Islamic, nationalist movement organized in British India in the late 1910s by Indian Muslims concerned on the one hand about their own fate in the British Empire in a Hindu-majority society and on the other about the status of the Ottoman Caliphate and their guardianship of Muslim holy sites, such as Mecca and Medina, following World War I. See Gail Minault, *The Kilafat Movement: Religious Symbolism and Political Mobilization in India* (New York: Columbia University Press, 1982) and Naeem Qureshi, *Pan-Islam in British Indian Politics: A Study of the Khilafat Movement, 1918–1924* (Leiden: Brill, 1999).

the hour had come to remove the seat of our [Sufi] Movement to a place such as Geneva, which has been chosen as an international centre by all.... I have always refrained from taking the side of any particular nation in my work, and have tried to keep my Movement free from any political shadows. Vast fields of political activity were laid open before me, during and after the war [World War I], in which I was quite capable of working at the time when there was a great demand for work of the kind, at the time of great upheaval in India and in the Near East. And if I hesitated to take interest in such activities, it was only that my heart was all taken by the need of a universal brotherhood in the world.[109]

Because the political activity that Inayat Khan mentions was against colonial rule and the achievement of sociopolitical equality, one has to assume that he was not preoccupied with attaining "universal brotherhood" in the here and now. He substituted sociopolitical equality for a message of metaphysical equality, which theoretically opposed racism and imperialism as manifestations of materialism and nationalism, but never called for getting one's hands dirty. The course Inayat Khan's mission took reveals the stakes embedded in the seemingly axiological division between a spiritual, emotive "East" and a materialist, rational "West" in the first half of the twentieth century. For "Eastern" religions to gain acceptance in the United States, they had to be depoliticized and privatized. Given the association that was made at the turn of the twentieth century between Protestantism and the imperial successes of the Anglo-Saxon race, Inayat Khan's decision to eschew politics in order to further his mission illustrates that the notion often associated with "Western" modernity, that religion is essentially a private affair, did not apply to all religions equally. Rather, the privatization of religion was a prerequisite for the participation of non-Protestants in American public life.

Inayat Khan's experiences in the United States demonstrate personally how the inclusionary theologies and practices of the late nineteenth century may have left the gate of religious pluralism ajar, but the non-Protestant religions that slipped in did not challenge Americans' triumphalist conflation of race, religion, and progress. Muslim newcomers, such as Inayat Khan, had to color their teachings with unspecific metaphysical claims of universality in order to cloak their stigmatized racial and religious backgrounds, and in the process they helped maintain the status quo.

Inayat Khan's experiences also draw attention to the role of gender in the conflation of the white race with Protestantism and civilizational

---

[109] Inayat Khan, *Biography*, 71.

progress. It is important to note that the conflation of race, religion, and progress left white, Protestant women in an ambiguous place. The World's Parliament of Religions, for example, sought to represent the religious accomplishment of women[110] as did the Columbian Exposition more generally with its Board of Lady Managers and Woman's Building. In both cases, however, women's participation, unlike men's participation, was marked by sex and thus marginal to the fair as a whole. There was, for example, no Men's Building nor a Men's Committee. Metaphysical interpretations of religion created a space of equality that allowed women to transcend the mark of gender in society just as they allowed individuals, such as Inayat Khan, to transcend race. It is thus not surprising that many of the founders of metaphysical religions (e.g., Helena Balvatsky and Mary Baker Eddy) and many of the most prominent disciples of spiritual teachers from "the East" were women.[111] Inayat Khan wrote, "Destiny made women understand my message and sympathize with me more readily than men, whose lives are absorbed in their daily occupations, and whose ideal and devotion is almost lost in the modern way of living. This made my life and work most difficult. I found on one hand a ditch, and on the other hand water."[112] Rationalism, modernity, and progress were not only seen as the domain of whites and Protestants but also of men. From the above citation, it appears that Inayat Khan begrudged the feminine appeal of his teachings in the West, but the success of his movement among white American and European women suggests that he reconciled himself to it.[113]

---

[110] John Henry Barrows, who chaired the Parliament, wrote in his history of the Parliament, "The Parliament of Religions gratefully recognized the supreme and splendid offices which woman has performed in the history of humanity's holiest development. The gracious lady, who is so worthy of her place in the fore-front of this gathering of the Nations, has said that, as Columbus discovered America, the Columbian Exposition discovered woman." Barrows, *World's Parliament of Religions: An Illustrated and Popular Story of the World's First Parliament of Religions, Held in Chicago in Connection with the Columbian Exposition of 1893* (Chicago, IL: The Parliament Publishing Company, 1893), vii–viii.

[111] For further discussion of this issue, see Ann Braude, *Radical Spirits: Spiritualism and Women's Rights in Nineteenth-century America*, 2nd ed. (Bloomington, IN: Indiana University Press, 2001).

[112] Inayat Khan, *Biography*, 119. While in the United States, Inayat Khan married a cousin of the founder of Christian Science Mary Baker Eddy, Ora Ray Baker (later known as Amina Begum), who at times practiced spiritual healing herself. See Inayat Khan, *Biography*, 116.

[113] For a discussion of the later development of his movement, see Karin Jironet, *The Image of Spiritual Liberty in the Western Sufi Movement Following Hazrat Inayat Khan* (Leeuven: Peeters, 2002).

SUMMARY

Post–Civil War America was a time of great social change, which raised many questions about the nature of American society and identity. In the late nineteenth and early twentieth centuries, as Americans came increasingly into contact with racial, ethnic, and religious diversity as a result of emancipation, territorial expansion, increased immigration, and urbanization, a powerful conflation of race, religion, and progress emerged. Through this conflation, Anglo-American, liberal Protestants triumphantly claimed America's industrial, cultural, political, and commercial achievements as the product of their particular racial and religious heritage. This conflation of the white race, Protestant Christianity, and progress allowed white native-born Protestants to define America as a white, Protestant nation thus maintaining their cultural and sociopolitical hegemony even as the nation itself became more racially, ethnically, and religiously diverse.

It was argued that the unique universality of Protestantism coupled with the military, scientific, and technological advancements of the so-called white race in the modern era proved the veracity of white Americans' religious beliefs and the superiority of their race. Race, religion, and progress thus came to constitute a matrix through which a triumphant American national identity was articulated. Ironically, insofar as this identity matrix was founded upon the concept of "universal religion," it left open the possibility for adherents of other religions to argue for theirs as the true universal religion, uniquely committed to modernity and progress. Indeed many representatives of "Eastern" religions at the World's Parliament of Religions in 1893, including the Muslim missionary Mohammed Alexander Russell Webb, made this precise claim, and some of them went on to found alternative religious movements among middle and upper-middle class white Americans. Prejudice against Islam, however, ran deep at this time. Webb faced grave difficulties gaining followers. His efforts to educate Americans about the rationality and universality of Islam were for the most part met with ridicule at worst and resentful tolerance at best. Another missionary, Inayat Khan, quickly realized that he faced a great deal of racial and religious prejudices as an Indian Muslim and opted to divorce his message of Sufi universalism from Islam. He adapted his teaching to the discourse of "universal religion" in order to gain acceptance. In the end, his relative success hinged upon his disavowal of any explicit connections between his Sufi inspired teachings and Islam.

In sum, given the general lack of recognition of the polyvalence of Islam, Webb's praise of Islam appeared as willful self-deception to most non-Muslim Americans and Khan's teachings had to be de-Islamicized. Both could only get their foot in the door as outsiders by contextualizing their teachings within a larger discourse of a universal, spiritual religion that emerged in nineteenth-century liberal Protestant thought. This "universal religion," as explained by James Freeman Clarke, was believed to encompass *essentially* the positive teachings of all other "ethnic religions." If African Muslims, as discussed in Chapter 2, drew on commonalities between Islam and Christianity to establish a common ground through which they could make sense of their new world and hold their white masters accountable for their behavior before God, the discourse on "universal religion" aimed at a higher ground through which it could establish the hierarchical relation between different religious beliefs and practices and to identify the "true religion," the religion most suited for "progress."

4

Race, Ethnicity, Religion, and Citizenship

Muslim Immigration at the Turn of the Twentieth Century

In the hagiographies of Inayat Khan, his arrival in the "West" is explained through a charge his Sufi master gave him when he attained enlightenment: "Go, my child, into the world, harmonize the East and the West with the harmony of thy music; spread the wisdom of Sufism, for thou art gifted by Allah, the most Merciful and Compassionate."[1] This otherworldly explanation of why Khan came to the United States in 1910 allowed Khan, as we have seen, to transcend the color of his skin and his stigmatized Islamic background. It situated him neatly within the contemporary universalizing discourses of liberal Protestantism and metaphysical religions. It concealed, however, the fact that he left India for the United States at a time when a few thousand north Indians were immigrating to the United States in search of economic opportunities.

The establishment's groping for a cohesive national identity and social order through such universalizing concepts as race, religion, and progress in the nineteenth and early twentieth centuries concealed the actual workings of American industry, commerce, culture, government, and science, most of which were advanced by the diligence and ingenuity not only of white native-born Protestants, but also of immigrants and natives who were not considered white (Irish Catholics, Eastern European Jews, African American Baptists, and others) who made up the mass of American workers, thinkers, and entrepreneurs. This chapter narrates the history of the arrival of a specific set of immigrants at the turn of the twentieth century, those who came from parts of the world

---

[1] Inayat Khan, *Sufi Message of Spiritual Liberty* (London: The Theosophical Publishing Society, 1914), 15.

with a significant Muslim population. Ten to fifteen percent, or about 60,000, of these immigrants (between 1890 and 1924) are estimated to have been Muslim. The history of America's successes in industry, science, and commerce in the nineteenth century were intimately intertwined with the history of immigration and emancipation. Today, this may seem like a truism to anyone familiar with American history, but the upshot of the conflation of race, religion, and progress in this period was that what is considered a truism today came as an epiphany in 1951 to Oscar Handlin, a pioneering historian of American immigration, who famously wrote: "Once I thought to write a history of the immigrants in America. Then I discovered that the immigrants were American history."[2]

This is not to suggest that white Protestants were blind to the contributions of members of other races and religions to the United States. They weren't. Rather, through the conflation of race, religion, and progress, they defined a triumphant paradigm for American identity that required others to imitate them and assimilate in order to participate in America's prosperity. This is how the establishment maintained its social preeminence and cultural authority. Josiah Strong, for instance, noted that the new immigration posed a danger only insofar as the new immigrants did not become part of "the amalgam which will constitute the new Anglo-Saxon race of the New World."[3] Similarly, James Freeman Clarke considered non-Protestant religions to be problematic only when they did not realize their limitations in comparison to Protestant Christianity's unlimited universality. "Christianity is adapted to take their place," he wrote, "not because they are false, but because they are true as far as they go."[4]

This conflation of race, religion, and progress affected immigrants from countries with a significant Muslim population at the turn of the twentieth century in two principal ways. At one level, it legally restricted, mainly through quotas, their entry to the United States and their eligibility for citizenship. At another level, it defined the paradigm of American identity through which they were expected to self-identify in order to be accepted as Americans. Since the stigma around Islam at this time would not have allowed for its inclusion within this national identity paradigm,

---

[2] Oscar Handlin, *The Uprooted: The Epic Story of the Great Migrations that Made the American People* (Boston, MA: Little, Brown and Company, 1951), 3.

[3] Josiah Strong, *Our Country: Its Possible Future and Its Present Crisis* (New York: The Baker and Tayor Co., 1885), 172.

[4] See James Freeman Clarke, *Ten Great Religions Religions: An Essay in Comparative Theology* (Boston, MA: James R. Osgood and Company, 1871), 29.

immigrant Muslims who sought inclusion did so primarily through an ethnic rather than a religious mode of self-identification.

Sometime around 1920, M. M. Aijian, an Armenian American Christian missionary to Muslim immigrants based in Chicago, wrote the Census Bureau to inquire about the number of Muslims in the United States. He was told that "[t]here have been various efforts to learn the number of Mohammedans in the United States, but so far without any satisfactory result. Of course there are Mohammedans from North India, as well as from Arabia and Turkey." Aijian later wrote that "at this time it is not possible to give, even approximately, the number of Moslems in North America." Nonetheless, based on his personal experiences with them, he surmised that their numbers in 1920 "reach up into the thousands" and that they were concentrated in the industrial centers of the East and the Midwest, such as Milwaukee, Chicago, Pittsburgh, Cleveland, Akron, New York City, Philadelphia, Baltimore, Boston, and Worcester.[5] Another American missionary and literary author, Mary Caroline Holmes, wrote in 1926 that Muslims themselves estimated that there were "as many as fifty or sixty thousand of them in this country." Holmes added St. Louis, Los Angeles, and San Francisco to Aijian's list of cities where Muslim enclaves could be found.[6]

There is no known way of accurately estimating the number of Muslims in the United States in this period. Census and immigration statistics provide data on the number of immigrants the United States received from Muslim-majority regions but offer little concrete data regarding their affiliation with Islam. The data for immigrants from Muslim-majority regions are also not very useful because of inconsistencies in record keeping and because they do not distinguish between immigrants by ethnicity. For example, prior to 1899, immigration officials lumped Syrians, Turks, Kurds, Armenians, and anyone else from the Asian Ottoman territories under the rubric of "Turkey in Asia."[7] Albanians, Macedonians, Bosnians, Herzegovinians, Croats, Serbs, and others living in European Ottoman

---

[5] M. M. Aijian, "Mohammedans in the United States," *Moslem World* 10 (1920), 30.

[6] Mary Caroline Holmes, "Islam in America," *Moslem World* 16 (1926), 264.

[7] For a discussion of the difficulties in using U.S. census and immigration records for estimating the number of immigrants from Muslim-majority regions, see Kemal Karpat, "The Ottoman Emigration to America, 1860–1914," *International Journal of Middle East*

territories were all categorized as coming from "Turkey in Europe." An unknown number of Muslim immigrants also came to the United States through other countries in North America illegally. Others came to the United States after having spent time in other European or South or Central American countries and were counted as nationals of the country of their last residence. This is particularly true of Albanians, many of whom came via Greece or Italy to the United States.

A concrete example of the general unreliability of official census data is found in the 1901 *Reports of the Industrial Commission on Immigration and on Education*. This is one of the few reports that made an effort to identify immigrants by their religious affiliation. According to this report, 110 "Mohammedans" arrived in the United States in 1899 by ship. Two of them were recorded to have come from France (including Corsica), one each from the Russian Empire and Finland, thirteen from Turkey in Europe, seventy-seven from other parts of Europe, and sixteen from Asia.[8] According to this report, the majority of Muslims who came to this country in 1899 were from parts of Europe normally not associated with Islam. While immigration officials made concerted efforts at the beginning of the twentieth century to distinguish between immigrants' nationalities and the countries from which they came, they were neither always accurate nor were they consistent. Despite these caveats, in what follows, I rely heavily on these official numbers because they represent the best known source for an actual headcount of immigrants from Muslim-majority countries. Future studies may compare these records with emigration records of the Ottoman Empire (as Kemal Karpat, mentioned below, has done) or Colonial India to provide us with more accurate data regarding the number of Muslims who immigrated to the United States at the turn of the twentieth century.

IMMIGRANTS FROM THE LEVANT

Arabic-speakers from the Ottoman province of Syria, more specifically from Mount Lebanon, comprised the largest group of immigrants from the Muslim-majority world. They were regarded as Syrians from the Levant until the early 1920s when the terms "Lebanese" and "Palestinian"

Studies 17, no. 2 (May 1985), 181 and Alixa Naff, *Becoming American: The Early Arab Immigrant Experience* (Carbondale, IL: Southern Illinois University Press), 108–109.
[8] U.S. House of Representatives Industrial Commission on Immigration and on Education, *Reports of the Industrial Commission on Immigration and on Education*, vol. XV (Washington, D.C.: Government Printing Office, 1901), 291.

gained political recognition as markers of modern national identities. In this chapter, I refer to the immigrants from the Levant prior to the 1920s as Syrians or Syrian Americans.

Syrian American narratives generally explain Syrian emigration as an escape from the oppressive nature of Ottoman rule. They cite complaints of heavy tax burdens, army conscriptions, government corruption, and unchecked sectarian violence between Muslims, Christians, and Druze.[9] Most of these factors, however, were exaggerated for the sake of an American public that had a very negative image of the Ottoman Sultans. In actuality, whatever oppressions Syrians faced in the Levant, they were not significant enough to stem their desire to return home. As Kemal Karpat has noted, "most of them were determined to return to Syria after accumulating some money, and a third of them did eventually return."[10] Indeed, poor economic conditions in Syria and the promise of wealth in the New World were more consequential in Syrians' decision to emigrate from the Ottoman Empire.[11]

Syrian immigration to the United States was facilitated by the presence of American missionaries in the region. Since some Syrian Christians had closer ties with these missionaries than did Syrian Muslims,[12] Syrian Christians arrived in the United States earlier and in larger numbers, and once in the Unites States they played a more prominent role as the face of the Syrian community. American Protestant missionaries arrived in the Levant as early as the 1820s. The missionaries made few converts, but they built schools, churches, and charities, all of which helped introduce and attract Syrians to the United States. American missionary schools were mostly established among Syria's non-Protestant Christian communities and played a significant role in developing a new professional and intellectual elite versed in "Western" ideas and modern sciences. "The proliferation of primary and secondary schools and the numerous graduates in medicine, the sciences, and humanities from the American University of Beirut, [formerly the Syrian Protestant College],

---

[9] Naff, *Becoming American*, 84–85; Gregory Orfalea, *The Arab Americans: A History* (Northampton, MA: Olive Branch Press, 2006), 66–68; Philip K. Hitti, *The Syrians in America* (New York: G. H. Doran and Company, 1924), 48–51.

[10] Karpat, "Ottoman Emigration to America," 178–179.

[11] For an overview of reasons why Syrians emigrated see Naff, *Becoming American*, 82–91; Karpat, "Ottoman Emigration to America," 176–186; Randa A. Kayyali, *The Arab Americans* (Westport, CT: Greenwood Press, 2006), 26–35.

[12] Ussama Makdisi, "Reclaiming the Land of the Bible: Missionaries, Secularism, and Evangelic Modernity," *American Historical Review* 102, no. 3 (June 1997), 705–706.

were testimony enough to the extent of American [Protestant missions] influence in Syria."[13]

Upon arrival in the United States, Syrian immigrants mostly peddled dry goods throughout rural parts of the United States. Later they opened their own retail stores and distribution centers for newcomers who took up their place in the pecking order as peddlers.[14] Some became homesteaders in places like North Dakota. Others took up farming in the Midwest.[15] When demand for labor in industries increased during and after World War I, many moved to urban centers to work in factories. The Ford Motor Company's commitment to pay five dollars a day for eight hours of work drew many Syrian immigrants to Detroit, which today hosts the largest population of Arab Americans in the United States.[16]

Even though the majority of immigrants from the Levant, generally referred to as "Syrian immigrants," were Christians (predominantly of the Eastern Orthodox churches), there was a substantial number of Muslims among them. Their numbers, as Kemal Karpat has convincingly argued, have generally been underestimated by scholars of Syrian immigration.[17] One of the earliest historians of Syrian-Americans, Philip Hitti, for example, wrote in 1924 that only about 8,000 (4 percent) of what he estimated to be 200,000 Syrians in the United States at that time were Muslim.[18] Alixa Naff, author of the most comprehensive study of early Syrian immigrants to date, stated that the presence of Muslims was so small that "they hardly warranted passing mention in the literature on Syrians at the turn of the century."[19]

One of the reasons why the number of Muslims among Syrian immigrants has been underestimated is that scholars of Syrian immigration to the United States have generally relied on Arabic sources and have not made extensive use of Ottoman sources, including the archives of

---

[13] Naff, *Becoming American*, 35. On the influence of American missions in Syria in the nineteenth century, see Naff, *Becoming American*, 34–37. For a more general discussion of American missions in the region, see Ussama Makdisi, *Artillery of Heaven: American Missionaries and the Failed Conversion of the Middle East* (Ithaca, NY: Cornell University Press, 2008).

[14] Naff, *Becoming American*, 128–160; Kayyali, *The Arab Americans*, 36–39; Nabeel Abraham and Andrew Shryock, eds., *Arab Detroit: From Margin to Mainstream* (Detroit, MI: Wayne State University Press, 2000), 95–96.

[15] William C. Sherman, Paul L. Whitney, and John Guerrero, *Prairie Peddlers: The Syrian Lebanese in North Dakota* (Bismarck, ND: University of Mary Press, 2002).

[16] Abraham and Shryock, *Arab Detroit*, 50 and Naff, *Becoming American*, 196.

[17] Karpat, "Ottoman Emigration to America."

[18] Hitti, *Syrians in America*, 108.

[19] Naff, *Becoming American*, 112.

the Ottoman consulates in the United States. By way of example, while scholars date the arrival of the first Muslim immigrants from the Levant to the early 1900s, a generation or so after the arrival of their Christian counterparts, "the Ottoman legation in Washington reported as early as 1892 that among Syrian immigrants there were 'considerable numbers' of Muslims," one of whom was an *imam* or religious leader who had come to join his son.

This 1892 Ottoman report mentions another crucial factor in the undercounting of Syrian Muslims in this period. Many Syrian Muslims sought to pass as Christians in order to be more easily accepted into the United States and to circumvent Ottoman regulations which forbade the emigration of Muslims. The Ottomans were not only concerned about losing some of their tax base and decreasing the pool of young men available for conscription, but they were also concerned about their public image. The conventional wisdom in the Ottoman government was that only the poor and uneducated emigrated to the Americas, and they did not want to be represented abroad by their underclass.[20] Consequently, Muslims who sought to come to the United States to improve their economic lot had to work around the state by dissimulating as Christians or bribing Ottoman officials.

In the United States, similar to previously discussed African Muslims who complied in their "de-Islamicization" and "de-negrofication" by white Christians in order to improve their social standing or to gain financial support for their repatriation to Africa, these immigrants disassociated themselves from Islam. Ostensibly "de-Islamicization" remained integral both to immigration and assimilation into the United States at the turn of the twentieth century. Many Muslim immigrants took Christian names to avoid the stigmatization associated with being a Turk or a Muslim. A. Joseph Howar, who came to New York in 1903, told a reporter in 1975:

My true name is Mohammed Asa Abu-Howah. But people I met on the boat told me I'd better change my name. They said it labeled me as a Muslim, and no immigration officer would allow a Muslim to enter the United States. I had two cousins who'd become American citizens. One had taken the name of Abraham and the other Joseph. So I took both those names, and since the British pronounced Howah as if it were Howar, I made my American name A. Joseph Howar. That's how I was naturalized in 1908.[21]

[20] Karpat, "Ottoman Emigration to America," 182 and 186–189.
[21] Philip Harsham, "One Arab's Immigration," *Saudi Aramco World* 26, no. 2 (March/April 1975), 14–15.

American press coverage of Greece's struggle for independence from the Ottoman Empire (1821–1832), sectarian strife in the Levant between Muslims, Christians, and Druze,[22] and the Armenian massacre of 1915 represented the Ottomans as despotic and intolerant oppressors of Christian minorities.[23] This image of the Ottomans was reinforced by American missionaries in the region and by Christian immigrants who exaggerated Ottoman corruption and oppression in order to bolster American support for Syrian immigration.[24] Moussa Daoud, a graduate of the Catholic College of Beirut who served as an interpreter for the British army before opening a small shop and rooming service in New York, told a reporter from the *New York Times* in 1894 about "the merits of the Syrian immigrants": "They are Roman Catholics and Protestants," he insisted, even though most Syrian immigrants were Orthodox, "persecuted by the Mohammedans, who have no other word to designate them than 'pigs.' They are taught by Jesuits and Presbyterians in Syria. The Sultan has issued orders that they shall not immigrate, but they escape the vigilance of the Sultan's officers."[25] A *Philadelphia Inquirer* article on a lecture on "the manners and customs of Syria" by Nageeb J. Arbeely, who founded the first Arabic newspaper in the United States, *Kawkab amrika (Star of America)*, in 1892, read: "Mr. Arbeely ... had retired to escape the cruelties of the Arabs and Druses in the great massacre [of 1860], during which they more than once sought his life. Mr. Arbeely was an object of special hatred on account of his services among the Christian missionaries. Being a member of the Greek Chruch, he had hailed with joy the arrival of his fellow Christians from the Western world."[26] The affable connection drawn between Syrian Christians and American missionaries simplified the complexities of the relations between American

[22] The Druze comprise a distinct ethnic and religious community in the Levant that emerged out of the Fatimid Isma'ili Shi'i movement in Islam in the eleventh century. For an overview of their religious beliefs and practices and historical presence in the United States, see Yvonne Y. Haddad and Jane I. Smith, *Mission to America: Five Islamic Sectarian Movements in North America* (Gainesville, FL: University of Florida Press, 1993).

[23] On the Greek War of Independence, see Timothy Marr, *The Cultural Roots of American Islamicism* (Cambridge: Cambridge University Press, 2006), 69–76, 113, and 147; on the Lebanon and Armenia issue, see the following *New York Times* articles: "Arms and Bombs for Zeitoun," December 15, 1895, 5 and "Christian Syrians Reported in Peril," July 6, 1920, 31.

[24] Karpat, "Ottoman Emigration to America," 178–179. See also, Nadim Makdisi, "The Moslems of America," *Christian Century* 76, no. 34 (August 26, 1959), 969–971.

[25] "Moussa Daoud Their Leader," *New York Times*, June 4, 1894, 2.

[26] "An Evening in the East," *Philadelphia Inquirer*, August 2, 1883, 2.

missionaries and the multireligious communities of the Levant,[27] but it demonstrates the cultural import of such a connection for the positive reception of Syrian immigrants in America.

A 1909 editorial in the *New York Times* questioned whether or not it made sense to deny Turks naturalization because they belong to the Mongolian or yellow race when for hundreds of years they have "freely intermingled with the Caucasian races." Salloum Mokarzel, a Maronite and co-publisher of one of the earliest Arabic newspapers in the United States, *al-Huda*, was quick to respond to urge Americans to distinguish between the freedom-loving, non-Muslim subjects of the Turkish empire and the oppressive empire itself. He stated that most of the people who are prejudicially assumed to be Turks are "none other than Turkish subjects of diverse nationalities who have through the succession of many centuries and in the face of the severest oppression clung to and kept alive their national characteristics, religions, and languages, and who, driven by that same oppression have sought a refuge in this free and hospitable country."[28]

General antipathy toward Muslims and Turks became more ensconced when the Ottomans joined forces with the Germans against the United States and its allies in World War I. The son of a Muslim peddler recounted that once in those years, when his father was lodging with a Catholic farmer during one of his peddling tours, "A prayer was said and they all crossed themselves, but my father did not. They asked him, 'Aren't you Christian?' He replied that no, he was a Muslim. They did not understand what a Muslim was and he proceeded to explain ... and he mentioned the Turkish government ... At this point, the farmer rose up in anger and, reaching for his gun, said, 'So, you are a Turk. I'll kill that Turk; get out of my house.' So my father left."[29] Hence, both Ottoman rules regarding the emigration of Muslims from the Empire and American prejudice against Muslims led Syrian Muslims to hide their religious identities and play a less prominent role as Muslims within their larger ethnic community. Using Ottoman sources, a number of which contained details of Syrian Muslims clandestinely leaving for the Americas, Kemal Karpat has estimated that 15 to 20 percent of the roughly 180,000 Syrians who immigrated to the United States between 1860 and 1914 were Muslim.[30]

---

[27] For an excellent discussion of American Missions in the Levant, see Makdisi, *Artillery of Heaven.*

[28] S. A. Mokarzel, "Turkish Subjects: Declares that Prejudice Exists Against Their Becoming American Citizens," *New York Times*, October 3, 1909, 12.

[29] Cited in Naff, *Becoming American*, 251.

[30] Karpat, "The Ottoman Emigration to America," 183, 185, and 195.

While Muslims from the Levant represent the largest number of Muslims
in the United States in this period, there was also a historically significant
presence of Muslims from Yemen, the Caucasus, Anatolia, the Balkans,
and the Punjab (in northern India). We know very little about the numbers
and activities of the Yemeni Muslims and Muslims from the Caucasus
and Anatolia in the United States. A Muslim missionary wrote of Yemeni
sailors on British ships who debarked in New York City to work on a
temporary basis before returning home.[31] Some Yemenis also arrived in
Detroit and were stranded in the city when Lake Detroit froze during the
winter. Some worked at the Ford factory until they could return home.
A few others began more long-term ventures, like starting coffee shops
which served as social centers for their co-ethnics.[32]

Eastern European Muslims began immigrating to the United States at
the turn of the twentieth century. Unfortunately, we do not know much
about their numbers or activities, but they must have been of some significance. Aijian, in 1920, reported that "Russian Tatar Moslems" had
established "the only real mosque" in the United States, known as the
Anglo-Mohammedan Association at 108 Powers Street in Brooklyn, New
York.[33] The association mentioned by Aijian was most likely the same as
the American Mohammedan Society, which was established by Muslim
immigrants of Poland, Russia, and Lithuania in 1907,[34] and by the mid-
1930s had two imams and about 200 members.[35]

Turkish- and Kurdish-speaking Muslims from Anatolia began to arrive
in the United States during the last decades of the nineteenth century, but
their mass immigration did not begin until the first decade of the twentieth
century. In 1899, twenty-eight immigrants classified as belonging to the
"Turkish race or people" were admitted to the United States. As previously

---

[31] Ahmed I. Abu Shouk, J. O. Hunwick, and R. S. O'Fahey, "A Sudanese Missionary to the
United States: Sāttī Mājid, '*Shaykh al-Islam* in North America', and His Encounter with
Noble Drew Ali, Prophet of the Moorish Science Temple Movement," *Sudanic Africa* 8
(1997), 143–144.
[32] Personal interview with Ron A., third-generation Arab American Muslim of Detroit,
Michigan (May 18, 2008).
[33] Aijian, "Mohammedans in the United States," 40.
[34] Marc Ferris, "To 'Achieve the Pleasure of Allah': Muslims in New York City, 1893–1991,"
in *Muslim Communities in North America*, ed. Yvonne Y. Haddad and Jane I. Smith
(Albany, NY: State University of New York Press, 1994), 211.
[35] National Council of the Churches of Christ in the United States of America, *Yearbook of
American Churches* (New York: Round Table Press, 1937), 9.

mentioned, official records were inconsistent in the way in which they iden-tified the ethnic and national background of immigrants from the Ottoman Empire. They made no distinction between Turks and Kurds, even though ethnographic studies among early Ottoman immigrants demonstrate that both Kurds and Turks immigrated to the United States in the early 1900s.[36] From 1903 to 1904, the number of "Turkish" immigrants jumped from 449 to 1,482. It remained in the low thousands until 1915 (following the onset of World War I), when it declined to 273. All in all between 1899 and 1931 a total of 22,942 immigrants classified as "Turkish" came to the United States. What percentage of these individuals were Muslim is difficult to say because this number most likely included many non-Muslim minorities in the Ottoman Empire. According to the 1930 Census, however, there were 10,457 Turkish speakers in the United States.[37] Some scholars of Turkish immigration, however, believe that immigration and census records under-count the number of Turkish immigrants and estimate that some 25,000 Muslim Turks immigrated to the United States between 1899 and 1924.[38]

The Turks and Kurds that came to the United States at this time were predominantly male, illiterate peasants seeking a better livelihood. Almost all intended to return to their country. According to one estimate, 86 per-cent of the Turks who came to the United States between 1899 and 1924 returned to Turkey after the fall of the Ottoman Empire and the estab-lishment of the modern Turkish republic.[39]

Bosnian Muslims also began immigrating to the United States around 1900 in order to find work. They were mainly illiterate, young, peasant men who intended to earn some money and return home. They mostly settled in Chicago and Gary, Indiana. They worked as common laborers in construction and played a noticeable role in digging Chicago's subway. Many also worked seasonally in the copper mines of Butte, Montana.

---

[36] See Barbara Bilgé, "Voluntary Associations in the Old Turkish Community of Metropolitan Detroit," in *Muslim Communities in North America*, 381–405.

[37] "Turkish" immigration numbers come from Table 86 in the U.S. Department of Labor's *Annual Report of the Commissioner General of Immigration* (Washington, D.C.: Government Printing Office, 1931); mother tongue data comes from the U.S. Bureau of the Census web site, "Table 6. Mother Tongue of the Foreign-Born Population: 1910–1940, 1960, and 1970," URL: http://www.census.gov/population/www/documentation/twps0029/tab06.html (accessed February 2, 2009).

[38] John J. Grabowski, "Prospects and Challenges: The Study of Early Turkish Immigration to the United States," *Journal of American Ethnic History* 25, no. 1 (2005), 85–86 and 95 ft. 4.

[39] Talat Sait Halman, "Turks," in *Harvard Encyclopedia of American Ethnic Groups*, ed. Stephan Thernstrom, Ann Orlov, and Oscar Handlin (Cambridge, MA: Harvard University Press, 1980), 993.

There are no census data or reliable estimates of their numbers in the United States, but they were significant enough to warrant the establishment of coffee houses and self-help organizations.[40]

ALBANIAN IMMIGRANTS

We know more about Albanian immigrants than we do about Tatars, Turks, Kurds, and Bosnians because Albanian immigrants left a larger footprint in the historical records as a result of their involvement in the nationalist movements in their homeland. As an ethnographic study of Albanian Americans in the 1930s has shown, "It is not too much to say that the creation of the Albanian state was largely their work."[41] Albanians lived under Ottoman rule until 1912, and their ethnic community was divided religiously between Muslims (70 percent) and Christians (30 percent).[42] The Muslims were further divided into Sunnis and members of the Bektashi Sufi Order; the Christians between the Greek Orthodox and Roman Catholic churches. Just as with Syrians, another religiously divided ethnic community under Ottoman rule, most of the early Albanian immigrants to the United States were Christian. More specifically, they belonged to the Greek Orthodox Church and joined Greek Orthodox congregations in the United States until they founded their own Albanian Orthodox Church in 1908 in Boston. Literature on Albanian Americans follows the same pattern as the sources on Syrian Americans. It focuses on the dominant Christian community, which had gained the sympathy of American Christian missionaries in the Ottoman Empire and whose welfare under Ottoman rule was of interest to the American public.[43] As with early Syrian Muslim immigrants, however, early Albanian Muslim immigrants were more likely than their Christian co-ethnics to downplay their religious identity in the United States, so it is likely that their numbers were greater than one would assume given the tangential references to them in the available English sources.[44]

---

[40] William G. Lockwood, "Bosnian Muslims," in *Harvard Encyclopedia of American Ethnic Groups*, 185–186.

[41] Federal Writers' Project–Works Progress Administration of Massachusetts, *The Albanian Struggle in the Old World and New* (New York: AMS Press, 1975), 81–82.

[42] Frances Trix, "'When Christians Became Dervishes': Affirming Albanian Muslim-Christian Unity through Discourse," *Muslim World* LXXXV, no. 3–4 (July-October 1995), 280.

[43] Constantine A. Demo, *The Albanians in America: The First Arrivals* (Boston, MA: Society "Fatbardhësia" of Katundi, 1960), 12.

[44] Albanian and Ottoman sources are likely to tell us more about the emigration of Albanian Muslims. Kemal Karpat's article on Ottoman immigration (cited above), which deals

The first Albanians began arriving in the United States individually in the 1880s, but it was not until the first decade of the twentieth century that Albanians immigrated to the United States in larger numbers. Albanian Christians from the Tosks region in southern Albania, who were economically and politically at a disadvantage to Albanian Muslims, came to the United States first. It was not until the outbreak of the Balkan Wars in 1912 that Albanian Muslims began immigrating to the United States in greater numbers.[45] This was the same year that Albania gained its independence from the Ottoman Empire, which had relied on Albanian Muslims for local administration of the region. The loss of this patronage coupled with Greece's invasion of southern Albania in 1913 hastened the immigrations of Albanian Muslims to the United States. [46] According to the U.S. Census Bureau, there were 2,312 foreign-born, Albanian-speaking individuals in the United States in 1910. By 1920, their number had more than doubled to 5,515.[47] By 1930, the first year for which we have Census data for Albanian Americans (as opposed to census data on foreign-born individuals who speak Albanian), there were 8,814 Albanians in the United States.[48] We do not know how many of these individuals were Muslim. Frances Trix, a scholar of the Albanian American Muslim community, has suggested that "a conservative estimate of the Muslim Albanians in the United States in the late 1930s is somewhere around 5,000."[49] This number, however, is at odds with the Census datum that counts 6,814 Albanians in total in the United States in 1930. Trix's estimate is derived from a 1939 ethnographic study of the Albanian American community in Massachusetts, *The Albanian Struggle*, which was sponsored by the Albanian Historical Society of Massachusetts and conducted by members of the Federal Writers' Project of the Works Progress Administration. *The Albanian Struggle* did not attempt to estimate how many Albanians in

with some of the Ottoman sources of emigration from the Ottoman Empire, does not discuss Albanian emigration in any detail.

[45] Federal Writers' Project–Works Progress Administration of Massachusetts, *The Albanian Struggle*, 42.

[46] Frances Trix, "Bektashi Tekke and the Sunni Mosque of Albanian Muslims in America," in *Muslim Communities in North America*, 363.

[47] http://www.census.gov/population/www/documentation/twps0029/tab06.html (accessed January 7, 2008).

[48] http://www.census.gov/population/www/documentation/twps0029/tab04.html (accessed January 7, 2008). The Census Bureau reported the presence of 7,528 foreign-born, Albanian-speakers in the United States in 1930. American-born Albanians most likely account for the difference between this number and the number of Albanians (8,814) reported in the 1930 U.S. Census.

[49] Trix, "Bektashi", 364.

the United States were Muslim, but it placed the number of Albanians as a whole in 1939 somewhere between 35,000 and 60,000, suggesting that 40,000 would be a conservative estimate.[50] Given that few Albanians immigrated to the United States between 1930, when the Census was conducted, and 1939, when *The Albanian Struggle* was completed, the 40,000 estimate seems too high. The discrepancy in the Census data and the Federal Writers' Project's estimate could be explained in part by the fact that Greek Orthodox Albanians were often counted in the official census as Greeks and Muslim Albanians as Turks.[51] Moreover, many Albanians came to the United States after having lived in other countries and may have been counted as citizens of these nations.[52] One would expect, however, that they would have remained Albanian speaking and thus would have been counted in the Census. Regardless, the differential between the 1930 Census and the estimate in *The Albanian Struggle* is still too great to justify the higher estimate. In all likelihood, the Federal Writers' Project relied on Albanian American informants who must have impressionistically overestimated their numbers. In the end we do not know exactly how many Albanian Muslims were in the United States in the first decades of the twentieth century. If we assume, given Trix's experience as an anthropologist of the Albanian American Muslim community, that the percentage of Albanians whom she estimates were Muslim is correct (even though her estimated number is most likely exaggerated), and if we raise the Census number to 10,000 to account for undercounting, then an educated guess would place the number of Albanian Muslims in the United States in the 1930s at around 1,300.

INDIAN IMMIGRANTS

Like their co-religionists from other parts of Asia and Eastern Europe, Indian Muslims began arriving in the United States in greater numbers during the first decade of the twentieth century. From 1820 to 1900, 696 Indians immigrated to the United States. Between 1901 and 1910, the number of Indian immigrants rose to 4,713. All in all, during the first three decades of the twentieth century, 8,681 Indians are on record as having immigrated to the United States, and of these 10 to 12 percent

---

[50] Federal Writers' Project–Works Progress Administration of Massachusetts, *The Albanian Struggle*, 5.
[51] Ibid., 41.
[52] Ibid. 5; Dennis L. Nagi, *The Albanian-American Odyssey: A Pilot Study of the Albanian Community of Boston, Massachusetts* (New York: AMS Press, 1988), 35–36.

(about 1,040) are estimated to have been Muslim. The majority (85 percent) were Sikhs, and the rest Hindus.[53] Indian immigrants came primarily from the Punjab province. Many Punjabis emigrated at this time due to increased population and economic pressures in their homeland. A significant portion of Punjabi immigrants in the United States had served in the British military and police and had held posts overseas. They were overrepresented in the British Indian armed forces in large part because when British rule in India was challenged during the Sepoy mutiny-rebellion of 1857, "the Punjab 'held for the Queen,' ... earning gratitude and preferential recruitment for its martial castes into the British Indian military service as a result."[54]

While serving on overseas assignments for the British army, these Punjabi Indians learned about opportunities available on the west coast of North America. Given their status as subjects of the British Empire, they first arrived into western port cities of Canada, which at that time was a dominion of the British Empire. As the Canadian government began enacting laws in the late nineteenth century to impede the immigration of Indians to Canada, Punjabi Indians began making their way south through Washington and Oregon, working in the mill and agricultural industries. Most, however, ended up settling in central California as farmers.

Indians who sought to immigrate to the United States faced numerous social, institutional, and legal obstacles aimed at barring "Orientals" from the country. Indians, for example, were violently forced out of Bellingham, Washington in 1907 by a group of 600 lumber mill workers.[55] As the numbers of Indians increased in California during the first decade of the twentieth century, the Asiatic-Exclusion League lobbied for restrictions on their entry. A report completed in 1921–1922 for the Bureau of Labor Statistics of the Department of Labor indicated that "due to their agitation the immigration officers became rather strict in their examination of the Hindustanees [i.e., Indians] and sent back many of those who applied for admission." According to this report, there was a clear correlation

---

[53] Karen Isaksen Leonard, *South Asian Americans* (Westport, CT: Greenwood Press, 1997), 43; and Karen Isaksen Leonard, *Making Ethnic Choices: California's Punjabi Mexican Americans* (Philadelphia, PA: Temple University Press, 1992), 30.

[54] Leonard, *Making Ethnic Choices*, 25.

[55] Gary R. Hess, "The 'Hindu' in America: Immigration and Naturalization Policies and India, 1917–1946," *Pacific Historical* Review 38, no. 1 (February 1969), 61; Gary R. Hess, "The Forgotten Asian Americans: The East Indian Community in the United States," in *The Asian American: The Historical Experience*, ed. Norris Hundley, Jr. (Santa Barbara, CA: Clio, 1976), 157–177.

between the political agitations of the Asian-Exclusion League and the number of Indians allowed into the country:

A[s] (sic) a result of this policy, the number of the Hindustanees who arrived in the United States fell from 1710 in 1908 to 337 in 1909. But the following year the policy of the Immigration Officers was somewhat modified and the number of immigrants rose to 1782 again. This rise in number led to fresh agitation by the press, the Asiatic Exclusion League and other organizations which protested against the Hindustani immigration to the Commissioner of Immigration at Washington, D. C. in 1910.[56]

Their protest led to another reduction of the number of Indians admitted (517) in 1911. There were 861 debarred from entry into the United States, 536 of them on account of the likelihood of them becoming a public charge.[57]

EXCLUSIONARY LEGISLATIONS AND MUSLIM IMMIGRATION

A number of exclusionary legislative acts also contributed to barring Muslim immigrants from entry into the United States. These acts were primarily intended to exclude East Asian immigrants but were later amended to impede the immigration of all non-Northwestern Europeans. On May 6, 1882, Congress passed the Chinese Exclusion Act which suspended Chinese immigration for ten years and barred Chinese immigrants from becoming naturalized. (This act was renewed in 1892 and remained in effect until 1943.) In 1908, President Theodore Roosevelt reached a Gentlemen's Agreement with Japan for the Japanese government to ban the emigration of its citizens to the United States. Congress instituted a literacy test for all new immigrants in 1917 and established an Asiatic Barred Zone that effectively stopped all immigration from East Asia.[58] Since by this time elementary education had become common in Northern and Western Europe and since East Asians were barred from immigration, the

---

[56] Rajani Kanta Das, *Hindustani Workers on the Pacific Coast* (Berlin: Walter de Gruyter and Company, 1923), 16.

[57] Das, *Hindustani Workers*, 11 and 13.

[58] This law reads "The following classes of aliens shall be excluded from admission to the United States...persons who are natives of islands not possessed by the United States adjacent to the Continent of Asia, situated south of the 20th parallel latitude north, west of the 160th meridian of longitude east from Greenwich, and north of the 10th parallel of latitude south, or who are natives of any country, province, or dependency situated on the Continent of Asia west of the 110th meridian of longitude east from Greenwich and south of the 50th parallel of latitude north."

literacy test was intended primarily to restrict immigration from Eastern and Southern Europe and secondarily from Western Asia and Africa.[59] Finally, the Immigration Acts of 1924 passed into law the desired effects of earlier immigration acts by establishing quotas that favored Northern and Western European countries. "The annual quota of any nationality shall be two per centum of the number of foreign-born individuals of such nationality resident in continental United States as determined by the United States Census of 1890, but the minimum quota of any nationality shall be 100." The law further restricted the total number of new immigrants to 150,000 beginning in 1927. Its quotas heavily favored those seeking to immigrate to the United States from Germany and Great Britain, each with a quota of 51,227 and 34,007 respectively. The 1924 Act effectively excluded immigration from the continent of Asia, where most Muslims live, and it barred any U.S. resident who is ineligible for immigration from becoming a naturalized U.S. citizen. All countries with a significant Muslim population outside of the 1917 Asiatic Barred Zone were given the minimum quota of 100 persons.[60]

Muslims more specifically were also barred from entry into the United States by the Immigration Act of 1891, which brought immigration under the purview of the federal government by establishing the Bureau of Immigration within the Treasury Department. This act added "polygamists; or persons who admit their belief in the practice of polygamy" to the inadmissible classes, which also included "all idiots, insane persons, paupers or persons likely to become a public charge, persons suffering from a loathsome or a dangerous contagious disease" and hosts of other individuals such as felons, anarchists and persons whose fares were funded by others. Since Islamic law allows men to marry up to four wives so long as they have the financial means to treat them all equitably, a number of Muslims were barred from entry into the United States on account of their religion allowing for polygamy. Between 1909 and 1917, 73 out of 2,457 Indians were barred from entry into the U.S. for this reason.[61] In 1920, when an Indian missionary from the Ahmadiyya Movement (discussed in Chapter 5), Muhammad Sadiq, was detained by immigration officials for being an adherent of a religion that

---

[59] Oscar Handlin, *The Uprooted: The Epic Story of the Great Migrations That Made the American People* (Boston, MA: Little, Brown and Company, 1951), 290.

[60] *Annual Report of the Commissioner General of Immigration to the Secretary of Labor* (Washington, D.C.: Government Printing Office, 1924), 27–29.

[61] Das, *Hindustani Workers*, 13. His numbers are adapted from Table XVIII of the *Annual Report of the Commissioner General of Immigration*.

allows for polygamy, he challenged his deportation orders and requested a hearing of his case in Washington, arguing, "I have not come here to teach plurality of wives. If a Moslem will ever preach or practice polygamy in America he will be committing a sin against his religion."[62] He then went on to explain the difference between legally permissible acts in Islam and divine commands. Polygamy, he explained, is not a commandment. It is a permissible act, "and that permission is taken away under the commandment that I must obey the Law of the Ruling Government of the country."[63] Sadiq's encounter with the polygamy law was extraordinary because he was affiliated with a movement and was versed enough in Islamic law and in English to defend himself. It is unlikely that average Muslim immigrants would have challenged their deportations. If asked about their religion, they most likely hid their religious affiliation from immigration officials to avoid debarment or were turned away at points of entry. On the whole, few were barred from entry to the United States on account of their belief in or practice of polygamy.

RACE, RELIGION, AND AMERICAN CITIZENSHIP

One of the most documented and best-known forms of discrimination against Muslim or "Oriental" immigrants in general is found in naturalization procedures. The Naturalization Act of 1790 granted citizenship only "to aliens being free white persons." Congress amended this law in 1870 to allow citizenship "to aliens of African nativity and to persons of African descent." The ambiguities surrounding the racial status of Turks, Indians, and Syrians resulted in challenges to their eligibility for citizenship. Since naturalization at this time was administered by local officials, not all Muslims or persons from the "Orient" were equally affected by these challenges. Different courts applied different standards of eligibility.[64] Nonetheless, all persons of questionable eligibility were gravely concerned about the consequences that challenges to their citizenship

---

[62] Richard Brent Turner, "Islam in the United States in the 1920's: The Quest for a New Vision in Afro-American Religion" (Ph.D. dissertation: Princeton University, 1986), 142.

[63] Mohammed Sadiq, "No Polygamy," *Moslem Sunrise* 1, no. 1 (July 1921), 9.

[64] A 1911 report by the Immigration Commission, for example, stated that "many courts have refused to naturalize East Indians, but there are others which admit them to citizenship." U.S. Senate Immigration Commission, "Part 25: Japanese and Other Immigrant Races in the Pacific Coast and Rocky Mountain States," vol. I: Japanese and East Indians, in *Immigrants in Industries* (Washington, D.C.: Government Printing Office, 1911), 348.

would have on their social status in the United States. Syrian Americans and Indian Americans put aside religious and caste differences among themselves to unite and mobilize a national response to governmental challenges to their right to citizenship. The pervasiveness of the con-flation of race, religion, and progress in the United States is evident in their responses. Immigrants from regions with significant Muslim popu-lations did not question the axiological assumption that participation in American modernity and progress was related to America's national character as a white, Christian nation.

This is ironic because, as we shall see in the following chapter, Muslim immigrants managed to do relatively well for themselves in the United States despite the xenophobia and institutional prejudices they faced. It was presumably because of the prosperity that these Indian and Syrian immigrants realized in the United States that they fought to maintain their right to American citizenship. Yet, despite the prosperity these immi-grants realized as non-whites and non-Protestants in the United States, they defended their eligibility to citizenship, not on the basis of their accomplishments and contributions to American society, but by arguing that they should be considered white, and, in the case of Syrians who were predominantly Christian, they appealed to the nation's Christian sensibilities to be considered eligible for U.S. citizenship. In other words, they did not challenge the racism and bigotry involved in the conflation of whiteness, Protestantism, and progress; rather, they argued for their inclusion within this matrix. They not only argued that they were "white" but they also believed it.

In response to legal challenges to their eligibility for American citizen-ship, both Syrians and Indians relied on contemporary ethnological clas-sifications of race to define themselves as white. Costa George Najour, a Christian from Mount Lebanon, became the first person to litigate his way to "free white person" status in this way in 1909.[65] The government had argued that based on the color of his skin and the fact that he was a subject of the Ottoman Empire, he did not meet the racial prerequisite for naturalization. District Judge Newman of Georgia rejected the gov-ernment's argument by making a distinction between race and skin color. Although he commented on Najour's appearance – "He is not particularly dark, and has none of the characteristics of appearance of the Mongolian race" – Newman interpreted "free white person" as a reference to racial

---

[65] Ian López, *White by Law 10th Anniversary Edition: The Legal Construction of Race* (New York: NYU Press, 2006), 48.

classification rather than skin complexion. He cited Dr. A. H. Keane's *The World's People: A Popular Account of Their Bodily and Mental Characters, Beliefs, Traditions, Political and Social Institutions* (1908), which "classifies, without question or qualification in any way, Syrians as a part of the Caucasian and white race." Newman further denied any significance to "the fact that the applicant was born within the dominions of Turkey, and was heretofore a subject of the Sultan of Turkey. I do not think this should cut any figure in the matter. If it did, the extension of the Turkish Empire over people unquestionably of the white race would deprive them of the privilege of naturalization."[66]

The establishment clause of the First Amendment made any religious litmus test for naturalization illegal. Nonetheless, one of the significant consequences of the conflation of race, religion, and progress in this period was that religion played a significant role in the way in which "whiteness" was judged both in the public square and in the courts. Syrian Christians, who had closer ties with American Protestant missionaries, were particularly mindful of the role religion could play in their argument for inclusion into America. For example, in reaction to the contestation of Syrians' eligibility for citizenship, Kalil A. Bishara, the editor of the popular Maronite Arabic newspaper *al-Huda*, researched the racial and ethnic origins of Syrians and wrote a formative book on the topic titled *Origin of the Modern Syrian* (1914). Bishara claimed in this book to familiarize Syrian Americans with their ethnic history, but in actuality, his project contributed to the making of a Syrian American identity that highlighted the Semitic origins of Christianity to argue for the inclusion of Syrians in the category of "white Americans."

The modern Syrian is an Asiatic in the sense that he is a native of the near section of the primitive home of all white peoples. Syria has always been a part of the Caucasian world. 'Asiatics' in the 'Asiatic exclusion laws' was clearly meant to be a synonym of 'Mongolians' as applied to the Chinese and the Japanese and other peoples of the far East who have a peculiar type of civilization of their own so radically different from our Christian civilization as to make racial amalgamation and national assimilation with respect to all Mongolian immigrants almost impossible....As a native of Asia, the Syrian is naturally to be classed with the Armenian, the Hebrew, the Greek (Asiatic), and the Persian. And to debar the Syrian alone from our American citizenship, would be as glaringly unjust and inconsistent as it would be imprudent to generalize the rule by excluding all Asiatics, White as well as Yellow, Christian and Heathen together. For, are not all American and European nations of Asiatic origin? ... The Syrian is pre-eminently the most popular man

[66] *In re Najour*, 174 F. 735.

in history. We can neither deny nor be blind to the significant role he has played (or, rather, earnestly worked out) in forming this wonderful civilization of which we are rightfully proud. Not to say anything of the actual human life of Jesus of Nazareth, (Syria), nor of the intrinsic value of the Holy Scriptures revealed to, proclaimed and penned by Syrians.... As a Semite myself, and as an American proud alike of his racial origin and his American citizenship, I most emphatically declare that our [i.e., American] national character, needs the Semitic element in it. That "pliability combined with iron fixity of purpose," which has developed a Moses, an Elijah, a Hannibal, an Amos, a Paul, a Peter, a John, not to begin to enumerate that large host of Fathers, Prophets, and Apostles.[67]

For the most part, Bishara's attempt to tie Syrians to white Christians' civilizational coattail speaks for itself. It is interesting, however, that Prophet Muhammad (not to mention other Arabic-speaking non-Christians) is missing from this list of religious luminaries. The omission of Muhammad, as Michael Suleiman has observed, "was no mere memory lapse, since the Arabic text of the same book includes Muhammad's name."[68] By including Muhammad in the Arabic text, Bishara, who was otherwise triumphantly Christian, nodded toward a broad, multireligious Syrian American identity. He and presumably his Syrian readers, both Christian and Muslim, must have been aware that for Americans, who would have read the English version of the text, the inclusion of Muhammad (and other Arabic-speaking Muslims) would have estranged Syrians from America rather than make the case for their inclusion.

In a 1914 hearing on the eligibility of George Dow of Charleston, South Carolina for American citizenship, the newly founded Syrian American Association also appealed to Americans' religious sentiments and argued that "the history and position of the Syrians, their connection through all times with the people to whom the Jewish and Christian peoples owe their religion, make it inconceivable that the statute could have intended to exclude them."[69] They further contended that if the statute was understood otherwise, it would mean that Jesus himself would not have been qualified for American citizenship on account of his birthplace. District Judge Smith dismissed this as an emotive argument: "The apostrophic argument that He cannot be supposed to have clothed His Divinity in

---

[67] Kalil A. Bishara, *The Origin of the Modern Syrian* (New York: Al-Hoda Publishing House, 1914), 40–44 in the English text, 62–70 in the Arabic.
[68] Michael Suleiman, "Early Arab-Americans: The Search for Identity," in *Crossing the Waters: Arabic-Speaking Immigrants to the United States before 1940*, ed. Eric J. Hooglund (Washington, D.C.: Smithsonian Institution Press, 1987), 45.
[69] *In re Dow*, 214 F. 355.

the body of one of a race that an American Congress would not admit to citizenship is purely emotional and without logical sequence."[70] Smith adopted skin color and "common knowledge" as the criteria for racial identification: "The pertinent statement rather is that a dark complexioned present inhabitant of what formerly was ancient Phoenicia is not entitled to the inference that he must be of the race commonly known as the white race in 1790."[71] Smith further rejected scientific definitions of race that classified Caucasians among the Aryan or Indo-European race by asserting that such definitions result in "the manifest absurdity of classing among whites the black Darvidian inhabitant of Ceylon or Southern India."[72] Smith denied Dow's application for citizenship, but his decision was overturned in 1915 by the Fourth Circuit Court of Appeals. That court adopted a "scientific" definition of race rather than one based on common knowledge or skin color to declare Dow a "free white person": "In the *Dictionary of Races*, contained in the *Reports of the Immigration Commission, 1911*, it is said: 'Physically the modern Syrians are of mixed Syrian, Arabian, and even Jewish blood. They belong to the Semitic branch of the Caucasian race, thus widely differing from their rulers, the Turks, who are in origin Mongolian.'"[73] This decision in 1915 settled the legality of Syrians' claims to American citizenship once and for all.

Until 1923 when the Supreme Court heard *United States v. Bhagat Singh Thind*, Indian Americans had successfully managed to define themselves legally as "free white persons" based on ethnological classification of Indians as Caucasians. As Ian Harvey López has noted, Thind had many reasons to be hopeful about his case in 1923. Four lower courts had recognized Indians as whites based on "scientific" classifications of race. Two months before Thind's hearing, the Supreme Court itself had relied on "scientific" classifications of race to deny naturalization to a Japanese emigrant, Takao Ozawa. The Indian American community had welcomed these decisions because of their implication for their own struggle for American citizenship. Thind must have also thought that his six months of service in the U.S. army should work to his advantage given Congress' decision to provide citizenship to anyone who had served in the army for at least three years.[74] In court, Thind's council argued that the people

---

[70] Ibid.
[71] Ibid.
[72] Ibid.
[73] *Dow v. United States et al*, 226 F. 145.
[74] López, *White by Law*, 62–63.

of the Punjab, where Thind came from, "belong to the Aryan race." The caste system prevented the people of the region from mixing with other races, thus maintaining the purity of the Aryan bloodline of the people of the region. "The high-class Hindu," Thind's defense contested, "regards the aboriginal Indian Mongoloit in the same manner as the American regards the negro, speaking from a matrimonial standpoint."[75]

The Supreme Court unanimously rejected Thind's petition for naturalization. In light of the fact that the court had presented an ethnological racial argument for denying Ozawa's petition for citizenship, its rejection of such an argument in Thind's case speaks to the confusion that surrounded issues of race and American identity and to the conflation of race, religion, and progress in the construction of American identity. The court must have been aware of the general "anti-Hindu"[76] sentiment of the American public. The judges also knew that in all but one case in which "scientific" classifications of race were used to define "free white persons," the courts had granted the right to naturalization to the petitioner. By reversing its own valuation of "scientific" classifications of race from *Ozawa* to *Thind* and adopting a "common knowledge" test for racial identification, the Supreme Court demonstrated it was not so much deliberating a jurisprudential point as it was legally affirming America's self-image as an essentially white nation and reaffirming race as a legitimate basis for exclusion.

I have not come across any direct reference to Muslims' religious identities in the federal appeals of naturalization cases prior to the 1940s. This does not mean, however, that Muslims from the Levant or India did not have their right to American citizenship challenged. They most likely did, but they did not appeal these decisions as Muslims. John Mohammad Ali's struggle to keep his American citizenship, which he received on May 26, 1921, illuminates the precarious position Muslims found themselves in at this time. In 1921, when Ali was given his certificate of citizenship, his eligibility was determined based on the immigration officials' belief that he was a "high-caste Hindu." At that time, Indians who could demonstrate that they were "high-caste Hindus" were still considered eligible for citizenship as members of the Caucasian race, and since the "high-caste Hindu" label worked to Ali's advantage, he did not deny it. However, after the Immigration Act of 1924 made "Asians" ineligible for

---

[75] *United States v. Bhagat Singh Thind*, 261 U.S. 204; 43 S. Ct. 338; 67 L. Ed. 616 (1923).

[76] "Hindu" at this time was a marker of ethnic rather than religious identity. It referred to a person from "Hindustan" or India and was synonymous with Indian.

citizenship, Ali sought to reclaim his Muslim identity. He told the court that "he is not a 'Hindu' of full Indian blood, but…an Arabian of full Arabian blood. While admitting that he is a native of India, as his ancestors for several centuries had also been, he contends that originally his ancestors were Arabians, who invaded the territory now known as India, and settled and remained there, but have been careful not to intermarry with 'the native stock of India,' and have 'kept their Arabian blood line clear and pure by intermarriage within the family'." The "Arabian" invasion of India to which Ali referred was in actuality a Muslim invasion of northern India by the Turkish Saljuqs. Ali seems to have conflated his Muslim identity with an Arab identity because Arabic-speaking Syrians, as Semites who have lighter skin, had not had their citizenship status challenged in courts since *Dow v. United States* declared them legally "white" in 1915. Tellingly, Ali seems to have not told the court that he was Muslim and that his alleged connection with Arabs was established through Islam. District Judge Tuttle was consequently confused:

I am unable to follow the argument thus sought to be made. No reason has been suggested, and I can discover none, why the mere fact that the early ancestors of the defendant came to India from Arabia, where they had been called Arabians, renders the defendant a white person. His skin is certainly not white, but unmistakably dark, like that of the other members of his race. He is a native of the continent of Asia, specifically of the country of India, and more specifically of the province of Punjab, the place of the nativity of the alien held, in the case of *United States v. Bhagat Singh Thind*, supra, not to be a white person.[77]

One presumes that Ali did not divulge his religion because he felt that it would hurt rather than help his case, given the popular prejudices against Islam. His intuition was apparently correct. When in 1942 District Judge Tuttle, who had heard Ali's case, received a petition from a Yemeni Muslim named Ahmed Hassan, he denied the petition. In that case, Tuttle argued that neither skin color nor religion could legally bar one from citizenship, given that there could be a dark-skinned Anglo-Saxon or light-skinned Chinese, but

when one seeking citizenship is in fact clearly not white of skin a strong burden of proof devolves upon him to establish that he is a white person within the meaning of the act….Apart from the dark skin of the Arabs, it is well known that they are a part of the Mohammedan world and that a wide gulf separates their culture from that of the predominantly Christian peoples of Europe. It cannot be

---

[77] *United States v. Ali*, 7 F.2d 728 (3 August 1925).

expected that as a class they would readily intermarry with our population and be assimilated into our civilization. The small amount of immigration of these peoples to the United States is in itself evidence of that fact.[78]

Ultimately, Tuttle decided that Hassan was not eligible for citizenship because he "is an Arab and...Arabs are not white persons within the meaning of the act." Regardless of what ethnological racial classification suggested, Tuttle argued, dark-skinned Muslims from Yemen were not among the people living in the United States whom Congress recognized as "white persons" when it first passed the citizenship act in 1790.

The courts' and immigration officials' estimation of Arab Muslims' race, however, remained inconsistent well into the 1940s. Two years after Tuttle received Hassan's petition in the East District Court of Michigan, Massachusetts District Court Judge Wyzanski permitted the naturalization of Mohamed Mohriez, "an Arab born in Sanhy, Badan, Arabia." Wyzanski had been told by local immigration officials that it is their practice "to regard Arabs ... born outside of the barred zone, as white persons." Wyzanski rejected Tuttle's assertion that Arab Muslims are culturally distinct from Europeans and thus unassimilable.

As every schoolboy knows, the Arabs have at various time inhabited parts of Europe, lived along the Mediterranean, been contiguous to European nations and been assimilated culturally and otherwise, by them. For the Battle of Tours to the capitulation of Granada, history records the wars waged in Europe by the Arabs. The names of Avicenna and Averroes, the sciences of algebra and medicine, the population and the architecture of Spain and of Sicily, the very words of the English language, remind us as they would have reminded the Founding Fathers of the action and interaction of Arabic and non-Arabic element of our culture. Indeed to earlier centuries as to the twentieth century, the Arab people stand as one of the chief channels by which the traditions of white Europe, especially the ancient Greek traditions, have been carried into the present.

Wyzanski's emphasis on the cultural and scientific achievements of non-Europeans reflects in part his own political beliefs. He found the "policies of rigid exclusion" "false to our profession of democratic liberalism" and "repugnant to our vital interests as a world power."[79] However, as we shall see later in the book, the conflation of race, religion, and progress, itself, as a predominant means of making sense of racial and religious diversity in the United States, also became indefensible in American public discourse after the United States entered World War II in December

[78] *In re Ahmed Hassan*, 48 F. Supp. 843 (1942).
[79] *Ex parte Mohriez*, 54 F. Supp. 941 (1944).

1941 and more and more Americans became aware of the racist atrocities the Nazis had committed in the name of Aryan superiority.

As these later naturalization cases involving Muslims demonstrate, the absence of Muslim identity claims in legal appeals of naturalization cases prior to the 1940s does not mean that Muslims were not invested in the outcomes of these cases in the 1910s and 1920s. The Ottoman embassy in Washington, D.C., for example, helped Syrians organize and petition the Najour's case in 1909. Muslim Syrians also contributed to legal funds established to fight challenges to Syrians' eligibility for citizenship.[80] Indeed, these challenges helped unite Muslims and Christians from the Levant under the banner of a new Syrian American ethnic identity.

ISSUES OF NATIONAL BELONGING OUTSIDE
OF THE COURTS

Outside of the courts, there were numerous other attempts at gaining inclusion into the matrix of American identity created by the conflation of whiteness, Christianity, and progress. Elizabeth Boosahda, for example, reports an oft-told story among Syrians in Worcester, Massachusetts about how Mitchell K. Maykel persuaded the Republican Senator Pehr G. Holmes (who served from 1931 until 1947) to help Syrians become legally classified as whites:

They were going to classify us, the Arab people, as Asian, but Mr. Maykel visited Congressman Pehr G. Holmes and asked him to fight this thing and make sure we are classified as white and not Asian. I'm as white as anybody who claims to be white is! Our people were going to be considered not of the white race but the senator made sure that we were classified *correctly* (emphasis added).[81]

Alixa Naff mentions that some of her informants indicated that Syrians who were friendly with African Americans were disliked by others in the community at the turn of the twentieth century, presumably because of the consequences that such an association would have had for the public image of their community.[82] An ethnographic study of Palestinian Muslims in the 1940s concluded that "they

[80] Naff, *Becoming American*, 255–257. "Turkey Protests," *The Independent...Devoted to the Consideration of Politics, Social and Economic Tendencies, History, Literature, and the Arts* 67, no. 3180 (November 11, 1909), 1105.

[81] Cited in Elizabeth Boosahda, *Arab-American Faces and Voices: The Origins of an Immigrant Community* (Austin, TX: University of Texas Press, 2003), 135.

[82] Naff, *Becoming American*, 250.

consider themselves much superior to the Negro although a few treat them kindly."[83] A study of Indian emigrants in the 1920s completed by an Indian emigrant Lecturer in Economics at New York University, Rajani Kanta Das, similarly concluded that Indians consciously avoided associating with African Americans, "partly due to their feeling of racial superiority and partly due to the fact that the negroes are socially ostracized by the Americans themselves and they do not like to be a party to the racial problem."[84]

As the following witty exchange in a Syrian American newspaper in 1898 demonstrates, Syrian and other immigrants from regions with a significant Muslim population deliberately proceeded to argue for their inclusion into the matrix of race, religion, and progress that defined American identity, and they were well aware of its cost.

Americanized Syrian:	Are you still a villager (i.e., backward, not modern)? Haven't you become civilized?
Syrian Nationalist:	Do good manners allow you to insult me this way when you are pretending to be civilized?
Americanized Syrian:	We alone know what it is to be civilized and we regret that you are not one of us.
Syrian Nationalist:	And what are the benefits of joining your kind?
Americanized Syrian:	Don't you understand that we are all intelligent? For when we become Americanized, we are able to earn more without working hard and we help each other by gaining greater prestige.
Syrian Nationalist:	But, I am from the East and I prefer to preserve the honor of my forefathers.
Americanized Syrian:	After what I have just told you, are you provoked because I called you a villager? Haven't you heard of Darwin who denies that man evolved from man? We are what we are as a result of the evolutionary process. And, your preserving the honor of your ancestors is pure ignorance and lack of education.
Syrian Nationalist:	I have not read Darwin and I gladly leave that honor to you. But you can be what you want to be; I am going to remain and Easterner. My original ancestor was Adam and it is likely that his language was Arabic. Long live the East! Down with its enemies.[85]

[83] Lawrence Oschinsky, "Islam in Chicago: Being a Study of the Acculturation of a Muslim Palestinian Community in That City" (Master's thesis: The University of Chicago, 1952), 25.

[84] Das, *Hindustani Workers*, 109–110.

[85] *al-Huda* (March 22, 1898), 16 (in Arabic), cited in Naff, *Becoming American*, 263–264.

THE PROMINENCE OF ETHNICITY OVER RELIGION
AS A MODE OF SELF-IDENTIFICATION

Whatever ambivalence Muslim and non-Muslim immigrants from Syria and India had about the loss of traditional identities and practices, legal challenges to their citizenship spurred them to argue for their right to naturalization based not on their accomplishments and merits as individuals, but as members of an ethnic community that could be "scientifically" classified as Caucasian. The institutional prejudices against Syrians and Indians led them to unite under the banner of ethnicity despite their differences in religion, tribe, class, and caste. These markers of identity did not fully disappear within the community. There were still, for example, instances of Muslim parents objecting to their children marrying non-Muslim co-ethnics and vice versa.[86] Nonetheless, religious identities became secondary. As Philip Hitti, a Syrian American who was a pioneering professor of Semitic Literature at Princeton University (1926–1954), observed, the people of Mount Lebanon self identified not through ethnicity or nationality but through "love for family and sect."[87] Once their eligibility for U.S. citizenship was challenged, however, they reacted by putting aside their religious differences and organizing multireligious ethnic associations, such as the Association for Syrian Unity and the Society of Syrian National Defense, to raise funds and rally support for Najour's and Dow's legal defenses, respectively. Christians, however, much more than Muslims served as leaders of these organizations not only because of their greater numbers and longer years of residence in the United States but also because of the stigmatization of Muslim identity.

A similar process of ethnic unification in the face of race-based prejudice was found among early Indian immigrants. In the face of the discrimination they encountered from the government and from nativist civic organizations along the Pacific Coast, they put aside caste and religious differences and united within ethnic and nationalist organizations. Funds were collected for Bhagat Singh Thind's legal defense from Indian farmers and workers throughout the Southwest.[88] In 1919, the Hindustani

---

[86] See for examples, Naff, *Becoming American*, 236–241; Leonard, *Making Ethnic Choices*, 156–159; Barbara Aswad and Barbara Bilgé, eds., *Family and Gender among American Muslims: Issues Facing Middle Eastern Immigrants and Their Descendants* (Philadelphia, PA: Temple University Press, 1996), 25–27.

[87] Hitti, *Syrians in America*, 25.

[88] Leonard, *Making Ethnic Choices*, 84.

Welfare and Reform Society of America was founded with its headquarters in El Centro, California. The Society aimed "to promote good will and fellow feeling" among different Indian groups both in the United States and abroad. It also sought "to protect and safeguard the material and moral interests" of Indians in the United States and "to create understanding and establish good relations between the Hindustanees and the Americans."[89] Even though discrimination against Indians increased during the 1920s, as evidenced by the enactment of immigration and naturalization policies that discriminated against Indians, the Society seems to have had some success countering discriminatory practices against Indians. In 1924, Ram Chand reported:

I have, however, had the privilege of seeing a great change in the sentiment toward the Hindus [i.e. Indians] in the Valley. A few years ago the lawyers in the courts would argue on the basis of race inferiority and would talk about the heathen Hindus and stuff of that sort.... During the time of the anti-Oriental agitation in 1918 the Hindustani Welfare Society was organized to be of assistance to the Hindu group. The Society gave assistance in the matter of contracts and gave out useful information. The occasion for this has now passed away to a considerable extent and so the Society does not function as it used to do. It now aids in case of sickness or other difficulties.[90]

SUMMARY

By the mid-1920s, some 60,000 Muslims had immigrated to the United States. For many of them, this was a feat because they had to bypass restrictions on emigration from their homeland and avoid being barred entry into the United States by exclusionary laws and practices in the United States. For those who arrived in the United States, prejudices against Islam and exclusionary practices did not impede their ability to find jobs as cheap laborers and peddlers. It also did not prevent them from achieving relative prosperity in the United States even though it made that success much more difficult to realize. Nonetheless, the prevalent conflation of race, religion, and progress necessitated that they argue for their inclusion into American society not in terms of the actual contributions they made to the nation, but rather through claims to the matrix of whiteness, Christianity, and progress that had come to constitute

---

[89] Cited in Das, *Hindustani Workers*, 90.

[90] Ram Chand, "Survey and Race Relations," no. 232 (June 1, 1924), cited in Leonard, *Making Ethnic Choices*, 59.

America's national identity. In the process of arguing that they should be considered white, Muslim immigrants put aside religious differences with their co-ethnics in order to form national self-help associations through which they could organize themselves and counter the government's challenges to their rights as U.S. citizens. As such, in this period, ethnicity played a greater role than did Islam in shaping their sense of national belonging and their representation of themselves on the national stage.

5

Rooting Islam in America

Community and Institution Building in the Interwar Period

The interval between the world wars was pivotal for the history of Islam in America because it marked a period in which American Muslims' institutions and community building efforts took root and thus helped shape future developments in the history of Islam in America. Among these American Muslim institutions were local mosques and benevolent societies and a number of prophetic movements, mainly: the Ahmadiyya missionary movement, founded by the Indian reformer Mirza Ghulam Ahmad; the Moorish Science Temple, founded by the African American religious leader Noble Drew Ali; and the Nation of Islam, founded by Fard Muhammad whose identity is shrouded in mystery.[1]

As the Muslim population in the United States became more diverse, particularly after the reformation of immigration and civil rights laws in the 1950s and 1960s, understanding of Islam and the character of Muslim institutions also changed and became more diverse. So, while the communities and institutions formed in the interwar period set roots for Islam in America and thus helped shape consequent developments in the history of Islam in America, they did not circumscribe the future practice of Islam nor the subsequent character of Islamic institutions in this country.

---

[1] The Sufi Order of the West founded by Inayat Khan in the 1910s has also had a continuing presence in the United States, but as I mentioned in Chapter 4, Inayat Khan disassociated his teaching from Islam. His organization has thus had limited influence on subsequent historical developments within self-identifying Muslim communities in the United States. His teachings, however, have been influential in the way in which Sufi teachings have been appropriated by New Age religious movements.

FROM SOJOURNERS TO SETTLERS

In the first stage of Muslims' voluntary immigration to the United States, which took place between the Civil War and World War I, the practice of Islam was generally ad hoc and improvisational. The social, legal, political, and economic challenges Muslim immigrants faced at the turn of the twentieth century relegated the practice of Islam largely to the private realm. Islam played a lesser role in shaping their lives than these challenges. The Ahmadiyya missionary Muhammad Sadiq, in a 1921 open letter to the American Muslim community, wrote, "I beg to be excused to say that in the majority of cases you are Moslems in name only – Islam not playing practical (sic) part in your every-day life. Nay, even your names are generally no more Moslem because you have adopted American names."[2] There were many incentives for foregoing Islamic practices and few for retaining them. The Muslim pioneers who came from the Levant, Eastern Europe, South Asia, and Anatolia to this country were predominantly young men in search of opportunities that would help them improve the economic lot of their families back home. Reportedly, Muslim immigrants at this time were often heard saying, "Of what were we to avail ourselves by not emigrating in search of a permissible (*halal*) living. Didn't God, the Exalted, say, 'Walk within the tracts [of the earth] and eat of His provisions. Ultimately, it is to Him one returns (67:15)?'"[3] The families back home relied heavily on the remittances their young men sent. In 1907 and 1908, the immigrant banks of Massachusetts alone sent $37,103 and $47,544 respectively to the Ottoman provinces in Europe and Asia. Banks in Pennsylvania sent $290,000 in 1907 and $860,000 in 1908 to Syria.[4] Philip Hitti reported that, up until March 20, 1920, individual Syrians had sent $168,100.79 back home through the Near East Relief, and by December 1919, they had remitted $2,250,362.07 to relatives and friends through the Presbyterian Board of Foreign Missions. Another $165,815.58 was sent through the Syrian Mt. Lebanon Relief Committee.[5] During the first half of 1908, Indians in northern California sent $34,000 to India. In

[2] Muhammad Sadiq, "My Advice to the Muhammadans in America," *Moslem Sunrise* 1, no. 2 (October 1921), 29.
[3] Maḥmūd Yūsuf al-Shawārbī, *al-Islām fī Āmrīkā* (al-Qāhira: Lajnat al-Bayān al-'Arabī, 1960), 17.
[4] William Dillingham, U.S. Immigration Commission, *Immigrant Banks* (Washington, D.C.: Government Printing Office, 1910), 73 and 78.
[5] Philip K. Hitti, *The Syrians in America* (New York: George H. Doran Company), 87.

the same year, Indians working in mills in Washington and Oregon each sent an estimated avarage of $140 to their families.[6]

The fact that early immigrants were preoccupied with accumulating wealth and returning home is evidenced by their frugal living arrangements, which were designed to maximize savings. The following is a description of typical Albanian living conditions during the 1910s:

> To save money on rent, men crowded together in tenements in the slums. Ten or fifteen men often lived together in a single flat, the *konak*. Existence in the *konak* was drab. In the homeland Albanians had been accustomed to an outdoor life; here they were cramped within the four walls of the most dilapidated houses in the worst slum areas of America's mill towns. After a long stretch at the work bench or the loom, they returned in the evening to dreary, cold tenements. Since there were no women, the immigrants had to clean the flat and cook their own meals. Different members took turns in the kitchen. Besides cooking they washed and mended their own clothes and repaired their own shoes.... The older members were bankers for the *konaks*. Wages were turned over to them for safe-keeping and placed in a *kemer*, a large money-pouch worn close to the flesh....If someone needed money the elder would decide whether the purpose was a worthy one before he opened his *kemer*.[7]

The details of daily life for Muslim immigrants of varying ethnicities may have differed, but cramped, communal living conditions designed to maximize savings were a common feature of immigrant Muslim life prior to World War I. A 1914 report by the Commission on Immigration in Massachusetts described the typical living conditions of Turkish Muslims at this time:

> [I]n the Turkish colony at Worcester, of 400 or more men, there is probably not one Turkish woman. Occasionally, the men club together and hire a cook, each paying usually $1 a month. In most of the groups visited, however, the men do their own cooking, either acting each one as his own commissary, or taking turns at buying and cooking the food.... As is expected under the circumstances, the living and sleeping conditions of these men are far from good. In most cases economy leads them to choose houses for which rents are low, and which consequently are often in a most dilapidated condition. These houses are planned for a family of four or five persons, and are totally unsuited for the purposes to which they are put. The sanitary conditions are far from adequate.... The sleeping quarters are, of course, crowded. Frequently, the floor is covered with mattresses

---

[6] U.S. Senate Immigration Commission, "Part 25: Japanese and Other Immigrant Races in the Pacific Coast and Rocky Mountain States," in *Immigrants in Industries*, vol. I: Japanese and East Indians (Washington, D.C.: Government Printing Office, 1911), 347.

[7] Federal Writers' Project–Works Progress Administration of Massachusetts, *The Albanian Struggle in the Old World and New* (New York: AMS Press, 1975), 9–10.

and pillows, and clothes are scattered about the rooms. Among the Turks beds are seldom used.... Police and health officers testify that day and night shifts are frequently found. In one case an investigator was told that a house of seven rooms was occupied by fourteen Turks, sleeping two in a room. On a visit at five in the afternoon he found eighteen men who apparently lived there, while four others who worked at night were sleeping in an adjoining room.[8]

Alixa Naff reports that early Syrian immigrants "lived in crowded cold rooms, walked miles to their jobs to save trolley fares, and zealously watched every cent."[9] Rajani Kanta Das wrote that only a few Indians "have a home life. Most of them live in a sort of club of from two to twenty men. They generally keep to themselves and have scarcely any intercourse with the Americans except in a business day." Even as their incomes rose over the years, their living conditions, Das reported, remained the same because they saved most of their money.[10] A 1911 immigration report showed that Indian farm laborers on average saved half of their earnings while using boxes as chairs and tables, cooking over a pit in the ground, and sleeping collectively in one dilapidated room.[11]

Between 1899 and 1910, 98 percent of the Indians, 96 percent of the Turks, and 68 percent of the Syrians who entered the United States were male (see Table 1). The majority of them were either farm or unskilled laborers (see Table 2). The number of Syrian women who came to this country was slightly higher because Syrian Christians, who had on the whole arrived about a decade earlier than Syrian Muslims, also brought their families to the United States earlier. The majority of the immigrants from Muslim-majority regions of the world at this time (about 84 percent) were 14 to 44 years old (see Table 3).

In the 1910s and 1920s, Muslim immigrants returned home for a variety of reasons. Albanians began to return home in large numbers following Albania's independence from the Ottoman Empire in 1912.[12] Many Syrians returned following the Ottomans' defeat in World War I when the Treaty of Sèvres (1920) placed the Levant within the dominion of the French Empire. Many Turks returned home during the war and after the

---

[8] Bernard J. Rothwell et al., Massachusetts Commission on Immigration, *Report of the Commission on Immigration on the Problem of Immigration in Massachusetts* (Boston, MA: Wright and Potter Printing, 1914), 66–67.

[9] Alixa Naff, *Becoming American: The Early Arab Immigrant Experience* (Carbondale, IL: Southern Illinois University Press), 196.

[10] Rajani Kanta Das, *Hindustani Workers on the Pacific Coast* (Berlin: Walter de Gruyter and Company, 1923), 77 and 100–101.

[11] *Immigrants in Industries*, vol. I, 341.

[12] Federal Writers' Project–WPA of Massachusetts, *The Albanian Struggle*, 54 and 65.

TABLE 1. *Number and percentage of male and female immigrants from regions with large Muslim populations between 1899 and 1910, by ethnicity.*

Ethnicity	Number		Percent (%)	
	Male	Female	Male	Female
Indian	5,673	113	98.0	2.0
Turkish	12,476	478	96.3	3.7
Syrian	38,635	18,274	67.9	32.1
Total	56,784	18,865	75.1	24.9

Note: Separate data on Albanians are not available from this period.

Source: William Dillingham, U.S. Immigration Commission, *Reports of the Immigration Commission. Statistical Review of Immigration, 1820–1910* (Washington, D.C.: Government Printing Office, 1910), 47.

TABLE 2. *Occupation of immigrants from regions with large Muslim populations between 1899 and 1910, by ethnicity.*

Ethnicity	Occupation (males and females)					
	Professional	Skilled	Farm laborer	Unskilled laborer	Other	Unemployed
Indian	359	93	636	3,649	728	321
Turkish	133	865	3,899	5,393	1,351	1,313
Syrian	441	8,349	10,901	7,744	9,287	20,187

Source: William Dillingham, U.S. Immigration Commission, *Reports of the Immigration Commission. Statistical Review of Immigration, 1820–1910* (Washington, D.C.: Government Printing Office, 1910), 95.

TABLE 3. *Age distribution of immigrants from regions with large Muslim populations between 1899 and 1910, by ethnicity.*

Ethnicity	Age (in years)		
	Under 14	14–44	45 and older
Indian	62	5,590	134
Turkish	284	12,459	211
Syrian	9,075	45,603	2,231
Total	9,421	63,652	2,576
Percentage of total (%)	12.5	84.1	3.4

Source: William Dillingham, U.S. Immigration Commission, *Reports of the Immigration Commission. Statistical Review of Immigration, 1820–1910* (Washington, D.C.: Government Printing Office, 1910), 89–91.

TABLE 4. *Number of male and female immigrants from regions with large Muslim populations who arrived or departed during the fiscal year 1920, by ethnicity.*

Ethnicity	Arrived		Departed	
	Male	Female	Male	Female
Indian	138	22	153	9
Turkish	118	22	1,314	26
Syrian	1,915	1,132	1,451	201

Source: "Report of the Commissioner General of Immigration," in *Reports of the Department of Labor, 1920* (Washington, D.C.: Government Printing Office, 1921), 373–374 and 376–377.

abolishment of the Ottoman Empire and again after the establishment of the Republic of Turkey in 1924. According to one estimate 86 percent of the Turks who immigrated to the United States between 1899 and 1924 repatriated.[13] Many Indian immigrants also returned as they raised enough money to purchase their own land in the Punjab and as prejudice against them made life in the United States more difficult. The inclusion of Indians in the Asiatic Barred Zone also prevented Indians who went home temporarily to marry or to visit their families from returning to the United States.

At the same time that many Muslim men were leaving the United States, the number of female immigrants from Muslim-majority regions of the world gradually increased (see Table 4). This suggests that the men who remained in the United States wished to settle and raise their families here. They either brought their families to the United States or went home to get married and returned. A sojourner mentality among the early immigrants gave way to a settler mentality in the aftermath of World War I.

Muslim immigrants' decision to remain and root themselves in the United States during the interwar period was made in large part because of the economic prosperity they experienced. Their lives are a testament to the fact that while white Protestants claimed this country as theirs by virtue of a conflation of race, religion, and progress, there were also Muslims from South Asia, Eastern Europe, the Levant, and Anatolia who

---

[13] Talat Sait Halman, "Turks," in *Harvard Encyclopedia of American Ethnic Groups*, ed. Stephan Thernstrom, Ann Orlov, and Oscar Handlin (Cambridge, MA: Harvard University Press, 1980), 993.

began, in modest ways, to lay claim on America as a country of progress. Presumably it was appreciation for the prosperity they experienced that motivated them to fight for citizenship rights as "white" Americans. Some Muslims also joined the United States military forces during this time and fought in World War I.[14] Their story, like the story of millions of other non-Anglo-American Protestant immigrants, is usually seen through the lens of assimilation into Anglo-American, Protestant society and culture, but their actions and words suggest that they did not see themselves as assimilating into someone else's America. Rather they were negotiating their own understanding of the relationship between Islam and America through the establishment of mosques and Muslim organizations and through their political activities.

We have very little specific data on the economic condition of Muslim immigrants in the United States in the interwar period. However, given the salience of ethnic over religious modes of self-identification (discussed in the previous chapter), it seems very reasonable to assume that they fared as well economically as their ethnic cohorts which, within a generation, went from peddling and factory or farm labor to becoming the proprietors of commercial real estate, retail stores, and farms. Most of their children became professionals.[15] Indian men who made 10 to 15 cents a day in India were able to make $2-$5 a day in North America.[16] Indians who had found employment in the railroad, mill, lumber, and agricultural industries upon their arrival managed, after about a decade, to purchase or rent their own land for the purpose of farming. According to a 1921–1922 Bureau of Labor Statistics report, their average annual income rose from $451 in 1908 to $900 in 1921. The report further indicated that Indians supplemented their measurable annual income by engaging in independent business or contract work, so "the average income of most of the Hindustanees is much higher than $900.00 per year."[17] In 1919, Indians leased or owned nearly 100,000 acres of farmland in California.[18]

[14] Hitti, *Syrians in America*, 102.

[15] al-Shawārbī, *al-Islām fī Āmrīkā* 18–22. Naff, *Becoming American*, 267f; Randa A. Kayalli, *The Arab Americans* (Westport, CT: Greenwood Press, 2006), 101; Karen Isaksen Leonard, *Making Ethnic Choices: California's Punjabi Mexican Americans* (Philadelphia, PA: Temple University Press, 1994), 50–54 and 161.

[16] Das, *Hindustani Workers*, 6; Lee M'Crae, "Self-Exiled in America," *Missionary Review of the World* 39 (July 1916), 526.

[17] Das, *Hindustani Workers*, 61–62.

[18] California State Board of Control, *California and the Oriental: Japanese, Chinese, and Hindus* (Sacramento, CA: California State Printing Office, 1922), 47.

In Massachusetts, many Albanians, who began their life in the United States as laborers in shoe factories and mills, made $30 a month in this country in a time when they would have had to work for their keep plus $3 or $4 a year in cash at home. By 1939, many of these laborers became proprietors of grocery stores, restaurants, bars, barber shops, furniture stores, and cleaning establishments. In the greater Boston area, they owned 300 grocery and fruit stores.[19]

Syrian Americans, whose numbers were greater, similarly came mostly from peasant backgrounds to improve their economic lot. Soon, they graduated from peddling and laboring in factories to become involved in a range of industries which ran the gamut from finance and retail to publishing and manufacturing. Many Syrians who went into business for themselves established dry goods stores.[20]

I do not mean to suggest that Muslim immigrants' entry into the lower echelon of the middle class in the interwar period was without its obstacles. Indians in particular had a difficult time. California's Alien Land Law, passed in 1913 and amended in 1920 and 1921, "barred aliens ineligible for citizenship from leasing or owning agricultural lands." East and South Asians, both Muslim and non-Muslim, tried to circumvent these laws by holding property under their American-born wives', children's, or white associates' names.[21] Immigration quotas, which reduced the number of immigrants from non-Northern European countries to a trickle, prevented Muslim immigrants from being joined by their families. The high unemployment rates and the financial crisis of the Great Depression in the 1930s also took their toll on Muslim immigrants as they did on the nation as a whole.[22] Statistics and personal stories of economic and educational achievements conceal the hardships of poor living and work conditions, which made individuals' achievements possible.

SATTI MAJID, "SHEIKH OF ISLAM IN NORTH AMERICA"

As the number of Muslims in the United States increased during the 1910s and 1920s and the "bird of passage" mentality waned among the early immigrants who remained in the United States, Muslim immigrants founded associations in order to meet the religious and social needs of

---

[19] Federal Writers' Project–WPA of Massachusetts, *The Albanian Struggle*, 9 and 93–99.

[20] Naff, *Becoming American*, 114 and 269.

[21] Leonard, *Making Ethnic Choices*, 21, 55–57, and 59.

[22] Gregory Orfalea, *The Arab Americans: A History* (Northampton, MA: Olive Branch Press, 2006), 109–115; Leonard, *Making Ethnic Choices*, 148.

their local communities. They also became more politically active. For the most part, the Muslim communities that emerged during the interwar period were small and locally organized. Their communal institutions were usually ad hoc and formed in response to their immediate needs. The practice of Islam within these institutions was improvisational and adapted readily to local circumstances. The variety of social, religious, and political activities in which Muslim engaged and the adaptive and improvisational nature of their religious institutions and practices can be gleaned from the activities of a Muslim missionary from Sudan named Satti Majid, who appointed himself "Sheikh of Islam in America."[23] While Satti's activities provide a window onto the historical development of Islam in America in this period, he was exceptional both in his efforts to become the public face of Islam in the United States and in his penchant to think nationally rather than locally about the presence of Muslims in the United States. Most American Muslims at this time were primarily concerned with their personal welfare and not with the public role of Islam in America.

Satti's claims to publicly represent Islam in the United States may have been highly exaggerated. He mentions, for example, that he sued the *New York Times* for anti-Islamic propaganda and for refusing to publish his editorials. There is no record of such a lawsuit in the *New York Times* or elsewhere.[24] Where there is corroborating evidence of Satti's activities, it is in relation to his local organizing efforts among Muslims in different parts of the United States. Pioneering immigrants from the Ottoman Empire in Detroit, for example, recalled him as "Sait Mahcit" to the anthropologist Barbara Bilgé as the person who in 1920 initiated the Detroit chapter of the Kizilay or the Red Crescent and purchased plots for Muslim burials at Roselawn Cemetery.[25] There is also an official

[23] The following biography of Satti Majid is based on Ahmed I. Abu Shouk, J. O. Hunwick, and R. S. O'Fahey, "A Sudanese Missionary to the United States: Sāttī Mājid, '*Shaykh al-Islam* in North America', and His Encounter with Noble Drew Ali, Prophet of the Moorish Science Temple Movement," *Sudanic Africa* 8 (1997), 137–191; Rogaia Mustafa Abusharaf, "The First to Arrive: Sati Majid, 1904–29," in *Wanderings: Sudanese Migrants and Exiles in North America*, (Ithaca, NY: Cornell University Press, 2002), 17–32; and 'Abd al-Ḥamīd Muḥammad Aḥmad, *Sāttī Mājid: al-dā'iyah al-Islāmī al-Sūdānī bī-Āmrīkā, 1904–1929* (al-Kharṭūm: Manshūrāt al-Kharṭūm 'Āsimat al-Thaqāfah al-'Arabīyah, 2005).

[24] Abu Shouk, Hunwick, and O'Fahey, "Sudanese Missionary to the United States," 142. Satti's claims of raising funds for the Ottoman Empire's navy may also be exaggerated, but I have not sought to corroborate this by searching through contemporary Ottoman sources.

[25] Barbara Bilgé, "Voluntary Associations in the Old Turkish Community of Metropolitan Detroit," in *Muslim Communities in North America*, ed. Yvonne Y. Haddad and Jane I. Smith (Albany, NY: State University of New York Press, 1994), 393.

record of one of the associations he founded in Pennsylvania, the Society of Muslim Africans, and of letters from some of the members of this society, which address him as their leader.[26] Despite Satti's seemingly grandiose claims to have been the public representative of Islam in the 1910s and 1920s, he was most likely a recognized activist among local Muslim communities in the Northeast and the Midwest.

Satti was born in al-Ghaddar in Old Dongola in 1883. He formally studied Islam in Sudan and seems to have wanted to continue his education at the renowned Sunni Muslim seminary, al-Azhar, in Cairo. At one point, he got sidetracked and emigrated to "the West." Prior to his arrival in the United States in 1904, he went to England, where he claimed to have founded an Islamic missionary society with the help of a Nubian and a Yemeni, who knew English and translated his sermons into English for him. In a 1935 interview with *al-Balagh* newspaper in Cairo, Satti explained:

Until 1908 we did not have an organized Muslim association in America to spread the mission of Islam. We used to act individually [missing word] in the field until the revolution against Sultan 'Abd al-Hamid and the abduction of the throne of the caliphate to Sultan Muhammad Rishad V. The idea developed among the subjects of the Ottoman State to act in order to bolster its naval warships by gathering subscriptions. This idea reached us in America, and we accepted it out of the desire to strengthen the government of the Islamic Caliphate. We organized the first meeting for this in order to collect donations. Many Lebanese and Syrian Christians who had arrived earlier in America worked with us. We had dispersed from our varying countries in search of a living and the accumulation of wealth. I remember that we collected a large enough amount of money toward the warship Rishadiyya, which the Ottoman State was having built in England. Later, at the onset of the World War, the British government seized it.[27]

As a result of his community organizing among Muslims, and to a lesser extent among Christians, from Syria and on account of his basic training in Islamic theology and law, Satti seems to have gained limited recognition as a Muslim leader:

When I saw the number of Muslims, I realized that religious duty necessitates undertaking what God has obliged us to do by way of the prescribed prayers, the fast of Ramadan, and the pilgrimage to the sacred House of God. I also realized

---

[26] Aḥmad, *Sāttī Mājid* 194–195. Letters to Satti are reprinted in Abu Shouk, Hunwick, and O'Fahey, "Sudanese Missionary to the United States."

[27] "Al-Islām fī Āmrīkā," *Al-Balagh* 3921 (August 14, 1935), cited in Aḥmad, *Sāttī Mājid*, 116–117.

that this noble work will not be completed without attaining consensus among Muslims and uniting them upon one view.[28]

Satti's statement suggests that most Muslim immigrants were not observant at this time. He further explains:

In 1911, we received a letter from the Islamic Society of Berlin in regard to the Italian occupation of Tripoli. We became active in America to form the Red Crescent Society, and we collected in its name a large sum to send to the Ottoman government at that time. Then the Balkan War started in 1912. This society worked also to help those afflicted in that war. We organized a gathering to aid Ottoman warships and the Red Crescent Society in America.[29]

Satti then explains that a Muslim died in Michigan, which made him and other Muslims realize that they needed to acquire land in order to assure their deceased co-religionists receive a proper Muslim burial. This was a particularly important endeavor because many Muslim immigrants had no family in the United States at this time. With Satti's help, Muslims in Detroit purchased a piece of land for $4,294, enough for 533 graves. Later, Satti continues:

We established a society by the name of Islamic Benevolence Society in Detroit, Michigan, and our first act was to build a mosque there next to Henry Ford,[30] the giant of the automobile industry. Then we organized another society in this city by the name of Islamic Union, and all of these societies worked together to spread the message of Islam under my leadership. We continued to work as such until 1914 when the war started and the organizations assisted with the aid of those who had been afflicted in the Ottoman State, and the number of Muslims at that time was around 100,000, of whom 20,000 were American converts.[31] Donations for the afflicted were given according to a system in which every Muslim gave from a four-day salary every week. We raised more than a quarter of a million dollars.[32]

In 1919, Satti's organizations came to the aid of the Egyptian independence movement. "We circulated the call [to aid Egypt] throughout Middle America," Satti told *al-Balāgh*, "and when the British forces arrested the

---

[28] Ibid., 117.

[29] Ibid., 120.

[30] There is no independent record of the existence of such a mosque prior to 1914.

[31] I have not been able to find corroborating evidence of these population estimates. The estimate given for immigrant Muslims (80,000) is fairly close to my own estimate of 60,000 (see Chapter 4). I have not, however, come across any evidence that would suggest the presence of such a large number of converts to Islam in America during or prior to World War I.

[32] "Al-Islām fī Amrīkā," cited in Ahmad, *Sāttī Mājid*, 122.

late Sa'd Zaghlul Pasha and exiled him in Malta, we sent a letter of protest to the League of Nations."[33] By 1919, Satti had clearly come to see himself as the pastoral representative of Muslims in the United States. On June 14, 1919, Satti wrote a letter to the French Embassy in Washington, D.C. on behalf of about 300 Syrian Muslims who wished to return to their homeland after World War I but could not afford to do so. In this letter he introduced himself as "the imam and sheikh of Muslims, who speaks on their behalf, and is a missionary of the religion of Islam in this country of freedom, the United States."[34] In another letter to the British Consulate-General on behalf of a number of Yemeni sailors who had served on British ships during World War I but in 1921 were desolate and jobless in New York City, Satti introduced himself as "the leader of Muslims in the state of New York."[35] In the headings to some of his letters to the British Consulate-General, he also referred to himself as "Rev. Majid Mohamed."[36]

Satti was addressed as "reverend" and "father" by a number of his African American converts in greater Pittsburgh. He in turn addressed them as "sons."[37] Given that Satti was from the Sudan, it is not surprising that he extended his mission to African Americans. He at one point founded the Islamic Benevolent African Society and in 1928 he registered the Society of Africans in America with the Commonwealth of Pennsylvania. In another place, he mentions that he founded the African Moslem Welfare Society of America.[38] A contemporary of Satti who heard him lecture in the Sudan in the mid-twentieth century about his missionary work (*da'wa*) in the United States recalls Satti indicating that "Black Americans were much impressed by the principles of Islam, and they developed a keen interest to find out, learn, and embrace all aspects of this religion. What they found more convincing and appealing to them is

---

[33] Ibid., 122.

[34] Ahmad, *Sāttī Mājid*, 134–135. Translated into English from 'Abd al-Ḥamīd Muḥammad Ahmad's Arabic translation of the original English. 'Abd al-Ḥamīd provides a photocopy of the original on p. 135, but it is illegible.

[35] Abusharaf, *Wanderings*, 25. This is presumably a reprint of the original letter that, according to Abusharaf, 'Abd al-Ḥamīd made available to her. Again a virtually illegible copy of this letter could be found in Ahmad, *Sāttī Mājid*, 137, with an accompanying Arabic translation. The English letter is also reprinted in part in Abu Shouk, Hunwick, and O'Fahey, "Sudanese Missionary to the United States," 143–144. There the first sentence translated here is omitted with the note that "there is a *lacuna* at the beginning" of the letter.

[36] See Ahmad, *Sāttī Mājid*, 141–153 (odd pages – original letters in English).

[37] See letters reprinted in Abu Shouk, Hunwick, and O'Fahey, "Sudanese Missionary to the United States," 183–187; Ahmad, *Sāttī Mājid*, 163, 165, 184, 189, 193.

[38] Abu Shouk, Hunwick, and O'Fahey, "Sudanese Missionary to the United States," 189–190 and Ahmad, *Sāttī Mājid*, 193, 194–195.

the principle, the ideal of social equality." Echoing African Muslim slaves' appeals for racial equality based on divine sovereignty, Satti asserted, "It was Islam that considers us as slaves of God, the Creator of the Universe, and respects man whether Black or White."[39]

It is unclear from the available evidence if Satti influenced Noble Drew Ali, the founder of the Moorish Science Temple (discussed below), or any of the black Muslim nationalist movements that emerged in the 1920s and 1930s in the United States. References to a "return back to our home-land Africa" and to a need to develop a colony near Abyssinia in a letter from one of Satti's followers in Wilkinsburg, Pennsylvania suggest that pan-African nationalists were attracted by him. On the other hand, since his surviving correspondences date from the 1920s and 1930s, it is possible that he himself decided to become a missionary to African Americans after witnessing the success the Ahmadiyya and Noble Drew Ali (both discussed below) had in preaching their versions of Islam in the United States. Whatever the case, Satti was extremely offended by Noble Drew Ali's claim to prophethood. His indignation led him to leave the United States on January 13, 1929 to attain *fatwa*s against Noble Drew Ali's heretical claims to prophethood and to have himself recognized as the official Muslim missionary in North America.[40] He obtained these *fatwa*s but was not officially recognized as a missionary. A scholar at al-Azhar wrote on December 17, 1934, "We declare that he does not have the scholarly qualifications to be appointed to a religious mission such as al-Azhar is accustomed to send abroad."[41] Having failed to receive an official recognition from al-Azhar, Satti attempted unsuccessfully to raise funds from other Muslims to return to the United States.[42]

---

[39] Abusharaf, *Wanderings*, 31.

[40] Satti also mentions the Baha'is and the Ahmadiyya as heretical Muslim movements claiming to represent Islam in the United States, but as his request for *fatwa* demonstrates, he was particularly concerned about Noble Drew Ali's movement which, unlike the Baha'i and Ahmadiyya movements, was unknown to Muslim scholars abroad. See his request for a *fatwa* and the *fatwa*s he received from al-Azhar and from Sudanese scholars in Abu Shouk, Hunwick, and O'Fahey, "Sudanese Missionary to the United States,", 155–182. On his departure from the United States, see Aḥmad, *Sāttī Mājid*, 199–203. He explains his motivation for leaving the United States for Egypt in "Al-Islām fī Āmrīkā," cited in Aḥmad, *Sāttī Mājid*, 204.

[41] Abu Shouk, Hunwick, and O'Fahey, "A Sudanese Missionary to the United States," 150–151.

[42] See the draft of the letter he addressed to Khan Bahadur Ahmed Alaadine requesting funds to return to the United States from the Sudan in Abu Shouk, Hunwick, and O'Fahey, "Sudanese Missionary to the United States," 188–189.

Satti's activities, which were geared toward fulfilling the emerging needs of both American and international Muslim communities, speak to the improvisational and adaptive nature of Islamic practice at the turn of the twentieth century in the United States. Satti addressed these needs from an American Muslim perspective. He founded associations modeled after numerous voluntary associations present in the United States at the time.[43] The pastoral duties Satti assumed in relation to Syrian and Yemeni immigrants are other examples of religious improvisation; through his representation of Muslim emigrants to British, American, and French government officials, Satti, who was only twenty-one years old when he came to the United States, became "Reverend Majid Mohamed, Sheik of Islam in North America."

THE ROLE OF NATIONALIST MOVEMENTS IN FOSTERING ETHNIC SELF-IDENTIFICATION AMONG IMMIGRANT MUSLIMS

Satti was not alone in his religious improvisations, but his activities were unique for their national outreach. Few Muslims in the pre–World War II period thought about establishing Islam nationally in the United States. Those who did were either foreign-sponsored missionaries (such as Muhammad Sadiq of the Ahmadiyya Movement in Islam) or prophetic founders of black nationalist movements (such as Noble Drew Ali and Fard Muhammad). The practice of Islam among most other Muslims in the interwar period was either individualistic or involved only their immediate community. Ethnicity continued to play a more prominent role than religion in the public self-representation of early immigrant Muslims who remained in the United States after World War I. As I argued in the previous chapter, challenges to Syrians' and Indians' eligibility for citizenship brought members of these ethnic communities together across religious divides. The unification behind an ethnic identity, however, was also fueled by political events abroad.

The Muslim-majority world witnessed enormous amount of change at the turn of the twentieth century. Numerous nationalist independence movements emerged in the Levantine and Eastern European provinces of

---

[43] See, for example, bylaws of the Islamic Society and the Muslim Benevolence Society (1922) in Aḥmad, *Sāttī Mājid*, 123–131. For a discussion of the rise of voluntary associations in the late nineteenth and twentieth centuries, see Jason Kaufman, *For the Common Good? American Civic Life and the Golden Age of Fraternity* (New York: Oxford University Press, 2002), 17–32.

the Ottoman Empire. Bosnia, Serbia, Bulgaria, and Romania all gained their independence in the 1870s and 1880s. Albania and Macedonia became independent in the 1910s. The Treaty of Sèvres in 1920 brought virtually all Ottoman territories outside of Anatolia under European rule. The empire itself was abolished in 1924 and was replaced by a republic. Meanwhile, there were growing Indian, Arab, and African nationalist movements rising against British rule in South Asia and the Middle East and against French rule in the Levant and North Africa. As Satti's fundraising on behalf of the Ottomans and the Egyptian independence movements demonstrates, Muslims in the United States, along with their co-ethnics, were watching these movements closely. Their newspapers reported on them in Arabic, Albanian, Hindi-Urdu, and later in English. Their responses to these world-altering events were wide and varied and deserve more scholarly analysis than they have received thus far or that I could provide here. What is particularly of interest to the present study is the way in which immigrants from the Muslim-majority world responded to these events by forming their own political paradigms through which they defined America. As the relative political freedoms and the prosperity they found in the United States allowed them to organize themselves into a variety of nationalist organizations, they gained an appreciation for the United States as a political entity. Satti, for example, referred to the United States on more than one occasion as "the land of freedom and justice."[44] A call to Arab unity by the Arab's Union Committee, published in the Arabic newspaper *al-Bayan*, read:

Today, you are in the greatest free republic in the New and the Old World. Will you not capture a spark from the flame of its freedom, brilliant to the eye? Will you not emulate the civilized peoples to whom you have sacrificed yourself by remaining in their nationality and citizenship? No doubt you drew nourishment from American freedom and learned what nationalism and patriotism demand. Then, we implore you by the nobility of Arabs not to neglect the opportunity to promote the Arab cause.[45]

While this call to unite Arabs of varying backgrounds for a nationalist cause seems suspiciously pro-American, it expressed a sentiment that was apparently widespread among not only Syrians in America but also among their compatriots in the Levant. In 1919, the King-Crane Commission

[44] See, for example, his letter to the French Council on pp. 133–135 of Aḥmad, *Sāttī Mājid*, and his handwritten description of his activities in the United States on pp. 102–103 of Aḥmad, *Sāttī Mājid*.

[45] *Al-Bayān*, May 3, 1919, 7.

surveyed opinions in Syria and Armenia to gain a sense of their political ambitions. The Commission concluded that most Syrians sought an autonomous state with a constitutional monarchy; short of that, however, they would welcome a temporary U.S. mandatory government.[46]

Of all the immigrant groups from the Muslim-majority world, Albanian immigrants' nationalist aspirations were perhaps most affected by their political experiences in the United States. While many Albanian nationalists at the turn of the twentieth century went into exile and settled in such places as Greece, Italy, Romania, Egypt, and Constantinople, they did not find the same freedom of movement and access to material resources to organize themselves in these countries as they did in the United States. When Albanian nationalists began to arrive in the United States, the *konak* (discussed above) and the Albanian coffee shops provided a ready-made network through which they could spread their nationalist ideology. The coffee shop was often the first destination for new immigrants who relied on their compatriots to help them find housing and work. In 1906, an Albanian nationalist, Sotir Petsi, established the first Albanian American newspaper, a weekly titled *Kombi* (Nation).[47] An early study of Albanian nationalist movements in the United States described how Albanian immigrants' social networks and print media worked to foster nationalist sentiments among Albanians in Massachusetts:

Kombi reached the *konak* on Friday or Saturday, and readers could absorb its contents in a leisurely fashion over the week-end. The literate man of the *konak* would first read every line of every article before the group, often including casual notices and advertisements. Then a heated discussion would burst forth as the entire group wrangled over the interpretation of the news. From time to time the *konaks* would receive a bundle of books from some colony abroad – Rumania, Bulgaria, or Egypt. There were elementary readers, small books of patriotic poems, political pamphlets, and translations from foreign languages. When one group exhausted its reading matter, it would pass the books and leaflets on to a neighboring *konak*.[48]

Since most Albanians in the United States at the time were illiterate, in order to increase their reach, nationalists also established classes to teach both Albanian and English. These classes were often led by a literate member of the *konak*.[49] In 1909, *Kombi* was succeeded by *Dielli* (Sun), which,

[46] Harry Nicholas Howard, *The King-Crane Commission: An American Inquiry in the Middle East* (Beirut: Khayats, 1963), 120.
[47] Federal Writers' Project–WPA of Massachusetts, *The Albanian Struggle*, 38.
[48] Ibid., 39.
[49] Ibid., 40.

in the spirit of interreligious cooperation that was becoming common-place in the Albanian nationalist movement, was founded by a Christian, Reverend Theofan S. Noli, better known as Fan Noli, and edited by a Muslim, Faik "Bey" Konitza.[50]

Albanian nationalist ideology was designed to appeal to both Christians and Muslims. Nationalist leaders urged all Albanians to take pride in their distinct Albanian cultural heritage and demand national rights. Christians were urged to cut their ties with the Greek Orthodox Church, which in addition to its religious functions also served as their political liaison to the Ottoman Empire. Muslims were called to fetter their ties from Albania's Turkish overlords, a proposition that seemed all the more appealing with the increasing loss of Ottoman territory in Eastern Europe at the turn of the twentieth century, including the loss of Albania in 1912. After 1912, Christian and Muslim immigrants from Albania participated in more or less equal numbers in Albanian nationalist organizations.[51]

When Albania became independent of the Ottoman Empire, many Albanian immigrants returned home. Those who could demonstrate their involvement in the Albanian nationalist movement in the United States, *Vatra*, were given political jobs. By around 1920, however, the old Turcophile and Hellenophile aristocracies came to power and the *Amerikani*s and their "visionary notions" were dismissed. They were reminded that they were peasants and that political activism and residence in the United States did not change their status in Albanian society: "So you dish-washers from America want to get the better of us, eh? ... Tell me, my American, why do you carry those pens in your coat pocket when you do not know how to write your name? ... Bah! These smart Americans! Donkeys of burden in America ... Peasants you were and peasant you remain!"[52] Many Albanians consequently returned to the U.S. where they set more permanent roots. They continued their nationalist activities as Albanian Americans and aspired toward cultural rather than political nationalism.

Indian immigrants' experiences with the United States as a political entity were mixed given the prejudices they faced as a result of their status as "barred Asians." Many Indians in the United States considered this country to be neutral in their fight for independence from Britain. A number of nationalist revolutionaries sought asylum in the United States.[53] We

---

[50] Ibid., 46–47.
[51] Ibid., 42.
[52] Ibid., 66.
[53] Gary R. Hess, "The Forgotten Asian Americans: The East Indian Community in the United States," in *The Asian American: The Historical Experience*, ed. Norris Hundley, Jr. (Santa Barbara, CA: Clio, 1976), 166.

have already seen this Indian ambivalence toward the United States displayed in Inayat Khan's description of the United States as a deeply racist country that nevertheless had the potential to "lead the world towards progress."[54] Similarly, the masthead of *The Free Hindustan*, an Indian nationalist paper which began its publication in the United States in 1908, cited Patrick Henry's words, "Resistance to tyranny is obedience to God," even as it called on Indian immigrants to fight their slavish treatment in North America and abroad by joining the cause of Indian Nationalism. The Ahmadi missionary Muhammad Sadiq, who was detained for seven weeks upon arrival in the United States for adhering to a religion that allowed for polygamy, derided racial prejudices in the United States but nonetheless argued that it was Islam, not Christianity, that offered a solution to the color problem "even right here in America, the very land of freedom, equality, and justice."[55]

Racial bigotry against Indians, particularly in California, led many Indian immigrants to join the Indian nationalist movement known as the Ghadar (mutiny) Party. Gobind Behari Lal, one of the founding members of the Ghadar Party recalled that anger over racial immigration issues "provided combustible material for [a founder of the movement] Har Dayal's revolutionary nationalism." Har Dayal impressed upon Indian immigrants that they could not gain respect in the United States until they gained independence from Britain and united despite their religious differences as Indians.[56] The immigrant farm laborers to whom Har Dayal lectured donated money to his cause, and in 1913 the movement's presence in the United States was officially announced. It began to publish a paper, *The Gadar*, in Hindi, Urdu, and Gurmukhi or Punjabi scripts. In fall of 1914, about 400 Indians returned to India on armed missions organized by the Ghadar Party to overthrow British rule. It is interesting to note that although the Ghadar appealed to Indian immigrants because of the prejudice they experienced in the United States, in its effort to arouse Indian nationalist pride, *The Gadar* published accounts of George Washington's struggle against the British along with accounts of the French Revolution and Bismarck's efforts to unify Germany.

The Ghadar Party was an international movement and its leaders are better characterized as cosmopolitan revolutionaries than American

[54] Inayat Khan et al., *Biography of Pir-o-Murshid Inayat Khan* (Madras: East-West Publications, 1979), 88.
[55] "The Only Solution of Color Prejudice," *Moslem Sunrise* 1, no. 2 (October 1921), 42.
[56] Tilak Raj Sareen, *Select Documents on the Ghadr Party* (New Delhi: Mounto Publishing House, 1994), 34.

immigrants. By 1917, support for the party had dissipated in large part because it accomplished little by way of addressing Indian immigrants' racial problems here in the United States and also because the British government urged American officials to curtail its activities, which they did by indicting some of its activists for conspiracy and violation of America's neutrality laws. Despite the failure of the Ghadar Party, Indian nationalists throughout the interwar period found a sympathetic audience among Indian Americans of varying religions and among some white, liberal Americans. They formed such associations as the India League of America and the India Welfare League to fight both on behalf of Indian independence and Indian American rights. In 1946, the India League and the India Welfare League managed to get a bill through Congress that established a quota that allowed Indians to immigrate to the United States once again and overturned the *Bhagat Singh Thind* decision by making Indians eligible for citizenship.[57]

While Anglo-American Protestants' experiences of America's political freedoms, scientific achievements, and economic power at the turn of the twentieth century led them to triumphantly celebrate the accomplishments of "our country," the experiences of immigrant Muslims with America's freedoms, scientific achievements, and economic power was coupled with experiences of racism, religious bigotry, and economic hardship. Consequently, immigrant Muslims' claims on America were not based on what they had already accomplished, as was the case for Anglo-Americans, but rather on the potential America held for them and their ethnic compatriots more so than for their co-religionists. Their activism at the national level in this period was thus expressed through ethnic self-help and nationalist organizations.

LOCAL MUSLIM RELIGIOUS ACTIVITY AND INSTITUTION BUILDING

In place of national religious activity, Muslims' religious activities were generally ad hoc and addressed the needs of local communities. An example of the local nature of organized American Muslim activity is found in Cedar Rapids, Iowa. The founders of the first mosque established in this city in 1934, for example, self-identified as a "league" that was intended to perform "benevolent duties,"[58] similar to numerous fraternal orders

---

[57] Hess, "Forgotten Asian Americans," 167 and 171–173.
[58] See the appendix of their bi-laws on p. 137 of Hussein Ahmed Sheronick, "A History of the Cedar Rapids Muslim Community: The Search for an American Islamic Identity" (BA thesis: Coe College, 1988).

and benevolent societies found throughout the United States at the time. While the League claimed that it was a religious duty for all Muslims within the Cedar Rapids area to join it, it controlled its membership by requiring new members "be admitted only by the majority vote of the present members."[59]

Islamic praxis was also predominantly individualistic and improvisational. By way of example, Imam Bakhesh, a rice farmer from India, used to teach religion to his work gang members, who were mostly illiterate.[60] Kalil Bazzi, a Syrian immigrant who was only 19 and illiterate when he began working for the Ford Motor Company in 1913, taught himself to read Arabic with the Qur'an and learned to perform burial and marriage ceremonies "because the Shi'a people had no one else to do this for them."[61] Bazzi later served as the imam of the Detroit Shi'i community in the 1920s. Lurey Khan, the daughter of a Punjabi Muslim man and an African American woman, recalls that her father who immigrated in 1912 could not find a mosque or a Muslim community in Boston, so in place of the noon congregational prayer and his five daily prayers, he "prayed alone on his rug every Friday at sunset. Then he would give alms in the form of fruit and candy to the neighbor's children."[62] A 1939 Works Progress Administration of Massachusetts study of Albanian immigrants noted that "Moslem Albanians in America neither built nor attended any mosques. Whatever influence Islam exerted upon its Albanian followers in America was exercised informally or through the channels of traditional sentiment."[63] In Cedar Rapids, most Muslim-owned grocery stores could not afford to lose business by closing around noon on Fridays for congregational prayers, so even as late as the 1930s and 1940s, they held their congregational prayers on Thursday night, and they followed it with some socializing and a 45-minute lecture or reading of the Qur'an.[64]

Many Muslims did not observe the ritual practices of Islam. An ethnography of early Palestinian immigrants in Chicago found that "although many of them do not adhere to Islamic ritual in Chicago, never once did I

[59] See article 11 and appendix of their by-laws on p. 135 and p. 138 of Sheronick, "History of the Cedar Rapids Muslim Community."

[60] Salim Khan, "Pakistanis in the Western United States," *Journal of Muslim Minority Affairs* 5, no. 1 (1983–84), 43.

[61] Naff, *Becoming American*, 303.

[62] Lurey Khan, "An American Pursues Her Pakistani Past," *Asia* (March/April 1980), 34.

[63] Federal Writers' Project–WPA of Massachusetts, *The Albanian Struggle*, 42.

[64] Sheronick, "History of the Cedar Rapids Muslim Community," 37.

hear a statement about the futility or unimportance of religion."[65] He found that only about 10 out of 128 individuals kept the fast during Ramadan, but all stayed away from the coffee shop, where they socialized, until after *iftar* (the break of the fast).[66] The children of Indian Muslim farmers on the West Coast report that few, if any, of them observed their daily prayers or fasted during Ramadan. They did, however, get together on the major feast days to socialize.[67] Even when South Asian Muslims built a mosque in Sacramento in 1947, they primarily used the building on the holidays.[68] Socializing was an important part of communal religious life. When Arab Muslims in Cedar Rapids established their mosque in 1934, it was suggested that it be called a *nadi* (or a "club"), so that its use would not be restricted to prayer. The goal was to have the mosque become the social center of the community.[69] The distinction between a mosque and a community center, however, was lost on their non-Muslim neighbors who knew their mosque as the "Moslem Temple."[70]

In addition to socializing, the need for proper burial of the deceased was a major impetus for the formation of local Muslim organizations. In 1918, Turkish and Albanian Muslims in Biddford, Maine got together to purchase a large burial plot in Biddeford's Woodlawn Cemetery for their co-religionists who had fallen victim to the Spanish Flu. It is believed that members of this community used to gather for communal prayers as early as 1915, but today no trace of their communal life remains aside from a few gravestones that identify them as "Muhamedan" or "Musluman."[71] Syrian and Turkish Muslims in Cleveland, Ohio founded the Association of Islamic Union of Cleveland in 1918 "to foster social relations and solidarity among the Moslems" and to purchase a burial plot in Highland Park Cemetery.[72] Long before

---

[65] Lawrence Oschinsky, "Islam in Chicago: Being a Study of the Acculturation of a Muslim Palestinian Community in That City" (Master's thesis: The University of Chicago, 1952), 42.

[66] Oschinsky, "Islam in Chicago," 33.

[67] Das, *Hindustani Workers*, 80.

[68] Khan, "Pakistanis in the Western United States," 44.

[69] Sheronick, "History of the Cedar Rapids Muslim Community," 35.

[70] "Federation of Islamic Association – First Convention program," 17, cited in Sheronick, "History of the Cedar Rapids Muslim Community," 35; "Boys Master Reading of Koran in Arabic Language," *Cedar Rapids Gazette*, January 12, 1936.

[71] Colleen Rost-Banik, "Woodlawn Cemetery – Muslim Burial Ground," www.pluralism.org/research/profiles/display.php?profile=73366 (accessed January 15, 2008); "Albanians," in *Harvard Encyclopedia of American Ethnic Groups*, 26.

[72] John J. Grabowski, "Turks in Cleveland," in *The Encyclopedia of Cleveland History* found at http://ech.case.edu/ech-cgi/article.pl?id=TIC (accessed July 17, 2009). *Annual*

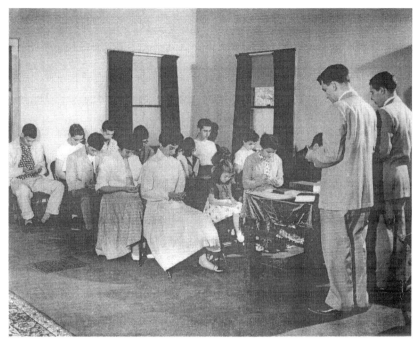

FIGURE 5. A children's class at the "Moslem Temple" of Cedar Rapids, Iowa, circa 1945. Their cupped hands and bowed heads suggest that they are reciting a prayer, most likely the first chapter of the Qur'an, *al-Fatiha*. Photo courtesy of Imam Taha Tawil of the Mother Mosque of America in Cedar Rapids, Iowa.

South Asian Muslims built their mosque in Sacramento in 1947, they formed the Moslem Association of America in 1919 in large part to establish proper burial grounds in central California for their deceased co-religionists. Their cemetery served Muslims throughout the West Coast, but it was not long after its founding that South Asian Muslims in El Centro, California, and Phoenix, Arizona decided to follow suit and bought their own burial plots.[73] In 1907, Polish, Russian, and

Report of the Secretary of State of the Governor and General Assembly of the State of Ohio for the Year Ending June 30, 1918 (Springfield, OH: The Springfield Publishing Company, 1918), 93. While Grabowski does not cite the participation of Syrian Muslims in this association, others do. See Robert Dannin, *Black Pilgrimage to Islam* (New York: Oxford University Press, 2002), 98.

[73] Das, *Hindustani Workers*, 89; Leonard, *Making Ethnic Choices*, 83; and Khan, "Pakistanis in the Western United States," 44.

Lithuanian Muslims founded the American Mohammedan Society[74] (also referred to as the Anglo-Mohammedan Association) in Brooklyn, New York. Contemporaries in 1920 took this to be "the only real mosque" in New York City,[75] and it maintained this reputation until the late 1930s, when it was also said to be the mosque that "claims most of the devout" Muslims in the city. By the mid-1930s, however, some Muslims were also said to attend the Mohammedan Unity Society in New York City.[76] In 1925, the Muslim community in Michigan City, Indiana, which reportedly numbered 200 families, founded the Society of the New Era and purchased a cemetery and a couple of buildings, one for the gratis use of those incapacitated in World War I and the other for social gatherings. Later, in 1934 it purchased another building for a mosque. The new building was divided into two parts, one intended for prayers and the other for socializing and Arabic instruction.[77] The Muslims of Ross, North Dakota, who were mainly homesteaders, used to congregate in one another's homes as early as 1900 in order to perform the congregational Friday prayer, but they did not build a mosque until around 1929,[78] presumably around the time that pioneers were beginning to pass away and the community had to think about funeral rites. The Ross mosque was built adjacent to a Muslim cemetery. The mosque seems to have gone out of use after World War II, but there were still Muslims buried at the cemetery as late as 1999.[79] The Detroit Muslim community, which Satti Majid had helped establish a Muslim cemetery in 1920,[80] founded a mosque in the Highland Park

[74] *Book of Conveyances*, Brooklyn City Register, Block 2781, Lot 12, cited in Marc Ferris, "To 'Achieve the Pleasure of Allah': Immigrant Muslim Communities in New York City 1893–1991," in *Muslim Communities in North America*, ed. Yvonne Y. Haddad and Jane I. Smith (Albany, NY: State University of New York Press, 1994), 211.

[75] M. M. Aijian, "Mohammedans in the United States," *Moslem World* 10 (1920), 40.

[76] Federal Writers' Project–Works Progress Administration of New York City, *New York Panorama: A Comprehensive View of the Metropolis, Presented in a Series of Articles Prepared by the Federal Writers' Project of the Works Progress Administration in New York City* (New York: Random House, 1938), 117.

[77] Sally Howell, "Mosques History," in *Encyclopedia of Islam in the United States*, ed. Jocelyne Cesari (Westport, CT: Greenwood Press, 2007), vol. I, 433. "An interview of Hussein Huseein Ayad: Early Immigrant to Michigan City, Indiana" (conducted by John P. Brennan, representing the Public Library of Michigan City, Ind., n.d., typescript), 8–10, cited in Naff, *Becoming American*, 300.

[78] "A Mosque in North Dakota," *Syrian World* 3, no. 10 (April 1929), 57.

[79] William C. Sherman, Paul L. Whitney, and John Guerrero, *Prairie Peddlers: The Syrian Lebanese in North Dakota* (Bismarck, ND: University of Mary Press, 2002), 99, 156 and 158.

[80] Bilgé, "Voluntary Associations in the Old Turkish Community of Metropolitan Detroit," 393.

area in 1921 with $55,000. The mosque was funded by Muhammad Karoub, a local real estate investor. Three religious leaders of different sects led the mosque – Hussein Karoub (Sunni), Kalil Bazzi (Shi'i), and Muhammad Sadiq (Ahmadi) – but Hussein Karoub was acknowledged as the official imam of the mosque.[81] The ecumenical arrangement of the mosque did not last very long. Quarrels first emerged when the local community discovered that Sadiq was a follower of a controversial movement known as the Ahmadiyya (discussed below). By 1922 Sadiq was forced to leave and moved the headquarters of his movement to Chicago. Later, when many Sunnis moved from Highland Park to Dearborn, Muhammad Karoub decided to turn the mosque over to his brother, Hussein, and the local community to support. The Shi'is, however, refused to support the mosque financially if it was to be led by a Sunni imam. Consequently, the building was sold to the city of Highland Park in 1926.[82]

Before the establishment of mosques, early immigrants who remained observant felt both isolated and empowered to pursue their religion as they saw fit:

Before, the [Highland Park] Muslims prayed in their homes. Each believer read his own Koran. He didn't need a leader.... This is a free country; no one asked you about your religion or faith. Personally, I prayed and fasted as I had done in the village. No one asked or bothered me. Nothing changed. I worked on Friday. It was not necessary to stop working to pray. This is a matter of choice; I worked and prayed on Friday. I prayed after work.... I fasted all day while working during Ramadan. Difficult? Don't ask how difficult! But I did, even when I felt very weak.[83]

A pious member of the early Palestinian Muslim community in Chicago described the behavior of the mostly non-observant Muslim community thusly:

The Arabs in Chicago behave more like Kafir (sic) [or unbelievers] rather than Muslims. They don't make the salat [or ritual prayer], they have forgotten the shahada [the confession of faith], drink like they were from Dublin, and eat ham sandwiches as if they were the food of paradise. All they have on their minds is women.[84]

---

[81] *Moslem Sunrise* 1, no. 2 (October 1921), 31.
[82] Howell, "Mosques History" 433; Mary Caroline Holmes, "Islam in America," *Moslem World* 16 (1926), 264.
[83] Naff, *Becoming American*, 301.
[84] Oschinsky, "Islam in Chicago," 29.

The condemning tone of this description expresses how isolating it was to be an observant Muslim in the 1920s and 1930s. Religious leaders recognized how alienating strict observance of Islamic precepts could be for Muslim immigrants. "An imam had to have elasticity, that is, flexibility in the American environment," according to Hussein Karoub's son who succeeded him. "My father was never rigid. Sometimes he was criticized for his liberalism. I believe, as my father did, that rigidity causes [immigrant] Muslims to shun Islam and [that] defeats the purpose of keeping Islam [alive in America]."[85]

MARRIAGE AND CHILDREARING

Another area of life in which Islamic practices were improvised and adapted was in the religious upbringing of children. This was particularly problematic because although communal observance of religion was rare, religion was still regarded as inherently valuable. Among Syrian immigrants, Alixa Naff states that "many, but by no means the majority," sent their kids back home for Islamic education.[86] A 1925 editorial in *al-Bayan* complained that the children of Syrian Muslim immigrants know little about their homeland, religion, and language not because of a lack of places of worship but because their parents do not teach them Islam or Arabic.[87] Some Muslims, however, did make a concerted effort to teach their children Islam. In fact, raising children within Islam was a major impetus behind the effort to build mosques and Islamic centers in the United States. By way of example, although Muslim men had settled in Cedar Rapids, Iowa, in the mid-1890s and even gathered at times at one another's houses to perform congregational prayers in the 1920s,[88] it was not until they were joined by their wives and families that their community of about 150 persons[89] began raising funds for a mosque. The women in the community founded a social club in 1933 named "Rose of Fraternity Lodge" through which they pushed the men in the community to raise funds for building a mosque.[90] Construction

[85] Naff, *Becoming American*, 246.

[86] Ibid., 301.

[87] "*Allimū awlādakum*," *al-Bayān*, March 28, 1925, 6.

[88] Yahya Aossey, Jr., *Fifty Years of Islam in Iowa, 1925–1975* (Cedar Rapids, IA: Unity Publishing, 1975). In *al-Islām fī Āmrīkā*, Shawarbi says Muslim families came to Cedar Rapids in 1895, p. 18; the families were the Igrams, the Khalils, and the Sheronicks.

[89] "Boys Master Reading of Koran in Arabic Language," *Cedar Rapids Gazette*, January 12, 1936.

[90] Sheronick, "History of the Cedar Rapids Muslim Community," 32; Naff, *Becoming American*, 287.

on the mosque was completed on February 15, 1934.[91] The edifice they built is the oldest, surviving mosque in the United States today, and it is affectionately known as the Mother Mosque of America. The "Rose of Fraternity Lodge" not only served as a center for social gatherings and prayer, but also housed classes taught by its imam, Kamil al-Hind of Damascus, every weekday evening in Arabic and Islam. In January 1936, an article in the *Cedar Rapids Gazette* announced that two boys from the community's founding families, Abdallah Igram and Hussein Sheronick, "are said to be the first in the United States to achieve a reading knowledge of the Koran in a temple class, practically all study of this type having been heretofore conducted privately."[92] Similarly when the Muslim community of Michigan City, Indiana established its first mosque in 1934, it set aside space for classes in Arabic and Islam.[93]

Given the scarcity of marriageable female co-religionists, exogenous marriages were common, particularly among non-Arab immigrants. An examination of marriages involving South Asians recorded in California in 1913–1949 found that out of 378 such marriages, 80 percent were with Hispanic women, 12.7 percent with Anglo-American women, 4 percent with African American women, 2.4 percent with other South Asians, and 0.5 percent with Native Americans.[94] Kurdish and Turkish Muslims from Anatolia generally abstained from marrying. According to one estimate, 95 percent of the men never married, but maintained contact with families back home. Out of the 5 percent that did marry, only 25 percent married Muslim wives. There was only one recorded instance of an American wife converting to Islam.[95]

Among the Syrian populations as a whole, outmarriages were not the norm. Many returned to the Levant to marry or to bring their families. The Shi'i imam Kalil Bazzi is reported to have said that very few Muslims in his small community in Highland Park married outside of their religion between the world wars.[96] A study of 128 Palestinian Muslims in Chicago in 1947 found that only seven had married outside of the Muslim

[91] "The Mother Mosque of America," http://www.mothermosque.org/page.php?2 (accessed January 28, 2010).

[92] "Boys Master Reading of Koran in Arabic Language," *Cedar Rapids Gazette*, January 12, 1936.

[93] "An interview of Hussien Hussien Ayad: Early Immigrant to Michigan City, Indiana" (conducted by John P. Brennan, representing the Public Library of Michigan City, Ind., n.d., Typescript), 8–10, cited in Naff, *Becoming American*, 300.

[94] Karen Isaksen Leonard, *South Asian Americans* (Westport, CT: Greenwood Press, 1997), 51, and Leonard, *Making Ethnic Choices*, 67.

[95] Bilgé, "Voluntary Associations," 388–389.

[96] Naff, *Becoming American*, 245.

community. Most had families back in Syria and traveled back and forth between the continents. A 1966 study of Arab Muslims in Detroit and Toledo showed that about half of the children of the early Syrian Muslim immigrants who had gotten married had married non-Muslims. Of these outmarriages almost all were with Christians, and a handful were with Jews. Roughly a third of the grandchildren of the early immigrants had married by the time this 1966 study was conducted; none had married Muslims.[97]

Outmarriages and pressures to conform socially, particularly in small rural communities, led some Muslims to employ poly-religious practices similar to the practices of enslaved African Muslims discussed in Chapter 2, which emphasized commonalities rather than differences between Islam and Christianity. One study, for example, found that the elderly among Arab Americans in Glenfield, North Dakota, admitted "to attending Christian services on Sunday, while saying Muslim prayers privately at home." The children of these older immigrants, however, ceased to be Muslim; most attended Lutheran churches and a few had become Methodist. Among the children of the Syrian Muslim pioneers of Ross, North Dakota, there were also those who attended both Protestant churches and selectively observed Muslim practices. Their grandchildren and great-grandchildren, who still live in Ross, attend Lutheran congregations. A descendent of Syrian Muslim immigrants in North Dakota, when asked to describe his ethnic heritage, said, "I'm Arab, Muslim, Chippewa, French, Catholic and Knights of Columbus."[98] Lurey Khan, who was born to an African American mother and an Indian father, indicated that her household was free of alcohol and "Pigmeat" and that her family "lived in a modified purdah" (separating the sexes). Khan's mother, however, took her and her siblings to a Methodist church on Sundays.[99] Many of the children of marriages between Punjabi Indians and Mexicans on the West Coast "claimed to be both Catholic and Sikh, or Catholic and Muslim."[100] As Karen Leonard discovered during her field research in this community, Indian husbands and their Mexican

---

[97] According to this study, 59 percent of second generation Arab American Muslims in Toledo had married other Muslims. Twenty-seven percent had married Christians, and 3 percent had married Jews. Fifty-four percent of second generation Arab American Muslims in Detroit had married Muslims. Twenty-one percent had married Christians and 1 percent had married Jews. The rest were unmarried. Abdo A. Elkholy, *The Arab, Moslems in the United States* (New Haven, CT: College & University Press, 1966), 33.

[98] Sherman, Whitney, and Guerrero, *Prairie Peddlers*, tables 9, 7, and 8.

[99] Khan, "American Pursues Her Pakistani Past," 34.

[100] Leonard, *South Asian Americans*, 58–59.

wives disagreed about many issues but the religious training of their children was not one of them. The men encouraged their wives to practice their own religion and supported them in their practice while they themselves continued to practice their own religion. "The men wanted to inculcate respect for Sikhism, Hinduism, or Islam, while they encouraged their children to practice Catholicism (or whatever form of Christianity their wives practiced)."[101] The type of religious instruction children of Muslim intermarriages received and the social and economic pressures that affected Muslim religious instruction during the first decades of the twentieth century has not been carefully studied. Based on the available anecdotal evidence, however, Leonard's observation regarding South Asians on the West Coast seems generalizable to all Muslim intermarriages in this period. A report in the *Minot Daily News* found a similar trend among Syrian Muslims in North Dakota, even after the building of the mosque at Ross: "As the children in the congregation grew to adulthood, many of them forsook the faith and adopted the Christian religion when they married a non-Muslim."[102]

The fact that educating children in Islam was difficult, if not impossible, does not mean that the practice was universally forsaken. "I would rather shoot the boy than have him brought up as a damn Catholic," said a Palestinian Muslim who immigrated in 1921 and had married a Christian Syrian woman.[103] The difficulties that would have resulted from religious intermarriages must have also been a part of the reason why most Muslims in this period, as discussed above, never married or returned to their home countries to marry.

Among those who intermarried, aspects of Islam were selectively observed. Households, like that of Lurey Khan mentioned above, avoided alcohol or pig-products but did not demand of members of the household such ritual activities as daily prayers or the fast of Ramadan. A similar household regiment existed among early South Asian immigrants in California. Mexican wives, for example, reportedly could distinguish between their South Asian husbands' religions only by whether or not they abstained from pork or beef in their household.[104] Second- and third-generation Arab Americans preserved prayer beads and copies of the Qur'an as reminders of their religious ancestry.[105] Like some of their

---

[101] Leonard, *Making Ethnic Choices*, 117.
[102] *Minot Daily News*, "Once Numerous Moslem Community," 12, cited in Naff, *Becoming American*, 246.
[103] Oschinsky, "Islam in Chicago," 29.
[104] Leonard, *Making Ethnic Choices*, 93.
[105] Sherman, Whitney, and Guerrero, *Prairie Peddlers*, table 8.

co-religionists who were brought to these shores as slaves, they generally downplayed differences observed through rituals and emphasized what their religions held in common: "all Gods are the same, but they are called different names because languages are different."[106] A second-generation resident of Stanley, North Dakota, who used to attend the Ross mosque but later became Lutheran, remarked that "the only thing is that there is a little different belief, but we're all humans."[107] In the end, children of intermarriages from this period became not so much Muslim but rather persons of Muslim heritage.

THE TURN TO ISLAM AMONG SOME AFRICAN AMERICANS

Concurrent with the growing influence of multireligious nationalist movements among immigrant Muslims and with the growth of local Muslim associations and mosques, there was an infusion of Islam in the public life of African Americans who had migrated to the metropolises of the Northeast and the Midwest after World War I in search of employment and an escape from Jim Crow laws. One of the outcomes of this migration was that during the 1920s and 1930s, black America experienced a mushrooming of religiously eclectic, spiritualist institutions similar to what white America had undergone in the nineteenth century with the founding of such religious movements as Mormonism, Shakerism, Spiritualism, Christian Science, and the Theosophical Society.[108] As we have seen, there was no shortage of religious eclecticism in the lives of African Americans in the nineteenth century, but it was not until the Great Migration of southern blacks to the North that African Americans had the financial resources and the freedom to form independent institutions around these beliefs and practices. Up until the 1920s, independent African American institutions were more or less limited to black versions of mainline churches and fraternal associations, both of which stood in an uneasy relation with their white counterparts because of racism. We saw tensions within the church exemplified in the two speeches given by African Americans at the World's Parliament of Religions. Members of African American fraternal organizations similarly found themselves in an uneasy and subservient position in relation to their white counterparts. In

---

[106] Leonard, *Making Ethnic Choices*, 116–117.
[107] Sherman, Whitney, and Guerrero, *Prairie Peddlers*, table 12.
[108] See Hans A. Baer, *The Black Spiritual Movement: A Religious Response to Racism*, 2nd ed. (Knoxville, TN: The University of Tennessee Press, 2001).

the early 1900s, William H. Grimshaw penned an *Official History of Freemasonry among the Colored People of North America* to respond to detractors of black or Prince Hall Freemasons who sought "to convince the world that negro Masonry in America did not emanate from the same source as white Masonry, hence it was of a spurious kind and could not be recognized."[109] In *Prince Hall and His Followers* (1914), George W. Crawford complained that an earlier attempt to legitimate Prince Hall's right to "the Royal Art" focused on white Lodges that claimed descent from him. "It is not surprising," he wrote in a telling statement about the racial tensions within Freemasonry, "that a white Mason is not able to conceive of the vindication of Negro Masonry without coupling it with 'recognition' by white members of the Fraternity."[110] The lack of recognition of Prince Hall Masonry excused white Masons from the privileges and hospitality that Masons were obliged to afford one another. There were also a number of court cases in which white Masons and Shriners challenged the right of black Masons and Shriners to use the orders' regalia. One of these cases was even settled in 1929 by the Supreme Court in favor of black Shriners.[111]

With the large migration of African Americans to the North, numerous independent African American eclectic religious institutions emerged in Northern metropolises, among them were Father Divine's Peace Mission movement, the United House of Prayer for All People, the Moorish Science Temple, and the Nation of Islam. These groups generally were not apologetic or deferential to white society in large part because they were innovative products of African America and not black offshoots of white organizations. As the following police officer's description of his encounter with the members of the Moorish Science Temple in Detroit shows, these new African American eclectic religious organizations relied on religion to institutionalize an identity outside of white society's racial hierarchies: "What a terrible gang! Thieves and cutthroats! Wouldn't answer anything. Wouldn't sit down when you told them. Wouldn't stand up when you told them. Pretending they didn't understand you, that they were Moors from Morocco. They never saw Morocco! Those Moors never saw anything before they came to Detroit

---

[109] William H. Grimshaw, *Official History of Freemasonry among the Colored People in North America* (New York: Broadway Publishing, 1903), vii.

[110] George W. Crawford, *Prince Hall and His Followers: Being a Monograph on the Legitimacy of Negro Masonry* (New York: The Crisis, 1914), 9.

[111] Susan Nance, "Respectability and Representation: The Moorish Science Temple, Morocco, and Black Public Culture in 1920s Chicago," *American Quarterly* 54, no. 4 (2002), 644–645.

except Florida and Alabama!"[112] Drew Ali deliberately chose to organize African Americans around a distinct Islamic national identity in part because he was aware of the legal protections afforded to religious organizations. "Whatever the reasons may be for their opposition [to the Moorish Science Temple]," he wrote, "the legal right to oppose citizens, individuals and organizations alike for their religious beliefs does not exist in the United States. The door of religious freedom made by the American Constitution swings open to all, and people may enter through it and worship as they desire."[113]

The waning of modernist optimism and white Protestant triumphalism in the aftermath of World War I helped eclectic, spiritualist movements flourish among African Americans. The destruction and fatalities caused by so-called progressive nations during World War I vividly demonstrated the shortcomings of evolutionary views of human progress, which saw history as an inevitable march toward advancement. The earlier conflation of the white race, Protestantism, and progress in these views of history no longer seemed invincible to people of color and non-Protestants in the face of World War I. Put differently, the identity paradigm that viewed modernity and progress as a result of liberal Protestant values championed by Anglo-Saxons, a paradigm that maintained the hegemony of white Anglo-Saxon Protestants, no longer held the same sway. Marcus Garvey, the Jamaican-born pan-Africanist founder of the Universal Negro Improvement Association, expressed this sentiment clearly when he said to his followers, "I am the equal of any white man; I want you to feel the same way. No one need think we are still the servile, bending, cringing people we were up to fifty odd years ago in this country. We are a new people, born out of a new day in this country. We are born out of the bloody war of 1914–18. A new spirit, a new courage has come to us."[114] Ahmadi missionaries saw similar opportunities for non-Christian, non-Protestant religions:

The great war ended five years ago, but the world is yet far from peace, and there can be no peace in the world unless there is a change in the hearts of men. Christianity has been tried in Europe, now let Islam have a trial. We hope that

---

[112] Arthur Huff Fauset, *Black Gods of the Metropolis: Negro Religious Cults of the Urban North* (Philadelphia, PA: University of Pennsylvania Press, 1944), 42–43n3.

[113] Noble Drew Ali, "Moorish Leader's Historical Message to America," *Moorish Literature* (n.p.: 1928), 13.

[114] Cited in Rollin Lynde Hartt, "The Negro Moses," *The Independent* (February 26, 1921), 205.

Islam which comes from the same root as **salam** which means peace, will prove to be the message of peace for Europe and the world. And we hope that Germany, the birth-place of Protestantism, will also be the centre for the new message of peace to Europe.[115]

The Nation of Islam also associated 1914 with the year in which white people's "time was up." According to the Nation of Islam's apocalyptic mythology, "[t]he United States was doomed to destruction in the year 1914 but that this time of destruction has been extended so that ELIJAH MOHAMMED can lead the black man out of the wilderness of North America and in turn the black man can become the rightful ruler of the world."[116]

What was an occasion for optimism and an opportunity for self-improvement and self-rule for many people of color, was an occasion of self-doubt and pessimism for many liberal Protestants. "When the war started I was a young man trying to be an optimist without falling into sentimentality," wrote the famed Neo-Orthodox theologian Reinhold Niebuhr. "When it ended and the full tragedy of its fratricides had been revealed, I had become a realist trying to save myself from cynicism."[117]

In American metropolises, the convergence of industrialism, cosmopolitanism, and the waning of modernist optimism created a social and cultural context for the relationship between race, religion, and progress to be rewritten in order to allow for non-whites and non-Protestants to claim their part in the making of American modernity. The fact that immigrants from Muslim countries sought to prove they were white and downplayed their affiliation with Islam in order to gain access to citizenship rights reminds us that the political and cultural hegemony of whites and Christians by no means disappeared after World War I. Nonetheless, its claim to represent the height of human civilization and divine providence became more difficult to defend after the tragic outcome of World War I. Islam played a significant role in the reconfiguring of the relationship between race, religion, and progress among a significant minority of African Americans who earnestly appropriated, to varying degrees, Islamic names, symbols, rituals, and concepts in an effort to participate in America's prosperity and modernity.

---

[115] *Moslem Sunrise* 3, no. 1 (January 1924), 13.
[116] Federal Bureau of Investigation file, CG 25–20607, March 17, 1943, 6 and 11.
[117] Reinhold Niebuhr, "What the War Did to My Mind," *Christian Century*, 45 (September 27, 1928), 1161.

MASONRY AND THE RISE OF ISLAM IN BLACK AMERICA

Prior to the 1920s, Islamic symbols and names had already been in use by Masonic orders. Freemason lodges were first established in the early eighteenth century in England. The secret societies of the Masons provided an institutional space in which Enlightenment ideals of meritocracy, equality, human progress, and self-governance could be experimented within a sociopolitical context that was still traditional, highly stratified, and aristocratic.[118]

Historical exchanges between Muslims in the United States and Freemasons have not yet been studied, but they date back at least to the time of the enslaved Fulbe Job Ben Solomon, whose encounters with the gentry of England following his emancipation in 1733 were mediated in some part by Freemasons. Job's principal patron in England was John the Duke of Montague, who had been elected the Grand Master of the Grand Lodge of England in 1721. Thomas Bluett also dedicated his biography of Job to the Duke of Montague. Furthermore, when Job was employed by the Royal African Company to advance English trade into the interior of Africa, he was entrusted to Francis Moore by Richard Hull, the Chief Merchant of the Royal African Company at James Fort, who was a Freemason and a Provincial Grand Master of Gambia. Hull instructed Moore that Job is to be used "with the greatest Respect, and all the Civility you possibly can."[119]

Another notable African Muslim associated with Freemasonry was 'Umar ibn Said. Accounts of his life as early as 1825 suggest that he was a Freemason in Africa before coming to America and that, on account of this association, he received special treatment. This is certainly a possibility because the presence of Masonic lodges on the coast of West Africa dates back to 1735, and, it seems that "there were at certain times specifically African and specifically European lodges as well as multiracial lodges in West Africa."[120] According to one report, when he was

---

[118] See Margaret Jacob, *The Radical Enlightenment* (Morristown, NJ: Temple Publishers, 2003) and *Living the Enlightenment: Freemasonry and Politics in Eighteenth-Century Europe* (Oxford: Oxford University Press, 1991).

[119] Francis Moore, *Travels into the Inland Parts of Africa: Containing a Description of the Several Nations* (London: Edward Cave, 1738), 21 and 205. Robert Freke Gould, *The History of Freemasonry: Its Antiquities, Symbols, Constitutions, Customs, Etc.* (London: Thomas C. Jack, 1887), vol. VI, 343.

[120] Augustus Casely-Hayford and Richard Rathbone, "Politics, Families and Freemasonry in the Colonial Gold Coast," in *People and Empires in African History: Essays in Memory of Michael Crowder*, ed. J. F. Ade Ajayi and J. D. Y. Peel (London: Longman, 1992), 146–147.

jailed as a runaway in South Carolina, a jail keeper found him to be "a bright mason" and threw the door open for him to escape. According to another account, he was said to have given the "Masonic sign of distress" to John Owen, who purchased him.[121] John Owen was a one-time governor of North Carolina (1828–1830) and was twice elected as deputy grand master of the Grand Lodge of North Carolina in 1829 and 1830.[122] Moreover, 'Abdul Rahman made use of both Prince Hall and white Freemasonry lodges to raise funds to purchase his family's freedom.[123]

Without more research in the archives of numerous Freemasonry lodges that dot the East Coast, it is difficult to know how extensive or historically significant the interactions between Muslims and Freemasons in antebellum America were. What seems certain, however, is that the appropriation of Islamic symbols, history, and rituals by such secret societies as Freemasons and Shriners played a significant role in the development of African American nationalist movements that were formed in the name of Islam in the 1920s and 1930s. Both Noble Drew Ali, the founder of the Moorish Science Temple, and Elijah Muhammad, the leader of the Nation of Islam, not to mention many of their early followers, had been initiated into Masonic orders.[124]

These fraternal orders were of significant social standing, and they provided a model of self-governance and institution building that was

---

[121] Gregory Townshend Bedell, "Prince Moro," *Christian Advocate* (July 1825), 306–307, reprinted in Allan Austin, *African Muslims in Antebellum America: A Sourcebook* (New York: Garland Publishing, Inc., 1984), 460; John Frederick Foard, "A True Story of an African Prince in a Southern Home," in *North American and Africa: Their Past, Present and Future and Key to the Negro Problem* (Statesville, NC: Brady, 1904), 65, reprinted in Austin, *African Muslims: A Sourcebook*, 478; A. M. Waddell's handwritten biography of 'Umar ibn Said found on the verso of a portrait of him in the DeRosset Paper of the Southern Historical Collection at the University of North Carolina at Chapel Hill, digital copy available at http://docsouth.unc.edu/nc/omarsaid/said_150.html (accessed August 20, 2009); and Margaret McMahan, "Bladen Slave Was Also a Prince," *Fayetteville News and Observer*, March 17, 1968, reprinted in Austin, *African Muslim: A Sourcebook*, 502.

[122] William R. Denslow, *10,000 Famous Freemasons from K to Z*, pt. II (Whitefish, MT: Kessinger Publishing, 2004), 298.

[123] "Abduhl Rahaman," *New York Journal of Commerce*, October 16, 1828, reprinted in Austin, *African Muslims: A Sourcebook* 169 and 257n124; Terry Alford, *Prince among Slaves: The True Story of an African Prince Sold into Slavery in the American South* (New York: Oxford University Press, 1977), 161–162.

[124] Claude Andrew Clegg III, *An Original Man: The Life and Times of Elijah Muhammad* (New York: Macmillan, 1998), 71–72. Peter Lamborn Wilson, *Sacred Drift: Essays on the Margins of Islam* (San Francisco, CA: City Lights Books, 1993), 20; Richard Brent Turner, *Islam in the African-American Experience*, 2nd ed. (Bloomington, IN: Indiana University Press, 2003), 95.

foundational for the development of African American Muslim nation-alist organizations, even though the latter organizations, unlike the Masonic orders, were not democratic.[125] Drew Ali, for example, upon founding the Moorish Science Temple, wrote of the need for "a national organization with a Rotarian complexion as it relates to branch Temples became obvious with the increasing numbers of inquiries from men and women in different sections of the country."[126] As seen in the formation of the first mosque in Cedar Rapids, which had membership dues and defined itself as a "lodge" and a "benevolent society" and was known as the "Moslem Temple," Masonry's administrative structure may also have exercised some influence in the early development of some immigrant Muslim mosques in the United States. Freemasonry had a presence in the Middle East since the mid-eighteenth century.[127] In the United States, fra-ternal orders provided immigrant Muslims with an entrée into American social and business networks.

In the late nineteenth and early twentieth centuries, Masonic orders, whose members were predominantly Christian, drew on the knowledge that was being amassed on "Oriental" and "ancient" cultures through such disciplines as archeology, ethnology, comparative religion, and phi-lology to construct their own myths and rituals in an effort to cohere their members through a civil religion of their own. They used sym-bols and sayings from an imagined "mystic Orient" in order to portray their own myths and rituals as representative of "perennial truths" and "ancient wisdoms" that had withstood the test of time. In reality, how-ever, their modern mimicry and satirizing of the ancients and the Orient were performances that on the one hand demonstrated their mastery and command over them and on the other distinguished them from their com-patriots as cosmopolitan citizens with access to ancient Oriental knowl-edge and regalia. In the process, they superficially familiarized Americans

---

[125] Robert Dannin advances this argument in *Black Pilgrimage to Islam*, 22–25. However, he pushes the dichotomy between the church and such fraternities too far, ignoring the fact that many African American church leaders were also involved in organizing and lead-ing fraternal orders. See Michael Gomez, *Black Crescent: The Experience and Legacy of African Muslims in the Americas* (Cambridge: Cambridge University Press, 2005), 243.

[126] Noble Drew Ali, "Moorish Leader's Historical Message to America," in *Moorish Literature*, 12; also in *Moorish Guide* (September 28, 1928), 2.

[127] On the presence of Freemasonry in the Middle East and South Asia, see Jessica Harland-Jacobs, *Builders of Empire: Freemasons and British Imperialism, 1717–1927* (Chapel Hill, NC: UNC Press, 2007); Hamid Algar, "An Introduction to the History of Freemasonry in Iran," *Middle Eastern Studies* VI (1970), 276–296; and Jacob M. Landau, "Muslim Opposition to Freemasonry," *Die Welt des Islams* 36, no. 2 (July 1996), 186–203.

with ostensibly "Oriental" and "ancient" symbols, rituals, and myths. In many ways, they had the same effect as evolutionary understandings of religions did. They allowed, at one level, the cultures and religions of "Eastern" peoples to be recognized as part of the cultural heritage of the modern world, without challenging Northern Europeans' prominence in the modern world. On another level, they were a Trojan Horse or a stealth conduit for the entry of "Eastern" religions into American culture. It is thus not surprising that the missionary Muhammad Sadiq sent 500 letters and copies of his paper, *The Moslem Sunrise*, to Masonic lodges in hopes of converting them to the Ahmadiyya Movement in Islam.[128]

Out of the varying Masonic orders, the Ancient Arabic Order, Nobles of the Mystic Shrine, or Shriners, made the most blatant and extensive use of Islamic symbols, history, and wisdom. The Shrine was founded in 1870 for an elite order of Masons holding advanced degrees. In 1893, the black version of the shrine, the Ancient Egyptian Arabic Order, Nobles of the Mystic Shrines, was founded, according to the order's own historical narrative, when John George Jones, a member of Chicago's Prince Hall Lodge No. 7, claimed to have the degrees of the Ancient Arabic Order of the Nobles and Mystic Shrine Masonry conferred upon him at Chicago's Columbian Exposition of 1893 by a Noble Rofelt Pasha. The Shrine, whether black or white, developed a reputation as "the playground of Masonry" well into the 1920s.[129] Shriners made playful use of Islamic regalia and symbols such as the crescent and the star and the black stone adjacent to the Kaaba in Mecca. They, who were mostly Christian, claimed to uphold Muhammad's creed and to obey his commands and moral teachings. They put on fezzes and turbans in their revelries and concocted legends about the origins of their order that they mapped onto Islamic history in a seemingly Islamic idiom:

The Order of the Nobles of the Mystic Shrine was instituted by the Mohammedan Kalif Alee (whose name be praised!), the cousin-german and son-in-law of the Prophet Mohammed (God favor and preserve him!), in the year of the Hegira 25 (A.D. 644) at Mecca, in Arabia, as an Inquisition, or Vigilance Committee, to dispense justice and execute punishment upon criminals who escaped their just deserts through the tardiness of the courts, and also to promote religious toleration among cultured men of all nations.[130]

---

[128] "A Brief Report on the Work in America," *Moslem Sunrise* (October 1921), 37.

[129] Lynn Dumenil, *Freemasonry and American Culture, 1880–1930* (Princeton: Princeton University Press, 1984), 204.

[130] George L. Root, *The Ancient Arabic Order of the Nobles of the Mystic Shrine for North America* (Whitefish, MT: Kessinger Publishing [1903], 1997), 11.

FIGURE 6. Members of the Moorish Science Temple at an annual meeting. From the Digital Collection of the Schomburg Center for Research in Black Culture at the New York Public Library.

The Shriners' influence on the Moorish Science Temple could be noted not only in the garb the "Moors" donned at their meetings and "costume balls" and the names (Ali, Hakim, Mustafa) and titles they adopted (Noble, Sheiks, Bey), but also in their religious literature. The Moorish Science Temple produced catechisms and initiation procedures similar to those found in Masonic lodges.[131] As I will discuss later, Drew Ali also cloaked occult religious writings used by some Masonic orders to "de-negrofy" African Americans (i.e., to disassociate them from contemporary stereotypes and stigma associated with being a "negro") and to create a foundation myth and a national identity for members of his organization.

Furthermore, the relative affluence and respectability of black secret societies created a prestige economy in African American communities in the North where black Muslim nationalist groups vied for adherents. Elijah Muhammad, for example, said in one of his radio addresses:

[131] See, for example, *History and Catechism of the Moorish Orthodox Church of America* (n.p.: Crescent Moon Press, 1986).

Never has any so-called American Negro been taught by white people to believe in Almighty God Allah and his true religion Islam. Only in higher organizations or we say Masonry, in the Masonics, there is a little teachings at the top mostly of the particular order [i.e., the Shriners] that mentions the teachings of Almighty God Allah. But you have to pay a lot of money to become a 33rd degree Mason; therefore, you are an absolute victim, as Isaiah teaches you, that you buy that which does not bring you any gain. To buy that king of teachings does not gain you the hereafter. We must have something that is pure. A Mason cannot be a good Mason unless he knows the Holy Qur'an and follows its teachings....I say, if you are a true Moslem friend, then alright, lets have it in the open and not in the secret.[132]

It is difficult to know whether or not Noble Drew Ali or Elijah Muhammad really believed that the Masonic performances of Islamic rituals and beliefs were the same as the rituals and beliefs of professing Muslims in other parts of the world. Whatever the case, they purported that their own teachings were a means for connecting with the global Muslim community.[133] Masonry provided them with the structural and mythological tools through which they could create and institutionalize their own understandings of religion. In this, Masonic orders played a parallel role in the development of black Muslim nationalist movements as Theosophy did in the development of liberal Protestant understandings of religion that were put on display at the World's Parliament of Religions in 1893. In fact, Noble Drew Ali's *Circle Seven Koran*, as we shall see later, was a product of metaphysical and theosophical religious writings popular with Masons. "There are many things about the history of Islam in America that people would not like to hear," recalled Wali Akram, a 1925 convert to the Ahmadiyya Movement who broke away in the 1930s to found the First Cleveland Mosque, to the anthropologist Robert Dannin. "The whole thing rested on the Masonic order! There's no use beating around the bush, that's how Islam came to America."[134]

THE UNIA, DUSE MOHAMED ALI AND THE RISE
OF ISLAM IN BLACK AMERICA

In addition to the cultural cachet that Islam – stereotypically reduced as exotic symbols and performances – had in certain Euro- and African American cosmopolitan circles after World War I, many African

[132] Reproduced in Elijah Muhammad, *The Secrets of Freemasonry*, 3rd ed. (Atlanta, GA: Secretarius, 2002), 2–3.
[133] Noble Drew Ali, "Moorish Leader's Historical Message to America," in *Moorish Literature*, 12; also in *Moorish Guide*, 2.
[134] Dannin, *Black Pilgrimage to Islam*, v–vi.

Americans, since the days of Edward Wilmot Blyden, also regarded Islam as an authentically African religion. Thus, they associated Islam with black nationalist causes, which in the early 1920s were represented most prominently in the streets of African America by Marcus Garvey's Universal Negro Improvement Association. The UNIA was founded in 1914 in Jamaica and established its first U.S. chapter in 1917 in Harlem. Its members believed that blacks would never find equality so long as they lived under the rule of white governments. They sought to establish a new world order by reclaiming Africa for blacks throughout the world.

Some of our leaders in the Negro race flatter themselves into believing that the problem of black and white America will work itself out, and that all the Negro has to do is to be humble, submissive and obedient, and everything will work out well in the "sweet bye and bye." ... The only wise thing for us as ambitious Negroes to do is to organize the world over, and build up for the race a mighty nation of our own in Africa.[135]

According to Garvey, an African nation needed an African religion. Garvey did not disavow Christianity but rather sought to Africanize it:

Whilst our God has no color, yet it is human to see everything through one's own spectacles, and since the white people have seen their God through white spectacles, we have only now started out (late though it be) to see our God through our own spectacles. The God of Isaac and the God of Jacob let Him exist for the race that believes in the God of Isaac and the God of Jacob. We Negroes believe in the God of Ethiopia, the everlasting God – God the Father, God the Son and God the Holy Ghost, the One God of all ages.[136]

While Garvey himself did not claim Islam for African Americans, Islam was nonetheless associated by some African Americans with his brand of African nationalism. This is evinced by Noble Drew Ali's claim that Garvey "was divinely prepared by the great God-Allah" as the forerunner "to the coming Prophet; who was to bring the true and divine Creed of Islam, and his name is Noble Drew Ali: who was prepared and sent to this earth by Allah, to teach the old time religion and the everlasting gospel to the sons of men."[137]

---

[135] Marcus Garvey, *Philosophy and Opinions of Marcus Garvey*, vol. 1, ed. Amy Jacques-Garvey (New York: Macmillan, 1992), 57–58.
[136] Ibid., 44.
[137] Noble Drew Ali, *The Holy Koran of the Moorish Science Temple of America* (Chicago, IL: Noble Drew Ali, 1927), 59.

Garvey's movement was influenced in part by the pan-Africanist Duse Mohamed Ali. Duse was born in 1866 in Alexandria, Egypt to an Egyptian army officer and his Sudanese wife. He was sent to England at the age of nine for his education, and went on to study history at King's College before getting involved in theater and journalism.[138] In 1912, he and John Eldred Taylor founded *The African Times and Oriental Review* (1912–1920), an influential monthly paper "devoted to the interests of the coloured races of the world." *The African Times and Oriental Review* was mostly in English with occasional articles or letters published in Arabic. It was distributed widely throughout the world and proclaimed itself as "a Pan-Oriental, Pan-African journal at the seat of the British Empire which would lay the aims, desires, and intentions of the Black, Brown, and Yellow races – within and without the Empire – at the throne of Caesar."[139] Duse associated with the mission of the Ahmadiyya in Britain which was led by Khwajah Kamel-ud-Din. The two often participated at events of the Central Islamic Society, and Duse published some of Kamel-ud-Din's writings in his journal.[140] In 1921,[141] Duse came to the United States on a business trip. He intended to find American buyers for products (particularly cocoa) which, the Inter-Colonial Cooperation, a West African cooperative he helped establish, sought to export.[142] Duse's business venture went awry, and he found himself in the position of having to start over in the United States. He spent the next ten years lecturing on issues related to Egypt and Africa throughout the United States, starting new business ventures, and promoting cultural activities related to Africa and the "Orient." In April 1922, he became a leading functionary in Garvey's Universal Negro Improvement Association, serving as the head of the African Affairs department.[143] This marked a turn in Duse and

[138] For an overview of Duse's life, see Ian Duffield, "Duse Mohamed Ali and the Development of Pan-Africanism 1866–1945," 2 vols. (Ph.D. thesis, Edinburgh University, 1971) and Khalil Mahmud, "New Introduction," in *In the Land of the Pharaohs*, by Duse Mohamed, 2nd ed. (London: Frank Cass and Company, 1968), ix–xxxiii. All autobiographical references to Duse's life in the following pages are from Duse Mohamed Ali, "Leaves from an Active Life, Chapter XV: American Activities" in *Comet*, February 5, 1938.

[139] "Foreward," *African Times and Orient Review* 1, no. 1 (July 1912), 1.

[140] For examples, see Khwaja Kamal-ed-Din, "Cross Versus Crescent" and "Jesus, an Ideal of Godhead and Humanity," *African Times and Orient Review* (December-January 1913), 197–198 and 217–222.

[141] Duse himself, writing later from memory, said that he came to the United States in 1920, but Duffield has shown based on external evidence that this was unlikely. Duffield, "Duse Mohamed Ali and the Development of Pan-Africanism 1866–1945," vol. 2, 650n1.

[142] Hakim Adi and Marika Sherwood, *Pan-African History: Political Figures from Africa and the Diaspora since 1787* (London: Routledge, 2003), 3–4.

[143] Duffield, "Duse Mohamed Ali," vol. 2, 660.

FIGURE 7. Duse Mohamed Ali. From *The African Times and Orient Review* (July 1912).

Garvey's relationship, because Garvey had been an employee of Duse's journal in 1913 and was heavily influenced by the journal's pan-African ideology. Indeed, in the 1930s it was often said that "Garvey was taught by a Muslim."[144] While working for Garvey, Duse contributed regularly to *The Negro World* and served as his liaison to African American leaders who deemed Garvey's ideology too radical to deal with him directly.[145]

[144] Turner, *Islam in the African-American Experience*, 86.
[145] Duffield, "Duse Mohamed Ali," vol. 2, 662.

While in the United States, Duse used to wear a fez to protect himself from racism. This act seems to suggest that despite the widespread
prejudice against Islam in white America, it continued to be significant
as a "semi-civilizing" and thus a liminal religion for African Americans.
According to one of Duse's biographers, "There is no doubt that he was
perfectly conscious that an exotic appearance, identifying a black man as
not a black American, could give protection."[146] As this suggests, black
Americans' adoption of Islamic symbols and sartorial practices helped
them escape to some degree the stigma of being black in a white society. It
gave them a liminal status by disassociating them from black stereotypes
or "de-negrofying" them, thus allowing them to identify themselves as a
new race, as "Moorish Americans" or members of "the Nation of Islam."
Testimonies by black converts to the Ahmadiyya Movement in Islam
(cited in Chapter 6) also confirmed the role Islam played in their lives
by ascribing to them a liminal racial identity between white and black,
which allowed them into white business establishment in the Jim Crow
South. "Come change your name," cried a prominent African American
convert who proselytized in the streets of St. Louis for the Ahmadiyya
in the 1920s, "get back your original language and religion, and you
won't be a nigger no more!" Another Ahmadiyya pamphlet produced by
African American converts in Cleveland in the early 1930s, read: "Abolish
Negro-ism! Nationality worries disappear! Learn the Arabic language,
the language of your ancestors, which is in daily use by more than one
third of the world's population."[147]

Around 1921, Duse reports that some Indian Muslims whom he had
met in New York asked him to come to Detroit to give a couple of lectures and to help them organize a Muslim society that would "be the
means of establishing a prayer room with a regular system of weekly
prayers which had been sadly neglected." Although he does not mention
who exactly invited him, given Duse's involvement with the Ahmadiyya
in London, it is very likely that his reference to "Indian Muslims" is
actually to the Ahmadiyya missionary Muhammad Sadiq, who came
to the United States in 1920 and was in Detroit in 1921–1922.[148] The
Muslim society to which he refers may very well have been the above-
mentioned Highland Park mosque, where Sadiq served as an imam

---

[146] Ibid., 665.
[147] Cited in Dannin, *Pilgrimage to Islam*, 92 and 104.
[148] The Ahmadiyya's paper, *The Moslem Sunrise*, carried few advertisements, but it did
carry an ad for "The Vision of Duse Mohamed Ali, The Egyptian Historian, President
American-African-Orient Corporation." See *Moslem Sunrise* 3, no. 2 (April 1924), 57.

and where he began the publication of his apologetic newspaper, *The Moslem Sunrise*.[149] While in Detroit, Duse also founded an American Asiatic Association which aimed to "call into being more amicable relations and a better understanding between America and the Orient in general." The Association provided him with opportunities to produce theatrical performances dealing with "the Orient" and to provide the community with lectures on "Oriental" literature, religions, societies, and politics. As a former Exalted Ruler of the Order of Elks, he was also involved with the Detroit branch of the Order.[150] It is likely that his involvement with fraternal orders was not limited to the Order of Elks. According to the April 1922 issue of the *Negro World* he attended gatherings of prominent Masons along with Marcus Garvey, Arthur Schomburg, and a Dr. Abdul Hamid of Khartoum, Egypt, a 96 degree Mason and a Shriner who was identified as a friend of Duse's.[151] Duse also associated with secret societies through his wife, Gertrude La Page; she was a white American actress and an "ardent Rosicrucian," and he himself had a deep interest in the "mysteries and secret lore of ancient Egypt," which he explored in some of his fictional writings.[152]

THE AHMADIYYA MOVEMENT AND THE RISE OF ISLAM IN BLACK AMERICA

Further research into Duse's activities in the United States should illuminate the history of American Muslim institution building in the interwar period. As a black, Egyptian, immigrant, pan-Africanist, Muslim, author-activist and a husband to a Rosicrucian and a former Exalted Ruler of the Order of Elks who had been involved with the Ahmadiyya missions in England and the United States, Duse stood at the intersection of several eclectic streams that were formative in immigrant Muslim institution building and in the introduction of Islam to African Americans in the North.

Even though the extant historical record is incomplete, there is some evidence that suggests Duse may have played an intermediary role in introducing the Ahmadiyya missionary Muhammad Sadiq to Graveyites in Chicago in 1922, which may help explain why Sadiq's propaganda became more nationalist in tone at this time. The Ahmadiyya Movement

---

[149] *Moslem Sunrise* 1, no. 1 (July 1921), 22, citing *Detroit Free Press*, June 8, 1921.
[150] Duse, "Leaves from an Active Life.
[151] *Negro World*, April 1922, cited in Turner, *Islam in the African-American Experience*, 95.
[152] Mahmud, "New Introduction," in *In the Land of the Pharaohs*, xxii.

in Islam was founded by Mirza Ghulam Ahmad (1835–1908) at the end of the nineteenth century. Although the Ahmadis affirm almost all fundamental Muslim beliefs and practices, they diverge significantly from most Muslims' understandings of Islam and are outlawed in some Muslim states, such as Pakistan and Saudi Arabia. The main theological source of contention between Ahmadi Muslims and their opponents is Mirza Ghulam Ahmad's claim to the station of prophethood, which most other Muslims believe ceased in the person of Muhammad ibn 'Abd Allah. Like the Baha'i Faith discussed in the previous chapter, the Ahmadiyya mission represents a Muslim response to modernity and the conflation of race, religion, and progress. The religious teachings of Mirza Ghulam Ahmad turned the table on exclusive Anglo-Protestant claims to rationalism, universalism, and progress by claiming these qualities for Islam. Unlike Inayat Khan's International Sufi Movement, the Ahmadiyya did not compromise on the details of Islamic beliefs and practices nor did they seek to harmonize a proverbial East with the West. They accepted "Western" political systems and rule and reminded the British that "you have most loyal subjects in the Muslims" of India, but also admonished the British that "they have their religious duties and have got feelings which should be respected by a wise ruler."[153] The Ahmadiyya saw their fight as a fight against Christian claims to superiority, not imperial political rule. By claiming to be the Christian Messiah, the Muslim Mahdi, and the final incarnation of Krishna for Hindus, Mirza Ghulam Ahmad sought to claim the evolutionary end of humanity's religious progress for Islam. In his prophecies, Ghulam Ahmad denied the historicity of Jesus' crucifixion and claimed that Jesus had fled to India where he died a natural death in Kashmir. In this way, he sought to neutralize Christian soteriologies of Christ and to demonstrate the superior rationality of Islam. Ironically, in his effort to demonstrate the superiority of Islam, he had to modify Islamic teachings, which regarded Muhammad as the "seal of the prophets" and the final authority on Islam. He also countered Muslims' belief in Jesus' ascension to heaven and redefined jihad as missionary activity rather than as warfare.

Most Indian Muslims at first welcomed Mirza Ghulam Ahmad's teachings and celebrated his rhetorical victories in debates with Christian missionaries and Hindu reformers. As his claims to prophethood became public, however, most Muslims disassociated themselves from his movement. In the 1910s, a number of his prominent followers rejected his

---

[153] Khwaja Kamal-ed-Din, "Cross versus Crescent," 198.

prophetic claims and accepted him as a religious reformer (*mujaddid*); they formed the Lahori branch of the Ahmadiyya and stood in contrast to the Qadiyani branch which accepted Ghulam Ahmad's prophetic claims and adhered to the *khalifa* or vicegerent who succeeded him.[154]

It was the Qadiyani Ahmadis who came to the United States as missionaries in the 1920s and 1930s. In Ahmadis' effort to turn the table on Christians' exclusive claims to universality, rationality, and progress, they dispatched missionaries to far-flung locales in Europe and North America to convert them. These Ahmadi missionaries emphasized the shortcomings of Christianity while idealizing Islam as the universal religion of humanity:

Islam in the Ahmadia Movement is the only religion for the uplift of human-ity in both the Eastern and Western worlds. Why? It bears all the virtues of the many religions and none of their flaws. Its beauty and substantiality lies in its truth and simplicity which transcend other religions and brings to humankind the ultimate in spiritual development. No religion presents to the seeker a greater nobility, a deeper sympathy, a warmer charity or a sweeter forgiveness toward man and womankind than Islam as taught by the blessed Prophet Ahmad.... As a guiding light for the world at large it is unexcelled in brightness and through the constant perpetuity of the divine laws of Islam it will mean for those who follow it, with even a degree of understanding, an easier road through life with its many entanglements.[155]

It is interesting to note that while Christians, as seen in the Columbian Exhibition of 1893, pointed to the economic and scientific attainments of European "civilization" as proof of the validity of their faith, the Ahmadiyya pointed to Mirza Ghulam Ahmad's prophetic reformation as proof of Islam's superiority. As I will argue at the end of this chapter, prophecy played a significant role in the reconfiguration of the confla-tion of race, religion, and progress in favor of non-Christian people of color.

Duse Mohamed Ali cared little about the "orthodoxy" of the Ahmadiyya. In his association with them, first in London and later in the United States, he was impressed with their activism as a positive expres-sion of "native" culture, for which he worked to gain respect: "The Black man, the Brown man, and the Yellow man all have religions, traditions, institutions and what not, which they love and admire, and for which

[154] Yohanan Friedmann, *Prophecy Continuous: Aspects of Aḥmadī Religious Thought and Its Medieval Background* (Berkeley, CA: University of California Press, 1989), 147–162.

[155] *Moslem Sunrise* 3, no. 1 (January 1924), 20.

FIGURE 8. Mufti Muhammad Sadiq. From *The Moslem Sunrise* (January 1923), 155.

they expect a little love and admiration."[156] Duse regarded Islam as a more proper religion for Africans and considered Christianity to be a corrupting influence on the progress of people of color because of its association with the colonial powers and their missionaries.[157]

In the spring of 1922, Sadiq moved the headquarters of the Ahmadiyya from Detroit to Chicago and later, with the help of Ahmadi funds from India, established a mosque next to it, adorned with a dome.[158]

After moving his headquarters to Chicago, Sadiq began to lecture at UNIA gatherings and to convert Garveyites to Islam in significant numbers. At one time, after five lectures at UNIA meetings in Detroit,

---

[156] Duse Mohamed Ali, "Foreword," *African Times and Orient Review* 1, no. 1 (July 1912), 1.

[157] Duffield, "Duse Mohamed Ali," vol. 2, 722.

[158] *Moslem Sunrise* 1, no.6 (October 1922), 138.

FIGURE 9. "Ahmadia Moslem Mosque and Mission House" at 4448 Wabash Avenue in Chicago. From *The Moslem Sunrise* (October 1922), 126.

he gained forty new converts.[159] Duse and Sadiq were in Chicago and Detroit around the same time, but whether or not Duse played a direct role in Sadiq adapting his message to a more pan-Africanist audience is not known for certain.[160] What is clear, however, as Richard Brent Turner has shown, is that after moving his headquarters to Chicago in 1922 and given his success in converting members of the UNIA, Sadiq placed greater emphasis on racial inequality in America and adopted a more nationalist tone in presenting Islam as a solution to America's "race problem."[161]

[159] *Moslem Sunrise* 2, no. 1 (January 1923), 167.
[160] Duffield presents evidence that suggests that Duse was in Chicago in 1922 and 1923. Duffield, "Duse Mohamed Ali," 678–679.
[161] Richard Brent Turner, "Islam in the United States in the 1920's: The Quest for a New Vision in Afro-American Religion" (Ph.D. dissertation: Princeton University, 1986), 154–162 and *Islam in the African-American Experience*, 127–130.

Before 1922, the Ahmadiyya appealed primarily to the gentry. It regularly sent "missionary epistles" to scientists, politicians, actors, authors, and royalty from all over the world.[162] Sadiq also wrote regularly to varying newspapers, including the *New York Times*, either to tout the virtues of Islam or to correct misperceptions about Islam. His preoccupation with national print media is further evidence that he was fishing for converts primarily among the gentry. Indeed, in the second issue of *The Moslem Sunrise* he ridiculed American Christian missionaries whose "converts in India chiefly come out of outcasts and illiterates who never understand what a religion is"(p. 43). Sadiq deemed the conversion of the educated elite as an indicator of the verity and superiority of his religion. The pages of *The Moslem Sunrise* ostentatiously displayed the titles and occupations of his "respectable" converts. He also sought to boast his own "respectability," printing copies of mail-order advanced degrees he received in such dubious fields as "Orientalistic Sciences" and "Mental Science" from some of the fake correspondence schools that popped up at this time.[163]

Through his connection with the UNIA, Sadiq found a community that, though not of the gentry, had the respect of average African Americans. Within this community he won not only converts but also "intelligent and enthusiastic" persons whom he then appointed as leaders to varying congregations in the cities he visited.[164] Consequently, his propaganda at times took on a more nationalist tone in order to map Islam onto Garvey's pan-Africanist project:

The spread of El Islam cannot help but benefit the UNIA, for they are desperately engaged in preparing for That Day – that day that we of the Universal are also preparing for. Great Britain, France, Spain – in fact all the white powers – fear Mohammedanism. None of them can afford to offend El Islam. With millions

---

[162] See, for example, "A Brief Report on the Work in America," *Moslem Sunrise* (October 1921), 37. Sadiq also sent 500 letters and copies of *The Moslem Sunrise* to Masonic lodges presumably because he felt they would be sympathetic to the proselytization of Islam.

[163] See, for example, his doctorate in literature from Lincoln Jefferson University in *Moslem Sunrise* 1, no. 1 (July 19221), 11; his doctorate in divinity from The College of Divine Metaphysics in *Moslem Sunrise* 1, no. 2 (October 1921), 35; his doctorate in "Orientalistic Sciences" in *Moslem Sunrise* 1, no. 3 (April 1922), 101; and his certificate in mental science from Robert S. Rawson in *Moslem Sunrise* 1, no. 5 (July 1922), 125. For news coverage of two of the so-called universities from which Sadiq received a diploma ("Oriental University" and "Lincoln Jefferson University"), see "Government Is Investigating Fake Universities" in *New York Times* August 27, 1911, SM5 and "Two 'Universities' in Room" in *New York Times*, May 14, 1926, 14.

[164] *Moslem Sunrise* 1, no. 6 (October 1922), 167. See also Turner, *Islam in the African-American Experience*, 127.

of Moslems in India, China, Arabia, Persia, Afghanistan, Turkey, Negroes would find valuable allies.[165]

Islam, however, was not new to the UNIA. In addition to his association with Duse, Garvey was thoroughly familiar with Blyden's *Christianity, Islam, and the Negro Race*. The UNIA, like the Shriners, made regular use of Islamic terms and symbols. A UNIA musical composition made references to "Allah-Hu-Akbar" and "May he our rights proclaim, In that most sacred Name Allah – one God, one Aim, one Destiny." In the end, however, the Ahmadiyya Movement in Islam was not a black nationalist movement nor were most Garveyites interested in Islam as anything more than a set of symbols that they could appropriate in the civic religion of their movement. Among 1,025 persons whose names were printed in *The Moslem Sunrise* as new converts between 1921 and 1925, the panoply of races were represented, even though African American converts were most prominent. It is thus not surprising that Sadiq's nationalist tone petered out as the UNIA began to decline in the mid-1920s.[166]

Given the continuing existence of racism in the United States in the 1920s and 1930s and given the Indian Ahmadi missionaries' own skin color, the "color problem" did not disappear from the Movement's discourses, but it was generally discussed in the more global terms of "universal brotherhood" and "democratic principles" rather than in terms of black nationalism and African Americans' specific struggles with racist laws and practices.[167] The Ahmadiyya's influence in the African American community further waned as black American nationalist Muslim organizations emerged in the late 1920s and early 1930s and as rifts grew between the national leadership of the Movement, which was exclusively South Asian, and some of the local African American leaders.[168] African Americans' splintering from the Ahmadiyya in Cleveland, Ohio and Pittsburgh, Pennsylvania are particularly noteworthy because they led to the formation of two of the earliest and best-known predominantly black "Sunni" Muslim mosques in the United States – the First Cleveland Mosque (1936) and the First Muslim Mosque of Pittsburgh (conceived in the late 1930s but founded in 1945).[169] It would be a misnomer to

---

[165] *Moslem Sunrise* 2, nos. 2 and 3 (April 1923), 263.

[166] Turner, *Islam in the African-American Experience*, 81–88, 124, 130 (quote on 88).

[167] See, for example, "Democracy in Islam," *Moslem Sunrise* 3 (January 1924), 21.

[168] Dannin, *Black Pilgrimage to Islam*, 38–40.

[169] For a history of the First Cleveland Mosque, see Dannin, *Black Pilgrimage to Islam*, 96–112. For a history of the First Muslim Mosque of Pittsburgh, see Jameela A. Hakim, *History of the First Muslim Mosque of Pittsburgh, Pennsylvania* (Cedar Rapids, IA: Igram Press, 1979) and Aminah Beverly McCloud, *African American Islam* (New York: Routledge, 1995), 24–27.

FIGURE 10. A gathering at the Auto-Worker's Hall in Detroit in February 1921 to hear Muhammad Sadiq lecture on Islam. From *The Moslem Sunrise* (January 1922).

FIGURE 11. Mirza Ahmad F. L. Andersen, touted as the first American Ahmadi Moslem from the First Scientific Station, in New York City. From *The Moslem Sunrise* (October 1921), 25.

FIGURE 12. Sheikh Ahmad Din (born Paul Nathaniel Johnson) of St. Louis, MO, an early convert to the Ahmadiyya Movement in Islam, who introduced Wali Akram of the First Cleveland Mosque to Islam in 1925. From *The Moslem Sunrise* (April 1924), 68.

FIGURE 13. Mrs. Rahatullah Thaha, an early convert to the Ahmadiyya Movement in Islam. From *The Moslem Sunrise* (October 1922), 146.

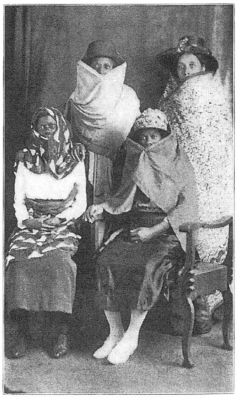

FIGURE 14. Some early converts to the Ahmadiyya Movement in Islam. From right to left: Mrs. Thomas (Sister Khairat), Mrs. Watts (Sister Zeineb), Mrs. Robinson (Sister Ahmadia), and Mrs Clark (Sister Ayesha). From *The Moslem Sunrise* (January 1923), 165.

call these communities strictly Sunni because they did not seek out Sunni teachings or consciously self-identify as such. Rather they rejected the Ahmadiyya Movement's centralized structure of authority and adopted what they assessed to be Islam based on their exposure to the religion through Ahmadiyya missionaries, the Qur'an and the Hadith (which were taught and distributed by the Ahmadiyya), and encounters with other immigrant Muslims in Cleveland and Pittsburgh at this time.[170] Over the years, however, as they learned more about Islam and communed with

---

[170] Wali Akram, the principal founder of the First Cleveland Mosque, for example, met Muslims from Yemen, Turkey, and the Levant in the Association of the Islamic Union of Cleveland. See Dannin, *Black Pilgrimage to Islam*, 97–98.

other Muslims, they came to regard their understanding of Islam as most closely affiliated with Sunni Islam, which has no central charismatic or institutional authority and considers the Prophet Muhammad bin 'Abd Allah to be the last prophet God sent to humanity.

These splits from the Ahmadiyya movement were motivated in part because the oath of allegiance (*bay'a*) that members of the Ahmadiyya Movement took to its *khalifa* or living leader made not only spiritual but also material demands on them. Whatever money local communities collected had to be sent to the regional Ahmadiyya headquarters and then redistributed among local communities. Some local, predominently black Ahmadi communities came to see themselves as financing the ventures and lifestyles of foreign missionaries and thus broke away. Some came to associate themselves with the Lahori branch of the Ahmadiyya movement which had no similar centralized authority and followed Mirza Ghulam Ahmad as a Muslim reformer rather than a prophet.[171]

Black members of the Ahmadiyya movement also faced the issue of racial solidarity and black economic advancement, both of which were central to the Moorish Science Temple and the Nation of Islam but were tangential to the mission of Ahmadis from India. Local African American leaders who sought to pursue such agendas soon realized that even though the Ahmadiyya trained converts to lead local communities, local leaders were subordinated to the international leadership of the movement, which was South Asian. Soon after declaring their independence from the Ahmadiyya, these groups thus sought to tend to the social and economic needs of the African American Muslim community. Wali Akram of the First Cleveland Mosque founded the Muslim Ten Year Plan in the late 1930s with precisely these aims in mind: "Our plan is to present the true doctrine of Islam to our fellow man and secure for its members the sole necessities of life here as well as in the Hereafter." According to a long time member of the Muslim Ten Year Plan who joined it in 1964, the plan was intended "to help those who had been disenfranchised and did not have economic strength. It was a way that we could form a commune and buy wholesale and bulk, and sell these items back to ourselves, and realize the profit in our community." In sum, the plan was intended to provide a communal structure for black Southerners who had migrated to the North in order to help them become self-sufficient, and this goal of self-sufficiency could not be realized if they remained subordinate to the interests of foreign missionaries. Once independent, however, they were confronted with

[171] Dannin, *Black Pilgrimage to Islam*, 102–103.

a lack of consensus. "[W]e are talking about people that were five years away from the plantation," retorted the above cited member of the plan. "Many of them came from Alabama, Georgia, Oklahoma, places like that, and they never ever participated in any group activity involving money other than donating to the Church. And these people were against it. And 'Negroism' came in. They argued, they bickered. Some just couldn't stay the course and left."[172] Such setbacks withstanding, it seems that the community Akram founded flourished in the 1960s and 1970s. When the Moroccan scholar Ali Kettani met with Akram as a representative of the Muslim World League in 1973, studying Muslim minority communities, he observed: "Hajj Wali Akram established the first Orthodox Sunni (*sunniyya mahda*) Islamic association in Cleveland in the early thirties, and it continues, till this day, to grow and expand. It is one of the best Islamic communities in terms of its organization, its understanding of Islam, and its adaptation to the land without undermining the religion. Hajj Wali Akram remains alive, continuing his silent struggle (*jihad*) on the path of Islam and cooperating with all Islamic organizations."[173]

NOBLE DREW ALI AND THE MOORISH SCIENCE TEMPLE

African Americans' exposure to Islam in the interwar period through Masonic lodges, the UNIA, the Ahmadiyya Movement, and immigrant Muslims, such as Duse Mohamed Ali, would not have had the historical impact it has had were it not for Noble Drew Ali's effective synthesis of Islamic and popular spiritualist practices into a prophetic nationalist movement that appealed to African American migrants from the South in search of a better livelihood in northern metropolises. The Moorish Science Temple of America (originally the Moorish Temple of Science) was organized in 1925 in Chicago and was legally incorporated in Illinois on November 29, 1926.[174] Noble Drew Ali (born Timothy Drew) was the founding prophet and the ultimate authority of the

[172] Ibid., 109 and 111.
[173] 'Alī ibn al-Muntaṣir al-Kittānī, *al-Muslimūn fī Ūrūbbā wa Āmrīkā*, vol. 2 (Beirut: Dār al-Kutub al-'Ilmiyya, [1976], 2005), 62.
[174] Noble Drew Ali, "Moorish Leader's Historical Message to America," in *Moorish Literature*, 11. Since Arthur Fauset's well-known study of the Moorish Science Temple in *Black God of the Metropolis* (1944), the founding of the Moorish Science Temple has been mistakenly dated to 1913. This mistake is based on the later mythology of the movement and is not borne out in the historical record. Edward E. Curtis IV, *Islam in Black America: Identity, Liberation, and Difference in African-American Islamic Thought* (Albany, NY: State University of New York Press, 2002), 47.

movement. He presented himself as the conduit of African Americans' "Forefathers' Divine and ancient Creed," Islam, which demonstrated to "Asiatics of America" that "they are not Negroes. Rather their true nationality is 'Moorish Americans'." In Ali's teachings, Islam became a means by which black Americans could strip themselves of the stigma associated with the color of their skin so that they could play a greater role in society. Through Islam, Ali "de-negrofied" his followers. As I argued in Chapter 1, white, Protestant Americans "de-negrofied" black Muslims in the antebellum period in order to demonstrate blacks' potential for "civilization" and thus argue for the abolition of slavery. In this discourse, enslaved black Muslims were portrayed as liminal figures who stood at the threshold of "civilization." While black Muslims in the antebellum period played a passive role, for the most part, in the processes of their "de-negrofication," in the interwar period, the prophetic founder of Moorish Science Temple (along with missionaries of the Ahmadiyya Movement and the prophetic founders of the Nation of Islam, Muhammad Fard and Elijah Muhammad) actively appropriated Islam in a "de-negrofying" process that was designed to ascribe to his followers a positive national identity. Noble Drew Ali signified and mytholigized this liminal national identity through his prophecies as "Moorish American." He urged Moorish Americans to return "the Church and Christianity back to the European Nations, as it was prepared by their forefathers for their early salvation. While we, the Moorish Americans are returning to Islam, which was founded by our forefathers for our earthly and divine salvation."[175]

In a social and cultural milieu in which race, religion, and progress were conflated, Drew Ali linked racial and religious identity within a national identity, arguing that a positive national identity was requisite to African Americans' advancement as citizens of the United States. "The object of our Organization," he wrote, "is to help the great program of uplifting fallen humanity and teach those things necessary to make our members better citizens."[176] These "things" could essentially be summed up as American middle-class values of honest hard work, sobriety, dedication to family and community, and entrepreneurship. Instilling such values, Ali taught, would bring about "economic security and power," which are necessary for progress. "A beggar people," he wrote, "cannot

---

[175] Ali, *Holy Koran of the Moorish Science Temple*, 59.
[176] Noble Drew Ali, "Moorish Leader's Historical Message to America," in *Moorish Literature*, 12.

develop the highest in them, nor can they attain to a genuine enjoyment of the spiritualities of life."[177] In these efforts, Ali considered Marcus Garvey as his divinely appointed harbinger.[178] By 1928, under Ali's leadership, some 15 Moorish Science Temples were founded throughout the United States with a collective membership of 3,000 persons.[179]

In 1927, he published a 64-page text titled *The Holy Koran of the Moorish Science Temple of America*, also known as the *Circle Seven Koran*. This text was said to have been "divinely prepared by the Noble Prophet Drew Ali." It was almost entirely a verbatim selection of two esoteric texts popular in spiritualist and mystical Masonic circles at the turn of the twentieth century. Chapters 1–19 of *The Circle Seven Koran* were copied from Levi Dowling's *The Antiquarian Gospel* (1907), an apocryphal biography of Jesus that presented him as a mystical figure who traveled to Europe, Egypt, India, and Tibet to uncover the mysteries and spiritual wisdoms of the religious traditions of these lands in order to demonstrate the metaphysical unity of existence as a form of divine emanation. The essential message of these chapters was that there is no distinction between man and God. "When man sees Allah as one with him, as Father Allah he needs no middle man, no priest, to intercede…He goes straight up to Him and says: 'My father God, Allah!' And then he lays his hands in Allah's own hand, and all is well."[180] For Ali and his followers this message of metaphysical unity fostered self-respect and emancipated one from the stigma associated with the black race. Along with this freedom, Ali taught, came responsibilities. These responsibilities were covered in chapters 20–45, and they were copied from *Unto Thee I Grant*, a text which purported to communicate ancient Chinese-Tibetan wisdom on moral behavior. The edition of this text with which Ali was familiar was most likely the 1925 edition published by the Ancient and Mystical Order of the Rosae Crucis or the Rosicrucians.[181] The purpose it served him was

---

[177] Noble Drew Ali, "Moorish Leader's Historical Message to America," in *Moorish Literature*, 13–14.

[178] Ali, *Holy Koran of the Moorish Science Temple*, 59.

[179] Debra Washington Mubashshir, "Forgotten Fruit of the City: Chicago and the Moorish Science Temple of America," *Cross Currents* (spring 2001), 13; and Nance, "Respectability and Representation," 628.

[180] Ali, *Holy Koran of the Moorish Science Temple*, 17.

[181] For further discussion of these texts in relation to the Moorish Science Temple, see Nance, "Mystery of the Moorish Science Temple: Southern Blacks and American Alternative Spirituality in 1920s Chicago," *Religion and American Culture: A Journal of Interpretation* 12, no. 2 (2002), 123–166; Frank T. Simpson, "The Moorish Science Temple and its 'Koran'," *Moslem World* 37 (1947), 56–61; Edward E. Calverley, "Negro Muslims in Hartford," *Muslim World* 55 (1965), 340–345; Wilson, *Sacred Drift*, 18–26.

to lay out a series of "holy instructions" on varying aspects of life including marriage, charity, character development, child rearing, treatment of parents, sincerity, social justice, and education. These chapters lay out the duties through which Moorish men and women who had come to realize the divine nature within themselves were supposed to purport themselves in order to advance in American society.

By appropriating the boilerplate of metaphysical religions as his own prophetic teachings, Ali sought to establish a national identity for African Americans' progress that centered on his authority. He began the concluding four chapters – which, along with a short preface, are his only original contributions to *The Circle Seven Koran* (save his replacing God with Allah in the other parts of the texts) – with the assertion that these teachings were "*civilizational*" teachings for "Moorish Americans":

The fallen sons and daughters of the Asiatic Nation of North America need to learn to love instead of hate; and to know of their higher self and lower self. This is the uniting of the Holy Koran of Mecca for teaching and instructing all Moorish Americans, etc. The key of civilization was and is in the hands of the Asiatic nations. The Moorish, who were the ancient Moabites, and the founders of the Holy City of Mecca.[182]

Noble Drew Ali then went on to assert his own authority over this Moorish nation: "These holy and divine laws are from the Prophet Noble Drew Ali, the founder of the uniting of the Moorish Science Temple of America. These laws are to be strictly preserved by the members of all the Temples, of the Moorish Science Temple of America. That they will learn to open their meanings and guide them according to the principles of Love, Truth, Peace, Freedom and Justice."[183]

It is of course difficult to see how these teachings could be *civilizational* rather than *civilizing* if they had not been attributed to a civilization. Islam, as a non-white, ancient creed of a once powerful "civilization," provided Ali with the connection to a civilization which his project demanded. To those who would challenge his teachings as the teachings of Islam, he retorted: "Moslems of India, Egypt, and Palestine had these secrets and kept them back from the outside world, and when the time appointed by Allah they loosened the keys and freed these secrets, and for the first time in ages have these secrets been delivered in the hands of the Moslems of America."[184]

---

[182] Ali, *Holy Koran of the Moorish Science Temple*, 56.
[183] Ibid., 58.
[184] Ibid., 3.

Ali's entrepreneurialism was not limited to the realm of spiritual nationalism. Like Garvey and Duse, he sought to promote black self-sufficiency by developing black businesses. He founded the Moorish Manufacturing Company, which sold bathing products, healing oils, and tonics. He published a newspaper, *Moorish Guide*, which sold for ten cents and served as the national mouthpiece of the organization. He also formed the Young Men Moorish National Business League to promote entrepreneurial activities among his followers. These business efforts were relatively successful in Ali's lifetime. In 1928, the Moorish Science Temple's varying businesses brought in about $36,000.[185]

On May 20, 1929, Ali was arrested along with nine of his followers for the murder of Claude D. Green, Ali's disenchanted business manager. Two months later, Ali died under unknown circumstances. Following his demise, several splinter groups emerged, but the bulk of the Moorish Science Temple Corporation elected Ali's chauffeur, Kirkman Bey, as its next leader.[186] The Moorish Science Temple is still in existence today.

One of Noble Drew Ali's followers, Muhammad Ezaldeen, who was familiar with the Ahmadiyya Movement, reportedly went to Cairo, Egypt in the early 1930s to study ancient Egyptian history and Islam. Upon his return to the United States he travelled in the Midwest and the East Coast proselytizing a version of Islam that combined the tenets of Sunni Islam with a myth of African American origins, which identified black Americans as a "Hamitic-Arab" people. According to Ezaldeen, through Islam, black Americans could reclaim their Hamitic-Arab identity and work collectively to improve their lot in life. Following the model of migration established by Prophet Muhammad who migrated from Mecca to Medina in 622 in order to escape persecution and establish the first Muslim polity, Ezaldeen encouraged his followers to migrate from cities to establish agricultural communes, where they could establish their own self-sufficient communities based on Islamic precepts. Between 1938 and 1941, he and some of his followers (around 140) founded such a community, called Jabul Arabiyya,[187] in rural West Valley of Cattaraugus County, New York. Soon after its founding Ezaldeen left West Valley for New Jersey, where he founded Addeynu Allahe[188] – Universal Arabic

---

[185] Gomez, *Black Crescent*, 269.

[186] Ibid., 269–271 and "Seize 60 After So. Side Cult Tragedy," *Chicago Daily Tribune*, September 26, 1929, 1.

[187] Based on the Arabic transliteration used by the community, it is impossible to render the exact meaning of this name. It is clear, however, that it was intended to convey that this is a "mountain" (*jabal*) with Arabs.

[188] Arabic for "the religion of God."

Association (AAUAA) and established the Ezaldeen Village near Camden, New Jersey. He continued his missionary work (*da'wa*) in other regions of the United States until his death in 1957. AAUAA survives till this day.[189]

THE FOUNDING OF THE NATION OF ISLAM

According to some accounts, another contender to Noble Drew Ali's mantle, known variously as David Ford, Wallace D. Fard, and Fard Muhammad, went to Detroit in 1930 where he began to preach his own version of Islam. This led to the formation of the Nation of Islam.[190] The identity of Ford or Fard is shrouded in mystery. According to the Nation of Islam's account of its origins, Fard Muhammad, who is God in person, was born on February 26, 1877 to a black man and a white woman in Mecca of the tribe of Quraysh, the tribe of the Prophet Muhammad ibn 'Abd Allah. According to the FBI's surveillance of the Nation of Islam beginning in the 1940s, Wallace D. Fard was a white man and a "racketeer" born either in Portland, Oregon or New Zealand. Others have suggested that he was of Indian descent and came to the West Coast of the United States illegally through Canada.[191] While Fard's biography would help shed light on the exact relation between Masonry, the UNIA, immigrant Muslims, metaphysical religions, the Moorish Science Temple, and the Nation of Islam, the details of his controversial biography need not concern us. As the above discussion I hope has shown, there was a synergy of ideas, techniques, and symbols between these groups in the interwar period. Whatever Fard's background, in 1930, he became a significant player in this dynamic field.

According to the sole field study of the Nation of Islam in the 1930s, Fard was a street peddler, who used his profession to enter people's homes and proselytize. He, like Noble Drew Ali, developed a foundation myth for African Americans that sought to "de-negrofy" his

---

[189] Margaret L. Fess, "Mohammedan Village Byproduct of Depression," *Buffalo Carrier Express* June 2, 1946. For further discussion of Ezaldeen and AAUAA, see Dannin, *Pilgrimage to Islam*, 47–55 and 121–131; www.aauaa.org/ezaldeen.html (accessed July 17, 2009); and Turner, *Islam in the African-American Experience*, xviii.

[190] Mubashshir, "Forgotten Fruit of the City," 16; and Clifton E. Marsh, *The Lost-Found Nation of Islam in America* (Lanham, MD: Scarecrow Press, 2000), 37.

[191] For some of the varying theories on Fard's origins, see Erdmann Doane Beynon, "The Voodoo Cult Among Negro Migrants in Detroit," *American Journal of Sociology* 43, no. 6 (May 1938), 896–897; Gomez, *Black Crescent*, 277–278; Karl Evanzz, *The Messenger: The Rise and Fall of Elijah Muhammad* (New York: Vintage Books, 2001), 402–407; Clegg III, *An Original Man*, 20–21.

followers by ascribing to them a new national identity founded on select Islamic beliefs and practices. He taught that African Americans were a godly race descended from the tribe of Shabazz. They had been stolen from the Holy City of Mecca about four centuries ago by whites, who represent the devil incarnate. Fard's mission was to restore blacks to their original religion, language, and culture through Islam and in doing so restore them to their original divine nature. Like Noble Drew Ali, Fard sought to instill discipline and middle-class values in his followers in order to uplift them in American society. He preached obedience to God's will, sobriety, abstinence from alcohol and certain types of "poison animals" such as "the hog." These ills, he taught, were part of the "tricknology" used by Caucasian devils to enslave blacks and keep them illiterate, economically destitute, and ignorant of their true selves. Fard's efforts met with success. By 1934, he reportedly had about 8,000 followers in Detroit. As the number of his adherents grew, they rented a hall for their meetings. Fard initiated a parochial school called the University of Islam, a training group to teach women to be "proper" wives and mothers called the Muslim Girls Training and General Civilization Classes (MGT and GCC), and an unarmed security force comprised of men called the Fruit of Islam (FOI). His followers also managed to improve their economic life during the Great Depression. At the time of their first contact with Fard, almost all of the members of the Nation of Islam were unemployed and receiving public welfare. By August 1937, practically all of these individuals were employed and living in economically better neighborhoods.[192]

In 1934, Fard mysteriously disappeared after some of his followers were accused of sacrificially killing four "Caucasian devils" in order to return to their homeland in Mecca.[193] After some controversy, Elijah Muhammad (originally Elijah Poole) emerged as the leader of the Nation of Islam. Technically Elijah did not succeed Fard. Rather, Fard came to be regarded in the Nation of Islam as God incarnate and Elijah Muhammad came to be known as his messenger. Under Elijah's leadership, and with the help of Malcolm X, the Nation of Islam in the 1950s and 1960s grew to become the most successful black nationalist movement in the United States.[194]

---

[192] Beynon, "The Voodoo Cult," 895–901.
[193] Ibid., 905.
[194] Clegg III, *An Original Man*, 157 and 163.

UNIVERSALIZING THE PARTICULAR: THE SIGNIFICANCE OF PROPHECY IN THE RISE OF ISLAM IN BLACK AMERICA

In the earliest scholarship on African American Islam, the Moorish Science Temple and the Nation of Islam were understood to have been nationalist movements that referred to Islam in order to signify a positive African American identity.[195] Islam was a means to deflect the stigma associated with the black race and to gain both recognition and self-respect. By teaching their adherents to adopt middle-class American values of sobriety, entrepreneurship, and hard work, the Moorish Science Temple and the Nation of Islam demonstrated to African American migrants from the South how "one could be racially proud and practically self-interested, without being 'uppity'."[196] In other words, references to Islam and the adoption of Masonic motifs, structures, and rituals paved a path to middle-class status for poor African Americans who had been left out of an American modernity that mapped progress onto the white race and Protestantism.

More recent scholars of these movements have argued that by interpreting these movements as pioneering appropriations of Islam for the sake of a positive, uplifting black national identity, we overlook the religious dimension of their movement and reduce them to political ideologies. In order to redeem the religious dimension of these movements in narratives of African American Islam, these scholars have argued that the history of African American Islam oscillates between particularist concerns (African nationalism) and religious universalism (Islamic religion).[197]

To these interpretations of the historical significance of the Moorish Science Temple and the Nation of Islam, I wish to add a third dimension, one that highlights the entrepreneurialism and synthetic eclecticism that were key to their success. A person walking on the south side of Chicago in 1927 was likely to learn about Noble Drew Ali by coming across a posted advertisement for "the great Moorish drama" in which Drew Ali was depicted in a regal Shriners custume with his right hand placed reverently over his heart. The poster invited people to attend the Moorish Holy Temple of Science at the community center to see the "Moorish drama" enacted by "men, women, and children" demonstrating "the need of a nationality." At the performance, Drew Ali lectured on "events

---

[195] C. Eric Lincoln, *The Black Muslims* (Boston, MA: Beacon, 1961); E. U. Essien-Udom, *Black Nationalism: A Search for an Identity in America* (New York: Dell, 1962); Marsh, *The Lost-Found Nation of Islam in America*.

[196] Nance, "Respectability and Representation," 628.

[197] Curtis, *Islam in Black America*, 12–20; McCloud, *African American Islam*, 3–5.

in the last days among the inhabitants of North America" and on "this Nationalistic topic." Madame Lomax Bey sang for the audience. Drew Ali was also bound at the event "as Jesus was bound in the Temple of Jerusalem and escaped before the authorities could take charge of Him; so will the Prophet Drew Ali, perform the same act, after being bound by anyone in the audience and will escape in a few seconds." The Prophet also promised to "heal many in the audience with touching them, free of charge…manifesting his divine power." Admission to the event was 50 cents for adults and 25 cents for children.[198]

The historical significance of this eclectic combination of entertainment, healing, salvation, nationalism, entrepreneurialism, and prophecy is distorted if it is reduced to the binary opposition of nationalist particularism and religious universalism. Such a binary approach to religion and politics obfuscates the centrality of prophecy in the Moorish Science Temple and the Nation of Islam. Noble Drew Ali, Master Fard Muhammad, and the Honorable Elijah Muhammad were all prophetic figures who, like all prophets, sought to *universalize* their *particular* experiences. They sought to universalize African American experiences in a way that would reconfigure the conflation of race, religion, and progress to "de-negrofy" their followers and to allow blacks to partake in American modernity. Prophecy was crucial in this process just as it was for the Ahmadiyya in their struggle against Christian claims of superiority in British India. Unlike white Protestants, none of these modern prophets of Islam could put on triumphant world expositions to celebrate their military, scientific, or industrial achievements. Their conflation of blackness, Islam, and progress rested on an argument for their divine potential for progress rather than the progress they had actually achieved. Noble Drew Ali, Wallace Fard, and Elijah Muhammad had to explain why historically African Americans had not achieved their potential given their divine nature. Why had they been dominated by whites and wrestled away from their ancestral lands, if they were truly a people with divine potential? Prophetic pronouncements by Ali, Fard, and Elijah regarding the divine origins of "lost-found nation" of African Americans, the innate divinity of humanity, the evil nature of whites whose end was prophesied to be at hand, and blacks' estrangement from their "original" religion of Islam, all went to address these dilemmas. These leaders explained that their followers' economic and political status was not what God had in mind for them. They vehemently rejected the notion of otherworldly conceptions of salvation that called for the

---

[198] A photocopy of this poster can be found in Wilson, *Sacred Drift*, 30.

disadvantaged to be content with their lot in this life in hopes of a better life in the hereafter. They also established prophetic laws and institutions, which they argued were divinely inspired and thus provided the means and knowledge by which African Americans could realize their divine potential in the here and now. Their efforts were eclectic because their prophetic project was instrumental. They had identified the pivotal role the conflation of race, religion, and progress played in America's national narrative and were motivated to employ whatever means were available to them to make religious sense of their own place in this narrative as African Americans. To say that Islam played an instrumental role in their prophetic missions does not mean that the founders or members of the Moorish Science Temple or the Nation of Islam did not wholeheartedly believe in the divine nature of their religion or in its claims to be truly Islamic. On the contrary, their appropriation of Islamic symbols, myths, and practices not only lent divine authority to their prophetic claims but Islam also provided a non-Christian, non-white context in which their prophetic teachings became all the more sensible as a religion.

6

Islam and American Civil Religion in the Aftermath of World War II

World War II significantly altered America's national identity. As Americans of varying ethnicities, religions, and gender united to fight a devastating war under the banner of liberty, American citizenship could hardly have been conceived through a conflated matrix of race, religion, and progress. The old white Protestant establishment was reconfigured and a new national identity emerged based on political loyalty to the founding liberal democratic values articulated in the Declaration of Independence and the Constitution. In response to this new American identity, immigrant Muslims began developing national organizations. The American-born children of Muslim immigrants took the lead in creating a national umbrella organization to complement and promote American Muslims' local activities. They were no longer satisfied with simply rooting Islam in America but wanted Islam recognized as an American religion.

Within African American Muslim communities, the chasm between the realities of discrimination and the democratic ideals through which America self-identified after World War II was a powerful example not only of hypocrisy but also of the fact that nearly a century after the Civil War, black Americans still remained outside America's national narrative. In this context, black nationalist Muslim movements' critique of Christianity as a "white man's religion" and their appropriation of Islam as the national religion of African America proved very appealing. It attracted numerous converts and ensconced Islam in black America as a religion of liberation. During the Civil Rights Movement, it Islamicized a significant segment of African America.

World War II also established the United States as a world power and increased America's involvement in Muslim-majority countries, particularly in the Middle East. Consequently, new channels of political and cultural exchange were established between Muslim-majority countries and the United States. The number of international students from Muslim-majority countries increased gradually throughout the 1950s and 1960s. Many of these students had been politicized by nationalist and Islamist movements at home, and like earlier immigrant activists, they took advantage of the freedoms found in the United States to organize around their varying ideologies. For those Muslim students who were influenced by such Islamist organizations as Jama'at-i Islami and the Muslim Brotherhood, the diversity of the American Muslim population provided an opportunity to put their utopian ideas of a pan-Islamic society into practice. *Islamism* is an ideal type that refers to the ideologizing of Islam. In this era of Islamic revival, Islamist organizations and their supporters reified Islam as a set of first principles derived from their readings of the Qur'an and the Prophetic traditions of Muhammad ibn 'Abd Allah (known as the Sunna and compiled in the Hadith), which they argued ought to govern every aspect of humans' lives. In the United States with its Muslim student population, these organizations found a more-than-adequate mix of material resources, enthusiasm, missionary impulse, and ethnic diversity to test the mettle of the Islamist ideology that inspired their activism.

WORLD WAR II AS A WATERSHED: THE SEARCH OF A NEW AMERICAN NATIONAL IDENTITY

World War II was a watershed in the multicultural history of the United States. The racist atrocities committed by the Nazis led Americans to take a more critical look at the racism within their own society. Social scientists wrote about the "fallacy of race." One politician argued, "Today it is becoming increasingly apparent to thoughtful Americans that we cannot fight the forces of imperialism abroad and maintain a form of imperialism at home.... Our very proclamation of what we are fighting for have rendered our own inequities self-evident. When we talk of freedom of opportunity for all nations, the mocking paradoxes in our own society become so clear that they can no longer be ignored."[1]

---

[1] Cited in Ronald Takaki, *A Different Mirror: A History of Multicultural America* (Boston, MA: Little, Brown, and Company, 1993), 373–374.

Such critical examination of race relations in the United States, coupled with the exigencies of war – which enlisted the manpower of Americans of all races, religions, and gender – forced a reframing of America's national character. It was difficult to think of "our country" as an Anglo-Saxon Protestant one when second-generation Jews, Catholics, Muslims, Buddhists, and Sikhs of varying ethnicities had fought and died for America's freedom. Perhaps the promise and the peril of this emerging new national character were most vividly embodied in the armed forces. Upon announcing the establishment of the 442nd combat team, which was composed mainly of Japanese-American soldiers, President Franklin D. Roosevelt asserted that "no loyal citizen of the United States should be denied the democratic right to exercise the responsibilities of citizenship, regardless of his ancestry. The principle on which this country was founded and by which it has always been governed is that Americanism is a matter of the mind and heart; Americanism is not, and never was, a matter of race or ancestry. A good American is one who is loyal to this country and to our creed of liberty and democracy."[2] Ironically, the 442nd combat team was a segregated unit in an army that also segregated its African American fighters and favored placing its colored soldiers under the command of white officers.[3] Moreover, "[t]he president's statement did not close the [Japanese-American] internment camps, offer reparations to internees, challenge U.S. laws restricting naturalized citizenship to 'white' immigrants, or contest state laws denying Japanese Americans the right to vote, to marry freely, or to own property."[4]

World War II necessitated a rethinking of racist practices in the United States and forged a multireligious and multiracial – though segregated – army, but it did not rid American society of racism. This fact was particularly visible to African Americans. "We are not exaggerating when we say that the American Negro is damned tired of spilling his blood for empty promises of better days," asserted the *Chicago Defender*. "Why die for democracy for some foreign country when we don't even have it here?"[5] Members of the Moorish Science Temple and the Nation of Islam resisted registering for selective service on the grounds that they would fight a white man's war. The FBI, which had begun its surveillance

---

[2] Cited in Austin Sarat and Thomas R. Kearns, *Cultural Pluralism, Identity, and the Law* (Ann Arbor, MI: University of Michigan Press, 2001), 135.
[3] Claude Andrew Clegg III, *An Original Man: The Life and Times of Elijah Muhammad* (New York: Macmillan, 1998), 83.
[4] Sarat and Kearns, *Cultural Pluralism, Identity, and Law*, 136.
[5] Cited in Takaki, *A Different Mirror*, 395.

of the Nation of Islam during World War II, intensified its scrutiny of the movement and arrested some of its members, including its leader, Elijah Muhammad, for draft-dodging in the early 1940s.[6] Aside from trying to quell black dissent, the FBI was concerned about any seditious influence that Satokata Takahashi, a Japanese national who sought to bolster support among blacks for the Japanese Empire as the "champion of the darker races," may have had on the Nation of Islam.[7] During their interrogations, however, members of the Nation of Islam laid to rest such concerns and informed the FBI that they refused to sign up for the draft because it "was contrary to the law of Allah."[8]

While the state read the Nation of Islam's separatist ideology as a sign of disloyalty and possible threat, the Nation of Islam's refusal to participate in the war had less to do with sedition than with its members' conversion to a new prophetic religion. In the Nation of Islam's mythology and prophetic teachings, the black self was defined not by African Americans' experiences in America, which were dehumanizing, but rather by their inherent divine nature, which they believed white America had stolen from them through slavery and Jim Crow. The Nation of Islam inculcated this new self-identity in its members not only through its mythology but also through rituals and practices that helped its members embody their new "superior" identity in their daily lives.[9] These rituals and practices were a result of a syncretistic synthesis of Islam, Christianity, and puritanical injunctions that were believed to help improve blacks' lot in America. In their sermons and writings, leaders of the Nation of Islam relied on the Bible as much as, if not more so, than the Qur'an. The Nation proscribed a ritual prayer for its members that was to be performed five times a day and consisted of the recitation of the first chapter of the Qur'an, *al-Fatiha*, in English. (*Al-Fatiha* is recited in the tradition Muslim ritual prayer in Arabic.) It also enjoined an annual fast to be observed during the Christmas season in December rather than during the month of Ramadan in the Islamic lunar calendar. The reason

---

[6] Clegg III, *An Original Man*, 84–85.

[7] Ernest Allen, Jr., "When Japan Was 'Champion of the Darker Race': Satokata Takahashi and the Flowering of Black Messianic Nationalism," *Black Scholar* 24, no. 1 (Winter 1994), 23–47.

[8] "Gulam Bogans," June 13, 1942, 2–3 (W. D. Fard FBI File), cited in Clegg III, *An Original Man*, 85.

[9] Edward E. Curtis IV, "Islamizing the Black Body: Ritual and Power in Elijah Muhammad's Nation of Islam," *Religion and American Culture* 12, no. 2 (Summer 2002), 167–196 and Edward E. Curtis IV, *Black Muslim Religion in the Nation of Islam* (Chapel Hill, NC: UNC Press, 2006), 95–174.

given for this was that December is the month during which Americans were most prone to fall victim to materialistic temptations and thus most in need of restraining themselves. The Nation also prohibited the use of alcohol, drugs, cigarettes, and pork products. It discouraged the use of fatty foods and overeating. It sought to instill a Puritan work ethic in its members by forbidding dancing, gambling, dating, attending movies, playing sports, taking long vacations, domestic quarreling, and any discourtesy. Whatever one may think of these rituals and injunctions, their disciplining effect in the lives of the members of the Nation was powerful. Malcolm X described the positive, liberating effect the quotidian routines in a Nation of Islam household had on him when he left prison:

There was none of the morning confusion that exists in most homes. Wilfred [his brother], the father, the family protector and provider, was the first to rise. 'The father prepares the way for his family,' he said. He, then I, performed the morning ablutions. Next came Wilfred's wife, Ruth, and then their children, so that orderliness prevailed in the use of the bathroom. 'In the name of Allah, I perform the ablution,' the Muslim said aloud before washing first the right hand, then the left hand. The teeth were thoroughly brushed, followed by three rinsings out of the mouth. The nostrils also were rinsed out thrice. A shower then completed the whole body's purification in readiness for prayer. Each family member, even children upon meeting each other for that new day's first time, greeted softly and pleasantly, 'As-Salaam-Alaikum' (the Arabic for 'Peace be unto you'). 'Wa-Alaikum-salaam' ('and unto you be peace') was the other's reply. Over and over again, the Muslim said in his own mind, 'Allahu-Akbar, Allahu-Akbar' ('Allah is the greatest'). The prayer rug was spread by Wilfred while the rest of the family purified themselves. It was explained to me that a Muslim family prayed with the sun near the horizon. If that time was missed, the prayer had to be deferred until the sun was beyond the horizon. 'Muslims are not sun-worshipers. We pray facing the East to be in unity with the rest of our 725 million brothers and sisters in the entire Muslim world.' All the family, in robes, lined up facing East. In unison, we stepped from our slippers to stand on the prayer rug…. No solid food, only juice and coffee, was taken for our breakfasts. Wilfred and I went off to work. There, at noon and again at around three in the afternoon, unnoticed by others in the furniture store, we would rinse our hands, faces and mouths, and softly meditate. Muslim children did likewise at school, and Muslim wives and mothers interrupted their chores to join the world's 725 million Muslims in communicating with God.[10]

The Nation of Islam's mythology and religious practices reconfigured African Americans' self-understanding by distancing them from their racist social and political context. As such, duty to God and duty to country

[10] Malcolm X and Alex Haley, *The Autobiography of Malcolm X* (New York: Ballantine Books, 1992), 193–194.

FIGURE 15. Cartoon by E. Majied from the newspaper of the Nation of Islam, *Muhammad Speaks*, September 16, 1965, 9.

for the members of the Nation of Islam were irreconcilable. For its members, going to war for the sake of America would have meant denying the sense of self-worth that the Nation of Islam sought to embody in them by estranging them from white America. For most other Americans at this time of war, however, the inherent tension between one's duty to God and one's duty to country were not to be maintained but reconciled. And given the inhumane practices of the Nazis, this reconciliation was not difficult to achieve. To go to war against fascist imperialist regimes was to do God's work on earth.

In fact, a religion of "Americanism" emerged from America's involvement in World War II that sought to unify Americans of varying ethnicities and religious backgrounds through the amorphous concept of loyalty to American democratic values. The perceived threat of Communism and the sense of doubt and moral ambiguity that resulted from the horrific acts of so-called civilized nations during two world wars made the quest of attaining some sort of religious consensus a societal imperative for most Americans. In 1948, the Executive Committee of the National Education Association of the United States charged its Educational Policies Commission, which included General Dwight D. Eisenhower, to recommend ways "to improve the teaching of moral and spiritual values." The commission accepted the charge, and it published its recommendations in a booklet titled *Moral and Spiritual Values in the Public Schools.*[11] As the members of this commission argued, the necessity of religion – dubbed "moral and spiritual values" – for American society at this time could not be clearer:

Whether we consider the social effects of recent wars, the remoteness of workers from the satisfaction of personal achievement, the mounting complexity of

[11] I am grateful to Emily B. Miller for bringing this book to my attention.

government, the increasing amount of aimless leisure, the changing patterns of home and family life, or current international tensions, the necessity for attention to moral and spiritual values emerges again and again. Moral decisions of unprecedented variety and complexity must be made by the American people. An unremitting concern for moral and spiritual values continues to be a top priority for education.[12]

The Commission further explained that "such an education must be derived, not from some synthetic patchwork of many religious views, but rather from the moral and spiritual values which are shared by the members of all religious faiths."[13] The content of these shared values, however, was a foregone conclusion: "By moral and spiritual values we mean those values which, when applied in human behavior, exalt and refine life and bring it into accord with the standards of conduct that are approved in *our democratic* culture" (emphasis mine).[14]

The notion that religion is essential to the political and national character of the United States was famously stated by President-elect Dwight Eisenhower in a speech he delivered to the directors of the Freedoms Foundation on December 22, 1952. Eisenhower tried to explain the difficulty Americans had explaining the founding principles of their government to the Soviets by recalling a conversation with his World War II friend Marshal Georgi K. Zhukov of the Soviet army: "Our Government has no sense unless it is founded in a deeply felt religious faith and I don't care what it is. With us of course it is the Judo-Christian (sic) concept, but it must be a religion that all men are created equal. So what was the use of talking to Zhukov about that? Religion, he had been taught, was the opiate of the people." Eisenhower further proclaimed that the struggle against Communism could only be won by going back to the fundamentals of our country, "and one of them is that we are a religious people. If we can sell ourselves this idea at home, we can win the ideological war.... We can then stand before the world in that strength, and all of the other nations will see that our leadership is not one of imperialism, but one of purity. It is one of integrity, with a belief in the dignity of man and they will go along."[15]

---

[12] Educational Policies Commission, *Moral and Spiritual Values in the Public Schools* (National Education Association, 1951), 12.

[13] Ibid., 6.

[14] Ibid., 3.

[15] "President-Elect Says Soviet Demoted Zhukov Because of Their Friendship," *New York Times*, December 23, 1952, 16.

As Eisenhower's famous statement regarding the essentially religious nature of America's national character demonstrates,[16] in the aftermath of World War II, the "universal religion" of Anglo-Saxon Protestantism through which a unified American national identity had been sought following the Civil War gave way to the "universal religion" of American democratic values and political institutions to which people of any race and religion could subscribe. In the aftermath of World War II, just as in the aftermath of the Civil War, religion played an important role in the way in which America redefined itself in light of its growing recognition of racial, gender, and religious diversity. Amidst competing interests of different religious and racial communities, religion was posited as a universal source of morality that could transcend these differences to provide unity at home and divinely guided action abroad.

Will Herberg powerfully described the unifying religious fervor and spirit of this age in his influential *Protestant-Catholic-Jew: An Essay in American Religious Sociology* (1955). Herberg was a theologian at Drew University who played a sociologist in this monumental book. His was "the most comprehensive and widely read analysis" of post–World War II religion at the time.[17] Herberg sought to explain the surge in religious life in the postwar era, but he is mostly remembered for his assertion that in following World War II, the old crucible of American society had become a "triple melting pot" of Protestantism, Catholicism, and Judaism. Herberg commented on how "religion has suddenly emerged as a major power in the 'hundred years of Cold War' that appears to confront mankind,"[18] but his analysis drew mainly on the work of the historian of immigration Marcus Hansen's argument that there were different generational processes of assimilation. While the children of immigrants generally eschewed their distinct cultural and linguistic heritage in order to assimilate into mainstream society, their grandchildren, who were more comfortable with their identity as Americans, were keen to "remember" what their parents were eager to "forget." What in particular attracted Herberg to Hansen's argument was that third-generation

---

[16] For a study of the legacy of Eisenhower's famous assertion, see Patrick Henry, "'And I Don't Care What It Is': The Tradition–History of a Civil Religion Proof-Text," *Journal of the American Academy of Religion* 49, no. 1 (March 1981), 35–49.

[17] William R. Hutchison, *Religious Pluralism in America: The Contentious History of a Founding Ideal* (New Haven, CT: Yale University Press, 2004), 201.

[18] Will Herberg, *Protestant-Catholic-Jew: An Essay in American Religious Sociology* (Chicago, IL: University of Chicago Press, 1955), 61.

immigrants could more readily revive the religion of their grandparents in their lives than any other aspect of their culture:

"What the son wishes to forget" – so runs "Hansen's law" – "the grandson wishes to remember." But what he can "remember" is obviously not his grandfather's foreign language, or even his grandfather's foreign culture; it is rather his grandfather's *religion* – America does not demand of him the abandonment of the ancestral religion as it does of the ancestral language and culture. This religion he now "remembers" in a form suitably "Americanized," and yet in a curious way also "retraditionalized." Within this comprehensive framework of basic sociological change operate those inner factors making for a "return to religion" which so many observers have noted in recent years – the collapse of all secular securities in the historical crisis of our time, the quest for a recovery of meaning in life, the new search for inwardness and personal authenticity amid the collectivistic heteronomies of the present-day world.[19]

The third generation remembered a religion that was stripped of its linguistic and cultural specificities. It was "Americanized." It entailed "a certain religious unity in terms of a common 'American religion' of which each of the three great religious communions is regarded as an equilegitimate expression." Herberg concluded, "Americanness today entails religious identification as Protestant, Catholic, or Jew in a way and to a degree quite unprecedented in our history. To be a Protestant, a Catholic, or a Jew are today the alternative ways of being an American." On the other hand, to "profess oneself a Buddhist, a Muslim, or anything but a Protestant, Catholic, or Jew, even when one's Americanness is otherwise beyond question" would "imply being foreign." "Or, it may imply being obscurely 'un-American', as is the case with those who declare themselves atheists, agnostics, or even 'humanists'."[20]

   In his portrayal of the new religious consensus on religious diversity, Herberg only identified as American those religions predominantly followed by whites. As evinced by the civil rights struggle of the 1950s and 1960s, race continued to play a problematic role in efforts to consolidate an American national identity following World War II. As his black contemporaries noted, Herberg overlooked black Protestant churches. He wrote, "The churches of the immigrants [i.e., white immigrants] ultimately became American churches and an integral, often indistinguishable part of the American denominational scheme. The Negro churches, entirely American to start with, still stand outside the general system, just

---

[19] Ibid., 257.
[20] Ibid., 257–258.

as the Negro still stands largely outside the general pattern of American life." He concluded his discussion of black churches by politely dismissing them from his project as "an anomaly of considerable importance in the general sociological scheme of the 'triple melting pot'."[21]

In addition to racial problems, what contemporaries who celebrated Herberg's work often overlooked was his theological critique of America's common-denominator religion as shallow and nationalistic. After a sociological discussion of how American identity was consolidated after World War II through religion, Herberg re-donned his theologian's hat in the last chapter of his book to highlight the perils of equating what a country demands of its citizens with what God demands of the faithful.

In its crudest form, this identification of religion with national purpose generates a kind of national messianism which sees it as the vocation of America to bring the American Way of Life, compounded almost equally of democracy and free enterprise, to every corner of the globe; in more mitigated versions, it sees God as the champion of America, endorsing American purposes, and sustaining American might.... Insensibly, this fusion of religion with national purpose passes over into the direct exploitation of religion for economic and political ends.[22]

Herberg described for his contemporaries the reconfiguration of the conflation of race, religion, and progress, which had resulted in catastrophic wars, into a conflation of nationalism, religion, and democracy, which he labeled as "Americanism" and condemned as "idolatrous."[23]

Robert Bellah's equally influential essay on "Civil Religion in America" sought to redeem "Americanism" as an essential unifying force in American society by distinguishing it as a "civil religion" that existed alongside the individual religions Americans practiced: "While some have argued that Christianity is the national faith, and others that church and synagogue celebrate only the generalized religion of 'the American Way of Life'," Bellah wrote, "few have realized that there actually exists alongside of and rather clearly differentiated from the churches an elaborate and well-institutionalized civil religion in America."[24] Bellah argued that what had unified American society over the years had not been its essentially religious character but its essentially poly-religious character, that Americans had participated in their own specific religions (Protestantism, Deism, Catholicism, Judaism, etc.) while simultaneously participating

[21] Ibid, 114.
[22] Ibid., 264.
[23] Ibid., 263.
[24] Robert Bellah, "Civil Religion in America," *Dædalus* 96, no. 1 (Winter 1967), 1.

in a civil religion in which democracy, freedom, and equality were not just political values but spiritual values organic to the experiences of the American body politic. Bellah acknowledged that Americans had often fallen short of living up to these values, but the American experience had been and continued to be shaped by a revolutionary effort to realize them. By distinguishing America's civil religion from the varying religions Americans practiced, Bellah sought to counter the notion that a commitment to America's national purpose adulterates or trivializes individual religious beliefs and commitments.

AMERICAN MUSLIMS AND AMERICAN NATIONAL IDENTITY AFTER WORLD WAR II

Whatever theological objections individual Americans may have had to "Americanism," most Americans, as evidenced by Eisenhower's, Herberg's, and Bellah's assessments of religion in the post–World War II era, agreed that America's national purpose was defined by its religious self-understanding, which *in theory* was no longer identified by a race or a particular religious tradition but rather by adherence to America's democratic values as defined by the Declaration of Independence and the Constitution.

American Muslims' response to this new definition of the national character, just as the society's response at large, tended to be polarized along racial lines. On the one hand, those immigrants, predominantly from the Levant, who had sought inclusion into America's matrix of race, religion, and progress understood Islam as yet another compartment that could be added to Herberg's tripartite melting pot of Protestantism, Catholicism, and Judaism. On the other, there were prophetic black nationalist voices that rejected America's civil religion as hypocritical by pointing to the structural inequities of race and class that continued to plague American society.

SEEKING INCLUSION IN THE NEW NATIONAL CONSENSUS

The Federation of Islamic Associations of the United States and Canada (FIA) was an umbrella organization that represented American Muslims' first significant attempt to define Islam as yet another of the monotheistic religions upon which American values were founded. While the FIA's membership and activities did extend into Canada, much of its work centered on developments in the United States. For this reason, and since its role in Canada is beyond the scope of this study, I discuss its activities in national terms. The FIA was the principal and most successful umbrella Muslim organization of immigrant Muslims in the 1950s and 1960s. It was the brainchild of Abdallah Igram, a second-generation Arab American Muslim who had served as an officer during World War II. Igram, like many other ethnic Americans who fought in World War II, felt that he had demonstrated his unquestionable loyalty to the United States and was no longer willing to tolerate the denial of his religious identity. A publication of the FIA read that "[w]hile in the service during World War II, Abdallah Igram recognized a lack of information and misinterpretation of the tenets of Islam, the second largest monotheistic faith in the world. As a solution to the problem, he envisioned an organization that would achieve equal recognition for the American Muslim."[25] Igram had envisioned a federation of local Muslim associations that would help foster national American Muslim unity while supporting and promoting the efforts of local American Muslim communities. It is not known exactly when Igram began work on achieving his vision, but seven years after the end of World War II his vision was first realized in the form of the International Muslim Society, which held its first convention of about 400 Muslims on June 28, 1952 in Cedar Rapids, Iowa. It was later renamed the Federation of Islamic Associations in the United States and Canada.[26] Once Igram realized his idea of an umbrella American Muslim association, he approached President Eisenhower in 1953 to ask, "Why is there no symbol for the Islamic faith on a Muslim serviceman's identification tags so that he might be given fitting burial rites if he's killed in action?" Igram's query led to the use of an "I" on the dog tags of American Muslim soldiers.[27] Igram served as the first president of the FIA (1952–1955). The second and third presidents of the FIA, Hassan Ibrahim (1955–1957) and Kassem Alwan (1957–1959), were also World War II veterans.[28] The fact that the first three presidents of the FIA were all veterans attests to the impact of the war on the development of a national American Muslim identity in the 1950s and the 1960s.

---

[25] Cited in Abdo A. Elkholy, *The Arab Moslems in the United States* (New Haven, CT: College & University Press, 1966), 46.

[26] This change occurred in 1954. Elkholy, *Arab Moslems in the United States*, 46–47.

[27] Philip Harsham, "Islam in Iowa," *Saudi Aramco World* 27, no. 6 (November/December 1976). The article is available online at the following www.saudiaramcoworld.com/issue/197606/islam.in.iowa.htm (accessed February 2, 2009).

[28] Gutbi Mahdi Ahmed, "Muslim Organizations in the United States" in *The Muslims of America*, ed. Yvonne Y. Haddad (New York: Oxford University Press, 1991), 13.

While the founders of the FIA were primarily second-generation American Muslims from the Levant, the organization also included some Albanian, South Asian, Iranian, and African American Muslims. The aims of the FIA, as articulated in the 1954 constitution and reiterated in its annual convention bulletins, was to unite the Muslim community in the United States and Canada "to promote and teach the spirit, ethics, philosophy, and culture of Islam among themselves and their children." The FIA also reflected the nation's mood as a whole by identifying unity and peace as social imperatives that could be attained through "spiritual and moral values." The FIA sought to "point out the common grounds, beliefs, and common ends which other religions share with Islam" and urged its member associations "in this age of international strife and unrest ... [to] draw on the spiritual, moral, and intellectual wealth of the Moslem civilization and contribute their proper share in the establishment of world peace."[29]

The FIA put a national face on American Islam as it was interpreted and practiced by Muslims of immigrant descent from the Levant, but its actual national activities were limited. Its primary activity was its annual convention. It was mainly a conduit through which individual Muslims reaffirmed their unity in Islam in order to help local Muslim communities flourish. Its constitution clearly placed the burden of organization on its constituent associations: "The Moslem communities in the United States and Canada should organize themselves into Local Associations to translate the above objectives within their communities. These local organizations should, beside the teaching and observance of the principles of Islam, administer to the religious needs of the members of their community. They should also provide media for the religious, intellectual, and social needs of their members, and tender them with moral, legal, and financial comfort."[30]

The annual conventions of the FIA were mainly social and fundraising events during which local Muslim communities reported on their individual activities, renewed their commitment to their faith as pioneers of American Islam, and partook in dances and musical performances. The convention was hosted each year by Muslim communities in different cities, which gave local Muslim associations an opportunity to showcase their progress.[31] Their goal was to root

---

[29] See a reprint of the constitution in Elkholy, *Arab Moslems in the United States*, 153–154.

[30] Ibid., 154.

[31] Sally Howell, "The Federation of Islamic Associations of North America and Canada," in *Encyclopedia of Islam in the United States*, ed. Jocelyne Cesari (Westport, CT: Greenwood Press, 2007), vol. I, 243.

Islam within local American communities and to make it an important aspect of their lives in America.

In all of its efforts from its founding until the 1970s, the FIA saw little to no contradiction between Islam and America's civil religion. On the contrary, as the preamble to its constitution clearly demonstrates, members of the FIA believed that Islam positively affirmed the democratic values of America's civil religion: "Moslems, wherever they are and in whatever age they live, are individually and collectively responsible to learn, exercise, and spread the ideals of Islam, such as the dignity and supreme worth of every human being, brotherhood, and love among all mankind, and the absolute equality of every person before God."[32] In short, Islam, rather than being an obstacle to American Muslims' participation in American life, was instrumental to it. This notion was confirmed by the best available sociological study of Arab American Muslims in Detroit and Toledo in the early 1960s, whose author, Abdo Elkholy, concluded: "Contrary to what was expected, assimilation worked hand in hand with religiosity; that is, the higher in religiosity, the more assimilated the community is to the American society."[33]

THE HYPOCRISY OF AMERICAN DEMOCRACY: THE NATION OF ISLAM, MALCOLM X, AND THE STRUGGLE FOR CIVIL RIGHTS

Elkholy's study, while highlighting the fact that Syrian and Lebanese Muslims were integrating into American society, also noted that these Muslims had been helped in this by "the absence of any physical or color traits to distinguish them from the American majority."[34] Indeed, race and skin color continued to play a significant role in the way in which Muslims experienced America in the aftermath of World War II.

As I mentioned earlier, unlike most Americans who viewed victory in the war as a crusade in which America triumphed over evil, members of the Nation of Islam viewed World War II as a "white man's war." They wanted no part of it. This did not mean that they disagreed with the ideals of America's civil religion. They did not. They were simply keenly aware of the hypocritical gap between these ideals and the realities they experienced:

[32] See a reprint of the constitution in Elkholy, *Arab Moslems in the United States*, 153.
[33] Elkholy, *Arab Moslems in the United States*, 149.
[34] Ibid., 151.

We believe that the offer of integration is hypocritical and is made by those who are trying to deceive the Black peoples into believing that their 400 year-old open enemies of freedom, justice and equality are, all of a sudden, their "friend." ... If the white people are truthful about their professed friendship toward the so-called Negro, they can prove it by dividing up America with their slaves. We believe that we who declare ourselves to be righteous Muslims, should not participate in wars which take the lives of humans. We do not believe this nation should force us to take part in such wars, for we have nothing to gain from it unless America agrees to give us the necessary territory wherein we may have something to fight for.... We believe that Allah (God) appeared in the Person of Master W. Fard Muhammad, July, 1930; the long awaited "Messiah" of the Christians and the "Mahdi" of the Muslims...and He will bring about a universal government of peace where in we all can live in peace together.[35]

At the heart of the Nation of Islam's critique of American society in the 1940s, 1950s, and 1960s was the notion that American idealism did not address the structural inequalities that persisted in the country. "If you can't do for yourself what the white man is doing for himself," Malcolm X exclaimed in one of his speeches, "don't say you are equal with the white man. If you can't set up a factory like he can set up a factory, don't talk that equality talk.... *This* is American democracy, and those of you who are familiar with it know that, in America, democracy is hypocrisy.... If democracy means freedom, then why don't we have freedom? If democracy means justice, then why don't we have justice? If democracy means equality, then why don't we have equality?"[36]

The Nation believed that racism was biologically entrenched in the "white devil," so the only way to address social inequalities in the United States was for black Americans to sever dependence on white institutions and attain their own land, form their own society, and govern themselves. For the Nation of Islam, religion was thus not an instrument of assimilation but a prophetic call for whites to repent by paying a penance (giving land to blacks) and for blacks to prepare for their divinely ordained salvation by joining the Nation of Islam.

The prophetic message of the Nation of Islam in the 1950s and early 1960s was powerfully voiced by one of its young, charismatic converts, Malcolm X. Malcolm X, born Malcolm Little, joined the Nation of Islam

---

[35] "What the Muslims Believe," printed regularly in the issues of *Muhammad Speaks*.
[36] Malcolm X, "Who are you?," Youtube video clip, http://www.youtube.com/watch?v=y7iHxAwPhpU (accessed January 28, 2010). A brief excerpt of the speech is cited in Benjamin Barber and Patrick Watson, *The Struggle for Democracy* (Boston, MA: Little, Brown, and Company, 1988), 91.

while he was in prison for robbery from 1946 to 1952. Upon leaving prison, Malcolm met with Elijah Muhammad and became one of the most active members of the Nation. He quickly rose through the ranks to become the national spokesperson for the Nation of Islam. Malcolm travelled throughout the country lecturing and organizing on behalf of Elijah Muhammad. He helped found *Muhammad Speaks*, which was first published in 1961 and served as the mouthpiece of the Nation of Islam. Within a few years, *Muhammad Speaks* became the best-selling black newspaper in the nation, claiming a circulation of 600,000 copies every other week.[37] During the 1960s, it served as the main sources of news from the Middle East and Africa for African Americans.[38]

Malcolm's publicity efforts were propelled by a 1959 PBS documentary on the movement called *The Hate that Hate Produced*.[39] This documentary introduced Malcolm, Elijah Muhammad, and the Nation of Islam to America. As the title of the documentary suggests, the film intended to condemn racism and segregation, but more significantly, it effected fear in white America by presenting the Nation of Islam as the angry, intractable monster child of white racism. White Americans assumed that, given black Americans' dehumanizing experiences in America, the Nation of Islam labeled whites the devil because of their suppressed anger against white brutality, and many feared the unleashing of this rage. This fear, however, was misplaced. As we saw in the previous chapter, the Nation of Islam was not so much concerned with taking revenge as it was with uplifting black Americans by fostering a new black self and society through religious beliefs and practices, with clear analogues in the Protestant work ethic of middle class America.

The sensational portrayal of the Nation of Islam in *The Hate that Hate Produced* brought national notoriety to the movement. The fiery speeches of its charismatic and articulate spokesperson attracted thousands of new members to the Nation of Islam and tens of thousands more sympathizers, who were not ready to convert to the Nation of Islam but certainly agreed with its assessment of race relations in the United States. Consequently, Malcolm X became a leading figure in the civil rights

---

[37] Clegg III, *An Original Man*, 160.

[38] Aminah Beverly McCloud, *African American Islam* (New York: Routledge, 1995), 53.

[39] The publication of C. Eric Lincoln's *The Black Muslims* (Boston, MA: Beacon, 1961) also brought much attention to the Nation of Islam. Lincoln's assertion that the popularity of the Nation of Islam pointed to the failures of the church to deal with the problem of racism shaped how the significance of this movement was interpreted for many years to come.

FIGURE 16. Cartoon by E. Majied from *Muhammad Speaks*, April 16, 1965, 8.

struggle of the 1950s and 1960s, and the Nation of Islam became one of the most successful black nationalist movement in American history.

In 1963–1964, Malcolm became increasingly disenchanted with Elijah Muhammad and the Nation of Islam. In April 1964, he went on the Hajj, where he met with a number of Muslim dignitaries and came face to face with the discrepancies between the teachings of the Nation and the Islamic beliefs and practices upheld by millions of Muslims outside of it. He recalled later, in rather romantic terms, how revelatory this experience had been for him:

My pilgrimage broadened my scope. It blessed me with a new insight. In two weeks in the [Muslim] Holy Land, I saw what I never had seen in thirty-nine years here in America. I saw all *races,* all *colors,* – blue-eyed blonds to black-skinned Africans – in *true* brotherhood! In unity! Living as one! Worshiping as one! No segregationists – no liberals; they would not have known how to interpret the meaning of those words. In the past, yes, I have made sweeping indictments of *all* white people. I never will be guilty of that again – as I know now that some white people *are* truly sincere, that some truly are capable of being brotherly toward a

FIGURE 17. From *Muhammad Speaks*, April 30, 1965, 1.

black man.... Yes, I have been convinced that *some* American whites do want to help cure the rampant racism which is on the path to *destroying* this country![40]

Malcolm X formally left the Nation of Islam in March 1964 and soon after founded an organization of his own, the Muslim Mosque, Inc., which, according to its incorporation filing, intended to propagate the "Islamic religion in accordance with the accepted Islamic Religious Principals."[41] Later, in 1965, he founded the Organization of Afro-American Unity as a vehicle for internationalizing the struggles of black Americans by finding common cause with independence and human rights movements abroad. Malcolm's founding of these two institutions, one religious, the other, political, points to what Edward Curtis has identified as his bifurcation of politics and religion following his adoption of mainstream Islamic beliefs

---

[40] Malcolm X and Haley, *Autobiography of Malcolm X*, 362.
[41] Louis A. DeCaro, Jr., *On the Side of My People: A Religious Life of Malcolm X* (New York: New York University Press, 1996), 340.

and practices.[42] Malcolm often asserted in the last years of his life that "[i]t is only being a Muslim which keeps me from seeing people by the color of their skin." For him, race was a deeply rooted reality in human society; he could thus hardly expect a racially blind religion to address the problems of racial inequality in political and economic terms. Put differently, Malcolm's adoption of mainstream Sunni beliefs and practices did not change his mind about the inability of American society to see past racial stereotypes. This fundamental belief about white America, which had originally attracted him to the racial mythology of the Nation of Islam, remained with him even after he became a Sunni Muslim. "Despite being a Muslim," he told an audience at Harvard Law School on December 16, 1964, "I can't overlook the fact that I'm an Afro-American in a country which practices racism against black people."[43]

Even though Malcolm X left the Nation of Islam and adopted a less radical ideology toward the end of his life, the publicity he brought to the Nation of Islam in the late 1950s and early 1960s resulted in the Nation's teachings having a disproportionate effect on the worldview of a generation of prominent black leaders, such as the poet, playwright, and activist Amiri Baraka.[44] Its accessible critique of the structures of racism provided the intellectual foundation and popular language of the Black Power movement. The media attention the Nation of Islam received helped ensconce Islam in black America as a religion of liberation. The Nation, whose flag bore the initials for "Freedom, Justice, Equality, and Independence," provided a way by which black Americans could uphold the values of America's post–World War II civil religion without forgetting the injustices faced by people of color.

RACE IN MUSLIM MOVEMENTS OUTSIDE OF THE NATION OF ISLAM

While the Nation of Islam was the most prominent organization to highlight the hypocrisy in Post-World War II American idealism and to uphold Islam as an alternative civil religion for black Americans, it was not the only one.

---

[42] Edward E. Curtis, IV, *Islam in Black America: Identity, Liberation, and Difference in African-American Islamic Thought* (Albany, NY: State University of New York Press, 2002), 99–104.

[43] Malcolm X, *Malcolm X: Speeches at Harvard*, ed. Archie Epps (New York: Paragon House, 1991), 164.

[44] Sherman Jackson, *Islam and the Blackamerican: Looking toward the Third Resurrection* (New York: Oxford University Press, 2005), 25 and 32.

Other groups have generally been overshadowed by the notoriety of the Nation of Islam, and their history in this period has yet to be adequately studied.[45] In addition to the continuing (though diminished) activities of the Moorish Science Temple in cities such as Detroit, Pittsburgh, and Chicago, some of the communities that emerged out of the Moorish Science Temple and the Ahmadiyya Movement began to organize themselves nationally based on their own understandings of Islam and their own visions for African American Muslims. As stated in the previous chapter, while these groups are generally associated with Sunni Islam because they eschewed the intermediation of any charismatic or institutional authority between God and man and emphasize the Qur'an and Islamic law, their proponents did not specifically articulate their beliefs in terms of Sunni tradition at this time. Their views of Islam evolved from what they learned over the years from varying sources on Islam: Islamic books (including the Qur'an and the Hadith), exchanges with other Muslims both here and abroad, encounters with Masonic orders, and the teachings of the Ahmadiyya, the Moorish Science Temple, and the Nation of Islam.

In 1943, some of these groups convened in Philadelphia to found their own umbrella organization called the Uniting Islamic Society of America. The aim of this organization was to coordinate the efforts of African American Muslims who were not officially affiliated with the Ahmadiyya, the Nation of Islam, or the Moorish Science Temple. According to one of its founders and the leader of the First Cleveland Mosque, Wali Akram, these Muslim converts feared that their fledgling movement will be subordinated to the interests of foreign Muslims unless they united and created their own national community. The communities most prominently represented in this national organization were the Cleveland and Pittsburgh African American Muslim communities who, under the leadership of Wali Akram and Nasir Ahmad respectively, had become independent of the Ahmadiyya Movement in the United States. Akram's community was represented on the handbill of the meeting by the Muslim Ten Year Plan. The gathering itself was hosted by the Addeynu Allahe-Universal Arabic Association, founded by Muhammad Ezaldeen, a former member of the Moorish Science Temple who reportedly went to Cairo to study Islam

---

[45] The most extensive study of African American Muslims who were not associated with the Moorish Science Temple and the Nation of Islam in this period is Robert Dannin's *Black Pilgrimage to Islam* (New York: Oxford University Press, 2002). Dannin, however, is not an Islamicist nor an Americanist. As such, this work should be approached with some caution. See also Jackson, *Islam and the Blackamerican* and McCloud, *African American Islam*, 9–72.

and ancient Egyptian history. On the gathering's handbill were two other lesser known organizations: Sheikh Omar Ali's Academy of Islam in Harlem and Moslems of America. The Uniting Islamic Society convened three more times before it was dismantled as a result of its members' competing visions of Islam for the African American community.[46]

Despite the splintering of some African American Muslims from the Ahmadiyya, the Ahmadiyya Movement made further pioneering inroads into black America in the 1940s and 1950s through the conversion of a number of jazz musicians, among them Ahmad Jamal, Yusef Lateef, Art Blakey, Fard Daleel, Nuh Alahi, McCoy Tyner, Sahib Shihab, Dakota Staton, and Talib Dawud. A 1953 *Ebony* article estimated that over 200 Jazz musician at this time were Muslim. They adopted Islam for a variety of personal, political, economic, and spiritual reasons, but all agreed that "Islam breaks down racial barriers and endows its followers with purpose and dignity." Lynn Hope and his all-Muslim orchestra, *Ebony* reported,

have been served in white restaurants in Atlanta, Birmingham, New Orleans, Nashville, Louisville, Charleston, W. Va. and Gadsden, Ala. Hope and his men, wearing their turbans, enter a restaurant with superb aplomb, and are usually told very quickly, 'We don't serve colored people here.' Hope's answer is swift, calm and always the same: 'We are not Negroes but members of the Moslem faith. Our customs are Eastern. We claim the nationality of our Arabic ancestors as well as their culture.' Almost invariably, they receive courteous treatment.[47]

Ebony and other non-Muslim contemporary observers often downplayed any influence the religion of Islam may have had on black converts by emphasizing its "de-negrofying" effect in white America. Dizzy Gillespie, whose big band hosted a number of African American Ahmadiyya converts, wrote in his autobiography that "they had no idea of black consciousness; all they were trying to do was escape the stigma of being 'colored'."[48] That Islam was instrumental in allowing some African Americans to participate more fully in American society during segregation, however, does not mean that African American Muslims did not take their new religious commitments seriously. Lynn Hope, for example, went on the Hajj in 1958 and changed his name to Hajj Rashid.[49] Talib Dawud, an Antiguan immigrant, gave up jazz to study Islam fulltime. In the 1950s

---

[46] Dannin, *Black Pilgrimage to Islam*, 48.
[47] "Moslem Musicians," *Ebony* (April 1953), 102 and 107.
[48] Dizzy Gillespie and Al Fraser, *To Be or Not...to Bop* (New York: Doubleday, 1979), 293, cited in Dannin, *Black Pilgrimage to Islam*, 59.
[49] Dannin, *Black Pilgrimage to Islam*, 58.

he, along with Mahmoud Alwan, an Egyptian immigrant and a member of the Muslim Brotherhood, and J. A. Rogers, the author of *Nature Knows No Color-Line*, formed the Islamic and African Institute in Philadelphia and New York. Their institute taught Islam, Arabic, and African history. It organized parades for visiting African dignitaries and raised funds and supplies for the Algerian independence movement. Later, Dawud affiliated his mosque with Harlem's International Muslim Brotherhood. As Dawud and his associates began expanding their efforts to the Midwest, they ran into territorial battles with the Nation of Islam. Dawud launched a campaign against what he regarded as the heretical teachings of the Nation of Islam through a black Chicago newspaper, the *New Crusader*, between August 1959 and March 1960. Elijah Muhammad in turn accused Talib Dawud of selling out to the "pale Arab."[50]

In addition to the Ahmadiyya, the Islamic Mission of America was also an influential organization that promoted Islam as the proper religion of African Americans. The Islamic Mission of America (originally the Islamic Mission of America for the Propagation of Islam and Defense of the Faith and the Faithful) was an influential Sunni organization established in the 1940s by another Caribbean immigrant, Daoud Ahmed Faisal (d. 1980). Faisal's early history in the United States is irretrievably mixed with legend.[51] We know that in 1947 he purchased a brownstone on 143 State Street in Brooklyn for a mosque (the State Street Mosque). The site may have had been rented for this purpose since 1939.[52] In 1950, the Islamic Mission of America published a primer on Islam by Faisal, titled *"al-Islam": The Religion of Humanity*. In this work Faisal thanks, in addition to his wife, an Iranian and two Pakistani Muslims, which suggests that his community was multiethnic. In his propagation of Islam,

---

[50] Ibid., 61–62. DeCaro, Jr., *On the Side of My People*, 147–150.

[51] A number of scholars date his activism on behalf of Islam to the 1920s based on the organization's own documents. See Richard Brent Turner, *Islam in the African-American Experience*, 2nd ed. (Bloomington, IN: Indiana University Press, 2003), 120 and McCloud, *African American Islam*, 21–24. I have not come across any outside evidence that corroborates such an early dating of Faisal's Islamic Mission of America. As Marc Ferris has suggested, Faisal most likely arrived in the United States in 1928 and gave this date as the start of his organized activity. It is not until the 1950s and beyond that Faisal appears as a notable American Muslim leader among the Muslim community of New York. Ferris, "To 'Achieve the Pleasure of Allah': Muslim Immigrant Communities in New York 1893–1991," in *Muslim Communities in North America*, ed. Yvonne Y. Haddad and Jane I. Smith (Albany, NY: State University of New York Press, 1994), 212.

[52] *Book of Conveyances*, Brooklyn City Register, Block 270, Lot 19, cited in Ferris, "To 'Achieve the Pleasure of Allah'," 212.

Daoud attacked Christianity as a white, racist religion, and argued that Islam is the only true "universal religion of humanity." He wrote:

Most assuredly, it [Christianity] was not established as a universal religion of humanity in which to worship God because one can only worship God in love, justice, truth, peace, fair play, human equality, fraternity and equal opportunity for all. This is righteousness, and such is "Islam." ... As Christians, they enslaved millions of people who are not white, and have deprived them of all things that a human being should enjoy, even the society of their own family. These are the Christian people who boast of being civilized.... White men are the only members of the human family who have openly and boastfully said to the whole world that they are superior and better than their human brothers who are not White. And why did they say this, because they have no true knowledge of what the true God hath revealed, and because they know not the true God. To them Jesus is their god, Lord and Saviour.... The Coloured people of the world who comprise more than two-thirds of the total population of the earth should never dislike a White person; instead they should sympathize with them and teach them the things they do not know. [53]

As a number of scholars have pointed out, Faisal and other African American Muslims who in the mid-twentieth century condemned Christianity for its legacy of slavery ignored the continuing legacy of slavery among Muslims. [54] This is a valid critique, but Faisal and other black American Muslims were not so much concerned with Islamic history as they were with the prophetic potential of Islam to close the gap between America's idealism and African Americans' experiences with racism (as I argued in the previous chapter). In the aftermath of World War II, when America began to develop a multiethnic and multireligious national narrative through a civil religion that upheld equality, freedom, and the pursuit of happiness as divinely endowed human rights, the discriminatory practices of American society served as a constant reminder to African Americans that they remained excluded from America's national narrative. When Faisal, the Nation of Islam, and others claimed Islam as the religion of peace, fraternity, freedom, justice, and equality – all values through which America publically self-identified after World War II – they were not appropriating the historical legacy of Islam. Rather, they were appropriating Islam as a "new" American religion for America's black citizens.

Ironically, as the success of the Nation of Islam's black nationalist rhetoric in this period illustrates, African Americans' adaptation of Islam to

---

[53] Daoud Ahmed Faisal, *"Al-Islam": The Religion of Humanity* (New York: Islamic Mission of America, 1950), 116.
[54] See, for example, Clegg III, *An Original Man*, 123–124.

the American context was directly related to the degree to which Islam was able to establish a national identity for African Americans separate from white America. Assertions by Faisal and other non-nationalist African American Muslims that one should not dislike whites but sympathize with them did not sit well with a number of African American converts. Some of Faisal's followers, for example, accused him of wanting to be "accepted by America." They charged that the State Street Mosque's leadership, which included some immigrants, was "either unaware of or unresponsive to the needs of the indigenous people in whose midst they had settled."[55] In 1962, three members of Faisal's mosque, Rajab Mahmud, Ishaq Abdush Shaheed, and Yahya Abdul Kareem, founded the Dar ul-Islam Movement in an effort to employ Islamist teachings to establish a separate black Muslim community governed by Islamic law (Shari'a). In the 1960s, Dar ul-Islam resembled the Nation of Islam in its efforts to uplift poor African Americans by establishing a separate Muslim community, but unlike the Nation of Islam, it relied on Islamic law, rather than the teachings of a contemporary prophet, to demarcate its boundaries. The membership pledge of the movement read:

In the name of Allah, the Gracious, the Merciful; Allah is the Greatest; bearing witness that there is no God but Allah and that Muhammad (peace be on him) is His Messenger, and being a follower of the last Prophet and Messenger of Allah, I hereby pledge myself to the Shariah and to those who are joined by this pledge. I pledge myself, by pledging my love, energy, wealth, life, and abilities. I also pledge myself to the Majlis (Imamate), whose duty is to establish, develop, defend, and govern according to the precepts of the Shariah. (Amen).[56]

In their call for building a black Muslim community based on strict observance of the Shari'a, the founders of Dar ul-Islam were influenced by the South Asian Islamist thinker and ideologue of the Pakistani Jama'at-i Islami (Islamic Society), Abul A'la Mawdudi (1903–1979).[57] Some of Mawdudi's works were translated into English and distributed in the United States by Muslim students who came to the United States in the 1950s and 1960s. At a time when Muslim-majority countries were gaining their independence, Mawdudi critiqued leaders of Muslim-majority states for aping the "West" and disparaging their Islamic heritage.

---

[55] "Dar-ul-Islam Movement," cited in R. M. Mukhtar Curtis, "Urban Muslims: The Formation of the Dar ul-Islam Movement," in *Muslim Communities in North America*, 54.
[56] Ibid., 55.
[57] Jackson, *Islam and the Blackamerican*, 49.

Unfortunately, however, political power and economic control have passed in all these [newly independent Muslim-majority] countries into the hands of people who have little knowledge of their religion and less pride in their cultural heritage. In their viewpoint all traditions of Muslims are contemptible and low, and they think that if they adopted a religious way of life and followed its values and principles, they would not progress and would not have an honorable position in this world. Furthermore, their thinking goes further – that if they can progress, they can only do so by adopting western thoughts and views of life.[58]

Like black nationalist Muslim movements in the United States, Mawdudi and ilk were dealing with the legacy of the conflation of race, religion, and progress after World War II. This conflation of race, religion, and progress underpinned what European empires viewed as their "civilizing" mission in their colonies. When the United States added the Philippines to its territories as a result of its victory in the Spanish-American War, Rudyard Kipling famously called this "the white man's burden" and admonished the United States:

> Take up the White Man's burden –
> Send forth the best ye breed –
> God bind your sons to exile
> To serve your captives' need;
> To wait in heavy harness,
> On fluttered folk and wild –
> Your new-caught, sullen peoples,
> Half-devil and half-child.[59]

For Mawdudi, Islam was a means by which newly independent Muslim-majority states could shed the stigmatization of their race and religion, which had been brought on by European colonialism and the conflation of whiteness, Christianity, and progress. In this, he found common cause with many Muslim black nationalists, which helps explain the appeal of his work for many African Americans in the 1950s and beyond. "The black American," wrote an African American Muslim to a primarily immigrant Muslim audience at this time, "has examined first-hand the sacred cow of Western civilization in its various forms and is far from enchanted by it. If some Afro-Americans have made great

---

[58] From a speech given at the 1967 annual convention of the Islamic Jama'at-ul-Talaba, printed under the title "Islam Today II," *al-Ittihad* 5, no. 1 (August 1968), 18.
[59] "The White Man's Burden," in *Rudyard Kipling's Verse, Inclusive Edition, 1885–1918* (New York: Doubleday, Page, and Company, 1920), 371. The poem was originally published in 1899.

achievements ... it has been in spite of centuries of harsh oppression and cruel discrimination against them by the white majority."[60]

Unlike movements such as the Nation of Islam or the Ahmadiyya, Mawdudi did not rely on prophecy to claim a new Islamic identity. He called for a revival of Islam based on strict observance of Islamic precepts. He defined Islam as an ethico-political ideology for a righteous society and blamed Muslims' subjugation by Europeans under colonial rule and their repression under secular nationalist regimes on their lack of adherence to Islam as a complete way of life:

Islam was always practicable in the past, and it is practicable today and will be practicable until '*Qiamah*' (the Day of Judgement). The actual problem is whether there is any nation which is prepared and ready to adopt Islam as a whole. Our history started from the fact that all of Arabia was prepared to establish economic, political, social and cultural life on the principles of Islam. They changed their individual character and social environment in accordance to Islam. This nation made the firm determination that it would raise the banner of Islam, that it would live for it and it would die for it. When a nation of this sort prepared itself, then one can see the epoch-making result. Similarly if a nation prepares itself today, the same result can be produced.[61]

As we have seen, however, Islam is polyvalent. In addressing the polyvalence of Islam, Mawdudi, like most Islamists, reduced the Islamic beliefs to an ideology and the practice of Islam to a strict adherence to the literal meaning of the Qur'an and the Prophetic Traditions (Hadith):

All those persons who thus surrender themselves to the will of God are welded into a community and that [is] how the "Muslim Society" comes into being. Thus, this is an ideological society – a society radically different from those which spring from accidents of races, colour or country. This society is the result of deliberate choice and effort; it is the outcome of a 'contract' which takes place between human beings and their Creator. Those who enter into this contract undertake to recognize God as their Sovereign, His Guidance as supreme, and His injunctions as absolute law. They also undertake to accept, without question, or doubt, His classification of Good and Evil, Right and Wrong, the Permissible and Prohibited.... When such a Society comes into existence, the Book [i.e., the Qur'an] and the Messenger [meaning the traditions of the Prophet Muhammad preserved in the Hadith] prescribe for it a code of life called *Shari'ah*, and this society is bound to conform to it by virtue of the contract into which it has entered.[62]

---

[60] Sulayman Shahid Mufassir, "Muslim Afro-Americans: The Forgotten Minority," *al-Ittihad* 7, no. 2 (December 1970), 11.

[61] Mawdudi, "Islam Today II," 20.

[62] Abul A'la Maududi (Mawdudi), *Islamic Law and Constitution*, ed. and trans. Khurshid Ahmad (Lahore: Islamic Pubicalions, 1986), 48–49.

As attractive as Mawdudi's *utopian* vision of an Islamic society was for many Sunni African American Muslims, members of the nascent Dar ul-Islam were neither familiar with Arabic nor had deep expertise in Islamic jurisprudence. Consequently, disputes broke out among them regarding what Islam permits and forbids. Without clear leadership or an organizational structure, the movement entered a state of disarray until 1968, when Yahya Abdul-Kareem emerged as the movement's leader and worked to spread the movement to other cities with significant African American populations.[63] Dar ul-Islam counted among its members the all-star basketball player, Kareem Abdul-Jabbar, and the former national chairman of the Student Nonviolent Coordinating Committee turned Black Panther, Jamil Abdullah al-Amin. Dar ul-Islam's adaptation of Mawdudi's thought to African American struggles with racism and poverty in the 1960s, 1970s, and 1980s earned it the reputation as "the most influential African American Islamic philosophy" among Sunni African American Muslims.[64]

AMERICAN MUSLIMS AND U.S. RELATIONS WITH MUSLIM-MAJORITY STATES

On the domestic front, World War II forged a new, more inclusive American national identity, which ironically politicized many people of color by highlighting the cleavage between America's democratic ideals and its discriminatory practices. Internationally, World War II thrust the United States on the world stage as a superpower. In the 1950s and 1960s, the collapse of European empires, the growing demand for oil, and the Cold War led the United States to become more directly involved in the internal affairs of Muslim-majority countries, particularly in the Middle East. The Roosevelt and Truman administrations forged an enduring alliance with Saudi Arabia to assure the United States uninterrupted access to the massive oil reserves in the Persian Gulf.[65]

The nature of the United States' new relationship with the Muslim-majority world could be indexed by the building of the Islamic Center of Washington, D.C. The idea for building a mosque for the growing number of diplomats and their families from the Muslim-majority world

---

[63] Curtis, "Urban Muslims", in *Muslim Communities in North America*, 56 and 59.
[64] McCloud, *African American Islam*, 69.
[65] Douglas Little, *American Orientalism: The United States and the Middle East Since 1945* (London: I.B. Tauris, 2003), 48–58.

in Washington, D.C. dates back to 1944 when Turkish Ambassador Münir Ertegün (the father of the co-founder of Atlantic Records, Ahmet Ertegün) passed away in the capital, where there was no suitable Islamic site to hold a prayer service for him. Following this event, a number of Muslim diplomats and American Muslims formed the Washington Mosque Foundation to raise money to build a mosque in Washington, D.C. Fourteen Muslim-majority countries, several prominent American Muslims, and a number of American Muslim organizations combined their efforts to fund the mosque.[66] The Islamic Center of Washington, D.C. was inaugurated on June 28, 1957. It was the first mosque in the United States built in the architectural vocabulary of the opulent mosques of the Muslim-majority world and it deliberately and artistically related architectural motifs from varying parts of the Muslim world to the landscape of America's capital. President Eisenhower attended the inauguration and his remarks sought to capture the new relationship the United States sought with the Muslim world. In this new international context, just as in the context of the development of a new American national identity, religion was not seen as a marker of difference but as an instrument of unity whose free expression the United States was bound to protect.

The countries which have sponsored and built this Islamic Center have for centuries contributed to the building of civilization. With their traditions of learning and rich culture, the countries of Islam have added much to the advancement of mankind. Inspired by a sense of brotherhood, common to our innermost beliefs, we can here together affirm our determination to secure the foundations of a just and lasting peace. Our country has long enjoyed a strong bond of friendship with the Islamic nations and, like all healthy relationships, this relationship must be mutually beneficial. From the time of the first brothers, the two sons of Adam, as reported in all our sacred writings, it has been clear that each man and each nation is also responsible for the welfare of others living outside the narrow limits of his own or their own special interest.... This fruitful relationship between peoples, going far back into history, becomes more important each year. Today, thousands of Americans, both private individuals and government officials, live and work – and grow in understanding – among the peoples of Islam. At the same time, in our country, many from the Muslim lands – students, businessmen,

---

[66] These countries were Afghanistan, Egypt, Indonesia, Iran, Iraq, Jordan, Kuwait, Libya, Morocco, Pakistan, Saudi Arabia, Syria, Turkey, and Yemen. Muhammad Abdul-Rauf, *History of the Islamic Center: From Dream to Reality* (Washington, D.C.: Colortone Press, 1978), 95. A list of the American Muslim organizations present at the opening ceremony can be found on p. 72. A. Joseph Howar, a contractor based in Washington, D.C., was one the prominent American Muslims of the time who helped facilitate the plans and construction of the mosque. William Geerhold, "The Mosque on Massachusetts Avenue," *Saudi Aramco World* 16, no. 3 (May/June 1965), 20–21.

FIGURE 18. The Islamic Center of Washington, D.C.

and representatives of states – are enjoying the benefits of experience among the people of the United States. From these many personal contacts, here and abroad, I firmly believe there will come a broader understanding and a deeper respect for the worth of all men; and a stronger resolution to work together for the good of mankind.... Under the American Constitution, this Center, this place of worship is as welcome as could be any similar edifice of any religion. Americans would fight with all their strength for your right to have your own church and worship according to your own conscience. Without this, we would be something else than what we are.[67]

Eisenhower's presence at the inauguration of the Islamic Center of Washington, D.C. brought national attention to the mosque. Local newspapers all across the country commented both on the oddity of having a grand mosque at the nation's capital and on the statement it made about America's religious tolerance.[68] Eisenhower's comments made clear that

---

[67] "Eisenhower's 1957 Speech at Islamic Center of Washington," available online at the U.S. Department of State web site, http://www.america.gov/st/texttrans-english/2007/June/20070626154822lnkaiso.6946985.html (accessed February 3, 2009).
[68] See, for examples, "Ike Presides at Opening of First Mosque in U.S.," *Oregonian*, June 29, 1957; "President Opens a Mosque Today," *New York Times*, June 28, 1957, 21; W. H. Lawrence, "President and Wife Doff Shoes at Rites Dedicating Mosque," *New*

there was room for Islam in the United States so long as Islam adhered to the precepts of America's civil religion. The challenge in his message was clearly heard and reciprocated by the Director of the Islamic Center:

The long cherished wish of American Muslims was realized when the minaret of this mosque was raised in one of the most beautiful spots in Washington. May this Islamic Center in Washington serve its purpose of shedding the light of truth about Islam as a universal religion, as a way of life, and as a culture which is essentially creative and humane.... May it thus help to realize mutual recognition and fuller understanding between peoples.... It is by exchange of views that men can reach an understanding; and it is our sincere hope that it will also help us to implement one of the most important concepts preached by Islam – the concept of the equality and universal brotherhood of men. Mr. President: The participation of the United States, as represented in your illustrious person, in the opening of this Islamic Center is not only a high honor, but a demonstration of the cooperation that exists between the Islamic World and the American people.[69]

The positing of religion as a medium for mutual understanding and cooperation at the opening ceremony of the Islamic Center of Washington, D.C. belied the political tensions between the United States and the people of the Muslim-majority world. U.S. support for the establishment of the state of Israel in 1948 and greater U.S. meddling in the Middle East at a time when Middle Eastern nations were becoming independent radically altered perceptions of the United States in the Muslim-majority world. Prior to World War II, the United States was generally viewed as a neutral "Western" power in Muslim-majority countries' struggles for independence from European colonial rule; in the aftermath of the war, U.S. interference in the internal affairs of Muslim-majority countries led to the portrayal of the United States as yet another Western imperial power.

The most marked example of the changing role of the United States in the Middle East can be traced through the evolution of U.S.–Iranian relations in the twentieth century. During the first half of the twentieth century, Iranians looked to the United States as a benevolent, non-interventionist power that supported the growth of developing nations. This image of America was cultivated by the positive work of American missionaries and other private citizens in Iran, such as Dr. Samuel M. Jordan's (1871–1952) largely successful efforts to create a modern education system in Iran, or Howard Baskerville (1885–1909), the young American teacher

---

York Times, June 29, 1957, 1; Walter Trohan, "Shoeless Ike Dedicates Islam Center," *Chicago Daily Tribune*, June 29, 1957, 15; Jean White, "Ike Stresses Free Religion at Mosque Rites," *Washington Post and Times Herald*, June 29, 1957, A2.

[69] Abdul-Rauf, *History of the Islamic Center*, 75 and 77.

who earned the respect of Iranians for giving his life in furtherance of the Iranian Constitutional Revolution. The espoused rhetoric of the United States as a champion of freedom and democracy also appealed to many Iranians. Consequently, during the Iranian Constitutional Revolution of the early 1900s, Iranian reformers looked to the United States for assistance in establishing Iran as a constitutional monarchy and protecting its sovereignty against Russian and British interests. Washington, however, stated that it had no interest in assisting Iran with its Constitutional Revolution and, internally, dismissed the movement and showed disdain for the country and its people. Nonetheless, America built up a reserve of goodwill among Iranians because of the work of various American missionaries and other private citizens.[70]

It was not until the 1950s that this image was shattered. In 1951, Mohammad Mossadeq, a democratically elected and extremely popular prime minister, came to power with an agenda to nationalize Iran's oil, which was then under the control of the British via the Anglo-Iranian Oil Company. By 1953, Mossadeq had nationalized Iran's oil and in effect exiled the king of Iran, Shah Muhammad Reza Pahlavi (r. 1941–1978). Fearing Soviet ties and the threat this nationalization would pose to world oil supplies, the U.S. Central Intelligence Agency and the British organized a successful coup against Mossadeq. The Shah returned to Iran in a CIA airplane. Following these events, Iran became widely recognized as a client state of the United States, and Iranians began to regard the United States as a neo-colonial power in their country.

In light of the United States' neo-imperial role in the Middle East, the presence of Muslims in the United States drew the attention of a number of governments from the region. Both government officials and American Muslims came to see the role that American Muslims could play in intermediating relations between Muslim-majority countries and the United States. The Federation of Islam Associations specifically stated in the preamble of its constitution that it sought to unite American Muslims by "establishing close contacts with all parts of the Moslem world and to participate in the modern renaissance of Islam."[71] In 1959, the FIA established formal relations with the United Arab Republic (a short-lived pan-Arab union between Syria and Egypt under the leadership of the populist Egyptian President Gamal Abdel Nasser). Abdel Nasser invited the first

---

[70] For an overview of U.S.-Iranian relations at this time, see Kamyar Ghaneabassiri, "U.S. Foreign Policy and Persia, 1856–1921," *Iranian Studies* 35, nos. 1–3 (winter 2002), 145–175.

[71] See reprint of the constitution in Elkholy, *Arab Moslems in the United States*, 154.

three presidents of the FIA to Cairo and contributed $44,000 for the building of an Islamic center in Detroit.[72] In 1961, the FIA held its tenth annual convention overseas in Lebanon and Egypt. Participants in the convention arrived in Cairo aboard two chartered airplanes and were greeted by representatives of the Egyptian government and the U.S. embassy.[73] The FIA received the Medal of Jumhuriyya (i.e., "the medal of the Republic") from Abdel Nasser. In the same year, King Saud ibn 'Abd al-'Aziz formally recognized the organization and promised Saudi cooperation and aid.[74]

Arab Muslim academics were also commissioned to study the presence of Muslim minorities throughout the world. In 1960, Mahmud Yusuf al-Shawarbi, a Fulbright visiting scholar at the universities of Maryland and Fordham and the head of the Islamic Center of New York Foundation, published the first book-length study of Muslims in the United States for the Society for the International Apprising of Islam based in Cairo.[75] Al-Shawarbi was the secretary for the society. He was also an intermediary between the American Muslim population and Muslim-majority nations who had established delegations in New York City since the United Nations was headquartered there in 1945. When Malcolm X applied for a visa to go on the Hajj, the Saudi embassy sent him to al-Shawarbi to obtain a written attestation of his conversion to Islam.[76]

During 1973 and 1974, the Muslim World League surveyed Muslim minority populations in Europe and the Americas in order to identify the type of missionary activities it ought to support. It commissioned M. Ali Kettani ('Ali ibn al-Muntasir al-Kattani), an electrical engineer from Morocco who was active both in the Muslim World League and the Organization of the Islamic Conference (OIC), to write a report on the state of Muslim minority communities in Europe and the Americas.[77] The intermediary role Muslim emigrants to Europe and North America hoped

---

[72] Elkholy, *Arab Moslems in the United States*, 48.

[73] Ibid., 6.

[74] The Federation of Islamic Associations in the United States and Canada, 11th Annual Convention bulletin (Philadelphia, PA: 1962).

[75] Maḥmūd Yūsuf al-Shawārbī, *al-Islām fī Āmrīkā* (al-Qāhira: Lajnat al-Bayān al-'Arabī, 1960).

[76] Malcolm X and Haley, *Autobiography of Malcolm X*, 319–320.

[77] "Muslims in America," *al-Ittihad* 11, no. 3 (spring 1974), 15–16, reprinted as excerpt from *Muslim World*, 13 April 1974. 'Alī ibn al-Muntasir al-Kattānī, *al-Muslimūn fī Ūrūbbā wa Āmrīkā*, 2 vols. (Bayrūt: Dār al-Kutub al-'Ilmiyya, [1976], 2005), 5. Later Kettani expanded this study to include Muslim minority communities throughout the world, see M. Ali Kettani, *Muslim Minorities in the World Today* (London: Mansell Publishing Limited, 1986).

to play in the global Muslim community is evidenced in Kettani's assertion that "the sorry state of affairs prevailing in the Muslim countries in general has ... driven him increasingly towards the Muslim minorities. He has felt inspired and thrilled by the idea that some of these minorities might one day produce those sons and daughters of Islam who might change the whole course of events of the entire Muslim *ummah*."[78]

Individual Muslim-majority governments and Muslim missionaries also took note of the conversion of African American Muslims to Islam. Malcolm X reported in the late 1950s that certain "African and Asian personages" privately encouraged and expressed support for the Nation of Islam. Abdul Basit Naeem, a Pakistani missionary affiliated with Jami'at al-Falah, who published *The Moslem World and the U.S.A*, sought common cause with the Nation of Islam in its effort to propagate Islam and drum up support for Islamist and anti-colonial movements in the Muslim-majority world.[79] Naeem was aware of the differences in the teachings of Islam and the Nation of Islam, but given the popularity of the Nation, he published some of Elijah Muhammad's writings in his magazine, which was read by Muslims not only in the United States but also in such distant places as Pakistan and South Africa.[80] He wrote, "both Mr. Muhammad and his Moslem movement have become an inseparable part of the overall picture of Islamic affairs in America, we consider it our duty to print periodical, detailed reports on their progress."[81] He further noted, "Mr. Muhammad's teachings (offered through his Temples) ... have enabled more Americans to form an acquaintance with Islam than the efforts of all other individuals seeking converts to Islam here put together." Naeem asserted that the "wisdom" of the Nation of Islam's presentation of Islam as "a religion of the black mankind" is readily comprehended. He reassured his readers that Mr. Muhammad is fully aware that his teachings differ from "those of Eastern Moslems. Mr. Muhammad readily concedes this, explaining that 'my people must be dealt with on a special basis, because their background and circumstances are different from those prevailing elsewhere in the world. You cannot use the same medicine to treat altogether different diseases'."[82]

[78] Kettani, *Muslim Minorities*, xvii–xviii.
[79] E. U. Essien-Udom, *Black Nationalism: A Search for an Identity in America*, 3rd ed. (New York: Dell, 1965), 302.
[80] Ibid., 415n46.
[81] *Moslem World and the U.S.A.* (October-November-December 1956), 8, cited in Essien-Udom, *Black Nationalism*, 303–304.
[82] *Moslem World and the U.S.A.* (October-November-December, 1956), 8–9, cited in Essien-Udom, *Black Nationalism*, 395n45.

Naeem's ties with the Nation of Islam seem to have been severed around 1957.[83] Nonetheless, the Nation's potential benefits to Muslim causes remained obvious to representatives of Islamic movements and Muslim-majority states. At a Nation of Islam rally in 1960, al-Shawarbi proclaimed, "We need you here to help bring the great truths of our faith to this country" and to create bridges of "understanding between the U.S. and Africa."[84] The Nation of Islam also benefited from the greater prestige and authenticity that such connections afforded. In 1957, Elijah Muhammad sent a letter to Abdel Nasser on the occasion of the Afro-Asian Solidarity Conference:

> Lt. President G. A. Nasser
>
> In the Name of Allah, the Beneficent, the Merciful, Beloved Brothers of Africa and Asia:
>
> As-Salaam-Alaikum. Your long lost Muslim Brothers here in America pray that Allah's divine presence will be felt at this historic African-Asian Conference, and give unity to our efforts for peace and brotherhood. Freedom, Justice and Equality for all African and Asians is of far reaching importance, not only to you of the East but also to over seventeen million of your long lost brothers of African and Asian descent here in the West. May Allah open and guide the hearts and minds of our people who are acting as our rulers and our leaders and especially those who are participating in this great Conference....
>
> All success is with Allah
As-Salaam-Alaikum
Your long lost brothers of the West
/signed/ Elijah Muhammad

Two years later, President Abdel Nasser reciprocated Elijah Muhammad's message of unity and goodwill. James R. Lawson, President of the United African Nationalist Movement, delivered a message on his behalf to the Nation of Islam's 1959 annual convention:

I would like you to convey my words to our brother peoples; namely, that unity and solidarity are the two indispensible factors for realizing our liberty. This lesson must be seriously taken to heart and maintained against imperialist forces seeking to undermine our integrity and convert us into disintegrated groups which can easily be victimized and made to serve their selfish interests....[O]ur

---

[83] Essien-Udom, *Black Nationalism*, 304–305.
[84] "Muslim from Cairo Lauds Muslims Here," *New York Amsterdam News*, November 15, 1960, 1 and 11, cited in DeCaro, Jr., *On the Side of My People*, 168.

great religion and traditions and ways of living will serve as the cornerstone in building the new society based on right, justice and equality.[85]

In that year, Abdel Nasser also invited Elijah Muhammad to Egypt (under the watchful eye of the FBI and the CIA, who secretly tried to prevent the trip in order to foil any attempt by the Nation to use it to claim greater clout and Islamic legitimacy).[86] Elijah Muhammad ended up sending Malcolm X on his behalf. Malcolm X visited with dignitaries in Egypt, Saudi Arabia, and Syria. A few months later, Elijah Muhammad himself went on a tour of the Middle East and Africa, with stops in Turkey, Syria, Lebanon, Jordan, Egypt, and Sudan.

There were many other examples of international Muslim organizations taking an interest in African American Muslims. The Lahori branch of the Ahmadiyya, who accepted the teachings of Mirza Ghulam Ahmad as a reformer rather than a prophet, came to the United States in 1949 and maintained close relations with members of the Nation of Islam throughout the 1950s, 1960s, and 1970s. The Pakistani Lahori missionary Muhammad Abdullah, who came to the United States in 1959, wrote a column for *Muhammad Speaks* and introduced Elijah Muhammad's son and successor, Wallace, to Urdu and to commentaries on the Qur'an. According to Richard Brent Turner, he became a confidant of Elijah Muhammad behind the scenes and in 1987 reported that Elijah Muhammad had told him, "Don't think I'm against prayer five times a day, making the hajj or fasting during Ramadan. Don't think I'm against following Islamic teachings. If I overload my followers, they will run away, so I'm teaching them bit by bit."[87]

When the Muslim World League was founded in 1962, it aimed to counter the spread of socialist ideology and secular Arab nationalism by the Ba'thists and pro-Nasserites. In countering these trends, the League sought to consolidate the efforts of Islamist groups including the Wahhabis, the Salafis, the Muslim Brotherhood, and Jam'at-i Islami. The Saudi government supported the League out of not only a sense of religious duty but also of self-interest. Its hope was that a consolidated and well-funded Islamist movement would quell the threat the rise of Arab nationalism and socialism presented to

---

[85] *Los Angeles Herald-Dispatch*, March 12, 1959, 1 and 5, cited in Essien-Udom, *Black Nationalism*, 305.
[86] Karl Evanzz, *The Messenger: The Rise and Fall of Elijah Muhammad* (New York: Vintage Books, 2001), 193–194.
[87] Cited in Turner, *Islam in the African-American Experience*, 195.

its kingdom.[88] In its efforts to propagate Islam, the Muslim World League reached out to Muslim minority communities throughout the world, including the United States. As the head of the Muslim Mosque, Inc., Malcolm X corresponded with Said Ramadan, a founding affiliate of the Muslim World League and a son-in-law of the Hasan al-Banna', the founder of the Muslim Brotherhood.[89] In September 1964, when Malcolm X went to Mecca again on the *'umra* (pilgrimage to Mecca outside of the Hajj season), he received missionary training at the Muslim World League and was offered scholarships to disseminate to American Muslims who may have wished to study at the University of Medina.[90] Since the 1960s, an unknown number of American Muslims have received funding to study Islam and Arabic in Saudi universities.

As the above examples make evident, the international connections of American Muslims in the 1950s and 1960s were numerous, complex, and diverse. Scholars have only recently begun to examine them, and we do not yet fully understand the extent of their influence on the historical development of American Islam.[91] Based on the available scholarship, however, it is apparent that as American Muslims began to organize nationally in the aftermath of World War II, they were in a position not only to relate Islam and America in their own lives but to mediate between the varying interests of Muslim-majority countries and the United States.

THE ARRIVAL OF FOREIGN MUSLIM STUDENTS IN SIGNIFICANT NUMBERS

Another effect of greater U.S. involvement in the Muslim-majority world after World War II was a significant increase in the number of foreign Muslim students in the United States. Prior to World War II, most students from the Middle East and South Asia who went abroad for their studies attended European schools. Shorter distances, colonial networks, and the prestige of European universities made Europe a much more attractive option for higher education than the United States. World

---

[88] For a brief but excellent overview of the Muslim World League, see Reinhard Schulze, "Muslim World League," in *The Oxford Encyclopedia of the Modern Islamic World*, ed. John L. Esposito (New York: Oxford University Press, 1995), vol. III, 208–210.

[89] DeCaro, Jr., *On the Side of My People*, 255–257; Edward E. Curtis IV, "Islamism and Its African American Muslim Critics: Black Muslims in the Era of the Arab Cold War," *American Quarterly* 59, no. 3 (September 2007), 695.

[90] Curtis, "Islamism and Its African American Muslim Critics," 695.

[91] See ibid. and Hisham D. Aidi, "Let Us Be Moors: Islam, Race and 'Connected Histories'," *Souls* 7, no. 1 (Winter 2005), 36–51.

War II, however, devastated Europe and shifted the economic and political center of international relations toward the United States. Many European academics fled to the United States during the war, which helped improve the quality of American universities. New colleges and universities were founded throughout the United States to serve numerous World War II veterans returning home on the G.I. Bill. The existence of these new institutions significantly increased the prospects of foreign students gaining admission into an American college or university. After the war, Congress also established new programs to attract more foreign students and scholars to the country. In 1946, for example, Congress established the Fulbright Program (named after Senator James William Fulbright) with the intent to "increase mutual understanding between the peoples of the United States and the people of other countries." The hope was that increased familiarity with the cultures, languages, and histories of other nations would help prevent another catastrophic world war. Foreign students were also excluded from the immigration quotas that restricted the entry of nationals from Muslim-majority countries. As such, higher education became a pathway for Muslims who wished to immigrate to the United States but were otherwise restricted from doing so. All in all, following World War II, the United States became one of the main destinations for students from Muslim-majority countries seeking an education abroad.

From 1948 to 1965, the number of students from Muslim-majority countries in the United States increased more than fivefold from 2,708 to 13,664.[92] The Muslim-majority country that sent the most students to the United States was Iran, followed by Egypt, Pakistan, and Turkey. A sizeable number of students also came from Lebanon, Syria, Jordan, Saudi Arabia, and Indonesia. Many of these students came to gain technical knowledge with the aim of meeting the technological, scientific, and bureaucratic needs of the new independent nation-states that emerged in the Middle East, Africa, and South Asia following World War II. Others had been politicized by the independence movements in their countries; many of them supported anti-colonial causes at home while studying in the United States. Still others belonged to Islamist movements and had fled to the United States to escape persecution from secular, nationalist regimes that came to power after independence and viewed Islamist organizations as a political threat.

[92] Data compiled from *Open Doors: Report on International Educational Exchange, 1948–2004.* CD-ROM, Institute of International Education.

MUSLIM STUDENTS ASSOCIATION OF THE
UNITED STATES AND CANADA

This latter group of Muslim students had a major impact on the development of national Muslim institutions in the United States by founding the Muslim Students Association of the United States and Canada (MSA) in January 1963 on the campus of the University of Illinois at Urbana-Champaign. In the ensuing two decades, the MSA became the most successful national Muslim organization founded by immigrants. When it was formed in 1963 it had only ten local affiliates. The next year, it counted 38 affiliates and had a representative on the Board of Directors of the FIA. By 1968, it had 105 local associations throughout colleges and universities in the United States and Canada. Already in the first three years of its operation, it began receiving funds from Muslim-majority countries such as Kuwait and Pakistan. It printed and distributed books and pamphlets on Islam to both Muslim and non-Muslim Americans. It published a newsletter and a journal titled *al-Ittihad* (Unity). It established a Zakat fund to help needy Muslims and non-Muslims in the United States and a relief fund to support Islamic causes abroad. Its members also visited prisons to proselytize, gave lectures on Islam to local Muslim and non-Muslim populations, and taught at Islamic Sunday schools. In 1965, the MSA sent a delegation to the meeting of the Muslim World League in Mecca with the hopes of creating a World Organization of Muslim Students. The majority of the MSA's members in the 1960s were male. A Women's Committee formed in 1966 comprised of "students' wives, mothers, daughters, and single girls, most of them studying at different institutes in this country." The Women's Committee met separately but alongside the national MSA convention and, in 1968, was considered not yet an essential part of the national organization but "very useful and important" to the organization of national and regional conferences. The Women's Committee determined and executed its own activities, which included hosting families, publishing a Muslim cookbook, forming a circulating library, providing family counseling, and fundraising.[93]

The early MSA, as a national organization, functioned for the most part on a small budget. It was financed by its membership dues ($2 per year), personal donations, donations from Muslim-majority countries, and the sale of books and Eid cards. It had no center for its operations

---

[93] Muslim Students Association, *The MSA Handbook* (Ann Arbor, MI: Muslim Students' Association of the U.S. and Canada, 1968), 28–33, 48, 51, 60, 92 and 97.

until the 1973 when it established its headquarters in al-Amin Mosque in Gary, Indiana. It later built its permanent headquarters – significantly, in the heartland – in Plainfield, Indiana.[94] It was essentially sustained by the free labor, expertise, and connections of its enthusiastic members. The 1968 *MSA Handbook* read, "We feel that if we find the most sincere, the most active and the most devoted workers, then the MSA can finance its activities without any difficulty" (56).

The Muslim students who came to the United States in the 1950s and 1960s founded the MSA in part because they were dispersed throughout the country, and some attended universities in places where there were no local Muslim communities. According to MSA documents, at the time of its founding there were no more than 15 local Muslim student associations in the country.[95] The MSA sought to consolidate their efforts and increase their numbers. By promoting the establishment of local associations, the MSA intended "to strengthen the fraternal bond among Muslim students" so that they might maintain their religious commitments while living in a non-Muslim society.[96] As such, the MSA was no different than any other international or cultural student association found on American university campuses. There was, however, another dimension to the MSA's activities. Most of its members – the majority of whom were students of engineering, the hard sciences, and medicine – saw themselves as participants in a historic Islamic "renaissance" ushered in by such Islamist thinkers as Abul A'la Mawdudi and Sayyid Qutb (1906–1966), the contemporary ideologues of Jama'at-i Islami and the Muslim Brotherhood respectively. Some of the founding members of the MSA were in fact members of these organizations.[97] This does not mean, however, that members of the MSA agreed with everything these ideologues had to say or that they agreed with every action these organizations undertook. Such an understanding misleads one to think of the MSA as an outreach of a foreign organization and overlooks the significant influence of the American context on the development of the MSA.

[94] Gutbi Mahdi Ahmed, "Muslim Organizations in the United States," 15.
[95] MSA, *The MSA Handbook*, 13.
[96] Constitution of the Muslim Student Association of the United States and Canada, printed in *The MSA Handbook*, 121.
[97] Yvonne Y. Haddad, "Arab Muslims and Islamic Institutions in America: Adaptation and Reform," in *Arabs in the New World*, ed. Sameer Y. Abraham and Nabeel Abraham (Detroit, MI: Wayne State University Press, 1983), 70; Larry Poston, *Islamic Da'wah in the West: Muslim Missionary Activity and the Dynamics of Conversion to Islam* (New York: Oxford University Press, 1992), 102.

For MSA activists, adherence to Islamic beliefs and practices was not only a religious duty but a transformative experience. Qutb's and Mawdudi's writings appealed to them because both of these authors began with the assumption that the religion of Islam is necessarily transformative both for individual Muslims and Muslim societies, and they went on to interpret Islam as an all-encompassing "way of life" for the modern world. As previously stated, in their interpretations, they eschewed classical Muslim scholarship and the formalities of Islamic disciplines. They went back to the Qur'an and the Prophetic Tradition (the Hadith) as the original and purest sources of Islam, the literal texts of which, they believed, trumped all ensuing interpretations and practices to which Muslims may be accustomed. In this sense, their approach seemed particularly suited for the modern, rational world. Moreover, these authors argued that "true Islam" is not found in existing Muslim-majority societies, which they generally considered to be un-Islamic, but in the positive transformation that is realized in human societies when individual Muslims and Muslim societies embody the ethical message of Islam. In one of the short books distributed by the MSA in the United States in the 1960s, Sayyid Qutb wrote: "The faith of Islam is divinely ordained path for human life. Its realization in the life of mankind depends on the exertions of men themselves, within the limits of their human capacities and the material realities of human existence in a given environment."[98]

This utopian understanding of Islam has since been encapsulated in the Muslim Brotherhood's motto, "Islam is the solution" to every problem facing humanity in any place and at any point in time.

It was this utopian vision of Islamic life that members of the MSA sought to realize in the United States:

In brief, the Association will carry on religious, charitable, educational, civic, social, literary, athletic, scientific and research activities and any other matter pertaining to the objectives of Islam as a *complete way of life* (emphasis mine). To help its members to live Islamically, the Association is ceaselessly trying to find better ways and means to practice Islam according to our changing situations and environment. In other words, the Association is endeavoring to establish a divinely guided community that enjoins good, preaches love and lives in peace.

Within the ethnically diverse context of North America, the MSA recognized a unique opportunity to attain its utopian, ideological, pan-Islamic society.

---

[98] Sayyid Qutb, *The Religion of Islam*, trans. "Islamdust" (Palo Alto, CA: al-Manar Press, 1967), 2.

The M.S.A. is unique in many ways. Its membership consists of students of many races, nationalities and languages. It is the *ideology of Islam* (emphasis mine) that brings them together and permits them to function as a single unit....The Association is unique in that its members form a community with its own identity, features and characteristics.[99]

Among its members in 1968, the MSA counted natives of Afghanistan, Albania, Algeria, Canada, China, Cuba, Cyprus, Egypt, India, Indonesia, Iran, Iraq, Jordan, Kenya, Kuwait, Lebanon, Libya, Malaysia, Mali, Mauritius, Morocco, Nigeria, Pakistan, Palestine, Saudi Arabia, Somalia, Sudan, Syria, South Africa, Tanzania, Thailand, Turkey, the United States, Yemen, and Yugoslavia.[100]

The absence of a Muslim-majority society coupled with the freedoms found in the United States made the United States a blank slate for the realization of the MSA's utopian, scripturalist vision of Islam. The fact that Muslims from all over the world had come to study in the United States also provided an opportunity for the organizers of the MSA to test this utopian vision, to see if the MSA could be the crucible to unify people of varying cultures and ethnic backgrounds to declare, "we are Muslims first, Muslims last, and Muslims forever. We should live as Muslims, we should act as Muslims and we should die as Muslims." The MSA saw its work in the United States and Canada as nothing less than historic: "Our ancestors have already created a history that one refers to with pride. We feel and we believe that it is our duty to CREATE a history for Islam all over the world. In order to achieve that idea we should SUPERVISE the molding of this history by sacrificing our money and wealth, our efforts and knowledge, and our time and lives so as we can see our history being written in the best way we love to see."[101]

Through its commitment to Islam as an ideology or a complete way of life, the MSA "melting pot" sought to create an organizational context in which Muslims in the United States transcended their ethnic, racial, and cultural differences to become what one scholar has aptly called, "normative *homo islamicus* subject[s]."[102] In practice, however, the MSA melting pot, just as the American melting pot, did not fully

---

[99] "The Muslim Students' Association of the U.S. and Canada: Purposes and Functions," *al-Ittihad* 4, no. 2 (March 1968), 3.

[100] MSA, *The MSA Handbook*, 34.

[101] "The Message of the M.S.A.," *al-Ittihad* 4, no. 2 (March 1968), inside cover.

[102] Behrooz Ghamari-Tabrizi, "Loving America and Longing for Home: Isma'il al-Faruqi and the Emergence of the Muslim Diaspora in North America," *International Migration* 42, no. 2 (2004), 61.

wash away cultural and ethnic differences; rather it created a context in which people of varying backgrounds could encounter, commune, and debate one another. In other words, there was considerable push-back against the unifying, normative ideology of the Muslim Students Association. Local chapters of the MSA were for the most part autonomous and did not necessarily follow the ideology of many of the national leaders. When ethnic and sectarian tensions could not be squared with the more utopian, normative vision of the MSA leadership, members split from the association to found either ancillary or separate organizations. A few years after its founding, in the 1970s, Arab students formed the Muslim Arab Youth Association (MAYA) and Malaysians, the Malaysian Islamic Study Group (MISG), both ancillary organizations of the Muslim Students Association. Also in the 1970s, some Iranian, Shi'i students formed the separate Muslim Students Association-Persian Speaking Group, and some South Asian students associated with the Jama'at-i Islami founded the Islamic Circle of North America, which has since ceased to be uniquely South Asian even though South Asians remain predominant within the organization.

Given the national MSA's conviction that it had arrived at *the* proper understanding of Islam, it should not be surprising that it paid little deference to earlier Muslim communities in the United States. It viewed local mosques and the Federation of Islamic Associations as conduits for its message and encouraged MSA members, almost none of whom were formally trained as Islamic scholars, to engage them and to lecture them on Islam: "For the communities that need assistance, the members of the MSA have extended their services to conduct of congregational prayers (sic), to deliver lectures and speeches on Islam, and teach children in Sunday Schools."[103] The MSA felt that the FIA had become too lax in its observance of Islamic precepts. The association frowned upon social gatherings and dances at older mosques and on communal prayers held on Sundays rather than on Fridays. It disapproved of the earlier immigrant community's widespread support for Gamal Abdel Nasser's nationalist-socialist project.[104] The MSA defined its role in relation to the FIA and earlier American Muslim associations, a number of which had been led by imams from Islamic seminaries, paternalistically: they "seek means and methods for helping the communities to adhere to their religion, preserve their Muslim identity and help educate their children on the

[103] MSA, *The MSA Handbook*, 59
[104] Poston, *Islamic Da'wah in the West*, 102.

main principles of Islam."[105] The MSA saw itself as the provider of these "means and methods" of maintaining a Muslim way of life for earlier established mosques and American Muslim organizations. While earlier Muslim immigrants were more concerned about mutual understanding and coexistence with others in American society, the founders of the MSA were gravely interested in the propagation of Islam. In sum, the MSA was a pan-Islamic, umbrella organization led by a utopian, mission-oriented immigrant Muslim student population which found in the United States fertile ground for the realization of its transformative, Islamizing project.

SUMMARY

In the aftermath of World War II, a new American national identity emerged that better reflected the religious and ethnic diversity of its citizens who had united in common cause and triumphed against the enemy. This national identity was founded upon a new conception of American civil religion which, rather than requiring membership in a particular religion or race, demanded loyalty to America's liberal democratic values. This new American national identity established a space in which American Muslims, particularly the veterans among them, could organize and begin developing a national American Muslim identity that insisted on the recognition of Islam as an American religion.

Yet the vast discrepancy between the democratic ideals underpinning America's new national identity and the persistence of racism in American society demonstrated to many people of color, particularly black Americans, that they continued to remain outside of America's national narrative even after they had fought for freedom under its flag in World War II. Consequently, black Muslim narratives that defined Islam as the original, national religion of black Americans found new purchase. Black Muslim critiques of Christianity as an essentially white religion and of American democracy as hypocritical became all the more sensible in an America that championed liberty while maintaining Jim Crow in the South and black ghettos in the North. As a result of the activities of black Muslim nationalist movements, Islam emerged as a prophetic, black, American religion of liberation within a large segment of the African American population in the 1950s and 1960s.

Meanwhile, World War II had made the United States a much more significant player on the world stage. The growing significance of oil to

---

[105] MSA, *The MSA Handbook*, 60.

the American economy and the perceived threat of Communism led the United States to become more involved in the affairs of Muslim-majority countries, particularly in the Middle East. This led to increased contact with Muslim-majority states and brought the presence of American Muslims to the attention of Muslim heads of state and Islamist missionaries who sought support in the United States for their individual causes.

The United States also became a major destination point for Muslim students wishing to complete their education abroad. Many of these students had been politicized by the nationalist or Islamist movements in their home countries. Some of them continued their activism in this country and sought to realize their utopian visions of an Islamic society among a diverse population of Muslims in the United States. Their Islamizing project found a fitting testing ground in the United States.

7

A New Religious America and a Post-Colonial Muslim World

American Muslim Institution Building and Activism, 1960s–1980s

In the mid-1960s Congress introduced landmark civil rights and immigration legislation intended to reconcile the reality of racial and gender discrimination in the United States with the nation's democratic ideals. These laws significantly altered the racial and religious landscape of the country by outlawing discrimination in immigration policy, educational institutions, the workplace, and the housing market. The old melting pot ideal came under assault and was replaced by a more pluralistic vision of America in which cultural and ethnic differences were not only recognized but increasingly valued for their distinct contributions to American society. White Protestant triumphalism in all of its varieties was taken to task as racist, sexist, and downright un-American.

As white, Protestant cultural and political hegemony receded, however, rivalries between different ethnicities surfaced, resulting in what is sometimes referred to as an era of "identity politics." These rivalries were fueled by governmental "affirmative actions" taken to correct the racist and sexist policies of the past. Social justice, it was argued, demanded more than the simple outlawing of discrimination; it also required giving assistance to those who had been wrongfully discriminated against so that they could finally establish a place for themselves in society. Since these "affirmative action" or "equal opportunity" programs were directed toward women and minorities, many male white ethnics felt left out. They believed that their success in overcoming prejudice by hard work and ingenuity had been overlooked. In the 1970s, they led a charge on two fronts. On one front, they put the melting pot ideal to bed and publicly celebrated America's diverse ethnic heritages in what is generally known as the "white ethnic revival." On the other, they articulated a "new conservative" public policy agenda to counter the welfare society that the new affirmative action policies were creating. The philosophy behind this public policy agenda was that every individual must earn her desert. Nothing in her background, not her race, not her gender, not her class, could entitle her to them. The government's job was thus not to correct past mistakes through special programs; it was to level the playing field in order to create a more perfect meritocracy. In this meritocracy, ethnic pride and solidarity was posited as a means by which hardworking minorities had prospered and could continue to prosper in America.

This new understanding of ethnic pride and solidarity shed a new light on the black Muslim movement's message of self-help, self-love, and discipline. The Nation of Islam's call for black self-sufficiency and its puritanical work ethic and mythology of black pride were no longer seen as a threat to America's national unity in the late 1960s and early 1970s. Rather, they were seen as teachings that, though racist, were uniquely American and could promote community building and self-help. Both middle-class black Americans and white Americans came to see the positive appeal of the Nation. As it gained greater acceptance, the Nation moved toward both the American and Islamic mainstreams. In fact, in 1975–1976 it was dismantled. Most of its leaders and members converted to mainstream Islam under the leadership of Elijah Muhammad's son, Warith Deen Mohammed and eventually came to regard themselves as yet another ethno-religious American community. The outlawing of racial discrimination had provided black Americans with more choices in their lives. More choices led to greater diversity within the black Muslim community. Warith Deen himself sought to accommodate the greater individualization of his community by decentralizing power and authority within the movement. Not all members of the Nation of Islam agreed with the changes instituted by Warith Deen Mohammed (who at that time was known as Wallace Deen Muhammad). In 1978, Louis Farakhan, who left Warith Deen Mohammed's organization in 1977, reconstituted the Nation of Islam along with its original practices and mythology.

Meanwhile, changes in immigration laws in 1965 allowed for Muslims from Asia and Africa to come once again to the United States in large numbers. Thanks to the Civil Rights Movement, however, these new Asian and African Muslim immigrants came to the United States in which they did not have to change their names or dissimulate their religion. And even if they had been asked to hide their cultural and religious identity, they would have been unlikely to do so willingly, given their own experiences and struggles with colonialism at home. They came from virtually

every part of the Muslim-majority world. They represented the enormous
ethnic and sectarian diversity of the Muslim world as a whole, and in
the United States they developed institutions and social networks that
reflected their diversity. Some of these new immigrants, many of them
students, were either involved with or inspired by Islamist movements,
mainly the Jama'at-i Islam and the Muslim Brotherhood, which sought to
establish modern Islamic states in Muslim-majority countries by deriving
a political ideology from Islamic scriptures. These Muslims were generally more active in building national Muslim institutions and in missionary work (*da'wa*). In the United States, their aim was to create an
ideal Islamic society based on the original teachings of the Qur'an and
the Hadith (the traditions of Prophet Muhammad). They sought to unite
Muslims of varying ethnicities and beliefs through the notion that Islam
is an ideology and a "comprehensive way of life" for the modern world
that transcends ethnic, racial, and cultural differences. Although these
individuals and the national organizations they founded have since been
the loudest Muslim voice in America, they do not represent the majority
of the American Muslim population as a whole.[1]

The United States saw a significant rise in the number of mosques
and Muslim associations in the 1970s and 1980s. While some of these
were constructed with funds from foreign countries or non-govern-
mental organizations, the majority resulted from local Muslim efforts.
Many served a specific ethnic or national Muslim community. National
Muslim organizations, from the Federation of Islamic Associations to
the Muslim Students Association and its successor, the Islamic Society of
North America, understood well the local nature of American Muslim
community building. They generally did not impose themselves upon
a community; rather they made themselves available as a resource for

---

[1] To put this statement in perspective, in the early 1980s, the number of Muslims who
attended the joint conventions of the Muslim Students Association and the Islamic Society
of North America, which were founded with the help of Islamist activists, were around
3,000–4,000, many of whom – as attested by the large size of the bazaars at these conventions – were there for socializing with other Muslims. Even within the membership
of groups that were specifically founded by members of international Muslim organizations, active members of the international organization are usually not in the majority.
For example, a leader of the Muslim American Society (MAS), which was founded by
members of the international Muslim Brotherhood indicated in 2004 that there are only
about 1,500 active members, including many women, in MAS, and of these 45 percent
are members of the Muslim Brotherhood. See Noreen S. Ahmed-Ullah, Sam Roe, and
Laurie Cohen, "American Muslims Divided over Group Aiming to Create Islamic States
Worldwide," *Chicago Tribune* (September 20, 2004). See also footnote 71 below.

local initiatives. They sought to increase their influence by distributing propaganda rather than getting involved in local decision making.

The legislative and social changes of the 1960s encouraged immigrant Muslims to define their Islamic identity as they saw fit. There were no general threats to their citizenship that would incite them to unite under a single national or racial banner. While most non-Muslim Americans' views of Islam were shaped by stereotypes, particularly in light of media reports of "Arab/Palestinian terrorism," the Arab oil crisis, and the Iranian hostage crisis, such public prejudices did not result in exclusionary laws as they had during the first decades of the twentieth century. Since new immigration laws created new categories of preference in favor of "professional" and "highly skilled" individuals, many of the new immigrants from the Muslim-majority world came from the middle or upper classes and thus more readily gained acceptance in the United States. In short, most immigrant Muslims in this period did not feel racialized in the United States.

The unifying threat American Muslims felt came from abroad in terms of the Palestinian-Israeli conflict and anti-colonial struggles. It was in this transnational context where they felt racialized and subject to injustice. The effect of this dual mode of self-identification – white at home and colored abroad – was most clearly seen among the Arab Americans after the 1967 Arab-Israeli war, when Arab Americans who had nearly assimilated themselves to extinction came to self-identify as a disadvantaged minority. America's changing attitudes toward minorities, of course, enabled their minority identity claims.

These conflicts, however, were cast in nationalist rather than religious terms. Islamist organizations participated in them but generally as members of a larger nationalist coalition. It was not until the Soviets invaded Afghanistan and an Islamic revolution took hold in Iran that American Muslims felt empowered to become more politically active in the United States for "Islamic causes."

DEBATING AND FRAMING DIVERSITY IN POST-1965 UNITED STATES

The landmark civil rights and immigration reforms of the 1960s were the culmination of a series of laws and court decisions, each of which chipped at the national image of America as an essentially Anglo-Saxon, Protestant country, dating back to World War II. In 1943 and 1946, Congress allowed for the naturalization of Chinese and Indian immigrants, respectively. In 1952, it passed the McCarren-Walter Act, which abolished the Asiatic Barred Zone, allowing entry to a limited number of immigrants from East Asia. In 1954, the Supreme Court in *Brown v. Board of Education* outlawed segregation in public schools by declaring that "separate education facilities are inherently unequal" and therefore unconstitutional. The Civil Rights Acts of 1957 and 1960 instituted a federal Commission on Civil Rights and gave the federal government authority to monitor and prosecute discriminatory voting practices. The egalitarian legislation of the mid-1960s was thus the outcome of a long and arduous struggle.

As civil rights and immigration laws changed the power dynamics between people of varying racial and religious backgrounds in the United States, the paradigms through which the relationship between politics and diversity was viewed also changed. Since the early twentieth century, ethnic and religious diversity was mainly understood through the problematic metaphor of the "melting pot."[2] Within this paradigm, the government's role was to manage the pot. It made sure through Americanization programs that the flame beneath the pot was hot enough to assure assimilation. It also managed the content of the pot by admitting only the "right" mixture of races and religions. The "unassimilable" were kept out through segregation and exclusionary immigration and naturalization laws.

The use of a melting pot metaphor to describe the emergence of an American identity out of varying ethnic European identities dates back at least to the beginning of the republic, when the French farmer M. G. St. Jean de Crèvecoeur (also known as J. Hector St. John de Crèvecoeur) wrote, "Here individuals of all nations are melted into a new race of men, whose labours and posterity will one day cause great changes in the world."[3] In 1908, Israel Zangwill popularized the metaphor in his successful Broadway play, *The Melting Pot*. In the play, David Quixano, a Russian Jewish immigrant who had been orphaned by a pogrom, acclaimed America as "God's Crucible, the great Melting Pot where all the races of Europe are melting and re-forming! Here you stand, good folk, think I, when I see them at Ellis Island, here you stand in your fifty groups, with your fifty languages and histories, and your fifty blood

---

[2] For a classic discussion of the problematic use of this metaphor to describe racial and religious diversity, see Philip Gleason, "The Melting Pot: Symbol of Fusion or Confusion?" *American Quarterly* 16, no. 1 (Spring 1964), 20–46.

[3] Michel-Guillaume Jean de Crèvecoeur, "Letters from an American Farmer," *The Monthly Review* (July 1782), 145.

hatreds and rivalries. But you won't be long like that, brothers, for these are the fires of God you've come to – these are the fires of God."[4]

Later in the mid-twentieth century, Will Herberg (see Chapter 5) argued that there was an American civil religion which melted away differences within the rubric of American Protestantism, Catholicism, and Judaism. During the first decades of the twentieth century, even among the few opponents of the melting pot ideal, the expectation was that a coherent society demands the harmonization, if not homogenization, of its diverse elements. Horace Kallen, for example, who famously rejected the notion that ethnic and cultural differences could or even should melt into an amorphous, homogenized "American," still argued for ethnic and cultural differences to harmonize into a form of "cultural pluralism" similar to the way different musical instruments in an orchestra harmonize to produce a symphony.[5]

In 1963, Nathan Glazer and Daniel Patrick Moynihan challenged the reality of the melting pot in their groundbreaking study of ethnicity in New York City, *Beyond the Melting Pot*. Glazer and Moynihan argued that although America had imagined itself "in terms of the Doric simplicity of New England, or the pastoral symmetry of the Virginia countryside," it was the longstanding heterogeneity and complexity of New York City that most accurately represented America. "Paris may be France, London may be England, but New York, we continue to reassure ourselves, is *not* America. But, of course, it *is* America: not all of America, or even most, but surely the most important single part."[6] Glazer and Moynihan argued that "the point about the melting pot ... is that it did not happen. At least not in New York and, *mutatis mutandis*, in those parts of America which resemble New York."[7] Although certain ethnicities, such as the Germans, did apparently melt away, in general, ethnic differences endured throughout U.S. history. They endured, however, not because they managed to "harmonize" individual ethnic communities with America as a whole, but because the forces of competition in the United States necessitated their existence. Glazer and Moynihan interpreted ethnic differences within the sphere of political and economic competition at the local level. "Social and political institutions," the authors wrote, "do not merely respond to

[4] Israel Zangwill, *The Melting Pot: Drama in Four Acts*, new and rev. edition (New York: The Macmillan Company, 1919), 33.

[5] Horace Kallen, "Democracy versus the Melting-Pot: A Study of American Nationality," *The Nation* 100, no. 2590 (February 18, 1915), 190–194.

[6] Nathan Glayer and Daniel Patrick Moynihan, *Beyond the Melting Pot: The Negroes, Puerto Ricans, Jews, Italians and Irish of New York City* (Cambridge, MA: M.I.T. Press, 1968), 2.

[7] Ibid., v.

ethnic interests; a great number of institutions exist for the specific purpose of serving ethnic interests. This in turn tends to perpetuate them."[8] The historical success of ethnic institutions in achieving their political and economic interests perpetuated ethnic identity socially and placed different ethnic groups in competition with one another politically and economically. Glazer and Moynihan thus concluded, "Religion and race define the next stage in the evolution of the American people."[9] Ultimately, upward mobility or economic inequity could be overcome by the political mobilization of ethnic and religious communities, which in turn would afford the members of these communities access to social and economic networks through which they could rise up the economic ladder.

By downplaying the role class differences play in shaping the American people, Glazer and Moynihan must have been aware that they were sidestepping one of the major reasons given by African American leaders in the North for why black Americans had not been able to attain the same level of economic prosperity as their white ethnic counterparts. The authors argued that ethnic mobilization among African Americans had effected some gains: "One can see the large mass of problems that are high up on the agenda of city government and civic groups – crime, delinquency, the breakdown of family responsibility. And one can see the increasing numbers who achieve middle-class status, and for whom the only problems are those created by the prejudiced and discriminatory behavior of others." The social problems blacks faced, Glazer and Moynihan contended, had less to do with economic inequities than with black leadership. The era of black "accommodation" of white racism was over, they declared, but so was the era of "protest," when blacks decried the social and institutional injustices they endured. What was now needed in the black community, they argued, was "a period of self-examination and self-help, in which the increasing income and resources of leadership of the group are turned inward." "It is probable that no investment of public and private agencies on delinquency and crime prevention programs will equal the return from an investment by Negro-led and Negro-financed agencies."[10]

By highlighting the economic and political successes of ethnic groups in New York City, Glazer and Moynihan moved the relation between government and diversity "beyond the melting pot" by demonstrating

[8] Ibid., 310.
[9] Ibid., 315.
[10] Ibid., 83–84.

concretely the achievements and contributions of ethnic minorities. The government, they showed, ought not to manage the melting pot; rather it ought to, to vary the metaphor, assure a level playing field on which people of diverse racial and religious backgrounds could compete with one another fairly. There were, however, many in the 1960s and 1970s who were unwilling to disassociate racial and religious conceptions of social justice from economic conceptions of social justice. Thus, they continued to see a distributive role for government in managing diversity beyond the outlawing of discrimination.

In addition to landmark civil rights and immigration legislations, the 1960s and 1970s also saw the beginning of affirmative action and social welfare programs designed to remedy the effects of many years of discrimination against people of color and to promote diversity in employment and education. "[F]reedom is not enough," President Lyndon Johnson explained in his 1965 speech at Howard University, just as Congress was about to pass the Voting Rights Act of 1965:

You do not wipe away the scars of centuries by saying: Now you are free to go where you want, and do as you desire, and choose the leaders you please. You do not take a person who, for years, has been hobbled by chains and liberate him, bring him up to the starting line of a race and then say, 'you are free to compete with all the others' and justly believe that you have been completely fair. Thus it is not enough just to open the gates of opportunity. All our citizens must have the ability to walk through those gates.[11]

The attempt to right the wrongs of the past for some at the possible expense of others proved controversial, particularly as quotas and statistical goals were established for the employment of women and minorities within public universities and government bureaucracies. White ethnic intellectuals and politicians (mainly of Catholic and Jewish origin) who, in the 1960s and 1970s, had begun to take pride in the distinct contribution their ethnic or religious community had made to the United States, led the charge against such programs. Believing that Catholic and Jewish immigrants had overcome discrimination through hard work and ingenuity, these intellectuals put forth a "new conservative" argument from within the Democratic Party in passionate support of individualism and meritocracy over minority entitlements and affirmative action. Glazer, for example, wrote in 1964:

---

[11] Cited in Ronald W. Walters, *Freedom Is Not Enough: Black Voters, Black Candidates, and American Presidential Politics* (Lanham, MD: Rowman & Littlefield, 2007), 16–17.

Negroes are acutely aware of how few of their young people even now get into the good colleges, and they see as a critical cause of this the small proportion of Negroes in good public elementary and high schools.... And since political pressure and organized group pressure have been effective in breaching segregation in the South, and in bringing about some of these entries in the North, they see no reason why similar pressures should not be equally effective in making up the deficiencies that continue to be apparent. If whites say, "But first you must earn your entry – through grades, or examinations," Negroes, with a good deal more knowledge of the realities of American society than foreign immigrants used to have, answer, "But we know how *you* got ahead – through political power, and connections, and the like; therefore, we won't accept your pious argument that merit is the only thing that counts." There is some truth to this rejoinder; there is, I believe much less truth when it is made to Jews. For the Jews have, indeed, put their faith in the abstract measures of individual merit – marks and examinations.[12]

The Catholic scholar Michael Novak took pride in how far America had come in terms of acknowledging the diversity within it.

Identification with an ethnic group is a source of values, instincts, ideas, and perceptions that throw original light on the meaning of America.... [M]illions of Americans who for a long time tried desperately even if unconsciously to become "Americanized," are delighted to discover that they no longer have to pay that price; are grateful that they were born among the people destiny placed them in; are pleased to discover the possibilities and the limits inherent in being who they are; and are openly happy about what heretofore they had disguised in silence. There is a creativity and new release, there is liberation, and there is hope. America is becoming America.[13]

Below the surface of Novak's celebration of white ethnics' rightful claims on America was a deep sense of anxiety about identity politics and about how "equal opportunity" and "affirmative action" programs were "changing the rules" through which white ethnic communities had prospered.

Blacks, for example, have been so deeply penalized in education, economic resources, and political organization that their social strategy has had to be unique. Jews fulfilled their own interests as an ethnic group by excelling individually in universities, merchandising, and new industries like television, cinema, and electronics. But blacks face their new possibilities with very little social leverage.

[12] Glazer, "Negroes and Jews: The New Challenge to Pluralism," *Commentary* (December 1964), reprinted in Glazer, *Ethnic Dilemmas: 1964–1982* (Cambridge, MA: Harvard University Press, 1983), 35–37.
[13] Michael Novak, *The Rise of the Unmeltable Ethnics: Politics and Culture in the Seventies* (New York: Macmillan, 1972), 290–291.

It is in their interest as an ethnic group to insist on high quotas for blacks in schools and jobs, and not to accept as valid the argument that equality is only for those who "qualify." For it is exactly in their lack of preparation to qualify that many blacks have born the weight of injustice. Hence blacks have seen fit to "change the rules." They have discovered that whites fear black rebellion and disruption.[14]

In many ways, the white ethnic revival of the late 1960s and the 1970s, in which Novak was but one of many participants, was a reaction to social welfare, from which white ethnics felt left out.[15] The resurgence of white ethnic identity affirmed the place of Catholics and Jews alongside Protestants in the America of the 1960s and 1970s and argued for meritocracy as the way through which the government should manage diversity. Any attempt to define social justice in economic terms or in terms of the redistribution of wealth was deemed subversive and "militant." Hence there were militant blacks, militant women, militant Chicanos, militant homosexuals, militant welfare mothers, and militant hippies.[16] "Militant" tactics, however, Novak warned, may work on white Anglo-Saxon Protestants but were of no use on "ethnic whites", who had also been victims of social prejudice: "Someone must make the argument in America, because it is true, that black militance can push some WASPS and some liberals around, but it will *not* push ethnics around."[17] Far from pushing ethnics around, the special status afforded to minorities by equal opportunity and affirmative action programs, which Novak viewed as WASP capitulations to black militancy, permitted white ethnics to shed the yoke of assimilation and to value their distinct contributions to America.

THE MAINSTREAMING OF THE NATION OF ISLAM IN AMERICAN SOCIETY

In many ways, Glazer and Moynihan articulated in sociological jargon what Noble Drew Ali, Fard Muhammad, Elijah Muhammad, Malcolm X and many other Southern black migrants to the northern cities had already intuited. Northern metropolises at the beginning of the twentieth century were home not only to large numbers of Catholic and Jewish "new immigrants" from southern and eastern Europe but also to "new

[14] Ibid., 285.
[15] Arthur Mann, *The One and the Many: Reflections on the American Identity* (Chicago, IL: University of Chicago Press, 1979), 36f.
[16] Mann, *The One and the Many*, 11–12.
[17] Novak, *Unmeltable Ethnics*, 168.

immigrants" from the Levant and East Asia. These communities, as Glazer and Moynihan demonstrated, formed colonies and self-help organizations. Most worked as wage laborers in the industrial and commercial labor markets of the North but some also started small businesses, which during the depression helped create a social network through which they provided jobs for their kin and co-ethnics. This "kind of clannishness," which allowed white ethnics to celebrate their contributions to American society in the late 1960s and 1970s, was precisely what the Moorish Science Temple and the Nation of Islam had sought for black migrants through their appropriation of Islamic symbols and practices.[18] Yet because they placed blacks' "original" identity outside of Christianity and, in the case of the Nation of Islam, outside of the predominantly white American nation-state, they were uniformly considered seditious. However, as the unifying ideal of the melting pot came under assault in the 1960s and 1970s as a symbol of American society, both northern whites and middle-class blacks came to view the message of self-discipline, ethnic pride, and independence advocated by black Muslim nationalist movements in a different light. Glazer and Moynihan, for example, wrote of the Nation of Islam, "It emphasizes traditional virtues, as do all storefront churches (no smoking, drinking, women), but less because these are sinful than because by saving his money and devoting himself to his business the Negro may make himself wealthy and successful. This is indeed a nationalist and racist movement. But it is surprising how much of Horatio Alger there is in it, too – and that reflects a great change in the Negro community."[19]

After the passage of civil rights legislation in the 1960s, the goals of the Civil Rights Movement and the Nation of Islam became more closely aligned. As Ronald Takaki has argued, the Civil Rights Movement at first focused primarily on the South and on abolishing Jim Crow. After the outlawing of discrimination, the movement turned its attention to the less overt racist practices of the North, which the Moorish Science Temple and the Nation of Islam had already begun confronting in the 1920s and 1930s. The goal of the Civil Rights Movement had been integration – a goal which Elijah Muhammad and Malcolm X denounced in favor of independence, self-help, and separatism. However, when faced with de facto rather than de jure racist practices in major cities – in which blacks found themselves on the lower end of the economic ladder and in competition

---

[18] Glazer and Moynihan, *Beyond the Melting Pot*, 30–31 and 33.
[19] Ibid., 82–83.

with other ethnic communities who had at their disposal established social, economic and political networks – separation, confrontation, and self-help appeared more viable options for advancement than integration. Shortly after Martin Luther King, Jr. spoke of his dream of racial integration in Washington, D.C. in August 1963, he confessed, "I watched that dream turn into a nightmare as I moved through the ghettos of the nation and saw my black brothers and sisters perishing on a lonely island of poverty in the midst of a vast ocean of material prosperity, and saw the nation doing nothing to grapple with the Negroes' problem of poverty."[20] As James H. Cone has noted, experiences in the ghettos of the North and the West following the passage of the Civil Rights Acts of the 1960s brought King face to face with "the world that created Malcolm X."[21]

The Nation of Islam during this period gained a new level of respect as its message of self-love and self-help – "Black is beautiful!" – resonated with many upwardly mobile African Americans who became involved in the Black Power movement and as its message of "do for self" appealed to white ethnics who decried equal opportunity quotas and affirmative action programs as forms of reverse discrimination. In the 1970s, the Nation of Islam came as close as it ever would to being mainstream without abandoning its mythology. Its message of separation and self-reliance, which was deemed deviant and subversive in the 1940s, 1950s, and early 1960s, was tempered as a message of ethnic pride, black community-building, and self-help. The group, though still deemed objectionable, was no longer seen as a threat. "It was strange," writes one of Elijah Muhammad's biographers, "how much the situation had changed in only the span of a decade." The Illinois state legislature, which had earlier sought to shut down the Nation of Islam's University of Islam, in 1973, recognized "the Honorable Elijah Muhammad and his organization for a distinct, positive community program." A year later, the mayor of Chicago declared March 29 "the Honorable Elijah Muhammad Day."[22] In 1975, Mayor Thomas Bradley proclaimed February 4 "the Honorable Elijah Muhammad Day" in Los Angeles.[23]

[20] Cited in James Melvin Washington, ed., *A Testament of Hope: The Essential Writings and Speeches of Martin Luther King, Jr.* (San Francisco, CA: Harper & Row, 1986), 257.

[21] James H. Cone, *Martin & Malcolm & America: A Dream Or a Nightmare* (Maryknoll, NY: Orbis Books, 1991), 222.

[22] Claude Andrew Clegg III, *An Original Man: The Life and Times of Elijah Muhammad* (New York: Macmillan, 1998), 272.

[23] *Muhammad Speaks*, February 21, 1975. The announcement can be viewed at the *Muhammad Speaks* website, http://www.muhammadspeaks.com/LosAngeles.html (accessed March 15, 2010).

WARITH DEEN MOHAMMED AND THE CONVERSION
OF THE NATION OF ISLAM

The Nation of Islam itself underwent radical changes in 1975–1976. On February 25, 1975, Elijah Muhammad passed away. His son Wallace Deen Muhammad, who later changed his name to Warith Deen Mohammed (literally, 'the inheritor of the religion of Muhammad'), was named his successor. Under W. D. Mohammed's leadership, the Nation of Islam was radically altered. It was de-mythologized, and most of its members were converted to a more mainstream understanding of Islam. The Nation of Islam's farms, restaurants, and other business ventures were sold to private parties, and its unarmed security force, the Fruit of Islam, was dismantled. All control over individual Muhammad Mosques went to the local community. If Elijah Muhammad had anticipated such an outcome when he appointed Wallace as his successor, he never made his intent public.

During the annual Nation of Islam gathering following the death of Elijah Muhammad, in what was called "the greatest expression of unity, loyalty and dedication," various high officials of the Nation of Islam, including Louis Farrakhan, champion boxer Muhammad Ali, National Secretary Abass Rassoull, and Supreme Captain Raymond Sharrieff, extended their support to W. D. Mohammed, who had at that time gained the title, "The Honorable Wallace Deen Muhammad," the Supreme Minister of the Nation of Islam.[24] This choice was somewhat surprising given that Wallace had been suspended several times from the Nation of Islam, mainly for his refusal to accept the divinity of Fard Muhammad and for questioning the teachings of the Nation of Islam based on what he had learned about Islam through his contact with different immigrant Muslims and through his travels in the Muslim world.[25] "Even on his best behavior," C. E. Lincoln wrote, "it is doubtful that he had ever accepted without reservation the doctrines laid down by his father and proclaimed by his fellow ministers in the mosques of Muhammad."[26] The dissidence between Wallace and his father was so widely known that even the FBI was aware of it. In 1969, the FBI headquarters wrote to its field office in Chicago: "The NOI appears to be the personal fiefdom of Elijah

---

[24] "Undying Support for Undying Leadership," *Muhammad Speaks*, March 14, 1975, 3.
[25] Richard Brent Turner, *Islam in the African-American Experience*, 2nd ed. (Bloomington, IN: Indiana University Press, 2003), 224–225; Edward E. Curtis IV, *Islam in Black America: Identity, Liberation, and Difference in African-American Islamic Thought* (Albany, NY: State University of New York Press, 2002), 110–112.
[26] C. Eric Lincoln, *The Black Muslims* (Boston, MA: Beacon, 1961), 264.

Muhammad. When he dies a power struggle can be expected and the NOI could change direction. We should be prepared for this eventuality. We should plan how to change the philosophy of the NOI." The FBI had identified Wallace D. Muhammad as "the only son of Elijah Muhammad who would have the necessary qualities to guide the NOI in such a manner as would eliminate racist teachings."[27] In any case, it was for the most part known within the higher circles of the Nation of Islam that Elijah Muhammad's fifth son, Wallace, born October 30, 1933, was to succeed him. According to W. D. Mohammed, he was the only child to be born during Fard Muhammad's tenure in the Nation of Islam, and Fard had predicted that he would be male and had indicated that he should succeed Elijah.[28]

Soon after assuming the mantle of the Nation of Islam, W. D. Mohammed began de-mythologizing and de-eschatologizing its doctrines. In 1975, he told his followers, "Brothers and sisters, you don't yet know the reality of God. But if you have patience and accept what I teach you of God, you will come into the reality of God. Then you will truly be a superior people in the earth."[29] He also instructed his followers to observe Islamic rituals, such as the Ramadan fast and the daily ritual prayers. By 1977, his community was so well versed in mainstream Islamic practices that some 300 of them attended the Hajj as guests of the Saudi government.[30]

Just as it was the case with earlier African Americans who split from the Ahmadiyya and the Moorish Science Temple to adopt more mainstream Muslim beliefs and practices, the conversion of the Nation of Islam could be characterized as a conversion to Sunni Islam because it entailed the adoption of practices and beliefs most commonly associated with Sunnism in Islamic history. W. D. Mohammed and his followers themselves, however, did not understand their conversion specifically in these terms. They did not contextualize their adoption of mainstream Islamic beliefs and rituals in the context of Sunni Islam or Islamic history; rather they contextualized their conversion in the context of African

---

[27] FBI file 100-448006-571, January 7, 1969 and Chicago FBI file 100-35635-Sub B, April 22, 1968, both cited in Mattias Gardell, *In the Name of Elijah Muhammad: Louis Farrakhan and the Nation of Islam* (Durham, NC: Duke University Press, 1996), 100–101.

[28] "Interview with Imam Wallace D. Muhammad," interview by Clifton E. Marsh (Chicago, July 25, 1979), in *The Lost-Found Nation of Islam in America* (Lanham, MD: The Scarecrow Press, 2000), 160.

[29] Wallace Deen Muhammad, "The Second Resurrection, Part 2: 'Baptism with the Water of Revelation'," *Muhammad Speaks*, April 18, 1975, 13.

[30] Curtis, *Islam in Black America*, 114–115.

American history. Put differently, they did not adopt a foreign, Sunni system of belief and praxis; rather, relying on the polysemous nature of religious beliefs and practices, they indigenized mainstream Islamic beliefs and practices and reinterpreted the teachings of Nation of Islam metaphorically in order to resignify them in terms of mainstream Islamic beliefs. Their Islam was thus understood to be distinctively and proudly African American. They saw themselves as "reverting"[31] to the original religion of their African ancestors rather than converting to a new religion. W. D. Mohammed wrote:

I believe firmly that Al-Islam ("Islam") is in America by Allah's Will to be our salvation and to establish African Americans.... If a child was taken from his parents by a kidnapper, and that parent was hurt and done a terrible injustice and so was the child; if no help comes to the child, and the parent also is being slandered and mistreated and lied against, then don't you know that if there is a God, that God should in time do something for that situation? The mercy and injustice would be to bring that child and that parent back together. Even if the parent is dead, if the child is still living, the justice would be to reconcile that child with its parents. But our parents are not dead; they are still alive. There are African Muslims still in Africa, and history reports that many of us were brought from African Muslim life and were enslaved here in America. Slave traders (buyers) did not go to churches in Africa to get slaves for America. When I was following my father's teachings (the late Honorable Elijah Muhammad), I felt it strongly. I felt that Allah had plans for us.... It is not popular for an African American race to embrace the religion of a White race, when that religion is imaged in a "White man," the "Word" and "God." The only way that could happen is that we were under them and could not express freedom of choice.[32]

Given this understanding of the divine role of Islam in African American history, neither W. D. Mohammed nor his followers denounced their twentieth-century, spiritual ancestors – Noble Drew Ali, Fard Muhammad, and Elijah Muhammad – as charlatans or false prophets who introduced them to a corrupt understanding of Islam. On the contrary, they held them in great esteem as individuals who gradually introduced a "lost-found

---

[31] In Islamic mythology, humanity is said to be born upon a divine nature (*fitra*) that predisposes it to the worship of God. This concept is expressed both in the Qur'an (7:172 and 30:30–31) and in a prophetic tradition (*hadith*) in which Prophet Muhammad is reported to have said that "Every child is born upon *fitra*, but then his parents make him into a Christian, a Jew, or a Zoroastrian." Based on this many converts to Islam in the United States, see themselves as "reverts" to their original nature. For followers of W. D. Mohammed at this time, however, it is clear that their adoption of Sunni beliefs and practices was not only a spiritual "reversion" but also a "reversion" to an ancestral religion.

[32] Warith Deen Mohammed, *al-Islam: Unity & Leadership* (Chicago, IL: The Sense Maker, 1991), 102–103.

nation" of black Americans to their ancestral path of salvation, which, in line with the teachings of earlier black nationalist Muslims, was to be achieved not only in the hereafter but also in the here and now in the form of economic and social advancement. "Because I am not believing in the theology of the Nation of Islam that we were in before," W. D. Mohammad retorted as late as 1995, "should not make anyone come to the conclusion that I don't like 'doing for self.' No one should come to the conclusion that I don't like seeing us work for business establishment and empowerment.... We want to get into situations where we can use our resources and improve our skills and become resourceful enough to produce for ourselves, so the White man won't have to carry us."[33]

W. D. Mohammed introduced his new teachings as the "Second Resurrection" of the Nation of Islam and the fulfillment of the original intent of the Nation:

We have been taught many things in the Teachings of the Great Master W. F. Muhammad [Wallace Fard Muhammad] and the Honorable Master Elijah Muhammad that have prepared us for this time – the time of the Second Resurrection. The Teachings have brought us along the road to a certain point towards our destination in scriptural interpretation. When we take it from that point and carry it on into the Second Resurrection, we will understand that this movement is a continuing movement and not a new movement.[34]

W. D. Mohammed also claimed to be divinely guided, but his divine guidance came not through prophecies but through the Islamic scripture. He presented himself as a *mujaddid* or a reviver of the Islamic faith. He argued that humans are defined by their minds, not by their physical appearance, so references to the divine nature of blacks and the devilish nature of whites should not be understood literally to mean that all black people are divine and all white people are the devil, but that there is a state of mind that is divine and a state of mind that is evil. "You can destroy a devil by destroying the mind that the person has grown within them. If you can destroy that mind, you will destroy that devil."[35]

W. D. Mohammed departed from his father's teachings by asserting that blacks were not the original humans who grafted the other races of people

[33] Warith Deen Mohammed, "The Priorities for an Advancing People," *Muslim Journal* 17 (March 1995), 3.

[34] Wallace Deen Muhammad, "The Second Resurrection, Part 1: 'The Light Behind the Veil'," *Muhammad Speaks*, April 18, 1975, 13.

[35] Wallace Deen Muhammad, "The Destruction of the Devil," *Muhammad Speaks*, July 11, 1975, 13.

from their lower nature; rather, they were original humans because they were ignorant of their origins and their potential as a people: "When we say that the Original man is the Asiatic Black man, what do we mean by 'Black?' We are referring to the man who was born in darkness and out of darkness and whose mind developed so strongly that it was able to bring light to darkness."[36] In other words, broadly construed, W. D. Mohammed replaced racial modes of self-identification with religious ones. This does not mean, however, that he abandoned the Nation of Islam's message of self-love and self-help. In October 1976, he renamed the Nation of Islam the World Community of al-Islam in the West (WCIW), which he claimed had around 70,000 members.[37] This change reflected a new outlook among his members; at a time when ethnic pride was on the rise, he sought to identify African American Muslims as yet another American ethnic community. African American Muslims were no longer to be viewed as a heretical movement within Islam nor were they to be referred to as "Black Muslims," a term adopted by outsiders for members of the Nation of Islam after the publication of C. E. Lincoln's *The Black Muslims in America* (1961). In 1978, the annual Nation of Islam gathering known as Saviour's Day (the day commemorating Fard Muhammad's birthday) was replaced by Ethnic Survival Week. Wallace also established the "New World Patriotism Day" to be observed on Independence Day. Over the years, W. D. Mohammed restructured his movement several times. The World Community of al-Islam in the West or Bilalians (after Bilal ibn Ribah, the black ex-slave who converted to Islam and made the call to prayer during Prophet Muhammad's lifetime) came to be known as the American Muslim Mission and later as the American Society of Muslims and finally as The Mosque Cares. In the absence of a critical biography of this immensely important figure in the history of Islam in America, it is difficult to ascertain the exact nature and significance of these changes. In general, they were intended to de-centralize power and religious authority among his adherents and to realize a hope he expressed in 1972 to have his community "be called American Muslims. I hope Muslims will be so comfortable in America that we won't have to introduce any structure or anything, just be American Muslims."[38] Despite the changes over the years, however, W. D. Mohammed remained a centrally revered figure

[36] Wallace Deen Muhammad, "Who Is the Original Man?" *Muhammad Speaks*, August 22, 1975, 16–17.
[37] Turner, *Islam in the African-American Experience*, 227.
[38] Marsh, "Interview with Imam Wallace D. Muhammad," in *Lost-Found Nation of Islam in America*, 168.

among his followers who, until his death on September 9, 2008, deferred to him on major religious questions and organizational issues.

After converting the Nation of Islam to mainstream Islam, W. D. Mohammed became a major beneficiary of funds from Muslim-majority countries. In 1978, a number of Persian Gulf states, including Saudi Arabia, Abu Dhabi, and Qatar designated him the "sole consultant and trustee" for their distribution of funds to Muslim missionary organizations in the United States.[39] He was also an American Muslim delegate at numerous international Islamic conferences in Saudi Arabia and elsewhere.

FARRAKHAN'S RECONSTITUTION OF THE NATION OF ISLAM

Whatever personal and religious reasons Warith Deen Mohammed may have had for converting the Nation of Islam to mainstream Islamic beliefs and practices, he would not have been successful if the economic conditions of its members and the nature of race relations in the United States had not changed in the 1970s. Indeed, some members of the Nation of Islam, who were not affected by these changes, broke away from the movement after its conversion. Chief among them was Louis Farrakhan (formerly Louis Eugene Walcott). Farrakhan left W. D. Mohammed's organization in 1977 and reestablished the Nation under Elijah Muhammad's teachings in 1978. He claimed that by moving away from the original teachings of the Nation of Islam, the uplifting message of the Nation of Islam was diluted and black Muslims were made subservient to Muslims from the Old World. During a speech at the "Welcome Home, Brother Farrakhan" rally in Harlem in 1980, Farrakhan explained why he believed it was necessary to return to the original teachings of the Nation: "You left the nation and its discipline. You have gone back to drinking alcohol, smoking reefers, eating pork, and boogie-ing. All the progress we made has been lost. The brothers are back on the street shooting dope and dying. The sisters are on the street corners hookin' for the White Man."[40] He also explained why he felt that Sunni Islam could not answer the problems of African Americans:

---

[39] C. Eric Lincoln, "The American Muslim Mission in the Context of American Social History," in *The Muslim Community in North America*, ed. Earle Waugh, Baha Abu-Laban, and Regula B. Qureshi (Edmonton, AL: The University of Alberta Press, 1983), 230–231.

[40] Louis Farrakhan, speech at "Welcome Home, Brother Farrakhan" rally at the City College of New York, May 18, 1980, Harlem, New York, cited in Lawrence H. Mamiya, "From Black Muslim to Bilalian: The Evolution of a Movement," *Journal for the Scientific Study of Religion* 21, no. 2 (June 1982), 144.

I am here as a servant of Allah and black people (not Mecca). I see Muslims taking advantage of Blacks in Arabia and Africa. I will not jump over one black Christian to find brotherhood with a Muslim.... If you [Sunni Muslims] are so interested in the Black Man in America, why don't you clean up the ghettoes in Mecca. The ghettoes in the Holy City where the Sudanese and other black African Muslims live are some of the worst I've seen anywhere.... I see racism in the Muslim world, clean it up![41]

It is not quite clear how many adherents of W. D. Mohammed transferred to Farrakhan's organization. What is clear, however, is that they did not flock in large numbers to Farrakhan; rather, Farrakhan had to rebuild both the economic foundation of the Nation of Islam and its membership. Indeed, throughout the 1980s (and later), the followers of W. D. Mohammed significantly outnumbered the members of the Nation of Islam.[42] Many members of the Nation adopted the changes initiated by W. D. Mohammed because they viewed him as their legitimate leader. Farrakhan himself defended these changes in 1976 by asserting that "for us to be alive we must be changing and growing. Unless you are changing and growing you are dead."[43] Nonetheless, as Lawrence Mamiya has argued, W. D. Mohammed retained a significant number of the members of the Nation of Islam after the establishment of Farrakhan's organization largely because the socioeconomic conditions of the Nation's members had changed over the years. "The Nation of Islam, which began as a lower-class movement," Mamiya wrote in 1982, "has become increasingly middle-class and ... this phenomenon has affected both groups. Wallace's American Muslim Mission has retained a largely middle-class membership, while Farrakhan's resurrected Nation is seeking to find its mass base again in its lower-class origins."[44] The Nation's Puritan work ethic and message of self-love paid its dividends. "Everybody who has been in the movement for 10 years or more has moved upward," said one of W. D. Mohammed's followers. "You can't help it because the Hon. Elijah Muhammad's message was strongly economic. If Elijah Muhammad was about anything, he

[41] Louis Farrakhan, speech at "Welcome Home, Brother Farrakhan" rally at the City College of New York (Harlem, New York, May 18, 1980), cited in Lawrence H. Mamiya, "Minister Louis Farrakhan and the Final Call: Schism in the Muslim Movement," in *Muslim Community in North America*, 238.

[42] Na'im Akbar, "Family Stability among African-American Muslims," in *Muslim Families in North America*, ed. Earle Waugh, Sharon McIrvin Abu-Laban, and Regula B. Qureshi (Edmonton, AL: University of Alberta Press, 1991), 222.

[43] James S. Tinney, "Bilalian Muslims," *Christianity Today*, March 12, 1976, 51.

[44] Mamiya, "Minister Louis Farrakhan and the Final Call," 245–246. See also Mamiya, "From Black Muslim to Bilalian."

was about uplifting people's education and economics."[45] Another one of W. D. Mohammed's followers said, "I was searching for spirituality and morals when I joined the Muslims [over five years ago]. I was looking for a strong family life.... Basically, I'm in my early 30s with a college education.... The transition to the Qur'an and the Prophet Muhammad under Wallace was a relief. Elijah Muhammad gave us discipline ... But I feel I don't need the security of a uniform anymore."[46]

These testimonies substantiate the claims made in the 1920s and 1930s that impoverished African Americans could participate in America's prosperity by comprising a distinct nation based on their "original" religion, Islam. By the 1970s, however, much had changed in America. Racial divides by no means disappeared, but by attaining greater freedom, African Americans also gained more choices. Consequently, the Nation of Islam could not have had the same appeal under Farrakhan as it did when Malcolm X was its national spokesperson. Once racial discrimination was outlawed and African American civil rights leaders turned their attention to community building and self-help, the message of nationalist mobilization through Islam was neither unique nor as attractive as it was during the height of the Civil Rights Movement. It is thus no wonder that Farrakhan's Nation of Islam gradually faded from the national scene as a black "Muslim" organization after the turn of the twenty-first century. Warith Deen Mohammed's community also became more disperse. Nonetheless, despite his efforts to de-centralize religious authority among his followers and promote individualization, W. D. Mohammed remained the principal authority of the community he inherited from the Nation of Islam at a time when America was availing more and more identity choices to African Americans.

Recently, Sherman Jackson lamented the fact that as a result of African American Muslims' reliance on charismatic leadership, they did not seek to master the sources of the Islamic tradition. The effect of this, he writes, was "a Blackamerican Muslim self-definition that was practically dysfunctional, enabling Blackamerican Muslims neither as blacks nor as Americans nor, ultimately, as Muslims in America."[47] While in Jackson's view this "dysfunctional" identity challenged African American Muslims to negotiate a more functional identity for themselves as "Blackamerican Muslims," the

---

[45] Lawrence H. Mamiya, personal interview with Sister Evelyn Akbar, Oakland Masjid, (Oakland, CA, April 30, 1980) cited in Mamiya, "Minister Louis Farrakhan and the Final Call," 248.

[46] Ibid., 249–250.

[47] Sherman Jackson, *Islam and the Blackamerican: Looking toward the Third Resurrection* (New York: Oxford University Press, 2005), 5.

truth of the matter was that the outlawing of institutional discrimination in the 1960s, the rise of ethnic pride in the 1970s, and the success of black Muslim nationalist movements in uplifting their members throughout the 1960s, 1970s, and 1980s created a new sociopolitical context in which it became less imperative, both socially and politically, for African American Muslims to have to choose between being Muslim, black, American or anything else. In short, the urgent call, first sounded by Noble Drew Ali, for African Americans to develop a distinct national identity through religion in order to prosper lost its urgency as African Americans gained more personal freedom and thus more choices in their lives. The limits of these freedoms and the extent of their choices, however, should not be exaggerated. As the relative popularity of Farrakhan in the late 1980s and early 1990s and the continued success of Muslim prison outreach programs attest, the appeal of Islam as a black nationalist solution to the problems of racism and poverty did not disappear, but it lost much of its shine and urgency.

INCREASED DIVERSIFICATION OF THE AMERICAN MUSLIM POPULATION

The increasing number of choices which the civil rights legislations afforded women and minorities had a major impact on the historical development of Islam in the post-1965 era. The Immigration and Nationality Act of 1965, also known as the Hart-Celler Act, abolished national-origins quotas established by the Immigration Act of 1924. Under these quotas, only 100 immigrants from most Muslim-majority countries were allowed entry into the United States. The quotas did not apply to visitors, foreign students, immediate family members of U.S. citizens, and members of certain professions, such as professors and religious workers. Congress also passed legislation between 1924 and 1965 that tweaked the criteria that distinguished "quota immigrants" from "non-quota" immigrants. The Hart-Celler Act abolished the nation-quota system completely and adopted new criteria which gave preference to family members of U.S. citizens or permanent residents, highly educated professionals, workers in fields in which there is a labor shortage, and refugees. While many saw the new immigration law as another step toward "abolishing discrimination" based on race and place of origin, Congress did not expect the bill to "upset the ethnic mix of our society."[48] The expectation was for the bill

---

[48] Senator Edward Kennedy, U.S. Senate, Subcommittee on Immigration and Naturalization of the Committee of the Judiciary, Washington, D.C., 10 February 1965, 1–3, cited

to improve the United States' relationship with non-European countries by altering the nation's laws to better reflect its democratic ideals. It was also expected, following the devastation caused by World War II, to allow immigrants from Southern and Eastern European countries to reunite in the United States with extended family members.

   In practice, the Hart-Celler Act radically altered the ethnic makeup of American society. Southern and Eastern Europeans did not immigrate in large numbers as anticipated. Rather, the majority of the post-1965 immigrants came from Latin American and Asia. These immigrants, as Diana Eck has argued, helped bring about a "new religious America," which today constitutes the world's most religiously diverse nation.[49] We do not have accurate statistics on the number of Muslims in the United States in this period, but a look at the number of foreign born individuals from Muslim-majority countries shows clearly that the number of Muslim immigrants in the United States increased dramatically after the passage of the Hart-Celler Act. According to the Bureau of Census, the number of immigrants from Muslim-majority parts of the world rose from 134,615 in 1960 to 871,582 in 1990 (see Table 5). Most of these new immigrants came from the Middle East and South Asia, but, by the 1980s, Muslims of virtually every national, ethnic, and sectarian background came to be represented in the United States. Unlike earlier immigrants from Muslim-majority countries who were predominantly young, single, uneducated, male laborers, post-1965 Muslim immigrants were generally older professionals who came either with their families or to join family members already here. Of the 181,036 immigrants who came to the United States from Muslim-majority countries between 1966 and 1982, for example, 20 percent came under the category of professional and technical workers, and 56 percent came as the dependents of these individuals.[50] Many were sponsored by family members already living in the United States. Others were students who decided to stay after completing their education. Another group consisted of refugees escaping military conflict or political persecution in their home countries. Almost all hoped to improve their lot by taking advantage of the economic and educational opportunities available in the United States.

     in Roland Takaki, *A Different Mirror: A History of Multicultural America* (Boston, MA: Little, Brown, and Company, 1993), 400–401.
[49] Diana Eck, *A New Religious America: How a 'Christian Country' Has Now Become the World's Most Religiously Diverse Nation* (San Francisco, CA: Harper SanFrancisco, 2001).
[50] Data compiled from the *Annual Report of the Immigration and Naturalization Service* (Washington, DC: U.S. Government Printing Office, 1966–1982).

TABLE 5. Foreign-born individuals from Muslim-majority countries and regions.

Country	1990	1980	1970	1960
Albania	5,627	7,381	9,180	9,618
Afghanistan	28,444	3,760	n/a	n/a
Bangladesh	21,414	4,989	n/a	n/a
Iran	210,941	121,505	n/a	n/a
Pakistan	91,889	30,774	6,182	1,708
Indonesia	48,387	29,920	n/a	n/a
Malaysia	33,834	10,473	n/a	n/a
Iraq	44,916	32,121	n/a	n/a
Jordan	31,871	21,587	n/a	n/a
Kuwait	8,889	4,337	n/a	n/a
Lebanon	86,369	52,674	22,396	22,217
Palestine	21,070	n/a	n/a	n/a
Saudi Arabia	12,632	17,317	n/a	n/a
Syria	36,782	22,081	14,962	16,717
Turkey	55,087	51,915	48,085	52,228
United Arab Emirates	1,656	534	n/a	n/a
Yemen	4,933	3,093	n/a	n/a
Middle East	n/a	n/a	52,752	23,811
Kenya	14,371	6,250	n/a	n/a
Somalia	2,437	691	n/a	n/a
Algeria	4,629	3,853	n/a	n/a
Egypt	66,313	43,424	20,666	8,316
Libya	4,037	6,427	n/a	n/a
Morocco	15,541	9,896	n/a	n/a
Sudan	4,423	2,711	n/a	n/a
Tunisia	4,101	3,466	n/a	n/a
Gambia	1,485	n/a	n/a	n/a
Senegal	2,287	762	n/a	n/a
Sierra Leone	7,217	1,963	n/a	n/a
Total	871,582	493,904	174,223	134,615

Source: U.S. Bureau of the Census, "Table 3: World Region and Country or Area of Birth of the Foreign-Born Population: 1960 to 2000" retrieved on July 21, 2009 from www.census.gov/population/www/documentation/twps0081/tables/tab03.xls.

By the turn of the 1990s, the United States was not only a microcosm of Muslims in the "Old World" but was also home to a variety of indigenous American Muslim populations and sects – the Nation of Islam, W. D. Mohammed's American Society of Muslims, and Dar ul-Islam – just to name a few. It is impossible to trace the historical development of each of these groups in any detail between the covers of a single book. Not only are the groups too numerous and dispersed, but most of the Muslims of varying national and sectarian backgrounds who came to the United States in this period did not participate in any organization or collectivity that left a historical footprint. This does not mean that they did not actively or collectively practice Islam. They just failed to leave us a verifiable record of their activities aside from a few national Muslim organizations. To learn more about Muslim activities in the 1960s and 1970s, an extensive effort is needed to collect oral histories of local Muslim communities. Today only a few oral histories of immigrant Muslims exist, and they often contain surprising data. In an inquiry into the oral history of Muslims in Portland, Oregon, for example, I learned that in the early 1970s Twelver Shi'is used to gather at individual homes on Thursday nights and then call other Shi'i households within the region on the phone to collectively listen to the recitation of the popular Shi'i devotional invocation known as *du'a al-kumayl*.[51]

Given how increasingly diverse the American Muslim community became after 1965 and given the dearth of historical research on Islam in America, narratives of Islam in America in this period have little choice but to nod to the multiplicity of Islamic beliefs and cultural practices while they focus their narratives on those Muslims who were involved in building national institutions like the Muslim Students Association, the Islamic Society of North America, the Islamic Circle of North America, and the ministry of Warith Deen Mohammed. Given the aim of these organizations to bring American Muslims under a single national umbrella, they published newsletters, journals, and propaganda. They also held national conventions. And their activities were all in English so that they could reach as wide a range of Muslims in the United States as possible. They thus left historians with an accessible record of American Muslim activity in the years following the passage of the Hart-Celler Act.

---

[51] Personal interview with a member of Islamic Society of Portland (Beaverton, OR, June 17, 2004). For examples of some extant personal histories see Steven Barboza, *American Jihad: Islam after Malcolm X* (New York: Doubleday, 1994) and Donna Gehrke-White, *The Face Behind the Veil: The Extraordinary Lives of Muslim Women in America* (Secaucus, NJ: Citadel Press, 2007).

Interpreting the history of American Islam after 1965 solely through the activities and publications of national Muslim organizations, however, would be misleading. Muslims involved in building these organizations were generally activists involved in the Islamic revival movements of the 1960s, 1970s, and 1980s. This is not to suggest that they were obedient foot soldiers of these pan-Islamic organizations, such as the Muslim Brotherhood or the Jama'at-i Islami; rather, they were inspired by their utopian interpretation of Islam as an ideology that trumped any other identity, including national, cultural, and professional identity. Focusing the history of Islam in America in this period on such groups provides only a glimpse of a small, unrepresentative – though influential – segment of the larger American Muslim population. It also homogenizes American Muslim beliefs and practices when the tendencies in the history of American Islam in this period in fact moved in the opposite direction, in increasing diversity of the American Muslim population and in American Muslims' attempts to come to terms with the cultural and sectarian differences among Muslims. This is not to say that national Muslim organizations have been insignificant in the history of Islam in America. On the contrary, no responsible historian of Islam in America could ignore them because they have become the public face of American Islam on national and international issues through assiduous institution building and activism. At this stage of scholarship on Islam in America, their record of their activities also constitutes the lion's share of our sources. My contention is simply that their homogenizing agendas should not obfuscate the broader history of Muslims in America and all of their differences. In view of this, while I discuss the activities of a few national Muslim organizations in the following pages, I seek to frame their endeavors in the context of the growing religious diversity of the United States and the changing relations between the United States and the Muslim majority, which had a direct impact on American Muslim lives and helped shape non-Muslims' views of Islam.

The increased diversity of the American Muslim population was largely the result of the fact that Muslims immigrated to the United States in large numbers at a time when institutional forms of discrimination had been outlawed and a new multicultural ethos was emerging in the nation. The country had moved "beyond the melting pot" and arrived at a place where differences were acknowledged, if not celebrated, as inherently valuable. Racism and religious bigotry, of course, did not disappear overnight. It just became more socially and economically costly since laws and federal bureaucracies were established to protect minorities' access to jobs, education, and housing.

The attitudes of post-1965 immigrants toward the United States had also changed. Since almost the entire Muslim-majority world had been under direct or indirect colonial rule during much of the first half of the twentieth century, most of the Muslim immigrants who came to the United States after 1965 had already experienced some form of "Westernization" in their own countries. Many were also participants in independence movements at home and had been exposed to leftist nationalist and Third-Worldist ideologies that sought to affix a "native" cultural identity for developing countries between the western capitalism of the First World and the Socialist Communism of the Second World. Consequently, they came to the United States with a much firmer sense of their national identity and a greater awareness of the political dynamics through which race, religion, and progress were conflated to justify white, Protestant superiority. For example, when the Iranian educator and author of *Gharbzadigi* ("westoxification" or "Euromania"), Jalal Al-e Ahmad, came to participate in the Harvard International Summer Seminar directed by Henry Kissinger, he told Ralph Ellison, "whose *Invisible Man* he considered a kind of manifesto for blacks,'I believe that the problem of American blacks comes from the two refuges they have constructed for themselves: Christianity and jazz'." As the historian Roy Mottahedeh has observed, "It would never have occurred to intellectuals of ... [the interwar] generation to travel to Europe or America in order to explain to the oppressed in the West the cultural factors that made for oppression."[52] As a result of their own experiences with colonialism, most of the post-1965 Muslim immigrants were thus unlikely to willingly change their names, dissimulate their religious beliefs, or forgo their cultural practices or identities.

Quite the reverse. Soon after their arrival Muslim immigrants began participating in existing mosques and national cultural organizations. Where such organizations were not available, they built their own mosques, Sufi centers, and cultural associations. According to one study, the number of mosques established in the 1970s was five times the number of mosques established in the 1950s or the 1960s, and the number of new mosques continued to grow, though more modestly (by about 25 percent), in the 1980s and 1990s.[53] In addition to mosques, cultural and social associations were formed in the 1970s and 1980s. A few examples

---

[52] Roy Mottahedeh, *The Mantle of the Prophet: Religion and Politics in Iran* (New York: Pantheon, 1985), 321.

[53] Ihsan Bagby, Paul M. Perl, and Bryan T. Froehle,*The Mosque in America: A National Portrait* (Washington, D.C.: Council on American Islamic Relations, 2001), 23.

of such organizations should suffice. The Pakistan Friendship Association in Indianapolis was founded in 1973. The United States saw few Bosnian Muslim immigrants from Communist Yugoslavia. Nonetheless Bosnians began to form their own Islamic centers, such as the Islamic Cultural Center of Greater Chicago which was built in the early 1970s. Albanian Sunnis, who had established the Albanian-American Muslim Society in Detroit in 1949, built other religious centers in Waterbury, Chicago, and Brooklyn in the 1970s. The religious life of the Albanian Bektashi Sufis centered around their lodge or *tekke*, which was established in Detroit in 1954.[54] In 1971, a number of South Asian members of the Muslim Students Association left to form the Islamic Circle of North America which, though not an exclusively South Asian organization, is still dominated by South Asians and generally ran its meetings at this time in Urdu.[55] Numerous Turkish American associations and Islamic centers were also established in the 1960s and 1970s, enough to justify the formation of the Assembly of Turkish American Associations in 1980.[56] Arab Americans also founded a number of national and local organizations in the 1970s and 1980s (discussed below).

The increasing diversity of Muslims in the United States also manifested itself in the establishment of Shi'i and Sufi mosques and centers. In 1963, first- and second-generation Levantine Shi'i Muslims, whose history in the United States dates back to the turn of the twentieth century, constructed a mosque in Detroit under the leadership of Mohamad Jawad Chirri (d. 1994). Chirri had immigrated to the United States in 1948 to serve this mostly Lebanese community, which prior to the establishment of this mosque worshiped in makeshift mosques. Soon after his arrival in the United States, Chirri became one of the most active spokespersons for Islam in the United States. Today, the mosque he helped found, the Islamic Center of America, is one of the largest and more opulent mosques in the United States.

Around 1970, Iranian Shi'i members of the Muslim Students Association formed the Muslim Students Association-Persian Speaking

---

[54] "Albanians" in *Harvard Encyclopedia of American Ethnic Groups*, ed. Stephan Thernstrom, Ann Orlov, and Oscar Handlin (Cambridge, MA: Harvard University Press, 1980), 26.

[55] Raymond Williams, *Religions of Immigrants from India and Pakistan: New Threads in the American Tapestry* (Cambridge: Cambridge University Press, 1988), 96.

[56] Delegates of 26 Turkish American associations were present at the founding meeting of this association. See the Assembly of Turkish American Associations website, http://www.ataa.org/about/ (accessed January 29, 2010).

FIGURE 19. The Islamic Center of America, Dearborn, Michigan (completed in 2005). Photo by the author.

Group.[57] In 1973, Yasin al-Jibouri founded the Islamic Society of Georgia, which published a newsletter, *Islamic Affairs*, which he claimed to be "the most powerful advocate for Shi'ism in the country." In 1976, the Khu'i Foundation of America was established by Muhammad Sarwar, a representative of Grand Ayatollah al-Khu'i, who was one of the world's leading Shi'i spiritual leader or *marja' al-taqlid* ("source of emulation") at the time. Numerous other Shi'i mosques also began dotting the country in the 1970s and 1980s.[58]

Many Isma'ili Shi'is also immigrated from South Asia and East Africa in this period. By 1975, members of the larger Nizari branch of the Isma'ili Shi'i community numbered around 10,000 in North America, and they had some twenty centers of worship, known as jamat khana, in the United States. Isma'ili communities are governed socially and religiously

[57] Kambiz GhaneaBassiri, *Competing Visions of Islam in the United States: A Study of Los Angeles* (Westport, CT: Greenwood Press, 1997), 30–33.
[58] Liyakat Takim, "Multiple Identities in a Pluralistic World: Shi'ism in America," in *Muslims in the West: From Sojourners to Citizens*, ed. Yvonne Y. Haddad (New York: Oxford University Press, 2002), 219–220.

by regional constitutions sanctioned by a leader or Imam, and in 1977, Agha Khan IV, the contemporary Imam of the world Isma'ili community, approved such a constitution for Isma'ilis in the United States.[59]

The 1960s and 1970s also saw the burgeoning of Sufi organizations that disassociated themselves from Islam and did not require their followers to either convert to Islam or observe normative Islamic rituals. Two such organizations were splinter groups from Inayat Khan's Sufi Order of the West. The Sufi Order International was formed in 1956 and led at this time by one of Inayat Khan's sons, Vilayat Khan (1928–2004). It is, today, led by his grandson, Zia Inayat-Khan (b. 1971). The International Sufi Movement was led by another of Inayat Khan's sons, Hidayat Inayat-Khan (b. 1917). These communities flourished as part of a larger "turning east," spiritual movement that brought numerous Zen masters, swamis, and gurus from South and East Asia to the United States in the 1960s and 1970s. Perhaps the most visible face of this type of Sufism at this time was Samuel Lewis (also known as Sufi Sam). Lewis dabbled widely in mystical religions and was a leading figure in Vilayat Khan's Sufi Order International. After Lewis died in 1971, his followers broke with Vilayat Khan and formed their own Sufi Islamia Ruhaniat Society in 1977.[60]

Alongside these Sufi communities, which disassociated themselves from normative Islam, a number of immigrant Muslims in the 1970s and 1980s also established Sufi communities.[61] One particularly noteworthy community among these is the Bawa Muhaiyaddeen Fellowship, founded by Muhammad Raheem Bawa Muhaiyaddeen (d. 1986). Bawa Muhaiyaddeen came to the United States from Sri Lanka in 1971 on behest of an American woman who had heard about his

---

[59] Zahra N. Jamal, "Isma'ilis," in *Encyclopedia of Islam in the United States*, vol. 1, ed. Jocelyne Cesari (Westport, CT: Greenwood Press, 2007), 348–351; Azim Nanji, "The Nizari Ismaili Muslim Community in North America: Background and Development" in *Muslim Community in North America*, 156–163.

[60] The organizational boundaries in these movements are extremely fluid and their histories both complex and controversial. For an attempt at a systematic overview, see Andrew Rawlinson, "A History of Western Sufism" *Diskus* 1, no. 1 (1993), 45–83. Available online at www.uni-marburg.de/religionswissenschaft/journal/diskus/ralinson. html (accessed December 23, 2003), and Andrew Rawlinson, *The Book of Enlightened Masters: Western Teachers in Eastern Traditions* (Chicago, IL: Open Court, 1997), 396–403 and 543–553.

[61] For a brief overview of Sufi communities in the United States, see Marcia Hermansen, "In the Garden of American Sufi Movements: Hybrids and Perennials," in *New Trends and Developments in the World of Islam*, ed. Peter B. Clarke (London: Luzac Oriental, 1997), 155–178.

reputation as a "holy man" from an anthropology graduate student at the University of Pennsylvania. Upon his arrival in Philadelphia, Bawa Muhaiyaddeen mainly addressed an audience of "seekers" about spirituality. It was not until 1976 that he introduced them to the *dhikr* (a Sufi ritual involving the recitation and remembrance of divine names). In 1981, he established the regular observance of the Islamic daily ritual prayer, and in 1984, his community built a mosque. The building of the mosque led some of his followers to leave the Fellowship because of its clear identification with Islam. On the other hand, the mosque attracted other, local non-Sufi Muslims, who began to frequent it to perform their communal prayers and observe the feasts (*'ids*) marking the end of Ramadan and the Hajj season. When Bawa Muhaiyaddeen died in 1986, a shrine (*mazar*) was built for him in the farmland the Fellowship had purchased in Chester County, Pennsylvania for communal gatherings and burial services. His shrine is regarded as the first Muslim pilgrimage site and is visited by American Muslims of varying ethnic and religious backgrounds in search of divine blessings (*baraka*).[62]

Another noteworthy Sufi order established in the United States in this period was the secretive 'Alawiyya Maryamiyya Order (generally shortened to Maryamiyya). The Maryamiyya Order is noteworthy because some of its leading members have greatly influenced the academic study of Islam in the United States and elsewhere. The Maryamiyya emerged in the mid-twentieth century out of a marriage achieved by the French thinker René Guénon (d. 1951) between Traditionalist-Perennialist philosophy and Sufism. Guénon's disciple and successor, Frithjof Schuon (also known as 'Isa Nur al-Din, d. 1998), came to the United States from Switzerland in 1981 but already in 1967 a branch of the Maryamiyya had been established around Indiana University in Bloomington by one of its professors of Arabic and Islamic Studies, Victor Danner. Today, the Maryamiyya Order, which has at least three centers in the United States, is led by Seyyed Hossein Nasr (b. 1933), a native of Iran who is currently a University Professor of Islamic Studies at George Washington University and one of the most widely recognized and influential scholars of Islam in the United States. The teachings of the Maryamiyya appealed to mid-twentieth-century intellectuals seeking religious certainty and universal truths within a diverse, modernizing world. At a time when the academic

[62] Gisela Webb, "Third-Wave Sufism in Ameica and the Bawa Muhaiyaddeen Fellowship," in *Sufism in the West*, ed. Jamal Malik and John Hinnells (London: Routledge, 2006), 90–98.

FIGURE 20. The shrine (*mazar*) of Bawa Muhaiyaddeen (d. 1986), foregrounded by the Bawa Muhaiyaddeen Fellowship Cemetery in Chester County, Pennsylvania. Photo courtesy of Lou Wilson.

study of religion was characterized by "mystocentricism,"[63] Maryamiyya scholars of Islam (and the scholars they influenced) wrote extensively about Sufi mystics and made their works available to students of religion in English. They popularized an understanding of Islam in which the eso-teric philosophical tradition of Islam came to define the universal, eternal "Truth" of Islam at the expense of its diverse historical expressions and ethico-legal traditions.[64] As with other universalist approaches to religion discussed thus far, the appeal of such an approach to Islam in particular and religion in general lied in its unifying vision of religion in a religiously and ethnically diverse society. For this reason, Maryamiyya scholars such as Schuon and Nasr found a wide readership not only among mystically oriented Muslims but also among non-Muslims attracted to perennial philosophy. By way of example, Huston Smith, who is a retired professor of comparative religion, an ordained Methodist minister, and the author of one of the most widely read American books on religion, *The Religions of Man* (1958), wrote of Nasr: "No other thinker that is still alive ... has influenced my thought as much as he has."[65]

---

[63] Steven M. Wasserstrom, *Religion after Religion: Gershom Scholem, Mircea Eliade, and Henry Corbin at Eranos* (Princeton, NJ: Princeton University Press, 1999), 239–41.

[64] For an overview of the Maryamiyya Order and its history in the United States, see Mark Sedgwick, *Against the Modern World: Traditionalism and the Secret Intellectual History of the Twentieth Century* (New York: Oxford University Press, 2004), 147–177. For a representative work of Seyyed Hossein Nasr, addressed specifically to an American Muslim audience, see *A Young Muslim's Guide to the Modern World* (Chicago, IL: Kazi Publications, 1994).

[65] Huston Smith, "Forward," in *The Essential Seyyed Hossein Nasr*, ed. William C. Chittick (Bloomington, IN: World Wisdom, 2007), vii.

ARAB AND MUSLIM AMERICANS AND CONFLICTS IN
THE MIDDLE EAST

Muslims who immigrated in 1960s-1980s were eager and able to establish their own understandings of Islam and places of worship. They arrived in the United States at a time when, even though they faced prejudice and social pressures to conform, there were no legal restrictions against their full participation in American life.[66] The Arab-Israeli conflict, the oil crisis of the 1970s, and the Iranian hostage crisis all fueled prejudice against Muslims in America, but unlike the first decades of the twentieth century, such public prejudices did not result in laws which excluded immigrant Muslims from citizenship, property ownership, or public life.

Nonetheless, the Arab-Israeli conflict and the oil crisis of the 1970s were factors that generated increased prejudice against Arabs and, through the association of Arabs with Islam (even though they comprise only about a fifth of the world's Muslim population), against Muslims in general. This increased prejudice against Arabs, coupled with the ascendency of ethnic pride and a vibrant social justice movement, led many Arab Americans who had previously assimilated as "whites" to claim minority status and to ally themselves with social justice movements. This was particularly true among younger Arab Americans, who were politicized through student movements on American university campuses.[67] One of the most influential Arab American national organizations at this time was the Association of Arab-American University Graduates (AAUG) founded in 1967, the same year in which Israel decisively defeated Egypt, Syria, Jordan, and Iraq in what has come to be known as the Six-Day War. The AAUG aimed to provide more accurate information about the Arab world through research and publications such as its flagship journal, *Arab Studies Quarterly*. It also served as a network for Arab American activism. It counted among its early members such prominent scholars as Ibrahim Abu-Lughod, Edward Said, and Elaine Hagopian.

In the 1960s and 1970s, American discourses on conflicts in the Middle East were generally framed in terms of nationality, in contrast to later framing of these conflicts in terms of Islam. This was in large part

---

[66] William R. Hutchison, *Religious Pluralism in America: The Contentious History of a Founding Ideal* (New Haven, CT: Yale University Press, 2004), 170–171.

[67] See, for example, "Maya Berry, telephone interview, April 20, 1998," in *Arab Detroit: From Margin to Mainstream*, ed. Nabeel Abraham and Andrew Shryock (Detroit, MI: Wayne State University Press, 2000), 350–351.

due to the popularity of nationalist movements in the 1960s and 1970s and the waning of their popularity in the 1980s and 1990s as many in the Middle East were disillusioned by the failures of nationalist governments and the region saw a revival of Islamic activism. In the United States, too, political activism for Arab and Arab American causes was led under a nationalist rather than an Islamic banner. The majority of Arab Americans in the United States at this time were Christian, and most Arab Americans, whether Muslim or Christian, held highly favorable views of Gamal Abdel Nasser. Islamist activists, as discussed in Chapter 5, however, mistrusted nationalism and were vehemently opposed to Abdel Nasser's socialist-nationalist project. They strongly advocated for Palestinian rights through an Islamic discourse mixed with an equally strong condemnation of the failures of Arab nationalist regimes. They only tacitly supported Arab American organizations in the 1970s, and when the shortcomings of Arab nationalist governments became apparent in the 1980s, they did not hold back their criticism:

It has been stated that when men stop believing in God, their minds, rather than continuing in a vacuum, will start entertaining new and strange concepts. Many of the AAUG members [the pan-Arab Association of Arab-American University Graduates] presented living examples of this ancient truth.... [T]hese intellectual guardians of Arabism made it clear that in their opinion Islamic fundamentalism was the real root cause of Arab humiliation. Echoes of Ataturk. Free the Arab world of Islam and the Arabs will be able to win a battle with the Israelis. Intellectual hogwash. In fact, the one fact that the Arab world had against Israeli aggression was masterminded in the name of Islam by the late King Faisel (sic).... Even in the current conflict, if we compare the games that nations play with poker, it is non-Arab Iran and outcasted Libya that were the only winners in Beirut.[68]

Whereas American Muslim activists became more politically active in the 1980s, in the 1970s, their own activities were explicitly aimed at missionary work and in establishing a just society based on Islamic precepts and transnational Muslim solidarity. In the 1970s, just as Arab Americans were organizing nationally to counter prejudice against them at home and to lobby Washington, D.C. in regard to the Israeli occupation of Arab territories, the Muslim Students Association met to reorganize itself based on a new set of priorities for "Islamic work" in North America:

[68] Muhammad Tahir, "Around and About Washington," *Islamic Horizons* 11, no. 12 (December 1982), 8.

1. Production and dissemination of Islamic knowledge (general and specific) in its original purity in all fields necessary for building an Islamic civilization.
2. Building and/or establishing institutes such as schools and community centers.
3. Daily requirements of Muslims. These include services as well as information concerning Friday prayers, Hajj, Zakat, marriage, funerals, etc.
4. Designing a program for recruitment. This covers recruitment of new members, training them to develop commitment to Islam and acquire leadership skills.
5. Producing a unity of Muslim conscience.[69]

For most Muslim activists in the United States the plight of Palestinians and the Muslim-majority world in general could not be separated from Muslims' estrangement from Islam:

The Palestine issue … is no doubt a human issue. Its human aspect, however, cannot preclude its religious aspect for Muslims. The emotional attachment of the world of Islam with the usurped holy land cannot be separated. The Muslim Ummah at present is in the whirlpool of non-Islamic waves. It is evident that the present age is a transitional age; for history bears testimony to the fact that political chaos, anarchism, social injustices and resultant upheavals have always been a feature of transition. The leadership of humanity will and must be changed…. Much to the alarm of some, in the Muslim countries the masses are awakening from slumber, trying hard to throw off the yoke of suppression and tyranny of conscience imposed upon them from within and without. Not only the present Muslim world but humanity at large needs a pious and God-obeying and God-fearing leadership. And we can say that the Muslim Ummah was erected and trusted only for that leadership. "Thus have We made you the community of the golden mean, so that you may be witness in regard to mankind and the messenger may be witness in regard to you." (Holy Qur'an: II-143)[70]

Muslim activists, however, constituted a small fraction of the American Muslim population.[71] The antipathy of Muslim activists

---

[69] *MSA News* 4, no. 12 (December 1975), 6.
[70] *Al-Ittihad* 5, no. 1 (August 1968), inside cover.
[71] There are no statistical studies of Muslim activism in 1960s–1980s that I could cite to substantiate this claim. It could, however, be readily gleaned from the fact that the attendance at the MSA and Islamic Society of North America conventions in the early 1980s numbered in the low thousands. This convention has been widely regarded as the biggest gathering of Muslims in North America, and it generally attracts Muslim activists along with other Muslims who attend with their families for community building

toward nationalism and leftist movements was not shared by the majority of American Muslims. Most Arab American Muslims participated in pan-Arab organizations founded in this period to support Arab causes both here and abroad. In addition to the AAUG, the Arab Community Center for Economic and Social Services was founded in Detroit in 1971 under the volunteer directorship of an Arab American Muslim woman named Aliyah Hassan.[72] In 1972, the National Association of Arab Americans was founded with the aim of improving relations between the United States and Arab countries and to lobby for issues of concern to Arabs and Arab Americans, first among them the Arab-Israeli conflict. In 1980, Senator James Abourezk of South Dakota (1973–1979), an Arab American Christian, founded the American-Arab Anti-Discrimination Committee to counter popular prejudices against Arabs as backward, unscrupulous, oil-rich sheiks. The deleterious influence of these unchecked stereotypes came to light in a powerful way when FBI agents in a sting operation called ABSCAM (short for Abdul Scam) stereotypically posed as rich Arab sheiks representing the fictitious company, "Abdul Enterprises," and tried to bribe U.S. congressmen. The operation received national attention when it was made public and led to the conviction of six house representatives and one senator. It raised many questions regarding police entrapment. It also led some to wonder whether Arabs were being singled out for their lobbying efforts. "This is the best thing the F.B.I. has ever done," read a letter to FBI Director William Webster (1978–1987). "My pet peave (sic) is the way Israel has bought and paid for our Congress. Israel continues to settle occupied Arab land against the wishes of every country in the World. But many of our congressman (sic) back Israel no matter what they do. I am positive the Jewish dollars have flowed to our senators so they must support Israel. Anyway thank you."[73]

---

or social reasons. In 1981, only about 4,000 people attended the MSA annual convention. In 1982, some 4,500 people were expected at the ISNA convention. See "Islam Alone Gives Full Expression to Human Rights: Over 4,000 Attend MSA Convention" in *Islamic Horizons* vol. X, no. 6 (June 1981) and "ISNA Convention May Draw 4,500 People" in *Islamic Horizons* vol. XII, no. 4 (April 1982), 1. See also footnote 1 above.

[72] "About us: A Brief History," available at the Arab Community Center for Economic and Social Services (ACCESS) web site, http://www.accesscommunity.org/site/PageServer?pagename=ACCESS_History2 (accessed August 29, 2009).

[73] Randa A. Kayalli, *The Arab Americans* (Westport, CT: Greenwood Press, 2006), 132–134; Jason Davis, "ABSCAM," in *Encyclopedia of White-Collar and Corporate Crime*, ed. Lawrence M. Salinger (Thousand Oaks, CA: SAGE, 2004), 4–5. For more detail on ABSCAM and the American public's reaction to it, see the FBI's report at their web site, http://foia.fbi.gov/foiaindex/abscam.htm (accessed February 7, 2009). The above-mentioned letter is the first document in Part 1a of the report.

FROM "ARAB TERRORISM" TO "ISLAMIC TERRORISM": THE
IDENTIFICATION OF ISLAM WITH VIOLENCE

In the 1980s, there was yet another marked shift in American discourse
on the Middle East: As Melani McAlister has argued, "What had been
understood, albeit incorrectly, as 'the Arab world' in the 1960s and
1970s became, again, incorrectly, 'the Islamic world' in the 1980s."[74]
The phrase "Arab terrorism" was exchanged for "Islamic terrorism,"
"militant Islam," "Islamic fundamentalism," or a variation thereof. The
1979 Islamic revolution of Iran and the Iranian hostage crisis played a
decisive role in this reframing of the cultural geography of the Middle
East. The revolution took pundits, academics, and policy-makers by
surprise. Iran, which had been a client state of the United States since
the early 1950s, was generally cited as a model of stability in the Middle
East. There was starry-eyed optimism among development theorists
regarding Muhammad Reza Shah's modernization programs.[75] The
conventional wisdom on development and modernization held that
with the greater individualization, democratization, and development
ushered in by modernity, religion would gradually fade from the public
sphere and become a matter of individual, private choice. Iran's Islamic
revolution proved a rude awakening. In their search for an explanation of this aberration in the conventional wisdom, pundits and scholars alike posited that there was a new reactionary type of religion
called "fundamentalism" that rejected modernism. *The Harper Collins
Dictionary of Religion* (1995), edited by one of the foremost scholars
of religion, Jonathan Z. Smith, defined fundamentalism as "the struggle against modernism by religious groups who claim the continued
relevancy of earlier time periods for models of truth and value and
reject what they perceive as forms of secularism." Although Judaism,
Christianity, and Hinduism were all said to have their fundamentalists, Islam, more specifically the Islam of the Iranian revolution, became
the poster child of fundamentalism in the 1980s, thus identifying Islam
with religious violence in the American public imagination.[76] This association was so pervasive that the author of the above-cited entry on

---

[74] Melani McAlister, *Epic Encounters: Culture, Media, and U.S. Interests in the Middle East
since 1945* (Berkeley and Los Angeles, CA: University of California Press, 2005), 200.
[75] See, for example, Leonard Binder, *Iran: Political Development in a Changing Society*
(Berkeley, CA: University of California Press, 1962).
[76] Numerous books and scholarly projects were written on religious fundamentalism in
the 1980s and early 1990s. See in particular Martin Marty and R. Scott Appleby, eds.,
The Fundamentalism Project (Chicago, IL: University of Chicago Press, 1991), and

fundamentalism felt it necessary to point out to its readers that "only a few Islamic fundamentalists are terrorists, and not all Arab terrorists are fundamentalists."

The association of fundamentalism with Islam was particularly ironic since the concept of fundamentalism emerged from within American Protestantism at the turn of the twentieth century as conservative Protestants sought to reaffirm the "fundamentals" of Christianity at a time when Christian doctrines regarding the inerrancy of the Bible, the divinity of Jesus, and the validity of the virgin birth were being questioned and revised in light of historical-critical studies of the Bible.

Neither Islam nor terrorism was ever properly defined in American discourses on "Islamic terrorism." Was there something specific about Islam that caused terrorism? If so, was America's "war on terror" during the Reagan administration a war on Islam or a particular understanding of Islam? If the latter, what was this particular understanding of Islam that was terrorist-forming? What made some acts of political violence terrorist and unjustifiable and others libratory and defensible? What objective criterion distinguished the terrorist from the freedom fighter? These difficult questions were generally evaded in preference of catchy phrases such as "war on terror," or sensationalist images of hijackings and suicide-bombings that captured Americans' attention.

Since the categories of Islam and terrorism were left undefined, they, like the other vague categories we have encountered thus far, race, religion, and progress, were manipulated and conflated to justify policies that were strategically in the interest of the United States but were not rationally consistent. To give but one salient, timely example, in the 1980s, just as the United States decried the threat of "Islamic fundamentalism" in the Middle East to justify its support for Iraq in the Iran-Iraq War and its military intervention in Lebanon in the 1980s, it provided logistical and financial support to "fundamentalist Muslims" in Saudi Arabia and Pakistan to help them organize the Islamist resistance movement in Afghanistan against the Soviets.[77] While the Palestinian resistance fighters were labeled Islamic terrorists, Islamist resistance fighters in Afghanistan were hailed as freedom fighters. In 1983, Congress and President Reagan declared March 21 "Afghanistan Day" in order to demonstrate U.S. support for

---

Bruce Lawrence, *Defenders of God: The Fundamentalist Revolt Against the Modern Age* (Columbia, SC: University of South Carolina Press, 1995).

[77] Fawaz Gerges, *America and Political Islam: Clash of Cultures or Clash of Interests?* (Cambridge: Cambridge University Press, 1999), 66–72.

"the resistance of the Afghan freedom fighters."[78] Later, in the 1990s, many of these fighters formed al-Qaeda, a militant Islamist movement that orchestrated the attacks of September 11, 2001, and the Taliban, an Islamist movement which took over the government of Afghanistan and gave safe haven to al-Qaeda. Yesterday's "freedom fighters" became today's "Islamic terrorists," even though their understandings of Islam and their obligations as Muslims did not change significantly.

RELATING ISLAM AND AMERICA: AMERICAN MUSLIM ACTIVISM FOLLOWING THE SOVIET INVASION OF AFGHANISTAN

The conflation of Islam, Arabs, and terrorism brought American Muslims and Arab Americans under suspicion as potential threats to national security. As early as the late 1960s, the FBI conducted surveillances of American Muslim and Arab American activists.[79] The vagaries of the notion of "Islamic terrorism," however, left spaces open for strategic alliances between Islamists and the United States. Indeed, it was in the 1980s, at a time when Islam was increasingly being associated with terrorism, that American Muslims became more politically active in the United States outside of Arab American organizations. The Soviet invasion of Afghanistan in 1979 was the turning point, because this is when the United States began to reach out to Islamist organizations indirectly via Saudi Arabia and Pakistan in order to fight the spread of Soviet influence in the Middle East and South Asia. Islamist organizations accepted the U.S. government's hand cautiously.

In 1980, Congress adopted a resolution recognizing the 1,400-year anniversary of the onset of Prophet Muhammad ibn 'Abd Allah's religious mission. In that year, while American employees of the U.S. embassy in Iran were being held hostage by presumed "Islamic fundamentalists" and America was brimming with anger and frustration, President Carter's State of the Union speech lauded the Muslim world's "justifiable outrage by this [Soviet] aggression against an Islamic people [of Afghanistan]." And he stated, "We believe that there are no irreconcilable differences between us and any Islamic nation. We respect the faith of Islam, and we are ready

---

[78] "Proclamation 5034 – Afghanistan Day, 21 March 1983," available online via the Ronald Reagan Presidential Library archives, http://www.reagan.utexas.edu/archives/speeches/1983/32183d.htm (accessed January 29, 2010).

[79] Gregory Orfalea, *The Arab Americans: A History* (Northampton, MA: Olive Branch Press, 2006), 216–217.

to cooperate with all Moslem countries [to counter Soviet advances]."
Three days after President Carter's speech, on January 26, 1980, the
Saudi-based missionary organization the Muslim World League met in
Newark, New Jersey and condemned Russia's invasion of Afghanistan
and issued a press release calling on Iran to release its American hostages. Around the same time, the Muslim Students Association expanded
its Afghan Relief Fund, which had been established in April 1979. The
fund's committee members travelled throughout local American Muslim
communities to gather money, clothes, medical supplies, and medical
doctors to send to Pakistan to boost Afghani relief efforts. By March
1981, the Muslim Students Association had also established a Jihad Fund
to help the "freedom fighters" or *mujahidun* (literally, "those who undertake jihad") in Afghanistan and wherever else Muslims' human rights
were being violated.[80] For its nineteenth annual convention in 1981 on
"Islam, Jihad and Human Rights," the MSA defined jihad as a struggle
for justice and liberation that is obligatory for every Muslim man and
woman. That this struggle has not only a spiritual, social, economic, and
political dimension but also a physical dimension was implied both by
the timing of the meeting – during the Soviet occupation of Afghanistan –
and by assertions that "Muslims, as well as non-Muslims, have growing
misconceptions about Jihad. Some even think that Jihad with one's self
(Jihad bi an nafs) is superior to other kinds of struggle. Such misconceptions need clarification."[81]

In 1981, in an interview at the Indiana headquarters of the Muslim
Students Association, two officials of the Jama'at-i Islami movement in
Pakistan who had come to the United States to attend the annual convention of the Islamic Circle of North America explained the Jama'at's
indirect alliance with the United States via Zia-ul-Haqq's government:

The Russian invasion of Afghanistan has changed the scenario of politics in
Pakistan. Zia ul-Haq has not only sympathized with the Afghan Islamic aspirations but also stood firmly behind them. Bring another government and the Afghan
situation may not be the same. As a policy, we don't divulge the decision-making
process in the Jama'at to the outsiders, but since so much is at stake and so many
are the misgivings that I am constrained to reveal at least part of it. When the
Jama'at decided to stay away from any combined opposition to Zia's rule, it was
Mian Tufail Muhammad's sensitivity to the Afghan issue and his perception of

---

[80] Emily Kalled Lovell, "Islam in the United States: Past and Present," in *Muslim Community in North America*, 107; "MSA's Afghan Relief Efforts in Full Swing," *Islamic Horizons* 9, no. 4 (April 1980), 2; *Islamic Horizons* vol. 10, no. 3 (March 1981), 11.
[81] *Islamic Horizons* 12, no. 2 (February 1982), 12.

the problem as a whole which influenced the historic decision.... With almost tears he pleaded for being patient to the internal political situation, 'If Russia succeeds in destroying Afghan Islamic resistance, what will be left of us? Would we be able to carry our program in Pakistan?' he asked.[82]

As the above examples indicate, U.S. overtures toward Islam were designed to appeal to Islamist organizations' agenda of reviving Islam and defending it against the socialist/nationalist regimes that came to power in the Middle East and South Asia in the post-colonial era. With the help of petrodollars, groups such as the Jama'at-i Islami and the Muslim Brotherhood, both of which were represented in the Saudi-based Muslim World League, had established an extensive missionary network to foster their vision of a utopian Islamic society founded on a puritanical reading of the Qur'an and the Hadith. They had also sought to influence government officials and agencies in Muslim-majority countries by positioning themselves as representatives of the people. They operated numerous charities and social services through which they contrasted themselves with the ruling powers by demonstrating their own competence and integrity. By assisting the needy, they both fulfilled a religious duty and gained political capital among the general public. The above-cited officials of the Jama'at-i Islami in Pakistan, for example, when questioned further about the Jama'at's association with Muhammad Zia-ul-Haqq's government (1978–1988), said: "The Jama'at is blessed that because of its consistent stand for Islamic programs and a plan of action, it is identified with Islam. So much so that any voice for Islam in the corridors of power is taken by our opponents as an echo of our voice."[83] Given their influence among the general Muslim population, particularly among the lower and lower-middle classes, their extensive networks, dedicated followers, and access to petrodollars, Islamist organizations appeared to be a convenient, strategic ally to the United States in its efforts to challenge Soviet advances in Afghanistan and elsewhere in the region. Such an alliance seemed to make all the more sense given that the United States' relation with these groups was generally mediated through Saudi Arabia, which has been a client of the United States since World War II and has been in cooperative political dealings with a number of pan-Islamic, Islamist organizations since the early 1960s.

---

[82] "Of Zia ul-Haq, Jama'at-e Islami and Afghanistan," *Islamic Horizons* 10, no. 10 (October 1981), 7.
[83] Ibid.

The Soviet invasion of Afghanistan thus opened a window between the American government and American Muslim activists, a number of whom, though by no means all, were Islamists. In the 1960s Muslim-majority governments had already seen the potential intermediary role American Muslims could play in their relations with the United States. In the 1980s, as American Muslim activists were slowly coming into their own, they began to organize as American citizens to advance pan-Islamic causes both in the United States and abroad.

One of the earliest examples of this is a meeting initiated by President Carter on December 5, 1979 between the president, National Security Advisor Zbingnion Brzezinski, and twelve representatives of varying American Muslim communities, including the Muslim Student Association, W. D. Mohammed's community, and the Shi'i community. The object of the meeting was to discuss the Iran hostage crisis. The American Muslim representatives expressed their desire for the release of the hostages and for the normalization of relations between Iran and the United States. They rejected any military action against Iran and conveyed their willingness "to offer any help in any way which will facilitate in resolving this crises (sic) in a peaceful manner." They also informed the President of the numerous attacks and assaults on American Muslims since the Iranian revolutionaries took the Americans hostage.[84]

The gradual maturing of American Muslim activism was exemplified in the incorporation of the Islamic Society of North America (ISNA) by the Muslim Students Association in 1981. In a letter to all members of the Muslim Students Association, the background to this change was explained as follows:

There is no longer any doubt, if there ever was, that Islam has come to North America to stay for good, insha'-Allah [God willing]. Islamic presence here must, therefore pervade all spheres of a Muslim's life in this societal environment and must exert a positive influence on the non-Muslim segments of this society. To do so, Islamic work must continually grow and come to grips with new challenges and opportunities. This requires evolution and adaptation of the organizational structure of Islamic organizations so that they may provide the right type of leadership to an increasingly sophisticated and comprehensive socioeconomic order among Muslims in North America.... Muslims in North America are truly at the cross-roads. The most sincere and persistent effort of every Muslim is needed to

[84] "Muslim Representatives Meet President Carter," *Islamic Horizons* vol. 8, no. 12 (December 1979), 1 and 9.

forestall fragmentation and forge a united and enlightened front of Muslims to serve the Cause of Allah.[85]

In 1983, the Muslim Students Association formally withdrew to university campuses where its efforts had begun and left to ISNA the impressive array of national and professional organizations it had created. These organizations included the Islamic Medical Association (1967), the Association of Muslim Scientists and Engineers (1969), the Association of Muslim Social Scientists (1972), the Islamic Teaching Center (1977), the Muslim Community Association (a federation of community-based Muslim organizations), the North American Islamic Trust (1973, an Islam trust or *waqf* that funds and secures titles for mosques and Islamic centers), and *Islamic Horizons* (the most widely distributed American Muslim magazine).

The decision of Muslim activists in America to participate more fully in American politics and society was riddled with controversy. While Islamist activists in general aspired to realize a utopian Islamic society, they disagreed about the practical means of attaining this goal. Beginning in the mid-1980s, American Muslim activists debated whether or not they should participate in American politics. "How many Muslims are there in America?" read a 1984 letter to the editor of *Islamic Horizons*. "Not even the Muslims know. To present a unified front against any further participation in Lebanon by American forces, we must have Islamic unity here. As former President Harry Truman once said, while he was assisting the Jews in stealing Jerusalem, 'I don't have Arab/Muslim voters in the United States, but I do have Jewish voters.' We must remember that."[86] Many leaders of ISNA agreed. In 1986, the Planning Committee of ISNA indicated, "In order to exert influence on the political decision-making and legislation in North America, ISNA should launch a campaign to educate Muslim citizens about their voting rights and mobilize them to vote on issues affecting Islam and Muslims."[87] Other members of ISNA, like Tariq Qureishi, the director of the North American Islamic Trust, disagreed, fearing that the political process would co-opt and adulterate the Islamist agenda.

---

[85] "New Organizational Structure Takes Shape," *Islamic Horizons* vol. 10, no. 8 (August 1981).

[86] *Islamic Horizons* 13, no. 1 (January 1984), 3.

[87] "Islamic Society of North America, Guidelines for Medium Range Planning, Report of the Planning Committee," December 22, 1986, 6, cited in Steve A. Johnson, "Political Activity of Muslims in America," in *The Muslims of America*, 111.

Those people who insist on entering U.S. politics say it on the presumption as if they are some kind of Jews who have to work for some state of Israel.... Some people think that one can distance himself or herself from the process, and then watch the process. But philosophically speaking it is not possible. The process will assimilate you, and then adopt you, and then change you to its own objective.... Even if you are ideologically very well indoctrinated, you will have to make compromises here and there.[88]

It is important to note that regardless of how American Muslims felt about the importance of greater political participation, they did not question the fundamental fairness of the political system itself. Even when they acknowledged a general prejudice against Islam and Muslims in the media and within policy circles, they operated on the assumption that such perceptions could change, and that America's foreign policies could change. The leaders of one of the most prominent Islamic centers in the United States, the Islamic Center of Southern California, expressed this sense of optimism in the late 1980s as they sought to persuade American Muslims to become more active in American social and political life.

Undoubtedly, many American foreign policy decisions have betrayed the ideals of international justice and fairness, alienating Muslim masses all over the world. Undeniably, a great majority of the American public looks at the realities of Islam through barriers of lingering historical prejudice, biased academia, sensational media, and sad and painful political events. On the other hand, Muslims have great difficulties in separating America, the people, the civilization, the progress and the pluralism, from America, the foreign policy, the superpower, the monopoly and the heartless competitive capitalism. But an analytical look at Muslims and at America will show clearly that the distance is being reduced and the barriers dismantled. There is an opportunity for Islam in America, and there is an opportunity for America in Islam. There exists mutual suitability between America and Islam and Muslims.... There is no doubt that Americans enjoy freedom and have an opportunity to pursue happiness. The majority appreciate free debate, and the country has an unmatched ability to change and to adapt to new ideas.... Those who describe America as good or bad fall into the trap of oversimplification that conceals the hard facts. America has the potential to offer an historical opportunity to Islam and Muslims.[89]

In 1986, the Islamic Center of Southern California founded the Muslim Political Action Committee. Two year later, it converted it to

[88] Amer Haleem, "Path to Peace: Calling to Allah in America," *Islamic Horizons* 16 (December 1987), 29, cited in Johnson, "Political Activity," 113.

[89] Hassan Hathout, Fathi Osman, and Maher Hathout, *In Fraternity: A Message to Muslims in America* (Los Angeles, CA: The Minaret Publishing House, 1989), 3–4 and 13–15.

a Muslim advocacy group and changed its name to the Muslim Public Affairs Council (MPAC). Since its founding MPAC has become one of the most widely recognized national Muslim advocacy groups in the country.

The background of leaders of the Islamic Center of Southern California was in the Muslim Brotherhood, but examples of American Muslim leaders' optimism about the future of Islamic political and religious activity span across the spectrum of Muslims' religious orientations. Isma'il al-Faruqi, who was a professor of Islamic Studies at Temple University, one of the most active members of the Muslim Students Association, and a proponent of the puritanical reformist theology of Wahhabism in the United States,[90] equated the arrival of Muslim immigrants with the advent of the original Calvinist Puritans in New England:

> The Islamic vision endows North America with a new destiny worthy of it.... [T]he continent cannot but be grateful to the immigrant with Islamic vision. It cannot but interpret his advent on its shores except as a God-sent gift, a timely divine favor and mercy. It will not fail to recognize in the person with Islamic vision a true son, though born overseas, whose spirit is nearly identical with that of the early founders of the New World, who ran away from oppression and tyranny seeking a haven where they would remold their lives under God, seek His bounty, and raise high His banner.[91]

On the other end of the spectrum, Muhammad Abdul-Rauf, a modernist Muslim, former director of the Islamic Center of Washington, D.C., and representative of the earlier generation of American Muslims who had helped found the Federation of Islamic Associations, also celebrated the future of Islam in America and acknowledged the compatibility of Islam with the American political system:

> Any system that upholds the Islamic ideals of liberty, equality, and human dignity, although it may not carry that label, need not necessarily be considered un-Islamic or anti-Islamic. Since any system, political, economic, or otherwise, that does not violate the Islamic religious and moral precepts can be incorporated into an "Islamic" structure, and since the American constitution guarantees religious

---

[90] Hamid Algar, *Wahhabism: A Critical Essay* (Oneonta, NY: Islamic Publications International, 2002), 14. Faruqi translated at least two of Muhammad ibn 'Abd al-Wahhab's treatises into English: *Three Essays on Tawhid* (Riyadh: International Islamic Publishing House, 1979) and Kitāb al-tawḥīd: *Essay on the Unicity of Allah, or, What is Due to Allah from His Creatures* (Riyadh: International Islamic Publishing House, 1991).

[91] Isma'il R. al-Faruqi, "Islamic Ideals in North America," in *Muslim Community in North America*, 270.

freedom, the American Muslims have great latitude in selecting features of the general American life to forge and nurture a viable American Muslim community. Admittedly, there are indeed some deep-seated misunderstandings about Islam, but it is up to the Muslims to work for the eradication of these misconceptions and to set up models of religious teachings of their faith.[92]

ASSIMILATION AND INCREASED AMERICAN MUSLIM ACTIVISM

The fact that American Muslim leaders, regardless of their religious orientation, had an optimistic outlook on Muslim participation in American politics and society was in part a result of the overtures made to Islamist causes during the Soviet occupation of Afghanistan. No doubt the outlawing of discrimination in the 1960s and the rise of ethnic pride also contributed to their optimism. However, the acceptance Muslims felt for their varying religious agendas, regardless of the content of those agendas, reminds us of the shallowness of Americans' engagement with the differences Muslims represented. The multicultural ideal which valued difference in the 1970s and 1980s generally reduced diversity to ethnicity or cultural practices. Most Americans thus tended to think of Islam in terms of dietary, sartorial and cultural practices (e.g., the Five Pillars, the prohibition of alcohol and pork products, the veil, the caftan). Very few thought of Islam as a distinct ethical system, even though what motivated American Muslim activists to participate in American politics and society was their distinct visions of Islam as an ethical system. Abdul-Rauf, for example, upheld the compatibility of American and Islamic political values as evidence that Muslims could consider the United States "Islamic." Al-Faruqi asserted:

Islam teaches an ethic of action.... The unity of God, Islam interprets as transcendence before which all humans are equal in creatureliness, and hence as equally subject to the law of God whether as agents or subjects of moral action.... Political action is viewed by Islam, to use the expression of Muhammad Iqbal, as the expression of its spirituality. Every individual, it holds, is a shepherd responsible for his circle; and the umma [the Muslim community] is responsible for mankind. The highest standard is justice. The Muslim is obliged to realize it in his person, his family, his country, the world, or on the other side of the moon.[93]

Similarly, leaders of the Islamic Center of Southern California contended, "The best that Muslims may offer to America are their Islamic values

[92] Muhammad Abdul-Rauf, "The Future of the Islamic Tradition in North America," in *Muslim Community in North America*, 277–278.
[93] Al-Faruqi, "Islamic Ideals in North America," 266.

and ethical norm.... To be American is not to blindly accept America as it is, but to strive to make it cleaner and better by using the available freedom, the constitutional rights and the democratic process persistently and relentlessly toward reaching that goal."[94]

While American Muslim leaders in the 1980s emphasized that the ethical imperatives of Islam require Muslims to become full participants in American society and politics, they never clearly specified the ends of Islamic ethical activity in the quotidian life of American Muslims. Their call for ethical action in Muslims' daily lives was vague because they were not as concerned with attaining justice in the United States as they were in attaining justice for Muslim causes abroad. The implications of ethical political activity for American foreign affairs were clear to most Muslims. Fighting for justice in the United States for Muslim causes abroad meant fighting for a Palestinian homeland or an end to the Soviet presence in Afghanistan.

American Muslim leaders' calls for unity and their assertions that American Muslims were "still insufficiently united as to be politically effective"[95] were also primarily the result of their concern with political causes abroad. There was no significant domestic threat against Muslims in the 1980s that required them politically to unite. The threat lied abroad and in American foreign policy. Fighting for social justice in the United States also did not require Muslims to unite nationally; rather it required them to pool their resources with other social justice advocacy groups at the local level.

The upshot of all of this is that since greater social and political engagement with American society leads to greater assimilation, immigrant Muslim activists' decision in the 1980s to become more involved in American politics and society in order to advance their causes abroad set them on a path toward greater assimilation. The civil rights achievements of the 1960s and the rise of multiculturalism in the 1970s and 1980s enabled them to enter this path willingly. The United States' indirect alliance with the Islamist resistance movement in Afghanistan helped push them further down the road of assimilation. In light of these historical developments, it is easy to see why a modernist like Abdul-Rauf, a Wahhabi-Islamist like al-Faruqi, and moderate members of the Muslim Brotherhood like the leaders of the Islamic Society of Southern California all wrote enthusiastically about the

---

[94] Hathout, Osman, and Hathout, *In Fraternity*, 25 and 29.
[95] Abdul-Rauf, "The Future of the Islamic Tradition in North America," 277.

suitability of America for Islam and argued for Muslims to become Americans through ethical political activism.

NON-ACTIVIST AMERICAN MUSLIM INSTITUTION AND COMMUNITY BUILDING

There was, however, a wide gap between the aims of Muslim activists in the United States and the larger American Muslim population in this period. Al-Faruqi was not alone among American Muslim activists in his derisive assessment of the aims and objectives of most Muslim immigrants: "Muslim immigrants have come to these shores to study or to seek livelihood and opportunity for professional advancement. In most cases, they are beggars at the Western altar of knowledge; or receivers of Western affluence and economic development. This is the way Muslim immigrants see themselves."[96] Muslim activists, who sought to mobilize American Muslims nationally for their causes, also chided the majority of the American Muslim population for its adherence to "cultural" religious practices. They upheld the Qur'an and the Hadith as the only "pure" sources of Islam, while all other practices and sectarian beliefs through which Muslims had indigenized and practiced Islam were deemed cultural and unnecessary. The desire for unity in the midst of America's diverse Muslim population necessitated a scripturalist understanding of Islam. "We gather as Muslims, and we are bound by Islam as revealed in the *Quran* and taught by the authentic *sunna* [or tradition] of Prophet Muhammad. We are united on issues of common concern. We do not allow divisive factors to creep into the community." Adopting an American identity further helped Muslim activists unify America's diverse Muslim population: "[W]e consider that being American is a significant turn of fate.... Some Muslim circles tend to imply that the process of Islamization should essentially lead to Arabization or Pakistanization, etc. It is regrettable that there exists a confusion between ethnicity and religion."[97] Despite such claims, in practice, there is of course no religion outside of a cultural or social context. Even divine revelations have to be revealed into a linguistic, cultural context. Muslim activists' assertion that the only "pure" sources of Islam are the Qur'an and the Hadith is a product of American Muslims' context, one in which the diversity of the Muslim population needs to be overcome in order to unify Muslims politically.

---

[96] Al-Faruqi, "Islamic Ideals in North America," 267.
[97] Hathout, Osman, and Hathout, *In Fraternity*, 24–25.

As one would expect, the overwhelming majority of Muslims who were not activists did not readily forgo their sectarian beliefs and cultural practices. Unlike Islamists, they did not reduce Islam to an ideology that could be separated from culture, work, family life, and community and then be imposed upon these aspects of life in order to conform them to some puritanical reading of the Qur'an and the Hadith. It is thus not surprising that most American Muslims in the 1970s and 1980s did not relinquish their cultural heritage to participate in the agendas of national Muslim organizations. The executive committee of the Muslim Students Association complained in the early 1980s that "[a]lthough the number of Islamic organizations and centers is increasing, there is a general tendency among Muslims to group themselves on the basis of ethnicity and nationality."[98] African American Muslim communities remained for the most part African American communities. Certain African American leaders, such as Warith Deen Mohammed and Siraj Wahhaj of Masjid al-Taqwa in Brooklyn, participated in executive boards of national Muslim organizations like ISNA, but they remained culturally and socially within the African American Muslim community. Although they were influenced by the Islamist writings of Hasan al-Banna', Sayyid Qutb, and Abul A'la Mawdudi, which were disseminated by these organizations, and even received funds from such organizations as the Muslim World League, they continued to practice Islam within the context of the heritage of Islam in African America and focused on the problems of their own communities. Despite the patronage many African American Muslim organizations received from Muslim-majority countries (such as Kuwait and Saudi Arabia) and pan-Islamic organizations (such as the Muslim World League), they did not blindly sign on to anyone else's agendas.[99] At a time when pan-Islamic organizations were decrying Egyptian President Anwar Sadat's peace agreement with Israel (1979), for example, W. D. Mohammed commented, "This is a very sensitive question for me.... What he's doing is inviting his people to come away from an emotional response to the presence of Israel on Muslim land to a more philosophical and rational strategy. To them it may look like Uncle Tomism, but to me it looks like

---

[98] *Islamic Horizons* 12, no. 12 and 13, no. 1 (December 1983/January 1984), 9.

[99] Curtis, "Islamism and Its African American Muslim Critics: Black Muslims in the Era of the Arab Cold War," *American Quarterly* 59, no. 3 (September 2007), esp. 703. See also W. D. Mohammad, *al-Islam*, in particular 85–119 and his *Focus on Al-Islam: A Series of Interviews with Imam W. Deen Mohammed in Pittsburgh, Pennsylvania*, with Ayesha K. Mustafa (Zakat, 1988).

wisdom."[100] Similarly, Turkish, Bosnian, Pakistani, Iranian, Albanian, Lebanese, Palestinian, Senegalese, Indonesian, Somali, and Kurdish Muslims who immigrated to the United States after 1965 all formed their own cultural and self-help organizations, and when their numbers and resources allowed, they also established their own mosques.

For the majority of non-activist Muslims, the building of mosques was a priority because it provided them with a local community through which they could socialize with other Muslims (usually of their own ethnic background) and to raise their children within an Islamic environment. Consequently, when Muslims came together to establish their own mosques, they did so as New Yorkers, Chicagoans, Angelinos, or Houstonians. They established the Islamic Society of Tampa, the Islamic Center of Greater Chicago, the Austin Mosque, the Islamic Community Center of Northern Virginia, the Islamic Center of Central Ohio, and so on. They became members of their local community before they pooled their resources to found a mosque. The local mosque was, and continues to be, the most central Islamic institution in American Muslims' lives. Although there is no single process through which local mosques were established in this period, generally speaking, most mosques began as gatherings in individuals' homes. When the community was large enough, amicable enough, and wealthy enough, a house was rented or purchased and converted into a mosque. Once the mosque had its own edifice, Sunday schools were usually formed. If the community continued to grow, then funds were raised locally or sought from national Muslim organizations. The majority of mosques had no paid staff. Members of the community volunteered to serve as imams and administrators of the mosque. A 1994 study of mosques in the United States found that 75 percent of nearly 1,000 mosques had no paid full-time staff and "only 11% had more than one paid staff."[101]

National Muslim organizations in the United States, such as the Federation of Islamic Associations and the Muslim Students Association (from which the Islamic Society of North America and the Islamic Circle of North America emerged in 1981 and 1971), long understood the local nature of Islamic practice and institution building. They rarely went into local communities to build mosques; rather, they offered themselves as a financial and organizational resource for local communities. That

[100] Marsh, "Interview with Imam Wallace D. Muhammad," in *The Lost-Found Nation of Islam in America*, 168.
[101] Bagby, Perl, and Froehle, *The Mosque in America*, 53.

institution building is largely a local affair for most American Muslims is evidenced by the fact that as the number of Muslims and their collective financial resources have increased over the years, fewer and fewer American Muslims have reached out to national Muslim organizations for funding.[102] When national organizations help fund a mosque, they generally hold the title to it. Since local Muslim communities run the day-to-day operations of mosques, holding the title usually does not afford the national organization a significant degree of influence over the mosque, but it does give the national organization the power to intervene in the affairs of the mosque if its sectarian or theological orientation radically changes.

THE IRANIAN REVOLUTION AS A MILESTONE

Despite the gap between how activist and non-activist Muslims understood and experienced Islam in the United States, there was a period at the turn of the 1980s when both were energized by the success of the Iranian revolution. Indeed, one of the reasons why American Muslim activists were successful in their organizational efforts during the 1980s was that the Iranian revolution invigorated, albeit briefly, the American Muslim community, just as it did many Muslim communities across the globe. It created a sense of Islamic solidarity among the United States' diverse Muslim population. Many American Muslims of varying backgrounds began to adopt a more Islamic lifestyle and to support Islamic resistance movements all over the world. The unexpected success of Iran's Islamic revolution signaled to many Muslims that providence and divine justice were at work: "[T]he revolution derives its strength from its belief in God and people's wills. Every government ... opposed it. Israel supported mercenaries for the Shah's regime; China dubbed the revolution as reactionary and against Iran's national interest, hoodlums and dark forces were unleashed within; but with God's will manifesting itself in people's resolve to struggle, they all failed to contain it."[103] An article in the MSA's *Islamic Horizons* chided the shortsightedness of pundits and scholars who interpreted the Islamic revival as a form of fundamentalism rather than the work of providence: "[T]hey presume that *Islamic*

---

[102] In 1994, only 24 percent of mosques surveyed by the Council of American-Islamic Relations were not associated with any national or international organization, but in 2000, 45 percent reported having no outside associations. Bagby, Perl, and Froehle, *The Mosque in America*, 57.

[103] "Islamic Revolution Begins When a Muslim Changes," *Islamic Horizons* 8, no. 3 (March 1979), 4.

fundamentalism is tied to ... a set of social, political, and economic conditions in whose absence there will be no upsurge of Islamic sentiments in a
Muslim people.... [I]t is the transcendental, all-embracing Islamic movement which determines the Muslim destiny."[104] Because Islamist activists
had been striving since the 1960s to develop and perfect pan-Islamic networks to advance Muslim causes in every corner of the globe, they were
poised to harness the community's energy and enthusiasm for Islam.

Contemporary Muslims of varying backgrounds and anti-colonial
activists alike saw, at least in part, the fulfillment of their own struggles
in the success of the Iranian revolution, which touted itself as a righteous
struggle for the "oppressed of the earth" (*mustad'ifun fi al-'ard*, mentioned in the Qur'an 8:26 and 4:75, see also 4:98). Many Iranian Muslims
involved in the revolution shared this sentiment. Shahryar Rouhani, one
of Khomeini's representatives, told an enthused audience of American
Muslims in February of 1979, "The Iranian revolution surpassed all such
revolutions; it drew all segments of society to action." He went on to
credit the spirit of a wide array of Muslim activists ranging from the pan-
Islamic Muslim thinker Jamal al-Din al-Afghani to the modernist ideologue of India's Islamic nationalist movement Muhammad Iqbal to the
founder of the Muslim Brotherhood Hasan al-Banna' to Malcolm X for
kindling Iranians' imagination and setting them on the path that ended in
revolution. The revolution, he concluded, was thus "for all Muslims."[105]

For Muslim activists in the United States, the revolution "vindicated
Islam as an instrument of change; it dignified Muslims."[106] For most other
Muslims, Shi'i and Sunni alike, the revolution was empowering. Yvonne
Haddad, who studied the impact of the revolution on North American
Muslims, wrote,

The joy expressed at the passing of the Shah's regime was shared by Muslims
I interviewed from 18 different countries then residing in North America. For
most of them (85 percent), the most significant aspect of the revolution was that
it demonstrated the ability of a people to withstand the pressures of the 'greatest
power in the world' and to be able to affirm its will in designing its own destiny. The Islamic nature of the revolution was seen by many as the guarantee of
the search for indigenous answers to local problems.... All Muslims questioned
about their reaction to the Iranian revolution said that it enhanced their pride and
provided them with a positive affirmation of identity. This was especially true of

[104] "Islamic Fundamentalism: Destiny or a Passing Phase?," *Islamic Horizons* 11, no. 11
     (November 1981), 1.
[105] "Islamic Revolution Begins When a Muslim Changes," 4.
[106] "Islamic Iran's Foreign Policy?," *Islamic Horizons* 12, no. 2 (February 1982), 1.

Muslims residing in North America who have encountered negative responses to their Islamic identity by the host culture.[107]

To Islamists, the revolution vindicated their ideological belief that "God will give the victory to the believers if they unite and strive to bring about an Islamic order in the world."[108] The average American Muslims whom Haddad interviewed became more religious after the revolution. Some who celebrated Christmas in 1978 did not do so in 1979, and those active in cultural clubs limited their participation in them in favor of organized religious activism. They also expressed a greater sense of Islamic solidarity and began collecting donations for Islamist struggles in other parts of the Muslim world including the Philippines, Ethiopia, Lebanon, and Afghanistan.

The Iranian revolution was thus another significant milestone in the history of Islam in America following the passage of the Immigration Act of 1965. Unlike the Soviet invasion of Afghanistan, however, it did not have an enduring impact on Muslim activists involved in national institution building. It did not prove to be the panacea for which they had hoped. Muslim activists complained about how Khomeini's pan-Islamic revolutionary rhetoric actually resulted in a Shi'i government that rather than promoting Islamic unity and Islamism, worked for its own national interests.[109] The revolution revived Islamic practices among the general Muslim population, but its impact was more enduring among Shi'i Muslims whose increased interest in religion bolstered support for the establishment of Shi'i mosques in the United States. It, along with the Israeli invasion and occupation of southern Lebanon in 1982, also politicized many Shi'i Muslims.[110]

Iran sought to export its revolution to the United States (along with other countries) by sending missionaries to the United States, who proselytized mostly among African Americans with a modicum of success. Islamic revolutionaries rightfully believed they would find kindred

---

[107] Yvonne Y. Haddad, "Syrian Muslims in Montreal," in *Muslim Community in North America*, 166.

[108] Ibid., 168.

[109] See, for examples, "Islamic Iran's Foreign Policy?," *Islamic Horizons* 12, no. 2 (February 1982), 1; and Maryam Magidi, "Iran's Foreign Policy: Another View," *Islamic Horizons* 12, no. 6 (June 1982), 3.

[110] Linda S. Walbridge, *Without Forgetting the Imam: Lebanese Shi'ism in an American Community* (Detroit: Wayne State University Press, 1997), 131–132; Sally Howell, "Finding the Straight Path: A Conversation with Mohsen and Lila Amen about faith, Life, and Family in Dearborn," in *Arab Detroit*, 250–252.

spirits among black Americans who had been victims of the conflation of Christianity, whiteness, and progress used to justify colonialism and exploitation. Two weeks after the Iranian hostage crisis began,
Khomeini called on revolutionary students who had taken over the U.S.
embassy to release women and black hostages so long as they were not
spies. "Islam has a special respect toward women," he explained, and
"blacks, who have spent ages under American pressure and tyranny,
may have come to Iran under pressure." The students complied and
indicated that through the freed hostages, they wished to "send the message of nobility, freedom, independence and humanity..., which is the
message of Islam, to the people of the world, in particular the women
and blacks of the U.S."[111]

SUMMARY

The outlawing of racial discrimination in the 1960s radically altered the
racial and ethnic makeup of American society. The Immigration Act of
1965 allowed Asians and Africans to come to the United States in large
numbers with their families. Civil rights legislations criminalized racist practices that had for many years prevented the full participation of
people of color in American society. The African American middle class
grew significantly in the 1970s and 1980s. In the aftermath of Jim Crow,
many civil rights leaders turned their attention to community development and the creation of self-help organizations. Consequently, black
Muslim nationalist movements came to be seen under a different light,
as they were recognized for the "do-for-self" mentality which they fostered among their adherents. As African Americans' lot slowly began to
improve, the separatist, nationalist ideology of the Nation of Islam was
toned down and finally eliminated when Warith Deen Mohammed converted the Nation to Sunni Islam in 1975–1976.

The development of affirmative action and equal opportunity programs incited a new conservative movement among white ethnics of
Jewish and Catholic backgrounds who felt that their struggles and contributions to America's history were being left out. They put the lie to
the notion that America was a white, Protestant country. They – recall
Oscar Handlin from Chapter 3 – re-wrote America's history as the history of immigrants. New York City, not New England nor Virginia, *was*
America.

[111] John Kifner, "Islamic Creed Cited," *New York Times*, 18 November 1979, 14.

The Muslim immigrants who came from Africa and Asia in the late 1960s, 1970s and 1980s came to a land that valued cultural differences and posed few legal obstacles to their progress. Many of these new immigrants were professionals and soon found their way economically in America's middle class. They built mosques and national Islamic institutions soon after their arrival. The overwhelming majority of these immigrants were concerned with such routine matters as education, work, and family. They worked to establish local Islamic institutions through which they could socialize with co-ethnics and raise their children in an Islamic environment.

Few, however, were activists who worked to build national Islamic organizations with the aim of creating a utopian Islamic society. They established Islamic networks within the United States and the Muslim world more generally. When the Soviets invaded Afghanistan in 1979 and the United States reached out to Islamists in order to counter the Soviet's influence in Central and South Asia, American Muslim activists began to organize themselves as American citizens. After a period of internal debate, they made a concerted effort to become more politically active. Their increased political activity, supported in part by petrodollars, was aided by the Iranian revolution which helped further an Islamic revival already on the way. Many American Muslims became more religious in this period. The revolution rejuvenated a sense of Islamic solidarity among average American Muslim and led to their greater politicization. Since Islamists had led the charge in creating national Islamic institutions in the 1960s and 1970s, they were poised to serve as leaders of this new revival.

To lead effectively and politically mobilize a population of varying ethnic and sectarian backgrounds, they distinguished between the "pure" Islam of the scriptures and "cultural" Islamic practices. They touted the Qur'an and the Hadith as the only "pure" sources of Islam. Muslims' allegiance to these sources, they argued, would obliterate any cultural differences that they may have had. They also argued that Islamic values were compatible with American values. Therefore, there was no reason why Muslims in America should not embrace their American identity and participate actively in American politics and society in order to advance Islamic causes in the United States and, more pointedly, abroad.

This did not mean, however, that the majority of Muslims in the United States abandoned their distinct cultural practices or varying understandings of Islam as they became more active in the pan-Islamic organizations led primarily by Islamist activists; rather, it meant that these organizations found themselves with a broader, more diverse Muslim constituency. Already by 1981, there were voices claiming, "In my opinion, MSA is a platform for Muslim Brotherhood. As Muslims, we should be together under Islam and not under political parties, even if these parties have the name of Islam."[112] In the early 1990s, Muslim leaders continued to observe that "there is such a diversity of opinions that people have on how things should be done that people have difficulty – even if they may tolerate each other – working towards common goals. They don't have common goals. They have entirely different objectives, not even remotely similar."[113] No single national Muslim organization was able to unite Muslims under a single cause or a single understanding of Islam.

[112] Bashir al-Zouby, "MAYA is Arabism," *Islamic Horizons*, February 1981, 4.
[113] Ghaneabassiri, *Competing Visions of Islam*, 96.

8

Between Experience and Politics

American Muslims and the "New World Order," 1989–2008

Since the late 1980s, the history of Islam in America has become increasingly more multifaceted. Between the time when the Berlin wall fell and when George W. Bush left office, many more Muslims immigrated to the United States. The United States became home to a large number of Muslim refugees from such war-torn regions as Afghanistan, Bosnia, Somalia, Iraq, and the Sudan.[1] The number of converts to Islam increased to include sizeable Latin and European American communities alongside a growing African American Muslim community. American Muslims of varying religious understandings and ethnic backgrounds established many more mosques, self-help organizations, and political and civil rights advocacy groups. They became more active in public service both in their local communities and in the federal government. American Muslims also became more visible participants in cultural ventures as comedians, musicians, actors, and authors. Acts of violence carried out by militant Muslims and the invasions of Afghanistan and Iraq brought American Muslims into America's collective conscience as a security threat – a potential enemy within. Consequently, hundreds of American Muslims have found their civil rights abused and an untold number have been deported.

---

[1] From 1990 to 2008, 17,541 refugees immigrated to the United States from Afghanistan, 143,772 from Bosnia Herzegovina, 48,289 from Iraq, 86,075 from Somalia, 29,271 from the Sudan. U.S. Department of Justice, *Statistical Yearbook of the Immigration and Naturalization Service: 1990–2003*, (Washington, D.C.: Office of Immigration and Naturalization Service, 1991–2004), and U.S. Department of Homeland Security, *Yearbook of Immigration Statistics: 2004–2008*, (Washington, D.C.: Office of Immigration Statistics, 2005–2009).

Most of the scholarship on Islam in America has focusesd on the activities of Muslims in this period. It is impossible for a single chapter to adequately represent the findings of this scholarship and to detail the complex developments that shaped Islam and Muslim lives in the United States at the turn of the twenty-first century. In this chapter, as with the book as a whole, I have not aimed to be comprehensive. What follows highlights the major themes in contemporary developments of Islam in America and situates them in their historical context.

For most Americans any mention of the presence of Muslims in the United States today is bound to conjure up thoughts of 9/11 and its aftermath. This was the first time since Pearl Harbor, that the United States was attacked on its own soil. In response to this attack, the Bush administration declared "war on terror(ism)" and invaded Afghanistan (2001), where the perpetrators of the attacks of 9/11 had found a safe haven. Later, the United States invaded Iraq (2003), accusing Saddam Hussein of assisting al-Qaeda and developing weapons of mass destruction, which the United States feared could fall in the hands of Muslim terrorists. On the domestic front, the federal government itself was restructured. The Department of Homeland Security was created, which subsumed and centralized the responsibility of several governmental agencies, including the Federal Emergency Management Agency, the U.S. Immigration and Customs Enforcement, the U.S. Citizenship and Immigration Services, the U.S. Customs and Borders Protection, the U.S. Coast Guard, and the Transportation Security Administration. Congress passed the USA PATRIOT Act (2001), which provided law enforcement and immigration authorities, along with the Treasury, greater powers of surveillance and regulation to combat terrorism. According to its opponents, the PATRIOT Act radically altered Americans' civil rights, allowed the government unchecked powers over its citizens whom it suspected of terrorist activity. Since 9/11, terrorism also became the subject of numerous television shows and Hollywood films. Overall, surveillance and the threat of terrorism became a much more routine part of Americans' lives. Reports and occasions of torture at the hands of the CIA and agents of the American army, of acts of governmental deception, and of civil rights abuses that accompanied the above-mentioned changes raised questions, once again, about the nature of American values and the nation's character.

Given that militant Muslims carried out the attacks that ushered these historic changes from within the United States, it is not surprising that, after 9/11, most Americans began to take stock of the presence of Muslims in the United States. The events of 9/11, however, did not mark a new epoch in the history of Islam in America; rather they amplified processes and tendencies that had already begun in the late 1980s.

At the end of the Cold War, Islam became deeply entangled in America's most recent search for a national identity. American Muslims played an intermediary role in this new context as individuals who are both Muslim *and* American. As earlier chapters have demonstrated, American Muslims were not new to this intermediary role. Over the years, however, they gradually came to play this role more independently and more publically. The days when enslaved black Muslims played a passive role as liminal figures in non-Muslim Americans' missionary, commercial, or abolitionist ventures were long gone. The institutions American Muslims built and the relations they formed with non-Muslim Americans throughout the twentieth century rooted them in America; and since the late 1980s, a number of events (the Rushdie Affair, the Gulf War, the first World Trade Center bombing, the attacks of September 11, 2001, the increased diversity of Muslim voices in the public square) pushed them (and continue to push them) toward greater independence and increased participation in American public life.

THE RUSHDIE AFFAIR

Enmity between European Americans and "the Turks" has a long history. In more recent years, however, the notion that Islam is incompatible with or opposed to American values gained special popularity when some Muslims acted hostilely and violently against Americans in the name of Islam. In particular, the Islamic revolution of Iran and the hostage crisis became emblematic of "the threat of Islam."[2] As we have seen, however, the United States also made overtures to Islamists in this same period in order to strengthen Afghanis' resistance against the Soviet Union. American society and government did not uniformly view Islam as a threat even though some Muslims acted hostilely toward Americans. The average American associated Islamic extremism in the early 1980s with "Iranian fundamentalists," even though the lines between Arab, Muslim, Iranian, and fundamentalist were not always clear to most Americans, who did not feel it necessary to familiarize themselves with the differences at that time. There were other events that helped advance the notion that Islam and "the West" may be inherently incompatible. After Salman

[2] For a contemporary discussion of this perceived Islamic threat, see John Esposito, *The Islamic Threat: Myth or Reality?* (New York: Oxford University Press, 1999).

Rushdie, a celebrated British author who was born to an Indian Muslim family, published *The Satanic Verses* (1988), many Muslims decried his work as blasphemous because of the negative attributions they believed it ascribed to Prophet Muhammad. Numerous Muslims demonstrated in European and Muslim-majority countries against the publication of the book. In Bradford, England in January 1989, some demonstrators burned copies of *The Satanic Verses* in protest. On February 14, 1989, the Supreme Leader of Iran, Rohollah Khomeini, issued a fatwa condemning Rushdie to death on the charge of blasphemy. These acts outraged many Europeans and Americans who saw them as symptomatic of Muslim fanaticism and illiberality. Conversely, a number of British Muslims accused their government of hypocrisy because its blasphemy laws only protected the Church of England. They sought inclusion and demanded that the state give legal protection against blasphemy to other religions and try Rushdie for blasphemy against Islam.

In the history of Islam in Europe, the Rushdie Affair is a major turning point in non-Muslims' relations with Muslims. Media coverage of the affair in Europe depicted Muslims in Europe as "uncivilized" and "intolerant."[3] Immediately following the affair, many Europeans came to believe that they could never integrate a population that disrupted their societies' peace simply because of an author's artistic expression. It is instructive to compare American and European reactions to the Rushdie Affair because it served as a training ground for independent American Muslim activism and demonstrated the potential of American Muslims to mediate between "Muslim" and "Western" sensibilities in a diverse society. In the United States, the Rushdie Affair rippled in the national media, but it did not mark a dramatic turning point in Muslims' relations with non-Muslims. American Muslim leaders defended Rushdie's right to freedom of expression even though most disapproved of what they considered to be his demeaning depictions of Prophet Muhammad.[4] There

---

[3] Steven Vertovec, "Islamophobia and Muslim Recognition in Britain," in *Muslims in the West: From Sojourners to Citizens*, ed. Yvonne Y. Haddad (New York: Oxford University Press, 2002), 23; Jocelyne Cesari, "Islam in France: The Shaping of a Religious Minority," in *Muslims in the West* 36; Thijl Sunier and Mira van Kuijeren, "Islam in the Netherlands," in *Muslims in the West*, 150.

[4] The *New York Times* titled an article on this topic, "U.S. Muslims Urge Ban," even though the body of the article reported on the coalition American Muslims formed with non-Muslim American authors in order to condemn violent Muslim protests against *The Satanic Verses* and to support free speech. The article was titled as it was because of a request made by American Muslims for Viking Penguin to voluntarily withdraw publication of the book. Edwin McDowell, "U.S. Muslims Urge Ban," *New York Times*, March 4, 1989, 3.

were no mass demonstrations. There were certainly no book burnings. Newspapers reported that a few bookstore chains had taken the novel off their shelves as a result of unspecified threats.[5] In general, however, as the *New York Times* reported, American Muslims "contended that the uproar over the book was a painful chapter in the wrenching history between Islam and the West." On the one hand, they were indignant about "Westerners'" attacks against Islam as a result of the affair; on the other, they were "outraged at the pronouncements of Khomeini and the fundamentalists."[6] As one American Muslim public intellectual, Ali Mazrui, observed: "At least for a while the debate was a classic case of the dialogue of the deaf between the West and the world of Islam. The West was bewildered by the depth of Muslim anger. The Muslims were bewildered by Western insensitivity." More personally, Mazrui wrote: "In the debate concerning Rushdie's *The Satanic Verses*, I have had a number of conflicting emotions of my own. I have been torn between believing in Islam and believing in free society, between being myself a writer and being a religious worshipper, between being a believer in the *Shari'a* and an opponent of all forms of capital punishment in the modern age."[7]

During the Rushdie Affair, most American Muslims, like Mazrui, found themselves interpolated between an "Islam" that did not reflect their religious understandings and experiences but nonetheless shaped the external context of their lives in the United States and a "West" that was foreign to their experiences as Muslims in the United States. Non-Muslim Americans on the whole, being more religious than non-Muslim Europeans, sympathized with American Muslims, who, keep in mind, did not overreact to the publication of *The Satanic Verses*. Some non-Muslim Americans even reached out to Muslims for greater understanding.[8] There were some who concluded that "[t]he lesson of Salman Rushdie's ordeal, as of the Islamic revolution [of Iran], is that the world of Islam is far different from that of the West," but the majority of non-Muslim Americans sympathized with American Muslims who were hurt by what they considered to be others' insensitivity toward their religious sentiments. Many Christian leaders, newspapers reported, "beyond their

---

[5] Edwin McDowell, "Furor Over 'Satanic Verses' Rises as 2 More Chains Halt Sales," *New York Times*, February 18, 1989.

[6] Eric Pace, "U.S. Muslims Embarrassed, Indignant," *New York Times*, February 20, 1989, A1 and A6.

[7] Ali A. Mazrui, "Satanic Verses or a Satanic Novel? Moral Dilemmas of the Rushdie Affair," *Third World Quarterly* 12, no. 1 (January 1990), 116.

[8] See footnote 4 above.

unanimous condemnation of the Ayatollah Ruhollah Khomeini's call for Mr. Rushdie's assassination ... appear[ed] caught between their concern for religious liberty and free speech, their desire to respect the feelings of Muslims, and their own divided reactions to ... the movie 'The Last Temptation of Christ'."[9] President George H. W. Bush captured the sentiment of most Americans who strived for a balance between respect for religious differences and for freedom of speech. "This country was founded on the principles of free speech and religious tolerance. I want to make it perfectly clear that the United States will not tolerate any assault on these rights."[10] Bush's statement validated both Muslims' religious right to feel offended and Rushdie's right to express his views. If there was a clash between Islam and "the West," neither Muslim nor "Western" responses to the Rushdie Affair in the United States testified to it.

THE GULF WAR OF 1990–1991

The event that most significantly affected the history of Islam in America at the outset of the 1990s was the Persian Gulf War. In August 1990, Iraqi President Saddam Hussein invaded Kuwait and annexed it as a province of Iraq. The invasion was roundly condemned throughout the world. The United States immediately deployed troops to protect its Arab allies in the region. This operation came to be known as "Desert Shield." After about five months of unsuccessful diplomatic negotiations, "Desert Shield" became an offensive war, known as "Desert Storm." Under the leadership of the United States, a loose coalition of 28 countries, including a number of Muslim-majority countries – Saudi Arabia, Egypt, Syria, Oman, Qatar, the United Arab Emirates, Pakistan, Morocco, Kuwait, and Bangladesh – attacked Iraq in order to drive Iraq out of Kuwait.

Saddam Hussein, who was the leader of Iraq's socialist, national-ist Ba'th Party, adopted an Islamist posture in order to peddle his war as a jihad against "Western imperialism." He added the Arabic phrase, *allahu akbar* ("God is greater") to the Iraqi flag. He purported himself as the champion of the Palestinian struggle for liberation. He backed this claim by firing Scud missiles at Israel during the war. He claimed to be the religious warrior or *mujahid* who was going to unfetter Mecca from its American shackles. The Saudi government, he claimed, had

---

[9] Peter Steinfels, "Many Clergymen Quiet in Rushdie Case," *New York Times*, February 26, 1989, 16.
[10] "Bush Denounces Violence," *New York Times*, 1 March 1, 1989, A10.

relinquished its responsibilities as a Muslim state by allowing non-Muslim troops in the sacred land and by making Mecca a "hostage of the Americans."[11]

American Muslims were not fooled by Saddam's sudden conversion to Islam nor did they approve of his invasion and annexation of another sovereign country. "Disingenuous sloganeering that uses Islamic terminology in an attempt to legitimize personal ambition, regional power, and national economic interests is hollow rhetoric that should deceive no one, least of all world Muslims," read a statement released by the Islamic Society of North America (ISNA) in August 1990. Nonetheless, American Muslims were troubled by the presence of foreign troops in Saudi Arabia. As James Piscatori has noted: "When Saddam asked why his troops should withdraw from Arab land when the Israelis remained unopposed in their occupation of Arab land, he found a sympathetic hearing."[12] This sympathetic hearing, however, should not be confused with assent. Saddam's posturing simply highlighted for many Muslims the double-standards and hypocrisy involved in American discourses on liberation and the right to self-determination. Many were aware that Saddam had been an ally of the United States and had received much of his arsenal from the United States during the Iran–Iraq War (1980–1988). Desert Storm was seen as a U.S. attempt to tame a rogue ally and to control the oil supply in the region. The above-mentioned statement released by ISNA prior to the U.S. attack on Iraq made this point plainly:

Worldwide Muslim sentiment rejects in principle the presence of foreign military forces in the birthplace of Islam. It is a dangerous precedent, sparking memories of colonialism, the lasting repercussions of which remain devastating to the life, liberty, and culture of the region and its ecology. It is more resented since it is seen as emanating from a principal ally of the Israelis as well as a superpower that cannot readily be compelled to withdraw. A continuing policy of categorical support for Israeli occupation, ambitions, and oppression of the Palestinian people, coupled with an overriding focus on controlling energy resources, opens a serious credibility gap between the American decision-makers and the Muslim and Arab peoples. Present concerted international measures [taken against Iraq] stand in clear contrast to actions taken against Israeli aggressions.[13]

---

[11] James Piscatori, "Religion and Realpolitik: Islamic Responses to the Gulf War," in *Islamic Fundamentalisms and the Gulf Crisis*, ed. James Piscatori (Chicago, IL: Fundamentalism Project, American Academy of Arts and Sciences, 1991), 3–11.

[12] Ibid., 11.

[13] "A Statement on the Recent Conflict in the Middle East," *Islamic Horizons* (July/August 1990), 8–9.

The enthusiastic support of the Arab Gulf states for American intervention in Middle Eastern affairs led to greater feelings of antipathy on the
part of many American Muslims toward these monarchies. Consequently,
American Muslim organizations came to view petrodollars as a toxic
asset. Because the Gulf states, particularly Saudi Arabia and Kuwait,
helped fund many missionary and Islamist organizations throughout the
world, including the United States, they asked the Islamist and conservative organizations they financially supported to endorse the U.S.-led
war against Iraq. In the United States, according to the historian Yvonne
Haddad, the only leader of a national Muslim organization to do so was
Warith Deen Mohammed.[14] As a representative of indigenous American
Muslims, W. D. Mohammed sought to reassure Muslims in the Middle
East that the United States was not an enemy of Islam. In a statement
made to the Saudi Arabia National Radio before the International Islamic
Conference on the Current Situation in the Gulf in Mecca September 10,
1990, W. D. Mohammed introduced himself as an authoritative imam
from the United States of America:

I am a member of the indigenous African-American or 'black' converts to the
religion. I was born to parents who had accepted the religion. I have followed
the religion and accepted the purity of the religion and the Sunnah [traditions]
of the Prophet (PBUH) as the guide to us on how to live this religion. I am a
member now, thanks to Allah, of several bodies (organizations) of Muslims representing the interests of Muslims in the United States and also throughout the
international world. I am a member of Rabita's [i.e., the Muslim World League's]
Council of Masajid representing Muslim masajid (mosques) of America. I have
come here in the interest of Muslims all over the world, as well as in the interest
of Muslims in America.

After establishing his authenticity as an American *and* a Muslim,
W. D. Mohammed asserted that even though Muslims and the government of the United States do not always have the same interests, this was
a case in which those interests intersected. Muslims, he sought to convey
to his Saudi audience, need not be wary of American intentions.

We have Islamic interest (sic) first, and then other interests come second, not
before Islamic interests.... I am comfortable with the decision which Saudi Arabia
has taken to defend its borders and to accept the support of its friends – not only

---

[14] Yvonne Y. Haddad, "Muslims in U.S. Politics: Recognized and Integrated, or Seduced
and Abandoned?" *SAIS Review* 21, no. 2 (Summer/Fall 2001), 93; Peter Skerry,
"America's Other Muslims," *Wilson Quarterly* (Autumn 2005), 23; Piscatori, "Religion
and Realpolitik," 11–12.

America but other friends, Muslim nations and non-Muslim friendly nations. As an American, I compliment my government for protecting its interest, the interest of the American people, the global interest, for being friendly to the Kingdom of Saudi Arabia, and for respecting the religion of Al-Islam ("Islam"). I am convinced, for I have met with presidents myself; I met with two presidents in my life as a representative of the religion of Al-Islam in America, and I am convinced that President Bush has great respect for the major religions of the world, Al-Islam included. Also I am told that many Muslims are believing that the military of the United States, the American or U.S. army is occupying the Sacred Places. This is not true. We arrived in Jeddah, and I haven't seen the military yet. We are now in Mecca, and I haven't seen the military.[15]

W. D. Mohammed's statement appears to have been the dividend on the investments the Saudis and other Gulf states had made in American Muslim organizations. The Saudis, however, were not able to collect the same type of return on their investments in other American Muslim organizations. On the contrary, the Saudis' beckoning of American Muslim national organizations to support their cause led these organizations toward greater independence from Saudi money and influence. Even W. D. Mohammed declared that since the mid-1990s, he no longer received funding from Saudi Arabia because there were "some strings attached." Those who refused to endorse the Saudis' acceptance of the large presence of foreign troops in the Arabian Peninsula saw the flow of petrodollars to their organizations dry up.[16] A director of United Muslims of America in Sunnyvale, California (established 1982) described the first Gulf War as "a watershed event for Muslim leaders taking Saudi money." He told the *San Francisco Chronicle*: "Most of those who did not openly come out and condemn Saddam (Hussein) received no more money.... They (the Saudis) are trying to have influence here, but many American Muslims are professionals now and have their own money. Many say they do not want Saudi money. They want independence."[17] At the annual convention of the Islamic Society of North America in 1991, the major issue discussed during the open session was ISNA's source of funding. Members wanted to know whether or not ISNA was under the influence of Arab states in the Persian Gulf since it received funds from them. One attendee was reported to have said, "Please make sure that you do not depend on

---

[15] Warith Deen Mohammed, *Al-Islam: Unity and Leadership* (Chicago, IL: The Sense Maker, 1991), 162–164.
[16] Skerry, "America's Other Muslims," 23.
[17] Don Lattin, "Some U.S. Muslims Question Saudi Largess" *San Francisco Chronicle* (January 12, 1994), A1.

those people because they are corrupted [sic]. We are more than happy to donate. Just organize yourselves and ask us for money. Believe me, you will get more than you need." The chairman of the North American Islamic Trust suggested that if foreign funds are sought, their use be restricted to capital improvement projects, so that the day-to-day decision-making processes of the organization could not be influenced by outsiders.[18] In 1994, Mahboob Khan, a leader of the ISNA, claimed that the organization "no longer accepts money from the Saudis or other Islamic governments." This, of course, did not mean that they ceased to receive funds from wealthy individuals from the Persian Gulf countries. Khan further retorted, "We are trying to establish an infrastructure so we don't have to accept foreign donations.... They [individual, wealthy Saudis] lavishly spend millions on their personal lives – on things like gambling. One view has been that they are just wasting their money, so why not use it for a good cause and ignore their political views?"[19]

As with the Rushdie Affair, the media coverage of the Gulf War interpolated American Muslims within an "external Islam" and an "external America" that had little to do with the way in which American Muslims actually led their lives or operated their local and national institutions. This "external Islam" was fashioned by the highly nationalist media coverage of the war, which pitted a freedom-loving United States against a barbaric Muslim tyrant.[20] American Muslims, as we have seen, saw a much more complicated picture. Immediately after the war, at a time when strict economic sanctions were being placed on Iraq, American Muslim activists set up a Gulf Humanitarian Fund and sought to house Iraqi refugees and orphans. They also urged the U.S. government to "lift economic sanctions against the people of Iraq." Their contention was that the sanctions had caused undue hardship on the people, particularly the children, of Iraq without weakening Saddam's regime.[21]

This "external America" was one in which the United States was represented as the opponent of Islamism and Middle Eastern tyrants. In reality, however, the U.S. government had no clear policy position on Islamist

---

[18] "What You Had to Say about ISNA," *Islamic Horizons* (Winter 1991), 35–36.
[19] Lattin, "Some U.S. Muslims," A1.
[20] For a cultural analysis of the media coverage of the first Gulf War, see Melani McAlister, "Military Multiculturalism in the Gulf War and After, 1990–1999," in *Epic Encounters: Culture, Media, and U.S. Interests in the Middle East since 1945* (Berkeley and Los Angeles, CA: University of California Press, 2005), 235–265.
[21] See, for example, the insert titled, "Help the Children of Gulf War," *Islamic Horizons* (winter 1991).

organizations or on Middle Eastern dictators. As Fawaz Gerges has argued, U.S. officials "gave little thought to the aftermath of the Afghan struggle." They never asked, "Could the jihad genie be put back into the bottle? ... [N]o systematic assessment of the potential repercussions of the Afghan jihad seems to have been undertaken. Obviously, American officials reckoned that the mujahedeen and foreign guests and veterans could be contained and kept under control by their local clients once the Afghan conflict was over."[22] These U.S. clients in the Middle East consisted mainly of politically repressive regimes, such as Saudi Arabia and Egypt.

THE WORLD TRADE CENTER BOMBING OF 1993

An attempt to trace the contemporary history of jihadist movements after the Soviets withdrew from Afghanistan would go beyond the purview of this book. Of concern is how that history intersected with the history of Islam in America in the 1990s in the first World Trade Center bombing in New York City. On February 26, 1993, jihadists detonated a moving truck filled with explosives in an underground parking lot of the World Trade Center in New York City. A number of the men accused of involvement in the bombing were American Muslims who had previously been involved in the jihad in Afghanistan.[23] Chief among them was the radical Egyptian preacher, Sheikh Omar Abdel-Rahman (b. 1938), who received a lifetime prison sentence in 1995 for masterminding the bombing. Sheikh Abdel-Rahman had been an active member of the Islamic Group in Egypt (al-Jama'a al-Islamiyya, pronounced al-Gama'a al-Islamiyya in Egyptian Arabic) and had traveled on multiple occasions to Pakistan to support the jihad in Afghanistan. During that war, he, with the help of a Mustafa Shalabi, raised funds and recruited young men in New York City for the jihad in Afghanistan through Al Kifah Refugee Center (known locally as the "Jihad Center"), which had been established in Brooklyn to help Afghani refugees. After the Soviet withdrawal from Afghanistan, Abdel-Rahman had returned to Egypt where at one point he learned he was going to be arrested for his association with militant Islamist organizations. He

---

[22] Fawaz Gerges, *The Far Enemy: Why Jihad Went Global* (New York: Cambridge University Press, 2005), 73–74.
[23] Chris Hedges, "Muslim Militants Share Afghan Link," *New York Times*, March 28, 1993, 15; Francis X. Clines, "U.S.-Born Suspect in Bombing Plots: Zealous Causes and Civic Roles," *New York Times*, June 28, 1993, B2; Colin Miner, "Sources Claim CIA Aid Fueled Trade Center Blast," *Boston Herald*, January 24, 1994, 4.

fled to the Sudan, where he received a tourist visa from the U.S. embassy and came to the United States. A year later, he was granted permanent residence status. When the State Department was asked how an accused terrorist, wanted by the Egyptian government, ended up receiving a visa to come to the United States, they gave a stupefying explanation – "computer error."[24] Was he permitted into the country, eventually as an immigrant, as a form of compensation for his efforts in Afghanistan? Was he of some potential strategic use to the United States? It should be noted that a few militant Islamists (including Abdullah Azzam (1941–1989), a Palestinian Islamist scholar and a fundraiser and recruiter for the Afghan jihad) were also allowed into the United States in the 1980s to recruit American Muslims to support the mujahedeen in Afghanistan.[25] After the Soviet's withdrawal, they returned to raise money for varying local Muslim struggles that such groups sought to support in places like Bosnia and Chechnya. Before he helped rationalize a global jihad to be launched by al-Qaeda, Ayman Zawahiri, for example, visited Silicon Valley, California in the early 1990s, while under secret FBI surveillance, for fundraising.[26]

While in the United States, Abdel-Rahman preached at mosques in Brooklyn and Jersey City. In 1990, one of his followers, El-Sayyid A. Nosair, was arrested and convicted for the murder of the anti-Arab, militant Israeli Rabbi Meir Kahane. All the men arrested in connection with the 1993 World Trade Center bombing also had connections with Abdel-Rahman. Prior to the bombing, Abdel-Rahman had been under FBI surveillance. As a result of these connections between the Afghani jihad and the World Trade Center bombing, some began to wonder whether or not the Afghan jihad had come home to roost. An unidentified CIA agent involved in the Afghan operation told The *Boston Herald*, "By giving these people the funding we did, a situation was created in which it could be safely argued that we bombed the World Trade Center." The CIA had used Al Kifah Refugee Center to funnel aid to the mujahedeen in Afghanistan through Gulbuddin Hekmatyar, the leader of the Hizb-i Islami (the Islamic Party), and an internal investigation by the CIA revealed that they were "partly culpable" for the World Trade Center bombing in 1993.[27]

---

[24] Mary Anne Weaver, "The Trail of the Sheikh," *New Yorker*, April 12, 1993, 72.
[25] Personal interview with a leader of the Muslim community in Virginia, (Monterey, CA, August 3, 2009). See also, Gerges, *Far Enemy*, 135, and John K. Cooley, *Unholy Wars: Afghanistan, America and International Terrorism*, 3rd ed. (London: Pluto Press, 2002), 69.
[26] Gerges, *The Far Enemy*, 77.
[27] Colin Miner, "Sources Claim CIA Aid Fueled Trade Center Blast," *Boston Herald*, January 24, 1994, 4.

While the exact role of the United States in dealing with the global dispersion of the Afghan jihad is not yet clear, what is clear is that the United States did not adopt a specific stance against so-called Muslim extremists, some of whom had been involved in the Afghan jihad. Wisely or otherwise, the United States vacillated between confrontation and accommodation, depending on its strategic interests at any given time and place. After the 1993 World Trade Center bombing, for example, it bolstered its support for its client states such as Egypt and Saudi Arabia in order to help them fight militant Islamists, but it also engaged the Taliban in Afghanistan in order to promote the construction of a gas pipeline from Turkmenistan to Pakistan.[28] A Unocal spokesman explained that "[t]he U.S. government was encouraging our engagement there to bring stability to the country." In December 1997, Unocal, with the consent of the State Department, arranged for Taliban officials to visit the United States to win support for Unocal's cooperation with the Taliban.[29]

During the 1990s, the United States deliberately sought not to vilify Islam or Islamic political movements while it worked to obstruct the activities of militant Islamist organizations. The Clinton administration overtly rejected the notion made popular by Samuel Huntington (discussed below) that there is a "clash of civilizations" between "Islam and the West." In what had become a tendency of U.S. administrations to conceptualize Islam for Muslims, President Bill Clinton, in a 1994 address to the Jordanian Parliament, eschewed the notion that there is an "Islamic threat" by disassociating Islam as a religion from acts of terror carried out by Muslims: "the forces of terror and extremism, cloak themselves in the rhetoric of religion and nationalism, but behave in ways that contradict the very teachings of their faith and mock their patriotism." "[T]he traditional values of Islam – devotion to faith and good works, to family and society – are in harmony with the best of American ideals. Therefore, we know our cultures can live in harmony with each other."[30]

Domestically, Clinton, who was a child of the civil rights and women's rights struggles of the 1950s and 1960s, made a concerted effort to include Muslims in America's national consensus. He was the first

---

[28] Ahmad Rashid, *Taliban: Islam, Oil and the New Great Game in Central Asia* (London: I.B. Tauris, 2002), 6 and 45–46.

[29] Michael J. Berens, "Center for Afghanistan Studies Has Hosted Taliban Leaders," *Chicago Tribune*, October 19, 2001.

[30] "Remarks by President Bill Clinton to the Jordanian Parliament," The White House: Office of the Press Secretary (Amman, Jordan, October 26, 1994) 3, cited in Gerges, *America and Political Islam*, 92–93.

president to include mosques alongside churches and synagogues as American centers of worship.[31] On February 20, 1996, First Lady Hillary Rodham Clinton hosted the first celebration of *'Id al-fitr*, which marks the end of Ramadan, at the White House. Such celebrations gradually became a regular affair at the White House and on Capitol Hill.

On June 15, 1991, Siraj Wahhaj, the imam of Masjid at-Taqwa, became the first Muslim to open a session of the House of Representatives with a prayer. On February 6, 1992, Warith Deen Mohammed offered a prayer on the Senate floor. The army ordained its first Muslim chaplain, Abdul Rasheed Muhammad, to the delight of many American Muslims on December 3, 1993. Abdul Rasheed Muhammad, an African American convert, was to be the pastoral representative of some 2,500 Muslims in the U.S. military at that time.[32] That the first imams chosen to lead prayers in the Congress and to serve as army chaplains were African American is of course no coincidence. Since the rehabilitation of the public image of "black Muslims" in the late 1970s, African American Muslims had become familiar to non-Muslim Americans through such figures as Malcolm X, Muhammad Ali, and Kareem Abdul-Jabbar.

INCREASED AMERICAN MUSLIM POLITICAL ACTIVISM AND
INDIGENIZATION OF ISLAM IN AMERICA

The Gulf War and the 1993 World Trade Center bombing increased prejudice and violence against American Muslims.[33] Nonetheless, American Muslims, both activists and non-activists, held on to the popular convention that, in America, through greater political organizing efforts, they, just as any other minority group, would be able to counter the prejudices they faced and play a more influential role in shaping U.S. policies both at home and abroad. Muslim activists accepted the inclusive gestures of the government. They, too, made a concerted effort to define cooperation

---

[31] According to Emily Kalled Lovell, Gerald Ford was the first president to acknowledge mosques as American centers of worship in 1976, but I have not been able to confirm this information. "Islam in the United States: Past and Present," in *The Muslim Community in North America*, ed. Earle Waugh, Baha Abu-Laban, and Regula B. Qureshi (Edmonton, AL: The University of Alberta Press, 1983), 107.

[32] *Islamic Horizons* (December 1993), 4.

[33] For reports of such incidents see, Council on American-Islamic Relations, *Unveiling Prejudice: The Status of Muslim Civil Rights in the United States* (CAIR, 1997).

rather than confrontation as their goal. In 1993, several national Muslim organizations held a day-long conference at the National Press Club called "Islam and the West: Cooperation not Confrontation." The conference featured four sessions titled: "Political Economy of Islamism," "Western Approaches to Islam," "Congressional Perspectives on Relations between Islam and the West," and "Islam and Human Rights." The third of these sessions on "Congressional Perspectives" entailed an off-the-record meeting on Capitol Hill with the Chairman of the House Foreign Affairs Committee, Lee H. Hamilton, and a banquet, during which Robert Torricelli, another member of the House Foreign Affairs Committee, delivered a keynote address.

The organizers of the conference explained to their constituency that American Muslims had two choices before them. They could either keep a low profile and ignore the public discourses and political decisions that had created the external contexts into which American politics and the media interpolated them or they could organize and actively participate in American society and politics in order to rectify these stigmatizing discourses.

Many American-Muslims have been forced to assume a low profile while their religion is vilified by some policy makers in the United States. Disintegration of the Soviet bloc, and then the Gulf War, signaled to many Muslims the beginning of a New World Order which identified them as the enemy. Since then, we have read stories about Hamas being operated and funded by [Muslims in] the U.S., and that America was in danger of attack from 'Islamic militants.' Of course, the bombing of the World Trade Center only made matters worse and created more suspicion, mistrust, intolerance and disdain. What we are left with is a public relations disaster. As American-Muslims, we have two choices: avoid attracting attention or challenge those who orchestrate this political spectacle. Four Muslim organizations saw the former option as a precarious approach to a volatile situation and coalesced to host a one-day conference, Islam and the West: Cooperation not Confrontation, to reintroduce policy makers, both inside and outside the halls of government, and in the press corps, to Islam without assigning blame for existing misrepresentations.

The description of the problem American Muslims faced as a "public relations disaster" and the title of the conference, "Islam and the West," clearly illustrate that national Muslim organizations viewed prejudice against Islam both in American society and in policy circles as an outcome of constructed images of Islam, which they sought to deconstruct through their own utopian constructions of Islam. They thus argued that "Islam" endorses democracy and pluralism by emphasizing the rule of law and due process; it promotes economic development; it lays a foundation for the observance of human rights.[34]

This depiction of an encounter between "Islam" and "the West," without any interrogation of the referents of these constructed categories or their relation to any local context (Whose Islam? Whose West?), would appear totally farcical were it not for the fact that the United States, after the success of the Afghan jihad, had come to realize that international Islamist organizations constituted a significant political and social force in the Muslim-majority world. "Islam" in the binary construct, "Islam and the West," stood for Islamist movements, and in the early 1990s, the United States explored ways through which it could engage these movements. As I stated earlier, the United States never adopted a coherent policy toward conservative, ideological understandings of Islam or Islamist activism. Part of the reason for this is that there are many different Islamist organizations with varying agendas and orientations. While they share a utopian vision of creating an Islamic society based on their understanding of Islam as a political ideology, they disagree among one another about the means by which such a vision should be attained and about what exactly constitutes Islam's ethical principles. Moreover, local Islamist organizations face varying social and political contexts. The Muslim Brotherhood in Palestine in the 1990s, for example, faced challenges that were very different from those faced by the Muslim Brotherhood in Egypt. The former, living under occupation, adopted a more militant understanding of Islamic activism, while the latter found that it could advance its cause from within by participating in existing political structures. There was thus no monolithic Islamist organization with whom the United States could engage, just as there was no monolithic West with which Islamists could engage.[35] In sum, what at first glance appeared to have been a farcical encounter between two constructed entities without referents in the real world was in actuality an improvised exercise in reestablishing a relationship between the United States and Islamist organizations in the absence of a common enemy – Soviet expansionism.

---

[34] Omar Jabara, "The Unwilling Scapegoat: Muslim-Americans Take on the Challenge," *Islamic Horizons* (December 1993), 12–13.

[35] For a thoughtful and accessible discussion of the diversity of Islamist ideologies and organizations, see Mohammed Ayoob, *The Many Faces of Political Islam: Religion and Politics in the Muslim World* (Ann Arbor, MI: The University of Michigan Press, 2008).

Oil and gas reserves in Muslim-majority countries continued to make the stability of the Middle East and South and Central Asia a significant priority for American foreign policy. In addition to sharing a common interest in access to oil and gas, the United States and a number of Muslim-majority states cooperated with Islamists in the effort to liberate Afghanistan from Soviet occupation. In this instance, the United States did not treat Islamist ideology in and of itself as a militant threat in the way it did Communism. For these and other factors, Islamist organizations rose to prominence as political players in the region. However, the United States and Islamist organizations ultimately did not reach a state of accommodation, even if they shared various common interests in dealing with other regions of conflict involving Muslims, such as the Balkans and Central Asia. The Israeli occupation of Palestinian territories and the United States' unyielding alliance with Israel along with U.S. support for oppressive regimes in the Middle East are the reasons most frequently cited on both sides to explain this retardation of positive relations between Islamists and the American government.

As I will show later, those who cried "clash of civilizations" and portended the violent outcome of Muslims' "rage" at this time were mainly neoconservative intellectuals and pro-Israel activists who were apprehensive about the future of U.S.-Israeli relations if the United States entered into constructive relations with Islamist organizations in the post-Soviet era. They were joined by more militant pro-Israelis, like Daniel Pipes and Steve Emerson, who launched an anti-Islamism propaganda campaign of their own in the 1990s. Steve Emerson produced and narrated a documentary that aired nationwide on PBS in 1994 titled, "Jihad in America." Daniel Pipes, a historian of Islam turned pro-Israel activist, began writing about American Muslims as early as 1990 in a cover article published in the *National Review* titled, "The Muslims Are Coming! The Muslims Are Coming!" In this article, he argued that while Muslims often advanced their causes through numbers (high birth-rate and immigration), there was no reason to fear Muslim immigration to "the West" as long as "we" checked the advancement of Islamist ideology.[36] His writings throughout the 1990s on the internal threat that Islamists presented in the United States culminated in an I-told-you-so book, *Militant Islam Reaches America* (2002). Although the title of his book refers to "militant Islam," what he means by "militant Islam" is Islamism in general and Islamist organizations. He

---

[36] Daniel Pipes, "The Muslims Are Coming! The Muslims Are Coming!," *National Review*, November 19, 1990, 28–31.

thus considers such organizations as the Muslim Students Association and the Islamic Society of North America to be proponents of "militant Islam" even though they have not carried out or advocated any militant actions. The aim of Pipes and his ilk has been to define Islamist ideologies and organizations as a militant threat to "the West" similar to Communism.

The most notable American Muslim political organization that emerged at this time to negotiate Islamist-U.S. relations was the Council on American-Islamic Relations (CAIR). CAIR was originally established as a political advocacy organization in Washington, D.C. in 1994. It aimed to educate the American public about Islam, challenge defamatory depictions of Muslims, protect American Muslims' civil liberties, and lobby for issues of concern to Muslim activists. It was founded mainly by Arab American Muslims, some of whom had roots in Islamist organizations associated with the Palestinian rights movement and the Palestinian struggle against Israeli occupation, mainly the Islamic Association for Palestine. For this reason, it has been attacked by staunch pro-Israel advocacy groups, who claim that it is an American front for Hamas and "Islamic terrorists" despite CAIR's repeated and categorical condemnations of terrorism.[37]

Soon after its founding, CAIR gained national notoriety for its advocacy on behalf of American Muslims after the Oklahoma City bombing on April 19, 1995. It published *A Rush to Judgment*, a report which recorded more than 200 incidents of harassment and hate crimes against Muslims in the days following the bombing.[38] Since then CAIR has become one of the most prominent Muslim advocacy and civil rights groups because of its quick response to issues involving prejudice or discrimination against American Muslims. Coming into existence during the digital age, CAIR has been successful in maintaining an e-mail blast service and a website through which it communicates regularly and rapidly with Muslims and non-Muslims interested in issues involving American Muslims. Over the years, CAIR has developed more than 30 local branches throughout the United States in order to monitor local news and events relating to Muslims

---

[37] Daniel Pipes and Sharon Chadha, "CAIR founded by 'Islamic Terrorists'?," *Front Page Magazine* online, http://www.danielpipes.org/2811/cair-founded-by-islamic-terrorists (accessed July 20, 2009); Anti-Defamation League, "Council on American-Islamic Relations," available at the ADL web site, http://www.adl.org/Israel/cair.asp (accessed July 20, 2009); CAIR has compiled a list of its statements against terrorism at its web site, http://www.cair.com/AmericanMuslims/AntiTerrorism.aspx (accessed July 20, 2009).

[38] Mohamed Nimer, *The North American Muslim Resource Guide* (New York: Routledge, 2002), 133.

and to develop relations with local media, government officials, and Muslim leaders through which it could more rapidly and effectively carry out its advocacy work.[39] Its support of American Muslims, whose civil liberties were compromised in the name of national security after 9/11, also made CAIR the premier Muslim advocacy group in America.

While CAIR has become the most prominent Muslim civil rights and political advocacy group, it was one of numerous national Muslim organizations that were founded in the 1990s with the aim of educating the American public about Islam, monitoring discrimination against Muslims, and increasing Muslims' participation in American society and politics. American Muslim women became more politically active in this period in order to empower Muslim women and to bring attention to women's issues. In 1992, the Muslim Women's League (MWL) was founded in Los Angeles as an offshoot of the Muslim Public Affairs Council in order, in its own words, "to implement the values of Islam and thereby reclaim the status of women as free, equal and vital contributors to society" and to inform "the American public, Muslims and non-Muslims alike, of the perspectives of Muslim women."[40] In 1993, a group of Muslim women lawyers founded KARAMAH (literally, 'dignity' in Arabic) under the leadership of Azizah al-Hibri with the aim of promoting Muslim women's rights in the United States and abroad and to educate Muslim women in Islamic law and community leadership.[41] Muslim women had always been active in local and national American Muslim organizations and some even came to national leadership positions. Aliya Hassan, an active member of the Federation of Islamic Associations, for example, went on to serve as the founding director (1972–1981) of one the most prominent Arab American self-help organizations known as the Arab Community Center for Economic and Social Services (ACCESS).[42] Nonetheless, the founding of distinctly women organization in the early 1990s brought American Muslim women and their issues more prominently into the public sphere. Soon after their founding, both MWL and KARAMAH, for example, went on to represent American Muslim women in the U.S.

---

[39] Council on American-Islamic Relations, "CAIR chapters," http://www.cair.com/Chapters. aspx (accessed February 9, 2009).

[40] http://www.mwlusa.org/about/about.html (accessed August 12, 2009).

[41] http://www.karamah.org/about.htm (accessed August 12, 2009).

[42] "Aliya Hassan" in *Arab Detroit: From Margin to Mainstream*, ed. Nabeel Abraham and Andrew Shryock (Detroit, MI: Wayne State University Press, 2000), 317–318. http://www.accesscommunity.org/site/PageServer?pagename=ACCESS_History2 (accessed August 12, 2009).

delegation to the Fourth World Conference on Women (1995), which was led by First Lady Hillary Rodham Clinton. These organizations served as catalysts for increasing American Muslim women's participation in American public life.[43]

Local Muslim institution building and activism also increased in the 1990s. The number of mosques in the United States grew by 25 percent in this period, while the number of people associated with mosques quadrupled.[44] By 2008, according to the Harvard Pluralism Project, there were about 1,600 mosques and Islamic centers in the United States. These mosques and Islamic centers, similar to those founded in the 1980s, were mainly founded to meet the needs of local communities. They were primarily centers for worship, Islamic education, and socializing. Throughout the 1990s and the first decade of the twenty-first century, nearly 200 Islamic private schools were established serving some 20,000 Muslim children.[45] Meanwhile, American Muslims also continued to organize around their ethnic backgrounds and sectarian beliefs.[46] Kosovar nationalists in particular actively organized and lobbied the Clinton administration. They also played a significant role in financing and arming the Kosovo Liberation Army in the 1990s.[47] Varying virtual communities also appeared and disappeared online.

The increase in the number of American Muslim institutions was in part a response to the increase in the number of Muslims in the United States. Census data shows that between 1990 and 2000, the number of foreign-born individuals from Muslim-majority countries increased from 871,582 to 1,717,132. While this number includes many

---

[43] For a select list of these organizations public activities, see http://www.mwlusa.org/news/list.html and http://www.karamah.org/archives.html (accessed August 12, 2009).

[44] Ihsan Bagby, Paul M. Perl, and Bryan T. Froehle. *The Mosque in America: A National Portrait* (Washington, D.C.: Council on American-Islamic Relations, 2001), 3.

[45] Louis Francis Cristillo, "'God Has Willed It': Religiosity and Social Reproduction at a Private Muslim School in New York City" (Ph.D. dissertation, Columbia University, 2004), 51–52.

[46] Mohamed Nimer, "Ethnic Associations," in *North American Muslim Resource Guide*, 81–93. See also Frances Trix, "Bektashi Tekke and the Sunni Mosque of Albanians in America," in *Muslim Communities in North America*, ed. Yvonne Y. Haddad and Jane I. Smith (Albany, NY: State University of New York Press, 1994), 359–380; Jonathan Friedlander, "The Yemenis of Delano: A Profile of a Rural Islamic Community," in *Muslim Communities in North America*, 423–444; Georges Sabagh and Mehdi Bozorgmehr, "Secular Immigrants: Religiosity and Ethnicity in Among Iranian Muslims in Los Angeles," in *Muslim Communities in North America*, 445–473.

[47] See the documentary *The Brooklyn Connection: How to Build a Guerrilla Army* (New Video Group, 2005).

non-Muslim immigrants from Muslim-majority countries, it gives us a sense of the growth of the Muslim population in the United States. It, of course, does not include the hundreds of thousands of American-born Muslims, including African American Muslims who, according to a statistical study of American Muslims made up around 20 percent of the American Muslim population in 2007.[48] Muslims from Muslim-minority countries also came to the United States. For example, between 1990 and 2000 the number of Indian immigrants increased from 450,406 to 1,222,552; undoubtedly, a significant number of these immigrants were Muslim. While there is no consensus on the number of Muslims in the United States at this time, the existing surveys suggest that there were about three million Muslims in the United States by 2008.[49] National Muslim organizations, however, cited numbers as high as six to eight million.

The mushrooming of American Muslim institutions and communities was met with a desire on the part of national Muslim organizations to unite Muslims for political leverage. Organizations, such as the American Muslim Alliance (AMA, founded in 1994) were established to provide civic education for Muslims and to empower Muslims in American politics. At the local level, a concerted effort was made by American Muslim organizations to "identify and train American Muslims to run for public offices."[50] American Muslims ran to serve as mayors and state legislators and on city councils and school boards. A few succeeded, paving the way for others. In 2006, Keith Ellison (from Minnesota's fifth district) became the first popularly elected American Muslim in the U.S. Congress. He was joined in 2008 by André Carson (from Indiana's seventh district).

During the 1996 presidential elections, for instance, five national Muslim organizations met with both the Clinton and Dole campaign staffs in order to reach a consensus on which candidate to support. The diversity of opinions and interests within the Muslim population, however, came to the surface as the American Muslim Council (founded in 1990) and the Muslim Public Affairs Council (founded in 1988) endorsed Bill Clinton, the National Council on Islamic Affairs (formed in the

---

[48] Pew Research Center, *Muslim Americans: Middle Class and Mostly Mainstream* (Pew, May 2007), 1.

[49] For an overview of existing surveys that have sought to determine the number of American Muslims, see Pew Research Center, *Muslim Americans: Middle Class and Mostly Mainstream* (Pew, May 2007), 9–14. See also footnote 2 of the Introduction.

[50] American Muslim Alliance, "Mission Statement," http://www.amaweb.org/images/special/Mission%20Statement.pdf (accessed July 28, 2009).

1960s) endorsed Dole, and the American Muslim Alliance (founded in 1994) and CAIR took no position. In the end this particular coalition fell apart because each group worried about how its membership base would view its endorsement of a presidential candidate.[51] Indeed American Muslims, at this time, did not share a common political philosophy nor did they strongly support one party over another. According to one poll, in 2001, 23 percent of Muslims identified as Republicans, 40 percent as Democrats, and 28 percent as independents. Nonetheless, 42 percent of Muslims voted for George W. Bush in 2000 and 31 percent for Al Gore.[52] In light of this disparity, American Muslim activists decided strategically to organize American Muslims politically around issues rather than parties. In fall of 2003, they formed a new national coalition called the American Muslim Task Force on Civil Rights and Elections (AMT).[53] "'What is the most effective way to conceptualize and organize Muslim politics?' was the question that the newly formed AMT faced," wrote a reporter covering the organization in 2004. "They decided to conceptualize Muslim politics around key issues, later labeled as 'the Civil Rights Plus' agenda."[54] AMT's multiparty strategy and emphasis on civil rights was stimulated in large part by Arab, South Asian, and Muslim Americans' complaints of civil rights abuses after September 11, 2001. These abuses stimulated the political coalescing of American Muslims, which contributed to the success of AMT. According to the abovementioned poll, 81 percent of some 1,700 American Muslims' surveyed indicated that they supported the AMT civil rights agenda and 69 percent indicated that an AMT endorsement for a candidate was important

---

[51] Richard H. Curtiss, "Dr. Agha Saeed: Dynamic Leader of Expanding American Muslim Alliance," *Washington Report on Middle East Affairs*, no. 1297 (December 1997), 23–25.

[52] Zogby International, "American Muslims Overwhelmingly Backing Kerry," www.zogby.com/search/readnews.cfm?ID=869 (accessed July 28, 2009).

[53] The following American Muslim national organizations are represented in the AMT coalition: American Muslim Alliance (AMA), Council on American-Islamic Relations (CAIR), Islamic Circle of North America (ICNA), Muslim Alliance of North America (MANA), Muslim American Society (MAS), Muslim Students Associaiton – National (MSA), Muslim Ummah of North America (MUNA), and United Muslims of America (UMA). The following organizations have an observer status within the coalition: Islamic Society of North America (ISNA), Muslim Public Affairs Council (MPAC), and American Muslims for Palestine (AMP). See "American Muslims in the American Mainstream" at www.americanmuslimvoter.net/images/special/ABOUT US AMT2008.pdf (accessed July 28, 2009).

[54] Lisette Poole, "Election 2004, Milestones of Muslim Activism," *Pakistan Link*, November 12, 2004, 7.

in their own decision-making. Following 9/11, both the AMT's and the larger American Muslim population's support for the Republican Party declined sharply. In 2004, only 12 percent of American Muslims identi-fied as Republicans while 50 percent indicated that they were Democrats and 31 percent said they were independents.[55] Seventy-one percent voted for the Kerry/Edwards ticket in 2004 versus 14 percent who voted for Bush/Cheney.[56]

In 2008, 49 percent of American Muslims self-identified as Democrats, 8 percent as Republicans, and 37 percent as independents.[57] They again overwhelmingly (79 percent according to a Gallup poll) supported the Democratic candidate, but, as *Newsweek* reported, "many Muslims kept their presidential preference a secret in the months leading up to Super Tuesday, fearing that an endorsement from them might in fact work against Barack Obama. After all, this was an election year in which the word 'Muslim' was used as shorthand to connote anti-American leanings and a hidden love of terrorism."[58] Such fears were heightened when false rumors spread in far-right media circuits about Obama being a "secret Muslim." American Muslim organizations, aware of the stigma associated with Islam, remained for the most part silent on this issue. It was former Secretary of State Colin Powell who, as a rather isolated voice, raised the question of what if Obama was Muslim in the national media:

I am also troubled by, not what Senator McCain says, but what members of the [Republican] party say. And it is permitted to be said such things as, "Well, you know that Mr. Obama is Muslim." Well, the correct answer is, he is not a Muslim.... But the really right answer is, what if he is? Is there something wrong with being a Muslim in this country? The answer's no; that's not America. Is there something wrong with some seven-year-old Muslim-American kid believing that he or she could be president? Yet, I have heard senior members of my own party drop the suggestion, "He's Muslim and he might be associated with terrorists." This is not the way we should be doing it in America.[59]

55 Zogby International, "American Muslims Overwhlmingly Backing Kerry," www.zogby. com/search/readnews.cfm?ID=869 (accessed July 28, 2009). Laurie Goosteing, "American Muslims Back Kerry," *The New York Times*, October 22, 2004.
56 Pew Research Center, *Muslim Americans: Middle Class and Mostly Mainstream* (2007), 8.
57 The Muslim West Facts Project, *Muslim Americans: A National Portrait* (*Gallup*, Inc., 2009), 49–50.
58 Lorraine Ali, "Islam and Obama: American Muslims Overwhelmingly Voted Democratic," *Newsweek*, November 7, 2008.
59 Colin Powell interview on "Meet the Press," October 19, 2008, transcript at www.msnbc. msn.com/id/27266223/page/2/ (accessed July 29, 2009).

American Muslim leaders' and organizations' silence in regard to questions raised about Obama's affiliation with Islam, while perhaps politically smart, demonstrated once again how the discourse on Islam in America was disembedded from American Muslims' actual experiences in 2008. Just as American Muslims became more politically active and influential in American politics, they faced an external reality in which their legitimacy in American politics was unabashedly questioned.

SHIFT TOWARD LOCAL ACTIVISM

National Muslim organizations' move toward greater financial independence after the Gulf War and their aim to become more politically influential by uniting American Muslims as a voting bloc led them to consult more with local Muslims and to pay more attention to issues of local concern. We already saw this in AMT's strategic decision to focus on civil rights issues, which, after 9/11, became a salient concern for Muslims of varying religious and political orientations. One of the presidents of the Islamic Society of North America, for example, when expressing his wish for ISNA to have 100,000 members (instead of the 3,000 members it had in 1991), asserted, "That would truly say that we are actively involved in consultation with the Muslims at large."[60] In formulating its "Civil Rights Plus" agenda, the AMT distributed a four-page survey to more than 10,000 American Muslims at some 50 town hall meetings.[61] In this process of appealing to the larger, more diverse American Muslim population, national Muslim organizations, which were predominantly led by Islamist activists, began to function less as intermediaries between the United States and Muslim causes abroad and more as intermediaries between American Muslims and their local and national governments and the media. Put differently, they went from being Islamist activists in America to being American Muslim activists. A study of the content of a national Muslim publication, *The Minaret*, found that between 1984 and 1994, the ratio of articles dealing with politics, society, and history in the context of life in America was four or five times greater than the number of articles on Palestine, Bosnia, or the Middle East.[62] A study of the *Islamic Horizons* from the early 1980s through the 1990s similarly found that this mouthpiece of the Islamic Society of North America

---

[60] "What You Had to Say about ISNA," in *Islamic Horizons* (Winter 1991), 37.
[61] Poole, "Election," 2004, 7.
[62] Juan Campo, "Islam in California: Views from the Minaret," *Muslim World* LXXXVI, no. 3–4 (July-October 1996), 294–312.

had begun "to envision itself as a vehicle for Americanization. Even as it warned its readers against succumbing to 'anti-Islamic' Western influences, *Islamic Horizons* encouraged them to think of themselves as full-fledged Americans, and to invest, both on a personal and a political level, in their adopted country."[63]

In the late 1980s and early 1990s, American Muslims had already begun to fund non-profit relief organizations aimed at assisting Muslims abroad through their obligatory charity contributions (*zakah*). Some of these organizations (among them Benevolence International Foundation, Holy Land Foundation, and Global Relief Foundation, founded in 1987, 1989, and 1992, respectively) were raided by the U.S. Treasury Department after 9/11 and were shut down for allegedly aiding terrorist organizations. While charges were filed against the founders of all of these organizations, only the founders of the Holy Land Foundation have been convicted in court.[64] As immigrant Muslims became more established in the mid-1990s, however, they joined African American Muslim organizations in establishing local social service and community building organizations. They did so not only to meet the growing needs of their increasingly diverse local communities but also to counter the negative image of Islam and Muslims that had become more pervasive in American society following the Gulf War of 1990–1991 and the World Trade Center bombing of 1993. Just as the large number of Muslim immigrants who came to the United States in the 1970s and 1980s were becoming more established in different American cities, the negative coverage of Muslims and Islam in the national media at this time estranged Muslims from their local communities. American Muslims responded by becoming more involved in local community-building efforts and by trying to educate non-Muslims in their communities about Islam. When the Muslim Education Trust was founded in

[63] Nadia Malinovich, "Americanization of Islam in the Contemporary United States," *Revue française d'études américaines* 3, no. 109 (2006), 101.

[64] U.S. Treasury, "The Holy Land Foundation for Relief and Development," http://www.ustreas.gov/offices/enforcement/key-issues/protecting/charities_Execorder_13224-e.shtml#h; "Benevolence International Foundation," http://www.ustreas.gov/offices/enforcement/key-issues/protecting/charities_Execorder_13224-b.shtml#b; "Global Relief Foundation," http://www.ustreas.gov/offices/enforcement/key-issues/protecting/charities_Execorder_13224-e.shtml (accessed July 28, 2009). On the conviction of the founders of the Holy Land Foundation, see Carrie Johnson, "Muslim Charity's Ex-Leaders Convicted," *Washington Post*, November 25, 2008, A6. On the trial of the leader of the Benevolence International Foundation, see Eric Lichtblau, "Threats and Responses: The Money Trail," *New York Times*, 11 February 11, 2003.

Portland, Oregon in 1993, for example, it explicitly said that it aimed to promote educational efforts that would build bridges between Muslims and non-Muslims in Portland as a response to the backlash the community felt after the Gulf War.[65]

The shift from national organizing to grassroots community-building efforts was perhaps most significantly marked by the formation of the Muslim American Society (MAS) in 1992 and its incorporation in Illinois in 1993. The founding leaders of MAS were mainly of Arab descent and associated with the international Islamist movement of the Muslim Brotherhood (*ikhwan al-muslimin*). As one of its officials said in 2004, "Ikhwan [Brotherhood] members founded MAS, but MAS went way beyond that point of conception."[66] MAS traced its history back to "the Islamic revival movement which evolved at the turn of the twentieth century." This is when the Muslim Brotherhood was founded (1928) by Hasan al-Banna'. "The call and the spirit of the movement," proclaimed MAS's website in 2009, reached the shores of North America with arrival of Muslim students and immigrants in the late 1950s and early 1960s." These students affiliated with the Muslim Brotherhood, as previously stated, went on to help found such organizations as the Muslim Students Association and the Islamic Society of North America.[67] They participated in the operation of these organizations but over the years, as these organizations came to define themselves in relation to the needs and events shaping American Muslims' lives, they took on a life of their own.

At the start of the 1990s, members of the Muslim Brotherhood, who operated privately and behind the scenes of these national organizations, met and debated how they should reform their "Islamic work" in light of their new, post-Gulf War, American context. They decided rather than working from the top down – forming national organizations that supported local Muslim communities – they would build a grassroots Muslim organization that represented and was supported by local Muslim communities. As Mohamed Nimer reports, "They came to the conclusion that

---

[65] Anne Marie Armentrout, "Muslim Education Trust," Portland Muslim History Project of the Harvard Pluralism Project, available online at http://pluralism.org/research/profiles/display.php?profile=73551 (accessed August 12, 2009).

[66] Noreen S. Ahmed-Ullah, Sam Roe, and Laurie Cohen, "American Muslims Divided Over Group Aiming to Create Islamic States Worldwide," *Chicago Tribune*, September 20, 2004.

[67] http://www.masnet.org/aboutmas.asp (accessed August 7, 2009).

American and Canadian societies are diverse enough to accommodate Islam, that North America is a land in which Islam may grow.... They also conceded that, rhetoric aside, the essence of the contemporary, mainstream Islamic movements has been largely educational."[68] To this end, they sought to reconcile their ideological understandings of Islam with their American context by focusing on grassroots community building and social service, with the aim "to encourage the participation of Muslims in building a virtuous and moral society," "to promote understanding between Muslims and non-Muslims," and "to offer a viable Islamic alternative to many of our society's prevailing problems."[69] These Muslim activists, who previously tended to work behind the scenes of national Muslim organization, publically formed the aptly named Muslim American Society, which consisted of chapters throughout the United States that promoted the founding of local mosques, Islamic schools, youth camps, and social service organizations. In adopting this new bottom-up approach, however, the founding leaders of MAS did not clearly break from, nor did they clearly appropriate, the heritage of the Muslim Brotherhood. Their local community-building efforts stood in tension with their national leadership, which historically emerged from the Muslim Brotherhood. They did not intellectually or ideologically resolve the contradiction present in being both a grassroots American organization and an offshoot of an international, Islamist organization founded with the aim of promoting the creation of Islamic states in Muslim-majority countries. Consequently, many founding leaders of MAS broke from it in the mid-1990s in order to advance their own integrated visions of Islamic life in America through their local communities.[70]

The Islamic Circle of North America (founded in 1971), which like MAS emerged from an international Islamist organization, Jama'at-i Islami, also increased its community building and social service efforts in the United States in the 1990s. It formed the ICNA Relief in 1994 with the aim of addressing "the basic human and social service needs of the underserved communities with in (sic) the United States."[71]

---

[68] Nimer, *North American Muslim Resource Guide*, 70.
[69] http://www.masnet.org/aboutmas.asp (accessed August 7, 2009).
[70] Personal interview with a founding member of MAS, August 3, 2009. See also Nimer, *North American Muslim Resource Guide*, 70.
[71] "Mission Statement," available at the ICNA Relief USA web site, http://www.icnarelief. org/ (accessed February 9, 2009).

Another national organization that in this time shifted its focus onto grassroots community-building efforts was the Nation of Islam, under the leadership of Louis Farrakhan. On October 16, 1995, the Nation of Islam organized the Million Man March, which brought hundreds of thousands of black men of varying religious backgrounds to the Mall on Capitol Hill to promote service and African American community-building. Farrakhan told the gathering,

> Black man, you don't have to bash white people. All we got to do is go back home and turn our communities into productive places. All we got to do is go back home and make our communities a decent and safe place to live. And, if we start dotting the black community with businesses, opening up factories, challenging ourselves to be better than we are, white folk, instead of driving by using the N-word, they'll say, 'Look! Look at them! Oh, my God! They're marvelous! They're wonderful! We can't say, they are inferior any more.'[72]

While the number of mosques associated with the ministry of Warith Deen Mohammed remained more or less the same in the 1990s,[73] numerous other African American-dominated mosques and Islamic organizations were founded to propagate Islam and to assist with community-building efforts in African American neighborhoods.

Independent local Muslim communities, like the aforementioned Muslim Education Trust in Portland, also began developing social and health service organizations in the mid-1990s. By way of example, the Inner-City Muslim Action Network (IMAN) was formed in 1995 and incorporated in 1997 in Chicago as a community service organization with a vision "to foster a dynamic and vibrant space for Muslim in Urban America by inspiring the larger community towards critical civic engagement exemplifying prophetic compassion in the work for social justice and human dignity ... particularly for marginalized people of color."[74] In 1996, a number of Muslim medical and graduate students at the University of California, Los Angeles and Charles Drew University of Medicine and Science, in conjunction with their universities and Los Angeles City Council member Rita Walters, founded the UMMA Community Clinic to provide health care, often at no cost, to underserved populations of Los Angeles.[75]

---

[72] Cited in Kambiz GhaneaBassiri, *Competing Visions of Islam in the United States: A Study of Los Angeles* (Westport, CT: Greenwood Press, 1997), 156.

[73] Bagby, Perl, and Froehle, "The Mosque in America," 57.

[74] www.imancentral.org/about.html (accessed July 28, 2009).

[75] http://www.ummaclinic.org/?cls=Our_Story (accessed July 29, 2009).

REFLECTING THE DIVERSITY OF ISLAM IN THE
PUBLIC SQUARE

While the majority of American Muslims, at this time, did not associate
with any Islamic institution and while those who did associate with
Islamic institutions usually did so through their local mosques,[76] Islamist
activists, because of the national institutions they helped found (e.g.,
ISNA and CAIR), became the face of American Islam to the larger non-
Muslim society and the government. In the late 1990s, some American
Muslims objected to this reality in an effort to have the diversity of the
American Muslim population better reflected in its national image. One
example of such an effort was a widely reported comment made in 1999
by Sheikh Muhammad Hisham Kabbani, the founder of the Islamic
Supreme Council of America (founded in 1998) and the U.S. representative of the Naqshbandi-Haqqani Sufi Order. At a public forum at the
State Department, Kabbani said that 80 percent of the Muslim leadership
in the United States was made up of "extremists." He explained that of
the 114 mosques he visited when he came to the United States, "Ninety
of them were mostly exposed, and I say exposed, to extreme or radical
ideology." Kabbani's condemnation of the American Muslim leadership
as "extremist" was no doubt due in part to their rejection of Sufism as
un-Islamic. Most national Muslim organizations, like Islamists in general, regard the master-discipline relationship and varying mystical rites
of Sufism, which date back to the earliest centuries of Islamic history, to
be heretical innovations in Islam. In the modern period, there has been
a significant anti-Sufi sentiment among both modernist and Islamist
Muslims, who believe Sufi practices are idolatrous, irrational, and too
otherworldly.[77] These organizations had not publicly denounced Kabbani
but had marginalized him. Following his comments, they asked him "with
a heavy heart" to retract his comment. Kabbani refused, and he was further shunned by the national American Muslim leadership, who viewed
his statement as an endeavor to carve a place for himself on the national

---

[76] A 2001 poll of American Muslims conducted by Project MAPS (Muslims in American
Public Square) of Georgetown University and Zogby International found that 71 percent
of its survey participants indicated they are involved in a mosque or a local religious
organization while only 33 percent indicated that they are involved in any political action
or public affairs organization, see *American Muslim Poll* (Project MAPS and Zogby
International, 2001), 15.

[77] For a discussion of this topic, see Elizabeth Sirriyeh, *Sufis and Anti-Sufis: The Defence,
Rethinking and Rejection of Sufism in the Modern World* (New York: Routledge,
1999).

scene. "He wanted to have a voice among the Muslim leaders," explained Sulayman Nyang, an American Muslim scholar, "so when American government (sic) talked to Muslims, the Sufis would have a voice, and he, Kabbani, will be the voice of the Sufis."[78]

Another scathing condemnation of American Muslim leaders came from Khaled Abou El Fadl, a professor of Islamic Law at UCLA. In 1996, when Denver Nuggets basketball player Mahmoud Abdul-Rauf refused to stand for the national anthem because he believed that it constituted a form of idolatry, questions arose regarding Muslims' loyalty to the United States and their willingness to integrate into America society. There was also a great deal of debate within the American Muslim community, which according to Abou El Fadl came to a halt when the Society for the Adherence to the Sunnah asked for a *fatwa* on the matter. Abou El Fadl was appalled by the stultifying effect the invocation of a *fatwa* had on the debate. From his point of view, the whole edifice of Islamic jurisprudence was constructed to encourage debate and to force Muslims to hone their intellects in order to better apply Islam's moral principles in their lives. Abou El Fadl saw American Muslims' reactions to the invocation of Islamic law as an index of the widespread influence of "Wahhabi puritanism" among American Muslims. He did not pull any punches. It is important to note that when he refers to Muslims in the United States in the following passage, he is referring mainly to Muslims active in establishing and administering local mosques and national institutions. (Abou El Fadl characterized these individuals by their theological orientation, while I have identified them mainly through their activism.)

[W]hat one found among Muslims in the United States was a remarkably arid intellectual climate. Far from freeing themselves from the burdensome baggage of their homelands, American Muslims reflected all the predicaments of their countries of origin, but in a sharply exasperated and pronounced form.... The immigrant Muslim community in the United States is comprised largely of professionals who immigrated to the United States primarily for economic reasons. There are no serious Muslim institutions of higher learning, and the field of Islamic Studies does not attract the brightest Muslims. The few Muslims who do become accomplished in Islamic Studies are often perceived by the Muslim community to be a part of the secular paradigm, and are therefore alienated and marginalized. Once in the West, Muslims struggle to be rooted in a tradition, and

---

[78] Laurie Goodstein, "Muslim Leader Who Was Once Labeled an Alarmist Is Suddenly a Sage," *New York Times*, October 28, 2001, B5. See also Paul M. Barrett, *American Islam: The Struggle for the Soul of a Religion* (New York: Farrar, Straus and Giroux, 2007), 179–215.

Wahhābī puritanism offers a convenient, easy, and effective package. The package roots the Muslim in an irreproachable ideal that fits well in a social context that treats religious practice as an extracurricular activity. One could be an objectified professional in the day practicing 'real life' in one manner, and go to the mosque on the weekends to practice his extracurricular activity in an entirely different manner. Therefore, one could work and talk to non-Muslim women during the day, but insist that the voice of women should not be heard in an Islamic center or that women sit behind a curtain when attending an Islamic lecture.[79]

Unlike Kabbani, whose comments were geared for the government and the national media, Abou El Fadl's criticism of the "Wahhabi puritanism" of American Muslims was mainly written for a Muslim audience that did not usually associate with Islamic institutions. It was first published by a Muslim press in 1997.[80] It was not until 2001 that it was revised and published by an academic press for a wider audience. Both Kabbani and Abou El Fadl had sought to gain national recognition in the American public square for the Islam that they knew and practiced. Many mystically minded Americans have joined the Naqshbandi-Haqqani order under Kabbani's leadership. Abou El Fadl's writings have also been very influential for many younger, college-educated American Muslims.

In the aftermath of 9/11, more American Muslim intellectuals and activists sought to introduce their varying understandings of Islam to the American public square. As with Abou El Fadl and Kabbani, they have sought both to challenge the hegemony of more conservative national American Muslim organizations and to counter negative perceptions of Islam in American society. A group of American Muslim professors of Islamic studies, including feminists and proponents of gay rights, published a well-received book, *Progressive Muslims: On Justice, Gender, Pluralism*. While they offered varying views of Islam and the struggle for social justice, gender equity, and religious pluralism, they all admonished Muslims to act critically both on the Islamic tradition and their American context. Omid Safi, the editor of the volume, wrote:

Walk into any Islamic Center, and there is likely to be a table in the hallway or in the library that features a wide selection of pamphlets. The pamphlets bear titles like "The Status of Women in Islam," "Concept of God in Islam," "Concept of Worship in Islam." Printed in pale yellow, pink, and green shades,

---

[79] Khaled Abou El Fadl, *And God Knows the Soldiers: The Authoritative and the Authoritarian in Islamic Discourses* (Lanham, MD: University Press of America, 2001), 20 and 12–14.

[80] Khaled Abou El Fadl, *The Authoritative and the Authoritarian in Islamic Discourses: A Contemporary Case Study* (Austin, TX: Dar Taiba, 1997).

they promised truth in black and white. I hate these pamphlets. I think we are in imminent danger – if we are not there already – of succumbing to "pamphlet Islam," the serious intellectual and spiritual fallacy of thinking that complex issues can be handled in four or six glossy pages. They simply cannot. The issues involved are far too complicated, and the human beings who frame the issues are even more so. I recently saw a bumper sticker that proclaimed, "Islam is the answer." If Islam is the answer, pray tell, what is the question? Modernity? Existence? God? (p. 22)

In 2004, some of the academic contributors to *Progressive Muslims*, along with some progressive Muslim activists founded the Progressive Muslim Union of North America (PMUNA) as a network for progressive Muslims in the United States and Canada with a mouthpiece called www.muslimwakeup.com. During the two years that the PMUNA was functional, it helped organize a mixed-gender congregational prayer led by a woman imam, Amina Wadud, a professor of Islamic Studies at Virginia Commonwealth University. The prayer took place on March 18, 2005. "Fundamentally, this event is about Muslim women reclaiming their rightful place in Islam," read a statement released by organizers of the prayer. "Our sole agenda is to help create Muslim communities that reflect the egalitarian nature of Islam."[81]

There were varying responses from American Muslims to the prayer. Most American Muslim organization and mosques disapproved of the act overtly. Others dismissed it as an unnecessarily provocative publicity stunt. Some offered their support. The congregational prayer itself was not hosted by any mosque; rather it took place at the Episcopal Cathedral of St. John the Divine in New York City and was attended by about 100 Muslim men and women. The worldwide publicity generated by this event led several national Muslim organizations (including CAIR, ICNA, ISNA, and the MSA) to widen their vision of their constituency and to publish and distribute a booklet to mosques in the United States and Canada on "Women Friendly Mosques and Community Centers: Working Together to Reclaim Our Heritage."

The contrast in national American Muslim organizations' silent response to Kabbani's and Abou El Fadl's critiques of Muslim activists in the United States in the 1990s and their more engaged response to the more controversial, women-led, congregational prayer of 2005 is

---

[81] "A Statement from the Organizers of the March 18th Woman-Led Jum'ah Prayer", reproduced in *Encyclopedia of Islam in the United States*, vol. 2, ed. Jocelyne Cesari (Westport, CT: Greenwood Press, 2007), 969.

indicative of the change that took place in these organizations after 9/11. In the 1990s, while national organizations became more responsive to the local needs of Muslims, they did not come to reflect the diversity of the American Muslim population either in terms of religious understandings or of ethnicities. African American national Muslim organizations and immigrant national Muslim organizations continued to meet separately because they served separate constituencies with different interests and experiences. Arabic-speakers and South Asians also dominated national Muslim organizations. It was not until September 11, 2001 that the diversity of the American Muslim population came to be a bit more widely reflected in these national organizations and in the American public square.

In the face of these horrific events committed in the name of Islam and the ensuing backlash against Muslims, many ordinary Muslims – women prominent among them – felt the need to come out and speak more publicly about their varying understandings of Islam.[82] Concurrently, the American public sought to learn more about Islam, and the media made a concerted effort to go beyond the talking heads of national Muslim organizations who found their Islamist assumptions fundamentally challenged by the murder of thousands of innocent people in the name of Islamic activism. The federal government similarly made an effort to recognize and officially represent the diversity of Muslims in the United States. The U.S. Institute of Peace published a report titled "The Diversity of Muslims in the United States" (2006). The U.S. Department of State profiled the diversity of American Muslims in a website titled "Muslim

---

[82] Many of these ordinary Muslims spoke publically about their faith at events at universities, local churches, community organizations, and the workplace. Some of their voices have been preserved in print. See, for examples, Michael Wolfe, ed. *Taking Back Islam: American Muslims Reclaim Their Faith* (n.p.: Rodale, 2002); Saleemah Abdul-Ghafur, ed. *Living Islam Outloud: American Muslim Women Speak* (Boston, MA: Beacon Press, 2005); Aslam Abdullah and Gasser Hathout, *The American Muslim Identity: Speaking for Ourselves* (Los Angeles, CA: Multimedia Vera International, 2003); Michael Muhammad Knight, *Blue-Eyed Devil: A Road Odyssey through Islamic America* (New York: Autonomedia, 2007); and Eboo Patel, *Acts of Faith: The Story of an American Muslim, the Struggle for the Soul of a Generation* (Boston, MA: Beacon Press, 2007). In addition to these works in which ordinary American Muslims expressed their religious experiences and understandings, there were also new public Muslim voices that were highly critical of Islam. See, for example, Irshad Manji, *The Trouble with Islam Today: A Muslim's Call for Reform in Her Faith* (New York: St. Martin's Griffin, 2003). Manji is Canadian Pakistani, but she has become a public figure in the United States since 9/11. For a critical analysis of her work, see Tarik El-Ariss, "The Making of an Expert: The Case of Irshad Manji," *The Muslim World* 97, no. 1 (January 2007), 93–110.

Life in America" and later in a glossy booklet called "Being Muslim in America."[83] The introductory essay in "Being Muslim in America" was written by Eboo Patel, who comes from an Isma'ili Shi'i background, which many Sunnis and other Shi'is consider to be heretical. Patel was not identified as an Isma'ili in the booklet, but the fact that he, rather than the leader of some national Sunni organization, introduced the booklet clearly demonstrated an official recognition of the wider diversity of the Muslim community. The State Department recognized this diversity mainly because it helped weave the story of American Muslims within the larger narrative of America as a nation of diverse immigrants:

Immigrants have come to America from every corner of the globe.... They arrived with hope, and often little else. Their initial reception was frequently mixed. These new Americans found a vast new land hungry for their labor. But some, unfamiliar with these newcomers' customs and religions, treated the new Americans as outsiders and believed they could never be real Americans. They were wrong. With freedom, faith, and hard work, each successive wave of immigrants has added its distinctive contributions to the American story, enriched our society and culture, and shaped the ever-dynamic, always-evolving meaning of the single word that binds us together: American. And today, this story is the Muslim American story too.[84]

It was of course no accident that this official recognition of the diversity of Muslims in the United States followed 9/11. At home, where the booklet was distributed to mosques and Muslim organizations, it reminded Muslims that not all non-Muslim Americans associate Muslims with terrorism. It also outlined for Muslims in the United States the self-understanding they needed to adopt to gain acceptance. Abroad, where this booklet was distributed out of U.S. embassies in Muslim-majority countries and European countries with significant Muslim populations, the presentation of American Muslims' story as a quintessentially American story was intended to demonstrate that America is not at war with Muslims at a time when many in the global Muslim community saw the Bush administration's "war on terror" as a "war on Islam." American Muslims, once again, became intermediaries for U.S. interests in the Muslim-majority world.

[83] http://usinfo.org/enus/education/overview/muslimlife/homepage.htm (accessed June 26, 2006). The content of this web site was also published as a booklet. I came across a copy distributed out of the U.S. embassy in Stockholm in 2007.

[84] Bureau of International Information Programs, "Being Muslim in America" (United States State Department, n.d.), 5–6. Electronic copy available at http://www.america.gov/media/pdf/books/being-muslim-in-america.pdf (accessed July 31, 2009).

Post-9/11 the entertainment industry also literally staged the diversity of American Muslims. Some American Muslim comedians, for example, went on a nationwide "Allah Made Me Funny" tour and on "The Axis of Evil Comedy Tour." Some of these comedians were later featured in a 2008 PBS documentary, "Stand up: Muslim American Comics Come of Age." "We can't define who we are on a serious note because nobody will listen," retorted Ahmed Ahmed, one of the comedians featured in the documentary; the only way to do it is to be funny about it." As, Max Brooks, one of the non-Muslim producers of Muslim comedy shows made clear, he was motivated to help Muslims enter into the mainstream entertainment industry in order to further their stake in the future of this country in view of the events of 9/11:

In a strange way, I feel like we are heading off potential terrorism at home. When you grow up in your own country that doesn't want you, of course, you are going to turn to something radical. The only way to head that off in this country is to embrace everyone.... Give everyone as much piece of the pie and to give everyone something to lose.

America came to recognize a newer set of spokesmen for Islam, who as Karen Leonard has observed, "were not builders of political movement" and "represent a wider range of Islam's sectarian, intellectual, artistic, and legal traditions than do the political spokesmen."[85] To meet the challenge posed to their status as *the* representatives of American Islam, Islamist activists found themselves after 9/11 having to further widen their reach to embrace a more diverse constituency and to take more strident measures to promote pluralism and counter extremism among the Muslims within their organizations. By way of example, Farid Esack, a celebrated progressive Muslim theologian, was invited for the first time to take part in a panel at the 42nd national convention of the Islamic Society of North America.

After 9/11, Muslim organizations took a second look at their activities and the points of view represented within mosques and national gatherings. Many mosques adopted a no-tolerance policy toward the expression of anti-American or anti-Semitic views. Some established guidelines for the topics on which members of the community could and could not offer sermons. In 2005, the Muslim Public Affairs Council launched a National Anti-Terrorism Campaign that was endorsed by

[85] Karen Leonard, "American Muslims, before and after September 11, 2001" *Economic and Political Weekly* 37, no. 24 (June 15–21, 2002), 2299.

the Department of Justice and the Islamic Society of North America. The Muslim Public Affairs Council explained that given the possibility of another terrorist attack on the United States and the grave consequences such an attack would have on the Muslim community, "it is obvious that Muslims should be at the forefront of the effort to prevent this from happening. While we find ourselves in the same line with most American citizens, there is the fear that those who are hateful fanatics or special interest opportunists will insist to marginalize Muslims and depict them as suspects to be watched. We owe it to our religion, our country, and our new generation to expose this fallacy and to change this perception." To this end, the National Anti-Terrorism Campaign recommended a set of guidelines for mosques to follow in order to assure that they did not become centers for terrorist recruitment and activity. The campaign urged mosques to maintain their financial records and to do so in a professional manner. They were asked to be cognizant of the flow of people through the mosque and to not allow any guest speakers at mosque with whom they were not familiar. "Talks should focus on harmony," one of the guidelines read, "emphasizing the fact that we are Muslims and Americans. We need to represent the great values of our religion and constructively engage our country in dialogues leading to improved life for all people. Irresponsible rhetoric should be avoided." Mosques were also encouraged to maintain a relationship with the regional FBI office, local law enforcement, and the media. It was also "highly recommended that the mosque be part of an interfaith dialogue and civic alliance and activities." In addition to training American Muslims to be more vigilant against possible extremist activity, the National Anti-Terrorism Campaign also sought to educate American law enforcement officials about mosque etiquette and about Muslim attitudes toward law enforcement officials.[86]

In many ways, 9/11 tested the mettle of American Muslim institutions at both the local and national level. These institutions played a fundamental role in helping American Muslims weather the backlash of 9/11. Members of local mosques and Islamic centers nearly uniformly came to see themselves as ambassadors of Islam to the larger non-Muslim community. Those communities that had preferred to remain insular opened up to the public. Many mosques set aside a time during the year when they held "open houses" during which their non-Muslim

---

[86] Muslim Public Affairs Council, *Grassroots Campaign to Fight Terrorism* (Los Angeles, CA: Muslim Public Affairs Council, 2005), 9.

neighbors could visit the mosque and learn about Muslim beliefs and practices. In concert with the guidelines suggested by the Muslim Public Affairs Council, they formed relations with the media and law enforcement agencies. They formed interfaith alliances and joined civil rights organizations. They brought members of civil rights organizations to their mosques to inform them of their rights. Whereas before 9/11 they may have gone about their religious life as an extracurricular activity, to use Abou El Fadl's phrase, after 9/11 they actively sought to integrate themselves more fully within their local communities. Where such relations existed prior to 9/11, they had resulted in friendships, which proved indispensible to American Muslims' ability to respond to the backlash of 9/11. A leader of one of the mosques in Portland, Oregon, Shahriar Ahmad, for example, reported that one of the first phone calls he received on 9/11 was from a local rabbi from a Muslim-Jewish interfaith dialog group; the rabbi invited him and his family to stay at his house for their own protection that evening. This Muslim leader also recalls that a seemingly threatening "big white guy with a big pickup truck" approached the mosque at prayer time the first Friday after 9/11 and offered to stand guard at the mosque while they prayed.[87] As hate crimes and Muslim surveillance increased nationally after 9/11,[88] American Muslims sought and found allies among local law enforcement agencies, civil rights activists, and liberal Christians and Jews. In this process, American Muslims became more involved in local issues and local community-building. Whereas prior to 9/11 Muslim activists were generally involved in American politics, after 9/11 local Muslim communities, through their mosques, began to become more involved in both local and national politics. They organized voter registration drives in mosques and invited local and national political candidates to address them.[89] Because local mosques and Islamic associations better reflect the diversity of the American Muslim population, their increased participation in American politics and integration in American society also helped further diversify the public image of Islam in America.

[87] Personal interviews with the author, (Beaverton, OR, summer 2004).

[88] For a discussion of hate crimes after 9/11 and a detailed time line of government initiatives, see Anny Bakalian and Mehdi Bozorgmehr, *Backlash 9/11: Middle Eastern and Muslim Americans Respond* (Berkeley, CA: University of California Press, 2009), 1–6, 125–155 and 253–262.

[89] Amaney Jamal, "The Political Participation and Engagement of Muslim Americans: Mosque Involvement and Group Consciousness," *American Politics Research* 33, no. 4 (July 2005), 521–544.

At the national level, untold numbers of American Muslims were detained after 9/11 without charges and many immigrants were deported.[90] The invasions of Afghanistan and Iraq, particularly the preemptive attack on Iraq, further exacerbated the sense of siege many Muslims felt at this time. In the midst of such threats to American Muslims' sense of belonging and civil rights, national Muslim organizations found their niche as Muslim advocacy groups. The increase in hate crimes and prejudice against Muslims created an atmosphere in which all American Muslims felt as though they were suspect. According to a 2002 Zogby poll, 66 percent of Arabs and Muslims in the United States worried about their future in this country and 81 percent thought that they were being profiled.[91] In such an atmosphere, American Muslims, regardless of their level of religiosity or religious orientations, were glad that these organizations existed in order to protect their civil liberties. Concurrently, national Muslim organizations actively sought to embody their new American identity. John Esposito, a renowned professor of Islam and the director of Georgetown's Center for Christian-Muslim Understanding, advised a group of Muslims at a CAIR fundraiser in October 2001 "to put forward more women and young people who spoke unaccented American English to articulate their community's message. Unless you tap the next generation, you are not going to make it through the next few months."[92] In 2001, Ingrid Mattson, a European Canadian Muslim convert and professor of Islamic Studies at Hartford Seminary who had been an active member of the Islamic Society of North America, was elected as its first female vice president. In 2006, Mattson became its first female president.

---

[90] In addition to the above-mentioned sections of Baklian and Bozogmehr's *Backlash 9/11*, see U.S. Department of Justice, *The September 11 Detainees: A Review of the Treatment of Aliens Held on Immigration Charges in Connection with the Investigation of the September 11 Attacks* (Office of the Inspector General, 2003); Nancy Murray, "Profiled: Arabs, Muslims, and the Post-9/11 Hunt for the 'Enemy Within' in *Civil Rights in Peril: The Targeting of Arabs and Muslims*, ed. Elaine C. Hagopian (Ann Arbor, MI: Pluto Press, 2004), 26–68; Louise Cainkar, "Post 9/11 Domestic Policies Affecting U.S. Arabs and Muslims: A Brief Review," *Comparative Studies of South Asia, Africa and the Middle East* 24, no. 1 (2004), 245–248. Amaney Jamal, "Civil Liberties and the Otherization of Arab and Muslim Americans," in *Race and Arab Americans Before and After 9/11: From Invisible Citizens to Visible Subjects*, ed. Amaney Jamal and Nadine Naber (Syracuse, NY: Syracuse University Press, 2007), 114–130.

[91] Jamal, "Civil Liberties," 115.

[92] Karen Isaksen Leonard, *Muslims in the United States: The State of Research* (New York: Russell Sage Foundation, 2003), 24.

THE FRAMING OF ISLAM IN AMERICA AND THE
SEARCH FOR A NEW AMERICAN NATIONAL IDENTITY

Between 1989 and 2008, American Muslims, at both the local and national level, further integrated themselves into American society as Muslims, and after 9/11, American Muslim organizations came to represent a wider spectrum of Muslims' diversity – in terms of theology, politics, and gender – in the American public square. These historical changes occurred against the backdrop of growing mistrust of American Muslims and their values as well as a struggle to define America's national identity in view of U.S. relations with Muslims, both within and outside its borders, after the Cold War.

In 2007, American Sunni and Shi'i leaders signed an "Intra-faith Code of Honor" in which they pledged to respect one another's differences, prevent hateful and condescending speech or acts, and to avoid sectarian propagandizing.[93] The import of such pluralistic acts for America's efforts to settle sectarian violence in Iraq at this time and to make sure that this sectarian violence did not spill over to the United States was obvious. The authors of the code acknowledged it themselves: "In recognition of our communal duty to promote goodness and peace, we remain eager to offer any help we can and to join hands with all those who wish well for the family of Believers (*ummah*) in stopping the senseless inhumane violence in Iraq and elsewhere in the world. In our view, we must begin by preventing such tragic sectarianism from spilling over into our Muslim communities in the United States."[94] What was not obvious to many non-Muslim Americans who grappled with how Muslims could fit within a new American national consensus was whether political expediency or religious principles motivated these acts. Were they outcomes of an Americanized Islam or of political posturing?

Polls of American attitudes toward Muslims conducted after 9/11 attest to the widespread mistrust of the religious beliefs and values that many non-Muslim Americans believed motivated Muslims' behavior. A three-year national survey conducted by sociologist of religion Robert Wuthnow found 47 percent of the Americans thought Muslims were "fanatical." Forty percent thought Muslims "violent," and 57 percent said Muslims

---

[93] The Intra-faith Code of Honor can be viewed online at http://files.e2ma.net/2785/assets/docs/muslim_intrafaith_code_of_honor.jpg (accessed February 9, 2009).

[94] Cited from a statement released by the Council of Islamic Organizations of Michigan, "Detroit Muslim Leaders to Sign Sunni-Shia Code of Honor," http://www.mpac.org/article.php?id=505 (accessed February 9, 2009).

were "closed-minded."[95] To put this in a comparative perspective, only about a quarter of the individuals surveyed thought Hindus or Buddhists were "fanatical." About 15 percent thought Hindus or Buddhists were "violent," and less than a third thought them closed minded. Another survey of American attitudes toward Muslims conducted in 2004 found that 47 percent of Americans believed "the Islamic religion is more likely than others to encourage violence among its believers." It also found that about a quarter of Americans would support governmental restrictions on Muslims.[96] About half of Americans believed "Islamic countries and peoples" are "violent," "fanatical," or "dangerous." Three-quarters of Americans believed that they are "oppressive toward women," and only a quarter believed that they are "tolerant of different faiths and beliefs." Twenty-two percent of Americans indicated that they believed that the primary reason why foreign Muslims were hostile to the United States was because there was "a fundamental difference between Western and Muslim values and culture."[97]

It goes without saying that these attitudes toward Muslims resulted largely from the terrorist acts a handful carried out against the United States. What is interesting from the perspective of this study, however, is that such mistrust of American Muslims as a collective persisted despite the fact that at the turn of the twenty-first century, non-Muslim Americans were in greater contact with American Muslims than ever before, and the overwhelming majority described their contact with Muslims, despite their mistrust of and prejudices against Islam, as positive. Wuthnow's study found that 24 percent of Americans "had a fair amount of contact with Muslims." Only 32 percent of Americans had no contact with Muslims, which means that 68 percent of the country had at least some contact with Muslims in the United States. Of these, 64 percent indicated that their contacts were "mostly pleasant."[98]

The scholarship on American Islam, which I critiqued at the outset of this book, was in many ways a product of this contemporary history of Islam in America. By inquiring into how well Muslims were faring in the United States and by aiming to familiarize non-Muslims with Muslims'

---

[95] Robert Wuthnow, *America and the Challenges of Religious Diversity* (Princeton, NJ: Princeton University Press, 2005), 213.

[96] The Media & Society Research Group, Cornell University, "Restrictions on Civil Liberties, Views of Islam, & Muslim Americans" (December 2004).

[97] The Media & Society Research Group, Cornell University, "U.S. War on Terror, U.S. Foreign Policy, and Anti-Americanism" (December 2004).

[98] Wuthnow, *America and the Challenges of Religious Diversity*, 216.

religious beliefs and practices, many scholars of American Islam sought to redress the cloud of mistrust that hanged over non-Muslim Americans' interactions with American Muslims. I have contended that this type of "get-to-know-your-neighbor" scholarship, though *highly* admirable and humanizing, neglected to examine the dynamic development of Muslim institutions and communal relations in the history of this country. Whatever the motives behind the greater inclusivity of American Muslim organizations or the greater integration of Muslims in American society after 9/11, the fact of the matter is that these were responses to historical events that concretely altered the way in which American Muslims organized their institutions and communal relations.

This chapter has shown that non-Muslim Americans' distrustful perceptions of Islam at this time did not mesh with the historical experiences that shaped Islamic institutions and Muslims' communal lives in the United States in the aftermath of the Cold War. Why then their persistence? These perceptions persisted and continued to shape the external context of American Muslims' lives because of politically motivated, discursive processes through which Americans sought to define a new national identity in the aftermath of the Cold War and in the midst of an increasingly multicultural, multi-religious society. These discourses framed Islam essentially as a monolith derived from a closed set of religious texts and beliefs that stood outside of the historical workings of Muslims' lives. We generally identify the inaccurate ways in which outsiders generalize about the characteristics of an ethnic, racial, or religious group as *stereotypes*. Stereotyping, however, as a cognitive process through which people interpret information about others, falls short of capturing the tangible *reality* of the "external Islam" and the "external America" that confronted American Muslims in this period.

The external reality in which American Muslims were interpolated was formed largely by a bifurcating discourse on "Islam and the West" through which the United States and Islamist organizations actively sought to negotiate their relationship with one another since the end of the Cold War. When Islam (a religion) and the West (a political territory) are juxtaposed, they signify conceptual categories that have no clear referent in the real world or in people's actual experiences. Most Americans simply reproduced this dichotomy without much critical thought. Others did so with forethought and for ideological reasons.

For Islamist activists, who adhered to Islam as an ideology derived from the Qur'an and the Hadith, the equating of Islam with "the West" as monoliths brought their transnational organizations, which had no state, no army, and no clear governing body, on par with powerful nation-states. Islamist activists thus had a stake in maintaining the bifurcating discourse on the ahistorical construct of "Islam and the West." Deconstructing the phrase "Islam and the West" would have deprived Islamist activists, particularly those involved in the Afghan resistance, of their clout after the collapse of the Soviet Union. In the 1990s, National Muslim organizations that were formed with the help of Islamist activists by and large ignored such efforts by progressive Muslims and sought to marginalize them as inauthentic representatives of Islam. Rather than abolishing the discourse on "Islam and the West," leaders of national Muslim organizations and Islamist activists sought to reframe "Islam" in the discourse. They, in what Omid Safi called "pamphlet Islam," replaced Islam as a religion of violence with Islam as a religion of peace. Islam as a religion oppressive toward women was replaced with Islam as a religion that honors and respects women. Islam as an intolerant religion was replaced with Islam as a religion of human rights. One such pamphlet on Islam produced by the Foundation for Islamic Knowledge under the direction of Ahmad Sakr, one of the founding members of the Muslim Students Association, began its 350-word summary of Islam with a definition of Islam as "peace" and "submission to the One God, and to live in peace with the Creator, within one's self, with other people and with the environment." It ended with the assertion that "[Muslims] do respect parents, elders, teachers and women. They observe morality and family values as well. They try to live in peace and harmony with all people of the world irrespective of color, nationality, creed or religion."

For non-Muslim Americans who adopted the discourse on "Islam and the West" for ideological reasons, America's national identity as a liberal democracy, which is fundamentally a product of Western European thought and Christianity, and the U.S. alliance with Israel was at stake in this bifurcating construct. After the collapse of the Soviet Union, Americans sought to configure a new, unifying national identity in light of their multicultural and multi-religious society and their new role as the world's only superpower. The Rushdie Affair and the Gulf War of 1990–1991, brought Muslims in direct confrontation with the United States as it grappled with its role in what President George H. W. Bush famously dubbed "the new world order." When George H. W. Bush announced that he had ordered a coalition of twenty-eight countries led by the United States to attack Iraqi forces in Kuwait and Iraq, he reminded Americans that "this is a historic moment. We have in this past year made great progress in ending the long era of conflict and cold war. We have before us the opportunity to forge for ourselves and for future generations a new world order, a world where the rule of law, not the law of the jungle, governs the conduct of nations." Bush envisioned this "new world order" as "an order in which a credible United Nations can use its peace-keeping role to fulfill the promise and vision of the U.N.'s founders."[99] Concurrently, American political scientists debated the contours of this new world. Of the varying theories proposed, Samuel Huntington's "clash of civilizations" thesis (1993) gained a lot of traction, particularly among neoconservatives, who later came to power during George W. Bush's presidency. Huntington himself, however, as attested by his opposition to the U.S. invasion of Iraq, was not one of these neoconservatives. His thesis was significant because it is the most influential articulation for the *cultural* lens through which Muslims' relations with "the West" were viewed in the contemporary period.

A fundamental assumption of Huntington's thesis was that human relations are essentially marked by conflict because of limited resources and competing interests. He thus searched to discover how nations will seek to organize themselves to manage their competing interests in the new world order, and he hypothesized that "the fundamental source of conflict in this new world will not be primarily ideological or primarily economic. The great divisions among humankind and the dominating source of conflict will be *cultural* (emphasis mine). Nation states will remain the most powerful actors in world affairs, but the principal conflicts of global politics will occur between nations and groups of different civilizations. The fault lines between civilizations will be the battle lines of the future."[100] More specifically in regard to the clash between Islamic and Western civilizations after the first Gulf War, Huntington wrote,

This centuries-old military interaction between the West and Islam is unlikely to decline. It could become more virulent. The Gulf War left some Arabs feeling proud that Saddam Hussein had attacked Israel and stood up to the West. It also left many feeling humiliated and resentful of the West's military presence in the Persian Gulf, the West's overwhelming military dominance, and their apparent inability to shape their own destiny.... On both sides the interaction between Islam and the West is seen as a clash of civilizations.[101]

---

[99] "George H.W. Bush Announces U.S. Attack on Iraq," U.S. Department of State web site, http://usinfo.org/enus/government/overview/bush_iraq.html (accessed February 9, 2009).

[100] Samuel P. Huntington, "The Clash of Civilizations," *Foreign Affairs* 72, no. 3 (Summer 1993), 22.

[101] Ibid., 31–32.

Huntington's assertion that post-Cold War international relations will be shaped by civilizational conflicts was influenced largely by his understanding of the enmities between Islam and "the West."

There are multiple intellectual genealogies of the polarizing construct encapsulated in the phrase, "Islam and the West." Huntington's articulation, however, relied on the widely-discussed work of the Orientalist scholar of Islam, Bernard Lewis. In an article, published in September 1990, after the fall of the Berlin Wall and in the midst of the Rushdie Affair, Bernard Lewis argued (in a passage cited by Huntington),

> We are facing a mood and a movement [among contemporary Muslims] far transcending the level of issues and policies and the governments that pursue them. This is no less than a clash of civilizations – the perhaps irrational but surely historic reaction of an ancient rival against our Judeo-Christian heritage, our secular present, and the world wide expansion of both.[102]

To explain Muslims' "anti-Westernism" and "anti-Americanism," Lewis invoked the history of Muslims' interactions with the United States. He argued that while Americans saw themselves as distinct from Europe, the rest of the world saw America essentially as a European project: "Though people of other races and cultures participated, for the most part involuntarily, in the discovery and creation of the Americas, this was, and in the eyes of the rest of the world long remained, a European enterprise." He explained, Muslims have turned the anger they felt toward European colonial powers toward the United States, not because of any imperial policies the United States employed, but because the United States, as the world's only superpower, represented to Muslims what European colonial powers had represented in the past. European colonialism emasculated the Muslim, according to Lewis. It stripped him (yes, *him*, because Muslim women were seen as passive actors in this civilizational struggle between men) of his "domination in the world" and undermined "his authority in his own country, through an invasion of foreign ideas and laws and ways of life." It challenged "his mastery in his own house, from emancipated women and rebellious children. It was too much to endure." The "outbreak of rage" was "inevitable." This "rage," Lewis argued, arrived at the United States' doorstep in the 1970s and 1980s with the ascendency of Islamist ideology.

---

[102] Bernard Lewis, "The Roots of Muslim Rage," *Atlantic Monthly* 266 (September 1990), 60.

And then came the great change, when the leaders of a widespread and widening religious revival sought out and identified their enemies as the enemies of God, and gave them 'a local habitation and a name' in the Western Hemisphere. Suddenly, or so it seemed, America had become the archenemy, the incarnation of evil, the diabolic opponent of all that is good, and specifically, for Muslims, of Islam.

In case the point may have been lost on the reader that in the absence of the Communist threat in the last decade of the twentieth century, "the West" should have focused its energies on the Islamist threat, Lewis went on to equate Islamism with Nazism and Communism. He asserted that the intellectual roots of Muslims' "mood of anti-Americanism" could be traced to Germany's negative view of America which was "by no means limited to the Nazis," but included such authors as Rainier Maria Rilke, Ernst Jünger, and Martin Heidegger. After the fall of the Third Reich, the German influence on "Arabs" was supplanted by "the Soviet version of Marxism." When the Soviet's influence faded, Arabs were influenced by "the new mystique of Third Worldism" coming out of a socialist France. Since Muslims' anti-Americanism was visceral, the causes of their "rage," Lewis explained, were "deeper" than any intellectual tradition. "[T] hese imported philosophies helped to provide intellectual expression for anti-Westernism and anti-Americanism, they did not cause it." The root source of Muslims' anger against "the West" was ultimately irrational and incomprehensible, according to Lewis, because it was based on religion.

As numerous critics of Huntington and Lewis have ably demonstrated, there is no historical or theological reason to assume that there is an *inherent* conflict between "Islam and the West."[103] As we have seen, in this chapter and throughout this book, both Islam and "the West" have been defined and redefined varyingly in relation to one another. They are interdependent. Indeed, historians of religion, such as myself, spend our professional lives studying such relationalities as a driving force in the historical development of religions. The polysemy and relationality of religions and cultures preclude the notion that they are inherently incompatible. Those who insist otherwise do so generally for reasons that have more to do with politics than religious beliefs and practices themselves. For Samuel Huntington, who followed his projects on "the Clash of Civilizations" with a book titled *Who Are We?* and for his supporters,

---

[103] For a pointed and erudite critique of Huntington's thesis, see Roy Mottahedeh, "The Clash of Civilizations: An Islamicist's Critique," *Harvard Middle Eastern and Islamic Review* 2 (1996), 1–26. The most well-known critique of Lewis's scholarship on Islam is Edward Said, *Orientalism* (New York: Vintage Books, 1979), esp. 314–321.

America's national identity was at stake. "Conflicts over what we should do abroad," Huntington himself observed, "are rooted in conflicts over who we are at home." The way we understood and defined American Muslims' place in American society thus affected the way America acted abroad.

> When Osama bin Laden attacked America and killed several thousand people, he also did two other things. He filled the vacuum created by Gorbachev with an unmistakably dangerous new enemy, and he pinpointed America's identity as a Christian nation.... Muslim hostility encourages Americans to define their identity in religious and cultural terms, just as the Cold War promoted political and creedal definitions of that identity.... As the Communist International once did, militant Muslim groups maintain a network of cells in countries throughout the world.... Muslim migrant communities in western Europe and the United States provide a nonthreatening and often sympathetic environment comparable to that provided by left-wing admirers of the Soviet Union. Mosques can serve as a base and a cover, and the struggles between moderates and militants to control them duplicate struggles between pro- and anti-communists in American unions in the 1930s and 1940s.... In recent decades, Muslims have fought Protestant, Catholic, and Orthodox Christians, Hindus, Jews, Buddhists and Han Chinese.... Superimposed on these local wars, however, has been a broader conflict between Islamist governments in Iran and Sudan, militant non-Islamist regimes (Iraq, Libya), and Muslim terrorist organizations, most notably Al Qaeda and its affiliates, on the one hand, and the United States, Israel, plus, on occasion, Britain and other Western countries, on the other.... The antagonism of Muslims toward the United States stems in part from American support for Israel. It also has deeper roots in the fear of American power, envy of American wealth, resentment of what is perceived as American domination and exploitation, and hostility to American culture, secular and religious, as the antithesis of Muslim culture.... Recent history suggests that America is likely to be involved in various sorts of military conflicts with Muslim countries and groups, and possible others, in the coming years. Will these wars unite or divide America?[104]

Huntington's dismissal of wars between Muslim countries (Iraq's invasions of Iran and Kuwait, for example) or conflicts between Muslims (Muslim opposition to the Taliban in Afghanistan and elsewhere, for example) in this same era points to the fact that such misleading assertions about Islam's relation with "the West" had more to do with ideology than with actual events or religions themselves. Huntington's history may have been selective but there is no mistaking what was at stake for him in the binary construct of "Islam and the West." At home, America's

---

[104] Samuel Huntington, *Who Are We? The Challenges to America's National Identity* (New York: Simon & Schuster, 2004), 10 and 357–361.

national identity as a united, Christian nation of Western European heritage was at stake, and abroad, America's alliance with Western Europe and Israel – the supposed "West" – was at stake.

How Americans defined their relations with Islam in light of their daily contact with Muslims in the United States was particularly important not only for scholars, such as Huntington and Lewis, but also for neoconservative activists and pro-Israel Zionists (both Christian and Jewish) because of the impact it could have had on U.S. support for Israel. Given the polarizing attitudes toward Israel's occupation of Palestinian territories in the Muslim Middle East, these groups regarded any conception of America's national identity that included Muslims as a potential threat to America's alliance with the only non-Muslim country in the region. Indeed, as the above-cited passage by Huntington shows, the lynchpin in these groups' framing of America's national identity within the polarizing construct of "Islam and the West" was U.S. support for Israel.

However one understands the intellectual genealogies and the political motivations underlying the binary construct of "Islam and the West," there is no denying the reality that this was the frame through which most contemporary Americans came to relate Islam and America to one another after 9/11. A major consequence of adopting such a frame without critical examination was that to be Muslim meant to have only two principal choices in America: one could either follow the "good Islam" that was compatible with "the West," or adhere to the "bad Islam" that stood in conflict with "the West." On September 20, 2001, President George W. Bush employed this distinction in his explanation of the difference between "Muslims" and members of al-Qaeda to a joint-session of the Congress.

Al Qaeda is to terror what the Mafia is to crime. But its goal is not making money, its goal is remaking the world and imposing its radical beliefs on people everywhere. The terrorists practice a fringe form of Islamic extremism that has been rejected by Muslim scholars and the vast majority of Muslim clerics; a fringe movement that perverts the peaceful teachings of Islam. The terrorists' directive commands them to kill Christians and Jews, to kill all Americans and make no distinctions among military and civilians, including women and children. This group and its leader, a person named Osama bin Laden, are linked to many other organizations in different countries, including the Egyptian Islamic Jihad and the Islamic Movement of Uzbekistan. There are thousands of these terrorists in more than 60 countries.[105]

As Mahmood Mamdani noted "[f]rom this point of view, 'bad Muslims' were clearly responsible for terrorism." "Good Muslims" were appalled

---

[105] George W. Bush, address to a joint session of Congress, September 20, 2001.

by these acts and sought to clear their name by representing Islam as peaceful and by demonstrating their political loyalty by joining us against "the war on terror." "But this could not hide the central message of such discourse: unless proved to be 'good,' every Muslim was presumed to be 'bad.' All Muslims were under obligation to prove their credentials by joining in a war against 'bad Muslims'."[106] In this speech and other variations thereof, President Bush essentially defined the "Muslims" whose citizenship rights the United States would acknowledge. By pitting a "peaceful Islam" that acknowledged the status quo against an "extremist Islam" that sought to subvert the status quo through unjustifiable violence, the President defined Islamic identity in terms of political loyalty to the United States, effectively closing the door on legitimate Muslim critiques of U.S. policies that had a devastating effect on the lives of Muslims in such places as Iraq, Afghanistan, Pakistan, and Palestine in recent years.

Putting aside the problem of a non-Muslim with very little knowledge of Islamic beliefs and practices expounding what is Islam (as I mentioned earlier, President Clinton employed a similar discourse), President Bush's definition of Islam further stigmatized Muslims. One's religious beliefs become stigmatized when one has to work to accommodate one's beliefs to the demands of the state or its official representatives. It is important to note that this stigmatizing discourse was not limited to the corridors of power; it pervaded contemporary American public discourse on American Muslims. In a popular book on Islam in America, the reporter and editor Paul M. Barrett wrote: "Intolerance versus broad-mindedness.... Reform versus reaction ... Integration with American society versus retreat into foreign antagonisms.... Muslims face critical choices as they struggle for the soul of their faith in the United States."[107] Here Barrett too set conditions upon Muslims' participation in American society; in order to be active participants in American society, Muslims had to make certain choices imposed on them by an "external America" that was disembedded from their experiences in this country. As we have seen throughout this book, Muslims, historically, had been active participants to varying degrees in American society and in American politics, and those who led the charge on greater participation since the late 1980s were generally activists with Islamist leanings. In fact, it was through participation in

[106] Mahmood Mamdani, *Good Muslim, Bad Muslim: America, the Cold War, and the Roots of Terror* (New York: Pantheon, 2004), 15.
[107] Barrett, *American Islam*, 277.

Islamic politics that many of the national Muslim organizations founded by immigrant Muslims were indigenized.

To offset the stigmatizing effects of the "good Muslim/bad Muslim" discourse in which American Muslims found themselves after 9/11, they increased their participation in American society. By doing so, they invited non-Muslim Americans into the interior reality of their lives and the lives of their institutions and out of the polarizing contexts in which they were interpolated. As one would expect, this had a humanizing effect. In an effort that testifies to the importance of institution and community building in relating Islam and America throughout the history of Muslims in this country, mosques across the nation following 9/11 hosted open-houses, literally bringing their non-Muslim neighbors into the interior of their lives. Conversely non-Muslim Americans, after 9/11, hosted and initiated numerous inter-religious dialogues, allowing Muslims and non-Muslims to break bread and to learn more about one another's religions. In my study of the history of the Muslim community in Portland, Oregon, I found that such efforts did not so much result in deep understanding of others' religions as they did in strengthening civil society bonds within local communities. American Muslims felt anxious about belonging to America after 9/11, "the War on Terror," and the invasion of Iraq, but most did not feel anxious about belonging to their local communities. As a number of scholars have recently shown, American Muslims "change their local realities through critical engagement with these larger publics, they do so in collusion with local allies – not only political activists, but also the keeper of rather staid mainstream institutions – who stand ready to facilitate these efforts." Through local institutions and allies, American Muslims gained a stake in America, which some (evoking Michel Foucault) argue had a "disciplinary" function by laying out for Muslims the ways in which they needed to understand their religion and to represent themselves in order to become part of the mainstream.[108] (Recall the State Department's "Being Muslim in America" booklet.)

Such a view, however, seems unduly cynical and does not fully recognize American Muslims' agency. Some Muslims responded to the post-9/11 stigma surrounding Islam by transforming (or "disciplining") themselves – regardless of age, gender, level of religiosity or religious knowledge – into

---

[108] See Katherine P. Ewing, ed., *Being and Belonging: Muslims in the United States Since 9/11* (New York: Russell Sage, 2008). Quote from Andrew Shryock, "Epilogue: On Discipline and Inclusion," in *Being and Belonging*, 203.

"ambassadors" of "good Islam" to non-Muslim Americans. There was, however, another response adopted by some Muslim activists who sought to turn the tables on the "good Muslim/bad Muslim" discourse during the Bush Presidency by arguing that there were also two Americas. There was "America the democracy" and "America the colonial power." M. A. Muqtedar Khan explained,

[American Muslims] are deeply enamored of what they call 'Islamic values in action,' such as consultative governance (democratic processes), religious freedom, and cultural and political pluralism. For these Muslims the relative opportunity to practice Islam and build Islamic movements and institutions in America, when compared to the presently autocratic Muslim world, remains the most thrilling aspect of American life.... There is also a competing image of America. Muslims who focus primarily on U.S. foreign policy see America as an evil force – a colonial power dominating the Muslim world, stealing its resources, and depriving it of its freedoms and right to self-determination. Many Muslims also believe that the United States is anti-Islam and seeking to globalize its immoral culture. They find America's uncritical support of Israel, even as Israel oppresses the Palestinian population and massacres its young people, to be proof of its evil motives. The complete devastation of Iraq and the incredible hardship caused by the U.S.-sponsored sanctions [during Saddam's era] are seen as further evidence of American intentions to destroy and eliminate Islam and Muslims. These Muslims have trouble reconciling America's benign attitude toward Muslims at home with the consequences of its malevolent foreign policy.[109]

Khan suggested that America too had to make a choice in the aftermath of 9/11 between democratic values and imperial ambitions. Just as the discourse on "good Muslims/bad Muslims" sought to define the Muslim who belonged in American society, Khan sought to define the America deserving of American Muslim's loyalties. We were thus, once again, at a junction when the United States and Islamist activists sought to negotiate their relation with one another by redefining "Islam" and "the West." As Khan himself stated, however, this America, torn between democracy and empire, was an "external America" that American Muslims did not recognize based on their personal experiences in the United States.[110]

---

[109] M. A. Muqtedar Khan, "Constructing the American Muslim Community," in *Religion and Immigration: Christian, Jewish, and Muslim Experiences in the United States*, ed. Yvonne Y. Haddad, Jane I. Smith, and John Esposito (Lanham, MD: Rowman–Altamira, 2003), 178–179.

[110] The most extensive scientific survey of American Muslims to date, for example, found that American Muslims are generally "middle class and mostly mainstream." Pew Research Center, *Muslim Americans: Middle Class and Mostly Mainstream*.

The challenge which emerged out of American Muslims' history at the turn of the twenty-first century, thus, was *not* a choice between a "good Islam" and a "bad Islam" or between a "good America" and a "bad America." Politically-driven discourses, external to Muslims actual experiences, resulted in these judgments of Islam and America. The more organic challenge American Muslims faced was to construct institutions, communities, discourses, and relations that reflected their actual lives and history in the United States. This chapter's examination of Muslims' experiences and history in America suggests that, unlike what some contemporaries suggested, there was not a "struggle for the soul of Islam" in America since the late 1980s, but rather that American Muslims struggled to create contexts in which they could live their religion neither in its Islamist idealized form nor in its stigmatized form. It is, of course, perilous for a historian to portend the future. Another attack by Muslim terrorists, increased discrimination against Muslims, or an equitable settlement of the Palestinian-Israeli conflict are all external events that could change the future of Islam in America, but given the fact that almost all American Muslims situated the challenges they faced after 9/11 in the context of the battles for civil rights[111] rather than the battles for independence from colonial rule suggests that American Muslims, during the first decade of the twenty-first century, believed they could shape the future of America by narrowing the gap between their lived experiences and their negative public representation and between their history and their politicized identities.

---

[111] Peter Skerry, "Political Islam in the United States and Europe," in *Political Islam: Challenges for U.S. Policy*, ed. Dick Clark (Aspen Institute: Second Conference, June 27–July 3, 2003), 43.

Epilogue

In the last chapter I argued that the challenge facing American Muslims in the future is not to settle a struggle between a "good Islam" and a "bad Islam," but to bridge the gap between the reality of their lives and the stigmatizing context in which they were interpolated by a polarizing discourse on "Islam and the West." Just as Muslims face the challenge of conforming their circumstances to the realities of their day-to-day lives, the academic study of Islam in America also faces a challenge in developing effective analytical categories and a vocabulary that allows for a representation of the historical realities of Islam in America. Much of the existing scholarship furthers the politicized dichotomy of "Islam and the West" by inquiring primarily into the assimilation of Muslims in the United States rather than focusing on the histories of their institution and community building efforts, which, as I have shown, were persistent and significant.

In the nineteenth century, increased travel and communication between cultures and the greater accessibility of visual and textual sources on the lives of others forced any understanding of an American national identity to necessarily grapple with alterity. During this time, however, very few Americans interacted meaningfully with the non-Christian other. Americans' contact with Muslims at this time was limited for the most part to their interactions with enslaved West African Muslims. Most Americans only encountered non-Christians in the abstract, in books and magazines. Over the years, as Muslims and other non-Christians immigrated to this country and as African Americans converted to Islam in noticeable numbers and as they built American Muslim communities and institutions, contact between Muslims and non-Muslims increased dramatically, to the point that at the turn of the twenty-first century, two-thirds of Americans indicated that they had some contact with Muslims in the United States.

Regardless of what one thinks of members of other religions theologically or what role they play in one's ideological vision of America, there is no escaping the fact that Americans encounter people of other religious traditions on a regular basis. In the midst of this diversity, the practical processes of institution and community-building play a much more significant role in shaping Muslims' lives than we have thus far acknowledged. The question of how Muslims are faring in the United States given their particular religious beliefs and the demands of Islamic law has received much attention in the past two decades, but as this study has shown, American Muslims' historical experiences in the United States have not been shaped so much by the way in which their religion and culture, abstractly conceived, allow for their assimilation into American society. Rather, their lives have been shaped more concretely by the institutions and communal relations they have formed since the colonial period and the ways in which they have adapted these institutions and relations to major national and international events, such as slavery and its abolition, industrialization, urbanization, colonialism, the world wars, the Cold War, the Civil Rights Movement, the Gulf War of 1990–1991, and 9/11.

Throughout this study we have seen Muslims in America occupy some sort of liminal space as semi-civilized, not-quite-black, not-quite-white, not-quite-American, not-quite-Muslim individuals. While the reality of their lives challenged the polarizing structures flanking them, their liminality served to reinforce the differences in these structures. The semi-civilized status of enslaved African Muslims, for example, reinforced the notion that black Africans are in need of the commerce and Christianity that accompanies white civilization. American Muslims' improvised religious practices in the first half of the twentieth century focused attention on the boundary between Islamic and non-Islamic praxis. Their liminal presence in America between "Islam and the West" was used to promote U.S. policies in the Muslim-majority world by differentiating between "good Muslims" who get along with the United States and "bad Muslims" who do not. While the history of American Muslim institution and community-building challenges these binary categories, the study of Islam in America has persistently framed American Muslims within them. Historically, Islam in America has been characterized by syncretism, eclecticism, heterogeneity, and complexity. In their history, American

Muslims repeatedly, and under varying circumstances, have related Islam and America to one another successfully. And they have done so because both Islam and America (as a national identity) have been diverse and polysemous. American Muslim experiences have spoken out of a poly-religious, poly-ethnic world in a polysemous tongue, one which we have yet to comprehend.

Select Bibliography

'Abd al-Karīm al-Maghīlī, Muhammad ibn. *Sharī'a in Songhay: The Replies of al-Maghīlī to the Questions of Askia al-Hājj Muhammad*, ed. and trans. John O. Hunwick. Oxford: Published for the British Academy by the Oxford University Press, 1985.

Abd-Allah, Umar F. *A Muslim in Victorian America: The Life of Alexander Russell Webb*. Oxford: Oxford University Press, 2004.

Abdul Rauf, Feisal. *What's Right with Islam Is What's Right with America: A New Vision for Muslims and the West*. San Francisco, CA: HarperSanFrancisco, 2004.

Abdul-Rauf, Muhammad. *History of the Islamic Center: From Dream to Reality*. Washington, D.C.: Colortone Press, 1978.

Abdul-Ghafur, Saleemah, ed. *Living Islam Outloud: American Muslim Women Speak*. Boston, MA: Beacon Press, 2005.

Abdullah, Aslam and Gasser Hathout. *Speaking for Ourselves: The American Muslim Identity*. Los Angeles, CA: Multimedia Vera International, 2003.

Abou El Fadl, Khaled. *The Authoritative and the Authoritarian in Islamic Discourses: A Contemporary Case Study*. Austin, TX: Dar Taiba, 1997.

And God Knows the Soldiers: The Authoritative and the Authoritarian in Islamic Discourses. Lanham, MD: University Press of America, 2001.

Speaking in God's Name: Islamic Law, Authority, and Women. Oxford: Oneworld Publications, 2001.

Abraham, Nabeel and Andrew Shryock, eds., *Arab Detroit: From Margin to Mainstream*. Detroit, MI: Wayne State University Press, 2000.

Abú Bekr eṣ-Ṣiddík. "Routes in North Africa." *Journal of Royal Geographical Society of London* 6 (1836), 100–113.

Abu Shouk, Ahmed I., J. O. Hunwick, and R. S. O' Fahey. "A Sudanese Missionary to the United States: Sāttī Mājid, 'Shaykh al-Islam in North America', and His Encounter with Noble Drew Ali, Prophet of the Moorish Science Temple Movement." *Sudanic Africa* 8 (1997), 137–191.

Abusharaf, Rogaia Mustafa. *Wanderings: Sudanese Migrants and Exiles in North America*. Ithaca, NY: Cornell University Press, 2002.

Adams, Hannah. *An Alphabetical Compendium of the Various Sects.* Boston,
    MA: B. Edes & Sons, 1784.
    A View of Religions in Two Parts, 2nd ed. Boston, MA: John West Folsom,
    1791.
    A View of Religions in Two Parts, 3rd ed. Boston, MA: Manning & Loring,
    1801.
    The Truth and Excellence of the Christian Religion Exhibited. Boston,
    MA: John West, 1804.
    *A Concise Account of the London Society for Promoting Christianity amongst
    the Jews.* Boston, MA: John Eliot, 1816.
    *A Dictionary of All Religions and Religious Denominations: Jewish, Heathen,
    Mahometan, Christian, Ancient and Modern,* 4th ed. [1817], intro. Thomas
    Tweed. Atlanta, GA: Scholars Press, 1992.
    *Memoir of Miss Hannah Adams, Written by Herself with Additional Notices
    by a Friend.* Boston, MA: Gray and Bowen, 1832.
Adi, Hakim and Marika Sherwood. *Pan-African History: Political Figures from
    Africa and the Diaspora since 1787.* London: Routledge, 2003.
Adorno, Rolena and Patrick Charles Pautz. *Alvar Núñez Cabeza de Vaca: His
    Account, His Life, and the Expedition of Pánfilo de Narváez,* 3 vols. Lincoln,
    NE: University of Nebraska Press, 1999.
Ahlstrom, Sydney E. *The American Protestant Encounter with World Religions.*
    Beloit, WI: Beloit College, 1962.
Aḥmad, 'Abd al-Ḥamīd Muḥammad. *Sāttī Mājid: al-dā'īyah al-Islāmī al-
    Sūdānī bi- Āmrīkā, 1904–1929.* Khartoum: Manshūrāt al-Khartūm 'Āṣimat
    al-Thaqāfah al-'Arabīyah, 2005.
Ahmad, Aziz and G. E. von Grunebaum. *Muslim Self-Understanding in India and
    Pakistan 1857–1968.* Wiesbaden: Otto Harrassowitz, 1970.
Al-e Ahmad, Jalal. *Plagued by the West,* trans. Paul Sprachman. New
    York: Columbia University Press, 1982.
Ahmed, Frank. *Turks in America: The Ottoman Turk's Immigrant Experience.*
    Greenwich, CT: Columbia International, 1993.
Ahmed, Gutbi Mahdi. "Muslim Organizations in the United States." In *The
    Muslims of America,* ed. Yvonne Y. Haddad, 11–24. New York: Oxford
    University Press, 1991.
Aidi, Hisham. "Jihadis in the Hood: Race, Urban Islam and the War on Terror."
    Middle East Report 224 (autumn 2002), 36–43.
    "Let Us Be Moors: Islam, Race and 'Connected Histories'." *Souls* 7, no. 1
    (winter 2005), 36–51.
Aijian, M. M. "The Mohammedans in the United States." *Moslem World* 10
    (1920), 30–35.
Alba, Richard D. *Ethnic Identity: The Transformation of White America.* New
    Haven, CT: Yale University Press, 1990.
Alba, Richard and Victor Nee. *Remaking the American Mainstream: Assimilation
    and Contemporary Immigration.* Cambridge, MA: Harvard University Press,
    2003.

Albanese, Catherine L. *A Republic of Mind and Spirit: A Cultural History of American Metaphysical Religion*. New Haven, CT: Yale University Press, 2007.

Alford, Terry. *Prince among Slaves: The True Story of an African Prince Sold into Slavery in the American South*. New York: Oxford University Press, 1977.

Algar, Hamid. "An Introduction to the History of Freemasonry in Iran." *Middle Eastern Studies* 6 (1970), 276–296.

Ali, Noble Drew. *The Holy Koran of the Moorish Science Temple of America*. Chicago, IL: Noble Drew Ali, 1927.

Alim, H. Samy. "A New Research Agenda: Exploring the Transglobal Hip Hop Umma." In *Muslim Networks from Hajj to Hip Hop*, ed. Miriam Cooke and Bruce B. Lawrence, 264–274. Chapel Hill, NC: The University of North Carolina Press, 2005.

Allen, Ernest, Jr. "When Japan Was 'Champion of the Darker Race': Satokata Takahashi and the Flowering of Black Messianic Nationalism." *Black Scholar* 24, no. 1 (winter 1994), 23–46.

Allison, Robert J. *The Crescent Obscured: The United States and the Muslim World, 1776–1815*. New York: Oxford University Press, 1995.

Allitt, Patrick. *Religion in America since 1945: A History*. New York: Columbia University Press, 2003.

Almond, Philip C. *Heretic and Hero: Muhammad and the Victorians*. Wiesbaden: Otto Harrassowitz, 1989.

Anderson, Benedict. *Imagined Communities: Reflections on the Origin and Spread of Nationalism*, rev. ed. London: Verso, 1991.

Anway, Carol L. *Daughters of Another Path: Experiences of American Women Choosing Islam*. Lee's Summit, MO: Yawna Publications, 1995.

Aossey, Yahya, Jr. *Fifty Years of Islam in Iowa, 1925–1975*. Cedar Rapids, IA: Unity Publishing, 1975.

Aossey, Yahya William. "The First Mosque in America." *Journal Institute of Muslim Minority Affairs* 5, no. 1 (1983–1984), 60–63.

Armitage, David and Michael J. Braddick, eds. *The British Atlantic World, 1500–1800*. New York: Palgrave Macmillan, 2002.

Aswad, Barbara and Barbara Bilgé, eds. *Family and Gender among American Muslims: Issues Facing Middle Eastern Immigrants and their Descendants*. Philadelphia, PA: Temple University Press, 1996.

Atterbury, Anson P. *Islam in Africa: Its effects – Religious, Ethical, and Social – upon the People of the Country*. New York: G. P. Putnam's Son, 1899.

Austin, Allan D. *African Muslims in Antebellum America: A Sourcebook*. New York: Garland Publishing, Inc., 1984.

"Islamic Identities in Africans in North America in the Days of Slavery (1731–1865)." *Islam et sociétés au Sud du Sahara* 7 (November 1993), 205–219.

African Muslims in Antebellum America: Transatlantic Stories and Spiritual Struggles. New York: Routledge, 1997.

Ayoob, Mohammed. *The Many Faces of Political Islam: Religion and Politics in the Muslim World.* Ann Arbor, MI: The University of Michigan Press, 2008.

Baepler, Paul, ed. *White Slaves, African Masters: An Anthology of American Barbary Captivity Narratives.* Chicago, IL: University of Chicago Press, 1999.

Baer, Hans A. *The Black Spiritual Movement: A Religious Response to Racism,* 2nd ed. Knoxville, TN: The University of Tennessee Press, 2001.

Bagby, Ihsan Abdul-Wajid, "Reflections on the Hijrah: Lessons for Muslims in North America." *al-Ittihad* 21 (September 1986), 61–68.

Bagby, Ihsan, Paul M. Perl, and Bryan T. Froehle. *The Mosque in America: A National Portrait.* Washington, D.C.: Council on American-Islamic Relations, 2001.

Bakalian, Anny and Mehdi Bozorgmehr. *Backlash 9/11: Middle Eastern and Muslim Americans Respond.* Berkeley, CA: University of California Press, 2009.

Bakhtiar, Laleh. *Sufi Women of America: Angels in the Making.* Chicago, IL: Institute of Traditional Psychoethics and Guidance, 1996.

Baldwin, James. *The Fire Next Time.* New York: Dell Publishing Company, 1962.

Balgamiş, A. Deniz and Kemal H. Karpat, eds. *Turkish Migration to the United States from Ottoman Times to the Present.* Madison, WI: The University of Wisconsin Press, 2008.

Banchoff, Thomas, ed. *Democracy and the New Religious Pluralism.* New York: Oxford University Press, 2007.

Barboza, Steven. *American Jihad: Islam after Malcolm X.* New York: Doubleday, 1994.

Barrett, Paul M. *American Islam: The Struggle for the Soul of a Religion.* New York: Farrar, Straus and Giroux, 2007.

Barringer, Paul B. *The Natural Bent: The Memoirs of Dr. Paul B. Barringer.* Chapel Hill, NC: The University of North Carolina Press, 1949.

Barrows, John Henry. *World's Parliament of Religions: An Illustrated and Popular Story of the World's First Parliament of Religions, Held in Chicago in Connection with the Columbian Exposition of 1893.* Chicago, IL: The Parliament Publishing Company, 1893.

Bayly, Christopher Alan. *The Birth of the Modern World, 1780–1914: Global Connections and Comparisons.* Malden, MA: Blackwell Publishing, 2004.

Bayoumi, Moustafa. "East of the Sun (West of the Moon): Islam, the Ahmadis, and African America." *Journal of Asian American Studies* 4, no. 3(October 2001), 251–263.

   How Does It Feel to Be a Problem? Being Young and Arab in America. New York: Penguin Press, 2008.

Ba-Yunus, Ilyas and Kassim Kone. *Muslims in the United States.* Westport, CT: Greenwood Press, 2006.

Bazan, Rafael Guevara. "Muslim Immigration to Spanish America." *The Muslim World* 56, no. 3 (1966), 173–187.

Bellah, Robert. "Civil Religion in America." *Dædalus* 96, no. 1 (winter 1967), 1–21.

Bennett, Norman Robert. "Christianity and Negro Slavery in Eighteenth-Century North Africa." *The Journal of African History* 1, no. 1 (1960), 65–82.

Benson, Kathleen and Philip M. Kayal, eds. *A Community of Many Worlds: Arab Americans in New York City*. Syracuse, NY: Syracuse University Press, 2002.

Beoku-Betts, Josephine. "'She Make Funny Flat Cake She Call Saraka': Gullah Women and Food Practices Under Slavery." In *Working Toward Freedom: Slave Society and Domestic Economy in the American South*, ed. Larry E. Hudson, Jr. Rochester, NY: University of Rochester press, 1994, 211–231.

Bergen, Teunis G. *In Alphabetical Order, of the Early Settlers of Kings County, Long Island, N.Y., from Its First Settlement by Europeans to 1700*. New York: S. W. Green's Son, 1881, 154–156 and 209.

Berger, Morroe. "The Black Muslims." *Horizon* 6, no. 1 (winter 1964), 48–64.

El-Beshti, Bashir M. "The Semiotics of Salvation: Malcolm X and the Autobiographical Self." *The Journal of Negro History* 82, no. 4 (Autumn 1997), 359–367.

Beynon, Erdmann Doane. "The Voodoo Cult Among Negro Migrants in Detroit." *American Journal of Sociology* 43, no. 6 (May 1938), 894–907.

Bilgé, Barbara. "Voluntary Associations in the Old Turkish Community of Metropolitan Detroit." In *Muslim Communities in North America*, ed. Yvonne Y. Haddad and Jane I. Smith, 381–405. Albany, NY: State University of New York Press, 1994.

Binder, Leonard. *Iran: Political Development in a Changing Society*. Berkeley, CA: University of California Press, 1962.

Bishara, Kalil A. *The Origin of the Modern Syrian*. New York: Al-Hoda Publishing House, 1914.

Blakely, Thomas D., Walter E. A. van Beek, and Dennis L. Thomson, eds. *Religion in Africa*. London: James Currey, 1994.

Blassingame, John W. "Using the Testimony of Ex-Slaves: Approaches and Problems." *The Journal of Southern History* 41, no. 4 (November 1975), 473–492.

Bluett, Thomas. *Some Memoirs of the Life of Job, the son of Solomon, the High Priest of Boonda in Africa;* London: Printed for Richard Ford, at the Angel in the Poultry, 1744.

Blyden, Edward Wilmot. *Christianity, Islam and the Negro Race*. Edinburgh: Edinburgh University Press, 1887.

Boosahda, Elizabeth. *Arab-American Faces and Voices: The Origins of an Immigrant Community*. Austin, TX: University of Texas Press, 2003.

Bose, Sugata and Ayesha Jalal. *Modern South Asia: History, Culture, Political Economy*. London: Routledge, 1998.

Botte, Roger. "Révolte, pouvoir, religion: Les Hubbu du Fūta-Jallon (Guinée)." *The Journal of African History* 29, no. 3 (1988), 391–413.

Bozorgmehr, Mehdi and Alison Feldman, ed. *Middle Eastern Diaspora Communities in America: Proceedings of the 17th Annual Summer Institute of the Joint Center for Near Eastern Studies of New York University and*

Princeton University. New York: Hagop Kevorkian Center for Near East Studies at New York University, 1996.

Braden, Charles S. "Islam in America." *The International Review of Missions* 48 (1959), 309–17.

Braude, Ann. *Radical Spirits: Spiritualism and Women's Rights in Nineteenth-century America*, 2nd ed. Bloomington, IN: Indiana University Press, 2001.

Bray, Thomas. *Apostolic Charity, Its Nature and Excellence Consider'd in a Discourse Upon Dan. 12. 3…to which is Prefixt A General View of the English Colonies in America, with Respect to Religion; in Order to Shew What Provision is Wanting for the Propagation of Christianity in Those Parts*. London: William Hawes, 1699.

A Memorial, Representing the Present State of Religion, on the Continent of North-America. London: John Brudenell, 1701.

Braziel, Jana Evans and Anita Mannur, eds. *Theorizing Diaspora*. Malden, MA: Blackwell Publishing, 2003.

Brenner, Louis. "The Jihad Debate between Sokoto and Borno: An Historical Analysis of Islamic Political Discourse in Nigeria." In *People and Empires in African History: Essays in Memory of Michael Crowder*, ed. J. F. Ade Ajayi and J. D. Y. Peel, 21–43. London: Longman, 1992.

ed. *Muslim Identity and Social Change in Sub-Saharan Africa*. Bloomington, IN: Indiana University Press, 1993.

Brittingham, Angela and G. Patricia de la Cruz. *We the People of Arab Ancestry in the United States*. U.S. Census Bureau, 2005.

Brodeur, Patrice. "The Changing Nature of Islamic Studies and American Religious History, Parts 1 and 2." *The Muslim World* 91 (spring 2001), 71–98 and 92 (spring 2008), 185–208.

Brooks, Joanna. *American Lazarus: Religion and the Rise of African-American and Native American Literatures*. New York: Oxford University Press, 2003.

Brooks, Joanna and John Saillant. *"Face Zion Forward": First Writers of the Black Atlantic, 1785–1798*. Boston, MA: Northeastern University Press, 2002.

Brown, Giles T. "The Hindu Conspiracy, 1914–1917." *The Pacific Historical Review* 17, no. 3 (August 1948), 299–310.

Bukhari, Zahid H., Sulayman S. Nyang, Mumtaz Ahmad, and John L. Esposito, eds. *Muslims' Place in the American Public Square: Hope, Fears, and Aspirations*. Walnut Creek, CA: AltaMira Press, 2004.

Bullock Steven C. *Revolutionary Brotherhood: Freemasonry and the Transformation of the American Social Order, 1730–1840*. Chapel Hill, NC: The University of North Carolina Press, 1996.

Burkett, Randall K. *Garveyism as a Religious Movement: The Institutionalization of a Black Civil Religion*. Metuchen, NJ: Scarecrow Press, 1978.

Burckhardt, J. L. *Travels in Nubia*. London: Association for Promoting the Discovery of the Interior Parts of Africa, 1819.

Burckhardt, Titus. *Introduction to Sufism*, trans. D. M. Matheson. [1976] San Francisco, CA: Thorsons, 1995.

Butler, Jon. *Awash in a Sea of Faith: Christianizing the American People*. Cambridge, MA: Harvard University Press, 1990.

Butler, Jon, Grant Wacker, and Randall Balmer. *Religion in American Life: A Short History*. New York: Oxford University Press, 2003.

Butt-Thompson, Frederick William. *West African Secret Societies: Their Organisations, Officials and Teaching*. London: H. F. & G. Witherby, 1929.

Cabeza de Vaca, Alvar Núñez. *Relación de los Naufragios y Comentarios de Alvar Núñez Cabeza de Vaca*, vol. 1. Madrid: Libreía General de Victoriano Suárez, 1906.

"The Narrative of Alvar Nuñez Cabeça de Vaca," ed. Frederick W. Hodge. In *Spanish Explorers in the Southern United States, 1528–1543*, ed. J. Franklin Jameson, 12–126. New York: Charles Scribner's Sons, 1907.

Adventures in the Unknown Interior of America, trans. and ed. Cyclone Covey. Albuquerque, NM: University of New Mexico Press, 1983.

Cainkar, Louise. "Post 9/11 Domestic Policies Affecting U.S. Arabs and Muslims: A Brief Review." *Comparative Studies of South Asia, Africa and the Middle East* 24, no. 1 (2004), 245–248.

"The Social Construction of Difference and the Arab American Experience." *Journal of American Ethnic History* 25, nos. 2–3 (winter-spring 2006), 243–278.

Calhoun, John C. "Slavery a Positive Good." Speech to U.S. Senate. February 6, 1837. In *The Works of John C. Calhoun*, ed. Richard Kenner Crallé, vol. 2, 626–633. New York: D. Appleton, 1888.

California State Board of Control. *California and the Oriental: Japanese, Chinese, and Hindus*. Sacramento: California State Printing Office, 1922.

Calverley, Edward E. "Negro Muslims in Hartford." *Muslim World* 55 (1965), 340–345.

Campo, Juan. "Islam in California: Views from the Minaret." *Muslim World* 86, nos. 3–4 (July–October 1996), 294–312.

Carroll, Bret E. *The Routledge Historical Atlas of Religion in America*. New York: Routledge, 2000.

Carter, Paul A. *The Spiritual Crisis of the Gilded Age*. DeKalb, IL: Northern Illinois University Press, 1971.

Casely-Hayford, Augustus and Richard Rathbone. "Politics, Families and Freemasonry in the Colonial Gold Coast." In *People and Empires in African History: Essays in Memory of Michael Crowder*, ed. J. F. Ade Ajayi and J. D. Y. Peel, 143–60. London: Longman, 1992.

Castañada, Pedro de. "The Narrative of the Expedition of Coronado," ed. Frederick W. Hodge. In *Original Narratives of Early American History: Spanish Explorers in the Southern United States, 1528–1543*, ed. J. Franklin Jameson, 281–387. New York: Charles Scribner's Sons, 1907.

Castries, Henri de la Croix, ed. *Les Sources inédites de l'histoire du Maroc: première série – Dynastie Sa'dienne – archives et bibliothèques d'Angleterre*, 3 vols. Paris: Paul Geuthner, 1918–1935.

Les Sources inédites de l'histoire du Maroc: archives et bibliothèque des Pays-Bas, vol. 6. Paris: Paul Geuthner, 1923.

Les Sources inédites de l'histoire du Maroc: premiére série – Dynastie Saadienne, archives et bibliothèques de France. Paris: Paul Geuthner, 1926.

Çelik, Zeynep. *Displaying the Orient: Architecture of Islam at Nineteenth-Century World's Fairs*. Berkeley, CA: University of California Press, 1992.

Cesari, Jocelyne. *When Islam and Democracy Meet: Muslims in Europe and in the United States*. New York: Palgrave Macmillan, 2004.

ed. *Encyclopedia of Islam in the United States*, 2 vols. Westport, CT: Greenwood Press, 2007.

Chalkley, Lyman. *Chronicles of the Scotch-Irish Settlement in Virginia Extracted from the Original Court Records of Augusta County, 1745–1800*. Rosslyn, VA: The Commonwealth Printing Co., 1912.

Child, L. Maria. *The Progress of Religious Ideas, through Successive Ages*, vols. 1 and 3, New York: C. S. Francis & Co., 1855.

Chireau, Yvonne P. *Black Magic: Religion and the African American Conjuring Tradition*. Berkeley, CA: University of California Press, 2003.

Christy, Arthur. *The Orient in American Transcendentalism: A Study of Emerson, Thoreau, and Alcott*. New York: Columbia University Press, 1932.

ed. *The Asian Legacy and American Life*. New York: The John Day Company, 1945.

Clark, Andrew F. "The Fulbe of Bundu (Senegambia): From Theocracy to Secularization." *The International Journal of African Historical Studies* 29, no. 1 (1996), 1–23.

Clark, G. N. "The Barbary Corsairs in the Seventeenth Century." *Cambridge Historical Journal* 8, no. 1 (1944), 22–35.

Clarke, James Freeman. "Condition of the Free Colored People of the United States" [1859], reprint. *The Free People of Color*. New York: Arno Press, 1969.

Ten Great Religions: An Essay in Comparative Theology. Boston, MA: James R. Osgood and Company, 1871.

Autobiography, Diary and Correspondence, ed. Edward Everett Hale. Boston, MA: Houghton, Mifflin, 1891.

Clasby, Nancy. "The Autobiography of Malcolm X: A Mythic Paradigm." *Journal of Black Studies* 5, no. 1 (September 1974), 18–34.

Clawson, Mary Ann. *Constructing Brotherhood: Class, Gender, and Fraternalism*. Princeton, NJ: Princeton University Press, 1989.

Clegg, Claude Andrew, III. *An Original Man: The Life and Times of Elijah Muhammad*. New York: Macmillan, 1998.

Cleveland, William L. *A History of the Modern Middle East*, 3rd ed. Boulder, CO: Westview Press, 2004.

Cole, David M. *The Development of Banking in the District of Columbia*. New York: The William-Frederick Press, 1959.

Cole, Juan. *Modernity and the Millennium: The Genesis of the Baha'i Faith in the Nineteenth-Century Middle East*. New York: Columbia University Press, 1998.

Collins, Dr. *Practical Rules for the Management and Medical Treatment of Negro Slaves in the Sugar Colonies*. London: J. Barfield, 1803.

Cone, James H. *Martin & Malcolm & America: A Dream or a Nightmare*. Maryknoll, NY: Orbis Books, 1991.

Conrad, Georgia Bryan. "Reminiscences of a Southern Woman." *Southern Workman* 30, no. 5 (May 1901), 252–259.

Cook, Anthony E. "Encountering the Other: Evangelicalism and Terrorism in a Post 911 World." *Journal of Law and Religion* 20, no. 1 (2004–2005), 1–30.

Cooley, John K. *Unholy Wars: Afghanistan, America and International Terrorism*, 3rd ed. London: Pluto Press, 2002.

Cooper, Frederick. "The Problem of Slavery in African Studies." *The Journal of African History* 20, no. 1 (1979), 103–125.

Council on American-Islamic Relations. *Unveiling Prejudice: The Status of Muslim Civil Rights in the United States.* Washington, D.C.: Council on American-Islamic Relations, 1997.

A Decade of Growth: CAIR Tenth Anniversary Report, 1994–2004. Washington, D.C.: Council on American-Islamic Relations, 2004.

American Muslim Voters: A Demographic Profile and Survey Attitudes. Washington, D.C.: Council on American-Islamic Relations, 2006.

The Status of Muslim Civil Rights in the United States 2007. Washington, D.C.: Council on American-Islamic Relations, 2007.

American Muslim Voters and the 2008 Election: A Demographic Profile and Survey of Attitudes. Washington, D.C.: Council on American-Islamic Relatins, 2008.

Cox, Harvey. *Turning East: Why Americans Look to the Orient for Spirituality – and What that Search Can Mean to the West.* New York: Touchstone, 1977.

Cranston, Sylvia. *HPB: The Extraordinary Life and Influence of Helena Blavatsky, Founder of the Modern Theosophical Movement.* New York: G. P. Putnam's Sons, 1993.

Crawford, George W. *Prince Hall and His Followers.* New York: The Crisis, 1914.

Crèvecoeur, J. Hector St. John de. *Letters from an American Farmer.* [1782]. Gloucester, MA: Peter Smith, 1968.

Cristillo, Louis Francis. "'God Has Willed It': Religiosity and Social Reproduction at a Private Muslim School in New York City." Ph.D. Dissertation: Columbia University, 2004.

Cronon, E. David. *Black Moses: The Story of Marcus Garvey and the Universal Negro Improvement Association.* Madison, WI: The University of Wisconsin Press, 1955.

Curtin, Philip D., ed. *Africa Remembered: Narratives by West Africans from the Era of the Slave Trade.* Madison, WI: Univ. of Wisconsin Press, 1967.

Curtis, Edward E., IV. *Islam in Black America: Identity, Liberation, and Difference in African-American Islamic Thought.* Albany, NY: State University of New York Press, 2002.

"Islamizing the Black Body: Ritual and Power in Elijah Muhammad's Nation of Islam." *Religion and American Culture* 12, no. 2 (summer 2002), 167–196.

"African-American Islamization Reconsidered: Black History Narratives and Muslim Identity." *Journal of the American Academy of Religion* 73, no. 3 (September 2005), 659–684.

Black Muslim Religion in the Nation of Islam. Chapel Hill, NC: UNC Press, 2006.

Curtis, Edward E., IV. "Islamism and Its African American Muslim Critics: Black Muslims in the Era of the Arab Cold War." *American Quarterly* 59, no. 3 (September 2007), 683–709.

——. ed. *The Columbia Sourcebook of Muslims in the United States.* New York: Columbia University Press, 2008.

Curtiss, Richard H. "Dr. Agha Saeed: Dynamic Leader of Expanding American Muslim Alliance." *Washington Report on Middle East Affairs*, no. 1297 (December 1997), 23–25.

Daniel, Norman. *Islam and the West: The Making of an Image.* Edinburgh: Edinburgh University Press, 1960.

Dannin, Robert. *Black Pilgrimage to Islam.* New York: Oxford University Press, 2002.

Das, Rajani Kanta. *Hindustani Workers on the Pacific Coast.* Berlin: Walter de Gruyter and Company, 1923.

Davenport, John. *An Apology for Mohammed and the Koran.* London: J. Davy and Sons, 1869.

Davis, David Brion. *Inhuman Bondage: The Rise and Fall of Slavery in the New World.* Oxford: Oxford University Press, 2006.

Davis, John. *The Landscape of Belief: Encountering the Holy Land in Nineteenth-Century American Art and Culture.* Princeton, NJ: Princeton University Press, 1996.

Dawisha, Adeed, ed. *Islam in Foreign Policy.* Cambridge: Cambridge University Press, 1983.

Decaro, Louis A., Jr. *On the Side of My People: A Religious Life of Malcolm X.* New York: New York University Press, 1996.

Demo, Constantine. *The Albanians in America: The First Arrivals.* Boston, MA: The Society "Fatbardhesia" of Katundi, 1960.

Denny, Frederick Mathewson. "Islamic Theology in the New World: Some Issues and Prospects." *Journal of the American Academy of Religion* 62, no. 4 (winter 1994), 1069–1084.

——. "The *Umma* in North America: Muslim 'Melting Pot' or Ethnic 'Mosaic'?" In *Christian-Muslim Encounters*, ed. Yvonne Yazbeck Haddad and Wadi Zaidan Haddad. Gainesville, FL: University Press of Florida, 1995.

Denslow, William R. *10,000 Famous Freemasons from K to Z*, pt. II. reprint Whitefish, MT: Kessinger Publishing, 2004.

Deutsch, Nathaniel. *Inventing America's "Worst" Family: Eugenics, Islam, and the Fall and Rise of the Tribe of Ishmael.* Berkeley, CA: University of California Press, 2009.

Dicarlo, Lisa. *Migrating to America: Transnational Social Networks and Regional Identity among Turkish Migrants.* London: Tauris Academic Studies, 2008.

Dillingham, William, U.S. Immigration Commission. *Immigrant Banks.* Washington, D.C.: Government Printing Office, 1910.

——. *Reports of the Immigration Commission. Statistical review of immigration, 1820–1910.* Washington, D.C.: Government Printing Office, 1910.

Dimock, Hedley S. "Trends in the Redefinition of Religion." *The Journal of Religion* 8, no. 3 (July 1928), 434–452.

Diouf, Sylviane A. *Servants of Allah: African Muslims Enslaved in the Americas.* New York: New York University Press, 1998.

"American Slaves Who Were Readers and Writer." *The Journal of Blacks in Higher Education* 24 (summer 1999), 124–125.

"Ṣadaqa among African Muslims Enslaved in the Americas." *Journal of Islamic Studies* 10, no. 1 (1999), 22–32.

Dirks, Jerald F. *Muslims in American History: A Forgotten Legacy.* Beltsville, MD: Amana Publications, 2006.

Doche, Viviane. *Cedars by the Mississippi: The Lebanese-Americans in the Twin-Cities.* San Francisco, CA: R & E Research Associates, Inc., 1978.

Dodd, Werter D. "The Hindu in the Northwest." *The World To-Day* 8 (November 1907), 1157–1160.

Dougherty, Kevin D., Byron R. Johnson, and Edward C. Polson. "Recovering the Lost: Remeasuring U.S. Religious Affiliation." *Journal for the Scientific Study of Religion* 46, no. 4 (2007), 483–499.

Douglass, Frederick. *The Narrative and Selected Writings,* ed. and intro. Michael Meyer. New York: The Modern Library, 1984.

Doutté, Edmond. *Magie et religion dans l'Afrique du Nord.* Algiers: A. Jourdan, 1909.

DuBois, W. E. B. *The Souls of Black Folk.* [1903] New York: Dover Publications, 1994.

Dubuisson, Daniel. *The Western Construction of Religion: Myths, Knowledge, and Ideology,* trans. William Sayers. Baltimore, MD: The Johns Hopkins University Press, 2003.

Duffield, Ian. "Duse Mohamed Ali and the Development of Pan-Africanism 1866–1945," 2 vols. Ph.D. thesis, Edinburgh University, 1971.

Dumenil, Lynn. *Freemasonry and American Culture, 1880–1930.* Princeton, NJ: Princeton University Press, 1984.

Dwight, Theodore Jr. "Condition and Character of Negroes in Africa." *The Methodist Quarterly Review* (January 1864), 77–93.

The People of Africa: A Series of Papers on their Character, Condition, and Future Prospects, ed. Henry M. Schieffelin. New York: Anson D.F. Randolph, 1871.

Dyson, Michael Eric. *Making Malcolm: The Myth & Meaning of Malcolm X.* New York: Oxford University Press, 1995.

Earle, Edward Mead. "Early American Policy Concerning Ottoman Minorities." *Political Science Quarterly* 42, no. 3 (September 1927), 337–367.

Ebaugh, Helen Rose and Janet Saltzman Chafetz, eds. *Religion and the New Immigrants: Continuities and Adaptations in Immigrant Congregations.* Walnut Creek, CA: AltaMira Press, 2000.

Eck, Diana L. *A New Religious America: How a "Christian Country" Has Now Become the World's Most Religiously Diverse Nation.* San Francisco, CA: HarperSanFrancisco, 2001.

Educational Policies Commission. *Moral and Spiritual Values in the Public Schools.* National Education Association, 1951.

Edwards, Bryan. *The History, Civil and Commercial, of the British Colonies in the West Indies,* 2nd ed., vol. 2. London: J. Stockdale, 1794.

Ehrman, John. *The Rise of Neoconservatism: Intellectuals and Foreign Affairs, 1945–1994.* New Haven, CT: Yale University Press, 1995.

El-Amin, Mustafa. *Al-Islam, Christianity, and Freemasonry.* Jersey City, NJ: New Mind Productions, n.d.

Elkholy, Abdo A. *The Arab Moslems in the United States.* New Haven, CT: College & University Press, 1966.

Elliott, Paul and Stephen Daniels. "The 'School of True, Useful and Universal Science'? Freemasonry, Natural Philosophy and Scientific Culture in Eighteenth-Century England." *British Journal for the History of Science* 39, no. 2, 207–229.

Ellis, John Tracy. *American Catholicism*, 2nd rev. ed. Chicago, IL: The University of Chicago Press, 1969.

Ellwood, Robert S., Jr. *Alternative Altars: Unconventional and Eastern Spirituality in America.* Chicago, IL: The University of Chicago Press, 1979.

Ellwood, Robert S. and Donald E. Miller. "Questions Regarding the CUNY National Survey of Religious Identification." *Journal for the Scientific Study of Religion* 31, no. 1 (March 1992), 94–96.

Eltis, David. *The Rise of African Slavery in the Americas.* Cambridge: Cambridge University Press, 2000.

Emerson, Steven. *American Jihad: The Terrorists Living among Us.* New York: Free Press, 2002.

Enayat, Hamid. *Modern Islamic Political Thought.* London: I. B. Tauris, 1982.

Ernst, Carl W. and Bruce B. Lawrence. *Sufi Martyrs of Love: The Chishti Order in South Asia and Beyond.* New York: Macmillan, 2002.

Esack, Farid. *On Being a Muslim: Finding a Religious Path in the World Today.* Oxford: Oneworld Publications, 1999.

Esposito, John L., *The Islamic Threat: Myth or Reality?* New York: Oxford University Press, 1999.

Essien-Udom, E. U. *Black Nationalism: A Search for an Identity in America*, 3rd ed. New York: Dell, 1965.

Evanzz, Karl. *The Judas Factor: The Plot to Kill Malcolm.* New York: Thunder's Mouth Press, 1992.

   The Messenger: The Rise and Fall of Elijah Muhammad. New York: Vintage Books, 2001.

Ewing, Katherine P., ed. *Being and Belonging: Muslims in the United States since 9/11.* New York: Russell Sage, 2008.

Faisal, Daoud Ahmed. *"Al-Islam": The Religion of Humanity.* New York: Islamic Mission of America, 1950.

Falola, Toyin. "The Lebanese in Colonial West Africa." In *People and Empires in African History: Essay in Memory of Michael Crowder*, ed. J. F. Ade Ajayi and J. D. Y. Peel, 121–141. London: Longman, 1992.

Fanon, Frantz. *The Wretched of the Earth*, trans. Constance Farrington. New York: Grove Press, 1963

   Black Skin, White Masks, trans. Charles Lam Markmann. New York: Grove Press, 1967.

Farber, David. *Taken Hostage: The Iran Hostage Crisis and America's First Encounter with Radical Islam.* Princeton, NJ: Princeton University Press, 2005.

Farrakhan, Louis. *Back Where We Belong: Selected Speeches by Minister Louis Farrakhan*, ed. Joseph D. Eure and Richard M. Jerome. Philadelphia, PA: PC International Press, 1989.

A Torchlight for America. Chicago, IL: FCN Publishing, 1993.

al-Faruqi, Isma 'il Ragi. *Christian Ethics: A Historical and Systematic Analysis of Its Dominant Ideas*. Montreal: McGill University Press, 1967.

Trialogue of the Abrahamic Faiths. Beltsville, MD: Amana Publications, 1982.

Islam. Brentwood, MD: International Graphics, 1984.

Fauset, Arthur Huff. *Black Gods of the Metropolis: Negro Religious Cults of the Urban North*. Philadelphia, PA: University of Pennsylvania Press, 1944.

Federal Writers' Project – Works Progress Administration of New York City. *New York Panorama: A Comprehensive View of the Metropolis, Presented in a Series of Articles Prepared by the Federal Writers' Project of the Works Progress Administration in New York City*. New York: Random House, 1938.

Federal Writers' Project – Works Progress Administration of Massachusetts. *The Albanian Struggle in the Old World and New*. New York: AMS Press, 1975.

Fischer, Michael M. J. and Mehdi Abedi. *Debating Muslims: Cultural Dialogues in Postmodernity and Tradition*. Madison, WI: The University of Wisconsin Press, 1990.

Fisher, Humphrey J. *Slavery in the History of Muslim Black Africa*. New York: New York University Press, 2001.

Frazier, E. Franklin. "Rejoinder [to Herskovits] by E. Franklin Frazier." *American Sociological Review* 8, no. 4 (August 1943), 402–404.

The Negro Church in America. New York: Schoken Books, 1963.

Freedom House. *Saudi Publications on Hate Ideology Invade American Mosques*. Washington, D.C.: Center for Religious Freedom, 2005.

Freeman, F. *Yardee: A Plea for Africa*. Philadelphia, PA: J. Whetham, 1836.

Friedlander, Jonathan, ed. *Sojourners and Settlers: The Yemeni Immigrant Experience*. Salt Lake City, UT: University of Utah Press, 1988.

Frothingham, Octavius B. *The Religion of Humanity: An Essay*. New York: Asa K. Butts, 1873.

Fulop, Timothy E. and Albert J. Raboteau, eds. *African-American Religion: Interpretive Essays in History and Culture*. New York: Routledge, 1997.

Gardell, Mattias. *In the Name of Elijah Muhammad: Louis Farrakhan and the Nation of Islam*. Durham, NC: Duke University Press, 1996.

Gartenstein-Ross, Daveed. *My Year Inside Radical Islam: A Memoir*. New York: Jeremy P. Tarcher/Penguin, 2007.

Garvey, Marcus. *Philosophy and Opinions of Marcus Garvey*, ed. Amy Jacques-Garvey. New York: Macmillan, 1992.

Geaves, Ron, Theodore Gabriel, Yvonne Haddad, and Jane Idleman Smith. *Islam and the West Post-9/11*. Burlington, VT: Ashgate, 2004.

Geerhold, William. "The Mosque on Massachusetts Avenue." *Saudi Aramco World* 16, no. 3 (May/June 1965), 20–21.

Gehrke-White, Donna. *The Face behind the Veil: The Extraordinary Lives of Muslim Women in America*. Secaucus, NJ: Citadel Press, 2007.

Gelvin, James L. *The Modern Middle East*. New York: Oxford University Press, 2005.

Georgia Writers' Project – Savannah Unit (Work Projects Administration). *Drums and Shadows: Survival Studies among the Georgia Coastal Negroes*, ed. Mary Granger. New York: Anchor Books–Doubleday, 1972 ed.

Gerges, Fawaz. *America and Political Islam: Clash of Cultures or Clash of Interests?* Cambridge: Cambridge University Press, 1999.

The Far Enemy: Why Jihad Went Global. New York: Cambridge University Press, 2005.

Ghamari-Tabrizi, Behrooz. "Loving America and Longing for Home: Isma'il al-Faruqi and the Emergence of the Muslim Diaspora in North America." *International Migration* 42, no. 2 (2004), 61–86.

Ghayur. M. Arif. "Muslims in the United States: Settlers and Visitors." *Annals of the American Academy of Political and Social Science* 454 (March 1981), 150–163.

"Demographic Evolution of Pakistanis in America: Case Study of a Muslim Group." *The American Journal of Islamic Studies* 1, no. 2 (August 1984), 113–132.

GhaneaBassiri, Kambiz. *Competing Visions of Islam in the United States: A Study of Los Angeles*. Westport, CT: Greenwood Press, 1997.

"Iranian American Muslims." In *Encyclopedia of Muslim-American History*, ed. Edward E. Curtis, IV. New York: Facts on File, forthcoming.

Ghaneabassiri, Kamyar. "U.S. Foreign Policy and Persia, 1856–1921." *Iranian Studies* 35, nos. 1–3 (winter 2002), 145–175.

Gillis, Chester. *Roman Catholicism in America*. New York: Columbia University Press, 1999.

Glazer, Nathan and Daniel Patrick Moynihan. *Beyond the Melting Pot: The Negroes, Puerto Ricans, Jews, Italians and Irish of New York City*. Cambridge, MA: M.I.T. Press, 1968 ed.

Gleason, Philip. "The Melting Pot: Symbol of Fusion or Confusion?" *American Quarterly* 16, no. 1 (spring 1964), 20–46.

Goff, Philip & Paul Harvey, eds. *Themes in Religion & American Culture*. Chapel Hill, NC: The University of North Carolina Press, 2004.

Goldman, Peter. *The Death and Life of Malcolm X*, 2nd ed. Urbana, IL: University of Illinois Press, 1979.

Gomez, Michael A. *Pragmatism in the Age of Jihad: The Precolonial State of Bundu*. Cambridge: Cambridge University Press, 1992.

"Muslims in Early America." *The Journal of Southern History* 60, no. 4 (Nov. 1994), 671–710.

Exchanging our Country Marks: The Transformation of African Identities in the Colonial and Antebellum South. Chapel Hill, NC: University of North Carolina Press, 1998.

Black Crescent: The Experience and Legacy of African Muslims in the Americas. Cambridge: Cambridge University Press, 2005.

Goody, Jack. "Introduction" and "Restricted Literacy in Northern Ghana." In *Literacy in Traditional Societies*, ed. Jack Goody, 16–19 and 199–264. Cambridge: Cambridge University Press, 1968.

Gordon, Milton M. *Assimilation in American Life: The Role of Race, Religion, and National Origins.* New York: Oxford University Press, 1964.

Gould, Robert Freke. *The History of Freemasonry: Its Antiquities, Symbols, Constitutions, Customs, Etc.* London: Thomas C. Jack, 1887.

Grabowski, John J. "Prospects and Challenges: The Study of Early Turkish Immigration to the United States." *Journal of American Ethnic History* 25, no. 1 (fall 2005), 85–100.

Grant, Douglas. *The Fortunate Slave: An Illustration of African Slavery in the Early Eighteenth Century.* London: Oxford University Press, 1968.

Greenberg, Joseph. "The Decipherment of the 'Ben-Ali Diary,' A Preliminary Statement." *Journal of Negro History* 25 (July 1940), 372–374.

Greene, Evarts B. "The Anglican Outlook on the American Colonies in the Early Eighteenth Century." *The American Historical Review* 20, no. 1 (October 1914), 64–85.

Grewal, Inderpal. "Transnational America: Race, Gender and Citizenship after 9/11." *Social Identities* 9, no. 4 (2003), 535–561.

Grimshaw, William H. *Official History of Freemasonry among the Colored People in North America.* New York: Broadway Publishing, 1903.

Gualtieri, Sarah M. A. "Becoming 'White': Race, Religion and the Foundations of Syrian/Lebanese Ethnicity in the United States." *Journal of American Ethnic History* (summer 2001), 29–58.

   Between Arab and White: Race and Ethnicity in the Early Syrian American Diaspora. Berkley, CA: University of California Press, 2009.

Haddad, Yvonne Y. "The Muslim Experience in the United States." *The Link* 12, no. 4 (September–October 1979), 1–12.

   "Muslims in U.S. Politics: Recognized and Integrated, or Seduced and Abandoned?" *SAIS Review* 21, no. 2 (summer/fall 2001), 91–102.

   "Islam in America: A Growing Religious Movement." *The Muslim World League Journal* 9, no. 9 (July 1982), 30–34.

   A Century of Islam in America. Washington, D.C.: Middle East Institute, 1986.

   "The Challenge of Muslim Minorityness: The American Experience." In *Integration of Islam and Hinduism in Western Europe*, ed. W. A. R. Shadid and P. S. van Kongingsveld. Kampen, the Netherlands: Kok Pharos Publishing House, 1991.

   ed. *The Muslims of America.* New York: Oxford University Press, 1991.

   ed. *Muslims in the West: From Sojourners to Citizens.* New York: Oxford University Press, 2002.

   "The Study of Women in Islam and the West: A Select Bibliography." *Hawwa* 3, no. 1 (2005), 111–157.

Haddad, Yvonne Y. and Adair T. Lummis. *Islamic Values in the United States: A Comparative Study.* New York: Oxford University Press, 1987.

Haddad, Yvonne Y. and Jane I. Smith. *Mission to America: Five Islamic Sectarian Movements in North America.* Gainesville, FL: University of Florida Press, 1993.

   eds. *Muslim Communities in North America.* Albany, NY: State University of New York Press, 1994.

Haddad, Yvonne Y. and John L. Esposito, eds. *Muslims on the Americanization Path?* New York: Oxford University Press, 1998.

Haddad, Yvonne Y., Byron Haines, and Elison Findly, eds. *The Islamic Impact.* Syracuse, NY: Syracuse University Press, 1984.

Haddad, Yvonne Y., Jane I. Smith, and John Esposito. *Religion and Immigration: Christian, Jewish, and Muslim Experiences in the United States.* Lanham, MD: Rowman–Altamira, 2003.

Haddad, Yvonne Y., Jane I. Smith, and Kathleen M. Moore. *Muslim Women in America: The Challenge of Islamic Identity Today.* New York: Oxford University Press, 2006.

Hagopian, Elaine. "Minority Rights in a Nation-State: The Nixon Administration's Campaign against Arab-Americans." *Journal of Palestine Studies* 5, nos. 1–2 (autumn 1975–winter 1976), 97–114.

  ed. *Civil Rights in Peril: The Targeting of Arabs and Muslims.* Chicago, IL: Haymarket Books, 2004.

Hagopian, Elaine C. and Ann Paden, eds. *The Arab Americans: Studies in Assimilation.* Wilmette, IL: Medina University Press International, 1969.

Hagy, James W. "Muslim Slaves, Abducted Moors, African Jews, Misnamed Turks, and an Asiatic Greek Lady: Some Examples of Non-European Religious and Ethnic Diversity in South Carolina Prior to 1861." *Carologue: Bulletin of the South Carolina Historical Society* 9, 1993.

Hahn, Lewis Edwin, Randall E. Auxier and Lucian W. Stone, Jr, eds. *The Philosophy of Seyyed Hossein Nasr.* Chicago: Open Court, 2001.

Hakim, Jameela A. *History of the First Muslim Mosque of Pittsburgh, Pennsylvania.* Cedar Rapids, IA: Igram Press, 1979.

Haley, Alex. *Roots.* Garden City, NY: Doubleday & Co., 1976.

Hall, Gwendolyn Midlo. *Africans in Colonial Louisiana: The Development of Afro-Creole Culture in the Eighteenth Century.* Baton Rouge, LA: Louisiana State University Press, 1992.

  Slavery and African Ethnicities in the Americas: Restoring the Links. Chapel Hill, NC: The University of North Carolina Press, 2005.

Hamdani, Abbas. "Ottoman Response to the Discovery of America and the New Route to India." *Journal of the American Oriental Society* 101, no. 3 (July–September 1981), 323–330.

  "An Islamic Background to the Voyages of Discovery." In *The Legacy of Muslim Spain,* ed. Salma Khadra Jayyusi. Leiden: E.J. Brill, 1992, 273–306.

Hamet, Ismaël. "Nour-El-Eulbab (Lumière des Coeurs) de Cheikh Otmane ben Mohammed ben Otmane dit Ibn-Foudiou." *Revue africaine* 41 (1897), 297–320, and 42 (1898), 58–70.

Handlin, Oscar. *The Uprooted: The Epic Story of the Great Migrations that Made the American People.* Boston, MA: Little, Brown and Company, 1951.

Handy, Robert T. *A Christian America: Protestant Hopes and Historical Realities,* 2nd rev. ed. New York: Oxford University Press, 1984.

Haque, Amber, ed. *Muslims and Islamization in North America: Problems and Prospects.* Beltsville, MD: Amana Publications, 1999.

Harland-Jacobs, Jessica. *Builders of Empire: Freemasons and British Imperialism, 1717–1927.* Chapel Hill, NC: UNC Press, 2007.

Harsham, Philip. "One Arab's Immigration." *Saudi Aramco World* 26, no. 2 (March/April 1975), 14–15.

"Islam in Iowa." *Saudi Aramco World* 27, no. 6 (November/December 1976), 30–36.

Hasan, Asma Gull. *American Muslims: The New Generation*, 2nd ed. New York: Continuum, 2002.

Hashaw, Tim. *Children of Perdition: Melungeons and the Struggle of Mixed America*. Macon, GA: Mercer University Press, 2006.

Hashem, Mazen. "Assimilation in American Life: An Islamic Perspective." *The American Journal of Islamic Social Sciences* 8, no. 1 (March 1991), 83–97.

Hathout, Hassan. *Reading the Muslim Mind*. Plainfield, IN: American Trust Publications, 1995.

Personal Memoirs. Los Angeles, CA: Multimedia Vera International, 2000.

Hathout, Hassan, Fathi Osman, and Maher Hathout. *In Fraternity: A Message to Muslims in America*. Los Angeles, CA: The Minaret Publishing House, 1989.

Hawie, Ashad. *The Rainbow Ends*. New York: Theo. Gaus' Sons, Inc. 1942.

Helweg, Arthur Wesley. *Asian Indians in Michigan*. East Lansing, MI: Michigan State University Press, 2002.

Henriksen, Thomas H. "African Intellectual Influences on Black Americans: The Role of Edward W. Blyden." *Phylon* 36, no. 3 (1975), 279–290.

Henry, Patrick. "'And I Don't Care What It Is': The Tradition–History of a Civil Religion Proof-Text." *Journal of the American Academy of Religion* 49, no. 1 (March 1981), 35–49.

Herberg, Will. *Protestant-Catholic-Jew: An Essay in American Religious Sociology*. [1955] Chicago, IL: The University of Chicago Press, 1983.

Hermansen, Marcia. "In the Garden of American Sufi Movements: Hybrids and Perennials." In *New Trends and Developments in the World of Islam*, ed. Peter Bernard Clarke. London: Luzac Oriental, 1997, 155–178.

"What's American about American Sufi Movements?" In *Sufism in Europe and North America*, ed. David Westerlund. New York: Routledge, 2004, 36–63.

"Literary Productions of Western Sufi Movements." In *Sufism in the West*, ed. Jamal Malik and John R. Hinnells. New York: Routledge, 2006, 28–48.

"Sufism and American Women." *World History Connected* (November 2006), http://www.historycooperative.org/journals/whc/4.1/hermansen.html, accessed April 18, 2008.

Hershkowitz, Leo. "The Troublesome Turk: An Illustration of Judicial Process in New Amsterdam." *New York History* 46 (1965), 299–310.

Herskovits, Melville J. *The Myth of the Negro Past*. Boston, MA: Beacon, 1958.

"African Gods and Catholic Saints in New World Negro Belief." In *The New World Negro*, ed. Frances S. Herskovits, 321–29. Bloomington, IN: Indiana University Press, 1966.

"What Has Africa Given America?" In *The New World Negro*, ed. Frances S. Herskovits, 168–74. Bloomington, IN: Indiana University Press, 1966.

Herskovits, Melville J. and Frances S. Herskovits. *Rebel Destiny*. New York: McGraw-Hill, 1934.

Hess, Gary R. "The 'Hindu' in America: Immigration and Naturalization Policies and India, 1917–1946." *Pacific Historical* Review 38, no. 1 (February 1969), 59–79.

"The Forgotten Asian Americans: The East Indian Community in the United States." In *The Asian American: The Historical Experience*, ed. Norris Hundley, Jr., 157–177. Santa Barbara, CA: Clio, 1976.'

al-Hibri, Azizah Y. "Islamic and American Constitutional Law: Borrowing Possibilities or a History of Borrowing?" *University of Pennsylvania Journal of Constitutional Law* (spring 1999), 492–527.

al-Hibri, Azizah Y., Jean Bethke Elshtain, and Charles C. Haynes. *Religion in American Public Life: Living with Our Deepest Differences*. New York: W. W. Norton, 2001.

Higginson, Thomas Wentworth. "Sympathy of Religions." *The Radical* 8 (February 1871), 1–23.

Hirschman, Elizabeth. *Melungeons: The Last Lost Tribe in America*. Macon, GA: Mercer University Press, 2005.

Hiskett, Mervyn. *The Development of Islam in West Africa*. New York: Longman, 1984.

Hitti, Philip K. *The Syrians in America*. New York: G. H. Doran and Company, 1924.

Hodge, Frederick Webb. *History of Hawikuh, New Mexico: On of the So-Called Cities of Cíbola*. Los Angeles, CA: The Southwest Museum, 1937.

Hodgson, William B. *Notes on Northern Africa: The Sahara and Soudan*. New York: Wiley and Putnam, 1844.

Höfert, Almut and Armando Salvatore, eds. *Between Europe and Islam: Shaping Modernity in a Transcultural Space*. Brussels: P.I.E.-Peter Lang, 2000.

Hoff, Henry B. "Frans Abramse van Salee and His Descendants: A Colonial Black Family in New York and New Jersey." *The New York Genealogical and Biographical Record* 121, no. 2 (April 1990), 65–71.

Holmes, Mary Caroline. "Islam in America." *The Moslem World* 16 (1926), 262–266.

Houghton, Louise Seymour. "Syrians in the United States," 4 pts. *Survey* 26 and 27 (July 1, 1911), 480–495; (August 5, 1911), 647–665; (September 2, 1911), 786–803; and (October 7, 1911), 957–968.

Houghton, Walter R., ed. *Neely's History of the Parliament of Religions and Religious Congresses at the World's Columbian Exposition*. Chicago, IL: F. T. Neely, 1893.

Hourani, Albert. *Islam in European Thought*. Cambridge: Cambridge University Press, 1991.

Howard, Harry Nicholas. *The King-Crane Commission: An American Inquiry in the Middle East*. Beirut: Khayats, 1963.

Howell, Sally and Andrew Shyrock. "Craking Down on Diaspora: Arab Detroit and America's 'War on Terror'." *Anthropological Quarterly* 76, no. 3 (summer 2003), 443–462.

Huda, Qamar-ul. *The Diversity of Muslims in the United States: Views as Americans*. Washington, D.C.: United States Institute of Peace, 2006.

Hughes, Richard T. *Myths America Lives By*. Urbana, IL: University of Illinois Press, 2003.

Humphreys, David. *An Historical Account of the Incorporated Society for the Propagation of the Gospel in Foreign Parts – to the Year 1728*. London, 1730.

Hunter, Shireen, ed. *Islam, Europe's Second Religion: The New Social, Cultural, and Political Landscape*. Westport, CT: Praeger, 2002.

Huntington, Samuel P. "The Clash of Civilizations?" *Foreign Affairs* 72, no. 3 (summer 1993), 22–49.

  The Clash of Civilizations and the Remaking of World Order. New York: Simon & Schuster, 1996.

  Who are We?: The Challenges to America's National Identity. New York: Simon and Schuster, 2004.

Hunwick, John. "'I Wish to Be Seen in Our Land Called Āfrikā': 'Umar b. Sayyid's Appeal to Be Released from Slavery (1819)." *Journal of Arabic and Islamic Studies* 5 (2003), 62–77.

Hunwick, John and Even Troutt Powell. *The African Diaspora in the Mediterranean Lands of Islam*. Princeton, NJ: Markus Wiener Publishers, 2002.

Hussaini, Hatem I. "The Impact of the Arab-Israeli Conflict on Arab Communities in the United States." In *Settler Regimes in Africa and the Arab World*, ed. Ibrahim Abu Lughod and Baha Abu Laban. Wilmette, IL: Medina University Press International, 1974.

Hutchison, William R., ed. *American Protestant Thought in the Liberal Era*. Lanham, NY: University Press of America, 1968.

  Errand to the World: American Protestant Thought and Foreign Missions. Chicago: The University of Chicago Press, 1987.

  The Modernist Impulse in American Protestantism. Durham, NC: Duke University Press, 1992.

  Religious Pluralism in America: The Contentious History of a Founding Ideal. New Haven, CT: Yale University Press, 2004.

Ibrahim, Saad. "American Domestic Forces and the October War." *Journal of Palestine Studies* 4, no. 1 (Autumn 1974), 55–81.

Inayat-Khan, Zia, ed. *A Pearl in Wine: Essays on the Life, Music, and Sufism of Hazrat Inayat Khan*. New Lebanon, NY: Omega Publications, 2001.

  "A Hybrid Sufi Order at the Crossroads of Modernity: The Sufi Order and Sufi Movement of Pir-o-Murshid Inayat Khan." Ph.D. Dissertation: Duke University, 2006.

Irving, Washington. *Mahomet and His Successors*. New York: The Co-operative Publication Society, 1849.

Jackson, Carl T. *The Oriental Religions and American Thought: Nineteenth-Century Explorations*. Westport, CT: Greenwood Press, 1981.

Jackson, Sherman. *Islam and the Blackamerican: Looking toward the Third Resurrection*. New York: Oxford University Press, 2005.

Jacob, Margaret. *Living the Enlightenment: Freemasonry and Politics in Eighteenth-century Europe*. Oxford: Oxford University Press, 1991.

The Radical Enlightenment. Morristown, NJ: Temple Publishers, 2003.

The Origins of Freemasonry: Facts and Fictions. Philadelphia, PA: University of Pennsylvania Press, 2006.

Jacobs, Jaap. *New Netherland: A Dutch Colony in Seventeenth-Century America*. Leiden: Brill, 2005.

Jacoby, Harold S. *A Half-Century Appraisal of East Indians in the United States*. Stockton, CA: College of the Pacific, 1956.

Jalal, Ayesha. *Self and Sovereignty: Individual and Community in South Asian Islam since 1850*. London: Routledge, 2000.

Jamal, Amaney. "Mosques, Collective Identity, and Gender Differences among Arab American Muslims." *Journal of Middle East Women's Studies* 1, no. 1 (winter 2005), 53–78.

"The Political Participation and Engagement of Muslim Americans: Mosque Involvement and Group Consciousness." *American Politics Research* 33, no. 4 (July 2005), 521–544.

Jamal, Amaney and Nadine Naber, eds. *Race and Arab Americans before and after 9/11: From Invisible Citizens to Visible Subjects*. Syracuse, NY: Syracuse University Press, 2008.

Jameson, John Franklin, ed. "Autobiography of Omar ibn Said, Slave in North Carolina, 1831." *American Historical Review* 30, no. 4 (July 1925), 787–795.

Jensen, Joan M. "Apartheid: Pacific Coast Style." *The Pacific Historical Review* 38, no. 3 (August 1969), 335–340.

Passage from India: Asian Indian Immigrants in North America. New Haven, CT: Yale University Press, 1988.

Jironet, Karin. *The Image of Spiritual Liberty in the Western Sufi Movement Following Hazrat Inayat Khan*. Leeuven: Peeters, 2002.

Johnson, Marion. "The Economic Foundations of an Islamic Theocracy: The Case of Masina." *The Journal of African History* 17, no. 14 (1976), 481–495.

Johnson, Samuel. *Oriental Religions and Their Relation to Universal Religion: India*. Boston, MA: James R. Osgood and Company, 1873.

Oriental Religions and Their Relation to Universal Religion: Persia. Boston, MA: Houghton, Mifflin, and Company, 1885.

Jones, Charles Colcock. *The Religious Instruction of the Negroes in the United States*. Savannah, GA: Thomas Purse, 1842.

Jones, J. Lynn. *Believing as Ourselves*. Beltsville, MD: Amana Publications, 2002.

Jordan, Louis Henry. *Comparative Religion*. [1905] Atlanta, GA: Scholars Press, 1986.

Joyner, Charles. *Down by the Riverside: A South Carolina Slave Community*. Urbana and Chicago, IL: University of Illinois Press, 1984.

Judy, Ronald. *(Dis)Forming the American Canon: African-Arabic Slave Narrative and the Vernacular*. Minneapolis, MN: University of Minnesota Press, 1993.

Kahera, Akel Ismail. *Deconstructing the American Mosque: Space, Gender, and Aesthetics*. Austin, TX: University of Texas Press, 2002.

Kallen, Horace. "Democracy Versus the Melting-Pot: A Study of American Nationality." *The Nation* 100, no. 2590 (February 18, 1915), 190–194.

Kammen, Michael. *Colonial New York: A History.* New York: Charles Scribner's Sons, 1975.

Karim, Jamillah. "Voices of Faith, Faces of Beauty: Connecting American Muslim Women through *Azizah*." In *Muslim Networks from Hajj to Hip Hop*, ed. Miriam Cooke and Bruce B. Lawrence, 169–188. Chapel Hill, NC: The University of North Carolina Press, 2005.

American Muslim Women: Negotiating Race, Class, and Gender within the Ummah. New York: New York University Press, 2009.

Karpat, Kemal. "The Ottoman Emigration to America, 1860–1914." *International Journal of Middle East Studies* 17, no. 2 (May 1985), 175–209.

"Commentary: Muslim Migration: A Response to Aldeeb Abu-Sahlieh." *International Migration Review* 30, no. 1 (spring 1996), 79–89.

al-Kattānī, 'Alī bin al-Muntaṣir [M. Ali Kettani]. *al-Muslimūn fī Ūrūbbā wa Āmrīkā*, 2 vols. Bayrūt: Dār al-kutub al-'Ilmiyya, [1976] 2005.

Kaufman, Jason Andrew. *For the Common Good? American Civic Life and the Golden Age of Fraternity*. New York: Oxford University Press, 2002.

Kaya, Ilhan. "Turkish-American Immigration History and Identity Formations." *Journal of Muslim Minority Affairs* 24, no. 2 (October 2004), 295–308.

Kayal, Philip M. and Joseph M. Kayal. *The Syrian-Lebanese in America: A Study in Religion and Assimilation*. Boston, MA: Twayne Publishers, 1975.

Kayalli, Randa A. *The Arab Americans*. Westport, CT: Greenwood Press, 2006.

Keddie, Nikki R. *An Islamic Response to Imperialism: Political and Religious Writings of Sayyid Jamāl ad-Dīn "al-Afghānī" with a New Introduction.* Berkeley, CA: University of California Press, 1983.

"The Revolt of Islam, 1700 to 1993: Comparative Considerations and Relations to Imperialism." *Comparative Studies in Society and History* 36, no. 3 (July 1994), 463–487.

Kellogg, Samuel H. *A Handbook of Comparative Religion*. Philadelphia, PA: Westminster Press, 1899.

Kennedy, N. Brent. *The Melungeons: The Resurrection of a Proud People, An Untold Story of Ethnic Cleansing in America*, 2nd rev. and corr. ed. Macon, GA: Mercer University Press, 1997.

Kepel, Gilles. *Muslim Extremism in Egypt: The Prophet and Pharaoh*, trans. Jon Rothschild. Berkeley, CA: University of California Press, 1984.

Allah in the West: Islamic Movements in America and Europe, trans. Susan Milner. Stanford, CA: Stanford University Press, 1997.

The War for Muslim Minds: Islam and the West, trans. Pascale Ghazaleh. Cambridge: The Belknap Press, 2004.

Kerr, Malcolm. *The Arab Cold War, 1958–1967: A Study of Ideology in Politics*, 2nd ed. London: Oxford University Press, 1967.

Kettani, M. Ali [Alī bin al-Muntaṣir al-Kattānī]. *Muslim Minorities in the World Today*. London: Mansell, 1986.

Khalidi, Tarif, ed. and trans. *The Muslim Jesus: Sayings and Stories in Islamic Literature*. Cambridge, MA: Harvard University Press, 2001.

Khan, Inayat. *Sufi Message of Spiritual Liberty* London: The Theosophical Publishing Society, 1914.

    The Heart of Sufism: Essential Writings of Hazrat Inayat Khan. Boston, MA: Shambhala, 1999.

Khan, Inayat, et al. *Biography of Pir-o-Murshid Inayat Khan.* Madras: East-West Publications, 1979.

Khan, Lurey. "An American Pursues Her Pakistani Past." *Asia* (March/April 1980), 34–39.

Khan, Muqtedar M. A. *American Muslims: Bridging Faith and Freedom.* Beltsville, MD: Amana Publications, 2002.

    "American Muslims and the Rediscovery of America's Sacred Ground." *Taking Religious Pluralism Seriously: Spiritual Politics on America's Sacred Ground*, ed. Barbara A. McGraw and Jo Renée Formicola. Waco, TX: Baylor University Press, 2005, 127–147.

Khan, Salim. "Pakistanis in the Western United States." *Journal Institute of Muslim Minority Affairs* 5, no. 1 (1983–84), 34–46.

Khan, Vilayat Inayat. *Thinking Like the Universe: The Sufi Path of Awakening*, ed. Pythia Peay. San Francisco, CA: Thorsons, 1999.

Khomeini, Ruhollah. *Islam and Revolution: Writings and Declarations of Imam Khomeini*, trans. Hamid Algar. Berkeley, CA: Mizan Press, 1981.

Kidd, Thomas S. *American Christians and Islam: Evangelical Culture and Muslims from the Colonial Period to the Age of Terrorism.* Princeton, NJ: Princeton University Press, 2009.

Kingsley, Mary H. *West African Studies.* New York: Macmillan and Co., 1899.

Kippenberg, Hans G. *Discovering Religious History in the Modern Age*, trans. Barbara Harshav. Princeton, NJ: Princeton University Press, 2002.

Klein, Martin A. "The Impact of the Atlantic Slave Trade on the Societies of the Western Sudan." *Social Science History* 14, no. 2 (summer 1990), 231–253.

Kly, Y. N. "The African-American Muslim Minority: 1776–1900." *Journal Institute of Muslim Minority Affairs* 10, no. 1 (January 1989), 152–159.

Knight, Michael Muhammad. *Taqwacores.* New York: Automedia, 2005.

    The Five Percenters: Islam, Hip Hop and the Gods of New York. Oxford: Oneworld Publications, 2007.

    Blue-Eyed Devil: A Road Odyssey through Islamic America. New York: Automedia, 2007.

Kosmin, Barry A., Egon Mayer, and Ariela Keysar. *American Religious Identification Survey 2001.* New York: The Graduate Center of the City University of New York, 2001.

Kosmin, Barry A. and Ariela Keysar. *American Religious Identification Survey 2008.* Hartford, CT: Trinity College, 2009.

Kosmin, Barry A. and Seymour P. Lachman. "Reply to Comments on the CUNY National Survey of Religious Identification (NSRI)." *Journal for the Scientific Study of Religion* 31, no. 1 (March 1992), 97–99.

Köszegi, Michael A. and J. Gordon Melton, eds. *Islam in North America: A Sourcebook.* New York: Garland Publishing, 1992.

Kudsi-Zadeh, A. Albert. "al-Afghānī and Freemasonry in Egypt." *Journal of the American Oriental Society* 92, no. 1 (January–March 1972), 25–35.

Kuklick, Bruce. *Puritans in Babylon: The Ancient Near East and American Intellectual Life, 1880–1930*. Princeton, NJ: Princeton University Press, 1996.

Laer, Arnold J. F. van, trans. and annot. *New York Historical Manuscripts: Dutch, Council Minutes, 1638–1649*, vol. 4. Baltimore, MD: Genealogical Publishing Co., 1974.

Laird, Lance and Wendy Cadge. "Constructing American Muslim Identity: Tales of Two Clinics in Southern California." *The Muslim World* 99, no. 2 (April 2009), 270–293.

Lambert, Frank. *The Barbary Wars: American Independence in the Atlantic World*. New York: Hill and Wang, 2005.

Landau, Jacob M. *The Politics of Pan-Islamism: Ideology and Organization*. Oxford: Clarendon Press, 1990.

  "*Muslim Opposition to Freemasonry*." *Die Welt des Islams* 36, no. 2 (July 1996), 186–203.

Laroui, Abdallah. *The Crisis of the Arab Intellectual: Traditionalism or Historicism?* trans. Diarmid Cammell. Berkeley, CA: University of California Press, 1976.

Laue, James H. "A Contemporary Revitalization Movement in American Race Relations: The 'Black Muslims'." *Social Forces* 42, no. 3 (March 1964), 315–323.

Launay, Robert. *Beyond the Stream: Islam and Society in a West African Town*. Berkeley, CA: University of California Press, 1992.

Law, Robin and Paul E. Lovejoy, eds. *The Biography of Mahommah Gardo Baquaqua: His Passage from Slavery to Freedom in Africa and America*. Princeton, NJ: Markus Wiener Publishers, 2003.

Lawrence, Bruce B. *Shattering the Myth: Islam Beyond Violence*. Princeton, NJ: Princeton University Press, 1998.

  New Faiths, Old Fears: Muslims and Other Asian Immigrants in American Religious Life. New York: Columbia University Press, 2002.

Leaming, Hugo P. "The Ben Ishmael Tribe: A Fugitive 'Nation' of the Old Northwest." In *The Ethnic Frontier: Essays in the History of Group Survival in Chicago and the Midwest*, ed. Melvin G. Holli and Peter d'A. Jones. Grand Rapids, MI: Wm. B. Eerdmans Publishing Company, 1977, 98–141.

Lee, Martha F. *The Nation of Islam: An American Millenarian Movement*. [1988] Syracuse, NY: Syracuse University Press, 1996.

Lee, Martha and Thomas Flanagan. "The Black Muslims and the Fall of America: An Interpretation Based on the Failure of Prophecy." *Journal of Religious Studies* 16, nos. 1–2 (1990), 140–156.

Leonard, Karen Isaksen. *Making Ethnic Choices: California's Punjabi Mexican Americans*. Philadelphia, PA: Temple University Press, 1992.

  South Asian Americans. Westport, CT: Greenwood Press, 1997.

  "American Muslims, before and after September 11, 2001." *Economic and Political Weekly* 37, no. 24 (June 15–21, 2002), 2292–2302.

  "American Muslim Politics: Discourses and Practices." *Ethnicities* 3, no. 2 (2003), 147–181.

Muslims in the United States: The State of Research. New York: Russell Sage Foundation, 2003.

Locating Home: India's Hyderabadis Abroad. Stanford, CA: Stanford University Press, 2007.

Leonard, Karen I., Alex Stepick, Manuel A. Vasquez, and Jennifer Holdaway, eds. *Immigrant Faiths: Transforming Religious Life in America*. Walnut Creek, CA: AltaMira Press, 2005.

Leopold, Anita Maria and Jeppe Sinding Jensen. *Syncretism in Religion: A Reader*. New York: Routledge, 2004.

Lesko, Kathleen M., Valerie Babb, and Carroll R. Gibbs. *Black Georgetown Remembered: A History of its Black Community from the Founding of "The Town of George" to the Present Historic District*. Washington, D.C.: Georgetown University Press, 1991.

Levtzion, Nehemia and Randall L. Pouwels, eds. *The History of Islam in Africa*. Athens, OH: Ohio University Press, 2000.

Lewis, Bernard. *Race and Slavery in the Middle East: A Historical Enquiry*. New York: Oxford University Press, 1990.

"The Roots of Muslim Rage." *Atlantic Monthly* 266 (September 1990), 47–60.

Liggins, Edith M. "The Moslem Movement in America." *The Moslem World* 20, no. 3 (July 1930), 309–315.

Lin, Phylis Lan. *Islam in America: Images and Challenges*. Indianapolis, IN: University of Indianapolis Press, 1998.

Lincoln, C. Eric. *The Black Muslims in America*. Boston, MA: Beacon, 1961 and 3rd ed. Grand Rapids, MI: William B. Eerdmans Publishing, 1994.

The Black Church since Frazier. New York: Schocken Books, 1974.

"The American Muslim Mission in the Context of American Social History." In *The Muslim Community in North America*, ed. Earle Waugh, Baha Abu-Laban, and Regula B. Qureshi, 215–233. Edmonton, AL: The University of Alberta Press, 1983.

Race, Religion, and the Continuing American Dilemma. New York: Hill and Wang, 1984.

"The Muslim Mission in the Context of American Social History." In *African American Religious Studies: An Interdisciplinary Anthology*, ed. Gayraud Wilmore. Durham, NC: Duke University Press, 1989.

Lincoln, C. Eric and Lawrence H. Mamiya. "Daddy Jones and Father Divine: The Cult as a Political Religion." *Religion in Life* 49 (spring 1980), 6–23.

The Black Church in the African American Experience. Durham, NC: Duke University Press, 1990.

Lippman, Walter. *Public Opinion*. New York: Harcourt, Brace, and Co., 1922.

Lippy, Charles H. *Pluralism Comes of Age: America's Religious Culture in the Twentieth Century*. Armonk, NY: M. E. Sharpe, 2000.

Little, Douglas. *American Orientalism: The United States and the Middle East since 1945*. London: I.B. Tauris, 2003.

Lo, Mbaye. *Muslims in America: Race, Politics, and Community Building*. Beltsville, MD: Amana Publications, 2004.

Lomax, Louis E. *When the Word Is Given: A Report on Elijah Muhammad, Malcolm X, and the Black Muslim World.* Westport, CT: Greenwood Press, 1963.

Long, Burke O. *Imagining the Holy Land: Maps, Models, and Fantasy Travels.* Bloomington, IN: Indiana University Press, 2003.

López, Ian Haney. *White by Law: The Legal Construction of Race,* rev. and updated. New York: New York University Press, 2006.

Lotfi, Abdelhamid. *Muslims on the Block: Five Centuries of Islam in America.* Ifrane, Morocco: Al Akhawayn University Press, 2002.

Lovejoy, Paul E. "Plantations in the Economy of the Sokoto Caliphate." *The Journal of African History* 19, no. 3 (1978), 341–368.

"The Characteristics of Plantations in the Nineteenth-Century Sokoto Caliphate." *The American Historical Review* 84, no. 5 (December 1979), 1267–1292.

"The Impact of the Atlantic Slave Trade on Africa: A Review of the Literature." *The Journal of African History* 30, no. 3 (1989), 365–394.

Transformations in Slavery: A History of Slavery in Africa, 2nd ed. Cambridge: Cambridge University Press, 2000.

Lovell, Caroline Couper. *The Golden Isles of Georgia.* Boston, MA: Little, Brown, and Co., 1933.

Lovell, Emily Kalled. "A Survey of the Arab-Muslims in the United States and Canada." *The Muslim World* 63, no. 2 (April 1973), 139–154.

Luker, Ralph E. *The Social Gospel in Black and White: American Racial Reform, 1885–1912.* Chapel Hill, NC: University of North Carolina Press, 1998.

Lyell, Charles. *Second Visit to the United States of America,* 2 vols. New York: Harper and Brothers, 1849.

Lynch, Hollis R. *Edward Wilmot Blyden: Pan-Negro Patriot, 1832–1912.* London: Oxford University Press, 1970.

ed. *Black Spokesman: Selected Published Writings of Edward Wilmot Blyden.* New York: Humanities Press, 1971.

Madden, R. R. *A Twelvemonth's Residence in the West Indies, During the Transition from Slavery to Apprenticeship.* London: James Cochrane and Co., 1835.

Mahmud, Khalil. "New Introduction." In *In the Land of the Pharaohs,* by Duse Mohamed, 2nd ed., ix–xxxiii. London: Frank Cass and Company, 1968.

Makdisi, Nadim. "The Moslems of America." *Christian Century* 76, no. 34 (26 August 1959), 969–971.

Makdisi, Ussama. "Reclaiming the Land of the Bible: Missionaries, Secularism, and Evangelic Modernity." *American Historical Review* 102, no. 3 (June 1997), 680–713.

Artillery of Heaven: American Missionaries and the Failed Conversion of the Middle East. Ithaca, NY: Cornell University Press, 2008.

Malik, Iftikhar H. *Islam and Modernity: Muslims in Europe and the United States.* London: Pluto Press, 2004.

Malik, Jamal and John Hinnells, eds. *Sufism in the West.* London: Routledge, 2006.

Malinovich, Nadia. "Americanization of Islam in the Contemporary United States." *Revue française d'études américaines* 3, no. 109 (2006), 100–112.

Mamdani, Mahmood. *Good Muslim, Bad Muslim: America, the Cold War, and the Roots of Terror*. New York: Pantheon Books, 2004.

Mamiya, Lawrence H. "From Black Muslim to Bilalian: The Evolution of a Movement." *Journal for the Scientific Study of Religion* 21, no. 2 (June 1982), 138–152.

———. "The Black Muslims as a New Religious Movement: Their Evolution and Implications for the Study of Religion in a Pluralistic Society." In *Conflict and Cooperation between Contemporary Religious Groups*. Tokyo: Chuo Academic Research Institute, 1988.

Manji, Irshad. *The Trouble with Islam Today: A Muslim's Call for Reform in Her Faith*. New York: St. Martin's Griffin, 2003.

Mann, Arthur. *The One and the Many: Reflections on the American Identity*. Chicago, IL: University of Chicago Press, 1979.

Mansur, W. A. "Syrians' Loyalty to America." *The Syrian World* 3, no. 10 (April 1929), 3–9.

[Markoe, Peter]. *The Algerine Spy in Pennsylvania; or, Letters Written by a Native of Algiers on the Affairs of the United States of America, from the Close of the Year 1783 to the Meeting of the Conventions*. Philadelphia, PA: Prichard and Hall, 1787.

Marmon, Shaun E., ed. *Slavery in the Islamic Middle East*. Princeton, NJ: Markus Wiener Publishers, 1999.

Marr, Timothy. *The Cultural Roots of American Islamicism*. Cambridge: Cambridge University Press, 2006.

Marsden, George M. *Religion and American Culture*. Fort Worth, TX: Harcourt Brace College Publishers, 1990.

Marsh, Clifton E. *The Lost-Found Nation of Islam in America*. [1984] Lanham, MD: The Scarecrow Press, 2000).

Martin, B. G. "Sapelo Island's Arabic Document: The 'Bilali Diary' in Context." *Georgia Historical Quarterly* 77, no. 3 (Fall 1994), 589–601.

Martin, Lucinda [Maria Martin], *History of the Captivity and Sufferings of Mrs. Maria Martin, Who was Six Years a Slave in Algiers*. Boston, MA: W. Carary, 1807.

Marty, Martin E. *A Nation of Behavers*. Chicago, IL: The University of Chicago Press, 1976.

Masterton, Rebecca. "Islamic Mystical Resonances in Fulbe Literature." *Journal of Islamic Studies* (2007), 1–23.

Masuzawa, Tomoko. *The Invention of World Religions: Or, How European Universalism Was Preserved in the Language of Pluralism*. Chicago, IL: The University of Chicago Press, 2005.

Matar, Nabil. *Turks, Moors, and Englishmen in the Age of Discovery*. New York: Columbia University Press, 1999.

Matory, J. Lorand. *Black Atlantic Religion: Tradition, Transnationalism, and Matriarchy in the Afro-Brazilian Candomblé*. Princeton, NJ: Princeton University Press, 2005.

Maurice, Frederick Denison. *The Religions of the World and Their Relation to Christianity*, 3rd rev. ed. Boston, MA: Gould and Lincoln, 1854.

Mawdudi, Abul A'la [also, Maudoodi]. *Come Let Us Change This World: Selections from Sayyid Maudoodi's Writings*, trans. Kaukab Siddique. Karachi: Salma Siddique, 1971.

Towards Understanding Islam, trans. and ed. Khurshid Ahmad. Lahore: Idara Tarjuman-ul-Quran, 1974.

Let Us Be Muslims, ed. Khurram Murad. Kuala Lumpur: The Islamic Foundation, 1985.

The Islamic Law and Constitution, trans. and ed. Khurshid Ahmad. Lahore: Islamic Publications Ltd., 1986.

Mazrui, Ali A. "Satanic Verses or a Statanic Novel? Moral Dilemmas of the Rushdie Affair." *Third World Quarterly* 12, no. 1 (January 1990), 116–139.

"Between the Crescent and the Star-Spangled Banner: American Muslims and US Foreign Policy." *International Affairs* 72, no. 3 (July 1996), 493–506.

"Islam and the United States: Streams of Convergence, Strands of Divergence." *Third World Quarterly* 25, no. 5 (2004), 793–820.

McAlister, Melani. *Epic Encounters: Culture, Media, and U.S. Interests in the Middle East since 1945*, updated ed. Berkeley, CA: University of California Press, 2005.

McClain, Edward L. *The Washington Ancestry and Records of the McClain, Johnson, and Forty Other Colonial American Families*. Greenfield, OH: Privately Printed, 1932.

McCloud, Aminah Beverly. *"A Method for the Study of Islam in America through the Narratives of African American Muslim Women."* Ph.D. Dissertation: Temple University, 1993.

African American Islam. New York: Routledge, 1995.

Transnational Muslims in American Society. Gainesville, FL: University Press of Florida, 2006.

McDonald, Dedra S. "Intimacy and Empire: Indian-African Interaction in Spanish Colonial New Mexico, 1500–1800." *American Indian Quarterly* 22 (1998), 134–156.

McFeely, William S. *Sapelo's People: A Long Walk into Freedom*. New York: W. W. Norton & Co., 1994.

McGinty, Anna Mansson. *Becoming Muslim: Western Women's Conversions to Islam*. New York: Palgrave Macmillan, 2006.

M'Crae, Lee. "Self-Exiled in America: Something about the Hindus in California." *Missionary Review of the World* 39 (July 1916), 525–526.

Meade, Bishop William. *Old Churches, Ministers and Families of Virginia*. Philadelphia, PA: J.B. Lippincott Company [1857], 1891.

"Selim, or the Algerine in Virginia." *Graham's American Monthly Magazine of Literature, Art, and Fashion* 51, no. 5 (November 1857), 433–438.

Mead, Sidney E. *The Lively Experiment: The Shaping of Christianity in America*. New York: Harper & Row, 1963.

Melki, Henry. *"Arab American Journalism and Its Relation to Arab American Literature."* Ph.D. Dissertation: Georgetown University, 1972.

Metcalf, Barbara D., ed. *Making Muslim Space in North America and Europe*. Berkeley, CA: University of California Press, 1996.

Metcalf, Barbara and Thomas R. Metcalf. *A Concise History of Modern India*, 2nd ed. Cambridge: Cambridge University Press, 2006.

Metcalf, Thomas R. *Ideologies of the Raj*. Cambridge: Cambridge University Press, 1994.

Middleton, Arthur Pierce. "The Strange Story of Job Ben Solomon." *The William and Mary Quarterly* 5, no. 3 (July 1948), 342–350.

Miles, George H. *Mohammed, the Arabian Prophet: A Tragedy in Five Acts*. Boston: Phillips, Sampson and Company, 1850.

Miller, Lucius Hopkins. *Our Syrian Population: A Study of the Syrian Communities of Greater New York*. San Francisco: R & E Research Associates, 1968.

Miller, Timothy, ed. *America's Alternative Religions*. Albany, NY: State University of New York Press, 1995.

Minault, Gail. *The Khilafat Movement: Religious Symbolism and Political Mobilization in India*. New York: Columbia University Press, 1982.

Mitchell, Richard P. *The Society of the Muslim Brothers*. New York: Oxford University Press, 1960.

Mitchell, Timothy. *Colonising Egypt*. Berkeley, CA: University of California Press, 1991.

Miyakawa, Felicia M. *Five Percenter Rap: God Hop's Music, Message, and Black Muslim Mission*. Bloomington, IN: Indiana University Press, 2005.

Mohamed, Duse. *In the Land of the Pharaohs: A Short History of Egypt from the Fall of Ismail to the Assassination of Boutros Pasha*, 2nd ed. London: Frank Cass & Co. [1911], 1968.

[Muḥammad 'Alī Dus.] Hayāh mawāra fī tārīkh al-'amal al-siyāsī al-'Arabī al-Afrīqī, trans. [into. Arabic] Aḥmad Muḥammad al-Badawī. Al-Qāhira: Markaz al-Buḥūth al-'Arabī, 1991.

Mohammad-Arif, Aminah. *Salaam America: South Asian Muslims in New York*. London: Anthem Press, 2002.

Mohammed, Warith Deen (also, Wārithuddīn Muḥammad and W. D. Muhammad). *The Man and the WoMan in Islam*. Chicago, IL: The Hon. Elijah Muhammad Mosque No. 2, 1976.

Prayer and al-Islām. Chicago, IL: Muhammad Islamic Foundation, 1982.

Focus on al-Islam: A Series of Interviews with Imam W. Deen Mohammed in Pittsburgh, Pennsylvania, ed. Ayesha K. Mustafa. Chicago, IL: Zakat Publications, 1988.

Al-Islam: Unity and Leadership. Chicago, IL: The Sense Maker, 1991.

Montgomery, Benilde. "White Captives, African Slaves: A Drama of Abolition." *Eighteenth-Century Studies* 27, no. 4 (summer 1994), 615–630.

Moore, Francis. *Travels into the Inland Parts of Africa: Containing a Description of the Several Nations*. London: Edward Cave, 1738.

Moore, Kathleen. "The Case for Muslim Constitutional Interpretive Activity in the United States." *The American Journal of Islamic Social Sciences* 7, no. 1 (March 1990), 65–75.

Al-Mughtaribûn: American Law and the Transformation of Muslim Life in the United States. Albany, NY: State University of New York Press, 1995.

Moore, R. Laurence. *Religious Outsiders and the Making of Americans.* New York: Oxford University Press, 1986.

Moore, Samuel. *Biography of Mahommah G. Baquaqua, A Native of Zoogoo, in the Interior of Africa.* Detroit, MI: By the author, 1854.

Moses, John G. *Annotated Index to the Syrian World, 1926–1932.* St. Paul, MN: Immigration History Research Center, the University of Minnesota, 1994.

Moses, Wilson Jeremiah, ed. *The Golden Age of Black Nationalism, 1850–1925.* New York: Oxford University Press, 1978.

Moses, Wilson Jeremiah, ed. *Classical Black Nationalism: From the American Revolution to Marcus Garvey.* New York: New York University Press, 1996.

Mottahedeh, Roy. *The Mantle of the Prophet: Religion and Politics in Iran.* New York: Pantheon, 1985.

"The Clash of Civilizations: An Islamicist's Critique." *Harvard Middle Eastern and Islamic Review* 2 (1996), 1–26.

Mubashshir, Debra Washington. "Forgotten Fruit of the City: Chicago and the Moorish Science Temple of America." *Cross Currents* (spring 2001), 6–20.

Mufassir, Sulayman Shahid. "Muslim Afro-Americans: The Forgotten Minority." *al-Ittihad* 7, no. 2 (December 1970), 13–15.

Muhammad, Amir Nashid Ali. *Muslims in America: Seven Centuries of History (1312–2000), Collections and Stories of American Muslims.* Beltsville, MD: Amana Publications, 1998.

Muhammad, Elijah. *Message to the Blackman in America.* Chicago, IL: Muhammad Mosque of Islam No. 2, 1965.

How to Eat to Live. Atlanta, GA: Messenger Elijah Muhammad Propagation Society, 1967.

The Fall of America. Chicago, IL: Muhammad's Temple of Islam No. 2, 1973.

The Theology of Time. Newport, VA: UBUS Graphics & Printing, 1992.

The Secrets of Freemasonry, 3rd ed. Atlanta, GA: Secretarius, 2002.

Murray, Nancy. "Profiled: Arabs, Muslims, and the Post-9/11 Hunt for the 'Enemy Within,'" 27–68. In *Civil Rights in Peril: The Targeting of Arabs and Muslims,* ed. Elaine C. Hagopian. Ann Arbor, MI: Pluto Press, 2004.

Muscati, Sina Ali. "Arab/Muslim 'Otherness': The Role of Racial Constructions in the Gulf War and the Continuing Crisis with Iraq." *Journal of Muslim Minorities Affairs* 22, no. 1 (2002), 131–148.

Muslim Public Affairs Council. *Grassroots Campaign to Fight Terrorism.* Los Angeles, CA: Muslim Public Affairs Council, 2005.

Activate 2008: MPAC's Policy Guide to the 2008 Election. n.p.: Muslim Public Affairs Council, 2008.

Muslim Students Association. *The MSA Handbook.* Ann Arbor: Muslim Students' Association of the US and Canada, 1968.

Muslim West Facts Project. *Muslim Americans: A National Portrait, an In-Depth Analysis of America's Most Diverse Religious Community.* n.p.: Gallup, 2009.

Nadwi, Syed Abul Hassan Ali. *Muslims in the West: The Message and Mission,* ed. Khurram Murad. Leicester, England: The Islamic Foundation, 1983.

Naff, Alixa. *Becoming American: The Early Arab Immigrant Experience.* Carbondale, IL: Southern Illinois University Press, 1985.

Nagi, Dennis L. *The Albanian-American Odyssey: A Pilot Study of the Albanian Community of Boston, Massachusetts.* New York: AMS Press, 1989.

Nance, Susan. "Mystery of the Moorish Science Temple: Southern Blacks and American Alternative Spirituality in 1920s Chicago." *Religion and American Culture: A Journal of Interpretation* 12, no. 2 (2002), 123–166.

"Respectability and Representation: The Moorish Science Temple, Morocco, and Black Public Culture in 1920s Chicago." *American Quarterly* 54.4 (2002), 623–659.

Nash, Gary B. *Red, White, and Black: The Peoples of Early North America,* 4th ed. Upper Saddle River, NJ: Prentice Hall, 2000.

Nasr, Seyyed Hossein. *Ideals and Realities of Islam.* London: G. Allen and Unwin, 1966.

Sufi Essays. London: G. Allen and Unwin, 1972.

Islamic Life and Thought. Albany, NY: State University of New York Press, 1981.

Traditional Islam in the Modern World. London: Kegan Paul International, 1987.

Knowledge and the Sacred. Albany, NY: State University of New York, 1989

A Young Muslim's Guide to the Modern World, 2nd ed. Chicago: Kazi Publications, Inc. 1994.

The Heart of Islam: Enduring Values for Humanity. San Francisco, CA: HarperSanFrancisco, 2002.

The Essential Seyyed Hossein Nasr, ed. William C. Chittick. Bloomington, IN: World Wisdom, 2007.

Nasr, Vali Reza Nasr. *The Vanguard of the Islamic Revolution: The Jama'at-i Islami of Pakistan.* Berkeley, CA: University of California Press, 1994.

Mawdudi & the Making of Islamic Revivalism. New York: Oxford University Press, 1996.

Neusner, Jacob, ed. *World Religions in America: An Introduction.* Louisville, KY: Westminster/John Knox Press, 1995.

Newby, Robert G. "Afro-Americans and Arabs: An Alliance in the Making?" *Journal of Palestinian Studies* 10, no. 2 (Winter 1981), 50–58.

Niebuhr, Reinhold. "What the War Did to My Mind." *Christian Century* 45 (September 27, 1928), 1161–1163.

Niebuhr, H. Richard. *The Kingdom of God in America.* New York: Harper & Brothers, 1937.

Nieuwkerk, Karin van, ed. *Women Embracing Islam: Gender and Conversion in the West.* Austin, TX: University of Texas Press, 2006.

Niles, H., et al, eds. *Niles' Weekly Register Containing Political, Historical Geographical, Scientific, Statistical, Economical, and Biographical Documents, Essays and Facts, Together with Notices of the Arts and Manufactures, and a Record of the Events of the Times from September, 1829, to March, 1830,* vol. 37.

Nimer, Mohamed. *The North American Muslim Resource Guide.* New York: Routledge, 2002.

Nomani, Asra Q. *Standing Alone: An American Woman's Struggle for the Soul of Islam*. San Francisco, CA: HarperSanFrancisco, 2005.

Novak, Michael. *The Rise of the Unmeltable Ethnics: Politics and Culture in the Seventies*. New York: The Macmillan Company, 1971.

Nu'man, Fareed H. *The Muslim Population in the United States: "A Brief Statement."* n.p.: American Muslim Council, 1992.

Nyang, Sulayman. "Islam in the United States of America: A Review of the Sources." *Islamic Culture* 55, no. 2 (1981), 93–109.

"Challenges Facing Christian-Muslim Dialogue in the United States." In *Christian-Muslim Encounters*, ed. Yvonne Yazbeck Haddad and Wadi Zaidan Haddad. Gainesville, FL: University Press of Florida, 1995.

Islam in the United States of America. n.p: ABC International Group, 1999.

Nyang, Sulayman and Mumtaz Ahmad. "The Muslim Intellectual Émigré in the United States" *Islamic Culture* 59, no. 3 (July 1985), 277–290.

Obenzinger, Hilton. *American Palestine: Melville, Twain, and the Holy Land Mania*. Princeton, NJ: Princeton University Press, 1999.

Office of International Programs. *Muslim Life in America*. U.S. State Department, n.d.

Olupona, Jacob K., ed. *African Spirituality: Forms, Meanings, and Expressions*. New York: Crossroad, 2000.

Olupona, Jacob K. and Regina Gemignani, eds. *African Immigrant Religions in America*. New York: New York University Press, 2007.

Orfalea, Gregory. *The Arab Americans: A History*. Northampton, MA: Olive Branch Press, 2006.

Oschinsky, Lawrence. "Islam in Chicago: Being a Study of the Acculturation of a Muslim Palestinian Community in That City." Master's thesis, the University of Chicago, 1952.

Osman, Ghada and Camille F. Forbes. "Representing the West in the Arabic Language: The Slave Narrative of Omar ibn Said." *Journal of Islamic Studies* 15, no. 3 (2004), 331–43.

Owen, Roger. *The Middle East in the World Economy, 1800–1914*. London: I. B. Tauris, 1993.

Owusu-Ansah, David. *Islamic Talismanic Tradition in Nineteenth-century Asante*. Lewiston, NY: Edwin Mellen, 1991.

"Prayer, Amulets, and Healing." In *The History of Islam in Africa*, Nehemia Levtzion and Randall L. Pouwels, eds. 477–488. Athens, OH: Ohio University Press, 2000.

Parker, Kenneth. *Early Modern Tales of the Orient: A Critical Anthology*. London: Routledge, 1999.

Parker, Richard B. *Uncle Sam in Barbary: A Diplomatic History*. Gainesville, FL: University Press of Florida, 2004.

Parramore, Thomas C. "Muslim Slave Aristocrats in North Carolina." *The North Carolina Historical Review* 77, no. 2 (2000), 127–150.

Patel, Eboo. *Acts of Faith: The Story of an American Muslim, the Struggle for the Soul of a Generation*. Boston, MA: Beacon Press, 2007.

Pew Forum on Religion and Public Life. *U.S. Religious Landscape Survey*. Washington, D.C.: Pew Research Center, 2008.

Pew Research Center. *Muslim Americans: Middle Class and Mostly Mainstream.* Washington, D.C.: Pew Research Center, 2007.

Phillips, Ulrich Bonnell. *American Negro Slavery: A Survey of the Supply, Employment and Control of Negro Labor as Determined by the Plantation Régime.* New York: D. Appleton and Company, 1929.

Pimienta-Bey, Jose V. "Some Myths of the Moorish Science Temple: An Afrocentric Historical Analysis." Ph.D. Dissertation: Temple University, 1995.

Pipes, Daniel. *Militant Islam Reaches America.* New York: W. W. Norton, 2002.

Piscatori, James. "Religion and Realpolitik: Islamic Responses to the Gulf War." In *Islamic Fundamentalisms and the Gulf Crisis.* Chicago: Fundamentalism Project, American Academy of Arts and Sciences, 1991.

Piven, Frances Fox and Richard A. Cloward. *Regulating the Poor: The Functions of Public Welfare.* New York: Pantheon Books, 1971.

Porteous, Laura L. "The Gri-Gri Case." *The Louisiana Historical Quarterly* 17 (January 1934), 48–63.

Porterfield, Amanda. *The Transformation of American Religion: The Story of a Late Twentieth-Century Awakening.* New York: Oxford University Press, 2001.

Portes, Alejandro and Rubén G. Rumbaut. *Immigrant America: A Portrait.* Berkeley, CA: University of California Press, 1990.

Poston, Larry. "The Future of Da'wah in North America." *The American Journal of Islamic Social Sciences* 8, no. 3 (December 1991), 501–511.

Islamic Da'wah in the West: Muslim Missionary Activity and the Dynamics of Conversion to Islam. New York: Oxford University Press, 1992.

Project MAPS and Zogby International. *American Muslim Poll* 2001.

American Muslim Poll 2004: Muslims in the American Public Square, Shifting Political Winds & Fallout from 9/11, Afghanistan, and Iraq. Washington, D.C.: Center for Muslim–Christian Understanding, Georgetown University, 2001.

Prothero, Stephen. "From Spiritualism to Theosophy: 'Uplifting' a Democratic Tradition." *Religion and American Culture* 3, no. 2 (summer 1993), 197–216.

The White Buddhist: The Asian Odyssey of Henry Steel Olcott. Bloomington, IN: Indiana University Press, 1996.

Puckett, Newbell N. *Folk Beliefs of the Southern Negro.* Chapel Hill, NC: University of North Carolina Press, 1926.

Puskar, Samira. *Bosnian Americans of Chicagoland.* Chicago, IL: Arcadia Publishing, 2007.

Qāsim, Jamāl Zakariyyā. *al-'Arab fī Āmrīkā: dirāsa li-tārīkh al-hijra al-'arabiyya ilā al-Wilāyāt al-Muttaḥida al-Āmrīkiyya.* al-Qāhira: Ma'had al-Buḥūth wa al-Dirāsāt al-'Arabiyya, 1988.

Qazwini, Hassan. *American Crescent: A Muslim Cleric on the Power of His Faith, the Struggle Against Prejudice, and the Future of Islam and America.* New York: Random House, 2007.

Quick, Abdullah Hakim. *Deeper Roots: Muslims in the Americas and the Caribbean from before Columbus to the Present.* London: Ta-Ha Publishers, Ltd., 1996

Quinn, David B. "Turks, Moors, Blacks, and Others in Drake's West Indian Voyage." *Terrae Incognitae* 14 (1983), 97–104.

Quiring-Zoche, Rosemarie. "Bei den male in Brasilien das Reisebuch des 'Abdarrahmān al-Baġdādī." *Die Welt des Islams* 40 (2000), 196–273.

Quli-Pūr, Maḥmūd Khudā and Fahīmah Vazīrī. *Islām va musalmānān dar Āmrīkā.* Qum, Iran: Markaz-i Intishārāt-i Daftar-i Tablīghāt-i Islamī-i Ḥawzah-i 'Ilmiyyah-i Qum, 1379 A.H.

Quraishi, M. Tariq. *Isma'īl al-Farūqi [sic]: An Enduring Legacy.* Plainfield, IN: A MSA Publication, 1987.

Qureshi, Naeem. *Pan-Islam in British Indian Politics: A Study of the Khilafat Movement, 1918–1924.* Leiden: Brill, 1999.

Qutb, Sayyid. *The Religion of Islam,* trans. "Islamdust." Palo Alto, CA: al-Manar Press, 1967.

Hādhā al-dīn, ed. Muḥammad al-Mu'allim. Al-Qāhira: Dār al-Shurūq, 1968.

Raboteau, Albert J. *Slave Religion: The "Invisible Institution" in the Antebellum South.* New York: Oxford University Press, 1978.

A Fire in the Bones: Reflections on African-American Religious History. Boston, MA: Beacon Press, 1995

Canaan Land: A Religious History of African Americans. Oxford: Oxford University Press, 2001.

Ramadan, Tariq. *Western Muslims and the Future of Islam.* New York: Oxford University Press, 2004.

Rashid, Ahmad. *Taliban: Islam, Oil and the New Great Game in Central Asia.* London: I.B. Tauris, 2002.

Rashid, Samory. "Islamic Influence in America: Struggle, Flight, Community." *Journal of Muslim Minority Affairs* 19, no. 1 (1999), 7–31.

"Divergent Perspectives on Islam in America." *Journal of Muslim Minority Affairs* 20, no. 1 (2000), 75–90.

Rawlinson, Andrew. "A History of Western Sufism." *Diskus* 1, no. 1 (1993), 45–83.

The Book of Enlightened Masters: Western Teachers in Eastern Traditions. La Salle, IL: Open Court, 1997.

Read, Jen'nan Ghazal. "The Sources of Gender Role Attitudes among Christian and Muslim Arab-American Women." *Sociology of Religion* 64, no. 2 (summer 2003), 207–222.

Reddick, L. D. "The Negro Policy of the United States Army, 1775–1945." *The Journal of Negro History* 34, no. 1 (January 1949), 9–29.

Rice, Benjamin H. "The Converted Algerine." *The Panoplist and Missionary Magazine* 12, no. 12 (December 1816), 544–551.

Richardson, E. Allen. *East Comes West: Asian Religions and Cultures in North America.* New York: The Pilgrim Press, 1985.

Rightmyer, Nelson Waite. *The Anglican Church in Delaware.* Philadelphia, PA: Church Historical Society, 1947.

Rippy, J. Fred. "The Negro and the Spanish Pioneer in the New World." *The Journal of Negro History* 6, no. 2 (April 1921), 183–189.

Rizk, Salom. *Syrian Yankee.* Garden City, NY: Doubleday & Company, Inc., 1952.

Roberts, Richard L. "Production and Reproduction of Warrior States: Segu Bambara and Segu Tokolor, c. 1712–1890." *The International Journal of African Historical Studies* 13, no. 3 (1980), 389–419.

Rodgers, Raymond and Jimmie N. Rogers. "The Evolution of the Attitude of Malcolm X toward Whites." *Phylon* 44, no. 2 (1983), 108–115.

Rodney, Walter. *A History of the Upper Guinea Coast, 1545–1800.* Oxford: Clarendon Press, 1970.

Roof, Wade Clark and William McKinney. *American Mainline Religion: Its Changing Shape and Future.* New Brunswick, NJ: Rutgers University Press, 1987.

Root, George L. *The Ancient Arabic Order of the Nobles of the Mystic Shrine for North America.* Whitefish, MT: Kessinger Publishing, 1997.

Rothwell, Bernard J., et al, Massachusetts Commission on Immigration. *Report of the Commission on Immigration on the Problem of Immigration in Massachusetts.* Boston, MA: Wright and Potter Printing, 1914.

Rouse, Carolyn Moxley. *Engaged Surrender: African American Women and Islam.* Berkeley, CA: University of California Press, 2004.

Roy, Olivier. *Globalized Islam: The Search for a New Ummah.* New York: Columbia University Press, 2004.

Secularism Confronts Islam. New York: Columbia University Press, 2007.

Rudolph, Susanne Hoeber and James Piscatori, eds. *Transnational Religion & Fading States.* Boulder, CO: Westview Press, 1997.

Ryan, Patrick J. "African Muslim Spirituality: The Symbiotic Tradition in West Africa." *African Spirituality: Forms, Meanings, and Expressions*, ed. Jacob K. Olupona. New York: The Crossroad Publishing Company, 2000.

Rydell, Robert W. *All the World's a Fair: Visions of Empire at American International Expositions, 1876–1916.* Chicago, IL: University of Chicago Press, 1984.

Sadīq, 'Īsā Khān. *Yaksāl dar Āmrīkā.* Tehran, 1311 A.H.

Safi, Omid, ed. *Progressive Muslims: On Justice, Gender and Pluralism.* Oxford : Oneworld Publications, 2003.

Safwat, Najdat Fathi. *Freemasonry in the Arab World.* London: Arab Research Center Publication, 1980.

Said, Edward W. *Orientalism.* New York: Vintage Books, 1979.

Covering Islam: How the Media and the Experts Determine How We See the Rest of the World. New York: Pantheon Books, 1981.

Said, Nicholas. *The Autobiography of Nicholas Said, A Native of Bornou, Eastern Soudan, Central Africa.* Memphis, TN: Shotwell and Co., 1873.

Said, 'Umar ibn. "The Life of Omar ibn Said (1831)." trans. and intro. Ala A. Alryyes In *The Multilingual Anthology of American Literature: A Reader of Original Texts with English Translations*, ed. Marc Shell and Werner Sollors, 58–93. New York: New York University Press, 2000.

Saliba, Najib E. "Emigration from Syria." *Arab Studies Quarterly* 3, no. 1 (winter 1981), 56–67.

Sanneh, Lamin. *The Crown and the Turban: Muslims and West African Pluralism.* Boulder, CO: Westview Press, 1997.

Sarat, Austin and Thomas R. Kearns. *Cultural Pluralism, Identity, and the Law.* Ann Arbor, MI: University of Michigan Press, 2001.

Sareen, Tilak Raj. *Select Documents on the Ghadr Party.* New Delhi: Mounto Publishing House, 1994.

Sarna, Jonathan D. "The American Jewish Experience and the Emergence of the Muslim Community in America." *The American Journal of Islamic Social Sciences* 9, no. 1 (spring 1992), 370–382.

American Judaism: A History. New Haven, CT: Yale University Press, 2004.

Sarroub, Loukia K. *All American Yemeni Girls: Being Muslim in a Public School.* Philadelphia, PA: University of Pennsylvania Press, 2005.

Sawaie, Mohammed, ed. *Arabic-Speaking Immigrants in the United States and Canada: A Bibliographical Guide with Annotation.* Lexington, KY: Mazda Publishers, 1985.

Schmidt, Garbi. *Islam in Urban America: Sunni Muslims in Chicago.* Philadelphia, PA: Temple University Press, 2004.

Schmidt, Gary D. *A Passionate Usefulness: The Life and Literary Labors of Hannah Adams.* Charlottesville, VA: University of Virginia Press, 2004.

Scholten, J. H. *A Comparative View of Religions,* trans. Francis T. Washburn. Boston, MA: Crosby & Damrell, 1870.

Schuon, Frithjof. *The Essential Frithjof Schuon,* ed. Seyyed Hossein Nasr. Bloomington, IN: World Wisdom, 2005.

Scolnick, Joseph M. and N. Brent Kennedy, eds. *From Anatolia to Appalachia: A Turkish American Dialogue.* Macon, GA: Mercer University Press, 2003.

Seager, Richard H. "Pluralism and the American Mainstream: The View from the World's Parliament of Religions." *The Harvard Theological Review* 82, no. 3 (July 1989), 301–324.

The Dawn of Religious Pluralism: Voices From the World's Parliament of Religions, 1893. La Salle, IL: Open Court Publishing, 1993.

The World's Parliament of Religions: The East/West Encounter, Chicago, 1893. Bloomington, IN: Indian University Press, 1995.

Sedgwick, Mark. *Against the Modern World: Traditionalism and the Secret Intellectual History of the Twentieth Century.* New York: Oxford University Press, 2004.

Sernett, Milton C., ed. *Afro-American Religious History: A Documentary Witness.* Durham, NC: Duke University Press, 1985.

Sewall, Gilbert T. *Islam in the Classroom: What the Textbooks Tell Us.* New York: American Textbook Council, 2008.

Sha'ban, Fuad. *Islam and Arabs in Early American Thought: The Roots of Orientalism in America.* Durham, NC: Acorn Press, 1991.

Shafiq, Muhammad. *The Growth of Islamic Thought in North America: Focus on Isma'il Raji al Faruqi.* Brentwood, MD: Amana Publications, 1994.

Shain, Yossi. "Ethnic Diasporas and U.S. Foreign Policy." *Political Science Quarterly* 109, no. 5 (winter 1994–1995), 811–841.

"Arab-Americans at a Crossroad." *Journal of Palestine Studies* 25, no. 3 (spring 1996), 46–59.

Shakir, Zaid. *Scattered Pictures: Reflections of an American Muslim.* Hayward, CA: Zaytuna Institute, 2005.

Sharafuddin, Mohammed. *Islam and Romantic Orientalism: Literary Encounters with the Orient.* London: I. B. Tauris Publishers, 1994.

Shari'ati, 'Ali. *On the Sociology of Islam: Lectures*, trans. Hamid Algar. Berkeley, CA: Mizan Press, 1979.

　Marxism and Other Western Fallacies: An Islamic Critique, trans. R. Campbell. Berkeley, CA: Mizan Press, 1980.

al-Shawārbī, Maḥmūd Yūsuf. *al-Islām fī Āmrīkā. al-Qāhira: Lajnat al-Bayān al-'Arabī*, 1960.

Shepard, William E. *Sayyid Qutb and Islamic Activism: A Translation and Critical Analysis of Social Justice in Islam.* Leiden: E. J. Brill, 1996.

Sherman, William C., Paul L. Whitney, and John Guerrero. *Prairie Peddlers: The Syrian Lebanese in North Dakota.* Bismarck, ND: University of Mary Press, 2002.

Sheronick, Hussein Ahmed. "A History of the Cedar Rapids Muslim Community: The Search for an American Islamic Identity." B.A. Thesis: Coe College, 1988.

Siddiqui, Zeba. *The Dilemma of Muslim Youth in America.* Plainfield, IN: The MSA of U.S. and Canada, 1978.

Silk, Mark. *Spiritual Politics: Religion and America since World War II.* New York: Simon & Shuster, 1988.

Silverstein, Paul A. *Algeria in France: Transpolitics, Race, and Nation.* Bloomington, IN: Indiana University Press, 2004.

　"The New Barbarians: Piracy and Terrorism on the North African Frontier." *CR: The New Centennial Review* 5, no. 1 (2005), 179–212.

Simpson, Frank T. "The Moorish Science Temple and Its 'Koran'." *Moslem World*, no. 37 (1947), 56–61.

Singleton, Brent D. "The Ummah Slowly Bled: A Select Bibliography of Enslaved African Muslims in the Americas and the Caribbean." *Journal of Muslim Minority Affairs* 22, no. 2 (2002), 401–412.

　"African Bibliophiles: Books and Libraries in Medieval Timbuktu." *Library & Culture* 39, no. 1 (winter 2004), 1–12.

Sirin, Selcuk R. and Michelle Fine. *Muslim American Youth: Understanding Hyphenated Identities through Multiple Methods.* New York: New York University Press, 2008.

Sivertsen, Karen. "Babel on the Hudson: Community Formation in Dutch Manhattan." Ph.D. Dissertation: Duke University, 2007.

Skerry, Peter. "Political Islam in the United States and Europe." *Political Islam: Challenges for U.S. Policy*, ed. Dick Clark (Aspen Institute: Second Conference, June 27–July 3 2003), 39–43.

　"America's Other Muslims." *Wilson Quarterly* (Autumn 2005), 16–28.

Skinner, David E. "Mande Settlement and the Development of Islamic Institutions in Sierra Leone." *The International Journal of African Historical Studies* 11, no. 1 (1978), 32–62.

Smith, Jane I. *Islam in America.* New York: Columbia University Press, 1999.

Smith, Peter. "The American Bahá'í Community, 1894–1917: A Preliminary Survey." In *Studies in Bábí & Bahá'í History*, vol. 1, ed. Moojan Momen, 85–224. Los Angeles, CA: Kalimat Press, 1982.

Smith, R. Bosworth. *Mohammed and Mohammedanism*, 2nd ed. London: Smith, Elder, & Co., 1874.

Smith, Tom W. "Religious Diversity in America: The Emergence of Muslims, Buddhists, Hindus, and Others." *Journal for the Scientific Study of Religion* 41, no. 3 (2002), 577–585.

Smock, David and Qamar-ul Huda. *Islamic Peacemaking since 9/11*. Washington, D.C. : United States Institute of Peace, 2009.

Social Science Institute. *God Struck Me Dead: Religious Conversion Experiences and Autobiographies of Negro Ex-Slaves*. Nashville, TN: Fisk University, 1945.

Sostre, Martin. *Letters from Prison: A Compilation of Martin Sostre's Correspondence from Erie County Jail, New York; and Green Haven Prison, Stormville, New York*. Buffalo, NY: State University of Buffalo, 1968.

Soysal, Yasemin Nuhoğlu. *Limits of Citizenship: Migrants and Postnational Membership in Europe*. Chicago, IL: The University of Chicago Press, 1994.

Starobin, Paul. "Crescent Conflict." *National Journal* 37, nos. 47–48 (19 November 2005), 3612–3618.

Stevens, Michael E., ed. *Journals of the House of Representatives 1789–1790*. Columbia, SC: University of South Carolina Press, 1984.

Stevenson, David. *The Origins of Freemasonry*. Cambridge: Cambridge University Press, 1988.

Stork, Joe and Rene Theberge. "'Any Arab or Others of a Suspicious Nature...'" *MERIP Reports*, no. 14 (February 1973), 3–6 and 13.

Stout, Harry S. and D. G. Hart, eds. *New Directions in American Religious History*. New York: Oxford University Press, 1997.

Strong, Josiah. *Our Country: Its Possible Future and Its Present Crisis*. New York: The Baker and Tayor Co., 1885.

Strum, Philippa and Danielle Tarantolo, eds. *Muslims in the United States: Demography, Beliefs, Institutions*. Washington, D.C.: Woodrow Wilson International Center for Scholars, 2003.

Stuckard, Kocku von. *Western Esotericism: A Brief History of Secret Knowledge*. London: Equinox, 2005.

Stucky, Sterling. *Slave Culture: Nationalist Theory and the Foundations of Black America*. New York: Oxford University Press, 1987.

Suleiman, Michael W., ed. *Arabs in America: Building a New Future*. Philadelphia, PA: Temple University Press, 1999.

    "Early Arab-Americans: The Search for Identity." In *Crossing the Waters: Arabic-Speaking Immigrants to the United States before 1940*. Washington, D.C.: Smithsonian Institution Press, 1987.

Summers, Martin. "Diasporic Brotherhood: Freemasonry and the Transnational Production of Black Middle-Class Masculinity." *Gender & History* 15, no. 3 (November 2003), 550–574.

Swanson, Jon C. "Sojourners and Settlers: Yemenis in America" In *MERIP Middle East Report*, no. 139 (March–April 1986), 5–21.

Sypher, Wylie. "The African Prince in London." In *Journal of History of Ideas* 2, no. 2 (April 1941), 237–247.

al-Tahir, Abdul Jalil. "The Arab Community in the Chicago Area: A Comparative Study of the Christian-Syhrians and the Muslim-Palestinians." Ph.D. Dissertation: The University of Chicago, 1952.

Takaki, Ronald. *Strangers from a Different Shore: A History of Asian Americans.* New York: Penguin Books, 1989.

  A Different Mirror: A History of Multicultural America. Boston, MA: Little, Brown, and Company, 1993.

Takim, Liyakat. "Multiple Identities in a Pluralistic World: Shi'ism in America." In *Muslims in the West: From Sojourners to Citizens*, ed. Yvonne Y. Haddad, 218–232. New York: Oxford University Press, 2002.

  "Preserving or Extending Boundaries: The Black Shi'is of America," in progress.

Temple-Raston, Dina. *The Jihad Next Door: The Lackawanna Six and Rough Justice in the Age of Terror.* New York: Public Affairs, 2007.

Tesdell, Lee S., Joel T. Fey, Judy L. Frohlich, Tarita L. Henry, and William Heyland. *The Way We Were: Arab-Americans in Central Iowa, An Oral History.* Iowa City, IA: Iowa Humanities Board, 1993.

Thernstrom, Stephan, Ann Orlov, and Oscar Handlin, eds. *Harvard Encyclopedia of American Ethnic Groups.* Cambridge, MA: Harvard University Press, 1980.

Thornton, John Kelly. *Africans and African Americans and the Making of the Atlantic World*, 2nd ed. Cambridge: Cambridge University Press, 1999.

Timmerman, Kenneth R. "Islamic Iran's American Base." *The American Spectator* (December 1995).

Tocqueville, Alexis de. *Democracy in America*, trans. George Lawrence, ed. J. P. Mayr. New York: Harper & Row, 1966.

Train, George Francis. *My Life in Many States and in Foreign Lands: Dictated in My Seventy-Fourth Year.* New York: D. Appleton and Company, 1902.

Trix, Frances. "Bektashi Tekke and the Sunni Mosque of Albanian Muslims in America." In *Muslim Communities in North America*, ed. Yvonne Y. Haddad and Jane I. Smith, 359–380. Albany, NY: State University of New York Press, 1994.

  "'When Christians Became Dervishes': Affirming Albanian Muslim-Christian Unity through Discourse." *Muslim World* LXXXV, nos. 3–4 (July–October 1995), 280–294.

  Albanians in Michigan. East Lansing, MI: Michigan State University Press, 2001.

Troll, Christian W. *Sayyid Ahmad Khan: An Interpretation of Muslim Theology.* New Delhi: Vikas Publication House, 1978.

Trulear, Harold Dean. "Sociology of Afro-American Religion: An Appraisal of C. Eric Lincoln's Contributions." *Journal of Religious Thought* 42, no. 2 (winter 1986), 44–55.

Tunison, Emory H. "Mohammed Alexander Russell Webb: First American Muslim." *The Arab World* 1, no. 3 (1945), 13–18.

Turner, Richard Brent. "Islam in the United States in the 1920's: The Quest for a New Vision in Afro-American Religion." Ph.D.issertation: Princeton University, 1986.

"The Ahmadiyya Mission to Blacks in the United States in the 1920's." *Journal of Religious Thought* 44 (spring 1988), 50–66.

"What Shall We Call Him? Islam and African American Identity." *Journal of Religious Thought* 51, no. 1 (summer–fall 1994), 25–53.

Islam in the African American Experience, 2nd ed. Bloomington, IN: Indiana University Press, 2003.

Turner, Victor. *The Ritual Process: Structure and Anti-Structure.* New York: Aldine de Gruyter, 1969.

Tweed, Thomas A. *The American Encounter with Buddhism, 1844–1912: Victorian Culture and the Limits of Dissent.* Bloomington, IN: Indiana University Press, 1992.

ed. *Retelling U.S. Religious History.* Berkeley, CA: University of California Press, 1997.

Tweed, Thomas A. and Stephen Prothero, eds. *Asian Religions in America: A Documentary History.* New York: Oxford University Press, 1999.

U.S. Congress, House of Representatives. Industrial Commission on Immigration and on Education. *Report of the Industrial Commission on Immigration and on Education,* vol. 15. Washington, D.C.: Government Printing Office, 1901.

U.S. Congress. Senate. Immigration Commission. "Part 25: Japanese and Other Immigrant Races in the Pacific Coast and Rocky Mountain States." In *Immigrants in Industries,* vol. 1: Japanese and East Indians. Washington, D.C.: Government Printing Office, 1911.

U.S. Congress. Senate. Subcommittee on Terrorism, Technology, and Homeland Security. *Two Years after 9/11: Keeping America Safe.* 108th Cong., 1st sess., March 2004.

U.S. Department of Commerce and Labor, Bureau of the Census. *Religious Bodies: 1906.* Washington, D.C.: Government Printing Office, 1910.

U.S. Department of Labor. "Report of the Commissioner General of Immigration." In *Reports of the Department of Labor, 1920.* Washington, D.C.: Government Printing Office, 1921.

U.S. Department of Justice. *The September 11 Detainees: A Review of the Treatment of Aliens Held on Immigration Charges in Connection with the Investigation of the September 11 Attacks.* Office of the Inspector General, April 2003.

Annual Report of the Commissioner General of Immigration. Washington, D.C.: Government Printing Office, 1931.

van Deburg, William L. ed. *Modern Black Nationalism from Marcus Garvey to Louis Farrakhan.* New York: New York University Press, 1997.

van der Veer, Peter. *Imperial Encounters: Religion and Modernity in India and Britain.* Princeton, NJ: Princeton University Press, 2001.

van Dyke Roberts, Hazel. "Anthony Jansen van Salee 1607–1676." *The New York Genealogical and Biographical Record* 103, no. 1 (January 1972), 16–28.

van Tubergen, Frank. "Religious Affiliation and Attendance among Immigrants in Eight Western Countries: Individual and Contextual Effects." *Journal for the Scientific Study of Religion* 45, no. 1 (2006), 1–22.

Vanzi, Max et al. *The Patriot Act, Other Post-9/11 Enforcement Powers and the Impact on California's Muslim Communities*. Senate Office of Research, March 2004.

Voll, John Obert. "The Mistaken Identification of 'the West' with 'Modernity'." *The American Journal of Islamic Social Sciences* 13, no. 1 (1996), 1–12.

Waddell, Jos. A. *The Annals of Augusta County, Virginia*. Richmond, VA: Wm. Ellis Jones, 1886.

The Annals of Augusta County, Virginia, from 1736 to 1871, 2nd ed. Staunton, VA: C Russell Caldwell, Publisher, 1902.

Walbridge, Linda S. *Without Forgetting the Imam: Lebanese Shi'ism in an American Community*. Detroit, MI: Wayne State University Press, 1997.

Walker, Dennis. "The Black Muslims in American Society: From Millenarian Protest to Trans-Continental Relationships" In *Cargo Cults and Millenarian Movements: Transoceanic Comparisons of New Religious Movements*, ed. G. W. Trompf. New York: Muton de Gruyter, 1990.

Islam and the Search for African-American Nationhood: Elijah Muhammad, Louis Farrakhan, and the Nation of Islam. Atlanta, GA: Clarity Press, Inc., 2005.

Walters, Ronald W. *Freedom Is Not Enough: Black Voters, Black Candidates, and American Presidential Politics*. Lanham, MD: Rowman & Littlefield, 2007.

Warren, William Fairfield. *The Religions of the World and the World-Religion*. New York: Eaton & Mains, 1911.

Wasfi, Atif A. *An Islamic-Lebanese Community in U.S.A.: A Study in Cultural Anthropology*. n.p.: Beirut Arab University, 1971.

Washington, Booker T. *Up from Slavery*. [1901]. New York: Dover Publications, 1995.

Washington, James Melvin, ed. *A Testament of Hope: The Essential Writings and Speeches of Martin Luther King, Jr*. San Francisco, CA: Harper & Row, 1986.

Washington, Joseph R. *Black Religion: The Negro and Christianity in the United States*. Boston, MA: Beacon Press, 1964.

Black Sects and Cults. Garden City, NY: Doubleday & Company, 1972.

Wasserstrom, Steven M. *Religion after Religion: Gershom Scholem, Mircea Eliade, and Henry Corbin at Eranos*. Princeton, NJ: Princeton University Press, 1999.

Waters, Mary C. *Ethnic Options: Choosing Identities in America*. Berkeley, CA: University of California Press, 1990.

Watts, Jill. *God, Harlem U.S.A.: The Father Divine Story*. Berkeley, CA: University of California Press, 1992.

Waugh, Earle H. "The Imam in the New World: Models and Modifications" In *Transitions and Transformations in the History of Religions: Essays in Honor of Joseph M. Kitagawa*, ed. Frank E. Reynolds and Theodore M. Ludwig. Leiden: E. J. Brill, 1980.

Waugh, Earle H., Baha Abu-Laban, and Regula B. Qureshi, eds. *The Muslim Community in North America*. Edmonton, AL: The University of Alberta Press, 1983.

Waugh, Earle, Sharon McIrvin Abu-Laban, and Regula B. Qureshi, eds. *Muslim Families in North America*. Edmonton, AL: University of Alberta Press, 1991.

Weaver, Mary Anne. "The Trail of the Sheikh." *The New Yorker* (April 12, 1993), 71–89.

Webb, Gisela. "Third-Wave Sufism in America and the Bawa Muhaiyaddeen Fellowship." In *Sufism in the West*, ed. Jamal Malik and John R. Hinnells. New York: Routledge, 86–102.

   ed. *Windows of Faith: Muslim Women Scholar-Activists in North America*. Syracuse, NY: Syracuse University Press, 2000.

Webb, Mohammed Alexander Russell. *The Three Lectures of Mohammed Alexander Russell Webb, Esq., Delivered at Madras, Hyderabad (Deccan) and Bombay, with a Brief Sketch of His Life*. Madras: Hassan Ali, Lawrence Asylum Press, 1892.

   Islam in America: A Brief Statement of Mohammedanism and an Outline of the American Islamic Propaganda. New York: Oriental Publishings, 1893.

   Yankee Muslim, ed. and intro. Brent D. Singleton. Rockville, MD: Borgo-Wildside Press, 2007.

Weisbrot, Robert. *Father Divine and the Struggle for Racial Equality*. Urbana, IL: University of Illinois Press, 1983.

Weslager, Clinton Alfred. *Delaware's Forgotten Folk: The Story of the Moors and Nanticokes*. Philadelphia, PA: University of Philadelphia Press, 1943.

Westerlund, David, ed. *Sufism in Europe and North America*. London: RoutledgeCurzon, 2004.

White, Ronald C., Jr. and C. Howard Hopkins. *The Social Gospel: Religion and Reform in Changing America*. Philadelphia, PA: Temple University Press, 1976.

Whitehurst, James Emerson. "The Mainstreaming of the Black Muslims: Healing the Hate." *Christian Century* (27 February 1980).

Whyte, Abbie. "Christian Elements in Negro American Muslim Religious Beliefs." *Phylon* 25, no. 4 (1964), 382–388.

Wigle, Laurel D. "An Arab Muslim Community in Michigan." In *Arabic Speaking Communities in American Cities*, ed. Barbara C. Aswad. Staten Island, NY: Center for Immigration Studies of New York, 1974, 155–167.

Williams, Loretta J. *Black Freemasonry and Middle-Class Realities*. Columbia, MO: University of Missouri Press, 1980.

Williams, Peter W. *Popular Religion in America: Symbolic Change and the Modernization Process in Historical Perspective*. Englewood Cliffs, NJ: Prentice-Hall, Inc., 1980.

   America's Religions: Traditions and Cultures, 2nd ed. Urbana, IL: University of Illinois Press, 2002.

Williams, Raymond. *Religions of Immigrants from India and Pakistan: New Threads in the American Tapestry*. Cambridge: Cambridge University Press, 1988.

Willis, John Ralph. "*Jihād fī Sabīl Allāh* – Its Doctrinal Basis in Islam and Some Aspects of Its Evolution in Nineteenth-Century West Africa." *Journal of African History* 8, no. 3 (1967), 395–415.

Wilmore, Gayraud S. and James H. Cone. *Black Theology: A Documentary History, 1966–1979.* Maryknoll, NY: Orbis Books, 1979.

Wilson, G. R. "The Religion of the American Negro Slave: His Attitude Toward Life and Death." *The Journal of Negro History* 8, no. 1 (January 1923), 41–71.

Wilson, Gary E. "American Hostages in Moslem Nations, 1784–1796: The Public Response." *Journal of the Early Republic* 2, no. 2 (summer 1982), 123–141.

Wilson, Peter Lamborn. *Sacred Drift: Essays on the Margins of Islam.* San Francisco, CA: City Lights Books, 1993.

Pirate Utopias: Moorish Corsairs and European Renegadoes, 2nd ed. Brooklyn, NY: Autonomedia, 2003.

Windley, Lathan, ed. *Runaway Slave Advertisements: A Documentary History from the 1730s to 1790,* 4 vols.: Georgia. Westport, CT: Greenwood Press, 1983.

Winkler, Wayne. *Walking Toward the Sunset: The Melungeons of Appalachia.* Macon, GA: Mercer University Press, 2004.

Winters, Clyde-Ahmad. "Afro-American Muslims: From Slavery to Freedom." *Islamic Studies* 17, no. 4 (winter 1978), 187–203.

Wolf, C. Umhau. "Muslims in the American Mid-West." *The Muslim World* 50, no. 1 (January 1960), 39–48.

Wolfe, Alan. *One Nation, after All: What Middle-Class Americans Really Think about: God, Country, Family, Racism, Welfare, Immigration, Homosexuality, Work, the Right, the Left, and Each Other.* New York: Penguin Books, 1998.

The Transformation of American Religion: How We Actually Live Our Faith. Chicago, IL: The University of Chicago Press, 2003.

Wolfe, Michael. *The Hadj: An American's Pilgrimage to Mecca.* New York: The Atlantic Monthly Press, 1993.

ed. *Taking Back Islam: American Muslims Reclaim Their Faith.* n.p: Rodale, 2002.

Wormser, Richard. *American Islam: Growing Up Muslim in America.* New York: Walker & Company, 1994.

Wuthnow, Robert. *After Heaven: Spirituality in America since the 1950s.* Berkeley CA: University of California Press, 1998.

America and the Challenges of Religious Diversity. Princeton, NJ: Princeton University Press, 2005.

Wyatt-Brown, Bertram. "The Mask of Obedience: Male Slave Psychology in the Old South." *The American Historical Review* 93, no. 5 (December 1988), 1228–1252.

X, Malcolm. *The End of White World Supremacy: Four Speeches by Malcolm X,* ed. Benjamin Karim. New York: Arcade Publishing, 1971.

X, Malcolm and Alex Haley. *The Autobiography of Malcolm X.* New York: Ballantine Books, 1965.

Malcolm X: Speeches at Harvard, ed. Archie Epps. New York: Paragon House, 1991.

Yaghmaian, Behzad. *Embracing the Infidel: Stories of Muslim Migrants on the Journey West*. New York: Delacorte Press, 2005.

Yee, James. *For God and Country: Faith and Patriotism under Fire*. New York: Public Affairs, 2005.

Younis, Adele L. "The First Muslims in America: Impressions and Reminiscences." *Journal Institute of Muslim Minority Affairs* 5 (January 1984), 17–28.

The Coming of the Arabic-Speaking People to the United States, ed. Philip M. Kayal. Staten Island, NY: Center for Migration Studies, 1995.

Yusuf, Imtiyaz. "Islam in America: A Historical-Social Perspective." *Hamdard Islamicus* 12, no. 4 (winter 1989), 79–86.

Zangwill, Israel. *The Melting Pot: Drama in Four Acts*, new and revised edition. New York: The Macmillan Company, 1919.

Zwierlein, Frederick J. *Religion in New Netherland, 1623–1664*. New York: Da Capo Press, 1971.

Index

51118705R00255

Made in the USA
San Bernardino, CA
30 August 2019